Portugal

THE ROUGH GUIDE

written and researched by

**Mark Ellingham, John Fisher
and Graham Kenyon**

this edition updated by

Jens Finke, Matthew Hancock,
Amanda Tomlin and Susan Grimshaw

THE ROUGH GUIDES

TRAVEL GUIDES • PHRASEBOOKS • MUSIC AND REFERENCE GUIDES

 We set out to do something different when the first Rough Guide was published in 1982. Mark Ellingham, just out of university, was travelling in Greece. He brought along the popular guides of the day, but found they were all lacking in some way. They were either strong on ruins and museums but went on for pages without mentioning a beach or taverna. Or they were so conscious of the need to save money that they lost sight of Greece's cultural and historical significance. Also, none of the books told him anything about Greece's contemporary life – its politics, its culture, its people, and how they lived.

So with no job in prospect, Mark decided to write his own guidebook, one which aimed to provide practical information that was second to none, detailing the best beaches and the hottest clubs and restaurants, while also giving hard-hitting accounts of every sight, both famous and obscure, and providing up-to-the-minute information on contemporary culture. It was a guide that encouraged independent travellers to find the best of Greece, and was a great success, getting shortlisted for the Thomas Cook travel guide award, and encouraging Mark, along with three friends, to expand the series.

The Rough Guide list grew rapidly and the letters flooded in, indicating a much broader readership than had been anticipated, but one which uniformly appreciated the Rough Guide mix of practical detail and humour, irreverence and enthusiasm. Things haven't changed. The same four friends who began the series are still the caretakers of the Rough Guide mission today: to provide the most reliable, up-to-date and entertaining information to independent-minded travellers of all ages, on all budgets.

We now publish 100 titles and have offices in London and New York. The travel guides are written and researched by a dedicated team of more than 100 authors, based in Britain, Europe, the USA and Australia. We have also created a unique series of phrasebooks to accompany the travel series, along with an acclaimed series of music guides, and a best-selling pocket guide to the Internet and World Wide Web. We also publish comprehensive travel information on our Web site:

http://www.roughguides.com

HELP US UPDATE

We've gone to a lot of effort to ensure that this new edition of *The Rough Guide to Portugal* is accurate and up-to-date. However, things change – places get "discovered", opening hours are notoriously fickle, restaurants and rooms raise prices or lower standards, extra buses are laid on or off. If you feel we've got it wrong or left something out, we'd like to know, and if you can remember the address, the price, the time, the phone number, so much the better.

We'll credit all contributions, and send a copy of the next edition (or any other Rough Guide if you prefer) for the best letters. Please mark letters: "Rough Guide Portugal Update" and send to:
Rough Guides, 1 Mercer St, London WC2H 9QJ, or
Rough Guides, 375 Hudson St, 9th floor, New York NY 10014.
Or send email to: mail@roughguides.co.uk
Online updates about this book can be found on Rough Guides' Web site at http://www.roughguides.com

Mark Ellingham set up Rough Guides in 1981, writing the first title in the series on Greece, and the original edition of this book the following year. He has updated various editions of the Portugal guide since then but is currently doing time developing Rough Guides' Internet publishing. He claims he'd be a lot happier back in Portugal, roaming around Trás-os-Montes, hanging out in Lisbon's bars or watching a Benfica match. He lives in London with his partner, Natania Jansz (co-author of *The Rough Guide to Greece*), and their toddler, Miles.

John Fisher has also been involved with Rough Guides from the start and has been inextricably involved with the series and with Portugal

ever since. The author of several other Rough Guide titles, John can normally be found at Rough Guide HQ in London, where work takes up far too much good travelling time. He lives in South London with his wife and two young sons.

Graham Kenyon became involved in *The Rough Guide to Greece* during a year off after studying classics at Oxford. He went on to co-write the Rough Guides to Spain and Portugal before retiring from travel writing to pursue a career in information technology. He now works in the City of London, specializing in business systems development. He still travels widely and his interest in ancient civilizations continues to provide a focal point for trips.

READERS' LETTERS

Thanks to all the readers who took the time and trouble to write in advising us of changes, errors, and suggestions for this edition. Apologies to anyone whose name we missed or whose signature we couldn't quite decipher.

Clare Alderson & James Corson, John & Bryony Allen, Fergal Altman, L. Aspinall, George Atkinson, K. Attema, Mark Baker, Ann M Bartlett, C.M. Beckman, Philip Beech, L. Binterhuis, Daniëlle Borger & Ivo Bastings, H. Bradley, Moira Byrne, Peter Calingaert, Carmen Stevens, Lisa Carroll, Una Clarke, Mike Colquhoun, Stefan Coppens, Chrisol Correia, David Crossland & Wendy Davies, Alfred Cutts, Ailsa Edge, Øyvind Ellingsen, C. Embrey, B.J. Evison & R.F. Lear, Jean Ferrie, James Fitzsimons, W. & J.Fox, Fulvio Garofalo, Chris Giles, Barbara Gill & Al Scarlett, R.K.V. Gillet, Jennie Glover, Vivienne & Alex Gray, Hanson family, Charles & Sarah Harmer, Angela Harris, Stephen Heneghan, Steve Henwood, Sion Hill, R.L. Hislop, Johanna & Paul Hofstee, Rosslyn Hyams, E. Hyland, Sophie Jacobs & Frederik Vekeman, John Jarvis, Bernard M. Jones, Neil Jones &

Amanda Thomas, A. Kay, Theresa Kemp, Jeff Klepper, Alison Knowles & Mark Wilson, Leslie Koerner, Wilma Kohler, David & Johnny Larcombe, Keddie & Isobel Law, Nick & Mary Llewellin, Max Louwerse, Bernard Luckhurst, S. Machado, Sasha Marques, Christina Marshall, Biddy & Matthew Martin, Gillian Mellors, Finlay Moodie, P.W. & M.A. Moody, Maurice Moore, Gillian More, Rosemary Morlin, Sean Neville, Joan Norton, John O'Farrell, E. Ogborn, Anne & Phil Riley Parker, A. Paterson, Chris & Helen Walsh Patient, Caroline Paul, Howard Quayle, C. Rebello, Helen & Peter Risk, Sue Roberts, Louise Ross, Heather Rowarth, M. Rutherford, Jennifer Rylands, Bruce Samuel, Franic Schaer, Jonathan Sear, Carole & Stephen Sherry, R. Sidhu, Linda Skinner, S.A. Skinner, Ann Smith, Melissa Smith, Stella Smith, T.J. Snow, Nick Speed & Gabriel Roberts, Gerard Stalenhoef, Mark Stobbs, Ivor Sweigler, B. Szczypka-Elyachouti, L. Tham, Richard D. Tucker, Barbara Tyrell, Hans van der Lubbe, W.J. Wall, Robert J. Wedum, Gina Westbrook, Paul J.T. Whittard, Gillian Whitworth, Gary Willis, Kevin Woods, Reg Woodward, Harvey & Leila Woolf, Ken Wuschke, J.D. Young.

CONTENTS

Introduction x

PART THREE CONTEXTS 489

LIST OF MAPS

MAP SYMBOLS

Railway	● Cave
Motorway	▲ Peak
Road	Mountains
Path	Viewpoint
Ferry route	Waterfall
Waterway	✕ Airport
Chapter division boundary	★ Bus stop
International borders	Ⓜ Metro station
∴ Ruins	ⓘ Tourist office
▲ Campsite	⊠ Post office
⌂ Refuge	Building
▣ Restaurant	Church
✡ Synagogue	Cemetery
♀ Lighthouse	Park
♦ Church (regional maps)	Beach
+ Chapel (regional maps)	

INTRODUCTION

I am very happy here, because I loves oranges, and talks bad Latin to the Monks, who understand it as it is like their own. And I goes into society (with my pocket pistols) and I swims in the Tagus all across at once, and I rides on an ass or a mule and swears Portuguese, and I have got a diarrhoea, and bites from the mosquitoes. But what of that? Comfort must not be expected by folks that go a-pleasuring.

Byron in Portugal, July 1809.

P ortugal is an astonishingly beautiful country, the rivers, forests and lush valleys of the north a splendid and complementary contrast to its contorted southern coastline of beaches, cliffs and coves. If you've come from the arid plains of central Spain, Portugal's dry southern Alentejo region doesn't promise any immediate relief, but – unlike Spain – you don't have to travel very far to witness so total a contrast that it's hard, at first, to take in. Suddenly the landscape is infinitely softer and greener, with flowers and trees everywhere. Life also seems easier-paced and the people more courteous; the Portuguese themselves talk of their nation as a land of *brandos costumes* – gentle ways.

For so small a country, Portugal sports a tremendous cultural diversity. There are highly sophisticated resorts along the coast around Lisbon and on the well-developed Algarve in the south, upon which European tourists have been descending for around thirty years. Lisbon itself, in its idiosyncratic, rather old-fashioned way, has enough diversions to please most city devotees; as 1994 European City of Culture it endured an infrastructural overhaul that locks it into modern Europe without quite jettisoning its most endearing, ramshackle qualities. Whether it will be able to maintain this traditional side in the face of the massive development projects that have accompanied the 1998 Lisbon Expo has yet to be seen. But in the rural areas – the Alentejo, the mountainous Beiras, or northern Trás-os-Montes – this is often still a conspicuously underdeveloped country. Tourism and European Union membership have changed many regions – most notably in the north, where new road building scythes through the countryside – but for anyone wanting to get off the beaten track, there are limitless opportunities to experience smaller towns and rural areas that still seem rooted in the last century.

In terms of population, and of customs, differences between the **north and south** are particularly striking. Above a roughly sketched line, more or less corresponding with the course of the Rio Tejo (River Tagus), the people are of predominantly Celtic and Germanic stock. It was here, in the north at Guimarães, that the "Lusitanian" nation was born, in the wake of the Christian reconquest from the North African Moors. South of the Tagus, where the Roman, and then the Moorish, civilizations were most established, people tend to be darker-skinned (*moreno*) and maintain perhaps more of a "Mediterranean" lifestyle (though the Portuguese coastline is, in fact, entirely Atlantic). **Agriculture** reflects this divide as well, with oranges, figs and cork in the south, and more elemental corn and potatoes in the north. Indeed, in the north the methods of farming date back to pre-Christian days, based on a mass of tiny plots divided and subdivided over the generations.

More recent events are also woven into the pattern. The 1974 **Revolution**, which brought to an end 48 years of dictatorship, came from the south – an area of vast estates, rich landowners and a dependent workforce – while the later conservative backlash came from the north, with its powerful religious authorities and individual

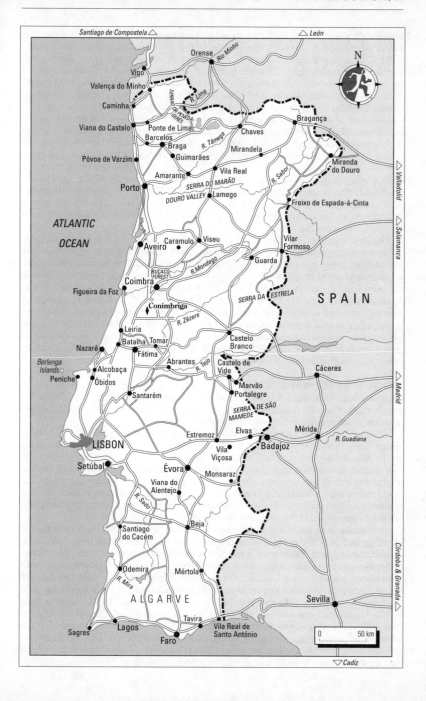

Santiago de Compostela △   △ León

N

Orense · Rio Minho

Vigo

Valença do Minho

R. Lima

Caminha

Bragança

Viana do Castelo · Ponte de Lima   Chaves

Barcelos   R. Tâmega

Braga   Mirandela

Póvoa de Varzim   Guimarães

Miranda
do Douro

Amarante   Vila Real   R. Sabor

Porto   SERRA DO MARÃO

DOURO VALLEY · Lamego   Freixo de Espada-à-Cinta

ATLANTIC

OCEAN

Caramulo · Viseu

Aveiro   Vilar
Formoso

BUÇACO
FOREST   R. Mondego   Guarda

Coimbra   SERRA DA ESTRELA   S P A I N

Figueira da Foz

Conímbriga   R. Zêzere

Leiria

Batalha · Tomar   Castelo
Branco

Nazaré   Fátima

Berlenga
Íslands ○   Abrantes · R. Tejo   Castelo de
Vide   Cáceres

Alcobaça

Peniche   Óbidos   Marvão
Portalegre

Santarém   SERRA DE SÃO
MAMEDE

Mérida

LISBON   Estremoz · Elvas   R. Guadiana

Setúbal   Vila
Viçosa · Badajoz

Évora

Viana do
Alentejo   Monsaraz   R. Sado

Beja

Santiago
do Cacém

Odemira   Mértola

R. Mira

A L G A R V E   Sevilla

Sagres   Lagos   Tavira

Faro   Vila Real de
Santo António

0   50 km

△ Valladolid

△ Salamanca

△ Madrid

Córdoba & Granada ▷

▽ Cadiz

smallholders wary of change. But more profoundly even than the Revolution, it is **emigration** that has altered people's attitudes and the appearance of the countryside. After Lisbon, the largest Portuguese community is in Paris, and there are migrant workers spread throughout France, Germany and North America. Returning, these emigrants have brought in modern ideas and challenged many traditional rural values. New ideas and cultural influences have arrived, too, through Portugal's own **immigrants** from the old African colonies of Cape Verde, Mozambique and Angola.

The greatest of all Portuguese influences, however, is **the sea**. The Atlantic seems to dominate the land not only physically, producing the consistently temperate climate, but mentally and historically, too. The Portuguese are very conscious of themselves as a seafaring race; mariners like Vasco da Gama led the way in the discovery of Africa and the New World, and until comparatively recently Portugal remained a colonial power, albeit one in deep crisis. Such links long ago brought African and South American strands into the country's culture: in the distinctive music of fado, blues-like songs heard in Lisbon and Coimbra, for example, or the Moorish-influenced Manueline, or Baroque "Discovery", architecture that provides the country's most distinctive monuments.

This "glorious" history has also led to the peculiar national characteristic of *saudade*: a slightly resigned, nostalgic air, and a feeling that the past will always overshadow the possibilities of the future. The years of isolation under the dictator Salazar, which yielded to democracy after the 1974 Revolution, reinforced such feelings, as the ruling elite spurned "contamination" by the rest of Europe. Only in the last decade or so, with Portugal's entry into the European Union, have things really begun to change. A belated industrial revolution is finally underway, and the Portuguese are becoming increasingly geared toward Lisbon and the cities. For those who have stayed in the countryside, however, life remains traditional – disarmingly so to outsiders – and social mores seem fixed in the past. Women still wear black if their husbands are absent, as many are, working in France, or Germany, or at sea.

Where to go and when

Since Portugal is so compact, it's easy to take in something of each of its elements – northern river valleys, southern coast, and mountains – even on a brief visit, whether you rent a car or make your own way by public transport.

Scenically, the most interesting parts of the country are in the north: the **Minho**, green, damp, and often startling in its rural customs; the sensational gorge and valley of the **Rio Douro**; the remote **Trás-os-Montes**; and the wild, mountainous *serras* of **Beira Alta**. For contemporary interest, spend at least some time in both **Lisbon** and **Porto**, the only two cities of real size. And if it's monuments you're after, the whole centre of the country – above all **Coimbra**, **Évora** and the **Estremadura** region – retains a faded grandeur dating from the Age of the Discoveries in the sixteenth century and from the later gold and diamond wealth of Brazil.

The **coast** is virtually continuous beach – some 800km of it – and only on the **Algarve** and in a few pockets around Lisbon and Porto has there been large-scale tourist development. Elsewhere, a number of beach areas have seen casual development on a relatively small scale, these resorts remaining thoroughly Portuguese, with great stretches of deserted sands between them. Perhaps the loveliest beaches are along the northern **Costa Verde**, around Viana do Castelo, or, for isolation, the wild stretches of **southern Alentejo**. It must be added, however, that the Portuguese coast is the Atlantic and can often be windswept and exposed. If you like your swimming warm, the only area where the water approaches Mediterranean temperatures is the **eastern Algarve**, where a series of sandbank islands, the *ilhas*, protect the shore.

Swimming aside, **when you go** matters little. The entire country is warm from **April to October**, if slightly erratically so in the rainy north, while the Algarve is amazingly mild throughout the year – it hardly has a winter and January can be delightful when the almond blossom is out. The **Serra da Estrela**, in contrast, features winter snow for skiers, while further north winter is wet and the wind bitingly cold – this is no time for extended journeys around Trás-os-Montes. Throughout the year, escaping the crowds, outside the Algarve and Lisbon, is little problem. Especially on the Algarve, booking accommodation is essential in high season; elsewhere, however, you should find rooms with little difficulty throughout the year except at festival times when even the smallest towns and villages can fill up quickly.

DAYTIME TEMPERATURES (°C) AND AVERAGE MONTHLY RAINFALL (MM)						
	JAN	MARCH	MAY	JULY	SEPT	NOV
LISBON						
Max °C	14	18	22	27	25	17
Min °C	8	10	13	17	16	12
Rainfall	111	109	44	3	33	93
PORTO (Costa Verde)						
Max °C	13	15	19	25	24	17
Min °C	5	7	10	15	14	8
Rainfall	159	147	87	20	51	148
FARO (Algarve)						
Max °C	15	18	22	28	26	19
Min °C	9	11	14	20	19	13
Rainfall	70	72	21	1	17	65

THE

BASICS

GETTING THERE FROM BRITAIN

It takes at least thirty hours to travel overland from Britain to Portugal, so the majority of visitors find flying is the most viable option. There are scheduled year-round flights to Lisbon, Porto and Faro (in the Algarve) from London and from several regional British airports, including Birmingham, Edinburgh, Glasgow, Manchester and Newcastle. Numerous package companies also sell significantly cheaper charter flights (mostly to Faro) from a variety of British regional airports. Alternatively, if time isn't the most important factor, you can approach Portugal overland from Spain, to which there are many more, and often cheaper, charter deals.

Road or rail alternatives are worth considering if you plan to visit Portugal as part of an extended trip through Europe. There is no direct ferry from Britain to Portugal but drivers can knock off much of the journey by taking the ferry from Plymouth or Portsmouth to Santander or from Portsmouth to Bilbão, both in northern Spain.

BY AIR

Most of the cheaper flights to Portugal are **charter** deals, sold either with a package holiday or as a flight-only option. They have fixed and unchangeable outward and return dates, and allow a maximum stay of one month. Obviously the more flexible you can be about departure dates, the better your chances of a rock-bottom fare. Last-minute summer flights go for as little as £100 return, occasionally even less, though more realistically you'll pay around £160.

Travel agents throughout Britain sell charter flights to Portugal (see p.4 for agents' addresses) and even the major high-street chains frequently promote "flight-only" deals, or heavily discount their all-inclusive holidays. The greatest variety of flights, however, tends to be from the **London airports to Faro**; there are fewer charters to Lisbon and Porto. Flying from other **British regional airports**, you'll find flights often have a connection in London or Manchester. From Manchester, the new Portuguese airline, Portugália, has daily flights (except Sat) to both Porto and Lisbon, for £189 standard return.

Student/youth charters are also sporadically available to Lisbon, though it's usually easier (and cheaper) to pick up flights to Madrid or Málaga (see below). The main student/youth operator for charters is Campus Travel (see p.4 for address).

Scheduled flights (with British Airways or TAP, the Portuguese national airline) are generally more expensive than charters, but can be booked well in advance and remain valid for three months, sometimes longer. There are various classes of scheduled ticket and occasional special offers, but with most of the cheaper tickets you'll have to stay at least one Saturday night and you won't be allowed to change your flight once it's booked. As with charters, discount deals are available from high-street travel agents, as well as specialist flight and student/youth agencies.

TAP flies from London (Heathrow) to Lisbon, Porto and Faro. **British Airways** operates services to Lisbon and Porto from London (Heathrow), and from London (Gatwick) to Faro, using the independent carrier **GB Airways** for the Faro and Porto routes. TAP and BA work in conjunction with each other, so you can book a flight to Portugal from any airport in Britain, with a low-cost add-on fare for the routing through London. Fares vary widely depending on time of year and length of stay; economy-class **fares** range from £176 to £193 return in low season and from £299 to £314 in high season. Flights from elsewhere in Britain will cost you a little more.

An alternative is to **fly to Spain** and travel on to Portugal from there. You can pick up relatively inexpensive charter flights to Madrid or Málaga throughout the summer (and scheduled flights year-round), from where train and bus (Internorte to northern Portugal, EVA to the south) connec-

AIRLINES, AGENTS AND OPERATORS

AIRLINES

British Airways 156 Regent St, London W1R 5TA; 101–102 Cheapside, London EC2V 6DT; Victoria Place, Victoria Station, London SW1W 9SJ; 146 New St, Birmingham B2 4HN; 19–21 St Mary's Gate, Market St, Manchester M1 1PU; 66 New Broadmead, Bristol BS1 2DL; 66 Gordon St, Glasgow G1 3RS; 32 Frederick St, Edinburgh EH2 2JR; 209 Union St, Aberdeen AB1 2BA (all enquiries ☎0345/222 111; Web site: *http://www.british-airways.com*).

Iberia 27–29 Glasshouse St, London W1R 6SU (☎0171/830 0011).

Portugália Olympic House, 1st Floor, Room 1006, Manchester Airport, M90 1QX (☎0161/489 5040).

TAP (Air Portugal), Gillingham House, 38–44 Gillingham Street, London SW1 V1JW (☎0171/630 0900; Web site: *http://www.TAP-AirPortugal.pt*).

FLIGHT AGENTS

Avro Vantage House, 1 Weir Rd, London SW19 8UX (☎0181/715 0000). *Good value flight-only deals to Lisbon (summer only) and Faro.*

Campus Travel 52 Grosvenor Gardens, London SW1W 0AG (☎0171/730 3402); 541 Bristol Rd, Selly Oak, Birmingham B29 6AU (☎0121/414 1848); 61 Ditchling Rd, Brighton BN1 4SD (☎01273/570 226); 37–39 Queen's Rd, Clifton, Bristol BS8 1QE (☎0117/929 2494); 5 Emmanuel St, Cambridge CB1 1NE (☎01223/324 283); 53 Forest Rd, Edinburgh EH1 2QP (☎0131/225 6111, telesales 668 3303); 122 George St, Glasgow G1 1RS (☎0141/553 1818); 166 Deansgate, Manchester M3 3FE (☎0161/833 2046, telesales 273 1721); 105–106 St Aldates, Oxford OX1 1DD (☎01865/242 067). *Student/youth travel specialists, with branches also in YHA shops and on university campuses all over Britain.*

Eclipse Direct First Choice House, Peel Cross Rd, Salford, Manchester M5 2AN (☎01293/554 400). *Discount fares from Gatwick to Faro.*

Flightbookers 177–178 Tottenham Court Rd, London W1P 0LX; Gatwick Airport, South Terminal inside the British Rail Station (☎01293/568 300); 34 Argyle Arcade, off Buchanan Street, Glasgow G1 1RS (☎0141/204 1919). *Discounted TAP tickets.*

North South Travel Moulsham Mill Centre, Parkway, Chelmsford, Essex CM2 7PX (☎01245/492 882, fax 356 612). *Friendly, competitive travel agency, offering discounted fares worldwide – profits are used to support projects in the developing world, in particular the promotion of sustainable tourism.*

Portugalicia 110b Ladbroke Grove, London W10 5NE (☎0171/221 0333). *Discounted scheduled flights (BA/TAP from Gatwick and Heathrow; Portugália from Manchester).*

---

tions to Portugal are simple enough – see the feature on p.6 for more details.

Besides the operators above, try the classified sections of newspapers like *The Independent* and *The Guardian*, the *Sunday Times* and *Observer* or, in London, *Time Out* and the *Evening Standard*.

PACKAGE HOLIDAYS

Although **package holidays** tend to concentrate on the Algarve, there is a fair range of other possibilities as well. In addition to beach-and-villa or beach-and-hotel holidays, there are companies which arrange rooms in manor houses and *pousadas* (see p.29) and others which operate weekend breaks to Lisbon or organize sporting (mainly tennis and golf) holidays.

Standard villa/hotel breaks to the Algarve start at around £300 per person for a week in high season, although some companies will take only two-week bookings at this time; in winter, you can get some very good deals and may pay around £50–60 less than this. **Specialist holidays** come a little pricier, say from around £400 for a week's golfing holiday based in a four-star hotel; though a three-night **weekend break** in Lisbon can be had for as little as £180 in winter, more like £300–350 in high season.

Virtually every UK holiday company operates in Portugal. There's a list of recommended specialist operators in the box on p.5, most of which are smaller companies, whose holidays tend to be directed towards individuals; all should be able to

STA Travel 86 Old Brompton Rd, London SW7 3LH; 117 Euston Rd, London NW1 2SX; 38 Store St, London WC1E 7BZ (☎0171/ 361 6161); 25 Queen's Rd, Bristol BS8 1QE (☎0117/929 4399); 38 Sidney St, Cambridge CB2 3HX (☎01223/366 966); 75 Deansgate, Manchester M3 2BW (☎0161/834 0668); 88 Vicar Lane, Leeds LS1 7JH (☎0113/244 9212); 36 George St, Oxford OX1 2OJ (☎01865/792 800); and branches in Aberdeen, Birmingham, Canterbury, Cardiff, Coventry, Durham, Glasgow, Loughborough, Nottingham, Warwick and Sheffield. *Worldwide specialists in low-cost flights and tours for students and under-26s, though other customers welcome. Also offices abroad.*

SPECIALIST OPERATORS

Abreu Travel 109 Westbourne Grove, London W2 4UL (☎0171/229 9905). *Portuguese-run agency – always worth a call for flights or accommodation.*

Allegro Holidays Vanguard House, 277 London Rd, Burgess Hill, West Sussex RH15 9Q (☎01444/248 222). *Holidays in the Lisbon area, Minho and Algarve.*

Caravela Tours 38–44 Gillingham St, London SW1V 1JW (☎0171/630 5148). *Charter wing of TAP. Offers stays in manor houses in the north, plus pousadas throughout the country.*

Destination Portugal Madeira House, 37 Corn St, Witney, Oxfordshire OX8 7BW (☎01993/773 269). *This agent claims to accommodate any Portuguese needs, including discount flight-only deals, car rental, villa and manor house lets, bird-watching, sailing and national park hiking holidays. They're also handling trips to Expo 98 in Lisbon. Highly recommended.*

Explore Worldwide 1 Frederick St, Aldershot, Hants GU11 1LQ (☎01252/319 448). *Hiking specialist that offers small group tours in the Douro and Gerês.*

Mundi Color 276 Vauxhall Bridge Rd, London SW1V 1BE (☎0171/828 6021). *Specializes in a range of holidays, from city breaks in Lisbon and Porto to tailor-made stays in pousadas and manor houses.*

Portuguese Travel Centre 13 Beauchamp Place, London SW3 1NQ (☎0171/581 3104). *Flights, car rental, hotels and villas.*

Something Special 10 Bull Plain, Hertford, Herts SG14 1DT (☎01992/552 231). *Algarve villas.*

Sunvil Holidays 7–8 Upper Square, Old Isleworth, Middlesex TW7 7BJ (☎0181/568 4499). *Tailor-made itineraries to suit most budgets, including fly-drive options and stays in pousadas and manor houses.*

Travel Club of Upminster Station Rd, Upminster, Essex RM14 2TT (☎017082/25000). *Long-established villa operator.*

Travelscene 11–15 St Ann's Rd, Harrow, Middlesex HA1 1AS (☎0181/427 8800). *Weekend breaks in Lisbon, Porto and elsewhere.*

arrange flights and car rental. For a full list of companies offering holidays in Portugal, contact the Portuguese National Tourist Office (see p.21 for addresses).

BY TRAIN

To get **from London to Lisbon** by train is quicker now thanks to the Channel Tunnel, but the journey still takes at least thirty hours. Also, as Eurostar will take bookings only as far as Paris it is a comparatively expensive way of getting to Portugal and you will almost certainly be able to fly there for less.

Most cheap tickets, however, still route you via the ferries and it's closer to forty hours setting out from Victoria Station, crossing the Channel at either Newhaven–Dieppe (the cheapest route) or Dover–Calais, changing trains in Paris (and transferring stations, from Nord to Austerlitz) and again at the Spanish border (at Hendaye/Irún). It's a good way to travel if you want to stop off in France or Spain on the way. But even if you qualify for under-26 or over-65 discounts, you are likely to pay more than you would for a charter flight. For full details and information on fares, call Rail Europe (see box on p.6).

There are two main **routes into Portugal**: from Paris via Irún, San Sebastián, Vilar Formoso, Guarda and Pampilhosa to Porto, Coimbra and Lisbon; and from Madrid via Cáceres to Marvão-Beirã, Abrantes and Entroncamento (where the line splits to Lisbon, or to Coimbra and Porto). A

TRAIN CONNECTIONS FROM SPAIN

Flying to **Madrid** or **Málaga** may well work out cheaper than flying to Portugal, and from either place train connections west are routine, with rewarding stops en route.

From Madrid, the most direct trains leave from the Estación Atocha, reaching **Lisbon** (Santa Apolónia Station) ten hours later. The fastest route is **via Badajoz**, the "gateway to Portugal", a close neighbour of Elvas (see p.407), the first stop the train makes in Portugal. Other stops along this line, such as the lofty towns of Portalegre (p.411) and Abrantes (p.171), make this the recommended route through the country.

From Málaga you are well placed to head for the **Algarve** and, if you have the time, you could take in a loop through the great Andalucian cities of Granada, Córdoba and Seville (though note that the Málaga–Granada and Granada–Córdoba journeys are quicker and easier by bus). At Córdoba, you're back on the main train line to Seville, with services to Huelva, from where buses run to the Portuguese border at Ayamonte-Vila Real de Santo António. Buses from Ayamonte take you across the border to the Portuguese town of Vila Real, where you can join the Algarve train line, towards Faro and Lagos, or catch one of the frequent local buses.

If you want to explore central Portugal, the line **from Salamanca**, which enters Portugal at Vilar Formoso, has useful connections to Guarda and Coimbra and is currently being upgraded. From northern Spain, trains connect **from Vigo** in Galicia (3hr to Porto, 9hr to Lisbon).

secondary route runs across northwestern Spain, through Santiago de Compostela to Vigo in Galicia, crossing the border at Tuy-Valença, from where it's an easy journey south to Porto.

The current standard **fare** from London to Lisbon is £220 return (£205 with Wasteels). If you're under 26, you can get a **discounted BIJ ticket** on the same route for £184, from Eurotrain or Wasteels. For trains to Faro, in the Algarve, you'll have to go via Lisbon and the standard return fare is £250; it will almost certainly be cheaper, and quicker, to buy a ticket to Lisbon, then get an express coach on to Faro. All these tickets are valid for two months and stops are allowed anywhere along the way on a pre-specified route.

TRAIN INFORMATION

British Rail International Rail Centre, Victoria Station, London SW1V 1JY (European information line ☎0990/848 848).

Eurostar EPS House, Waterloo Station, London SE1 8SE (reservations ☎0345/303 030; Web site: *www.eurostar.com/eurostar/*).

Eurotrain Campus Travel, 52 Grosvenor Gardens, London SW1W 0AG (☎0171/730 3402).

Le Shuttle Customer Services Centre (☎0990/353535).

Rail Europe 179 Piccadilly, London W1V 0BA (☎0990/300 003).

Wasteels Victoria Station (by platform 2), London SW1V 1JY (☎0171/834 7066).

However, none is a particularly good deal when compared to an **InterRail** pass, available from British Rail or a travel agent. If you're under 26, a two-zone pass covering all countries between the UK and Portugal will cost you £209 for a month, and gives discounts in Britain and on various ferry services. The 26 and over version costs £279. Alternatively an under-26 one-zone ticket (covering only Portugal, Spain and Morocco) costs £159 for 22 days; £229 for those 26 and over. To qualify for an InterRail pass, you have to have been resident in Europe for six months. Non-UK passport-holders who have not been resident in the UK for longer than six months can purchase a **Eurail pass** (see p.25 for details).

Senior citizens holding a British Rail Senior Card can buy a **Rail Europe Senior Card** for £5, which gives a thirty percent discount on rail travel between – but not within – 25 European countries, and includes Eurostar and rail-connected sea crossings.

BY BUS

If you can tolerate the long journey (40–45hr depending on your destination), **Eurolines**, the foreign travel wing of National Express, operates a service three times weekly from London to Coimbra, Fátima and Lisbon, and another to Faro and Lagos. The current fare to Lisbon is £139 return (£83 for under-12s); there are no student discounts. Tickets are available in Britain from any National Express or Eurolines agent (in effect most travel agents), or from the Eurolines office at 52 Grosvenor Gardens, London SW1W 0AU (☎0990/143 219), opposite Victoria Station. You have to change buses in Paris, where there's a wait of around three hours between connections.

Alternatively, if you make your own way to **Paris**, there are buses six days a week (not Mon) to Lisbon, and fairly regular services to most other towns in Portugal. Coming back, providing you've made bookings in advance, you can join these buses at any stage. In Paris, tickets are sold at the Porte de Charenton terminus, and by a Portuguese agent at Boulevard Poniatowski 75, Paris (☎01.43.07.44.58).

Tiring though these journeys are, they're comfortable enough, and broken by frequent rest and meal stops. As long as you take plenty to eat, drink and read, as well as a certain amount of French and Spanish currency to use along the way, you should emerge relatively unscathed.

BY CAR: FERRIES AND LE SHUTTLE

Driving through France, your route obviously depends on what you want to see along the way. The quickest route is to take the coast road via Nantes and Bordeaux, entering Spain at Irún. This can be followed from the standard **Channel ports** (Calais, Boulogne or Dieppe) or, further to the west, off the **ferries** from Portsmouth–Cherbourg (5hr; P&O), Poole–Cherbourg (4hr 15min; Brittany Ferries), Poole–St Malo (8hr; April–Sept only; Brittany Ferries), Portsmouth–Caen (6hr; Brittany Ferries), Portsmouth–St Malo (8hr 45min; Brittany Ferries) or Plymouth–Roscoff (6hr; Brittany Ferries).

Ferry costs vary enormously and depend on the size of car, number of passengers and, especially, the season – from October to March there are very good deals on all the longer crossings. You're looking at around £140–320 return for a car (plus up to five passengers), depending on the season. Crossing from Portsmouth or Plymouth is a little more expensive, but may of course be much more convenient if you live west of London. For all of the above options, full details can be

FERRY COMPANIES AND LE SHUTTLE	
Brittany Ferries	☎0990/360 360
Hoverspeed	☎0990/240 241
Le Shuttle	☎0990/353 535
P&O European Ferries	☎0990/980 980
Sally Line	☎01843/595 522
Stena Sealink Line	☎0990/707 070

obtained from travel agents or from the ferry companies themselves (see box above).

Another alternative is to take your car on Le Shuttle, the freight trains which carry coaches, cars and motorbikes in the Channel Tunnel. Le Shuttle runs every 15–30 minutes and the journey takes 35 minutes between the terminals at Folkestone and Calais. Fares start at £89 for a car and passengers, going up to £308 at peak times. Call Le Shuttle Customer Services Centre (see box above) for further information.

The only way of substantially cutting down on the driving time to Portugal is to take the ferry from **Plymouth** (March–Nov) or **Portsmouth** (Oct–April) **to Santander** in northern Spain, though this is an expensive route – and it still means a long day's drive before you reach Portugal itself. The ferry crossing takes 24 hours from Plymouth, around 30 hours from Portsmouth, and the boat runs twice weekly for most of the year (once a week in January, and with a three-week gap around Christmas) carrying cars and passengers. Passenger-only prices for a one-way trip cost up to £82 according to the season, cars (with an obligatory seat reservation) from £229–378. Details and tickets are available from most travel agents or direct from Brittany Ferries.

An alternative, but pricier, route is the ferry from **Portsmouth to Bilbão**, also in northern Spain. There are twice-weekly crossings and the journey takes 35 hours. Passenger-only prices start at £100 single and £185 return (both include a cabin). With a car, fares start from £245 single and £460 return, for four people. Details and tickets are available from P&O.

GETTING THERE FROM IRELAND

Summer charter flights to Faro are easy to pick up from either Dublin or Belfast, while year-round scheduled services operate to Lisbon, usually via London or Manchester.

TAP has direct **scheduled flights** in the summer only from Dublin to Lisbon and Faro starting from £IR225; all BA flights to Portugal (services to Lisbon, Oporto and Faro) are from Belfast via London with high-season fares starting from £IR291. Summer **charters** from Dublin to Faro cost around £IR200 return. Or you can fly from Belfast to Faro for around IR£250 return. Taking a package holiday may cut costs, although one week's villa or hotel holiday in the Algarve costs from around £IR400 (from Dublin) or IR£500 (from

---

USEFUL ADDRESSES IN IRELAND

AIRLINES

Aer Lingus Northern Ireland reservations (☎0645/737 747); 40–41 O'Connell St, Dublin 1; 13 St Stephen's Green, Dublin 2; 12 Upper St George's St, Dun Laoghaire (centralized reservations at Dublin airport ☎01/705 3333); 2 Academy St, Cork (☎021/327 155); 136 O'Connell St, Limerick (☎061/474 239); Minicom/Text telephone ☎01/705 3994.

British Airways 1 Fountain Centre, College St, Belfast BT1 6ET (reservations ☎0345/222 111, bookings and travel agency services ☎0345/326

566). BA does not have a Dublin office; Aer Lingus acts as their agents (reservations ☎1800/626 747).

British Midland Northern Ireland reservations ☎0345/554 554; Nutley, Merrion Rd, Dublin 4 (☎01/283 8833).

Ryanair Phoenix House, Conyngham Rd, Dublin 8 (☎01/609 7800, flight information ☎1550/200 200).

TAP (Air Portugal) 1st Floor, 54 Dawson St, Dublin 2 (☎01/679 8844).

SPECIALIST AGENTS AND TOUR OPERATORS

Abbey Travel 44–45 Middle Abbey St, Dublin 1 (☎01/872 4188). *City breaks to Lisbon.*

Joe Walsh Tours 34 Grafton St, Dublin 2 (☎01/671 8751); 69 Upper O'Connell St, Dublin 2 (☎01/872 2555); 8–11 Baggot St, Dublin 2 (☎01/676 3053); 117 St Patrick St, Cork (☎021/ 277 959). *General budget fares agent.*

Neenan Travel 12 South Leinster St, Dublin 2 (☎01/676 5181; email gk@neenan.sprint.com). *Portuguese city break specialists.*

Selective Travel 146 Lisburn Road, Belfast BT9 6AJ (☎01232/663 303). *Specialists in charter flights from Belfast.*

Trailfinders 4–5 Dawson St, Dublin 2 (☎01/677 7888). *Competitive fares out of all Irish airports,*

as well as deals on hotels, insurance, tours and car rental worldwide.

Travel Shop 35 Belmont Rd, Belfast (☎01232/471 717). *Offers packages and flight-onlys to the Algarve, as well as city breaks to Lisbon.*

USIT Fountain Centre, College St, Belfast BT1 6ET (☎01232/324 073); 10–11 Market Parade, Patrick St, Cork (☎021/270 900); 33 Ferryquay St, Derry (☎01504/371 888); 19 Aston Quay, Dublin 2 (☎01/602 1600 or 679 8833); Victoria Place, Eyre Square, Galway (☎091/565 177); Central Buildings, O'Connell St, Limerick (☎061/415 064); 36–37 Georges St, Waterford (☎051/872 601). *Student and youth specialists for flights and trains.*

Belfast). If you book for two weeks, it can work out cheaper.

If you're really trying to get there in the cheapest possible way, you might find budget flights from Dublin (with Ryanair, Aer Lingus and British Midland) or from Belfast (British Airways and British Midland) to London, plus a last-minute London–Faro charter flight, will save you a few pounds, but don't count on it. Buying a Eurotrain ticket from Dublin to London will slightly undercut the plane's price, but by this time you're starting to talk about a journey of days and not hours.

GETTING THERE FROM NORTH AMERICA

Flying to Portugal directly from the US is more feasible than it used to be. TAP (the Portuguese national airline) has a range of flights available, while deals and routes have opened up in general. However, at present, there are no direct flights from Canada to Portugal. Most scheduled and charter flights originate in New York or Montréal, and you'll generally do best to buy an add-on ticket to one of these "gateway" cities.

Until quite recently, travellers from North America were better off buying a flight to Spain and then making their own way to Portugal by train or bus. But with more competition on the US/Portugal route, particularly since Contintental entered the market in 1997, this is now no longer the case. Similarly, where once you might have made substantial savings (particularly on flights from Canada) by taking a scheduled flight to London and picking up a British charter flight to Portugal, there are now competitive charter carriers serving the US (Azores Express and Suntrips) and Canada (Sata Express, Lawson Tours and Munditravel).

If you're making Portugal part of a longer European trip, you may want to check out details of the Eurail pass, which must be purchased in advance of your arrival and can get you by train to Portugal from anywhere in Europe (see "European rail passes" on p.12 for details).

SHOPPING FOR TICKETS

Discounted tickets aside, the cheapest way to go is with an **Apex** (Advance Purchase Excursion) ticket, although this carries certain restrictions: you'll most likely have to book – and pay – 21 days before departure, be restricted as to the time you spend abroad (minimum seven days, maximum three months, must include a Saturday night, etc) and face penalties if you change your schedule. There are also winter **Super Apex** tickets, sometimes known as "Eurosavers" – slightly cheaper than an ordinary Apex, but limiting your stay to between 7 and 21 days. Some airlines issue **Special Apex** tickets to those under 24, often extending the maximum stay to a year. It's worth looking in the newspapers for any limited offers from the major carriers. The catch with these, apart from the usual Apex restrictions, is that you often have only a small window of time to make your bookings, which may be several months before departure.

The discount outlets advertised in Sunday newspaper travel sections, such as that in the *New York Times*, can usually do better than any Apex fare. They come in several forms. **Consolidators** buy up large blocks of tickets that airlines don't think they'll be able to sell at their published fares, and sell them at a discount. Besides being cheap, consolidators normally don't impose advance purchase requirements (although in busy times you'll want to book ahead to be sure of getting a ticket), but they do often

USEFUL ADDRESSES IN NORTH AMERICA

AIRLINES

Air Canada (in Canada call ☎800/555-1212 for local toll-free number). *Flies from Toronto and Montréal to Lisbon (via Paris or Frankfurt).*

Air France (☎800/237-2747). *Flies from many cities to Paris and then on to Lisbon, Porto and various Spanish destinations.*

British Airways (☎800/247-9297; in Canada, ☎800/668-1059). *Flies from many cities to London, with connections to Lisbon, Faro and Porto and Spanish cities.*

Continental Airlines (☎800/231-0856). *Daily flights from Newark, NJ to Lisbon.*

Delta Airlines (☎800/241-4141). *New York (JFK) and Newark to Lisbon.*

Iberia (☎800/772-4642). *Flights from many cities to Madrid, with connections to Lisbon, Porto and Spanish cities.*

KLM (☎800/374-7747). *Flights, via Amsterdam, to Lisbon, Porto and Spanish cities.*

Lufthansa (☎800/645-3880). *Flights from many cities to Lisbon, Porto, Faro and Spain, all via Frankfurt.*

Sabena (☎800/955-2000). *Flights from East Coast cities to Brussels and on to Lisbon, Porto and Spain.*

TAP (Air Portugal) (☎800/221-7370). *Daily flights from New York (JFK) or Newark to Lisbon with connections to Porto, Faro, Madeira and the Azores. Wednesday and Friday from Boston to Lisbon via the Azores.*

TWA (☎800/892-4141). *Flies daily from New York to Lisbon with connections from many US cities.*

CHARTER CARRIERS

Note that some charter companies will accept bookings only through a travel agent.

Azores Express (☎800/762-9995). *All year round from Boston to the Azores and on to Lisbon in the summer.*

Lawson Tours (☎416/977-3000). *From Toronto and Montréal.*

Munditravel (☎800/387-0365; 416/525-9198). *From Toronto and Montréal.*

Sata Express (☎800/387-0365; 416/515-7188). *From Toronto and Montréal.*

Suntrips (☎800/786-8747). *Daily flights from LA/San Francisco to Lisbon.*

CONSOLIDATORS, DISCOUNT AGENTS AND TRAVEL CLUBS

Council Travel Head Office, 205 E 42nd St, New York, NY 10017 (☎800/226-8624; 888/COUNCIL; 212/822-2700). Other branches at: 530 Bush St, Suite 700, San Francisco, CA 94108 (☎415/421-3473); 10904 Lindbrook Drive, Los Angeles, CA 90024 (☎310/208-3551); 1138 13th St, Boulder, CO 80302 (☎303/447-8101); 3300 M St NW, 2nd Floor, Washington, DC 20007 (☎202/337-6464); 1153 N Dearborn St, Chicago, IL 60610 (☎312/951-0585); 273 Newbury St, Boston, MA 02116 (☎617/266-1926). *Nationwide US organization. specializing in student travel.*

Encore Travel Club 4501 Forbes Blvd, Lanham, MD 20706 (☎800/444-9800). *East Coast travel club.*

Interworld 800 Douglass Rd, Miami, FL 33134 (☎800/468-3796; 305/443-4929). *Southeastern US consolidator.*

Moment's Notice 7301 New Utrecht Ave, Brooklyn, NY 11204 (☎718/234-6295; 212/486-0500). *Discount travel club.*

New Frontiers/Nouvelles Frontières 12 E 33rd St, New York, NY 10016 (☎800/366-6387; 212/779-0600); 1001 Sherbrook East, Suite 720, Montréal, PQ H2L 1L3 (☎514/526-8444). *French discount travel firm. Other branches in LA, San Francisco and Quebec City.*

STA Travel 10 Downing St, New York, NY 10014 (☎800/777-0112; 212/627-3111); 7202 Melrose Ave, Los Angeles, CA 90046 (☎213/934-8722); 51 Grant Ave, San Francisco, CA 94108 (☎415/391-8407); 297 Newbury St, Boston, MA 02115 (☎617/266-6014); 429 S Dearborn St, Chicago, IL 60605 (☎312/786-9050); 3730 Walnut St, Philadelphia, PA 19104 (☎215/382-2928); 317 14th Ave SE, Minneapolis, MN 55414 (☎612/615-1800). *Worldwide specialists in independent travel.*

Travac 989 6th Ave, New York, NY 10018 (☎800/872-8800). *Consolidator and charter broker.*

Travel Avenue 10 S Riverside, Suite 1404, Chicago, IL 60606 (☎800/333-3335). *Discount travel agent.*

Travel Cuts 187 College St, Toronto, ON M5T 1P7 (☎800/667-2887; 888/238-2887 from US; 416/979-2406); 180 MacEwan Student Centre, University of Calgary, Calgary, AB T2N 1N4 (☎403/282-7687); 12304 Jasper Av, Edmonton, AB T5N 3K5 (☎403/488-8487); 1613 Rue St Denis, Montréal, PQ H2X 3K3 (☎514/843-8511);

555 W 8th Ave, Vancouver, BC V5Z 1C6 (☎888 FLY CUTS; 604/822-6890); University Centre, University of Manitoba, Winnipeg, MB R3T 2N2 (☎204/269-9530). *Canadian student travel organization.*

Travelers Advantage 3033 S Parker Rd, Suite 900, Aurora, CO 80014 (☎800/548-1116). *Discount travel club.*

Unitravel 1177 N Warson Rd, St Louis, MO 63132 (☎800/325-2222). *Consolidator.*

Worldwide Discount Travel Club 1674 Meridian Ave, Miami Beach, FL 33139 (☎305/534-2082). *Discount travel club.*

TOUR OPERATORS

Abercrombie and Kent 1520 Kensington Rd, Oak Brook, IL 60523 (☎800/323-7308). *Upmarket joint tours of Portugal and Spain.*

Abreu Tours 25 W 45th St, New York, NY 10036 (☎800/223-1580). *Pousada bookings, tailor-made holidays and set land/air packages.*

Altamira Tours 860 Detroit St, Denver, CO 80206 (☎800/747-2869). *Specialists in food and wine tours.*

American Express Vacations PO Box 1525, Fort Lauderdale, FA 33301 (☎800/241-1700). *Land/air packages.*

Backroads 801 Cedar St, Berkeley, CA 94710 (☎800/462-2848). *Combined Spain/Portugal cycling tours.*

Contiki Holidays 300 Plaza Alicante, Suite 900, Garden Grove, CA (☎800/CONTIKI). *Spain/Portugal coach tours for under-35s.*

Different Strokes Tours 1841 Broadway, New York, NY 10023 (☎800/668-3301). *Customized tour service for gay/lesbian travellers.*

Elderhostel 75 Federal St, Boston, MA 02110 (☎617/426-8056). *Specialists in educational and activity programmes, cruises and homestays for senior travellers. Spain and Portugal combinations.*

Euro-Bike Tours PO Box 990, De Kald, IL 60115 (☎800/321-6060). *Cycling tours of Spain and Portugal.*

Europe Through the Back Door 120 4th Ave N, PO Box 2009, Edmonds, WA 98020 (☎206/771-8303). *Excellent travel club which publishes a regular newsletter packed full of travel tales and advice, sells its own guides and travel accessories, Eurail passes, and runs good-value bus tours to Spain and Portugal.*

Globus and Cosmos 5301 South Federal Circle, Littleton, CO 80123 (☎800/221-0090). *Offers a*

twelve-day motor-coach sightseeing tour "Portugal In Depth". Bookable through travel agents only.*

Gogo Worldwide Vacations 69 Spring St, Ramsey, NJ 07446. *City breaks, fly-drives, pousada holidays all over Portugal. Bookings through travel agents only.*

Golf International 275 Madison Ave, New York, NY 10016 (☎800/833-1389). *Customized golfing holidays and packages.*

Homeric Tours 55 E59th St, New York, NY 10022 (☎800/223-5570; 212/753-1100). *Customized tours and packages. Lisbon city breaks and programmes geared to Expo 98.*

Maupintour 1515 St. Andrews Drive, Lawrence, KS 66047 (☎800/255-6162). *Fifteen-day pousadas and paradors tour of the western Iberian peninsula.*

Mountain Travel-Sobek 6420 Fairmount Ave, El Cerrito, CA 94530 (☎888/MT SOBEK; 800/227-2384). *Ten days, easy kayaking, luxury hotel/farm inn/manor house accommodation.*

Odyssey Adventures 537 Chestnut St, Cedarhurst, NY 11516 (☎800/344-0013). *Customized tours and a wide range of packages featuring trekking, fishing, surfing, historical and religious programmes.*

Paragon Travel 100 East Broad St, Palmyra, NJ 08065 (☎888/783-3552; 609/786-6969). *City breaks, fly-drives, pousadas, manor houses, spas, cruises and open hotel vouchers.*

Petrabax Tours 9745 Queens Blvd, Rego Park, NY 11374 (☎800/634-1188). *Customized tours plus a variety of set packages.*

Portuguese Tours 321 Rahway Ave, Elizabeth, NJ 07202 (☎800/526-4047). *Customized tours.*

charge very stiff fees for date changes. Also, these companies' margins are tiny, so they make their money by dealing in volume – don't expect them to entertain lots of questions. **Discount agents** also wheel and deal in blocks of tickets offloaded by the airlines, but they typically offer a range of other travel-related services such as travel insurance, rail passes, youth and student ID cards, car rental, tours, and the like. These agencies tend to be most worthwhile to students and under-26s, who can often benefit from special fares and deals. **Travel clubs** are another option for those who travel a lot – most charge an annual membership fee, which may be worth it for discounts on air tickets and car rental.

Regardless of where you buy your ticket, the fare will depend on the season. **Fares** to Portugal are highest from June to mid-August; they drop during the "shoulder" seasons (mid-Sept to Oct & mid-March to May and the ten days or so before Christmas), and you'll get the best deals during the low season, November to early December and just after Christmas to mid-March. Note that flying on weekends ordinarily adds $50–70 to the return fare.

Prices quoted in the sections below assume midweek travel, exclude taxes and are subject to change.

FLIGHTS FROM THE US

TAP (the Portuguese national airline), **Delta** (in a code-sharing agreement with TAP), **TWA** and **Continental** are the operators of direct scheduled flights to Lisbon. TAP also offers flights to Porto, Faro, Madeira and the Azores (all via Lisbon). In addition it has a scheduled service between Boston and Lisbon, with a stop at Ponta Delgada in the Azores.

Iberia flies to Porto (via Madrid), and also to Santiago de Compostela in northwestern Spain, just a couple of hours by car or train from the Portuguese border. Several other European carriers fly to Lisbon and on to Porto and Faro via their respective capitals. However, given the competitive nature of the business, you'll find little if any difference in fares.

FROM EASTERN AND CENTRAL USA

With the exception of the limited offers that appear every now and then, TAP's cheapest return Apex fare **from New York or Boston** to Lisbon is currently $606 in low season, $760 in shoulder season and $904 in high season; fares to Porto and Faro (via Lisbon, but allowing no stopovers) are $60–65 more. **From Miami or Chicago** you can expect to pay an extra $100 and **from Houston** $160. Booking through a discount agent, you may be able to get low-season fares to Lisbon for as little as $408 (from New York) or $558 (from Chicago). The **flight time** from New York/Newark to Lisbon is 6 hours 40 minutes and from Lisbon to Porto or Faro, between 30 and 45 minutes.

FROM THE WEST COAST

All flights to Portugal from the West Coast involve changing planes, either in New York or somewhere in Europe. **From Los Angeles**, **San Francisco** or **Seattle** TAP (using feeder flights on other carriers to get to New York) adds $250 onto its fares from New York (see above). **From Denver** the extra cost is $200. A discount agent may find you a low-season Los Angeles to Lisbon fare for around $658.

FROM CANADA

There are no direct flights from Canada to Portugal, but Air Canada will fly you to Lisbon in conjunction with one of several European airlines, connecting in London, Paris, Frankfurt. Air Canada fares **from Toronto** and **Montréal** range from CDN$838 (low season) to CDN$1184 (high season); **from Vancouver** CDN$1111 (low) to CDN$1552 (high). A discount travel agent, however, might be able to find you a charter flight for as little as CDN$899 (from Toronto, high season) or CDN$1384 (from Vancouver, high season).

EUROPEAN RAIL PASSES

Eurail passes are only really worth looking into if you're intending to visit Portugal as part of a longer trip to Europe as you'll find it difficult to get your money's worth on a short trip to Portugal alone. The passes, which must be purchased before arrival in Europe, allow unlimited free train travel for specified periods of time in seventeen European countries and come in various forms.

The **Eurail Youthpass** (for under-26s) costs $365 for 15 days, $475 for 21 days, $587 for one month or $832 for two months; if you're 26 or over you'll have to buy a first-class pass, available in 15-day ($522), 21-day ($678), one-month ($838), two-month ($1188) and three-month ($1468) formats. You stand a better chance of getting your money's worth out of a Eurail **Flexipass**, which is good for a certain number of travel days in a two-month period. This, too, comes in under-26 and first-class versions: 10 days for $431/$616; and 15 days for $568/$812. Alternatively, the more specific **Portuguese Railpass** (see "Getting around" p.26) allows 4 days' travel out of 15 ($99, all ages). All these passes can be purchased through Rail Europe, 226 Westchester Ave, White Plains, NY 10604 (☎800/438-7245; Web site: *http://www.raileurope.com*) or youth-oriented travel agents (see p.10).

GETTING THERE FROM AUSTRALIA & NEW ZEALAND

There are no direct flights to Portugal from Australia or New Zealand, but changing planes a couple of times can get you there within 24 hours, via stopovers in Europe, Asia or the Pacific.

Currently, the cheapest **scheduled flights to Lisbon** are via Asia, with Garuda-Alitalia offering the best price. For a little more, there are the options of KLM, Air France, Singapore Airlines and Aeroflot, all of which fly via their home bases. More expensive but offering extras such as free onward travel to Lisbon from other European cities, fly-drive packages and stopover en route are Japan Airlines, Thai Airways, Cathay Pacific, Qantas and British Airways. Alternatively, you can find a rock-bottom fare to Amsterdam, London or other European hub city and then either pick up a cheap charter flight or travel overland by road (see p.7) or rail (see "European rail passes" on p.12). However, with the high living and transport costs in northwestern Europe, this rarely works out any cheaper in practice. **Round-the-World** (RTW) tickets (valid for a year) are a better choice; they are usually priced according to the

number of stopovers you make, but extras are not always expensive. Cathay Pacific-UA's "Globetrotter", Air New Zealand-KLM-Northwest's "World Navigator" and Qantas-BA's "Global Explorer" all offer six stopovers worldwide (including Lisbon), limited backtracking, and additional stopovers (around $120 each), from A$2499–3199/NZ$3089–3599.

Fares to Portugal vary according to the seasons which break down as follows: high season (mid-May to end-Aug & Dec to mid-Jan); shoulder season (March to mid-May & Sept); and low season (rest of the year). However, seasons vary slightly depending on the airline. You can expect to pay about A$400–600 more for high-season fares. Tickets purchased direct from the airlines tend to be expensive; you'll get much better deals on fares from your local **travel agent** (see box on p.15) as well as the latest information on limited specials, fly-drive, accommodation packages, stopovers en route and round-the-world fares. Some of the best discounts are through **Flight Centres** and **STA** (for students and under-26s), who can also advise on visa regulations. Seat availability on most international flights out of Australia and New Zealand is often limited so it's best to book at least three weeks ahead.

FROM AUSTRALIA

All the fares quoted below are from eastern Australian cities. Flights from Perth and Darwin via Asia are A$200-400 less.

Currently the lowest scheduled return fares to Lisbon are offered by Garuda-Alitalia flying three times weekly via Jakarta and Rome, at around A$1550 (low season) to A$2030 (high season). Other good options are KLM, which flies daily via Singapore and Amsterdam for A$1700–2410, and Aeroflot via Singapore and Moscow for

AIRLINES IN AUSTRALIA AND NEW ZEALAND

Aeroflot 24/44 Market St, Sydney (☎02/9262 2233). *Flights to Lisbon from Australia via Singapore and Moscow.*

Air France 12 Castlereagh St, Sydney (☎02/9321 1000); 2/143 Nelson St, Auckland (☎09/303 3521). *Daily from Sydney to Lisbon via Singapore and Paris.*

Air New Zealand, 5 Elizabeth St, Sydney (☎13 2476); 139 Queen St, Auckland (☎09/357 3000). *Daily flights to London via LA.*

Alitalia 32 Bridge St, Sydney (☎02/9247 1308); 6/229 Queen St Auckland (☎09/379 4457). *Three flights a week to Lisbon via a transfer in Rome from Sydney, Melbourne, Brisbane, Perth and Auckland: code share with Qantas/Cathay Pacific for the first leg.*

Britannia Airways 6/210 George St, Sydney (☎02/9251 1299). *Several flights per month (during their charter season Nov–April) from Sydney, Brisbane, Cairns and Auckland to London Gatwick and once a week to Manchester via Bangkok and Abu Dhabi.*

British Airways Level 26, 201 Kent St, Sydney (☎02/9258 3300 or 1-800 251 321); 154 Queen St, Auckland (☎09/356 8690). *Daily to London from Sydney with onward connections to Lisbon.*

Cathay Pacific 12/8 Spring St, Sydney (☎13 1747); 11/205 Queen St, Auckland (☎09/379 0861). *Several flights a week from major Australasian cities to Paris via Hong Kong. Onward connections to Lisbon.*

Garuda 55 Hunter St, Sydney (☎02/9334 9944 or 1-800 800 873); 120 Albert St, Auckland (☎09/366 1855). *Three times a week from Brisbane, Sydney, Perth and Auckland to Paris and twice weekly to Paris via Rome with a transfer in Jakarta or Denpasar: link with Alitalia for onward travel to Lisbon from Rome.*

Japan Airlines 14/201 Sussex St, Sydney (☎02/9272 1111); 12/120 Albert St, Auckland (☎09/379 9906). *Flies several times a week from Sydney, Brisbane, Cairns and Auckland to Tokyo*

and then onto Madrid (with overland connection to Lisbon); includes an overnight stop in Tokyo or Osaka.

KLM 5 Elizabeth St, Sydney (☎02/9231 6333 or 1-800/222 747). No NZ office. *Twice weekly to Faro and daily to Lisbon via Amsterdam from Sydney.*

Lauda Air/Lufthansa 11/143 Macquarie St, Sydney (☎02/9251 6155 or 9367 3888); 36 Kitchener St, Auckland (☎09/303 1529). *Several flights a week from Sydney, Brisbane and Melbourne to Vienna with onward connections to destinations in Portugal; use the free flight coupons (unalterable and must be booked with the main ticket).*

Malaysia Airlines 16 Spring St, Sydney (☎13 2627); 12/12 Swanson St, Auckland (☎09/373 2741). *Twice weekly, to Madrid via Kuala Lumpur and Istanbul, from Brisbane, Sydney, Melbourne, Perth and Auckland.*

Qantas 70 Hunter St, Sydney (☎13 1211); 154 Queen St, Auckland (☎09/357 8900 or 0800/808 767). *Three times a week from Auckland via Rome to Madrid with onward connections to Lisbon.*

TAP (Air Portugal) Mezzanine Level, 261 George St, Sydney (☎02/9221 8011). No NZ office. *Connecting flights from Singapore and Bangkok as well as most European gateway cities to Lisbon and other destinations in Portugal.*

Singapore Airlines 17 Bridge St, Sydney (☎13 1011); corner of Albert St & Fanshawe St, Auckland (☎09/379 3209). *Code share with TAP to provide daily service to Lisbon via Singapore and Frankfurt from Sydney, Melbourne, Brisbane, Perth and Auckland.*

Thai Airways 75 Pitt St, Sydney ☎13 1960; 22 Fanshawe St, Auckland (☎09/377 3886). *Three flights a week to London, Paris and Madrid, via Bangkok, from Sydney, Melbourne, Brisbane, Perth and Auckland. Onward connections to Lisbon.*

A\$1870–2120. For a little more – A\$1899 (low season), A\$2510 (high season) – Singapore Airlines-TAP (Air Portugal) flies several times a week via Singapore and Frankfurt, while daily Air France flights via Bangkok and Paris start from A\$2150.

More expensive (starting at A\$\$2399) but offering extras such as free onward flights to Lisbon from other European cities, fly-drive packages and stopover en route are British Airways and Qantas flying via Bangkok or Singapore to London, and Cathay Pacific flying via Hong Kong

DISCOUNT AGENTS AND SPECIALIST OPERATORS

DISCOUNT AGENTS

Anywhere Travel 345 Anzac Parade, Kingsford, Sydney (☎02/9663 0411).

Brisbane Discount Travel 260 Queen St, Brisbane (☎07/3229 9211).

Budget Travel 16 Fort St, Auckland, plus branches around the city (☎09/366 0061 or 0800/808 040).

Destinations Unlimited 3 Milford Rd, Auckland (☎09/373 4033).

Flight Centres Australia: 82 Elizabeth St, Sydney, plus branches nationwide (☎13 1600). New Zealand: 205 Queen St, Auckland (☎09/309 6171), plus branches nationwide. *Good discounts on fares.*

Northern Gateway 22 Cavenagh St, Darwin (☎08/8941 1394).

STA Travel Australia: 702 Harris St, Ultimo, Sydney; 256 Flinders St, Melbourne; other offices in state capitals and major universities (nearest branch ☎13 1776, fastfare telesales ☎1300/360 960). New Zealand: 10 High St, Auckland (☎09/309 0458, fastfare telesales ☎09/366 6673), plus branches in Wellington, Christchurch, Dunedin, Palmerston North, Hamilton and at major universities. email: *traveller@statravelaus.com.au*; Web site: *http://www.statravelaus.com.au*). *Fare discounts for students and under-26s.*

Thomas Cook Australia: 175 Pitt St, Sydney; 257 Collins St, Melbourne; plus branches in other state capitals (local branch ☎13 1771, Thomas Cook Direct telesales ☎1800/063 913). New Zealand: 96 Anzac Ave, Auckland (☎09/379 3920). *Travellers' cheques, bus and rail passes.*

SPECIALIST OPERATORS

Adventure Specialists 69 Liverpool St, Sydney (☎02/9261 2927). *Offers a selection of adventure holidays in Portugal.*

Adventure World 73 Walker St, North Sydney (☎02/9956 7766 or 1800/221 931), plus branches in Brisbane and Perth; 101 Great South Rd, Remuera, Auckland (☎09/524 5118). *Agents for rambles through "Vinho Verde" country.*

CIT Ground Floor, 123 Clarence Street, Sydney (☎02/9299 4754). *City tours and accommodation packages.*

European Travel Office 122 Rosslyn St, West Melbourne (☎03/9329 8844); 407 Great South Road, Penrose, Auckland (☎09/525 3074). *A*

wide selection of tours and accommodation from hotels to country inns, palaces and monasteries.

Exodus Expeditions Suite 5, Level 5, 1 York St, Sydney (☎02/925 5430 or 1800/800 724); book through *Adventure World* in New Zealand (☎09/524 5118). *Tours such as eight days in the Alentejo by mule, on foot and by minibus from Faro.*

Peregrine 258 Lonsdale St, Melbourne (☎03/9663 8611), plus offices in Brisbane, Sydney, Adelaide and Perth. *Guided and independent walking and cycling holidays in Portugal.*

Ya'lla Tours 1st Floor, West Tower, 608 St Kilda Rd, Melbourne (☎03/9510 2844). *Holidays to Portugal and other European destinations.*

---

to Paris. One of the best deals is with Japan Airlines which takes you as far as Madrid (from where you continue overland), with an overnight stop in Tokyo or Osaka included for A$1969–2499.

Another option is to look around for a bargain fare to a European hub city from where you can shop around for a cheap charter flight to Portugal. Currently the cheapest are to London – Britannia Airways flies several times a month during their charter season (Nov–April) via Singapore and Abu Dhabi. Low-season fares start at A$1299, going up to A$1899 in high season.

Via the US the best deals to Lisbon are with United Airlines-TAP which offers a through connecting service via LA and New York for A$2299–2899.

FLIGHTS FROM NEW ZEALAND

Most flights to Lisbon are out of **Auckland** (fares from Christchurch and Wellington are NZ$150–300 more) with the cheapest fares offered by Garuda-Alitalia, flying via Jakarta or Denpasar and Rome, for NZ$2110–2420. Singapore Airlines and TAP also fly several times a week from Auckland for around NZ$2605–3250. British

Airways and Air New Zealand fly daily via LA to London for NZ$2800–3500, with onward flights to Lisbon on BA included in the price.

Alternatively, you can pick up a rock-bottom flight to another European city and then look around for a cheap charter flight to Lisbon – one of the best deals is offered by Britannia Airways which runs several times a month from Auckland to London during their charter season (Nov–April) for NZ$1450–2150.

As with Australia the best deals to Lisbon via the US are with United Airlines starting at NZ$2599.

EUROPEAN RAIL PASSES

If you're planning to visit Portugal as an extension to a European trip it's worth looking into one of a variety of **Eurail** passes, which are valid in seventeen European countries. The **Eurail Youthpass** (for under-26s) costs A$485/NZ$580 for 15 days, A$635/NZ$856 for 21 days, A$785/NZ$932 for one month or A$1110/NZ$1259 for two months; if you're 26 or over you'll have to buy a **first-class pass**, available in 15-day A$695/NZ$829, 21-day

---

RAIL CONTACTS IN AUSTRALASIA

CIT 123 Clarence St, Sydney (☎02/9299 4754); other branches in Melbourne, Brisbane, Adelaide and Perth. No NZ office; all enquiries via Australian offices.

Thomas Cook Rail Direct Australia (☎1300/361 941); New Zealand (☎09/263 7260).

A$905/NZ$1077, one-month A$1115/NZ$1331, two-month A$1585/NZ$1795 and three-month A$1955/NZ$2165 increments.

Eurail Flexipass is good for a certain number of travel days in a two-month period and also comes in youth/first-class versions: 10 days cost A$575/820, NZ$685/978; and 15 days, A$755/1085, NZ$902/1289. A scaled-down version of the Flexipass, the **Europass** allows travel in France, Germany, Italy, Spain and Switzerland for (youth/first-class) A$280/420, NZ$334/502 for 5 days in 2 months, on up to A$665/980, NZ$794/1169 for 15 days in 2 months with the option of adding Portugal as an "associate" country. See the box above for relevant addresses.

RED TAPE AND VISAS

Citizens of the European Union need only a valid passport or identity card for entry to Portugal, and can stay indefinitely. Australian and New Zealand nationals can stay up to ninety days on production of a passport; American and Canadian nationals can stay up to sixty days.

An **extension** to your stay can be arranged once you're in the country. They are issued by the nearest District Police headquarters or the Foreigner's Registration Service (Rua Conselheiro José Silvestre Ribeiro 4, 1600 Lisbon; ☎01/714 10 27) which has branch offices – Serviço de Estrangeiros e Fronteiras – in most major tourist centres. You should apply at least a week before your time runs out and be prepared to prove that you can support yourself without working (for example by keeping your bank exchange forms every time you change money). One well-used way around the bureaucracy is simply to leave the country for a couple of days and get a new sixty- or ninety-day stay stamped in your passport when you return.

Visas or extended stay visas are also available through any **Portuguese Consulate** abroad; see below for addresses.

PORTUGUESE CONSULATES AND EMBASSIES ABROAD

Australia Embassy: 23 Culoga Circuit, O'Malley, Canberra (☎02/6290 1733); Consulate, 17 Lefroy Rd, South Fremantle, WA (☎08/9335 9458).

Britain Consulate: 62 Brompton Road, London SW3 1BJ (☎0171/581 8722/8723/8724).

Canada Embassy: 645 Island Park Drive, Ottawa, K1Y 0B8 (☎613/729-2922); for enquiries related to tourism call ☎416/360-8260. Consulates in several other cities.

Ireland Embassy: Knock Sinna House, Fox Rock, Dublin 18 (☎01/289 4416).

Netherlands Embassy: Bazarstraat 21, 2518 AGDEN, Haag (☎010/363 0217).

USA Embassy: 2125 Kalorama Rd NW, Washington, DC 20008 (☎202/328-8610). Consulates in nearly a dozen other cities.

There is no embassy or consulate in New Zealand.

HEALTH AND INSURANCE

No inoculations are required for Portugal, though, as throughout southern Europe, it's a sensible precaution to have a typhoid shot and an up-to-date polio booster. A hepatitis jab is also worth considering, as there have been outbreaks in the past along parts of the coastline around Porto.

Whatever you might hear from hypochondriacs, water is drinkable from the tap anywhere in the country, and from some freshwater sources, too. Be wary, however, of pools and streams in the south of the country. Otherwise, Portugal poses few health problems. **Mosquitoes** can be an intolerable menace at certain times of year and in certain areas, but there seems to be no pattern to this, though the north and the Lisbon coast are often cited as being particularly bad. December and January are usually mosquito-free. Mosquito-repellent lotion and coils are widely sold in towns and resorts.

MEDICAL MATTERS

For minor health complaints in Portugal you should go to a **farmácia** (pharmacy), which you'll find in almost any village; in larger towns there's usually one where English is spoken. Pharmacists are highly trained and can dispense many drugs that would be available only with a prescription in Britain or North America.

In the case of serious illness, you can get the address of an **English-speaking doctor** from a British or American consular office or, with luck, from the local police or tourist office, or a major

hotel. There's a British Hospital in Lisbon (see "Listings", p.106). In an **emergency** dial ☎115 (free).

TRAVEL INSURANCE

As an EU country, Portugal has free recipro-cal health agreements with other member states. To take advantage of this, EU citizens will need form E111, available from main post offices. Reassuring as the EU health agreements may sound, however, some form of travel insurance is still worthwhile – and essential for North Americans and Australasians, who must pay for any med-ical treatment in Portugal.

In many parts of Portugal public health care lags behind much of northern Europe and you may well prefer to get private treatment. With insurance you have to pay on the spot, but will be able to claim back the cost – along with any drugs prescribed by pharmacies. Be sure to keep all your receipts. Travel insurance usually pro-vides cover for your **baggage, money and tick-ets**, too, should they be stolen, though to reclaim from your insurance company you must register any theft with the police within 24 hours.

Before you buy your policy, however, be aware of the cover offered by various **credit card com-panies** for holidays bought on their account; Visa and American Express offer some medical and theft coverage on items and travel arrangements paid for with their cards.

TRAVEL INSURANCE COMPANIES

UK
Campus Travel (see p.4 for full list of branches).
Endsleigh Insurance Cranfield House, 97–107 Southampton Row, London WC1B 4AG (☎0171/436 4451).
Marcus Hearne & Co Ltd 65–66 Shoreditch High Street, London E1 6JL (☎0171/739 3444).
STA (see p.4 for full list of branches).

US
Carefree Travel Insurance PO Box 9366, 100 Garden City Plaza, Garden City, NY 11530 (☎1-800/323-3149).

Travel Assistance International 1133 15th St NW, Suite 400, Washington, DC 20005 (☎1-800/821-2828).
Travel Guard 1145 Clark St, Stevens Point, WI 54481 (☎1-800/826-1300).
Travel Insurance Services 2930 Camino Diablo, Suite 200, Walnut Creek, CA 94596 (☎1-800/937-1387).

AUSTRALASIA
Cover More Level 9, 32 Walker St, North Sydney (☎02/9202 8000).
Ready Plan 141 Walker St, Dandenong, Melbourne (☎03/9791 5077 or 1800/337 462) and 10/ 63 Albert St, Auckland (☎09/379 3208).

If you plan to participate in water sports, or do some hiking, you'll probably have to pay an extra premium; check carefully that any insurance policy you are considering will cover you in case of an accident.

EUROPEAN COVER
In Britain and Ireland, travel insurance schemes are sold by almost every travel agent or bank, and by **specialist insurance companies**. For standard cover, you can expect to pay around £17 for a basic two-week policy covering Portugal, and around £26.50 for a month. Cover varies, but a standard policy will include the cost of cancellation and curtailment of flights, medical expenses, travel delay, accident, missed departures, lost baggage, lost passport, personal liability and legal expenses.

Some insurance companies refuse to cover travellers over 65, or stop at 69 or 74 years of age, and most that do charge hefty premiums. The best policies for **older travellers**, with no upper age limit, are offered by Age Concern (☎01883/346964).

NORTH AMERICAN COVER
North Americans should check on existing cover (including bank and charge card benefits) before buying special travel insurance. For example, **Canadians** are usually covered for medical expenses by their provincial health plans. Holders of **ISIC** student identity cards are entitled to accident coverage and sixty days of hospital in-patient benefits for the period during which the card is valid. **University students** will often find

that their student health coverage extends for one term beyond the date of last enrolment. **Company** plans may take care of most contingencies, and **homeowners' or renters'** insurance may cover overseas theft or loss of documents, money, and valuables.

If, after exhausting the above possibilities, you feel you still need additional travel insurance, your travel agent can recommend a policy. Most offerings are quite comprehensive, though **premiums** vary widely. The policy offered by STA comes with or without medical cover. Rates are $60/$45 (8–15 days); $110/$85 (one month); $165/$130 (two months) and rise by $50/$35 for each extra month. It's worth knowing that policies offered through student/youth agencies are often available to everyone.

If you are travelling for some length of time in Europe, or if you are stopping en route in Britain, it is worth considering taking out a British travel insurance policy, which routinely covers thefts – sometimes excluded from the more health-based American policies.

AUSTRALASIAN COVER
Travel insurance is available from most travel agents or direct from insurance companies, for periods ranging from a few days to a year or even longer. Most policies are similar in premium and coverage. A typical policy covering medical costs, lost baggage and personal liability for Portugal will cost: A$100/NZ$110 for two weeks, A$170/NZ$190 for one month.

TRAVELLERS WITH DISABILITIES

Portugal is slowly coming to terms with the needs of travellers with disabilities, but you should not expect much in the way of special facilities. That said, the Portuguese themselves always seem ready to help and people will go out of their way to make your visit as straightforward as possible.

Facilities that do exist include adapted WCs and wheelchair facilities at airports and main train stations; a "dial-a-ride" system for wheelchair users in Lisbon (call ☎01/363 20 44; two days' notice required); and reserved disabled parking spaces in main cities, where the Orange Badge will be recognized. Portuguese national tourist offices abroad can supply a list of wheelchair-accessible hotels and campsites. Once there, your first port of call in any town should be the local tourist office, which will invariably find you a suitable hotel and, in smaller towns, may be able to organize personally your needs.

For other **information**, contact one of the organizations listed in the box below.

USEFUL ADDRESSES

PORTUGAL

ARAC Rua Dr António Cândido 8, 1097 Lisbon (☎01/56 37 37). *Provides information on hire companies that have cars with adapted controls.*

Secretariado Nacional de Reabilitação Avda. Conde de Valbom 63, 1000 Lisbon (☎01/793 65 17). *Provides information on transport facilities and Lisbon access, but in Portuguese only.*

Wheeling Around the Algarve (Rodando Pelo Algarve) Rua 5 de Outubro 181, Apartado 3421, 8136 Almancil, Algarve (☎089/39 36 36). *Private company organizing holiday accommodation, transport and sporting/leisure activities in the Algarve. All facilities are personally inspected before recommendation.*

BRITAIN

Access Travel 16 Haweswater Ave, Astley, Lancashire M29 7BL (☎01942/888 844, fax 891 811). *Small tour operator able to arrange flights, transfer and accommodation in several countries including Portugal. Accommodation is personally checked before recommendation.*

Holiday Care Service 2nd Floor, Imperial Building, Victoria Rd, Horley, Surrey RH6 9PZ (☎01293/774 535, fax 784 647; Minicom ☎776 943). *Provides free lists of accessible accommodation.*

ICEP 22–25a Sackville St, London W1X 2LY (☎0171/494 1441; 24hr brochure-request line ☎0891/600 370). *Publishes a list of hotels in Portugal that are "without barriers or with few obstacles to wheelchair users".*

RADAR (Royal Association for Disability and Rehabilitation) 12 City Forum, 250 City Rd, London EC1V 8AF (☎0171/250 3222; Minicom ☎250 4119). *A good source of advice on holidays and travel abroad.*

Tripscope The Courtyard, Evelyn Rd, London W4 5JL (☎0181/994 9294, fax 994 3618). *Provides a national telephone information service offering free advice on UK and international transport and travel.*

NORTH AMERICA

Directions Unlimited 720 N Bedford Rd, Bedford Hills, NY 10507 (☎1-800/533-5343). *Tour operator specializing in custom tours for people with disabilities.*

Mobility International USA Box 10767, Eugene, OR 97440 (Voice & TDD ☎541/343-1284). *Information, access guides, tours and exchange programmes. Annual membership $25 (includes quarterly newsletter).*

Society for the Advancement of Travel for the Handicapped (SATH) 347 Fifth Ave, New York, NY 10016 (☎212/447-7284). *Non-profit travel industry referral service that passes queries on to its members as appropriate.*

Travel Information Service (☎215/456-9600). *Telephone-only information service and referral service.*

AUSTRALIA

ACROD (Australian Council for Rehabilitation of the Disabled), PO Box 60, Curtin, ACT 2605 (☎02/6282 4333).

NEW ZEALAND

Disabled Persons Assembly 173–175 Victoria St, Wellington (☎04/811 9100).

INFORMATION AND MAPS

You can pick up a wide range of brochures and maps, for free, from the Portuguese National Tourist Office (see p.21 for addresses). Though some of their descriptions are best taken with a pinch of salt, it is well worth contacting one of their offices for information before you leave home.

In Portugal itself you'll find a tourist office, or **turismo**, in almost every town and village of any size. Most are detailed in the guide and are usually helpful and friendly. Aside from the help they can give you in finding a room (some will make bookings, others simply supply lists), they often have useful local maps and leaflets that you won't find in the national offices. **Opening hours** are given after each office in the text but don't be surprised if you find them closed when they should be open – times of opening are often totally dependent on staff available, especially in small towns and villages.

MAPS

The Portuguese National Tourist Office and the turismos in larger towns can provide you with a

---

PORTUGAL ON THE INTERNET

Escudos daily exchange rate
http://www.wiso.gwdg.de/ifbg/currency.html

Expo 98
http://www.expo98.pt
Up-to-date information on the site and events in English.

ICEP (Investments, Trade and Tourism of Portugal)
http://www.portugal.org
Run by the government agency responsible for promoting Portugal abroad, this site contains information on tourist attractions, sport and culture. Also has links to accommodation agencies, businesses, etc.

Jornal de Notícias
http://www.jnoticias.pt
Digital version of the established Portuguese daily.

Portugal for Travellers
http://nervo.com/pt
General information and practical advice on visiting Portugal, including a useful link to the latest
weather forecasts. "Traveller's Corner" features first-hand accounts sent in by recent visitors to the country.

Público
http://www.publico.pt
Digital version of one of Portugal's most popular daily national newspapers.

Solares de Portugal (formerly Turihab)
http://www.sidra.pt/turihab
On-line brochure with photographs and details of over ninety properties belonging to the scheme, ranging from simple farmhouses to former palaces. Full booking details.

The News
http://www.nexus-pt.com/news
Portugal's national English-language newspaper on-line. The site also features "Esc to Portugal" – the country's first English-language magazine on the Net.

Yahoo!: Portugal
http://www.yahoo.com/Regional_Information/Countries/Portugal/

PORTUGUESE TOURIST OFFICES ABROAD

Australia Portuguesa Agencia, 17 Lefroy Rd, South Fremantle (☎08/9335 9503).

Britain 2nd Floor, 22/25a Sackville Street, London W1X 1DE (☎0171/494 1441, fax 494 1868).

Canada 60 Bloor St West, Suite 1005, Toronto, Ontario, M4W 3B8 (☎1416/921-4925 or 7376, fax 921-1353).

Ireland 54 Dawson Street, Dublin 2 (☎01/660-1711, fax 660-8853).

Netherlands Paul Gabriëlstraat 70, 2596 VG Den Haag (☎070/326 4371, fax 328 0025).

Spain Gran Via 27-1, Madrid 28013 (☎91/522 4408, fax 522 2382); Calle Bruc 50-4a, 08010 Barcelona (☎03/301 4416, fax 318 5068); c/Asunción 84–11°D, Edificio Presidente Portal B1, 41011 Seville (☎05/428 4910, fax 428 4793).

USA 590 Fifth Avenue, 4th Floor, New York, NY10036 (☎212/354 4403, fax 764 6137); 1900 L Street NW, Suite 310, Washington, DC 20036 (☎202/331 8222, fax 331 8236).

There are no offices in New Zealand.

MAP OUTLETS IN THE UK

London Daunt Books, 83 Marylebone High St, W1M 3DE (☎0171/224 2295); 193 Haverstock Hill, NW3 4QL (☎0171/794 4006); National Map Centre, 22–24 Caxton St, SW1H 0QU (☎0171/222 2466); Stanfords, 12–14 Long Acre, WC2E 9LP (☎0171/836 1321; maps by mail or phone order are available on this number); The

Travel Bookshop, 13–15 Blenheim Crescent, W11 2EE (☎0171/229 5260).

Glasgow John Smith and Sons, 57–61 St Vincent St, G2 5TB (☎0141/221 7472). Specialist map department in long-established booksellers; full range of foreign maps; mail order service.

MAP OUTLETS IN NORTH AMERICA

Chicago Rand McNally, 444 N Michigan Ave, Chicago, IL 60611; (☎312/321-1751).

Montréal Ulysses Travel Bookshop, 4176 St-Denis, H2W 2M5 (☎514/843-9447).

New York The Complete Traveler Bookstore, 199 Madison Ave, NY 10016 (☎212/685-9007); Rand McNally, 150 E 52nd St, NY 10022 (☎212/758-7488); Traveler's Bookstore, 22 W 52nd St, NY 10019 (☎212/664-0995).

San Francisco The Complete Traveler Bookstore, 3207 Fillmore St, CA 92123 (☎415/923-1511); Rand McNally, 595 Market St, CA 94105 (☎415/777-3131).

Santa Barbara Map Link Inc, 30 S La Patera Lane, Unit 5, CA 93117 (☎805/692-6777).

Seattle Elliot Bay Book Company, 101 S Main St, Seattle, WA 98104 (☎206/624-6600).

Toronto Open Air Books and Maps, 25 Toronto St, Toronto, M5R 2C1 (☎416/363-0719).

Vancouver World Wide Books and Maps, 1247 Granville St, Vancouver, V6Z 1G3 (☎604/687-3320).

Washington DC The Map Store Inc, 1636 ISt NW, Washington, DC 20006 (☎202/628-2608).

Note: Rand McNally now has more than 20 stores across the US; call ☎1-800/333-0136 (ext 2111) for the address of your nearest store, or for direct mail maps.

MAP OUTLETS IN AUSTRALIA AND NEW ZEALAND

Adelaide The Map Shop, 16a Peel St, Adelaide, SA 5000 (☎08/8231 2033).

Auckland Speciality Maps, 58 Albert St, Auckland (☎09/307 2217).

Brisbane Worldwide Maps and Guides, 187 George St, Brisbane (☎07/3221 4330).

Melbourne Bowyangs, 372 Little Bourke St, Melbourne, VIC 3000 (☎03/9670 4383).

Perth Perth Map Centre, 891 Hay St, Perth, WA 6000 (☎09/9322 5733).

Sydney Travel Bookshop, 20 Bridge St, Sydney, NSW 2000 (☎02/9241 3554).

reasonable **map** of the country (1:600,000), which is fine for everything except mountain roads. However, if you're doing any real exploration, it's worth investing in a good **road map**. The best maps available abroad are Michelin's 1:400,000 *Portugal* (#440); or Geo Centre's Euro Map *Portugal and Galicia* at 1:300,000. Geo Centre also produces a 1:200,000 map of the Algarve and a 1:250,000 map of the Lisbon area; *Bartholomew's Algarve Holiday Map* (1:100,000) is good, too. If you're planning on spending more than a day or two in Lisbon, the German *Falk Plan* of the city is unequalled.

More detailed topographic **maps for walkers** can be obtained in Lisbon at the Instituto Geografica e Cadastral by the Basilica da Estrêla, or less conveniently at the Serviços Cartográficos do Exército (Avenida Dr. Alfredo Bensaúde, Olivais Norte), and in Porto at Porto Editora, Praça Filipe de Lancastre. Many of these topographic maps are disastrously out of date – none has been revised since Portugal began its motorway programme – but they're the best you'll get.

Most general and regional Portuguese maps can be ordered through one of the map suppliers in Britain and North America detailed on p.21.

COSTS, MONEY AND BANKS

The cost of living in Portugal has been edging up ever since entry into the EC in 1986 but, as a tourist, you're unlikely to feel the pinch. Accommodation, transport, food and drink are still cheaper than in northern Europe – or North America – and, on the whole, better value than in Spain.

A **European Under-26 card** (Euro<26) is well worth having if you're eligible – it'll get you free or reduced admission to many museums and sights, discounts on bus and train tickets, as well as reductions in numerous shops and restaurants (sometimes even hotels). Of much less use is the **International Student Identity Card** (ISIC), which is rarely accepted, even if you attempt an explanation in Portuguese. Both are available through STA and Campus Travel/USIT in Britain and Ireland, Council Travel in the US and Travel

CUTS in Canada (see the relevant "Getting there" sections for addresses). You will also find the Euro<26 card on sale in Portugal at post offices and banks.

COSTS

Costs for a **double room** in the cheaper pensions work out at about £10–20/$15–30, rising to around £20–40/$30–60 in two- or three-star hotels, £50–170/$75–265 in four- and five-star places, and upwards of £60/$96 in *pousadas*. **Campsites** are a bargain at around £2–4/$3–6 a night per person, tent included, in all but the fanciest coastal sites.

You should always be able to get a substantial basic **meal** for around £5/$7.50; even dinner in the smarter restaurants is unlikely to cost more than £20/$30 a head. **Drink** costs are more than reasonable, too – a bottle of house wine rarely comes to more than £3/$5, a glass of the local brew in a bar around 40p/60¢. Even **transport** is hardly going to break the bank, especially since most distances you'll travel are fairly short and fares (especially on trains) low. A second-class train journey from Porto to Lisbon, or Lisbon to the Algarve, for example, costs around £12/$18.

To sum up, then, in most places you can get by on a budget of **around £30/$45 a day**, which will get you a room for the night, picnic lunch, dinner with drinks in a restaurant, a bus or train ride, and a beer or two. By camping and being a little more frugal, you could reasonably expect to survive on much less than this; while on £35–40/$50–60 a day you'll be living pretty well. It's worth noting that prices in Lisbon and the Algarve are higher than anywhere else in the country; expect things to cost up to ten percent more in all the main tourist resorts.

CURRENCY

The Portuguese currency unit is the **escudo ($)**; 1000 *escudos* is called a **conto**. Prices are written with the $ sign in the middle: thus 2$50 is two *escudos* and fifty *centavos,* and 1000$00 is a thousand *escudos* or one *conto*. For the last few years, exchange rates have been edging up in the visitor's favour, currently around 300$00 to the pound sterling, 182$00 to the US dollar. You can buy *escudos* in advance at most European, US and Canadian banks. **Notes** come in denominations of 500$00, 1000$00, 2000$00, 5000$00 and 10,000$00; **coins** as 1$00, 2$50, 5$00, 10$00, 20$00, 50$00, 100$00 and 200$00.

You will often find that shops round up prices to the nearest 10$00, so don't feel you've been short-changed. When travelling in rural areas, avoid getting stranded without **small notes and change**: a 10,000$00 note can be hard to change on a bus or at a small village market.

BANKS AND EXCHANGE

By far the easiest way to get money in Portugal is to use a credit card or bank card to **withdraw cash** from any of the large number of Multibanco **ATMs**. You'll find them in even the most out-of-the-way small towns and you can withdraw up to 40,000$00 per day. Any card using the Cirrus or Eurocheque system will work, as will all major credit cards (Visa, American Express, Mastercard and Eurocard), though you'll be charged a hefty

cash advance fee with the credit and charge cards, in addition to the usual currency conversion fee. Most Portuguese banks will give cash advances on cards over the counter and will also charge a currency conversion fee. **Credit cards** are also accepted for payment in many hotels and restaurants.

It is very expensive to change **travellers' cheques** in Portugal, although it's probably worth taking a supply in case your credit card is lost, stolen or swallowed by an ATM. You can buy them at most banks (even if you don't have an account), or from offices of Thomas Cook and American Express. They are accepted by all Portuguese banks and by exchange bureaux (*câmbios*) at airports and major train stations. Alternatively, most British banks can issue current-account holders with a **Eurocheque** card and chequebook, with which you can pay for things in some shops and get cash from the majority of Portuguese banks; you'll pay around £7.50 service charge a year but only small currency conversion fees on each transaction. In fact, Portuguese banks are not supposed to charge you commission at all on Eurocheques but many do.

If you do use travellers' cheques, all banks now charge a hefty **commission**, often 2500$00 or upwards per transaction (and per cheque in some cases) – so it is worth changing a reasonable amount of money at a time. There are much lower commissions on foreign currency exchanges at *caixas* – savings banks or building societies.

You'll find a **bank** in all but the smallest towns. Standard **opening hours** are Monday to Friday 8.30am–3pm. In Lisbon and in some of the Algarve resorts they may also open in the evening to change money, while some banks have installed **automatic exchange machines** for various currencies and denominations.

GETTING AROUND

Portugal is not a large country and you can get almost everywhere easily and efficiently by train or bus. Trains are often cheaper, and some lines very scenic, but it's almost always quicker to go by bus – especially on shorter or less obvious routes. Approximate times and frequencies of most journeys are given in the "Travel details" section at the end of each chapter; local connections and peculiarities are pointed out in the text.

Car rental is also worth considering if time is limited and you want to cover a lot of ground, though you may find you need nerves of steel to drive on some Portuguese roads.

TRAINS

CP, the Portuguese railway company, operates all trains. Most are designated *Regional*, which means they stop at most stations en route and have first- and second-class cars. *Inter-regional* are faster, stopping only at major stations. The next category up, *Intercidades*, are twice as fast and twice as expensive, and you should reserve your seat in advance if using them. The fastest, most luxurious and priciest services are the *Rápidos* (known as "Alfa"), which speed between Lisbon, Coimbra and Porto – sometimes they have only first-class seats. Both these latter classes charge supplements for rail-pass holders (see below).

Always turn up at the station with time to spare since long queues often form at the ticket desk. On certain trains, even with a rail pass,

you'll need to queue up for seat reservations, too. If you end up on the train without first buying a ticket you could be liable for a huge supplement, payable to the ticket controller, or be kicked off the train by the guard at the next stop. However, smaller regional stations are sometimes unmanned, in which case just hop on and pay the ticket inspector on board.

Complete **train timetables** (600$00) and timetables for individual lines are available from information desks at main stations. These can also supply information about taking a **car train**, a service available on the main Lisbon to Porto, Faro and Paris routes.

Sadly, several of the old narrow-gauge **mountain railways** of the north have been phased out, with the Tâmega, Corgo, Tua Valley and Douro lines terminating, respectively, at Amarante, Vila Real, Mirandela and Pocinho. Several other minor lines have been closed, too, though some have at least been replaced by buses operated by CP. Regular train tickets and passes are valid on these bus lines.

Lastly, it's as well to note that train stations can be some miles from the town or village they serve – Portalegre station and town are 12km distant, for example – and there's no guarantee of connecting transport.

TICKETS AND PASSES

Train travel is relatively inexpensive and most visitors simply buy a ticket every time they make a journey; **children** under four go free, under 12s pay half price. **Senior citizens** (over-60s) can get thirty percent off travel if they produce their passport (or other form of ID proving their age) and ask for a *Bilhete Terceira Idade* (third-age ticket). On main lines it's cheapest to travel on the so-called "Blue Days" – ie: avoiding Friday afternoons, Sunday afternoons, Monday mornings, national holidays and the day preceding a national holiday.

If you're planning a lot of train travel, using a **rail pass** might save you money, though note that pass holders pay **supplements** on *Intercidades* and *Rápidos*. CP sells its own *Bilhete Turístico* rail pass (valid for first-class travel on all trains except the Lisbon–Madrid Talgo) for 18,200$00 (£65/$104) for 7 days, 36,000$00 (£130/$208) for 14 days, and 54,000$00 (£195/$312) for 21 days. There's also a

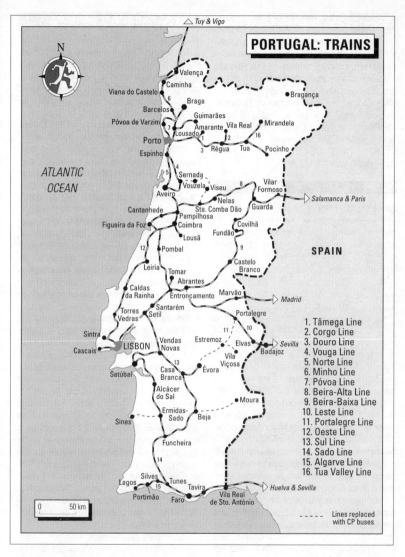

PORTUGAL: TRAINS

ATLANTIC
OCEAN

SPAIN

△ Tuy & Vigo
Valença
Caminha
Viana do Castelo
Braga
Barcelos
Póvoa de Varzim
Guimarães
Amarante Vila Real Mirandela
Porto
Lousado
Espinho
Régua Tua Pocinho
Sernada
Vouzela Viseu
Aveiro
Vilar Formoso
Nelas
Cantanhede
Sta. Comba Dão Guarda
Pampilhosa
Figueira da Foz
Coimbra
Lousã Fundão Covilhã
Pombal
Leiria
Tomar
Abrantes
Caldas da Rainha
Entroncamento Marvão
Torres Vedras
Santarém
Setil
Sintra
Portalegre
Cascais
LISBON
Vendas Novas Estremoz Elvas Badajoz
Setúbal
Casa Branca
Vila Viçosa
Évora
Alcácer do Sal
Moura
Ermidas-Sado
Sines
Beja
Funcheira
Silves
Lagos
Tunes Tavira
Portimão Faro
Vila Real de Sto. António

Bragança

▷ Salamanca & Paris

▷ Madrid

▷ Sevilla

▷ Huelva & Sevilla

1. Tâmega Line
2. Corgo Line
3. Douro Line
4. Vouga Line
5. Norte Line
6. Minho Line
7. Póvoa Line
8. Beira-Alta Line
9. Beira-Baixa Line
10. Leste Line
11. Portalegre Line
12. Oeste Line
13. Sul Line
14. Sado Line
15. Algarve Line
16. Tua Valley Line

0   50 km

- - - - - Lines replaced with CP buses

CP family card (*cartão de familia*) and group tickets (*bilhetes de grupo*), which offer varying reductions on tickets – more information can be obtained from local stations.

Both **InterRail** (see p.6) and **Eurail** passes (see p.6) are valid on Portuguese trains, though unless you're planning to travel extensively by train you're unlikely to be able to make them pay on a short trip just to Portugal. The following passes covering Portugal only (all of which must be purchased in your home country) may not give you your money's worth either given that the journey from Porto to Faro costs only 2000$00 (£7/$11) and takes the best part of a day. The **Eurodomino** pass allows three, five or ten days' rail travel in one month within Portugal; under-26 and over-26 fares are £79/£99 for 3 days, £99/£129 for 5 days and £139/£189 for 10 days. Alternatively, the **Portugal Explorer** pass entitles you to 7, 14 or 21 days of consecutive travel on the Portuguese rail network for £48, £81, and £120 respectively. Both are available in Britain from Eurotrain (see p.6). North Americans are eligible to purchase the **Portuguese Railpass**, allowing 4 days' travel out of 15 ($99 all ages). The Portuguese Railpass is obtainable through Rail Europe, 226 Westchester Ave, White Plains, NY 10604 (☎800/438-7245) or youth-oriented travel agents (see p.10).

BUSES

Buses shadow many of the main train routes as well as linking most of the country's smaller towns and villages. It's almost always quicker to go by bus if you can, though you'll pay slightly more than for the equivalent train ride. Comfortable express buses operate on longer routes, for which you'll usually have to reserve tickets in advance – certainly for the Lisbon–Algarve routes in summer.

All bus services are privatized, though a national network of express coaches (Rede Expressos) has been maintained, combining services from a number of different companies. Although the competition brought on by privatization has meant an increase in the number of buses on certain routes, it has also led to the inevitable reduction or phasing out of many local services. The variety of companies can also be a cause of confusion, as two buses going to the same destination may leave from different terminals (in the case of Porto almost all of the twenty companies operate out of different terminals) and companies may be unwilling to volunteer information about rival bus operators.

Local bus stations (detailed wherever possible in the text) are the place to pick up timetables and reserve seats on long-distance journeys but, as companies, addresses and routes change every year, it's advisable to check first with the local turismo – they can usually advise on where to book or catch specific buses. It's as well to be aware that bus services are considerably less frequent – occasionally non-existent – at weekends, especially on rural routes; while at other times, you'll find that departures can be frighteningly early in the morning. This is because bus services are often designed to fit around school and market hours.

DRIVING, CAR RENTAL AND TAXIS

With car rental rates among the lowest in Europe, driving around Portugal is an option worth thinking about, even for just a part of your travels. **Petrol** (*gasolina*), however, is not so cheap, at around 160$00 (about 55p/$1) a litre for Super. Unleaded petrol is now widely available (and most rental cars run on it).

Before you set out, bear in mind that Portugal has one of the highest **accident** rates in Europe. Road surfaces are improving, but even major roads are often potholed, narrow and full of dangerous bends. But it's not so much the quality of roads but the driving that is lethal – reckless overtaking being the main problem. Even on motorways, you'll need to check your mirror every few seconds to make sure someone isn't right up your exhaust pipe. August is especially dangerous, with Portuguese emigrant workers returning home in fast cars to show off to relatives.

A massive EU-funded **road construction programme**, now in its final stages, has made previously remote areas of the country such as Trás-os-Montes and Beira far more accessible, via a network of main highways (numbers prefixed "IP"), similar in speed to motorways. The **motorway network** itself (numbers prefixed with "A") is privately owned by BRISA and is a network of toll roads gradually expanding outwards from a central spine that links Setúbal and Lisbon with Porto. Recent developments include the completion of stretches heading east, from Porto to Amarante, and from Lisbon to Montemor-o-Novo in the Alentejo. In the south, it's now possible to travel between Lisbon and the Algarve by motorway, and the IP1 now passes through the eastern Algarve, crossing the Spanish border at Vila Real. Be warned, though, that the **tolls** can add significantly to the cost of your journey – as an indication, the stretch from Lisbon to Porto will set you back £10/$15. The advantages as usual are less traffic and a faster journey time.

Traffic on the **smaller roads** will be much heavier: slow journeys stuck behind trucks are common. In addition, as car ownership has increased massively over recent years, towns can no longer cope with the traffic. Travelling by car, you'll have endless problems finding central parking spaces – Coimbra is notoriously awful. Only the top hotels have car parks; otherwise you can expect to spend ages looking for a space, often ending up on the outskirts of town and having to walk to the centre.

CAR RENTAL AGENCIES

BRITAIN		Hertz US	☎800/654-3131;
Avis	☎0990/900 500.	Canada	☎800/263-0600.
Budget	☎0800/181 181.	Holiday Autos	☎800/442-7737.
Eurodollar	☎01895/233 300.	National Car Rental	☎800/CAR-RENT.
Europcar/InterRent	☎0345/222 525.	The Kemwell Group	☎800/678-0678.
Hertz	☎0990/996 699.		
Holiday Autos	☎0990/300 400.	**AUSTRALIA**	
		Avis	☎1800/225 533.
NORTH AMERICA		Budget	☎1300/362 848.
Auto Europe US	☎800/223-5555.	Hertz	☎13 3039.
Avis US	☎800/331-1084;		
Canada	☎800/879-2847.	**NEW ZEALAND**	
Budget	☎800/527-0700.	Avis	☎09/526 2847.
Europe by Car	☎ 800/223-1516.	Budget	☎09/375 2222.
		Hertz	☎09/309 0989.

Traffic drives on the right: **speed limits** are 50kph in towns and villages; 90kph on normal roads; and 120kph on motorways and inter-regional highways. At road junctions, unless there's a sign to the contrary, vehicles coming from the right have priority – a rule that wreaks havoc at roundabouts, effectively giving anyone cutting in the right of way. If you're **stopped by the police**, they'll want to see your documents – carry them in the car at all times and be courteous to the officers (see "Police and trouble", p.43).

If you **break down** you can get assistance from the Automóvel Clube de Portugal which has reciprocal arrangements with foreign automobile clubs. The head office is at Rua Rosa Araújo 24, Lisbon (☎01/942 50 95); in the north, phone their Porto service on ☎02/830 11 27.

CAR RENTAL

Car rental agencies can be found in all the major towns and at the airports in Lisbon, Porto and Faro. Local agencies usually charge less than the big three – Hertz, Avis and Europcar – and we've listed addresses and phone numbers for some of them in the Lisbon, Porto and Algarve chapters; tourist offices can give details of others.

Rates are reasonable, from around £100–120/$150–180 a week for the cheapest category car with unlimited mileage, though prices are inflated on the Algarve in high season. It's often a much better deal to **arrange rental before setting out**. In Britain, several of the specialist holiday companies detailed on p.5 will arrange car rental in conjunction with flights; or

call one of the major car rental outfits listed in the box above. In the US, you can get cheaper deals (as low as $120 a week) by booking your car through a wholesaler, such as Auto Europe, Europe by Car or The Kemwell Group (see box above). However, you must reserve and pay for the car in advance, before you leave the US.

When picking up your car, check such important details as brakes and, if you're renting locally, **insurance coverage**. As you might have gathered, collision insurance is a good idea and unless you pay a separate supplement the initial several thousand *escudos'* worth of damage may be on your head; if you're given the option of collision damage waiver, take it. Keep the receipts of any repairs you make along the way – you may be able to get some money back from the company.

Finally, it can't be stressed enough that hire cars are especially prone to **theft**. If at all possible detach any tell-tale stickers – the company might complain but at least the car and your belongings won't be a sitting target.

TAXIS

Travelling **by taxi** in Portugal is relatively cheap by European standards. It is worth considering for trips across major towns and for shorter journeys in rural areas where other means of transport may be limited. Generally, taxis are metered, with a minimum fare of 250$00. Additional charges are made for carrying baggage and fares are slightly higher between 10pm and 6am and at weekends. Outside major towns, you can also negotiate specific fares if you want to hire a taxi for a few hours.

BIKES, MOPEDS AND MOTORBIKES

Bicycles are a great way of seeing the country, though everywhere north of Lisbon is hilly and you'll find pedalling hard work in mountainous Beira Alta or across the burned plains of southern Alentejo. The bicycle-carrying service on trains is efficient, if expensive: prices are unpredictable, varying between 800$00 and 2000$00. Ask in advance which train to take, as not all take bicycles and it's advisable to arrange it in advance with the baggage office. On long-distance international trains, allow three days for the bike to arrive.

Although it's a hassle taking your own **bike by plane**, it really is worth it to have a decent machine with gears and brakes you can trust. Standard **spares**, such as tyres and inner tubes, are easy enough to get hold of but it's still worth taking your own, especially if you have a modern, specialized model.

If all that legwork is not to your taste, you can rent **mopeds** and low-powered (80cc) **motorbikes** in many tourist areas, especially on the Algarve. Go easy and check all the cables before setting off. A helmet and valid licence are obligatory.

ACCOMMODATION

In almost any Portuguese town you can find a *pensão* (pension) offering a double room for around 4000$00 (£13/$22) and singles for around 2500$00 (£8/$13) . The only accommodation that you're likely to find cheaper than this is rooms in a private home; most turismos have lists of those available in the area. You can expect to pay more in Algarve resorts in high season, or in Lisbon. If you have the money to move upmarket, you're often spoilt for choice, with some wonderful manor houses and a network of state-run *pousadas* scattered about the country.

Even in high season you shouldn't have much of a problem finding a bed in most Portuguese regions. However, parts of the Algarve are often a very different matter, with all rooms booked up for

days ahead. Try and reserve in advance where you can, especially if you're arriving late in Faro.

ROOMS AND PENSÕES

After hostels, the next rung up the accommodation ladder consists of **rooms** (*quartos* or *dormidas*) let out in private houses. Most commonly available in the seaside resorts, these are sometimes advertised, or more often hawked at bus and train stations. The local turismo may also have a list of rooms available. Rates should be a little below that of a *pensão*, say 3000–4000$00 (£10–13/$16–22), though on the Algarve, in high season, you can expect to pay up to twice as much. It's always worth haggling over prices, especially if you're prepared to commit yourself to a longish stay. And always ask where the room is before you agree to take it – in the resorts you could end up miles from the town centre or beach.

The main budget travel standby is a room in a *pensão* (plural, *pensões*) – which are officially graded from one to three stars (often, it seems, in a quite random fashion). Many serve meals, sometimes in a bargain-priced, all-inclusive package, but they rarely insist that you take them. *Pensões* that don't serve meals are sometimes called *residenciais* (singular *residencial* or *residência*), though in price and all other respects they are virtually identical. Similar to *pensões*, and generally at the cheaper end of the scale, are *hospedarias* or *casas de hóspedes* – boarding houses – which can be characterful places.

ACCOMMODATION PRICE CODES

Nearly all the accommodation prices in this book have been coded using the symbols below. The symbols represent the lowest prices you can expect to pay for a **double room in high season**. Effectively this means that most rooms in places with an ① or ② category will be *without* private bath or shower, though there's usually a washbasin in the room. In places with a ③ category and above, you'll probably be getting private facilities; while many of the cheaper places may also have more expensive rooms with bath/shower if you ask.

Price codes are not given for youth hostels and campsites (see p.30 and p.31 respectively for the rates at those).

① Under 3000$00	④ 5500$00–8500$00
② 3000$00–4000$00	⑤ 8500$00–12,500$00
③ 4000$00–5500$00	⑥ 12,500$00–20,000$00
⑦ Over 20,000$00	

Pensão **prices** for a double room range from around 4000–10,000$00 (£13–33/$22–55), depending on the season, and their location and facilities. Always ask to see the room before you take it, and don't be afraid to ask if there's a cheaper one (rooms without private showers or bathrooms are often considerably less) – especially if you're travelling alone, in which case you'll frequently be asked to pay more or less the full price of a double. *Tem um quarto mais barato?* ("Do you have a cheaper room?") is the relevant phrase.

HOTELS AND POUSADAS

A one-star **hotel** usually costs about the same as a three-star *pensão*, though quirks abound in the official grading systems, and establishments classified as one-star hotels often don't show any notable differences from *pensões*. Tourist offices sometimes downgrade hotels to *pensão* status, although it is rare for the hotel to change its sign accordingly. Indeed, it's not uncommon to find a two- or three-star *pensão* offering much better quality rooms than a one-star hotel. Prices for two- and three-star hotels, though, see a notable shift upscale, with doubles running from 8,000$00 (£27/$44) upwards.

There's a further and more dramatic shift in rates as you move into the four- and five-star hotel league, where you'll pay anything from 15,000–50,000$00 (£50–170/$82–274) for a double. The very fanciest places, on the Algarve and in Lisbon, can pretty much charge what they like. *Estalagems* and *albergarias* are other designations of hotels in the same range.

One fairly surprising bargain is the chain of 43 government-run **pousadas**, often converted from old monasteries or castles, or located in dramatic countryside settings. They're rated in four categories, and charge different prices in low, middle and high season; in some you'll pay as little as 10,300$00 a double a night in winter, 15,000$00 in summer, though on average you can expect to pay more like 16,900–23,500$00 for a double room. We've detailed many of them in the guide but for a full list of *pousadas*, contact the Portuguese National Tourist Office in your home country, or ENATUR, Avda. Santa Joana Princesa 10, 1749 Lisbon (☎01/848 12 21, fax 840 58 46).

COUNTRY AND MANOR HOUSES

An increasingly popular alternative in the three-to four-star hotel price range is to stay in one of the many properties throughout Portugal promoted by the tourist board as **country and manor houses**. Rivals to the *pousada*, there are now upwards of 150 of them, all of which have had their facilities and accommodation inspected and approved by the government tourist office. In terms of atmosphere and luxury, they are often unbeatable and their equivalent in other European countries would command in excess of double the price. The properties vary from simple farmhouses (*Casas Rústicas*) offering just two or three rooms on a bed-and-breakfast basis to country manors (*Quintas*) and estate houses (*Herdades*) and even palaces (*Casas Antigas*) owned by Portuguese aristocrats who have allowed their ancient seats to become part of the scheme. Their facilities have to conform to certain standards, categorized on a scale of A–C. Rates are currently the same throughout the year: category A doubles are around 16,500$00; B 12,500$00; and C 9500$00. In high season in certain areas you might find that stays are for a minimum of three nights. Facilities can vary from a simple room in a rustic house to a suite or annexe of a manor house with its own gardens and swimming pool. All properties which have been approved under this scheme are entitled to display a **green tree symbol**, although there are some unauthorized houses displaying their own symbols.

In general the scheme has given a new lease of life to properties which had begun to fall into decline through changing patterns of economics and lifestyles. The appeal – or not as the case may be – lies in the chance to stay with the owners of the properties. Many will provide typical dinners made from local ingredients, sometimes accompanied by wine made on the estate, and almost all are founts of advice and information about local matters. Even if dinner is not available – or you prefer not to eat with the family – large breakfasts are invariably included.

Once a property has passed the government inspection, its owners can choose to join one of the private marketing organizations, of which the first and best known is **Solares de Portugal** (formerly known as Turihab), based in Ponte de Lima where the scheme originated (Praça da República, 4990 Ponte de Lima; ☎058/74 16 72; fax 058/74 14 44; email: *turihab@mail.telepac.pt*; Web site: *http://www.sidra.pt/turihab*). It has some amazing country houses on its books as well as simpler, more basic properties. The success of Solares de Portugal has prompted the formation of similar marketing associations such as PRIVETUR, Rua de João Penha 10, Sala 15, 1200 Lisbon (☎01/69 05 49, fax 388 81 15), and ANTER, Quinta do Campo, Valado dos Frades, 2450 Nazaré (☎062/57 71 35, fax 57 75 55). All three can provide you with brochures detailing their properties; bookings can be made through the offices listed above or with the individual properties directly. If you want to book in advance, several of the specialist holiday operators detailed on pp.5, 11 or 15 can make arrangements for you, or the Portuguese National Tourist Office can send you the short *Guide to Country and Manor Houses*.

VILLAS

Holiday and tour operators are also the best sources if you want to rent a **villa** for your stay in Portugal. Summer sees most places booked solid months in advance, especially on the Algarve, but either side of the peak period you should be able to turn up in more out-of-the-way resorts like Tavira or Sagres and bag a self-catering apartment. The local turismo will probably be able to help. In winter, prices can be very reasonable indeed.

YOUTH HOSTELS

There are twenty **youth hostels** (*Pousadas de Juventude*) in Portugal, most open all year round. The price for a dormitory bed runs from around 1200–2350$00 a night, depending on the location and season; doubles cost between 3200$00 and 5700$00. Add on a little extra if you need to hire sheets and blankets. The most expensive hostels are in Lisbon, Porto and on the Algarve.

Most have a curfew (usually 11pm or midnight) and all require a valid Hostelling International (HI) card – available from your home-based youth hostel association (see below). In Portugal, the head office of the **Portuguese Youth Hostel Association** (Movijoven) is at Avda. Duque de Ávila 137, 1050 Lisbon (Mon–Fri 9.30am–12.45pm & 2–5.45pm; ☎01/355 90 81, fax 352 86 21).

YOUTH HOSTEL ASSOCIATIONS

Australia Australian Youth Hostels Association, Level 3, 10 Mallett St, Camperdown, 2050 NSW (☎02/9565 1699).

Canada Canadian Hostelling Association, Room 400, 205 Catherine St, Ottawa, ON K2P IC3 (☎613/237-7884).

England and Wales Youth Hostels Association (YHA), Trevelyan House, 8 St Stephen's Hill, St Albans, Herts AL1 (☎01727/855 215). London shop and information office: 14 Southampton St, London WC2 7HY (☎0171/836 1036).

Ireland An Oige, 61 Mountjoy St, Dublin 7 (☎01/830 4555).

New Zealand Youth Hostels Association of New Zealand, PO Box 436, Christchurch 1 (☎03/379-9970).

Northern Ireland Youth Hostels Association of Northern Ireland (YHANI), 22 Donegall Rd, Belfast BT12 5JN (☎01232/324 733).

Scotland Scottish Youth Hostels Association, 7 Glebe Crescent, Stirling, FK8 2JA (☎01786/451 181).

USA American Youth Hostels (AYH), 733 15th Street NW, Suite 840, Washington, DC 20005 (☎202/783-6161).

All of the hostels are detailed in the guide. Among the best are those at Vilarinho das Furnas (in the Gerês National Park), Penhas de Saúde (in the Serra de Estrêla), São Martinho do Porto, Areia Branca, Oeiras (on the seafront near Lisbon), Coimbra, Alcoutim (northeastern Algarve) and Leiria (perhaps the best of the lot).

CAMPING

Portugal has more than a hundred authorized **campsites**, many of them in very attractive locations and, despite their often large size, extremely crowded in summer. Charges are per person and per tent, with showers and parking extra; even so, it's rare that you'll end up paying more than 600–800$00 a person. Some are even cheaper than this, while those operated by the Orbitur chain are usually a little more expensive. For details of their sites, contact Orbitur, Rua Diogo do Couto 1-8°, 1100 Lisbon (☎01/811 70 70, fax 814 80 45; Web site: *http://www.orbitur.pt*). The most useful campsites are detailed in the text (unless otherwise stated they are open all year) but you can get a fairly complete list from any Portuguese tourist office, or a detailed booklet (700$00) called *Roteiro Campista* (with prices, exact locations, facilities, etc) from Portuguese bookshops or direct from Guia de Parques de Campismo, Apartado 3168, 1304 Lisbon Codex (☎01/364 23 74, fax 364 23 70).

There are only a few sites in Portugal for which you will have to produce an **international camping carnet**, but if you want to be on the safe side they are available from home motoring organizations, or, in Britain, from the Camping and Caravanning Club of Great Britain, Greenfields House, Westwood Way, Coventry CV4 8JH (☎01203/694 995), in the US from the Family Campers and RVers (FCRV), 4804 Transit Rd, Building 2, Depew, NY 14043 (☎1800/245-9755) and in Canada from FCRV, 51 W 22nd St, Hamilton, Ontario, LC9 4N5 (same phone as US). They serve as useful identification and cover you for third party insurance when camping.

Camping outside official grounds is legal, but with certain restrictions. You're not allowed to camp "in urban zones, in zones of protection for water sources, or less than 1km from camping parks, beaches, or other places frequented by the public". What this means in practice is that you can't camp on tourist beaches, but with a little sensitivity you can pitch a tent for a short period almost anywhere in the countryside. That said, in recent years a number of Portugal's natural parks have banned unofficial camping in an attempt to reduce littering and fire damage. Check first with the relevant park office as to whether it is permitted or not.

The **Algarve** is another exception, having banned freelance camping altogether. When staying on one of the region's campsites, be warned that thefts are a regular occurrence – over most of the rest of the country the locals are extremely honest and you can leave equipment without worrying.

EATING AND DRINKING

Portuguese food is excellent, inexpensive and served in quantity. Virtually all cafés, whatever their appearance, will serve you a basic meal for around 1500$00 (£5/$8), while for 1600–3000$00 (£5.50–10/$9–16) you have the run of most of the country's restaurants. Only a handful of top-class restaurants in Lisbon and the Algarve will cause a credit card crisis. Do beware, however, of eating anything you haven't explicitly asked for and expecting it to be free, or included: it won't be.

BREAKFAST, SNACKS AND SANDWICHES

For **breakfast** it's best to head for a café or *pastelaria* (pastry shop) for the usual Continental basics – a croissant or pastry of some kind washed down with a coffee. The latter is usually taken espresso-style (*uma bica*), though the milky version (*um galão*) served in a glass, is also popular at breakfast time.

You'll often find a whole range of dishes served at a café, but classic Portuguese **snacks** include *prego no pão* (steak sandwich), which is usually served with a fried egg (*prego no prato*) or with sliced ham (*prego no fiambre*); *rissóis* (deep-fried meat patties); and *pastéis de bacalhau* (cod fish-cakes). In the north you may also find *lanches* (pieces of sweetish bread stuffed with ham) and *pastéis de carne* or *pastéis de chaves* (puff pastries stuffed with sausage meat). If cafés cook in a big way you'll probably see blackboard lists of dishes, or perhaps just a sign reading *Comidas* (meals).

Among **sandwiches** (*sandes*) on offer, the most common fillings include *queijo* (cheese), *fiambre* (ham), *presunto* (smoked ham) and *chouriço* (smoked sausage). *Sandes mistas* are usually a combination of ham and cheese. If there's food displayed on café counters and you see anything that looks appealing, just ask for *uma dose* (a portion). *Uma coisa destas* (one of those) can also be a useful phrase.

Markets – often held in indoor covered sites – are always good hunting grounds for snacks. At many of them you'll find stands serving complete meals, or at least some local delicacy. In the north, especially, the most delicious standby is a chunk of *broa* (corn/rye bread) with local cheese and *marmelada* (thick quince – *marmelo* – spread).

MEALS AND RESTAURANTS

Even those on the tightest of budgets won't need to depend exclusively on snacks and picnics. The country is awash with accessible and affordable **restaurants** and, in addition, servings tend to be huge. Indeed, you can usually have a substantial **meal** by ordering a *meia dose* (half portion), or *uma dose* between two. Meals are often listed like this on the menu and it's normal practice; you don't need to be a child.

It is worth checking out the *ementa turística*, too – not a "tourist menu", but the set meal of the day, sometimes with a choice of two starters and two main courses, plus beer or wine. It can be very good value, particularly in *pensões* that serve meals, or in the cheaper workers' cafés. Smarter restaurants, however, sometimes resent the law that compels them to offer the *ementa turística*, responding with stingy portions, excessive prices or, where there's any deviation from the set fare, declaring your meal to be *à lista* (à la carte) and consequently twice as expensive. If you feel strongly enough to want to make a formal complaint, ask for the *livro de reclamações* (complaints book) – every restaurant, however humble, is obliged to keep one.

Otherwise, the one thing to watch for when eating out in Portugal – especially if you've grown happily complacent in Spain on a regular intake of free *tapas* – is the plate of **starters** usually placed before you when you take a table and before you order. These can be quite elaborate lit-tle dishes of olives, cheese, sardine spread and *chouriço*, or can consist of little more than rolls and butter, but what you eat is counted and you will be charged for every bite. Each item should be itemized on the menu, so you can see what you're spending.

Apart from straightforward restaurants – *restaurantes* – you could end up eating a meal in one of several other venues. A *tasca* is a small neighbourhood tavern; a *casa de pasto*, a cheap, local dining room usually with a set three-course menu, mostly served at lunch only. A *cervejaria* is literally a "beer house", more informal than a restaurant, with people dropping in at all hours for a beer and a snack. In Lisbon they are often wonderful old tiled caverns, specializing in seafood. Also specializing in seafood is a *maris-queria*, occasionally very upmarket, though as often as not a regular restaurant with a superior fishy menu.

Meal times are earlier than in Spain, with lunch usually served from noon–3pm, dinner from 7.30pm onwards; don't count on being able to eat much after 10pm outside the cities and tourist resorts. Simple cafés and restaurants don't charge for service, though you'll have paid a **cover charge** for bread and appetizers if you had any. People generally leave just small change as a **tip** in these places, though in more upmarket restaurants, you'll either be charged, or should leave, around ten percent.

DISHES AND SPECIALITIES

It's always worth taking stock of the *prato do dia* (dish of the day) if you're interested in sampling **local specialities**. They're often considerably cheaper than the usual menu fare as well. Some of the more common dishes are detailed in the food lists on p.34.

Soups are extraordinarily inexpensive, and the thick vegetable *caldo verde* – cabbage and potato broth sometimes with pieces of ham – is as filling as dishes come. The other soup served every-where is *sopa à alentejana*, a garlic and bread soup with a poached egg in it. Otherwise, fish and shellfish soups are always worth sampling.

On the coast, **fish and seafood** are pre-emi-nent: crabs, prawns, crayfish, clams and huge barnacles are all fabulous, while fish on offer always includes superb mullet, tuna and scabbard fish. The most typical Portuguese fish dish is that created from **bacalhau** (dried, salted cod), which

is much better than it sounds. It's virtually the national dish with reputedly 365 different ways of preparing it. Running it a close second are **sar-dines** (*sardinhas*), which – when grilled or bar-beuced outside – provide one of the country's most familiar and appetizing smells. On the coast, you shouldn't miss trying a **cataplana** – pres-sure-cooked seafood and strips of ham, named after the copper vessel in which it's cooked – or **arroz de marisco**, a bumper serving of mixed seafood served with a soupy rice. These are near-ly always served for a minimum of two people, though.

On the whole, **meat** dishes are less special, though they're often enlivened by the addition of a fiery *piri-piri* (chilli) sauce, either in the cooking or provided on the table. Simple grilled or fried steaks of beef and pork are common; while **chicken** is on virtually every menu – at its won-derful best when barbecued (*no churrasco*); cer-tain restaurants specialize in this and little else. Other, more exotic, specialities include smoked hams (*presunto*) from the north of the country (especially Chaves), and the ubiquitous and extremely tasty **porco à alentejana** (pork cooked with clams) – perhaps Portugal's most enterprising contribution to world cuisine – which originated, as its name suggests, in the Alentejo. However, steel yourself for a couple of special dishes that local Portuguese people might entice you into trying: Porto's **tripas** (tripe) dishes incor-porate beans and spices but the heart of the dish is still recognizably chopped stomach-lining; while **cozido à portuguesa**, widely served in restaurants on a Sunday, is a stomach-challeng-ing boiled "meat" stew in which you shouldn't be surprised to turn up a pig's ear or worse. And it's worth paying good money to avoid eating the unspeakable **papas de sarrabulho** (a blood and bread-based dish).

Accompanying most dishes will be potatoes (generally fried so ask if you want them boiled) and/or rice – calorific overkill is a strong feature of Portuguese meal times. Other **vegetables** rarely make an appearance, though you might find sliced fresh tomato served with your fish, and boiled carrots or cabbage and the like accompa-nying meat stews.

If you've had enough rich food, any restaurant will fix a **salada mista** (mixed salad), which usu-ally has tomatoes, onions and olives as a base, and you can ask for it to be served *sem óleo* (with-out oil), though it's nowhere near as tasty if you

PORTUGUESE FOOD GLOSSARY

BASICS

Acepipes	Hors d'oeuvres	mexido	scrambled
Arroz	Rice	cozido	boiled
Azeitonas	Olives	Pão	Bread
Batatas fritas	French fries	Pimenta	Pepper
Legumes	Vegetables	Piri-piri	Chilli sauce
Manteiga	Butter	Sal	Salt
Ovos	Eggs	Salada	Salad
estrelado	fried	Queijo	Cheese

IN THE RESTAURANT

Almoço	Lunch	Ementa	Menu	Jantar	Dinner
Colher	Spoon	Faca	Knife	Mesa	Table
Conta	The bill	Garfo	Fork	Pequeno almoço	Breakfast
Copo	Glass	Garrafa	Bottle		

SOUPS (SOPAS)

Caldo verde	Cabbage/potato broth	Sopa de feijão verde	Green bean soup
Canja de galinha	Chicken broth with rice and boiled egg yolks	Sopa de grão	Chickpea soup
		Sopa de legumes	Vegetable soup
Gaspacho	Chilled vegetable soup	Sopa de marisco	Shellfish soup
Sopa à alentejana	Garlic/bread soup with poached egg on top	Sopa de peixe	Fish soup

FISH (PEIXE) AND SHELLFISH (MARISCOS)

Ameijoas	Clams	Lulas	Squid
Anchovas	Anchovies	Mexilhões	Mussels
Atum	Tuna	Ostras	Oysters
Camarões	Shrimp	Pargo	Sea bream
Caranguejo	Crab	Peixe espada	Swordfish (often confused with the more common espadarte)
Carapau	Mackerel		
Cherne	Sea bream		
Chocos	Cuttlefish	Perceves	Goose barnacles
Enguia	Eel	Pescada	Hake
Espadarte	Scabbard fish (a long, thin fish, black or white in colour)	Polvo	Octopus
		Robalo	Sea bass
Gambas	Prawns	Salmão	Salmon
Garoupa	(Like) bream	Salmonete	Red mullet
Lagosta	Lobster	Sarda	Mackerel
Lampreia	Lamprey (similar to eel)	Sardinhas	Sardines
Linguado	Sole	Truta	Trout

MEAT (CARNE), POULTRY (AVES) AND GAME (CAÇA)

Almondegas	Meatballs	Costeleta	Chop	Pato	Duck
Borrego	Lamb	Dobrada	Tripe	Perdiz	Partridge
Cabrito	Kid	Fiambre	Cooked ham	Perú	Turkey
Carne de porco	Pork	Fígado	Liver	Presunto	Smoked ham
Carneiro	Mutton	Frango	Young chicken	Salpicão	Cured pork
Chouriço	Spicy sausage	Galinha	Chicken	Salsicha	Sausage
Coelho	Rabbit	Lombo	Loin of pork	Tripas	Tripe
Cordoniz	Quail	Morcela	Blood pudding	Vitela	Veal

SPECIALITIES

Açorda (de marisco)	Bread-based stew (cooked with shellfish and spices)	aldeirada	Fish stew, with a base of onions, tomatoes and potatoes
Arroz de marisco	Seafood paella	Cataplana	Shellfish or fish cooked with strips of ham, pepper and onion
Bacalhau	There are reputedly 365 ways of cooking dried salt cod, including *com batatas e grão* (with boiled potatoes and chickpeas), *à brás* (with egg, onions and potatoes), *na brasa* (roasted with sliced potatoes), *à Gomes de Sá* (sliced, with boiled eggs and potatoes), and *à minhota* (with fried potatoes)	Chanfana	Casserole of lamb or kid
		Cozido à portuguesa	Boiled casserole of chicken, lamb, pork, beef, sausages, offal and beans, served with rice and vegetables
		Espedeta mista	Mixed meat kebab
		Frango na churrasca	Barbecued chicken, nearly always superb; eat with the *piri-piri* (chilli) sauce provided
		Leitão assado	Roast suckling pig
Bife à Portuguesa	Beef steak, topped with mustard sauce and a fried egg	Porco à alentejana	Pork cooked with clams, an oily and salty dish from the Alentejo
		Tripas à moda do Porto	Tripe with beans and vegetables

SOME TERMS

Assado/no speto	Roasted/spit-roasted	Guisado	Stew
Cozido	Boiled/stewed	Molho	Sauce
Ensopado de . . .	Soup or stew of . . .	Na brasa	Charcoal-grilled
Frito	Fried	No forno	Baked
Fumado	Smoked	Piri-piri	With chilli sauce
Grelhado	Grilled	Salteado	Sautéed

VEGETABLES (*LEGUMES*) AND SALAD (*SALADA*)

Alcachofra	Artichoke	Espargos	Asparagus
Alface	Lettuce	Espinafre	Spinach
Alho	Garlic	Favas	Broad beans
Batatas	Potatoes	Feijão	Beans
Cebola	Onion	Grão	Chickpeas
Cenoura	Carrot	Pepino	Cucumber
Cogumelos	Mushrooms	Pimenta	Pepper
Ervilhas	Peas	Salada	Salad

FRUIT (*FRUTA*)

Ameixas	Plums	Maçã	Apple
Ananás	Pineapple	Melão	Melon
Cerejas	Cherries	Morangos	Strawberries
Figos	Figs	Pêra	Pear
Laranja	Orange	Pêssego	Peach
Limão	Lemon	Uvas	Grapes

do. Otherwise, strict **vegetarians** are in for something of a hard time outside Lisbon and the Algarve, where there's a bigger choice of non-Portuguese food. Eggs are mostly free-range in Portugal, but out in the sticks you'll soon tire of omelettes or fried eggs, chips and salad – though every restaurant will be happy to prepare this for you if you ask.

PASTRIES, SWEETS AND CHEESES

Pastries (*pastéis*) and cakes (*bolos*) are usually at their best in *casas de chá* (tearooms), though you'll also find them in cafés and in *pastelarias*, which themselves often serve drinks, too. Here, pastries are serious business and enthusiasts won't be disappointed. Among the best are the Sintra cheesecakes (*queijadas de Sintra*), *palha de ovos* (egg pastries) from Abrantes, *bolo de anjo* (angel food cake), *pastéis de nata* (delicious little custard tarts), and a full range of marzipan cakes from the Algarve. The incredibly sweet, egg-based *doces de ovos* – most infamously from Aveiro – are completely over-the-top.

Unfortunately, few of these delicacies are available in restaurants as **desserts**. Instead, you'll almost always be offered either fresh fruit, the ubiquitous Ola ice cream price list, *pudim flan* (crème caramel), *arroz doce* (rice pudding) or *torta da noz* (almond tart). **Cheese** is widely available in restaurants, the best being the *queijo da Serra* (from the Serra da Estrela). *Cabreiro* or *queijo de cabra* is a goat's cheese like Greek *feta*; and also worth looking out for are the soft cheeses of Tomar and Azeitão. Travelling in remoter areas, you're also in for a treat – the cheeses of northern Beira and southern Trás-os-Montes being especially worth mention.

ALCOHOLIC DRINKS

Portuguese table wines are dramatically inexpensive and of a good overall quality. Even the standard *vinho da casa* that you get in the humblest of cafés is generally a very pleasant drink. But it's fortified port, of course, and Madeira that are Portugal's best-known wine exports – and you should certainly sample both.

Beer choices are far less varied, with just two or three brands available country-wide, while the typical Portuguese measure of spirits is equivalent to at least two shots in Britain or North America, making drunkenness all too easy. Low prices, too, are an encouragement, as long as you stick to local (*nacional*) products.

WINES

Modern wine-making techniques are making fast inroads into Portugal's traditional wine-growing regions, with a corresponding growth in the number of internationally recognized and reputed Portuguese labels, such as **Bairrada**, from the region between Coimbra and Aveiro, and **Ribatejo**, **Arruda** and **Liziria** from the Ribatejo. Some of the best-known Portuguese table wines are reds from the **Dão** region, a roughly triangular area between Coimbra, Viseu and Guarda, around the River Dão. Tasting a little like burgundy, and produced mainly by local co-operatives, they're available throughout the country. Among other smaller regions offering interesting wines are **Colares** (near Sintra), **Bucelas** in the Estremadura (crisp, dry whites), **Valpaças** from Trás-os-Montes, **Reguengos** from Alentejo and **Lagoa** from the Algarve.

The light, slightly sparkling *vinhos verdes* – "green wines", in age not colour – are again produced in quantity, this time in the Minho. They're drunk early and don't mature or improve with age, but are great with meals, especially shellfish. There are red and rosé *vinhos verdes*, though the whites are the most successful – Casal Garcia is the one you'll find most often in restaurants. Otherwise, Portuguese **rosé wines** are known abroad mainly through the spectacularly successful export of Mateus Rosé. This is too sweet and aerated for most tastes, but other rosés – the best is Tavel – are definitely worth sampling.

Portugal also produces an interesting range of sparkling, champagne-method wines, known as *espumantes naturais*. They are designated *bruto* (extra dry), *seco* (fairly dry), *meio seco* (quite sweet) or *doce* (very sweet). The best of these come from the Bairrada region, north of Coimbra, though Raposeira wines are the most commonly available.

Even the most basic of restaurants usually has a decent selection of wines, many of which are available in half-bottles, too. The *vinho da casa* (house wine) is nearly always remarkably good value, but even ascending the scale and choosing from the wine list, you'll be surprised at the quality wines on offer at very moderate prices. Most **wine lists** don't just distinguish between *tinto* (red) or *branco* (white); they'll also list wines as either *verdes* (ie, young and slightly sparkling) or *maduros* (mature) – choose from the latter if you're after a red with a kick or a white with no bubbles.

FORTIFIED WINES: PORT AND MADEIRA

Port (*vinho do Porto*) – the famous fortified wine – is produced from grapes grown in the valley of the Douro and stored in huge wine lodges at Vila Nova de Gaia, facing Porto across the Rio Douro. You can visit these for tours and free tastings; see p.268 for all the details. Alternatively, you can try any of 300 types and vintages of port at the *Instituto do Vinho do Porto* (Port Wine Institute) bars in Lisbon (p.95) and Porto (p.267). But even if your quest for port isn't serious enough to do either, be sure to try the dry white aperitif ports, still little known outside the country.

Madeira (*vinho da Madeira*), from Portugal's Atlantic island province, has been exported to Britain since Shakespeare's time – it was Falstaff's favourite tipple, known then as sack. Widely available, it comes in three main varieties: Sercial (a dry aperitif), Verdelho (a sweeter aperitif) and Bual or Malmsey (sweet, heavy dessert wines). Each improves with age and special vintages are greatly prized and priced.

SPIRITS (*LICOR*)

The national **brandy** is arguably outflanked by its Spanish rivals – which are sold almost everywhere – but the native spirit is available in two varieties (Macieira and Constantino), each with loyal followings. It's frighteningly cheap. Portuguese **gin** is weaker than international brands but again ridiculously inexpensive.

Local **firewaters** – generically known as *aguardente* – are more impressive. They include Bagaço (the fieriest), Figo (made from figs, with which it shares similar qualities when drunk to excess), Ginginha (made from cherries), and the very wonderful Licor Beirão (a kind of cognac with herbs).

BEER

The most common Portuguese **beer** (*cerveja*) is Sagres in the south or Super Bock in the north, but there are a fair number of local varieties. If you're curious, they can all be tasted at the Silves Beer Festival, held in the town's castle for a week every June. For something unusual (and not recommended on a hot afternoon) try the Sagres Preta, which is a dark beer, resembling British brown ale.

When **drinking draft beer** order *um imperial* (or *um fino* in the north) if you want a regular glass; *uma caneca* will get you a half-litre. And when **buying bottles**, don't forget to take your empties back: they can represent as much as a third of the price!

COFFEE, TEA AND SOFT DRINKS

Coffee (*café*) comes either black, small, and espresso-strong (*uma bica* or simply *um café*); small and with milk (*um garoto* or *um pingo* in some parts of the north); or large and with milk but often disgustingly weak (*um galão*). For white coffee that tastes of coffee and not diluted warm milk, ask for "*um café duplo com um pouco de leite*".

Tea (*chá*) is usually plain; *com leite* is with milk, *com limão* with lemon, but *um chá de limão* is hot water with a lemon rind. *Chá* is a big drink in Portugal (which originally exported tea-drinking to England) and you'll find wonderfully elegant *casas de chá* dotted around the country.

All the standard **soft drinks** are available. Tri Naranjus is a good local range of fruit drinks (excellent *limão*, lemon), and the fizzy Sumol is extremely fruity and appetizing. Fresh orange juice is *sumo de laranja* – add the word *fresca* to ensure you get the real thing. Lastly, **mineral water** (*água mineral*) is available almost anywhere in the country, either still (*sem gás*) or carbonated (*com gás*).

COMMUNICATIONS: POST AND PHONES

POSTAL SERVICES

Portuguese postal services are reasonably efficient. Letters or cards take under a week to arrive at destinations in Europe, and a week to ten days to North America. The Correio Azul system guar-antees delivery in three to four days but, natural-ly, you pay for it – 310$00 for a letter to Europe compared to the standard 80$00.

Post offices (*correios*) are normally open Monday to Friday 8.30am–6pm, larger ones sometimes on Saturday mornings, too. The main Lisbon branches have much longer opening hours; see "Listings", p.106. **Stamps** (*selos*) are sold at post offices and anywhere that has the sign of a red horse on a white circle over a green back-ground and the legend *Correio de Portugal – Selos*. To send a card to Europe or the USA costs 80$00, 150$00 to anywhere else.

You can have **poste restante** (general delivery) mail sent to you at any post office in the country. Letters should be marked *Posta Restante*, and your name, ideally, should be written in capitals and underlined. To collect, you need to take along your passport – look for the counter marked *encomen-das*. If you are expecting mail, ask the postal clerk to check for letters under your first name and any other initials (including Ms, etc) as well as under your surname – filing can be erratic.

TELEPHONE CODES AND USEFUL NUMBERS

To phone abroad *from Portugal*

Dial the country code (given below) + area code (minus initial zero) + number

Australia 0061	Canada 001	Ireland 00353
New Zealand 0064	UK 0044	USA 001

To phone Portugal *from abroad*

Dial the international access code (see below) + 351 (country code) + area code (minus intitial zero; see below) + number

International Access Code

Australia 0011	Canada 001	Ireland 00
New Zealand 00	UK 00	USA 001

Portuguese Area Codes

Braga 053	Coimbra 039	Évora 066	Faro 089	Guarda 071
Lagos 082	Leiria 044	Lisbon 01	Odemira 083	Porto 02
Setúbal 065	Tavira 081	Viana do Castelo 058	Vila Real 059	Viseu 032

Useful Telephone Numbers

Directory enquiries 118	Emergency services 115
Operator (Europe) 099	Operator (rest of the world) 098
	Speaking clock 151

TELEPHONES

All calls, whether local or international, are most easily made using **card-operated public phones** called *credifones*, which you'll find in all but the most remote villages. Cards come in denominations of 50 and 120 units, costing 880$00 and 2100$00 respectively, and are available from post offices, newsagents, tobacconists and kiosks. The few coin-operated phones remaining are often broken.

You'll also find **pay phones** in bars and cafés (and, increasingly, in turismo offices and newsagents), usually indicated by the sign of a red horse on a white circle over a green background and the legend *Correio de Portugal – Telefone*. If you need quieter surroundings you'd be better off in one of the phone cabins found in most main post offices – simply tell the clerk where you want to phone, and pay for your call afterwards. Except in Lisbon and Porto, most telephone offices are closed in the evening. The **cheap rate for international calls** is between 10pm and 8am, and at weekends.

Reverse charge (collect) calls (*chamada cobrar ao destinatário*) can be made from any phone, dialling ☎099 for a European connection and ☎098 for the rest of the world. If you encounter difficulties, call ☎090.

THE MEDIA

The two most established **Portuguese daily newspapers** are the Lisbon-based *Diário de Notícias* and the *Jornal de Notícias* from Porto. They have their uses for listings information, even if you have only a very sketchy knowledge of the language. The stylish *Público* has good foreign news and regional inserts as well as fairly easy-to-read listings. For an interesting view of the country's culture, try *JL* (*Jornal de Letras*).

The *International Herald Tribune*, and most British **newspapers**, can be bought in the major cities and resorts, usually a day late. One or two domestic English-language magazines and newspapers pop up from time to time on the Algarve, none of them especially informative but occasionally useful for finding work.

Portuguese **television** imports many American and British shows – nearly always subtitled rather than dubbed. Increasingly, too, European **satellite TV** stations are spawning their dishes around the country; sports channels are popular in bars, showing televised bullfights among other things. You also get *telenovelas* – soaps – often from Brazil, and compelling viewing even if you don't understand a word.

On the **radio**, you can pick up the BBC World Service, with hourly news, on 648 KHz medium wave and 15.07 MHz short wave; *Voice of America* is sporadically audible on 6040 on the 49m short wave band. Portuguese radio also puts out an **English language programme** for tourists at 8.30am or 10am (between 558 and 720 KHz/87.9 and 95.7FM depending on where you are).

OPENING HOURS AND PUBLIC HOLIDAYS

Like Spain, Portugal has held onto the institution of the *siesta*. Most stores and businesses, plus smaller museums and rural post offices, close for a good lunchtime break – usually from around 12.30pm to 2.30 or 3pm.

Banks are a rare exception, opening Monday to Friday 8.30am to 3pm. **Shops** generally open around 9am, and upon re-opening after lunch keep going until 7 or 8pm; except in larger cities, they tend to close for the weekend at Saturday lunchtime. Larger shopping centres, however, stay open seven days a week, often until midnight. **Museums, churches and monuments** generally open from around 10am–12.30pm and 2–6pm, though the larger ones stay open through lunchtime. Almost all museums and monuments, however, are closed Mondays. The other thing to watch out for are national **public holidays** (see right) when almost everything is closed and transport services reduced. There are also **local festivals** and holidays (see opposite), when entire towns, cities and regions grind to a halt: for example June 13 in Lisbon and June 24 in Porto.

PUBLIC HOLIDAYS

January 1 New Year's Day

Good Friday

April 25 Commemorating the 1974 Revolution

May 1 Labour Day

Corpus Christi Usually early June

June 10 Dia de Camões e das Comunidades – Camões day: the community part was added after the Revolution

August 15 Feast of the Assumptio

October 5 Republic Day

November 1 All Saints' Day

December 1 Celebrating independence from Spain in 1640

December 8 Immaculate Conception

Christmas Day

FESTIVALS, BULLFIGHTS AND SPORTS

Portugal maintains a remarkable number of folk customs which find their expression in local carnivals (*festas*) and traditional pilgrimages (*romarias*). Some of these have developed into wild celebrations lasting days or even weeks and have become tourist events in themselves; others have barely strayed from their roots.

Every region is different, but in the **north** especially there are dozens of village festivals, everyone taking the day off to celebrate the local saint's day or the harvest, and performing ancient songs and dances in traditional dress for no one's benefit but their own. Look out, too, for the great **feiras**, especially at Barcelos (p.321). Originally they were markets, but as often as not nowadays you'll find a combination of agricultural show, folk festival, amusement park and, admittedly, tourist bazaar.

The festival list is potentially endless and only the major highlights are picked out below. For more **details** on what's going on around you, check with the local turismo or buy the monthly *Borda d'Água*, an information leaflet detailing saints' days, star signs, gardening tips and, most importantly, all the country's annual fairs. It is

MAJOR POPULAR FESTIVALS

Among the biggest and best known of the country's **popular festivals** are:

MAY

Queima das Fitas, celebrating the end of the academic year in Coimbra (mid-May).

Fátima (May 13), Portugal's most famous pilgrimage; also in October; see p.162.

JUNE

Feira Nacional at Santarém lasts for ten days (starting on the first Fri). Dancing, bullfighting and an agricultural fair; see p.174.

Festa de São Gonçalo in Amarante (1st weekend); see p.287.

Santos Populares (Popular Saints) in Lisbon – celebrations in honour of St Anthony (June 13), St John (24) and St Peter (29). Festival, too, in Porto for St John on the same date.

JULY

Festa do Colete Encarnado in Vila Franca de Xira, with Pamplona-style running of bulls through the streets (first two weeks); see p.178.

AUGUST

Romaria da Nossa Senhora da Agonia in Viana do Castelo (third weekend); see p.328.

SEPTEMBER

Romaria de Nossa Senhora dos Remédios in Lamego (pilgrimage from Sept 6–8, though events start in last week of Aug and run through to mid-Sept); see p.296.

"New Fairs" in Ponte de Lima (2nd and 3rd weekend); see p.342.

OCTOBER

Feira de Outubro in Vila Franca de Xira (first two weeks); more bull-running and fighting.

Fátima (Oct 13); second great pilgrimage of the year; see p.162.

NOVEMBER

Feira Nacional do Cavalo (National Horse Fair) in Golegã; see p.172.

---

often the obscure and unexpected event which turns out to be the most fun.

Among major national celebrations, **Easter Week** and **St John's Eve** (June 23/24) stand out. Both are celebrated throughout the country with religious processions. The former is most magnificent in Braga, where it is full of ceremonial pomp, while the latter tends to be a more joyous affair. In Porto, where St John's Eve is the highlight of a week of celebration, everyone dances through the streets all night, hitting each other over the head with plastic hammers.

BULLFIGHTS

The Portuguese **bullfight** is neither as commonplace nor as famous as its Spanish counterpart, but as a spectacle it's marginally preferable. In Portugal the bull isn't killed, but instead wrestled to the ground in a genuinely elegant, colourful and skilled display. After the fight, however, the bull is usually injured and it is always slaughtered later in any case.

If you choose to go – and we would urge visitors not to support the events put on simply for tourist benefit on the Algarve – these are the basics.

A *tourada* opens with the bull, its horns padded or sheared flat, facing a mounted *toureiro* in elaborate eighteenth-century costume. His job is to provoke and exhaust the bull and to plant the dart-like *farpas* (or *bandarilhas*) in its back while avoiding the charge – a demonstration of incredible riding prowess. Once the beast is tired the *moços-de-forcado*, or simply *forcados*, move in, an eight-man team which tries finally to immobilize it. It appears a totally suicidal task – they line up behind each other across the ring from the bull and persuade it to charge them, the front man leaping between the horns while the rest grab hold and try to subdue it. It's as absurd as it is courageous, and often takes two or three attempts, the first tries often resulting with one or more of the *forcados* being tossed spectacularly into the air.

The great Portuguese bullfight centre is **Ribatejo**, where the animals are bred. If you want to see a fight, it's best to witness it here, amid the local *aficionados*, or as part of the festivals in Vila Franca de Xira and Santarém. The season lasts from around April to October. Local towns and villages in the Ribatejo also feature **bull-running**, through the streets, at various of their festivals; see Chapter Two for further details.

SPORTS

Soccer is the Portuguese national sport, with a long and often glorious tradition of international and club teams. The leading clubs, inevitably, hail from Lisbon (Benfica and Sporting) and Porto (FC Porto). Just about every Portuguese supports one of these three teams, paying scant attention to the lesser, local teams. Of these, F.C. Guimarães are the most consistent challengers to the big-league boys, though Académica de Coimbra are worth watching too. If you want to see a league match, the season runs from September through to May. Tickets are inexpensive, and matches given due prominence in the local press. The spectacle of a packed capacity football stadium puts bullfights somewhat in the shade.

PARTICIPATORY SPORTS

Participatory sports on offer in Portugal include windsurfing, golf and tennis – all of which are promoted mainly on the Algarve. **Windsurf boards** are available for rent on most of the Algarve beaches and at the more popular northern and Lisbon coast resorts. The biggest windsurfing (and surfing) destination is **Guincho**, north of Lisbon (see p.113), though the winds and currents here require a high level of expertise.

Tennis courts are a common feature of most larger Algarve hotels – their attraction being that you can play year-round. If you want to improve your game, the best intensive coaching is under the instruction of ex-Wimbledon pro Roger Taylor at the **Vale do Lobo** resort complex. Arguably the country's best **golf course**, designed by Frank Penninck, is just up the road from here at **Vilamoura**, and several others are within reach.

Anyone interested in **fishing** should head to the trout streams of the Minho and other northern regions; licences are available from local town halls. For further information – and addresses of operators promoting **sporting holidays** – contact the Portuguese National Tourist Office for a copy of their *Sportugal* brochure.

TROUBLE, POLICE AND SEXUAL HARASSMENT

Portugal is a remarkably crime-free country, though there's the usual petty theft in larger tourist resorts. Although Lisbon is one of the safer European capitals, you should take care in the Alfama and parts of the Bairro Alto after dark; if you are robbed, whatever you do, don't resist. Hand over your valuables and run. Watch out also for pickpockets on public transport, something for which Lisbon is developing a bit of a reputation.

Rental cars, too, are always prey to thieves: remove any rental company stickers and wherever you park, don't leave anything visible in the car – preferably, don't leave anything in the car at all.

WHAT TO DO IF YOU'RE ROBBED

If you do have anything stolen while in Portugal, you'll need to go the **police** – primarily to file a report which your insurance company will require before they'll pay out for any claims made on your policy. Police stations in Lisbon and other major towns are detailed in the various "Listings" sections throughout the guide.

In an emergency, dial ☎115 for the police.

You can't count on English being spoken by most of the local police personnel you may have occasion to meet, and since tourists can usually muster only a few basic words of Portuguese, confusion can easily arise. To this end, showing deference to a police officer is wise: the Portuguese still hold respect dear, and the more respect you show a figure in authority, the quicker you will be on your way.

THE POLICE

There are three different authorities with which you might come into contact, though in an emergency, the first policeman you see will be able to point you in the right direction. In major towns, the police force most likely to be of assistance will be the **PSP** (Polícia de Segurança Pública), responsible among other things for incidents involving tourists. They wear distinctive blue uniforms, a beret and a badge on their jackets identifying themselves. Once you're away from the larger conurbations, you will have to rely on the **GNR** (Guarda Nacional Republicana) for help: they police the rural areas, patrol the motorways, and are responsible for overseeing all ceremonial occasions, like state visits, at which time they deck themselves out in magnificent dress uniforms. Ordinarily, though, they wear blue-grey uniforms and highly polished knee-length boots. If you require specialist help – work permits and the like – the local office of the **Serviço de Estrangeiros e Fronteiras** is the place to go.

SEXUAL HARASSMENT

The ruralism and small-town life of Portugal make it one of the most relaxed of the Latin countries for **women travellers**. Which is not to say that the Portuguese *machismo* is any less ingrained than in Spain or Italy: simply that it gets rather less of an outlet.

Portugal is rarely a dangerous place for women travellers, and only in the following few areas do you need to be particularly wary: parts of Lisbon (particularly around Cais do Sodré and the Bairro Alto by night), streets immediately around train stations in the larger towns (traditionally the red-light districts), and some of the Algarve resorts, where aggressive males congregate on the pick-up.

On the whole it's a rural country, intensely traditional and formal to the point of prudishness. People may initially wonder why you're travelling on your own – especially inland and in the mountains, where Portuguese women rarely travel unaccompanied – but once they have accepted that you are a crazy foreigner you're likely to be welcomed, adopted, and even offered food and lodging in their homes.

As far as transport goes, **hitching** is reasonably safe as long as there are two or more of you – but absolutely not recommended for lone women travellers. If you are on your own, you should be able to get around at night by **taxi**, which are very cheap anyway. By day **public transport** is good and quite safe; but remember to take the usual precautions at night on Lisbon's Metro and on the Cais do Sodré–Cascais coastal train line.

WORKING IN PORTUGAL

Portugal has employment problems of its own, and without a special skill you're unlikely to have much luck finding any kind of long-term work. One realistic option though is **teaching English**. For this a TEFL certificate is a distinct advantage, though you may find work without one. The biggest demand nowadays is for teaching English to children, probably in the smaller provincial towns. If you're already in Portugal you could just apply to individual schools or advertise your services privately, but even EU citizens should register with the Serviço de Estrangeiros e Fronteiras. Non EU passport holders must apply for a work permit before they enter Portugal.)

WORKING ON THE ALGARVE

As far as temporary jobs go, the only real opportunities are in tourist-related work **on the Algarve**, which offer a range of ways of getting money, all of them dependent to some extent on your self-confidence and/or lack of scruples.

Most obvious of the jobs is **bar work**. This is not easy to find – you'll stand the best chance in one of the many British-owned places – and even when you do, it often brings in barely enough money to live on. Better, at least in terms of time involved, is to try your hand walking the streets at night **giving out disco invitations** to holiday-makers. This work is available in most major resorts and is paid solely on a commission basis, but it does leave you free during the day – and much of the night – to seek your own entertainment.

Which leads nicely into the biggest scam in the country – perhaps in Europe – of **selling time shares**. Here possibilities exist for making really big bucks, though not everyone, of course, strikes it rich. The work involves walking the streets in the major resorts inviting British tourist couples to view time-share resorts and villas. It is extremely tiring, soul-destroying, and, at its most successful, pretty disreputable work, but earnings are on a commission basis and this can add up to a fair living if you're the type who enjoys selling your own grandmother. Just ask the people who are already doing the job on the street what to do. They'll tell you how to find work and how depressing it is.

One last option is to head for the huge yacht marina at **Vilamoura**, which holds around a thousand craft and is slowly being surrounded by trendy bars, boutiques and cafés. You could try some of these, but it's even better to approach the yachties themselves. Almost all boat owners have hundreds of little tasks that need doing and, given the opportunity, will pay a few thousand *escudos* to anyone presenting themselves as a handyman/woman. Mostly it's **painting** or **scrubbing down** decks – hardly skilled labour – but if you can convince someone you know what you're doing the quality of work you'll be given may improve. Between late September and early November, however, there's the chance of **crewing** to the Canaries or the Caribbean; for this sort of angle try the local bars as well as word of mouth. For the more menial odd jobs you just need persistence and a thick skin: spend a couple of days asking around and something should turn up.

If you do decide to stay on in the Algarve to work, the easiest (if unofficial) way to **extend** your sixty or ninety days is to cross the border at Vila Real de Santo António. The official way, if reliable long-term employment beckons, is to go to one of the Serviço de Estrangeiros offices in Portimão, Albufeira or Faro.

DIRECTORY

ADDRESSES Most addresses in Portugal consist of a street name and number followed by a storey number, eg, Rua de Afonso Henriques 34-3°. This means you need to go up to the third floor of no. 34 (US, fourth floor). An "esq" or "E" (standing for *esquerda*) after a floor number means you should go to the left; "dir" or "D" (for *direita*) indicates the apartment or office you're looking for is on the right. *Esquina* means corner or junction.

BAGGAGE You can often leave bags at a train or bus station for a small sum while you look for rooms. On the whole the Portuguese are highly trustworthy, and even shopkeepers and café owners will keep an eye on your belongings for you. Or try the local turismo, which may agree to look after your bags for a while.

BEACHES Beware of the heavy undertow on many of Portugal's western Atlantic beaches and don't swim if you see a red or yellow flag. The EU blue flag indicates that the water is clean enough to swim in – sadly, not always the case at many of Portugal's resorts. The sea is warmest on the eastern Algarve (ie, the beaches east of Faro).

CHILDREN Portugal is child-friendly and families should find it as easy a place to roam as any other country. Cheap hotels and *pensões* will only rarely charge extra for children in their parents' room and many of the more upmarket hotels give a fifty percent discount for children under eight. In restaurants small portions and extra plates are absolutely the norm for all who require them.

Lastly, museums and most sights don't usually charge for small children.

CONTRACEPTION Condoms – *preservativos* – are widely available from street vending machines, as well as in pharmacies and supermarkets. In more rural, traditional places, you may have to ask and the pharmacist will set out an array on the counter, in the best formal Portuguese manner.

DRESS Churches often require "modest dress" – which basically just means you shouldn't wear shorts or very flimsy tops.

DUTY-FREE GOODS If you're in the market for duty-free goods, try to check out prices when you arrive at the airport. Apart from standard *licor* brands, there are no great savings to be made relative to Portuguese high-street prices. For national specialities – including wine, port, and brandy – you're better off buying from local groceries and *licor* stores.

EMERGENCIES Phone ☎115 for the emergency services. If you're involved in a road accident, use the nearest roadside orange-coloured SOS telephone – press the button and wait for an answer.

FILM Going to the movies in Portugal is extremely cheap, and films are often shown with the original (usually English-language) soundtrack with Portuguese subtitles. Listings can be found in the local newspaper or on boards, invariably placed somewhere in the central square of every small town. Screenings are cheap, with reduced price matinées and at all Monday shows.

GAY LIFE The gay scene isn't especially prominent, or at least commercialized, though there's a fair sprinkling of clubs, and a gay beach, in Lisbon and one or two places to meet in Porto and the Algarve. Attitudes in the capital are fairly tolerant; elsewhere a gay consciousness has yet to make much impact. There is no explicit law against homosexuality.

LAUNDRY There are very few self-service launderettes, but loads of *lavandarias*, where you can get your clothes washed, mended, and ironed (overnight) at a fairly low cost. Some of these offer only a dry-cleaning service.

NATIONAL/NATURAL PARKS The head office in Lisbon (Rua da Lapa 73, 1200 Lisbon) has details on Portugal's parks and reserves, but generally neither head nor district offices have much time for foreign visitors, concentrating on awakening a spirit of wildlife conservation and protection in their compatriots.

SWIMMING POOLS Every sizeable town has a swimming pool, usually outdoors, but you'll find that they are often closed from September to May.

TIME Portugal now follows "British" time, ie GMT in winter and one hour ahead in summer. Clocks go forward one hour at the end of March and back an hour at the end of October.

TIPPING Hotels and restaurants include a service charge but porters and maids expect something; cab drivers don't.

TOILETS "Ladies" often charge and are clean, "Gentlemen" may look more aesthetic (lots of ironwork) and are free, but usually pretty unattractive inside. A sign that says *Retretes, Banheiro, Lavabos or WC* will head you in the right direction, then it's *homens* or *cabalheiros* for men and *senhoras* for women. Ask for "*um banheiro*" if in doubt.

WOMEN'S MOVEMENT There are relatively few women's organizations in Portugal. The best contact points are the IDM centre and the feminist bookshop Editora das Mulheres, both in Lisbon (see p.108). Also of interest is the Comissão para a Igualdade e para os Direitos das Mulheres (Avenida da República 32-1°, 1000 Lisbon), which maintains a watching brief on all aspects of women's lives in Portugal; members organize conferences and meetings, are very active in areas of social and legal reform, and are linked with other feminists throughout the country.

THE
GUIDE

LISBON AND AROUND

There are few cityscapes as startling and eccentric as that of **Lisbon** (Lisboa). Built on a switchback of hills above the broad **Tejo** estuary, its quarters are linked by an amazing network of cobbled streets with outrageous gradients, up which crank trams and funiculars. Down by the river, you are lured across towards the sea by a vast, Rio-like statue of Christ, arms outstretched, whose embrace encompasses one of the grandest of all suspension bridges and a fleet of cross-river ferries. For visitors, it's hard not to see the city as an urban funfair: a sense heightened by the castle poised above the Alfama district's medieval, whitewashed streets; the fantasy Manueline architecture of

Belém; the mosaics of the central Rossio square; and the multitude of Art Nouveau shops and cafés.

To Americans, San Francisco is an obvious counterpart: a city that exhibits parallels not only in its physical appearance but also in its fault-line location – Lisbon's Great Earthquake of 1755 levelled most of the old lower town. The two cities stand further comparison as Lisbon, too, is immediately likeable, gentler than any port or capital should expect to be, almost provincial in feel and defiantly human in pace and scale. For much of the present century, the city stood apart from the European mainstream, an isolation that ended abruptly with the 1974 Revolution, and still more so with Portugal's integration into the European Community (now the European Union) just over a decade later.

Over the past hundred years, central Lisbon's population has more than doubled to over a million, one tenth of all Portuguese, with numbers boosted considerably after the Revolution by the vast influx of **refugees** – *retornados* – from Portugal's former African colonies of Angola, Cabo Verde, São Tomé e Principe, Guinea Bissau and Mozambique. The *retornados* imposed a heavy burden on an already strained economy, especially on housing, but their overall integration is one of the chief triumphs of modern Portugal. Like the city's Brazilian contingent, the Portuguese Africans have also brought a significant **cultural** buoyancy. Alongside the traditional fado clubs of its Bairro Alto and Alfama quarters, Lisbon now has superb Latin and African bands, and a panoply of international restaurants and bars.

Conventional sights and monuments are arguably thin on the ground, largely as a result of the 1755 earthquake. The Romanesque **Sé** (cathedral) and the Moorish walls of the **Castelo de São Jorge** are fine early survivors, though hardly unique in Portugal. But there is one building from Portugal's Golden Age – the extraordinary **Mosteiro dos Jerónimos** at Belém – that is the equal of any in the country. Two museums demand attention, too: the **Fundação Calouste Gulbenkian**, a combined museum and cultural complex with superb collections of ancient and modern art, and the **Museu Nacional de Arte Antiga**, effectively Portugal's national art gallery. The latest highlight, however, is the high-tech **Expo 98** site and its star attraction, the futuristic **Oceanarium**. Beyond these sights, it's the central streets, avenues and squares, and their attendant comings and goings, that keep the interest level well topped up; watch out, too, for some adventurous contemporary architecture, such as Tómas Taveira's shopping complex at **Amoreiras**.

All of this makes for a city that demands at least a few days out of anyone's Portuguese itinerary. Better still, make the capital a base for a week or two's holiday, taking day trips and excursions out into the surrounding area. The sea is close by, with the beach suburbs of **Estoril** and **Cascais** just half an hour's journey away to the west by train; while to the south, across the Tejo, are the miles of dunes along the **Costa da Caparica**. Slightly further south lies the port of **Setúbal**, featuring one of the earliest Manueline churches, while nearby is the resort of Sesimbra – a popular day-trip for Lisboetas. Northwest of the city, again easily reached by train, lie the lush wooded heights and royal palaces of **Sintra**, Byron's "glorious Eden." And should you develop an interest in Portuguese architecture, there are the Rococo delights of the **Palácio de Queluz** and its gardens en route, or the extraordinary monastery of **Mafra** – a good first step into Estremadura, the region immediately to the north.

LISBON

Physically, **LISBON** is an eighteenth-century city: elegant, open to the sea and carefully planned. The description does not extend to its modern expanse, of course – there are suburbs here as poor and inadequate as any in Europe – but remains accurate within the old central boundary of a triangle of hills. This "lower town", the **Baixa**, was the product of a single phase of building, carried out in less than a decade by the dictatorial minister, the Marquês de Pombal, in the wake of the earthquake that destroyed much of central Lisbon in 1755.

The **Great Earthquake**, which was felt as far away as Jamaica, struck Lisbon at 9.30am on November 1 (All Saints' Day), when most of the city's population was at Mass. Within the space of ten minutes there had been three major tremors and the candles of a hundred church altars had started fires that raged throughout the capital. A vast tidal wave swept the seafront, where refugees were seeking shelter, and, in all, 40,000 of the 270,000 population died. The destruction of the city shocked the continent, prompting Voltaire, who wrote an account of it in his novel *Candide*, into an intense debate with Rousseau on the operation of providence. For Portugal, and for the capital, it was a disaster that in retrospect seemed to seal an age. Previously, eighteenth-century Lisbon had been arguably the most active port in Europe.

Indeed, the city had been prosperous since **Roman**, perhaps even Phoenician, times. In the Middle Ages, as **Moorish** Lishbuna, it thrived on its wide links with the Arab world, while exploiting the rich territories to the south: the Alentejo and Algarve. The country's reconquest by the Christians in 1147 was an early and dubious triumph of the Crusades, its one positive aspect being the appearance of the first true Portuguese monarch **Afonso Henriques**. It was not until 1255, however, that Lisbon took over from Coimbra as capital.

Over the following centuries, Lisbon was twice at the forefront of European development and trade, on a scale that is hard to envisage today. The first phase came with the great Portuguese **discoveries** of the late fifteenth and sixteenth centuries, such as Vasco da Gama's opening of the sea route to India. The second was in the opening decades of the **eighteenth century**, when the colonized Brazil was found to yield both gold and diamonds. These phases were the great ages of Portuguese patronage. The sixteenth century is dominated by the figure of **Dom Manuel I**, under whom the flamboyant national architectural style known as Manueline developed. Lisbon takes its principal monuments – the tower and monastery at Belém – from this era. The eighteenth century, more extravagant but with less brilliant effect, produced **Dom João V**, best known as the obsessive builder of Mafra, which he created in response to Philip II's El Escorial in Spain.

The city in the nineteenth and early twentieth centuries was more notable for its political upheavals (from the assassination of Carlos I to the Revolution in 1974) than for any architectural legacy, though the **Art Nouveau** movement made its mark on the capital. However, in the last decade, Lisbon has once more echoed to the sounds of incoming money and reconstruction on a scale not seen for two hundred years. After the influx of EU cash for economic regeneration in the 1980s came the recognition of Lisbon as **European City of Culture** in 1994, with new arts facilities and renovated buildings helping to give the city a higher European profile.

Lisbon is set to receive attention on an unprecedented scale when it hosts **Expo 98**. To coincide with the event, almost every monument has been spruced up and a major new transport infrastructure has been put into place, including the construction of Europe's biggest bridge, new rail and metro lines and a road network encircling the capital. If this activity has gone some way towards destroying the provincial feel of the city, it has also injected a wave of excitement and optimism that has made Lisbon one of Europe's most happening cities.

The **telephone code** for the Greater Lisbon area is ☎01.

Arrival and information

On **arrival**, the first place to head for is Rossio, which is easily accessible from all points of arrival, either on foot, by bus or by taxi. Most of the city's pensions (*pensões*) are within walking distance of the square, and on the western side of the adjoining Praça dos Restauradores, the English-speaking **turismo** (daily 9am–8pm; ☎346 33 14) in the Palácio da Foz can provide you with accommodation lists, bus timetables and **maps** of the city. You can arrange car rental here, too. For **departure information**, by air, bus and train, refer to the relevant sections of "Listings".

By air
The **airport** is just twenty minutes north of the city centre and has a tourist office (daily 6am–1am), exchange bureau and information desk that can help you find accommodation (see p.57). There are also car rental agencies at the airport; details in "Listings" on p.106.

The easiest way into the centre is by **taxi**, which should cost 1500–2000$00 to Rossio, depending on traffic conditions. Note that you'll be charged 300$00 extra for baggage, and that fares are slightly higher between 10pm and 6am, at weekends and on public holidays.

Alternatively, catch the #91 **Aerobus**, which departs every twenty minutes between 7am and 9pm from outside the terminal, and runs to Praça do Marquês de Pombal, Praça dos Restauradores, Rossio, Praça do Comércio and Cais do Sodré train station. The **ticket**, which you buy from the driver, gives you one day's travel on the city's buses and trams for 430$00 (available free from the Welcome Desk for TAP passengers) or three days' for 1000$00 – see p.53 for more information. Cheaper **local buses** (#44 or #45) leave from the main road outside the terminal to Praça dos Restauradores and Cais do Sodré station every ten to fifteen minutes between 4am and 1.40am (150$00), though these are less convenient if you have a lot of luggage.

By train
Long-distance trains from Coimbra, Porto and the north (and from Badajoz, Madrid and Paris) arrive at **Santa Apolónia station** (☎888 41 42), from where it's about fifteen minutes' walk west to Praça do Comércio, or a short ride on bus #9, #39, #46 or #90 to Praça dos Restauradores or Rossio. At the station there's a helpful information office (Mon–Sat 9am–7pm) and an exchange bureau.

Trains from the Algarve and south take a slightly more involved approach. The railway lines from the south terminate at the Barreiro station (☎207 30 28), on the far bank of the river, from where you catch a ferry (included in the price of the train ticket) to the Fluvial station (also known as Sul e Sueste), next to Praça do Comércio. Buses #9, #39, #80 and #90 run up from Fluvial to Rossio, through the Baixa.

Local trains from Sintra and some destinations in Estremadura emerge right in the heart of the city at Rossio station (☎346 50 22), a mock-Manueline complex with the train platforms an improbable escalator-ride above the street-level entrances. The station is complete with shops, bank exchange counters and left-luggage cabins. Services from Cascais and Estoril arrive at the other local station, Cais do Sodré (☎347 01 81), also fairly central – you can either walk the half a kilometre east along the waterfront to Praça do Comércio or take any of the buses heading in that direction. The station also has its own metro stop.

By bus

Various bus companies have terminals scattered about the city, but the main one is at Avenida Casal Ribeiro (metro Saldanha), north of the centre, which has an information office that can help with all bus arrival and departure details. This terminal is also where most international bus services arrive. You can usually buy tickets if you turn up half an hour or so in advance, though for the summer express services to the Algarve it's best to book a seat (through any travel agent) a day in advance. See "Listings" for other bus terminals in the city, and check with the turismo for the latest details.

By car

Driving into Lisbon can take years off your life, and if it's the beginning or end of a public holiday weekend should be avoided at all costs. Heading to or from the south on these occasions, it can take over an hour just to cross the Ponte 25 de Abril, a notorious traffic bottleneck that the new Vasco da Gama bridge will do little to alleviate. Parking is also very difficult in the centre and you'd be wise to head straight for an official car park: central locations include the underground one at Restauradores; Parque Mayer on Travessa do Salitre, off Avenida da Liberdade; Parque Eduardo VII; the underground car parks around the Gulbenkian such as Parking Berna on Rua M.D. Sá de Bandeira; and the Amoreiras complex on Avenida Eng. Duarte Pacheco. Wherever you park, do not leave valuables inside: the break-in rate is extremely high.

If you are renting a car on arrival, the best advice is to wait until the day you leave the city to pick it up; you really don't need your own transport to get around Lisbon and its surroundings. See "Listings" on p.106 for car rental companies if you remain undeterred.

City transport

Most places of interest are within easy walking distance of each other, but for those that are further away transport connections by tram, bus or metro are detailed in the text. Taxis are among the cheapest in Europe and a useful complement at all hours. Note that although it is one of the safer cities in Europe,

△ The Airport   △ Expo Site

△ Roma Metro

LISBON

ACCOMMODATION
1 Pensão Lar do Areeiro
2 Pensão Pátria
3 Residencial Canada
4 Hotel Impala
5 Pensão Embaixatrix
6 Residencial Pascoal de Melo
7 Residencial Luena
8 Residencial O Paradouro
9 Miraparque
10 Residencial Avenida Alameda
11 Ritz Lisboa
12 Capital Hotel
13 Hotel Fenix
14 Tivoli Lisboa
15 Hotel Britania
16 Hotel Lisboa Plaza
17 Residencial Alegria
18 Residencial Pemba
19 Pensão Monumental
20 Hotel Suisso-Atlántico
21 Pensão Iris
22 Residencial Florescente
23 Residencial Flor da Baixa
24 Pensão Imperial
25 Pensão Dona Maria II
26 Residencial York House
27 As Janelas Verdes
28 Hotel da Lapa

Entrecampos Station

Praça de Touros

Bus Station

Youth Hostel

Museu Gulbenkian

Centro de Arte Moderna

Estufas

Parque Eduardo VII

SALDANHA

ESTEFÂNIA

Lisbon has its share of **pickpockets**. Take special care on the metro and buses, and when walking around the main squares.

Public transport in the city is operated by Carris (☎363 20 44). If you're staying for more than a few days, it may be worth getting a **Lisboa Card** (1500$00 for one day, 2500$00 for two days or 3250$00 for three days), which entitles you to free bus and metro rides and entry to 25 museums, plus discounts of around 25 to 50 percent for other main sites. The card is available from Rua Jardim do Regedor 50, the Mosteiro dos Jerónimos and the Museu Nacional do Arte Antiga. The **Passe Turístico** (1600$00 for four days, 2265$00 for seven) might also be worth considering. It's valid on the metro, trams, buses and *elevadors*, and is obtainable, on production of a passport, at kiosks by the Elevador Santa Justa, in Praça da Figueira and in Restauradores metro station, among other places. For much longer stays, there is the **Passe Social** (3810$00), renewable each calendar month and purchased from the booths or at any metro station with a *venda de passes* sign; you'll need a photograph and there's the usual bit of form filling to do. Otherwise, just buy a ticket each time you ride: all the details are given below.

The metro and local trains

Lisbon's **metro** – the Metropolitano – covers a few useful routes (to the Gulbenkian museum, for example), and many new stations are opening around the city; the most central are those at Praça dos Restauradores and Rossio. **Hours of operation** are 6am–1am and **tickets** cost 70$00 per journey or 550$00 for a ten-ticket *caderneta* – sold at all stations. If you think you're going to use the metro a lot, you could buy a one-day (200$00), seven-day (620$00) or thirty-day (2070$00) **pass**.

There is a **local train** line west along the coast through Belém, to Estoril (p.109) and Cascais (p.110); trains depart from Cais do Sodré station, west of Praça do Comércio. Tickets to Estoril and Cascais are currently 185$00 one way. The other local train line you're likely to use is the service to Queluz (see p.122; 155$00 one way) and Sintra (see p.114; 185$00 one way), which departs from the central Rossio station.

Trams, elevadors and buses

At the slightest excuse you should ride one of the city's **trams** (*eléctricos*). Ascending some of the steepest gradients of any city in the world, many are worth taking for the sheer pleasure of the ride alone; **#28**, for example, is probably the best public transport ride in the city, running from São Vicente to the Estrêla gardens, passing through Rua da Conceição in the Baixa. Other useful routes include the **#12** from São Tomé in the Alfama to Largo Martim Moniz, near Praça da Figueira; and the new modern "supertram" **#15** from Praça da Figueira to Belém. Further suggestions are detailed in the text where appropriate.

The three funicular railways and one street lift – each known as an **elevador** – are also exciting forms of transport, offering quick access up to the Bairro Alto; see the box on p.57 for their routes. Otherwise, **buses** (*carris*) run just about everywhere in the Lisbon area and can prove valuable for getting to and from the more outlying attractions. Most of the trams, buses and *elevadors* run every ten to fifteen minutes throughout the day, from around 6.30am to midnight: stops are indicated by a sign marked *paragem*, which carries route details.

Individual **tickets** for a bus, tram or *elevador* bought on board cost 150$00; alternatively a ticket valid for two journeys can be bought from kiosks for the

---

ELEVADORS

Elevador da Bica: funicular linking Rua do Loreto/Rua Luz Soriano in Bairro Alto to Rua de São Paulo near Cais do Sodré station.

Elevador da Glória: a funicular to the Bairro Alto from the west side of Praça dos Restauradores.

Elevador de Santa Justa: a lift, rather than a funicular, taking you from Rua do Ouro, on the west side of the Baixa, up to a walkway by the ruined Carmo church.

Elevador do Lavra: funicular linking Rua São José, just off Avda. da Liberdade, to the back of the Institute of Medicine and Hospital de São José.

---

same amount. There are also one-day (430$00) or three-day (1000$00) **passes**, which you validate by punching in the machine by the driver the first time you ride; it's then valid for 24 or 72 hours.

A couple of **tram and bus tours** run during the summer months, departing from Praça do Comércio; for more information see "Listings".

Taxis

Lisbon's cream or black-and-green **taxis** are inexpensive, so long as your destination is within the city limits; there's a minimum charge of 250$00 and an average ride will run to around 600$00 (a little more from 10pm to 6am). Fares are higher at weekends and on public holidays. All taxis have meters, which are generally switched on, and tips are not expected. A green light means the cab is unoccupied – the only problem then is persuading them to stop. They can be found quite easily by day at the **ranks** in Rossio and Praça da Figueira and those at the southern end of Avenida da Liberdade and at Cais do Sodré. At night, however, when going home from a bar or restaurant, it's usually best to **phone**: try Rádio Taxis (☎815 50 61), Autocoope (☎793 27 56) or Teletaxi (☎815 20 76).

Ferries

Finally there are the **ferries**, which cross the Tejo at various points. From **Praça do Comércio** (Fluvial), there are crossings to Cacilhas (daily 6am–10.30pm; 90$00 one way), Barreiro (daily 6am–10.30pm; 155$00), Montijo (daily 6am–10.30pm; 275$00) and the Expo site at Olivais. They're worth taking for the terrific views of Lisbon alone, something you may prefer to see from a tourist river cruise (see "Listings" p.106). From **Cais do Sodré**, ferries also cross to Cacilhas (24-hour service, every 20–30min during day, 40–50min at night; 90$00). From **Belém** there are services to Trafaria (Mon–Sat 6.30am–11.30pm, Sun 7.30am–11.30pm, every 30 min–1hr; 125$00), from where you can catch buses to Caparica.

Accommodation

If you have enough money for mid-range *pensões* and the more expensive categories of hotels, you're probably best off using the **booking service** at the turismo (daily 9am–8pm) in Praça dos Restauradores; there is no commission charge. The **airport information desk**, facing you as you pass through Customs, will establish whether or not there's space at a city *pensão* or hotel, but they won't

ACCOMMODATION PRICE CODES

All the accommodation prices in this book have been coded using the symbols below. The symbols represent the lowest prices you can expect to pay for a **double room in high season**; for a full explanation, see p.29.

① Under 3000$00
② 3000$00–4000$00
③ 4000$00–5500$00
④ 5500$00–8500$00
⑤ 8500$00–12,500$00
⑥ 12,500$00–20,000$00
⑦ Over 20,000$00

reserve the room for you. For more information on the various types of accommodation available see "Basics" pp.28–31.

Lisbon has scores of small, inexpensive **pensões**, often in tall tenement buildings, in all the central parts of the city. The most obvious and accessible area, with dozens of possibilities, is around Rossio, Praça dos Restauradores and Praça da Figueira. Among cheaper *pensões*, the most likely to have space at busy times of year are those on either side of Avenida da Liberdade and on parallel streets, such as Rua das Portas de Santo Antão and Rua da Glória. The Baixa grid, to the south, has a fair selection of places, too, with a couple of more upmarket choices in the Chiado's shopping streets. Bairro Alto is probably the most atmospheric, if noisy, part of the city to stay in, though rooms in its few *pensões* can be hard to come by, and there are a couple of attractive places on the periphery of the Alfama, climbing up towards the castle. Finally, a number of more expensive places are located out of the historic centre: in the prosperous streets in the suburb of Lapa; around Parque Eduardo VII and Saldanha, where many places are geared to the business traveller; or to the east, in the area around Avenida Almirante Reis – in particular the streets between Anjos and Arroios metro stops.

When doing the rounds, be warned that the *pensões* tend to be on upper storeys (leaving one person with all your bags is a good idea if you're in company). **Addresses** – written below as 53-3° and so on – refer to the street number followed by the storey number. Don't be unduly put off by some fairly insalubrious staircases, but do be aware that rooms facing onto the street can be unbearably noisy.

At Easter, and even more so in midsummer, room **availability** is often stretched to the limit, with artificially inflated prices. At these times, be prepared to take anything vacant and, if need be, look around the next day for somewhere better, or possibly cheaper. Fortunately, for most of the year you should have little difficulty finding a room, and can even try knocking the price down at quieter times, especially if you're able to summon up a few good-natured phrases in Portuguese.

Lisbon has two **youth hostels**, one in the city centre and one out at Oeiras, overlooking the sea. For details of these, and the city's **camping** possibilities, see p.63.

Rossio and Praça da Figueira

All the hotels and pensões listed below are marked on the Baixa map on p.65.

Pensão Arco da Bandeira, Rua dos Sapateiros 226-4° (☎342 34 78). Friendly pension with half a dozen comfortable rooms, some overlooking Rossio. The separate bathrooms are spotless. The entrance is just through the arch at the southern end of the square. ③.

Hotel Avenida Palace, Rua 1° de Dezembro (☎346 01 51). Lisbon's grandest downtown hotel, tucked away between Rossio and Praça dos Restauradores. Elegant nineteenth-century style and very comfortable rooms sporting high ceilings, traditional furnishings and marble bathrooms. ⑦.

Pensão Beira Minho, Praça da Figueira 6-2° (☎346 18 46). Rooms (with and without bath) are small but clean and some have fine views, though the cheaper ones without windows may dissuade some. There are rooms on the fourth floor, too. ③.

Pensão Coimbra e Madrid, Praça da Figueira 3-3° (☎342 17 60, fax 342 32 64). Large, decently run (if faintly shabby) *pensão*, above the *Pastelaria Suíça*. Superb views of Rossio, Praça da Figueira and the castle beyond from (street-honkingly noisy) front-facing rooms, which come with shower or bath. Best choice on the square. Breakfast included. ③.

Pensão Estação Central, Calçada do Carmo 17-2° (☎342 33 08). To the side of Rossio station; climb the flight of stairs and head up the road to the left. Small, musty rooms, some with cubby-hole bathrooms, but you get what you pay for. ②.

Pensão Ibérica, Praça da Figueira 10-2° (☎886 70 26, fax 886 7412.). Central location and lots of rooms, most with TVs, but it's a bit ramshackle and has gloomy, uninspiring decor. The rooms overlooking the praça are the best, if noisiest. There's a breakfast room and a 24hr reception for those planning a late night out. ③.

Hotel International, Rua da Betesga 3 (☎346 64 01, fax 347 86 35). You know this is a smart central choice as soon as you see the red-carpeted lift, and if you get one of the rooms with a balcony overlooking the town, you won't be disappointed. Rooms have air-conditioning, TV and a safe. ⑤.

Residencial Montepuez, Rua Dom Duarte 2-4° (☎887 57 40). The friendly Mozambiquan owners offer big, clean rooms with washbasin and shower; some have balconies overlooking Praça da Figueira. Basic kitchen with fridge but bathrooms are communal. Breakfast not included. ③.

Hotel Mundial, Rua Dom Duarte 4 (☎886 31 01, fax 887 91 29). Central four-star hotel which is being expanded to contain nearly 300 plush rooms. Rooftop pool and all mod cons. Buffet breakfast included. ⑥.

Hotel Portugal, Rua João das Regras 4 (☎887 75 81, fax 886 73 43). An amazing old hotel that has suffered from an appalling conversion; the high decorative ceilings upstairs have been chopped up under wall partitions. For all that, there are comfortable rooms, a lovely ornate TV room and fine azulejo-lined stairs. ⑤.

Residencial do Sul, Praça Dom Pedro IV 59 (☎342 25 11, fax 813 26 97). Entered through a small shop, this is very close to the station, and a good first choice if you want a view of Rossio itself. It's very clean and there are quieter back rooms, though some are windowless. ③.

The Baixa and Chiado

All the hotels and pensões listed below are marked on the Baixa map on p.65.

Hotel Borges, Rua Garrett 108 (☎346 19 51, fax 342 66 17). Nice position near the *Brasileira* café in Chiado's main street, though the rooms are very ordinary and the hotel itself often filled with tour groups. Breakfast included. ⑤.

Hotel Duas Nações, Rua da Vitória 41 (☎346 07 10, fax 347 02 06). Classy, pleasantly faded, nineteenth-century hotel in the Baixa grid with a secure entrance and friendly reception. Rooms with bath are more attractive, but cost quite a bit more. ③.

Pensão Galicia, Rua do Crucifixo 50-4° (☎342 84 30). The entrance is through a shoe repair stall, which you may be in need of once you've been up and down the steep stairs a few times. Sweet little rooms – the best have sunny balconies and wooden floors – and a fine Baixa location. ③.

Residencial Insulana, Rua da Assunção 52 (☎342 76 25). Reached by a series of underwear shops, this has smart rooms, each with its own bath. The bar overlooks a quiet pedestrianized street. English-speaking staff. Good breakfasts, too. ④.

Pensão Moderna, Rua dos Correeiros 205-4° (☎346 08 18). The stairwell is offputting but rooms are big, clean and crammed with old furniture. Some have (rickety) balconies overlooking the pedestrianized street. Communal bathrooms. ②.

Residencial Nova Silva, Rua Vítor Cordon 11 (☎342 43 71, fax 342 77 70). A clean, friendly option, which is also good value. Make sure you get a back room, ideally on the top floor, for a stunning view over the Tejo. Rooms with bathrooms are more expensive. ③.

Pensão Prata, Rua da Prata 71-3° (☎346 89 08). You need mountaineering experience to climb the stairs to this place, which offers small rooms in a welcoming, family-run apartment with TV lounge. Some rooms have showers, others share a clean bathroom. It's in a handy location for Praça do Comércio. Book in advance as it's popular. ②.

Bairro Alto
All the pensões listed below are marked on the Bairro Alto map on p.69.

Casa de Hóspedes Atalaia, Rua da Atalaia 150-1° (☎346 44 59). Unprepossessing, though tolerable at the price. Standards vary and you can find yourself uncomfortably remote from the shared bathrooms. Very active nocturnal life – mostly human rather than insect. ②.

Residencial Camões, Trav. do Poço da Cidade 38-1° (☎346 75 10, fax 346 40 48). Small, pretty rooms, some with balcony and the more expensive ones with private bathroom. Situated right in the midst of the Bairro Alto action (which can up the noise level). Breakfast is served in a nice, light room. ③.

Casa de São Mamede, Rua da Escola Politécnica 159 (☎396 31 66, fax 395 18 96). Superb seventeenth-century town house with period fittings, bright breakfast room and even a grand stained-glass window. Rooms are rather ordinary but come with private bathrooms and TVs. ⑤.

Pensão Duque, Calçada do Duque 53, (☎346 34 44). Near São Roque church, down the steps off the square. Fairly basic rooms with separate bathrooms. ②.

Pensão Globo, Rua do Teixeira 37 (☎346 22 79). Up Travessa da Cara from the Elevador da Glória and first right. Located in an attractive house, the rooms are simple but clean and reasonably large (though those at the top are a little cramped). It's in a good location, near the clubs but in a quiet street. ② for rooms without shower or windows, up to ④ for showers and views.

Pensão Londres, Rua Dom Pedro V 53 (☎346 55 23). Great old building with high ceilings and pleasant enough rooms spread across several price ranges and floors. Some rooms come with cubby-hole bathrooms. Breakfast included. ②–⑤.

Pensão Luar, Rua das Gavéas 101-1° (☎346 09 49). Calm, polished interior whose decently furnished rooms (with and without shower) are somewhat noisy. Some are much larger than others, so ask to see. ③.

Lapa
To reach these superb hotels (marked on the general map of Lisbon on pp.54–55), take bus #40 or #60 from Praça do Comércio. Booking in advance is recommended.

As Janelas Verdes, Rua das Janelas Verdes 47, Lapa (☎396 81 43, fax 396 81 44). This discreet eighteenth-century town house, once the home of the novelist Eça de Queiróz, is just metres from the Museu de Arte Antiga. Well-proportioned rooms with marble-clad bathrooms, period furnishings and pictures, and a delightful walled garden to which wrought-iron staircases descend from the rear rooms. Top-floor rooms have river views. Breakfast served in the garden. ⑦.

Hotel da Lapa, Rua do Pau de Bandeira 4 (☎395 00 05, fax 395 06 65). A stunning nineteenth-century mansion with dramatic vistas over the Tejo. Rooms are luxurious, and if you opt to stay in the Palace Wing, there is a different styled decor in each, from Classical to Art Deco. In summer, grills are served in the gardens by the outside pool. ⑦.

Residencial York House, Rua das Janelas Verdes 32 (☎396 24 35, fax 397 27 93). Installed in a sixteenth-century convent, rooms come with rugs, tiles and four-poster beds. The best rooms are grouped around a beautiful interior courtyard, where drinks and meals are served in summer. The restaurant is highly rated and is also open to non-residents. ⑦.

Alfama and Castelo

All the hotels and pensões listed below are marked on the Alfama and Castelo map on p.73.

Pensão Beira-Mar, Largo do Terreiro do Trigo 16 (☎887 15 28). A 10min walk east of Praça do Comercio, at the foot of the Alfama. Reasonable top-floor rooms (communal showers & toilets), some with balcony facing the main street and others with bathrooms but no windows. ③.

Pensão Ninho das Águias, Costa do Castelo 74 (☎886 70 00). Beautifully sited in its own view-laden terrace-garden on the street looping around the castle. Climb up the staircase and past the bird cages. Rooms are bright, white and light; management capricious. Book in advance. ④.

Pensão São João de Praça, Rua São João de Praça 97-2° (☎886 25 91, fax 888 13 78). Located immediately below the cathedral in a beautiful town house with street-facing balconies. It's a clean, quiet and friendly choice. Rooms vary from en suite to sharing a shower. ②.

Sé Guest House, Rua São João de Praça 97-1° (☎886 44 00). In the same building as the *Pensão São João de Praça*. Wood floors and bright, airy rooms, but communal bathrooms. Breakfast not included. ④.

Albergaria Senhora do Monte, Calçada do Monte 39 (☎886 60 02, fax 887 77 83). Comfortable, modern hotel in a beautiful location with lovely views of the castle and Graça convent from its south-facing rooms. Breakfast included. Parking available or tram #28 passes close by. ⑥, or ⑦ with a terrace.

Avenida da Liberdade, Restauradores and Rua das Portas de Santo Antão

All the hotels and pensões listed below are marked on the general map of Lisbon on pp.54–55.

Residencial Alegria, Praça Alegria 12 (☎347 55 22, fax 347 80 70). Great position, facing the leafy square. Don't let the crumbly exterior put you off as this has spacious, spotless rooms with TVs. Those with bath are more than shower-only rooms. ①.

Hotel Britania, Rua Rodrigues Sampaio 17 (☎315 50 16, fax 315 50 21). A smart three-star hotel, just to the east of the avenida, with good-sized rooms and classic Deco interior style. Buffet breakfast included. Children under 12 stay free. ⑥.

Pensão Dona Maria II, Rua Portas de Santo Antão 9-3° (☎342 52 68). Rock-bottom prices for double rooms, some with views over Rossio, others with balconies above the action on Rua Portas. Fairly basic with communal bathroom, but the price and position can't be faulted. ①.

Pensão Flor da Baixa, Rua Portas de Santo Antão 81-2° (☎342 31 53). Almost opposite the Coliseu, and entered through an electrical supply shop. A friendly *pensão* with small rooms, each with a TV. ③.

Residencial Florescente, Rua Portas de Santo Antão 99 (☎342 66 09). One of this pedestrianized street's best-value establishments, whose best rooms are spick-and-span and come with TV and small bathroom (others are windowless and less appealing). Breakfast not included. ③.

Pensão Imperial, Praça dos Restauradores 78-4° (☎342 01 66). This *pensão* has a fine blue-tiled facade and is situated in a sunny position at the bottom of the avenue (by Rua Jardim Regedor). Enter through an optician's and climb to the top floor for small rooms, some with showers and a view up the avenue. ②.

Pensão Iris, Rua da Glória 2a-1° (☎342 31 57). Extremely off-putting entrance but has English-speaking proprietors and large, clean, if shabby rooms (triples available), some with shower and a couple overlook the main avenue. The ones at the side are a bit too close to the clanking street funicular for comfort. ②.

Hotel Lisboa Plaza, Trav. Salitre 7 (☎346 39 22, fax 347 16 30). Just off the avenida, and in front of a theatre park, this bright, polished, four-star hotel has marble bathrooms, bar, restaurant and botanical garden views from rear rooms. Good breakfast included. ⑦.

Pensão Monumental, Rua da Glória 21 (☎346 98 07). A backpackers' favourite with a mixed bag of rooms in a rambling old building; the hot water supply is a little erratic, but it's handy if you fancy a night out at the *Ritz Club* up the road. ③.

Residencial Pemba, Avda. da Liberdade 11-3° (☎342 50 10). Basic little rooms on the avenida, most with private showers, though that's about the only real comfort provided. But you're high enough up to escape much of the noise, and a couple of rooms have balconies. ③.

Hotel Suisso-Atlântico, Rua da Glória 3–19 (☎346 17 13, fax 346 90 13). Tucked around the corner from the *elevador*, just off the avenida, this is a clean and modern hotel in a good location. Standard mid-range accommodation; rooms with shower and and some with a balcony overlooking the seedy Rua da Glória. The intriguing mock-baronial bar is the best bit. ⑤.

Tivoli Lisboa, Avda. da Liberdade 185 (☎353 01 82, fax 357 94 61). Flash hotel with cavernous lobby-lounge. Three hundred sound-proofed rooms, outdoor pool, tennis courts, garden and a top-floor grill-restaurant with superb city views. Breakfast included. ⑦.

Praça Marquês de Pombal to Saldanha

All the hotels and pensões listed below are marked on the general map of Lisbon on pp.54–55.

Residencial Avenida Alameda, Avda. Sidónio Pais 4 (☎353 21 86, fax 352 67 03); metro Parque or Rotunda. Very pleasant three-star *pensão* with air-con rooms, all with bath and park views. Breakfast included. ⑤.

Residencial Canada, Avda. Defensores de Chaves 35-1–4° (☎352 14 55); metro Saldanha. Excellent value for money, largish, airy rooms with private bathrooms (and satellite TV). Sunny breakfast room and lounge area. Recommended. ⑤.

Capital Hotel, Rua Eça de Queiroz 24 (☎353 68 11, fax 352 61 65); metro Rotunda. Popular three-star hotel tucked down a hill near Rotunda. Some rooms have balconies. Breakfast included. ③.

Pensão Embaixatrix, Rua Pedro Nunes 45-2° (☎353 10 29); metro Picoas. Welcoming management make this a perennially popular place. Hardly luxurious but inexpensive (even less for a room with a shower instead of a bath), clean and respectable. ③.

Hotel Fenix, Praça Marquês de Pombal 8 (☎386 21 21, fax 386 01 31); metro Rotunda. Large four-star hotel on the Rotunda, with double-glazed rooms to keep out the noise. Popular with tour groups, some rooms overlook Rotunda or the park. ⑥.

Hotel Impala, Rua Filipe Folque 49 (☎314 89 14, fax 357 53 62); metro Picoas. Interesting choice if you want a longer Lisbon stay, offering small and simple apartments for one, two or three people. *Pensão*-standard bedrooms attached to small kitchen/living rooms with TVs. There are also laundry facilities. ④.

Miraparque, Avda. Sidónio Pais (☎352 42 86); metro Rotunda or Parque. An attractive building with a traditional feel overlooking Parque Eduardo VII. The reception can be a bit brusque, but there's a decent bar and restaurant. All rooms come with TV. ⑥.

Pensão Pátria, Avda. Duque d'Ávila 42-5–6° (☎315 06 20, fax 357 83 10); metro Saldanha. Highly convenient for the main bus station; plenty of nice little rooms with clean bathrooms in a cheerful establishment. Some rooms with rooftop views, others with small, glassed-in verandahs. ④.

Ritz Lisboa, Rua Rodrigo da Fonseca 88 (☎383 20 20, fax 383 17 83); metro Rotunda. On the west side of Parque Eduardo VII, this vast modern block is one of the grandest hotels in Lisbon. Huge airy rooms, terraces overlooking the park, and public areas replete with marble, antiques, old masters and overly attentive staff. The restaurant is highly thought of. ⑦.

Around Avenida Almirante Reis

All the hotels and pensões listed below are marked on the general map of Lisbon on pp.54–55

Pensão Lar do Areeiro, Praça Dr. Francisco de Sá Carneiro 4-1° (☎849 31 50); metro Areeiro. Respectable, old-fashioned, and well-run *pensão*, whose rooms all come with a bath. It's right on the praça, which means it's noisy; ask for a room at the back. Breakfast included. ④.

Residencial Luena, Rua Pascoal de Melo 9 (☎355 82 46); metro Arroios. A competent management maintains neat and welcoming rooms with private bathrooms. Breakfast included. ④.

Residencial O Paradouro, Avda. Almirante Reis 106-7° (☎815 32 56); metro Arroios. Smart, English-speaking establishment in a residential neighbourhood, opposite the fine *Portugalia* restaurant. All rooms with TV, some with balconies offering distant river views. Breakfast included. ④.

Residencial Pascoal de Melo, Rua Pascoal de Melo 127–131 (☎357 76 39); metro Arroios or Saldanha. Spotless and airy, this three-star residencial is characterful, with an azulejo-lined entry hall. Rooms have bathrooms, TVs and balconies. ④.

Youth Hostels

Pousada de Juventude de Lisboa, Rua Andrade Corvo 46 (☎353 26 96); metro Picoas. This is the main city hostel, with 200 beds, good facilities and no curfew; reception open at all times. There are doubles as well as hostel beds. The price includes breakfast; lunch and dinner are served at bargain prices. Doubles ④, dorm beds from 1800$00.

Pousada de Juventude de Catalazete, Estrada Marginal, Oeiras (☎443 06 38). A small attractive hostel, overlooking the beach at Oeiras, between Belém and Cascais. To reach it, take any train from Cais do Sodré and follow signs from Oeiras station under the coast road (Estrada Marginal) and through the park – around 1km. Reception open 6–11pm; midnight curfew. Phone before setting out. Pleasant double rooms are ③, dorm beds from 1300$00.

Campsites

Parque Municipal de Campismo, Parque Florestal de Monsanto (☎760 89 38). The main city campsite – well-equipped with a swimming pool and shops – is 6km west of the city centre, though buses run every 15min or so. The entrance is on Estrada da Circunvalação on the park's west side. Either take a train from Cais do Sodré to Algés, then bus #50 to the campsite; or bus #43 from Praça da Figueira. Take care in the park after dark.

Costa da Caparica, There are several small and lively campsites here, 30–50min away by bus from the Praça de Espanha terminal, or by ferry from Cais do Sodré to Cacilhas and then local bus on from there. See p.126.

The City

Eighteenth-century prints show a pre-quake Lisbon of tremendous opulence and mystique, its skyline characterized by towers, palaces and convents. There are glimpses of this still – the old Moorish hillside of Alfama survived the destruction, as did Belém – but these are isolated neighbourhoods and monuments. It is instead Pombal's perfect Neoclassical grid that covers the centre. Given orders, following the earthquake, to "Bury the dead, feed the living and close the ports", the king's minister followed his success in restoring order to the city with a complete rebuilding. The **Baixa** – still the heart of the modern city – was rebuilt according to Pombal's strict ideals of simplicity and economy; individual streets were assigned to each craft and trade and the whole enterprise was shaped by public buildings and squares.

One of the legacies of this visionary town planning is a city centre in which it could hardly be easier to get your bearings. At the Baixa's southern end, opening onto the Rio Tejo, is the broad, arcaded **Praça do Comércio** (also known as Terreiro do Paço), with its ferry stations for crossing the river, tram terminus for

Belém, and grand triumphal arch. At the Baixa's northern end – linked to the Praça do Comércio by almost any street you care to take – stands Praça Dom Pedro IV, popularly known as **Rossio**, the main square since medieval times and the only part of the rebuilt city to remain in its original place, slightly off-centre in the symmetrical design. Rossio merges with **Praça da Figueira** and **Praça dos Restauradores** and it is these squares, filled with cafés and lively with buskers, business people, and streetwise hawkers and dealers, that form the hub of Lisbon's daily activity. At night the focus shifts to the **Bairro Alto**, high above and to the west of the Baixa, and best reached by funicular (the Elevador da Glória) or by the great street elevator, the Elevador de Santa Justa. Between the two districts, halfway up the hill, **Chiado** is Lisbon's most elegant shopping area, largely rebuilt after being severely damaged in the fire that swept through the Baixa in 1988. East of the Baixa, the **Castelo de São Jorge**, a brooding landmark, surmounts a still taller hill, with the **Alfama** district – the oldest, most fascinating part of the city with its winding lanes and anarchic stairways – sprawled below.

From Rossio, the main, tree-lined **Avenida da Liberdade** runs north to the city's central park, **Parque Eduardo VII**, beyond which spreads the rest of the modern city: the **Gulbenkian** museum is to the north; the **Amoreiras** shopping complex to the west; and mundane shopping streets to the east. No stay in Lisbon should neglect the futuristic **Expo** site, 5km to the east, or the waterfront suburb of **Belém**, 6km to the west, which is dominated by one of the country's grandest monuments, the **Jerónimos** monastery. En route to Belém lies Lisbon's other main museum, the **Museu de Arte Antiga.**

However, it should be remembered that Lisbon's contemporary interest lies as much in the everyday aspects of the city as in any specific sights. The cafés, markets, trams, ferries across the Tejo: all these are sufficient stimulation for random wanderings; the most rewarding areas being, as you'd expect, the oldest – the aforementioned lower and upper towns of Baixa and Bairro Alto, and the Alfama district.

The Baixa

The lower town – the **Baixa** – is very much the heart of the capital, housing many of the country's administrative departments, banks and business offices. Europe's first great example of Neoclassical design and urban planning, it remains an imposing quarter of rod-straight streets, cobbled underfoot and either streaming with traffic or given over to pedestrians, street performers and pavement artists. This area was also the site of Lisbon's first settlers; building work on the Banco Comercial Português at Rua dos Correeiros 21 revealed Roman walls and a mosaic floor, which can be viewed from the tiny **Núcleo Arqueológico** museum (guided tours Thurs 3–5pm & Sat 10am–noon, 3–5pm, max 15 people; free). A major appeal of the Baixa is the survival of tradition. Many of the streets in the grid maintain their crafts and businesses as Pombal devised: in Rua da Prata (Silversmiths' Street), Rua dos Sapateiros (Cobblers' Street), Rua do Ouro (Goldsmiths' Street), Rua do Comércio (Commercial Street). These, along with the mosaic-sidewalked squares, are a visual delight, with tiled Art Deco shopfronts and elaborately decorated *pastelarias* still surviving here and there. Note, too, that in the upper reaches of the Baixa, from the western end of Rua de Santa Justa, the restored **Elevador de Santa Justa** (see p.57) provides easy access to the Bairro Alto.

THE BAIXA

Statues ●
Metro station Ⓜ

ACCOMMODATION

❶ Avenida Palace
❷ Residencial do Sul
❸ Pensão Estação Central
❹ Pensão Coimbra e Madrid
❺ Pensão Beira Minho
❻ Hotel Mundial & Residencial Montepuez
❼ Hotel Portugal
❽ Pensão Ibérica
❾ Pensão Arco da Bandeira
❿ Hotel International
⓫ Pensão Moderna
⓬ Residencial Insulana
⓭ Hotel Borges
⓮ Hotel Duas Nações
⓯ Pensão Galicia
⓰ Pensão Prata
⓱ Residencial Nova Silva

Elevador da Glória
Palácio do Foz
RESTAURADORES
Cinema & Events Kiosk
Teatro Nacional Dona Maria II
Rossio Station
PORTAS DE SANTO ANTÃO
STO. ANTÃO
JARDIM REGEDOR
PR. DOM JOÃO DA CÂMARA
LG. DOMINGOS
RUA B. QUEIRÓZ
São Domingos
RUA DO ARCO DA GRAÇA
TRAV. DO ARCO DA GRAÇA
RUA DA PALMA
LARGO MARTIM MONIZ
R. DA MOURARIA
R. JOÃO DO OUTEIRO
R.A.M. DO ALEGRETE
Praça
Dom Pedro IV
(Rossio)
ROSSIO Ⓜ
Praça da Figueira
TRAV. N.S. DOMINGOS
R. DUARTE
R. JOÃO DAS REGRAS
P. BORRATEM
RUA DO AMPARO
Café Nicola
Convento do Carmo
RUA BETESGA
LG. DUQUE CADAVAL
C. DO CARMO
RUA 1º DEZEMBRO
RUA DO CARMO
RUA NOVA DA TRINDADE
RUA DA OLIVEIRA
BECO DO DUQUE
R. DA CONCEIÇÃO
Elevador Sta. Justa
LG. DO CARMO
R. DA TRINDADE
LG. R. BORDALÓ PINHEIRO
TRAV. DO CARMO
CALÇ. DO SACRAMENTO
BAIXA
RUA DE SANTA JUSTA
RUA DO OURO
RUA DA ASSUNÇÃO
RUA DA PRATA
RUA AUGUSTA
RUA DOS SAPATEIROS
RUA DOS CORREEIROS
RUA DOS DOURADORES
RUA DA MADALENA
RUA DOS FANQUEIROS
RUA DE SÃO NICOLAU
RUA DA VITÓRIA
CHIADO
RUA GARRETT
BAIXA-CHIADO Ⓜ
Igreja dos Mártires
RUA SERPA PINTO
R. ANCHIETA
R. IVENS
R. CAPELO
RUA NOVA DO ALMADA
CALÇ. NOVA D.J. S. FRANCISCO
Teatro Nacional de São Carlos
Museu do Chiado
RUA SERPA PINTO
LRGO DA BIBLIOTECA
ARCO DA C. D. S. FRANCISCO
RUA VITOR CORDON
Núcleo Arqueológico
RUA DA CONCEIÇÃO
RUA DE SÃO JULIÃO
Sé
RUA DE SANTO ANTÓNIO DA SÉ
R. DA PADARIA
RUA DOS BACALHOEIROS
RUA DAS PEDRAS NEGRAS
RUA DE SÃO MAMEDE
City Hall
PRAÇA DO MUNICÍPIO
RUA DO COMÉRCIO
Conceição Velha
RUA DO ALFANDEGA
RUA DO ARSENAL
Praça do Comércio
AVENIDA DA RIBEIRA DAS NAUS
Rio Tejo
Fluvial (ferries to Cacilhas)

◁ Cais do Sodré
Castelo ◁
Alfama ◁

N

0   100 m

DEVELOPMENT AND DESTRUCTION

In recent years Lisbon has experienced some of the most radical **redevelopment** since the Marquês de Pombal rebuilt the shattered capital after the 1755 earthquake. This phase began with Portugal's relative economic stability – and extensive grants – in the wake of joining the European Community in 1986, when foreign investment poured into the capital. The building boom continued in the lead up to Expo 98 which has seen further chunks of old Lisbon disappearing under new roads and train lines; tramlines have gone to provide space for faster roads, and shanty towns have been hastily erased.

Ironically, it is beyond Pombal's statue at Rotunda that most of the redevelopment work is being done. Complicated **rent laws** mean that, at present, landlords whose tenants were installed before the Revolution get insufficient income to maintain properties, making the option of selling up to property developers a tempting one. As a result, many of the city's beautiful pre-war mansions and tenement buildings have been demolished to make way for office buildings while new property in Lisbon is some of the most expensive in Europe.

But not all of old Lisbon is lost and at least the **city centre** will retain its elegance. EU funding continues to help with restoration work of many historic buildings, including Lisbon's oldest quarter, the **Alfama**. However, the most obvious sign of renovation is in the streets of the **Chiado**, burned out in the 1988 fire and now beautifully restored to their original design.

At the southern, waterfront end of the Baixa, the **Praça do Comércio** was the climax to Pombal's design, surrounded by classical buildings and centred on an exuberant bronze of Dom José – the reigning monarch during the earthquake and the capital's rebuilding. The square is currently undergoing substantial redevelopment that will ultimately (estimated at some time around the millennium) see the area between the river and the Baixa pedestrianized, freeing this elegant space to host cultural and political functions once more. All traffic, barring public transport, will be sunk in a tunnel, just above a new metro station. New museums, galleries and cafés are planned for the arcades, though at present the only refreshment spot is the old-world café of *Martinho da Arcada*, one of the poet Pessoa's old haunts.

The Praça do Comércio metro will be named **Terreiro do Paço**, after the old royal palace that once stood here (its steps still lead up from the Tejo) and which played an important part in the country's history. In 1908, alongside the Central Post Office, King Carlos I and his eldest son were shot and killed, clearing the way to the declaration of the Republic two years later.

Rossio and around

Perhaps the most interesting places in the Baixa are the squares, of which **Rossio** – at the northern end of the Baixa grid – is the liveliest. The square itself is modest in appearance, but very much a focus for the city, sporting several atmospheric and popular cafés, most of which have outdoor seating.

The square's single concession to grandeur is the **Teatro Nacional de Dona Maria II**, built along the north side in the 1840s. Here, prior to the earthquake, stood the Inquisitional Palace, in front of which public hangings, *autos-da-fé* (ritual burnings of heretics) and even bullfights used to take place. The nineteenth-century statue atop the central column is of Dom Pedro IV (after whom the square is officially named), though curiously it's a bargain adaptation: cast originally as Maximilian of Mexico, it just happened to be in Lisbon en route from France when news came through of Maximilian's assassination.

São Domingos church, immediately to the east in Largo São Domingos, was where the Inquisition read out its sentences. It was blackened and gutted by a fire in the 1950s, but has now been fully restored. The road and square outside the church, at the bottom of Rua das Portas de Santo Antão, is a popular meeting place – the local African population hangs out on the street corner; businessmen get their shoes cleaned at the rank of little metal booths; and Lisbon's lowlife frequent the various **ginginha bars**, which specialize in lethal measures of cherry brandy. Resist the urge to eat the proffered cherry itself – they've been soaked in alcohol for years and provide a kick usually only available from expensive drugs.

South, past the church, the street runs into **Praça da Figueira**, the square adjacent to Rossio. It contains one of the main city bus stops and, like Rossio, is centred on a fountain and lined with shops and cafés.

Chiado

On the west side of the Baixa, stretching up the hillside towards the Bairro Alto, the area known as **Chiado** – the nom de plume of the poet António Ribeiro – suffered great damage from a fire that swept across the Baixa in August 1988. It destroyed all but the facade of the Grandella department store and many old shops in Rua do Crucifixo, though most buildings are now fully restored. Restoration is very much in keeping with the Chiado's traditions; new, soaring marble facades consciously ape those destroyed in the fire, though they now shelter designer shops and the new Chiado metro station.

Chiado remains one of the city's most affluent quarters, focused on the fashionable shops and old café-tearooms of the Rua Garrett. Of these, **A Brasileira**, Rua Garrett 120, is the most famous, having been frequented by generations of Lisbon's literary and intellectual leaders – the very readable Eça de Queiroz and Portugal's greatest twentieth-century poet, Fernando Pessoa (see box on p.71), among them. While on Rua Garrett, take a stroll past **Igreja dos Mártires** (Church of the Martyrs), which occupies the site of the Crusader camp during the Siege of Lisbon. As its name suggests, the church was built on the site of a burial ground, created for the English contingent of the besieging army. Music recitals are often held in the church; check the local press for details.

Just beyond, Rua Serpa Pinto veers steeply downhill to the **Museu do Chiado** (Wed, Fri & Sun 10am–6pm, Thurs & Sat 10am–8pm, Tues 2–6pm; 400$00). Opened in 1994, this stylish building with a pleasant courtyard café and rooftop terrace incorporates the former Museum of Contemporary Art, whose original home was damaged in the Chiado fire. The new museum was constructed around a nineteenth-century biscuit factory, which explains the presence of the old ovens. The three floors display the work of some of Portugal's most influential artists since the nineteenth century. Highlights include the beautiful sculpture *A Viúva* (The Widow) by **António Teixeira Lopes** and some evocative Lisbon area scenes by Carlos Botelho and José Malhoa. Look out also for the wonderful decorative panels by **José de Almada Negreiros**, recovered from the San Carlos cinema. There is also a small collection of French sculpture, including Rodin's *The Bronze Age*.

Around Cais do Sodré

Ten minutes' walk west of the Baixa grid, along the riverfront, is **Cais do Sodré** station, from where trains run out to Estoril and Cascais, and ferries cross to Cacilhas. It's not the most elegant, or inviting, of areas, but its various **markets** are wonderful, particularly the huge **fish market** (Mon–Sat) behind the station, which starts at dawn. Here you can still see *varinas*, fishwives from Alfama, who were joined a few years ago by groups from Cabo Verde, bargaining for and carting off great baskets of wares on their heads.

Take a look inside the **Ribeira market**, too, located in the domed building beyond Cais do Sodré. Even if you're not tempted by the food – least of all perhaps by the gruesome slabs of flesh and innards – the fruit, flower, spice and vegetable displays on the upper storey are impressive. On the way back into town, **Rua do Arsenal** is packed with shops selling fresh fish and dried cod, while grocers here are stocked with everything, including cheap wines, port and brandies.

Just as diverting, and perhaps more desirable after a long night out, is the **fruit and vegetable market** down by the waterfront further west, toward Belém. Four o' clock in the morning is the perfect time to share a glass of hot *cacão* with the traders in the market bar.

Bairro Alto

High above the central city, to the west of the Baixa, **Bairro Alto**, the upper town, is the natural place to wind up at night – in its *fado* houses, bars, excellent restaurants, or even in the refined and somewhat dauntingly named *Instituto do Vinho do Porto* (Port Wine Institute). By day, the quarter's narrow seventeenth-century streets have a very different character, with children playing and the old sitting in doorways. It is well worth a morning or afternoon's exploration, with two of the city's most interesting churches – Carmo and São Roque – on the fringes and a few approaches to the quarter that are a treat in themselves.

Approaches by elevador

Raul Mésnier's **Elevador de Santa Justa**, just off the northern end of Rua do Ouro (also known as Rua Aurea) on Rua de Santa Justa, is the most startling approach to the Bairro Alto. Built in 1902, it is one of the city's most extraordinary and eccentric structures, whisking you up through metal latticework, and depositing you on a platform high above the Baixa. Alternative, though hardly more conventional feats of engineering, are the two funicular-like trams, originally powered by water displacement, and then by steam, until electricity was introduced. One, the **Elevador da Glória**, built in 1885, links the quarter directly with Praça dos Restauradores, from where it takes off just behind the tourist office on the left. The other, **Elevador da Bica**, climbs up to Rua Loreto (west of Praça de Camões) from Rua de São Paulo/Rua da Moeda, northwest of Cais do Sodré. Tickets for these services cost 150$00 each way and the hours of operation are Monday to Saturday 7am–11pm, and Sunday 9am–11pm. Our account follows a route from the disembarkation point of the Elevador da Glória, and enables you to take in the main highlights of the area.

From the Elevador da Glória to São Roque

The Elevador da Glória drops you at the top of the hill on Rua de São Pedro de Alcântara, from whose adjacent **gardens** there's a superb view across the city

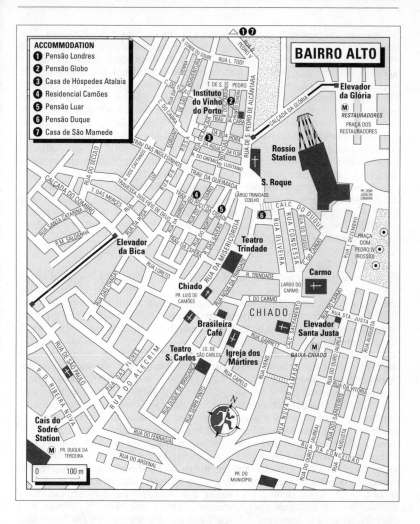

BAIRRO ALTO

ACCOMMODATION
1. Pensão Londres
2. Pensão Globo
3. Casa de Hóspedes Atalaia
4. Residencial Camões
5. Pensão Luar
6. Pensão Duque
7. Casa de São Mamede

to the castle. Immediately across the road is the **Instituto do Vinho do Porto**, a good place to stop and taste Portugal's finest tipple (see p.95), while a turn to the left from the *elevador* takes you downhill and round the corner to the **Igreja de São Roque** (daily 8.30am–6pm; free), in Largo Trindade Coelho. From the outside, this looks like the plainest church in the city, its bleak Renaissance facade (by Filipo Terzi, architect of São Vicente) having been further simplified by the earthquake. Neither does it seem impressive when you walk inside. But hang around in the gloom and the sacristan will come and escort you around, turning on lights to a succession of side chapels, each lavishly crafted with azulejos (some emulating reliefs), multicoloured marble, or Baroque painted ceilings.

However, the highlight of a visit is the **Capela de São João Baptista**. This chapel, for its size, is estimated to be the most expensive ever constructed and was certainly one of the most bizarre commissions of its age. It was ordered from Rome in 1742 by Dom João V to honour his patron saint and, more dubiously, to requite the pope, whom he had persuaded to confer a patriarchate upon Lisbon. Designed by the papal architect, Vanvitelli, and using the most costly materials available, including ivory, agate, porphyry and lapis lazuli, it was actually erected at the Vatican for the pope to celebrate Mass before being dismantled and shipped to Lisbon. The cost, then, was about £250,000 sterling, which is perhaps its chief curiosity. But there are other eccentricities. Take a close look at the four "oil paintings" of John the Baptist's life and you'll discover that they are in fact mosaics, intricately worked over what must have been years rather than months.

Next to the church, the associated **Museu de São Roque** (summer Tues–Sun 10am–5pm; winter daily 10am–noon & 1–5pm; free) displays sixteenth- to eighteenth-century paintings and the usual motley collection of vestments, chalices and bibles bequeathed to the church over the centuries, including treasure from the Capela de São João Baptista.

Convento do Carmo

Further south, it's a couple of minutes' walk down to the pretty, enclosed **Largo do Carmo**, with its outdoor café. From here you can regain the Baixa by using the Elevador de Santa Justa, whose entrance lies up an alley to the side of the ruined Gothic arches of the **Convento do Carmo**. Once the largest church in the city, this was half-destroyed by the earthquake but is perhaps even more beautiful as a result.

In the nineteenth century its shell was adapted as a chemical factory but these days it houses the splendid **Museu Arqueológico do Carmo** (Mon–Sat: April–Sept 10am–6pm; Oct–March 10am–1pm & 2–5pm; 500$00), whose miscellaneous collection is one of the joys of the city. At the time of writing, the museum was undergoing restoration though it is due to re-open shortly; assuming it will be much the same as it was, the entire nave is open to the elements, with roses growing up the aisle, columns and tombs and statuary scattered in all corners. Inside, on either side of what was the main altar, are the main exhibits, centering on a series of **tombs** of great significance. Largest is the beautifully carved stone tomb, 2m high, containing the bones of **Ferdinand I**; nearby, that of **Gonçalo de Sousa**, chancellor to Henry the Navigator, is topped by a prone statue of Gonçalo, his clasped arms holding a book, signifying his learning. Other noteworthy pieces include a jasper sculpture of the Virgin Mary, from Brazil, with cherubs clinging to the stand for dear life; more alarmingly, two pre-Columbian **mummies** lie curled up in glass cases, alongside the preserved heads of a couple of Peruvian Indians. Elsewhere there are flints, arrowheads, prehistoric ceramics, coins dating back to the thirteenth century, Roman inscriptions, church architecture – you name it – all well labelled in English and endearingly positioned cheek-by-jowl with little thought of thematic progression.

The Jardim Botânico

Heading right from the top of Elevador da Glória, it's around ten minutes' walk uphill to Rua Escola Politéctica, where towering palm trees on the right mark the entrance to the **Jardim Botânico** (daily: summer 10am–8pm; winter 10am–6pm; 250$00). Laid out in 1873, the gardens are almost completely invisible from the surrounding streets, and form an oasis of twenty thousand exotic plants from around the world, each one neatly labelled. Just beyond the gardens' entrance are the **museums of Natural History and Science** (Mon–Sat 10am–noon & 3–5pm; closed Aug; free, bus #15 or #58 from Cais do Sodré). The former traces the evolution of Iberian plant and animal life and the latter has a small interactive section amongst its geological and botanical displays, but neither museum is particularly inspiring.

Estrêla

Situated on another of Lisbon's hills, the district of **Estrêla** lies 2km west of Bairro Alto – a thirty-minute walk or a short ride on tram #28 from Praça Luís de Camões in Chiado, or bus #13 from Praça do Comércio. Its main point of interest for the visitor is the **Basílica da Estrêla** (Mon–Sat 8am–7pm, Sun 9am–7pm), a vast domed church and *de facto* monument to late-eighteenth-century Neoclassicism. Below the church is the **Jardim da Estrêla**: Lisbon takes its gardens seriously, even the small patches amid squares and avenues, and these are among the most enjoyable in the city, a quiet refuge often graced with an afternoon brass band. There's a pool of giant carp, too, and a café with outside tables.

   Through the park and on Rua de São Jorge is the gate to the post-Crusader **Cemitério dos Ingleses** (English Cemetery; ring loudly for entry) where, among the cypresses, lies Henry Fielding, author of *Tom Jones*, whose imminent demise may have influenced his verdict on Lisbon as "the nastiest city in the world".

A little uphill from here at Rua Coelho da Rocha 16 is the **Casa Museu Fernando Pessoa** (Mon–Wed & Fri 10am–6.30pm, Thurs 1–8pm; free), home to Portugal's best-known poet for the last fifteen years of his life. The building is now a cultural centre containing **Almada Negreiros'** famous painting of the writer, a few of Pessoa's personal belongings, such as his glasses and diaries, and exhibits of artists who have been influenced by Pessoa, such as **Paula Rego**.

FERNANDO PESSOA

In common with many other great artists, **Fernando Pessoa** was largely unrecognized until after his death, but he is now Portugal's most celebrated modern poet. Born in Lisbon in 1888, Pessoa spent most of his childhood in South Africa with his mother, and subsequently wrote many of his poems in English. When he returned alone to Lisbon aged 17, he lived mostly in spartan rented rooms, contributing poetry to literary magazines. With his distinctive gold-rimmed glasses, bow tie and hat, the quirky poet was a conspicuous figure in the Baixa cafés where he wrote and soon became known as a modernist, influenced by the European avant-garde, Cubists, Futurists and others.

   Unfortunately, his need to smoke and drink while he worked led to his premature death in 1935, a year after the appearance of *Mensagem*, his only work to be published during his lifetime. Since his death, researchers have unearthed several other previously unpublished works, many written under pseudonyms: Alberto Caeiro, Alvaro de Campos, Ricardo Reis and, for his prose, Bernardo Soares. Each of these pseudonyms represented a different persona and a different literary style, but each was equally learned and inspired, embodiments of the different personalities that the enigmatic Pessoa believed we all possess.

From the tram turnaround in front of the Basílica da Estrêla you can catch #25 down the steep Rua de São Domingos à Lapa, getting off where the tram veers left into Rua Garcia de Orta. Here, you're only a five-minute walk from the Museu de Arte Antiga (see p.81); staying with the tram takes you to Praça do Comércio and back into the Baixa.

From Praça do Comércio to the Sé and Castelo

A couple of blocks east of Praça do Comércio, along Rua do Alfandega, is the church of **Conceição Velha**, severely damaged by the earthquake but still in possession of its flamboyant Manueline doorway, an early example of the style and hinting at the brilliance that later emerged at Belém. It once formed part of the Misericórdia (almshouse) – you'll find one of these impressive structures in almost every Portuguese town or city. Five minutes' walk further east, at Campo das Cebolas, stands the curious **Casa dos Bicos**, set with diamond-shaped stones and again offering an image of the richness of pre-1755 Lisbon. The building is not routinely open, though it sees fairly regular use for cultural exhibitions.

The Sé
Lisbon's cathedral – the **Sé** (daily 8.30am–6pm) – stands stolidly above the Baixa grid. Founded in 1150 to commemorate the city's reconquest from the Moors, it has a suitably fortress-like appearance, similar to that of Coimbra, and in fact occupies the site of the principal mosque of Moorish Lishbuna. Like so many of the country's cathedrals, it is Romanesque – and extraordinarily restrained in both size and decoration. The great rose window and twin towers form a simple and effective facade, but inside there's nothing very exciting: the building was once splendidly embellished on the orders of Dom João V, but his Rococo whims were swept away by the earthquake and subsequent restorers. All that remains is a group of Gothic tombs behind the high altar and the decaying thirteenth-century **cloister**.

You need to buy tickets for admission to the cloister (Mon–Sat 10am–5pm, Sun 10am–noon; 100$00, free on Sun) and the Baroque *Sacristia* (same hours; 400$00) with its small **museum** of treasures, including the relics of Saint Vincent, brought to Lisbon in 1173 by Afonso Henriques in a boat piloted by ravens (see "Sagres"). For centuries the descendants of these birds were shown to visitors but the last one died in 1978, despite receiving great care from the sacristan. Nevertheless, ravens are still one of the city's symbols.

Opposite the Sé is the church of **Santo António**, said to have been built on the spot where the city's patron saint was born. His life is chronicled in the neighbouring **museum** (Tues–Sun 10am–1pm & 2–6pm; 165$00, free on Sun).

Up to the Castelo
From the Sé, Rua Augusto Rosa winds upward towards the castle, past sparse ruins of a **Roman theatre** (57 AD), set behind a grille just off to the left at the junction of ruas de São Mamede and Saudade. Further up the hill you reach the well-positioned **Igreja da Santa Luzia** and the adjacent **Miradouro da Santa Luzia**, from where there are fine views down to the river.

Just beyond, at Largo das Portas do Sol 2, is the Espírito Santo Silva Foundation, home of the **Museu Escola de Artes Decorativas** (10am–5pm; closed Tues; 900$00), a seventeenth-century mansion stuffed with what was once

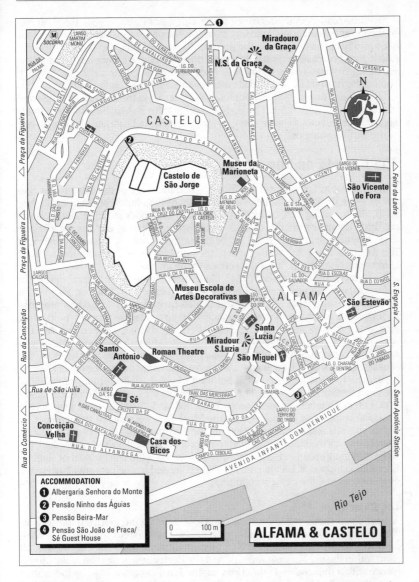

ALFAMA & CASTELO

ACCOMMODATION
1 Albergaria Senhora do Monte
2 Pensão Ninho das Águias
3 Pensão Beira-Mar
4 Pensão São João de Praca/
Sé Guest House

0   100 m

the private collection of Ricardo do Espírito Santo Silva, who offered it to the
nation in 1953. On display are unique pieces of furniture, major collections of silver and porcelain, paintings, textiles and azulejo panels – in short, some of the
best examples of seventeenth- and eighteenth-century applied art in the country.
The museum, which promotes traditional crafts, also contains a café and
restaurant.

Over the road from the **terrace-café** in Largo das Portas do Sol, the views are tremendous – a solitary palm rising from the stepped streets below, the twin-towered facade of Graça convent, the dome of Santa Engraçia, and the Tejo beyond. Catch your breath here for the final push up to the castle, higher up the hill to the northeast. You can enter the grounds from a couple of points and signposts keep you on the right track as the roads wind confusingly ever higher.

Incidentally, **tram** #28 runs from Rua da Conceição in the Baixa, past the Sé and Santa Luzia, to Largo das Portas do Sol; coming from Rossio, **bus** #37 from Praça do Comércio follows a similar route, cutting off at Santa Luzia and climbing to one of the castle entrances.

The Castelo de São Jorge

The conquest of Lisbon from the Moors – and the siege of the **Castelo de São Jorge** – are depicted in azulejos on the walls of the church of Santa Luzia (see p.72). An important victory, leading to Muslim surrender at Sintra and throughout the surrounding district, this was not, however, the most Christian or glorious of Portuguese exploits. A full account survives, written by one Osbern of Bawdsley, an English priest and Crusader, and its details, despite the author's judgmental tone, direct one's sympathies to the enemy.

The attack, in the summer of 1147, came through the opportunism and skilful management of Afonso Henriques, already established as "King" at Porto, who persuaded a large force of French and British Crusaders to delay their progress to Jerusalem for more immediate goals. The Crusaders – scarcely more than pirates – came to terms and in June the siege began. Osbern records the Archbishop of Braga's demand for the Moors to return to "the land whence you came" and, more revealingly, the weary and contemptuous response of the Muslim spokesman: "How many times have you come hither with pilgrims and barbarians to drive us hence? It is not want of possessions but only ambition of the mind that drives you on." For seventeen weeks the castle and inner city stood firm but in October its walls were breached and the citizens – including a Christian community coexisting with the Muslims – were forced to surrender.

The pilgrims and barbarians, flaunting the diplomacy and guarantees of Afonso Henriques, stormed into the city, cut the throat of the local bishop and sacked, pillaged and murdered Christian and Muslim alike. In 1190 a later band of English Crusaders stopped at Lisbon and, no doubt confused by the continuing presence of Moors, sacked the city a second time.

The Castelo

A triumphant statue of Afonso Henriques – who alone emerges from the account with honour – stands at the main entrance to the **Castelo** (daily 9am–sunset; free). Beyond stretch gardens and terraces, walkways, pools and caged birds, all lying within the old Moorish walls. At first the Portuguese kings had taken up residence within the castle – in the *Alcáçova*, the Muslim palace – but by the time of Manuel I this had been superseded by the new royal palace on Terreiro do Paço. Of the *Alcáçova* only a much-restored shell remains. But the castle as a whole is an enjoyable place to spend a couple of hours, wandering amid the ramparts and towers to look down upon the city.

Crammed within the castle's outer walls is the tiny medieval quarter of **Santa Cruz**, once very much a village in itself, while to the north sprawls the old

Mouraria quarter, to which the Moors were relegated on their loss of the town. This, despite a few grand old houses, is largely in decay, though currently undergoing substantial redevelopment.

Just below the castle's eastern entrance, at Largo Rodrigues de Freitas 19a, is the **Museu da Marioneta** (daily 10am–1pm & 2–7pm; 500$00, under 10s free), a surprisingly interesting puppet museum. There are weekend puppet shows here, too; ask at the museum. From the Museu da Marioneta, Calçada da Graça leads up to the Graça district, a worthwhile walk for the stunning views across the city from the **Miradouro da Graça**.

Alfama

The oldest part of Lisbon, stumbling from the walls of the castle down to the Tejo, **Alfama** was buttressed against significant damage in the 1755 earthquake by the steep, rocky mass on which it is built. Although none of its houses dates from before the Christian conquest, many are of Moorish design and the kasbah-like layout is still much as Osbern described it, with "steep defiles instead of ordinary streets . . . and buildings so closely packed together that, except in the merchants' quarter, hardly a street could be found more than eight foot wide".

In Arab-occupied times Alfama was the grandest part of the city but following subsequent earthquakes the new Christian nobility moved out, leaving it to the local fishing community. Today, it is undergoing some commercialization, with its cobbled lanes and "character", but although antique shops and restaurants are moving in, they are far from taking over. The quarter retains a largely traditional life of its own: you can eat at local prices in the cafés; the flea market (see below) engulfs the periphery of the area twice a week; and this is very much the place to be during the June "Popular Saints" festivals (above all on June 12), when makeshift *tavernas* appear on every corner.

The steep defiles, alleys and passageways are known as *becos* and *travessas* rather than *ruas*, and it would be impossible (as well as futile) to try and follow any set route. At some point in your wanderings around the quarter, though, head for the **Rua de São Miguel** – off which are some of the most interesting *becos* – and for the (lower) parallel **Rua de São Pedro**, the main market street leading to the lively **Largo do Chafariz de Dentro**, right at the bottom of the hill. Along all these streets and alleys, life continues much as it has done for years: kids playing ball in tiny squares and chasing each other up and down precipitous staircases; people buying groceries and bread from hole-in-the-wall stores; householders stringing washing across narrow defiles and stoking small outdoor charcoal grills; and elderly men idling away the hours on decrepit wooden benches.

The Feira da Ladra

The **Feira da Ladra**, Lisbon's rambling and ragged flea market, fills the Campo de Santa Clara, at the eastern edge of Alfama on Tuesdays and Saturdays (7am–6pm). Though it's certainly not the world's greatest – "you will find stalls with shabby ready-made clothes" advises the cautious turismo pamphlet – it does turn up some interesting things: oddities from the former African colonies, old prints of the country, and army-surplus gear. Out-and-out junk – broken alarm clocks and old postcards – is spread on the ground above Santa Engrácia, and half-genuine antiques at the top end of the *feira*.

To get here, tram #28 runs from Rua da Conceição in the Baixa to São Vicente (see below), and bus #12 runs between Santa Apolónia station and Praça Marquês de Pombal.

Santa Engrácia and São Vicente de Fora

While at the flea market, take a look inside **Santa Engrácia** (Tues–Sun 10am–5pm; free), the loftiest and most tortuously built church in the city. Begun in 1682 and once a synonym for unfinished work, its vast dome was finally completed in 1966. If you ask nicely, you may be allowed to take the elevator to the dome, from where you can look down on the empty church and out over the flea market, port and city.

More interesting, architecturally, is the nearby **São Vicente de Fora**, whose name – "of the outside" – is a reminder of the extent of the sixteenth-century city. It is also where Afonso Henriques pitched camp during his siege and conquest of Lisbon. Built during the years of Spanish rule by Philip II's Italian architect, Felipe Terzi, its severe geometric facade was an important Renaissance innovation. Through the **cloisters**, decorated with azulejos, you can visit the old monastic refectory, which since 1855 has formed the **pantheon of the Bragança dynasty** (Tues–Sun 10am–5.30pm; 300$00). Here, in more or less complete (though unexciting) sequence, are the bodies of all Portuguese kings from João IV, who restored the monarchy, to Manuel II, who lost it and died in exile in England in 1932. Among them is Catherine of Bragança, the widow of Charles II and (as the local guide points out) "the one who took the habit of the fifth o'clock tea to that country".

Further east: the Museu Militar, Museu da Água and Museu Nacional do Azulejo

There's not much call to head east beyond the Alfama, unless you're leaving by train from the dockside **Santa Apolónia station**, though there is a trio of museums of varying interest. Opposite the station, on Largo Museu da Artilharia, a couple of blocks south of Santa Engraçia, is the imposing Corinthian facade of the city's military museum, the **Museu Militar** (Tues–Sun 10am–5pm; 300$00, free on Wed), though this is very traditional in layout – old weapons in old cases – and lacks much appeal. However, some ten minutes' walk beyond Santa Apolónia station, off Calçada dos Barbadinhos at Rua do Alviela 12, stands the **Museu da Água** (Tues–Sat 10am–12.30pm & 2–5pm; 200$00, bus #105 from Praça da Figueira), a surprisingly engaging museum devoted to the evolution of the city's water supply. It is housed in an old pumping station, built in 1880 to pump water up Lisbon's steep hills, and is complete with working nineteenth-century steam engines. While here, you can arrange a visit to the Aqueduto das Águas Livres (see p.78).

A little under a kilometre to the east of Santa Apolónia (bus #104 from Praça do Comércio, bus #105 from Praça da Figueira), at Rua Madre de Deus 4, is the **Museu Nacional do Azulejo** (Tues 2–6pm, Wed–Sun 10am–6pm; 350$00, free on Sun). Installed in the church and cloisters of Madre de Deus, whose own eighteenth-century tiled scenes of the life of Saint Anthony are among the best in the city, it contains an impressive collection of azulejos from the fifteenth century to the present day. The highlight, however, is Portugal's longest azulejo – a wonderfully detailed 36-metre panorama of Lisbon, completed in around 1738. While here, don't miss the opportunity of a drink in the lovely garden café.

PORTUGUESE AZULEJOS

Though influenced by Moorish and Spanish glazed tiles, Portuguese **azulejos** developed their own style around the mid-sixteenth century when tile-making techniques were improved. By the seventeenth century, decadent and colourful images along the lines of the Spanish and Flemish models were all the rage, but by the end of the century they were replaced by images in blue and white only – at this time tiles were placed on the Palácio dos Marquêses de Fronteira (see p.81) and São Vicente de Fora (see p.76). However, competition with Dutch ceramics meant that the business had to turn professional in order to survive, and the early eighteenth century saw trained artist "masters" producing highly decorated ceramic mosaics, culminating in Rococo themes which continued in a more functional way after the Great Earthquake.

By the early nineteenth century, azulejos were being produced in factories to decorate residential buildings, often with Neoclassical designs, while the end of the century saw the appearance of figures on tiles, typified by the work in the *Cervejaria da Trindade* (see p.90). The nineteenth century also saw the arrival of individualists such as Rafael Bordalo Pinheiro (see p.80). Art Deco took hold in the 1920s, while more modern, contemporary works can be admired in Lisbon's underground stations – Colégio Militar, Cidade Universitária and others.

Avenida da Liberdade, Parque Eduardo VII and Amoreiras

To the north of the Baixa is the city's principal park – the Parque Eduardo VII. The easiest approach is by metro (to Rotunda or Parque) or bus (to Rotunda), though you could take an energetic twenty-minute walk up the main **Avenida da Liberdade**, which would give you the chance to make a couple of stops along the way. The bottom end of Avenida da Liberdade, just above the new metro interchange at Restauradores, has some of the city's nicest outdoor **cafés**, with esplanade tables in the green swathes that split the avenue. Running parallel, to the east, the pedestrianized **Rua das Portas de Santo Antão** is well known for the seafood restaurants that line it; their waiters lurk by every doorway attempting to entice you in. Despite the obvious tourist trappings, you can still have a good, reasonably inexpensive meal here (see p.88), and it's not a bad street to promenade up and down at least once anyway.

Parque Eduardo VII

At the top of the avenue, in the formal, elongated **Parque Eduardo VII**, the big attractions are the **Estufas** (daily 9am–5.30pm; 95$00) at the park's northern end – huge and wonderful glasshouses filled with tropical plants, flamingo pools and endless varieties of palms and cacti. Rock and classical concerts and an antiques fair are occasionally held in the **Estufa Fria**. Useful **bus links** from the park are #31, #41 and #46 to the Gulbenkian museum; #27 and #49 west to Belém; and #51, which runs from Belém to the Gulbenkian museum via the top of the park near the Estufa Fria.

Amoreiras

Leading west of the park from the Rotunda, Avenida J.A. de Aguiar becomes Avenida Duarte Pacheco, on which you will find Lisbon's post-Modernist shopping centre, **Amoreiras**, still visible on the city skyline from almost any approach despite the growing number of high-rise blocks around it. The complex, designed by Tomás Taveira, is Portugal's most adventurous – and most entertaining – modern building: a wild fantasy of pink and blue, sheltering ten cinemas, sixty cafés and restaurants, 370 shops and a hotel. Most of the shops here stay open until midnight (11pm on Sun); the heaviest human traffic is on Sunday, when entire families descend on the complex for an afternoon out. To get here directly by bus, take the #11 from Rossio/Restauradores.

The Aqueduto das Águas Livres

Buses #11 and #23 pass Amoreiras and then continue on the kilometre or so to the **Aqueduto das Águas Livres**. Opened in 1748, the aqueduct brought reliable drinking water to the city for the first time. It stood firm during the 1755 earthquake and later became notorious through one Diogo Alves, a nineteenth-century serial killer who threw his victims off the arches – a drop of 60m. If you'd like to visit it, enquire at the Museu da Água (see p.76), which arranges walking tours over the aqueduct every Thursday and Saturday. Once inside and up, you can make the very scenic walk across the aqueduct to the **Parque Monsanto**. Tours start from Mãe d'Água cistern at Rua das Amoreiras, close to Largo do Rato.

The Fundação Calouste Gulbenkian

The **Fundação Calouste Gulbenkian** is the great cultural centre of Portugal – and it is a wonder that it's not better known internationally. Housed in a superb complex, ten minutes' walk north of Parque Eduardo VII, the foundation is set in its own park, and features a museum whose collections seem to take in virtually every great phase of Eastern and Western art – from Ancient Egyptian scarabs to Art Nouveau jewellery, Islamic textiles to French Impressionists. In a separate building, across the park, the **Centro de Arte Moderna** sports excitingly displayed and exclusively Portuguese works, which touch on most styles of twentieth-century art. The complex has its main entrance at Avda. de Berna 45; to reach it, take **bus** #31 or #41 from Rossio, #51 from Belém, or the **metro** to Pahlavã or São Sebastião.

Astonishingly, all the main museum exhibits were acquired by just one man, the Armenian oil magnate **Calouste Gulbenkian** (1869–1955), whose legendary art-market coups included buying works from the Leningrad Hermitage after the Russian Revolution. In a scarcely less astute deal made during the last war, Gulbenkian literally auctioned himself and his collections to the European nations: Portugal bid security, an aristocratic palace home (a Marquês was asked to move out) and tax exemption, to acquire one of the most important cultural patrons of the century.

Today the Gulbenkian Foundation runs an orchestra, three concert halls and two galleries for temporary exhibitions in the capital alone. It also finances work in all spheres of Portuguese cultural life – there are Gulbenkian museums and libraries in the smallest towns – and makes charitable grants to a vast range of projects. The admissions desk of the museum has a schedule of current activities.

Anyone travelling with children may be equally impressed to know that the Gulbenkian maintains a **Centro Artístico Infantil** in its gardens (entrance just off Rua Marquês de Sá de Bandeira), well stocked with toys and offering free **childcare sessions** for four to twelve year-olds between 9.30am and 5.30pm.

The Museu Gulbenkian

The **Museu Gulbenkian** (main entrance on Avda. de Berna: June–Sept Tues, Thurs, Fri & Sun 10am–5pm, Wed & Sat 2–7.30pm; Oct–May Tues–Sun 10am–5pm; 500$00, free on Sun) is divided into two complete and distinct halves – the first devoted to Egyptian, Greco-Roman, Islamic and Oriental arts, the second to European art – and ideally you'll want to take them in on separate visits. The collections aren't immense in number but each contains pieces of such individual interest and beauty that you need frequent unwinding sessions – well provided for by the basement **café-bar and gardens**.

CLASSICAL AND ORIENTAL ART

It seems arbitrary to hint at highlights, but they must include the entire contents of the small **Egyptian room**, which covers almost every period of importance from the Old Kingdom (2700 BC) to the Roman period. Particularly striking are a carved ivory spoon from the time of Amenophis III and an extraordinarily lifelike sculpture *Head of a Priest* from the penultimate, Ptolomaic period. **Mesopotamia** produced the earliest forms of writing and two cylinder seals, one dating from before 2500 BC, are on display here, along with architectural sculpture from the Assyrian civilization.

Fine **Roman** statues, silver and glass and intricate gold jewellery from ancient **Greece** come soon after. There's also a particularly extensive collection of Greek coins, followed by remarkable illuminated manuscripts and ceramics from **Armenia**, porcelain from **China**, and beautiful **Japanese** prints and lacquerwork. Islamic arts are magnificently represented by ornamented texts, opulently woven carpets, glassware (such as the fourteenth-century mosque lamps from Syria) and precious bindings from **Persia** and **India**.

EUROPEAN ART

In the **European art** section you'll find work from all the major schools, beginning with a group of French medieval ivory diptychs (in particular the six scenes depicting the *Life of the Virgin*) and a thirteenth-century copy of Saint John's prophetic *Apocalypse*, produced in Kent and touched up in Italy under Pope Clement IX. From fifteenth-century Flanders, there's a pair of panels by van der Weyden, and from the same period in Italy comes Ghirlandaio's *Portrait of a Young Woman*. The seventeenth century collection yields two exceptional portraits – one by Rubens of his second wife, *Helena Fourment*, and Rembrandt's *Figure of an Old Man* – plus works by van Dyck, Frans Hals and Ruisdael. Eighteenth-century works featured include a good Fragonard, and a roll-call incorporating Gainsborough, Sir Thomas Lawrence and – most impressively, with no fewer than nineteen paintings – Francesco Guardi. Finally Corot, Manet, Monet, Degas and Renoir supply a good showing from nineteenth- to twentieth-century France.

Sculpture is poorly represented on the whole, though a French sixteenth-century religious statue of *Mary Magdalene*, a fifteenth-century medallion of *Faith* by Luca della Robbia, a 1780 marble *Diana* by Jean-Antoine Houdon, and a couple of Rodins all stand out. Elsewhere, you'll find **ceramics** from Spain and Italy; **furniture** from Louis XV to Louis XVI; eighteenth-century works from **French goldsmiths**; fifteenth-century Italian bronze **medals** (especially by Pisanello); and assorted Italian tapestries and textiles. An Art Nouveau collection with 169 pieces of fantasy jewellery by **René Lalique** is the best of the tail-end of this great collection.

The Centro de Arte Moderna

To reach the **Centro de Arte Moderna** (main entrance on Rua Dr. N. de Bettencourt: June–Sept Tues, Thurs, Fri & Sun 10am–5pm, Wed & Sat 2–7.30pm; Oct–May Tues–Sun 10am–5pm; 500$00, free on Sun) walk through the gardens, which are enlivened by some specially commissioned sculptures. The centre features some big names on the twentieth-century Portuguese scene, including **Almada Negreiros** (1873–1970), the founder of *modernismo* (his portrait of Fernando Pessoa, now in the Casa Museu Fernando Pessoa, is particularly well known; see p.71), Amadeu de Sousa Cardoso and Guilherme Santa-Rita (both of Futurist inclinations), Vieira da Silva (whose distinctive painting style is a criss-cross of lines) and **Paula Rego** (one of Portugal's leading contemporary artists, now resident in England). Next to the museum, don't miss the perennially popular self-service **restaurant** (see p.92).

North of the Gulbenkian

Few visitors explore anything of Lisbon **north** of the Gulbenkian, unless for a trip to the Sporting or Benfica football stadiums or the Campo Pequeno bullring. Out past the Cidade Universitária, though, are some mildly diverting **museums**, devoted to the city's history and to costume, plus a private **art collection**. They are all on the route of the #7 bus, which runs from Cais do Sodré via Praça da Figueira. Over to the northwest of the Gulbenkian, further peripheral attractions are provided by the **Jardim Zoológico** (the city's zoo), and by the nearby **Palácio dos Marquêses da Fronteira**. Buses #31 and #41 (or the metro, to Sete Rios) link Rossio with the Jardim Zoológico via Rotunda.

The Museu da Cidade, Museu Rafael Bordalo Pinheiro and Museu do Traje

Some 2km north of the Gulbenkian, the **Museu da Cidade** (Tues–Sun 10am–1pm & 2–6pm; 350$00) is installed in the eighteenth-century Palácio Pimenta, in the northwestern corner of Campo Grande. Its principal interest lies in an imaginative collection of prints, paintings and models of pre-1755 Lisbon. A death-defying crossing of the road leads you to another lovely mansion housing the **Museu Rafael Bordalo Pinheiro** (Tues–Sun 10am–1pm & 2–6pm; 260$00), dedicated to the caricaturist and ceramicist. Upstairs exhibits include his amazing collection of ornate dishes crawling with crabs and lobsters, frogs and snakes. The paintings, cartoons and sketches downstairs are of less interest.

The **Museu do Traje** (Tues–Sun: summer 10am–6pm; winter 10am–5pm; joint ticket with Museu do Teatro 400$00; free on Sun) occupies another eighteenth-century palace, the Palácio do Monteiro-Mor, some 2km further north of the Museu da Cidade. The museum's extensive collections are drawn upon for temporary thematic exhibitions – excellent if costume is your subject, less gripping if you're not an aficionado of faded fabrics. For more casual visitors, the surrounding **park** is at least as big an attraction – one of the lushest areas of the city, open daily until 5pm and with a good restaurant and café. The small **Museu do Teatro** (Tues 2–6pm, Wed–Sun 10am–6pm; joint ticket with Museu do Traje 400$00; free on Sun), containing theatrical memorabilia, is also sited in the grounds but is of truly specialist interest.

The Jardim Zoológico

The **Jardim Zoológico**, on Estrada de Benfica (daily 9am–7pm; 1600$00) has been spruced up but remains one of the least inspiring of European zoos, exhibiting overheated polar bears and other unhappy captives. On the other hand it's really as much a rambling garden as anything else and in this, and in its peculiarly Portuguese eruptions of kitsch (an extraordinary dogs' cemetery), makes for an enjoyable afternoon's ramble, with a small *téléférique* (daily 11am–7pm), a reptile house (10am–noon & 1–6pm) and performing dolphins as further diversions. You can get there by metro, to Sete Rios, or by bus #41 from Rossio.

The Palácio dos Marquêses da Fronteira

Palace enthusiasts might like to visit the seventeenth-century **Palácio dos Marquêses da Fronteira**, Largo de São Domingos de Benfica 1, which is around twenty minutes' walk west from the zoo; bus #41 from Rossio or bus #46 from Praça do Comércio pass nearby. After the view of the bland housing development on Rua de São Domingos de Benfica, the fantastic gardens of this small, pink country house feel like an oasis. The allegorical panels on the lower level, taken from Camões' tale of the *Doze da Inglaterra*, mark a historic moment in the history of azulejos when, in the mid-seventeenth century, the Portuguese dropped the formal Moorish methods of design and turned to painting straight onto tiles.

Because the palace is still inhabited, **visiting hours** are limited and by guided tour only (June–Sept Mon–Sat, tours at 10.30am, 11am, 11.30am & noon; Oct–May tours at 11.30am & noon; 500$00 gardens only or 1500$00 palace and gardens). Call ☎778 20 23 to check on the latest details.

The Museu Nacional de Arte Antiga

The **Museu Nacional de Arte Antiga** (Tues 2–6pm, Wed–Sun 10am–6pm; 500$00, free on Sun), Portugal's national gallery, certainly stands comparison with the Gulbenkian. The core of the museum – comprising fifteenth- and sixteenth-century Portuguese works by such artists as Nuno Gonçalves – is excellent and well displayed in a beautiful converted palace of the period; the garden and restaurant (hours as for museum, restaurant open till midnight) are worth a visit in their own right. It is situated at Rua das Janelas Verdes 95 in the wealthy suburb of **Lapa**, two kilometres west of Praça do Comércio. To get there, take bus #40 or #60 from Praça do Comércio, or bus #27 or #49 on the way to or from Belém.

Gonçalves and the Portuguese School

Gonçalves and his fellow painters of the so-called "Portuguese school" span that indeterminate and exciting period when Gothic art was giving way to the Renaissance. Their works, notably Gregório Lopes' *Martyrdom of São Sebastião*, and those by Frei Carlos, are exclusively religious in concept, and particularly interesting in their emphasis on portraiture – transforming any theme, even a martyrdom, into a vivid observation of local contemporary life. Stylistically, the most significant influences upon them were those of the Flemish, "Northern Renaissance" painters: Jan van Eyck, who came to Portugal in 1428, Memling and Mabuse (both well represented here) and Rogier van der Weyden.

The acknowledged masterpiece, however, is Gonçalves' **Panéis de São Vicente** (Saint Vincent Altarpiece; 1467–1470), a brilliantly marshalled canvas depicting the saint, Lisbon's patron, receiving homage from all ranks of its citizens. On the two left-hand panels are Cistercian monks, fishermen and sailors; on the opposite side the Duke of Bragança and his family, a helmeted Moorish knight, a Jew (with book), a beggar, and a priest holding Saint Vincent's own relics (a piece of his skull, which is still possessed by the Sé). In the epic central panels the mustachioed Henry the Navigator, his nephew Afonso V (in green), and the youthful (future) Dom João II, pay tribute to the saint. Among the frieze of portraits behind them, that on the far left is reputed to be Gonçalves himself; the other central panel shows the Archbishop of Lisbon. **Later Portuguese painters** – from the sixteenth to the eighteenth century – are displayed too, most notably António de Sequeira and Josefa de Óbidos (for more on whom, see p.144).

The rest of the collection

After Gonçalves and his contemporaries the most interesting works are by **Flemish and German** painters – Cranach, Bosch (represented by a fabulous *Temptation of St Anthony*) and Dürer – and miscellaneous gems by Raphael, Zurbarán, and, rather oddly, Rodin. But exhibits more likely to delay you are those in the extensive **applied art** sections. Here, on Level 1, you'll find **Portuguese furniture and textiles** to rival the European selection in the Gulbenkian and, on Level 2, an excellent collection of **silverware** and **ceramics**. Also on Level 2, the **Oriental Art** collection shows the influence of Indian, African and Oriental designs derived from the new trading links of the time. Other colonially influenced exhibits include inlaid furniture from Goa and a supremely satisfying series of late sixteenth-century **Japanese screens**, showing the Portuguese landing at Nagasaki.

Belém

It was from **Belém** in 1497 that Vasco da Gama set sail for India, and here too that he was welcomed home by Dom Manuel "the Fortunate" (O Venturoso). Da Gama brought back with him a small cargo of pepper, but it was enough to pay for his voyage sixty times over. The monastery subsequently built here – the **Mosteiro dos Jerónimos** – stands as a testament to his triumphant discovery of a sea route to the Orient, which amounted to the declaration of a "golden age". Built to honour the vow Dom Manuel made to the Virgin in return for a successful voyage, it stands on the site of the old Ermida do Restelo or Capela de São Jerónimo, a hermitage founded by Henry the Navigator, where Vasco da Gama and his companions had spent their last night ashore in prayer. Its funding also was a levy on the fruits of his discovery – a five percent tax on all spices other than pepper, cinnamon and cloves, whose import had become the sole preserve of the Crown.

The Rio Tejo at Belém has receded with the centuries, for when the monastery was built it stood almost on the beach, within sight of caravels moored ready for expeditions, and of the **Torre de Belém**, guarding the entrance to the port. This, too, survived the earthquake and is the other showpiece Manueline building in Lisbon. Both monastery and tower lie in what is now – despite the road and railway cutting it in half – a pleasant waterfront suburb, 6km west of the city centre, close to a small group of museums, and with some fine **cafés and restaurants**. Make time, in particular, for the *Antiga Confeitaria de Belém*, in Rua de Belém, by the tram stop, which bills itself as the "única fábrica de pasteis de Belém" – *pasteis de Belém* being delicious flaky tartlets filled with custard-like cream.

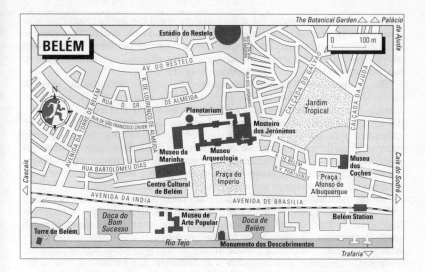

Belém is easily reached by **tram** (signed Algés) – the fast supertram #15 runs from Praça da Figueira via Praça do Comércio taking about twenty minutes – or by slow train from Cais do Sodré or bus #51 from the Gulbenkian museum. If you feel like escaping to a **beach** you can get a **ferry** across the Tejo from Belém to Trafaria, which is only 3km by bus from Costa da Caparica (see p.125); ferries leave on the hour and half hour (Mon–Fri 6.30am–11.30pm, Sun 7.30–11.30pm) from a terminus right by the train station (some five minutes from central Belém). Alternatively, **trains** from here continue to Cascais (see p.110). When planning your trip keep in mind that quite a few of the sights at Belém are closed on Mondays.

The Mosteiro dos Jerónimos

Even before the Great Earthquake, the **Mosteiro dos Jerónimos** (Tues–Sun: June–Sept 10am–6.30pm; Oct–May 10am–5pm; monastery free, cloister 400$00, 250$00 for students, free Sun morning) was Lisbon's finest monument: since then, it has stood quite without comparison. Begun in 1502 and more or less completed when its funding was withdrawn by João III in 1551, the monastery is the most ambitious and successful achievement of Manueline architecture. It is less flamboyantly exotic than either Tomar or Batalha – the great culminations of the style in Estremadura – but, despite a succession of master-builders, it has more daring and confidence in its overall design. This is largely the achievement of two outstanding figures, **Diogo de Boitaca**, perhaps the originator of the Manueline style with his Igreja de Jesus at Setúbal, and **João de Castilho**, a Spaniard who took over the construction from around 1517.

It was Castilho who designed the **main entrance** to the **church** (closed during Mass) a complex, shrine-like hierarchy of figures centred around Henry the Navigator (on a pedestal above the arch). In its intricate and almost flat ornamentation, it shows the influence of the then current Spanish style, Plateresque (literally, the art of the silversmith). Yet it also has distinctive Manueline features

– the use of rounded forms, the naturalistic motifs in the bands around the windows – and these seem to create both its harmony and individuality. They are also unmistakably outward-looking, evoking the new forms discovered in the East, a characteristic that makes each Manueline building so new and interesting and so much a product of its particular and expansionary age.

This is immediately true of the church itself, whose breathtaking sense of space alone places it among the great triumphs of European Gothic. Here, though, Manueline developments add two extraordinary and fresh dimensions. There are tensions, deliberately created and carefully restrained, between the grand spatial design and the areas of intensely detailed ornamentation. And, still more striking, there is a naturalism in the forms of this ornamentation that seems to extend into the actual structure of the church. Once you've made the analogy, it's difficult to see the six central columns as anything other than palm trunks, growing both into and from the branches of the delicate rib-vaulting.

Another peculiarity of Manueline buildings is the way in which they can adapt, enliven, or encompass any number of different styles. Here, the basic structure is thoroughly Gothic, though Castilho's ornamentation on the columns is much more Renaissance in spirit. So too is the semicircular apse (around the altar), added in 1572, beyond which is the entrance to the remarkable double cloister.

Vaulted throughout and fantastically embellished, the **cloister** is one of the most original and beautiful pieces of architecture in the country. Again, it holds in balance Gothic forms and Renaissance ornamentation and is exuberant in its innovations, such as the rounded corner canopies and delicate twisting divisions within each of the arches. These lend a wave-like, rhythmic motion to the whole structure, a conceit extended by the typically Manueline motifs drawn from ropes, anchors and the sea. In this – as in all aspects – it would be hard to imagine an artistic style more directly reflecting the achievements and preoccupations of an age.

In the wings of the monastery are two museums. The enormous **Museu da Marinha** (Tues–Sun: June–Sept 10am–6pm; Oct–May 10am–5pm; 300$00, free Sun morning), in the west wing, is more interesting than most of its kind, packed not only with models of ships, naval uniforms and a surprising display of artefacts from Portugal's oriental trade and colonies, but also with real vessels – among them fishing boats and sumptuous state barges – a couple of seaplanes and even some fire engines. In contrast, the **Museu de Arqueologia** (Tues 2–6pm, Wed–Sun 10am–6pm; 400$00, free Sun morning), in the east wing, seems sparse and, apart from a few fine Roman mosaics unearthed in the Algarve, thoroughly unexceptional.

The Torre de Belém

Still washed on three sides by the sea, the **Torre de Belém** (Tues–Sun: June–Sept 10am–6.30pm; Oct–May 10am–5pm; 400$00) stands 500m west of the monastery, fronted by a little park with a café. Whimsical, multi-turreted and with a real hat-in-the-air exuberance, it was built as a fortress to safeguard the approach to Lisbon's harbour and constructed over the last five years of Dom Manuel's reign (1515–20). As such, it is the one completely Manueline building in Portugal, the rest having been adaptations of earlier structures or completed in later years.

Its architect, **Francisco de Arruda**, had previously worked on Portuguese fortifications in Morocco and the Moorish influence is very strong in the delicately arched windows and balconies. Prominent also in the decoration are two great symbols of the age: Manuel's personal badge of an armillary sphere (representing the globe) and the cross of the military Order of Christ, once the Templars, who took a major role in all Portuguese conquests. The tower's interior is unremarkable except for a "whispering gallery"; it was used into the nineteenth century as a prison, notoriously by Dom Miguel (1828–34), who kept political enemies in the waterlogged dungeons.

Back towards the Monumento dos Descobrimentos
Walking back along the waterfront, towards the monastery, you'll pass the **Museu de Arte Popular** (Mon–Sat 10am–12.30pm & 2–5pm; 300$00), a province-by-province display of Portugal's still very diverse folk arts, housed in a shed-like building. Almost adjacent is the **Monumento dos Descobrimentos** (Monument to the Discoveries; Tues–Sun 9.30am–6pm; 320$00, students 160$00), an angular slab of concrete in the shape of a caravel which was erected in 1960 to commemorate the 500th anniversary of the death of Henry the Navigator. Henry appears on the prow with Camões and other Portuguese heroes. Within the monument is a small exhibition space, with interesting and changing exhibits on the city's history; the entrance fee also lets you climb right up to the top for some fine views of the Tejo and Torre de Belém.

The Centro Cultural de Belém and the Museu dos Coches
Across from the monument, on the western side of the Praça do Imperio, the controversial modern **Centro Cultural de Belém** (daily 11am–8pm; ☎361 24 00) puts on regular photography exhibitions and concerts as well as hosting some kind of live entertainment over the weekend – jugglers, mime artists and the like. For the best views of the surroundings, drop into the café, whose esplanade overlooks the river and the Monument dos Descobrimentos.

At the corner of Belém's other main square – Praça Afonso de Albuquerque, a few minutes' walk east from the monastery along Rua de Belém – you'll find the **Museu dos Coches** (Tues–Sun: June–Sept 10am–5.30pm; Oct–May 10am–1pm & 2.30–5.30pm; 450$00, free Sun morning), oddly the most visited tourist attraction in Lisbon. It consists of an interminable line of royal coaches – Baroque, heavily gilded and sometimes beautifully painted.

Palácio da Ajuda
Jump on bus #14, on Calçada da Ajuda behind the Museu dos Coches, for the short ride uphill to the **Palácio da Ajuda** (half-hour tours 10am–5pm; closed Wed; 400$00, free Sun morning). The palace was built by those crashingly tasteless nineteenth-century royals, Dona Maria II and Dom Ferdinand, and like their Pena Palace folly at Sintra (see p.117) is all over-the-top aristocratic clutter. The **banqueting hall**, however, is quite a sight; likewise the lift, decked out with mahogany and mirrors. Tram #18 will get you back from the palace to Praça do Comércio, or take bus #14 or #60 to Praça da Figueira.

Expo 98

Following its success as European City of Culture in 1994, Lisbon will once more be the focus of international attention when, from May 22 to September 30, 1998 it hosts **Expo 98**. This, the last Expo of the millennium, is the culmination of maslights of the **Knowledge of the Seas Pavilion**, which examines how mankind exploits the oceans and what we can do to protect them – a theme further explored in the **Pavilion of the Future**. After Expo, the Knowledge of the Seas Pavilion will become the Museum of the Sea and Technology. For those who fancy a temporary flight from reality, the **Utopia Pavilion** will broadcast a multimedia show five times daily recreating ocean myths and legends; its more down-to-earth post-Expo function will be as a sports and concert hall with a capacity of fifteen thousand.

Other countries and organisations will exhibit in the **International Areas**, divided into north and south, set to become eventually the new **Feira Internacional de Lisboa**, Lisbon's main exhibition hall and crafts emporium.

Practicalities

Transport connections have been an integral part of the whole development and like the site itself will continue to serve the city after Expo is over. The new station **Estação do Oriente**, designed by Spanish architect Santiago Calatrava, is a stunning building and is destined to become Lisbon's main train terminal, served by **trains** from Santa Apolónia station and a direct **metro** line (the Olivais line). The site can also be reached by a regular bus shuttle from the airport; all buses terminate at Estação do Oriente. A private **ferry** service also serves the River Gate with connections to Praça do Comércio.

The site will be **open** from 9am to 3am daily. An Expo **Day Ticket** (valid 9am–3am) will cost 5000$00 or 12,500$00 for a three-day ticket (days do not have to be consecutive). However, if it's the night-time entertainment that interests you, an **Expo night ticket** (lasting from 8pm to 3am) will set you back only 2000$00. There will be no admission charge to the site when Expo is over, although inevitably admission charges will be made for the permanent attractions. Further details of the event can be obtained from **Expo 98 Tourism Unit**, Avda. Marechal Gomes de la Costa, 37, 1800 Lisbon (☎01/831 98 98, fax 837 31 33) or from the Expo Web site at *http://www.expo98.pt*.

Eating

Lisbon has some of the best-value **cafés and restaurants** of any European city, serving large portions of good Portuguese food at sensible prices. A set menu (an *ementa turística*) at lunch or dinner will get you a three-course meal for 1800–2500$00, though you can eat for considerably less than this by sticking to the ample main dishes and choosing the daily specials. **Seafood** is widely available – there's an entire central street, Rua das Portas de Santo Antão, as well as a whole enclave of restaurants across the Rio Tejo at Cacilhas, that specialize in it. This is the only time you'll need to be careful what you eat as seafood is always pricier than other menu items. Several traditional restaurants still survive in Lisbon, most notably beautifully tiled **cervejarias** (literally beer halls) where the emphasis is often as much on drinking as eating; while the capital, naturally, also features some of the country's best (and most expensive) restaurants – specializing for the most part in a hybrid French-Portuguese cuisine. If you tire of all this, Lisbon has a rich vein of inexpensive **foreign restaurants**, in particular those featuring food from the former colonies: Brazil, Mozambique, Angola, Macão and Goa.

Gambrinus, Rua das Portas de Santo Antão 15 (☎342 14 66). One of Lisbon's top seafood restaurants, serving up dishes like broiled eel with bacon, lobster and dessert crepes in a smart, wood-panelled interior.

Gordos, Rua 1° de Dezembro 105 (☎346 94 95). Very attractive, azulejo-covered pizzeria, which also offers substantial salads and pasta dishes.

Martinho da Arcada, Praça do Comércio 3. Beautiful, traditional restaurant, in the arcade, little changed from the beginning of the century when it was frequented by writer Fernando Pessoa. Closed Sun.

Rei dos Frangos, Trav. de Santo Antão. On an alleyway connecting Restauradores with Rua das Portas de Santo Antão, this is the place for spit-roast chicken – whole ones with fries for about 1000$00. You may have to wait for a table, but it's worth it.

Solmar, Rua das Portas de Santo Antão 108 (☎342 33 71). A vast showpiece seafood restaurant, with fountain and marine mosaics, and generally deserving its reputation. Very slick service and fine seafood for up to and around 5000$00 a head.

Yin-Yang, Rua dos Correeiros 14-1°. Macrobiotic-vegetarian lunches (noon–1pm), including tofu dishes, fruit juices and crepes. Main dishes cost 600–1300$00, and it's open from 6–8pm for light snacks. Closed weekends.

Chiado

Associação Católica, Trav. Ferragial 1. Go through the unmarked door and head to the top floor for this self-service canteen offering different dishes each day. The chief attractions are the low prices and the fine rooftop terrace with views over the Tejo. Open Mon–Fri noon–3pm.

L'Entrecôte, Rua do Alecrim 121. The place to eat steaks washed down with fine wines. Relaxed, informal atmosphere in a spacious, wood-panelled interior with soaring ceilings.

Tágide, Largo Academia das Belas Artes 18–20 (☎342 07 20). One of Lisbon's priciest restaurants, serving superb regional dishes in a dining room with sweeping city views. Book ahead, especially for a window seat. At least 6000$00 per person. Open till 8.15pm; closed weekends.

Around Cais do Sodré

Cais da Ribeira, Armazem A, Porta 2 (☎346 36 11). Attractive converted warehouse with river views around the back of Cais do Sodré serving superior (and pricey) fish, meat and seafood dinners, straight from the market. Closed weekends.

Marisqueira do Cais do Sodré, Cais do Sodré (☎342 21 05). Big, expensive seafood restaurant by the station, complete with bubbling fish tanks. Try the *caldeirada de tamboril* (monkfish stew), the *caril de gambas* (curried prawns) or the seafood *parrilhada*.

Porto de Abrigo, Rua dos Remolares 16–18. Old-style tavern-restaurant serving market-fresh fish at reasonable prices. Closed Mon.

Bairro Alto

Restaurante Alfaia, Trav. de Queimada 18–24. Very good-value lunches and dinners turned out to a mixed local crowd in a dining room resembling a snake charmer's boudoir. Closed Sun.

Ali-a-Papa, Rua da Atalaia 95. Rare Moroccan restaurant in attractive interior. Good-value couscous and tajine dishes.

O Barrigas ("The Stomachs"), Trav. da Queimada 31. Titchy little tavern with friendly service and simple dishes such as steaks. Inexpensive if you settle for the half portions, which should suffice.

Bizarro, Rua da Atalaia 133. Fashionable spot with a limited, but adventurous, menu. The *ementa turística* is a good deal. Closed Mon.

Bota Alta, Trav. da Queimada 37 (☎342 79 59). This attractive old tavern restaurant attracts queues for its large portions of traditional Portuguese food – cod cooked in cream, among other things. The tables are crammed in cheek-by-jowl and it's always packed; try to get there before 8pm. Closed Sun.

Brasuca, Rua João Pereira da Rosa 7 (☎342 85 42). A lively restaurant set in an ageing mansion off Rua do Seculo, with great Brazilian food (and *caipirinhas*) as well as the Portuguese standards. Busy at the weekends; you may want to book. Expensive.

O Cantinho do Bem Estar, Rua do Norte 46. Friendly, authentic tiled Alentejan restaurant – get there before 9pm. Cheap and with a good-value tourist menu including local wine. Closed Mon.

Casa Faz Frio, Rua Dom Pedro V 96. A beautiful, traditional restaurant, replete with tiles and distinctive cubicles. Huge portions of *bacalhau*, quail, steaks and fish at inexpensive prices.

Fidalgo, Rua da Barroca 27 (☎342 29 00). This has long been a fashionable and cosy hangout for artists and media types, who are rewarded with delicious seafood creations such as *arroz de tamboril com camarão*. Closed Sun.

Hell's Kitchen, Rua da Atalaia 176 (☎342 28 22). Fashionable place with unusual and good-value dishes such as falafels and creole salmon.

Pap'Açorda, Rua da Atalaia 57–59 (☎346 48 11). Famous and popular restaurant with a dining room converted from an old bakery, now hung with chandeliers. An *açorda* – the house speciality – is a sort of bread and shellfish stew, seasoned with fresh coriander and a raw egg. Expensive. Closed Sun.

Patô Baton, Trav. Fiéis de Deus 28 (☎362 63 72). One of the most stylish interiors in Bairro Alto provides a backdrop for pleasant, French-inspired cooking. The *Bife Dijonais* is splendid. In summer there's terrace dining on the steps outside. Around 3500$00.

A Severa, Rua das Gavéas 51. Good, moderately-priced late-night eating option (open until 3.30am); its speciality is chicken *na púcara* – in the pot. Closed Fri & Sun.

Sinal Vermelha, Rua das Gavéas 89 (☎346 12 52). Roomy, split-level *adega* that's still popular with Lisbon's trendies. Try the rabbit or liver dishes.

Cervejaria da Trindade, Rua Nova da Trindade 20. Huge, vaulted beer hall-restaurant, with some of the city's loveliest azulejos on the walls. It specializes in shellfish, though go for the experience rather than the food, which is overrated.

Vá e Volte, Rua do Diário de Notícias 100. Excellent little family diner serving large plates of fried/grilled fish or meat at thoroughly modest prices. Closed Mon.

Vamos ao Norte, Rua do Norte 13. Cramped, split-level restaurant serving good northern Portuguese cooking, which means more meat than fish, and there are some heady northern wines to try as well. Closed Mon.

Estrêla and Lapa

Farah's Tandoori, Rua de Santana à Lapa 73. Between Lapa and Estrêla, this is one of Lisbon's more reliable Indian restaurants and is good for vegetarians, with dishes such as vegetable *tikka massala* and *palak paneer*. Meat dishes are also fragrant and delicious. Closed Tues.

Flor da Estrêla, Rua João de Deus 11. Neighbourhood restaurant around the back of the Estrêla basilica, serving all the usual dishes and cheap wine. There are a few outdoor tables, but the interior is attractive. Try the *feijoada de marisco*. Closed Sun.

Sua Excelência, Rua do Conde 42 (☎60 36 14). Small, intimate restaurant in the heart of Lapa specializing in Mozambiquan tiger prawns. Marvellously inventive Portuguese cooking,worth the high prices. Reservations advised. Expensive. Closed Wed & Sat, Sun lunch & Sept.

York House, Rua das Janelas Verdes 47, Lapa (☎396 81 43). Inside this sumptuous hotel is a surprisingly moderately priced restaurant serving delicious fish, meat, pasta and vegetarian options. In summer, you can dine in the tranquil courtyard. Closes at 7.30pm.

Around the Sé

Estrela da Sé, Largo S. António da Sé 4. Beautiful, azulejo-covered restaurant serving inexpensive and tasty dishes like *alheira* sausage and salmon. Closed Sun.

Mão de Ferro, Rua da Padaria 12, off Rua de São Julião. Budget meals in a subterranean vault of paper-topped tables. Some less usual options, too, such as octopus salad and curried chicken. Closed Sun.

Rio Coura, Rua Augusta Rosa 30. A couple of hundred metres up from the Sé, and despite the tourist trappings, this place offers good value, with full meals including rough house wine for around 2000$00, served in a traditional tiled dining room.

Solar da Padaria, Rua da Padaria 18–20. Attractive tiled restaurant offering Portuguese favourites such as *bacalhau com natas*, meat cataplana and squid kebabs.

Adega Triunfo, Rua dos Bacalheiros 129. One of several no-frills, paper-tablecloth café-restaurants along this street with a changing menu of meat and fish, pricier seafood, and cheap house wine. Try the *feijoada*. Closed Mon.

Alfama and around the Castelo

Arco do Castelo, Rua Chão da Feira 25. Cheerful place specializing in Goan dishes; tempting shrimp curry, Indian sausage and spicy seafood. Closed Sun.

O Cantinho do Aziz, Rua de São Lourenço 3–5. This is a little hard to find (easiest approach is up a couple of flights of stairs east of Rossio), but well worth the search. Run by a congenial Mozambiquan family, it offers a selection of African and Indian food (try the curried goat) at fairly low prices. Closed Sun.

Casa do Leão, Castelo de São Jorge (☎887 59 62). Couldn't be better sited, within the castle walls and offering a superb city view and slick service – which explains the outrageous prices. Good traditional Portuguese food for 5000$00 and upwards.

Lautasco, Beco do Azinhal 7. Tucked just off the Largo do Chafariz de Dentro, this has a lovely, fairy-lit courtyard and, accordingly, higher than average prices. Closed Sun.

Restaurante Malmequer-Bemmequer, Rua de São Miguel 23–25, at Largo de São Miguel. Charcoal-grilled meat and fish (try the sole) served up amidst cheery, flowery decor, all presided over by a friendly owner, who learned his craft aboard cruise liners. Closed Mon.

Marítima das Colunas, Largo do Chafariz de Dentro 16–17. Honest portions of Portuguese standards in tiled place that lures in the tourists. Closed Sun.

Mestré André, Calçadinha de Santo Estevão 4–6. A fine tavern with a bit of traditional colour about it, superb pork dishes and good *churrasco* (grills). Outdoor terrace seating in summer. Closed Sun.

Os Minhotos, Calçadinha de Santo Estevão 31. Average interior but attractive outdoor seating and a very reasonable tourist menu.

A Tasquinha, Largo do Contador Mor 5–7. Considering its position, on the main route up to the castle, this lovely *tasca* has remained remarkably unaffected by tourism, with a few tables in its traditional interior and a fine outdoor terrace. Closed Sun.

Via Graça, Rua Damasceno Monteiro 9b (☎887 08 30). Unattractive new building but an interior offering stunning panoramas of Lisbon. Specialities include spider crab and duck with moscatel. Closed Sun.

Along and around Avenida da Liberdade

Casa da Comida, Trav. das Amoreiras 1 (☎388 53 76); metro Rotunda. One of the city's top French-Portuguese restaurants set in one of the city's nicest squares, under the aqueduct. Superb mansion surroundings, an outdoor patio and meals costing a good 6000$00 and upwards. Closed Sun.

A Casa de Pompeia, Rua da Alegria 23; metro Avenida. Trendy Portuguese food, with good grilled meat dishes, and young, friendly staff. Moderate. Closed Sun.

Centro de Alimentção e Saúde Natural, Rua Mouzinho da Silveira 25; metro Rotunda. Self-service restaurant with light, bright upstairs dining rooms and a summer courtyard. Serves good, inexpensive vegetarian options such as chickpea stew, pepper rice and natural fruit juices. Open Mon–Fri till 6pm.

Cervejaria Choupal, Rua do Salitre 9; metro Avenida. Rather gloomy backstreet *cervejaria*, just off the avenida, but with tasty food and pleasant service. Try the *caril de marisco* or lobster curry. Inexpensive. Closed Sun.

Comida de Santo, Calçada Engenheiro Miguel Pais 39; metro Avenida. Rowdy, late-opening Brazilian restaurant serving cocktails and classic dishes. Off Rua das Escola Politecnica, opposite the entrance to the botanical gardens.

O Manel, Parque Mayer, Avda. da Liberdade; metro Avenida. The small group of theatres tucked off Trav. do Salitre also hides a cluster of restaurants, this one serving great *feijoada* and *bacalhau* in a log-cabin-style interior. There's even an open fire in winter. Closed Sun.

Os Tibetanos, Rua do Salitre 117; metro Avenida. Located in the Buddhist Centre, this stripped-pine restaurant has superb, unusual veggie food such as vegetarian paella. Closed Sun.

Restaurante 33, Rua Alex. Herculano 33. Fine old wood-beamed building where you can eat partridge stuffed with onions, duck rice, curried seafood and the like in some style but at moderate prices. Closed Sun.

Belém

Rua Vieira Portuense, a block back from the main Rua de Belém, off Praça Afonso de Albuqerque, is a terrace of little buildings housing a line of *tascas* and restaurants, all with outdoor seating. They're packed at lunchtime; either call in earlier to book a table or expect to wait in line if you want to sit outside.

Capsula, Rua Vieira Portuense 74. Cheap place with tiled interior, upstairs seating and outside tables catering to tourists tucking into tuna steaks, trout and the like.

Carvoeiro, Rua Vieira Portuense 66–68. An inexpensive little *tasca*, with good grilled fish and jugs of wine. A good-value choice with outdoor tables.

Ja Sei, Avda. Brasília 202. Prowling waiters see to your every need in this modern place with great views over the Discoveries monument and prices to match. International and Portuguese dishes. Closed Mon evenings.

São Jerónimo, Rua dos Jerónimos 12 (☎364 87 97). Classic formal dining by the side of the monastery. High prices but worth it for excellent fish dishes. Closed Sun.

Vela Latina, Doca de Bem Sucesso. Trendy smart option overlooking the docks. Expensive Portuguese cooking and a late-night bar open till 2am. It has a cheaper self-service café round the corner. Closed Sun.

Saldanha, Estefânia, Campo Pequeno and Alvalade

Centro de Arte Moderna, Fundação Calouste Gulbenkian, entrance by Rua Dr. N. de Bettencourt; metro São Sebastião. Join the lunchtime queues at the museum restaurant for good-value hot or cold dishes. There are excellent salads for vegetarians; you get a choice of four or six varieties. Open daily noon–4pm.

Restaurante Chimarrão, Praça do Chile 8; metro Arroios. If you're looking for quantity, 3800$00 spent here gets you unlimited stabs at twelve types of barbecued meat and various salads – you'll need to pace yourself. There are also branches at Campo Pequeno and on Avda. Roma 90.

Espiral, Praça Ilha do Faial 14a, off Largo de Dona Estefânia; metro Saldanha. Inexpensive, self-service macrobiotic restaurant downstairs (including vegetarian, Chinese and fish dishes) with adjacent snack bar and upstairs bookshop. The food isn't that great, but there's often live music at the weekend.

Grog, Praça de Alvalade 3; metro Alvalade. Long-standing snack bar and sandwich shop with a great range of homemade foods. Daily 8pm–1am.

Cervejaria Portugália, Avda. Almirante Reis 117; metro Arroios. Busy beer hall-restaurant where you can either snack and drink at the bar or eat fine *mariscos* or steak in the dining room. A popular family outing and always busy. Open till 1.30am.

Recanto da Bahia, Avda. Luís Bivar 7A; metro Saldanha. Good but pricey Brazilian restaurant serving *caipirinhas* and fruit shakes. Live music on Thurs, Fri & Sat nights.

Ser-Veja-Ria, Avda. João XXI 80C; metro Campo Grande. As it sounds: a decent modern town *cervejaria*, with moderate food and drink.

Cafés, bars and clubs

Drinking, at its most prosaic level, is done in bars and cafés throughout Lisbon; some of the older **cafés** and *pastelarias* (specializing in cakes) in particular are worth dropping in to at some stage during the day. For night-time drinking, there are a few good places in the **Alfama**, but the densest concentration of designer **bars and clubs** is found in the **Bairro Alto**, traditionally the centre of Lisbon's nightlife, with its cramped streets still sheltering around fifty or so of them, in addition to the fado houses and restaurants. As the night progresses, most Lisboetas seek out the nightlife along **Avenida 24 de Julho** and its surroundings, though this area is now less trendy than the docks a little further west at **Alcântara** and **Santo Amaro**, the latter right underneath the Ponte 25 de Abril.

Cafés

All the places listed below are good for breakfast, coffee and cakes or just a beer during the afternoon. Most stay open into the evening, too, with a few – like *A Brasileira* and *Cerca Moura* – also on the late-night bar-crawl circuit.

Academica, Largo do Carmo, Bairro Alto. Tables in one of the city's nicest, quietest squares, outside the ruined Carmo church. Also does light lunches – the grilled sardines are hard to beat.

Antiga Casa dos Pasteis, Rua de Belém 90, Belém. Excellent and cavernous tiled pastry shop and café with scrumptious *pasteis de Belém*.

Bernard, Rua Garrett 104, Chiado. Superb cakes, ice cream and coffees, which you can sample on the outdoor terrace on Chiado's most fashionable street. Open Mon–Sat until 2am.

A Brasileira, Rua Garrett 120, Chiado. Marked by a bronze of Pessoa outside, this is the most famous of Rua Garrett's old-style coffee houses. Livens up at night with a more youthful clientele swigging beer outside until 2am, though the interior is its real appeal.

A Camponeza, Rua dos Sapateiros 155–157, Baixa. Yester-year *leitaria* (dairy shop) with tiled walls, snacks and milk products. Closed Sun.

Casa Chineza, Rua Aurea 274, Baixa. Beautifully decorated pastry and coffee shop. Closed Sat evenings & Sun.

Cerca Moura, Largo das Portas do Sol, Alfama. Stunning views of the Alfama from its esplanade; a good resting place as you climb up and down the hilly streets. Open till late.

Martinho da Arcada, Praça do Comércio 3, Baixa. Traditional old stand-up café with outdoor tables under the arches, call in for a coffee and *pastel de nata*. Closed Sun.

Nicola, Praça Dom Pedro IV 26. On the west side of Rossio, this grand old place is a good stop for breakfast. Outdoor seats are always at a premium. It's been under restoration for some time, but should re-open in 1998.

Pastelaria São Roque, Rua D. Pedro V 57c, Bairro Alto. Relaxed, ornate corner café where you can enjoy coffee and croissants below a wonderfully high ceiling.

Suíça, Praça Dom Pedro IV 96, Bairro Alto. Famous for its cakes and pastries; you'll have a hard job getting an outdoor table here, though there's plenty of room inside – the café stretches across to Praça da Figueira.

Bars and clubs

Lisbon does not immediately strike visitors as a city for **nightlife**, largely because many of its clubs are somewhat discreet, get going late and are concentrated in select areas of the city. But once in the know, you'll find its clubs and bars hard to beat. The **Bairro Alto** hosts one of Europe's biggest weekly street parties, with up to 50,000 people descending on the maze of streets over the weekend, drifting from bar to club before heading out to those at the docks for the small hours. Several Bairro Alto clubs are extremely low key, revealing their presence simply by a street-light and a slot in the door for the attendant to inspect customers. Don't be intimidated by this: just knock and walk in – and straight out, if you don't like the look of the place. Also in Bairro Alto, and on its periphery, over towards **Rato**, is much of the city's gay scene. You'll be hard pushed to find a bar open late at night in the **Baixa**, though things are picking up further east in the **Alfama** and **Graça**, where a growing number of bars cater for the crowds leaving the excellent local restaurants.

Though some of the trendy action still takes place along **Avenida 24 de Julho**, around Santos station, this is no longer the "in" area. That accolade now belongs to the docks, in particular those at **Alcântara** and **Santo Amaro** under Ponte 25 de Abril, in whose tastefully done-up warehouses heaves a wealth of bars and clubs. The shift is partly the result of the local authority's plan to encourage clubs to move out of Barrio Alto into non-residential areas where they can stay open until 6am or later without disturbing the neighbours. Once some of the hippest operators had made the move, the transformation gathered momentum and now the districts attract a largely young, upmarket crowd, who flit from bar to bar before hitting the clubs. To get to the docks, you'll need to hop in a taxi or catch a train to **Alcântara Mar** from **Cais do Sodré**, which has a growing number or riverside clubs and bars itself. Committed clubbers, drinkers and low-life enthusiasts might try one of a dozen places along the nearby Rua Nova do Carvalho, which range from atmospheric to downright seedy.

Drinks are uniformly expensive in all fashionable bars and clubs – from 500$00 for a beer – but the plus-side is that very few charge admission. Generally, where there is an **admission charge**, you can expect to pay around around 3000$00, which usually includes a drink or two; if you're handed a ticket on entry, keep hold of it to claim your first drink. **Friday and Saturday nights** tend to be overcrowded and expensive everywhere; while on Sunday, especially in Bairro Alto, places often close to sleep off the weekend excesses. Note that none of the places listed below **opens** much before 10pm unless otherwise stated; all are open until at least 2am, with most doing business much later than that – 3–4am is normal, 7am not unheard of.

Baixa and Chiado

A Ginginha, Largo de São Domingos 8. Everyone should try *ginginha* – Portuguese cherry brandy – once. There's just about room in this microscopic joint to walk in, down a glassful and stagger outside to see the city in a new light.

Ninho Dourado, Rua Augusta 278. About the only café-bar in the Baixa grid to stay open at night – thus attracting a fleet of peddlers and beggars panhandling the mainly young crowd that packs its pavement tables. Beer, coffee, snacks and crackly rock and pop.

Café Rosso, *Galerias Garrett*, Rua Ivens 57, entrance on Rua Garrett. Courtyard bar that also serves coffee and snacks in the renovated shop galleries on Rua Garrett, a relaxed spot with seats under huge square canopies. Downstairs there's a huge room with modernist seats and lighting.

Around Cais do Sodré

Absoluto, Rua D. Luís I 5. Restaurant, bar and disco complex playing everything from the latest hits to Júlio Iglesias; occasional live bands too. Open till 6am on Fri & Sat, 5am on Thurs; closed Sun.

Irish Pub O'Gilins, Rua de Remolares 8. Despite the British prices, one of a growing band of popular Irish bars with a pleasant, light wooden interior and live music most nights.

Jamaica, Rua Nova do Carvalho 6. Predominantly Sixties' and Seventies' hard rock sounds, with reggae on Tuesday nights. Open till 4am.

Bar do Rio, Armazem 7, Cais do Sodré. Old riverside warehouse decked out as hip esplanade-bar. Open till 4am; closed Sun.

Rock City, Cais do Sodré. Flash new building just above Cais do Sodré station next to the river – just head for the palm trees. As well as the outdoor esplanade, there's a restaurant and live music most nights. Open till 3am.

Tokio, Rua Nova do Carvalho 12. Seventies-style decor and a young student crowd savouring rock and pop; you'll even hear a Portuguese disc or two. Regular live bands. Open till 4am; closed Sun.

Bairro Alto

The map on p.96 shows the whereabouts of the bars and clubs listed below.

Apollo XIII, Trav. da Cara 8. Most nights, a young, boisterous student crowd stuffs itself into this hard-to-spot aluminium sweatbox, a likeable place for a drink until 2am. Closed Sun.

Arroz Doce, Rua da Atalaia 117–119. Nice, normal bar in the middle of the mayhem. Friendly owners and a good spot for an early or late beer; or try "Auntie's" sangria. Closed Sun.

Bar Ártis, Rua do Diário de Notícias 95. A relaxed bar wallowing in the jazzy decor and music, with a fine range of snacks and dishes, too. Closed Mon.

Cafédiario, Rua do Diário de Notícias 3. Jazz and laid-back dance music in a basic bar with a heavy gay presence.

Cena de Copos, Rua da Barroca 103–105. Not a club to frequent unless you're under 25 and bursting with energy. If you are, this is the place – don't turn up until after midnight though.

Frágil, Rua da Atalaia 126. For a long time one of Lisbon's trendiest clubs, partly gay and can be oppressively pretentious, with anyone with an art degree or video camera talking up their careers for all they're worth. Mainly house, rap and soul. Open Mon–Sat till 3.30am.

Gráficos, Trav. da Água de Flor 40. Fashionable, metallic bar with infectious rock and pop music. Closed Sun.

Harry's Bar, Rua de São Pedro de Alcântara 57. A tiny little front-room bar, with waiter service, bar snacks and an eclectic clientele – often including a late-night contingent from the nearby gay discos. Ring bell for admission. Closed Sun.

Incógnito, Rua dos Poiais de São Bento 37. Appropriately named – the only indication is a pair of large metallic doors. The low-lit, plush dance floor downstairs is booming with alternative sounds. After-hours sessions until 7am on Tues, otherwise until 4am. Closed Sun.

Instituto do Vinho do Porto, Rua de São Pedro de Alcântara 45. This is firmly on the tourist circuit, with over 300 types and vintages of port, supposedly from around 160$00 a glass upwards, served at low tables in a comfortable old mansion. Waiters are notoriously snooty and the cheaper ports seem never to be in stock, but it's a good place to kick off an evening. Closed Sun.

Keops, Rua da Rosa 157–159. Small, fashionable nightspot with Egyptian decor and a tiny dance floor should you want to get to grips with the rap, soul and bit of jazz, as well as the odd revivalist sound from the Seventies and Eighties. Open till 3.30am; closed Mon.

BAIRRO ALTO
BARS & CLUBS

KEY

❶ Snob	❼ Instituto do Vinho do Porto	⓭ Arroz Doce	⓳ A Tasca
❷ Pavilhão Chinês	❽ O Tacão Grande	⓮ Portas Largas	⓴ Bar Ártis
❸ Cervejaria Real Fábrica	❾ Primas	⓯ Incógnito	㉑ Cena de Copos
❹ Bar Nova	❿ Gráficos	⓰ Sudoeste	㉒ Tertúlia
❺ Harry's Bar	⓫ Keops	⓱ Pintai	㉓ Café Targus
❻ Apollo XIII	⓬ Frágil	⓲ Os Três Pastorinhos	㉔ Cafédiario

Bar Nova, Rua da Rosa 261. The one with the matt black frontage, just down from *Keops*, and with a similar clientele, but not yet too pretentious. Hip rock and pop as you shuffle between the three rooms and terrace.

Pavilhão Chinês, Rua Dom Pedro V 89. A wonderfully decorated bar, completely lined with mirrored cabinets full of ludicrous and bizarre tableaux of artefacts from around the world. Drinks include a long list of speciality cocktails and there are two pool tables.

Pintaí, Largo Trindade Coelho 22, across the road from São Roque church. Bouncy Brazilian music and cocktails. Open till 3am; closed Sun.

Portas Largas, Rua da Atalaia 105. Black-and-white tiled *adega* with cheapish drinks, music from fado to pop and a funky clientele. The sangria starts flowing from around 8pm; later on there's a significant gay presence as the late-night move up to *Frágil* takes shape.

Primas, Rua da Atalaia 156. Basic drinking den hosted by boisterous bar staff and full of local youths skirmishing and flirting over the table-football and pool tables. Open till 3am; closed Sun.

Cervejaria Real Fábrica, Rua Escola Polítecnica 277. Some fifteen minutes' walk down the hill in Rato, this is famous for its own brewed beer, which you can enjoy at the long, curly wooden bar or at smart tables beneath huge mirrors. The upstairs restaurant is also recommended.

Snob, Rua do Século 178. Upmarket bar-restaurant on the *bairro* outskirts full of media people tucking into cocktails, steaks and light meals until 3am.

Sudoeste, Rua da Barroca 135. Still in the fast lane with Bairro Alto trendies. Ring for admission. Happy hour from 10pm–1am; that's quite an hour.

O Tacão Grande, Trav. da Cara 3. Next to the *Tacão Pequeno* restaurant, this barn of a bar serves up beer, snacks, pop and funk. Closed Mon.

Café Targus, Rua do Diário de Notícias 40. Very much on the night-out circuit for clubbers, this gets them in at midnight before they move on to the clubs.

A Tasca, Trav. da Quiemada 13–15. Cheerful and welcoming American-owned tequila bar, serving cocktails and Mexican specialities.

Tertúlia, Rua do Diário de Notícias 60. Laid-back café-bar, with papers to read, jazz in the background and occasional art exhibitions. If you fancy the urge to play, there's a piano for customers too. Open till 4am; closed Sun.

Os Três Pastorinhos, Rua da Barroca 111. Currently one of the "in" places, so very busy after midnight: music treads the line between dance and easy listening, funk and soul, with a policy of avoiding techno. Decor is a rather neat pinball theme. Open till 4am; closed Mon.

Alfama, Castelo and Graça

Chapitô, Costa do Castelo 1/7. Multimedia centre, incorporating an open-air bar with a marvellous river view, recording studios, circus tent, exhibition areas, a small theatre, a restaurant, and surreal decoration in the downstairs bar interior. It's youthful, highly fashion-conscious and there's no charge for admission. Closed Sun.

Costa do Castelo, Calçada do Marquês de Tancos 1B. Sunny terrace-café and bar with rooftop views, a long list of cocktails, and Brazilian rhythms and jazz. There's a good-value restaurant, too, serving fine Mozambiquan dishes. Closed Mon.

Esboço, Rua do Vigário 10. Tiny bar (press the bell to gain admission) with antique furnishings and tiles. Closed Sun.

Bar da Graça, Trav. da Pereira 43. Off the east side of Largo da Graça, this arty bar mixes live music with theatre and shows, and serves a mean range of Belgian beers. Closed Sun.

Graça Esplanado, Caraçol da Graça. Esplanade-bar underneath the Miradouro da Graça, with great views and, as it gets late, pumping music.

Sua Excelência O Marquês, Largo Marquês do Lavradio. Dark rock bar hidden away in a little square behind the Sé. Live music most nights. Closed Sun.

Tradicional, Rua Afonso de Albuquerque 4. Live Portuguese singing and a decent range of drinks, including some extremely powerful local firewaters. Closed Sun.

Avenida 24 de Julho and around

Kapital, Avda. 24 de Julho 68. One of the seriously trendy spots, with three sleekly designed floors full of *queques* (yuppies) paying high prices for drinks and listening tó techno, but it's hard work getting past the style police on the door. There's a great rooftop terrace. Wednesday night is rock night. Open till 4am.

Kremlin, Escadinhas da Praia 5. One of the city's most fashionable nightspots, this is packed with flash, young, raving Lisboetas. Tough door rules, and don't bother showing up before 2am. Techno still rules. Open till 7am; closed Sun & Mon.

Metalúrgica, Avda. 24 de Julho 110. The re-opened club is popular again, and a cheaper than usual venue dishing out pop, blues and soul for a happy, mixed crowd till 4am.

Plateau, Escadinhas da Praia 3–7. Gentle admission policy here, with more of a pop, rock and indie orientation in a venue designed by nightclub mogul Pedro Luz. This was one of the very first avenida bars. Wednesday is considered the best night. Open till 6am; closed Sun.

A Última Ceia, Avda. 24 de Julho 96. Rock and pop restaurant-bar where Thursday to Sunday is karaoke night with a vengeance. All the fun starts after midnight. Open till 4am; closed Mon.

Alcântara

Alcântara Café, Rua Maria Luísa Holstein 15. Designer bar-restaurant that is among the city's trendiest, in decor, clientele – and prices. Most people have a drink here and move onto the neighbouring *Alcântara-Mar* to dance.

Alcântara-Mar, Rua Cozinha Económica 11. Big, glitzy house-techno spot, attracting soccer stars, gays, executives and trendies amid the chandeliers, candelabras and country-house furnishings. Outside, the *Souk de Alcântara*, a line of food and snack vans, does great business. Open till 6am; closed Mon & Tues.

Banana-Power, Rua de Cascais 51–53. The clientele is dauntingly well-heeled, and the mixed music policy is impossible to pin down (salsa to techno with a growing African influence), but design enthusiasts will at least want to take a look at the bar and restaurant. Live music a couple of nights a week. Open till 6am; closed Mon.

Benzina, Trav. Teixeira Junior 6. Smart chrome-and-wood interior. Disco and funk night on Tuesday, slipping into underground sounds on Wednesday and Thursday. Considered a good spot to end the night for the Bairro Alto crowd. Closed Mon.

Gartejo, Avda. da Ceuta 38–48. Extremely trendy club, which is becoming a major venue for bands. Wednesday night is rock night. Closed Sun.

Pillon, Rua do Alvito 10. Cape Verdean disco sounds for a relaxed in-crowd. Best night is said to be Tuesday.

Rock Line, Rua das Fontainhas 86. Straight-down-the-line rock and roll in a small club mercifully free of the posturing going on all about it, which is perhaps why it's growing in popularity. Open till 6am; closed Mon.

Doca de Alcântara

Blues Café, R. Cintura do Porto de Lisboa. Cajun food in the restaurant plus dancing till 4am in what is claimed to be Lisbon's only blues bar. Closed Sun.

Cais de Alcântara. One of a row of bar-restaurants on boats in the docks, this one with moderately priced food, a pool table and lively music. Closed Sun.

Indochina, R. Cintura do Porto de Lisboa. Large, eastern-influenced restaurant in a converted warehouse done up in the style of a 1930s colonial mansion, which becomes a "dance club" when the eating's over. Thursday nights are the most lively, with soul, jungle, Latin and classics spinning till the small hours. Closed Sun.

Doca de Santo Amaro

Unless otherwise stated, all of the following are clustered around the small Doca de Santo Amaro, beneath Ponte 25 de Abril.

Cais S. Dancing till 4am combined with the chance to drink by the river in this minimalist bar decorated with giant metal insects.

Doca de Santo. Designed by nightclub mogul Pedro Luz, this large, palm-fringed club, bar and restaurant was one of the first places in the docks to attract – and keep – a late-night clientele. Closed Mon.

Doca 6. Rated as one of the best bars in the docks and also has good food. Restaurant tables get snapped up so it is best to reserve. Closed Mon.

Espalha Brasas. Enjoy tapas and beer to the accompaniment of a jukebox overloaded with Seventies' sounds. The upstairs room is bright and offers great views over the river. Closed Tues.

Café da Ponte. Bills itself as Lisbon's craziest café, serving everything from croissants to cocktails. The lively atmosphere is abetted by riverside seating. Sunday and Wednesday are karaoke nights. Closed Tues.

Salsa Latina, Gare Marítima de Alcântara. A bar-restaurant just outside the docks offering salsa nights Thursday to Saturday from midnight to 3am with riotous dancing to the live band serving up Brazilian rhythms, jazz, Dixieland and other sounds. Monday to Wednesday offers the chance to have salsa dance lessons, or just come and admire the terrace views. Food is moderate, but for the bar, minimum consumption is 5000$00.

Zonadoca. Worth a visit for its ice creams, though you can also enjoy coffee or alcohol inside or outside this friendly, family-oriented café. Open till 4am.

Lapa

Stones, Rua do Olival 1. A club that is on the up: good-time Sixties' and Seventies' rocking, pricey and endless list of drinks and grooving until 4am. Ring to enter. Closed Mon.

Belém

T-Clube, Edifício Espelho de Água, Avda. Brasília. Politicians dine here and the jet-set dance here so not the place for your average clubber. High-spending, high-flying, thirty-something crowd parties on down to live music, house, or Seventies' and Eighties' hits depending on the night (Thurs is best dance night). Very pricey drinks and members-only policy though day membership is an option if you have the funds. Great riverside terrace, too. Closed Sun.

Gay and lesbian bars, clubs and discos

While the Lisbon **gay and lesbian** scene doesn't yet have the high profile common to some other European capitals, there are some lively goings-on around the borders of the Bairro Alto and the Rato quarter to its northwest. Unless stated, listings below are in this area.

Finalmente, Rua da Palmeira 38 (☎347 26 52). Very busy, with first-class disco but lashings of kitsch. Weekend drag shows (2am) feature skimpily dressed young *senhoritas* camping it up to high-tech sounds. Open till 4am; closed Mon.

Kings and Queens, Alcântara docks. Lisbon's newest and most high-tech gay disco attracts a large following of beautiful people of all sexual persuasions; a huge, throbbing place with room for 2500 revellers.

Spartacus, Rua da Emenda 88. Long-established gay bar – go down to the bottom end of the Bairro Alto, towards Cais do Sodré.

Trumps, Rua da Imprensa Nacional 104b. The biggest gay disco in Lisbon with a reasonably relaxed door policy. Mostly techno and house with a drag show most nights at 3am. Packed with a broad mix of people from Thursday to Saturday, a bit cruisy midweek. Closed Mon.

Xeque-Mate, Rua de São Marçal 170. Exclusive and obnoxiously cruisy bar-disco, though it gets a bit more cosmopolitan in summer. Open till 2.30am.

Live music, the arts and other entertainments

Although tourist brochures tend to suggest that **live music** in Lisbon begins and ends with **fado** – the city's most traditional music – there's no reason to miss out on other forms. Portuguese **jazz** can be good (there's a big annual **International Jazz Festival** at the Gulbenkian in the summer), and **rock** an occasional surprise. **Brazilian** artists also tour frequently but, for Lisboetas, **African music** from the former colonies of Cabo Verde, Guinea Bissau, Angola and Mozambique is the happening sound.

There's often a crossover between music styles at many of the places listed below; it's always worth checking the listings magazines (see below) and posters around the city to see what's on. Note, too, that many of the bars listed in the previous section put on live bands on certain nights of the week. There's a charge to get into most music clubs, which usually covers your first drink, and most clubs stay open until around 4am, often later. In addition, big American and British rock bands on tour – not forgetting the top visiting Brazilian singers – play at a variety of **local halls and stadia** (listed below); you can usually get advance tickets from the APEB kiosk (☎347 58 23) at the corner of Praça dos Restauradores (near the post office), which also has ticket and programme details for all the city's cinemas and theatres.

Most major **cultural events** in the city – including just about every classical music concert – are sponsored either by the Fundação Calouste Gulbenkian (p.78) or the Centro Cultural de Belém (p.85), both of which have a full annual programme. Classical music aside, there's a fair amount of other cultural entertainment in Lisbon: several **theatres**, countless **cinemas**, three top-flight **soccer** teams, summer season **bullfights**, and a host of cultural and traditional **festivals** with which your visit might coincide (look out for the extra events laid on throughout Lisbon to coincide with Expo 98).

To find out **what's on**, pick up a schedule of exhibitions, concerts and events from the reception desks at the Gulbenkian and the Belém Cultural Centre. Most things are also listed, in English, in *Lisboa em*, a free monthly magazine, or in the *Agenda Cultural* booklet (in Portuguese), published monthly by the city council. Both are available from the tourist office. For other **listings and previews** of forthcoming events, concerts, bars, clubs and restaurants, get hold of the Friday editions of the *Diário de Notícias* or *O Independente* newspapers: both have pull-out listings magazines.

Fado

Fado is often described as a kind of working-class blues, although musically it would perhaps be more accurate to class it as a kind of light operetta, sung to a vaguely flamenco accompaniment. Alongside Coimbra (which has its own distinct tradition), Lisbon is still the best place to hear it, in one of thirty or so nightclubs in the Bairro Alto, Alfama and elsewhere – either at a *Casa de Fado* or in an *Adega Típica*. There's no real distinction between these places: all are small, all serve food (though you don't always have to eat), and all open around 9–10pm, get going toward midnight, and stay open until 3 or 4am.

Their drawbacks are inflated minimum charges – rarely, these days, below 3000$00 – and, in the more touristic places, extreme tackiness. Uniformed bouncers are fast becoming the norm, as are warm-up singers crooning Beatles' songs, and photographers snapping your table. Ask around to discover which are the most authentic current experiences. For more on the roots of fado, see p.510.

Taverna do Embuçado, Beco dos Cortumes 10, Alfama (☎886 50 78). Well-established *adega* with a nice feel. Gets some big-name visitors. Closed Sun.

Adega do Machado, Rua do Norte 91, Bairro Alto (☎342 87 13). One of the longest-established Bairro Alto joints; the minimum consumption of 3000$00 isn't too hard to notch up; you'll end up paying more like 5000$00 a head for fine Portuguese cooking and several styles of fado from Lisbon and Coimbra. Closed Mon.

Adega Mesquita, Rua do Diário de Notícias 107, Bairro Alto (☎346 20 77). Another of the big Bairro Alto names, with better-than-average music and meals, air-conditioning and traditional dancing as well as singing.

Parreirinha d'Alfama, Beco do Espírito Santo 1, Alfama (☎886 82 09). Just off Largo do Chafariz de Dentro, this has music by some renowned singers and food at fairly moderate prices. Closed Mon.

Adega do Ribatejo, Rua Diário de Notícias 23, Bairro Alto (☎346 83 43). Great little *adega*, with one of the lowest minimum charges and fado that locals describe as "pure emotion". Enjoyable also for its food, it remains popular with locals. The singers include a couple of professionals, the manager and – best of all – the cooks. There's a minimum charge of 1800$00; you'll spend around 3500$00. Closed Sun.

O Senhor Vinho, Rua do Meio à Lapa 18, Lapa (☎397 26 81). Famous Bairro Alto club sporting some of the best singers in Portugal, which makes the 4000$00 minimum charge (more like 5000$00 a meal) pretty good value. Closed Sun.

A Severa, Rua das Gáveas 55, Bairro Alto (☎346 40 06). A city institution, named after a nineteenth-century gypsy singer who had an affair with a Count, with big fado names and big prices. Closed Thurs.

Timpanas, Rua Gilberto Rola 24, Alcântara (☎397 24 31). This is one of Lisbon's most authentic options, away from the tourist scene. Minimum consumption is 2000$00. Closed Wed.

African music

B.leza, Largo Conde-Barão 50, Santos. Live music on most nights in this thriving second-floor club. Closed Sun.

Kandando, Centro Comércial Calendoscópio, Campo Grande (☎759 42 93). One of Lisbon's most boisterous clubs, with live music and a minimum consumption charge of around 3000$00. Open till 4am; closed Tues.

Kussunguila, Rua dos Lusiadas 5, Alcântara (☎363 35 90). Over-the-top African club with live bands on Monday nights – discos and extravaganzas on the others. Open till 6am.

Lontra, Rua de São Bento 157, Bairro Alto (☎369 10 83). You'll be hard pushed not to join in the animated dancing in this intimate African club with live music every night except Monday; come after midnight.

Monte Cara, Rua do Sol ao Rato 71, off Largo do Rato, Rato (☎388 87 38). There's a lively and relaxed atmosphere in this restaurant and club. You get sporadic live music – mainly Cabo Verdean bands – otherwise there's a disco; the restaurant on the ground floor serves Cabo Verdean food. Closed Mon.

Ritz Club, Rua da Glória 57 (☎342 51 40). Lisbon's largest African club occupies the premises of an old brothel-cum-music-hall, one block west of Avda. da Liberdade. It's a great place, with a resident Cabo Verdean band, plus occasional big-name concerts. Closed Mon.

Brazilian music

Bate Pato, Rua Alameda D. Afonso Henriques 63, off Avda. Almirante Reis (☎353 46 86). Fun-time bar with live music and cocktails to get you jigging along to the samba beat. Closed Mon.

Bipi-Bipi, Rua Oliveira Martins 6 (☎797 89 24); metro Roma. Uptown venue for Brazilian bands, exotic cocktails and dirty dancing. Closed Mon.

Chafarica, Calçada de São Vicente 81, Alfama (☎886 74 49). Tiny, old Brazilian bar with live music till late most nights. Closed Sun.

Pê Sujo, Largo de São Martinho 6–7, Alfama (☎886 56 29). The "Dirty Foot" is five minutes' walk from the Sé in Alfama; ring to gain admission. Drinks feature *caipirinhas*, the lethal Brazilian concoction of rum, lime, sugar and ice, which regularly results in massive audience participation and table-banging samba sessions in this tiny bar. Closed Mon.

Rock and pop

Alcool Puro, Avda. Dom Carlos I 59, Santos (☎396 74 67). Different bands every night in this rock bar. Closed Sun.

Anos Sessenta, Largo do Terreirinho 21, Alfama (☎887 34 44). This small club ("The Sixties") has different rock bands on Fridays and Saturdays; as you can guess, the music is retro. It's a few minutes' walk from Largo Martim Moniz, near the castle. Closed Sun.

Cinearte, Largo de Santos 2, Santos (☎396 53 60). Regular performances by Portuguese bands, and a decent bar too, in this cult media hideaway. Closed Sun.

Gartejo, Avda. da Ceuta 38–48, Alcântara (☎395 59 77). Regular gigs, including foreign bands. Closed Sun.

Johnny Guitar, Calçada do Marquês de Abrantes 72, Rato (☎396 04 15). Regular live music from 11pm most nights. Closed Sun.

Rock City, Cais do Sodré. Live music most nights by the river in one of Lisbon's newest venues.

Jazz

Hot Clube de Portugal, Praça de Alegria, off Avda. da Liberdade (☎346 73 69). The city's best jazz venue – a tiny basement club that hosts local and visiting artists. Closed Mon.

Café Luso, Trav. da Queimada 10, Bairro Alto (☎342 22 81). Touristy fado joint with regular weekend jazz sessions from 11pm. Closed Sun.

Large venues

Aula Magna, Reitoria da Universidade de Lisboa, Alamada da Universidade (☎796 76 24); metro Cidade Universitaria. The student union venue.

Coliseu dos Recreios, Rua das Portas de Santo Antão, Baixa (☎346 19 97 or 343 16 97). Main city centre indoor rock and pop venue set in a lovely old domed building.

Estádio José Alvalade, metro Campo Grande (☎758 90 21). The Sporting Lisbon soccer stadium stages concerts by huge international stars.

Estádio do Restelo, Restelo, Belém (☎301 04 61). Belenenses soccer stadium plays host to smaller rock and pop bands.

Classical, theatre and opera

There are three **concert halls** (including an outdoor amphitheatre) at the Gulbenkian, and both a large and small auditorium at the Centro Cultural de Belém. In addition, regular **classical music** concerts take place at the Teatro Nacional de São Carlos, Rua Serpa Pinto 9, Chiado (☎346 59 14); the Teatro Municipal de São Luís, Rua António Maria Cardoso 40, Baixa (☎342 17 72); the Coliseu dos Recreios, Rua das Portas de Santo Antão, Baixa (☎346 19 97 or 343 16 97) and at the university. Tickets range from 500$00 to 3000$00, though there are also **free concerts and recitals** at the Carmo and São Roque churches in Bairro Alto (every Sat night at the latter), the Sé, the Basílica da Estrêla, São Vicente de Fora and the Igreja dos Mártires.

For **theatre**, there are performances of Portuguese and foreign plays at the Teatro Nacional de Dona Maria in Rossio (Aug–June; ☎342 22 10) and an **opera** season (Sept–June) at the Teatro Nacional de São Carlos (see above).

Film

Cinema is an unsung glory of a stay in Lisbon. The city and its environs have dozens of **cinemas**, virtually all of them showing original-language films with Portuguese subtitles. Ticket prices are low (around 800$00; cheaper on Mon) and some of the theatres are beautiful in themselves – Art Nouveau and Art Deco palaces, often with original period bars. The tourist office should be able to tell you what's on, or consult the kiosk at the corner of Restauradores.

Among the most interesting **art-house** venues are Quarteto, Rua das Flores Lima 16 (☎797 13 78), off Avenida Estados Unidos (metro Entre Campos), with four screens; and the Instituto da Cinemateca Portuguesa (☎354 62 79), Rua Barata Salgueiro 39 (metro Avenida), the national film theatre, with twice-daily shows, ranging from contemporary Portuguese films to anything from Truffaut to Valentino.

Mainstream movies are on show at a clutch of cinemas around Praça dos Restauradores and Avenida da Liberdade: the São Jorge, Avda. da Liberdade 174 (☎357 91 44); Condes, Avda. Liberdade 2 (☎342 25 23); and the Xenon, Praça dos Restauradores (☎346 84 46). At the Amoreiras complex (see p.77; ☎69 12 75) there are no fewer than ten screens; all, unfortunately, are modest in size.

Sports

Soccer is the biggest game in Lisbon, and **Benfica** – Lisbon's most famous football team – have a glorious past (the great Eusébio played for the team in the 1960s), though they have been struggling of late to keep up with rivals Porto. Games take place at the huge Estádio da Luz, Avda. Gen. Norton Matos (☎726 61 29), north of the city centre, and you can buy tickets in advance from the kiosk in Praça dos Restauradores (at a small commission), or at kiosks (not the turnstiles) at the ground on the night. The best way to get to matches is on the metro – Colegio Militar is a short walk from the stadium. **Sporting Club de Portugal**, Benfica's traditional city rivals, play at the Estádio José Alvalade (☎758 90 21) – metro Campo Grande or bus #1 or #36. Top-division action can also be caught at Belenenses of Belém; a trip out to watch F.C. Estoril can also be fun. Details of all matches are printed in the daily papers – most of the regular league fixtures take place on Sunday afternoons (Sunday evenings for a few big events).

Bullfights take place most Thursdays and Sundays (June–Sept) at the principal **Praça de Touros do Campo Pequeno** (metro Campo Pequeno; ☎793 20 93), just off Avenida da República; tickets cost 3000–8000$00, depending on where you sit, and the performances start at 10pm. There are less frequent fights at Cascais in summer, or travel out of Lisbon to Vila Franca de Xira (see p.178) and surrounding towns and villages for more traditional events.

Golf is best enjoyed at the upmarket courses around Estoril (see p.109), which also hosts Portugal's Formula One **Grand Prix**. For those into **water sports**, good surfing opportunities can be found at Caparica and windsurfing at Guincho and Ericeira, both of which have previously held world windsurfing championships.

Festivals and events

Lisbon's main **popular festivals** are in June, with fireworks, fairground rides and street-partying to celebrate the **Santos Populares** – saints Anthony (June 13), John (June 24), and Peter (June 29). Celebrations of each begin on the previous evening; Saint Anthony's is the largest, taking over just about every square in Alfama.

Also in June, the **Festas da Lisboa** are a series of city-sponsored events, including free concerts, exhibitions and culinary contests, while from May to September there's a permanent fairground, the **Feira Popular**, opposite the Entrecampos metro station: eats, rides and a thoroughly Portuguese night out (Mon–Fri rides 7pm–midnight, Sat & Sun 3pm–midnight; 150$00; rides extra, restaurants open daily noon–midnight).

On the cultural front, there's the annual **Estoril Festival**, which takes place throughout July and August offering sometimes adventurous performances by internationally known orchestras, musicians and dance groups; various summer events in Cascais, mostly held in the Parque Palmela; and – again at Estoril, and a lot better than it sounds – the state-run **Handicrafts Fair**. Here, crafts of all kinds from every region of the country are displayed along Avenida Amaral: if you buy anything, bargain at length. The fair runs through July and August, from around 5pm until midnight, with foodstalls included in the attractions.

Shops and markets

The more interesting **shopping areas** are detailed in the preceding pages: the Chiado district (p.67); the markets around Cais do Sodré (p.68); the Amoreiras complex (p.77); and the Alfama flea market (p.75). Some of the better **shops** are picked out below, along with a handful of **markets**. The Bairro Alto is fast becoming a centre for designer clothes and furniture but the main shopping area for **clothes** is in the modern city, from Praça de Londres north along Avenida de Roma. Portuguese designers also have outlets in Amoreiras shopping centre, Chiado and in various fashionable stores in the Bairro Alto.

Other than traditional **ceramics and carpets**, perhaps the most Portuguese of items to take home is a **bottle of port**: check out the vintages at the *Instituto do Vinho do Porto* (see p.95), where you can also sample the stuff, and buy from one of the specialist shops listed on p.105, or from any delicatessen or supermarket.

Antiques, arts and crafts
Cheapish antique/junk shops are concentrated along **Rua do Alecrim** in Chiado and **Rua Dom Pedro V** in the Bairro Alto. None stands out above the others, but most make for some good browsing. Other interesting shops throughout the city include:

Antiquíssimo, Rua São Tiago 8, Alfama. One of many antique shops close to the Miradouro Santa Luzia, for bric-a-brac, old toys, azulejos and other bits and bobs. Closed Sun.

Deposito da Marinha Grande, Rua de São Bento 243, São Bento. Portuguese glassware at affordable prices.

Fábrica Sant'ana, Rua do Alecrim 95, Chiado. If you're interested in Portuguese tiles – azulejos – check out this factory-shop, which sells copies of traditional designs and a great range of pots and ceramics. Closed Sun.

Fábrica Viúva Lamego, Largo do Intendente 25; metro Intendente. Highly rated azulejo factory-shop producing made-to-order designs or reproduction antiques.

Filartesanato, Feira Internacional de Lisboa, on the waterfront, west of Ponte 25 de Abril. General Portuguese regional crafts emporium. Closed Mon.

SHOPPING HOURS

Traditionally, **shopping hours** have been Monday to Friday 9am–1pm and 3–7pm or 8pm, Saturday 9am–1am. However, many of the **Bairro Alto** shops are open afternoons and evenings only, usually 2–9pm or so, while the **Amoreiras** shops stay open daily 9am–11pm. Many larger shops now open all day, some even on Sundays.

Olaria do Desterro, Rua Nova do Desterro 14; metro Intendente. Old family firm that's been turning out excellent Portuguese pottery for over 150 years – most of it by the owner, who is now 93.

Pessoa de Carvalho, Costa do Castelo 4, Alfama. Cool old Alfama town house with candles, glassware, jewellery, carvings, umbrellas and the like.

Ratton, Rua da Academia Ciencias 2, Bairro Alto. Hand-painted tiles by famous artists, including Paula Rego. Closed weekends.

Books and maps

Livraria Bertrand, Rua Garrett 73; Chiado Loja 1129; Amoreiras; Avda. de Roma 13B. Good general bookshops with novels in English, plus a range of foreign magazines.

Livraria Buchholz, Rua Duque Palmela 4, Pombal. Good range of English-language books and very helpful staff.

Livraria Portugal, Rua do Carmo 70–74, Baixa. Excellent Portuguese bookshop that features – among other fine books – *Rough Guides*.

Serviços Cartográficos do Exército, Avda. Dr. Alfredo Bensaúde, Olivais Norte (bus #25 from Praça do Comércio to Laboratório Química Militar). The army's map office is the place to go for ordnance survey maps for hiking. If at all possible, take a Portuguese friend along to facilitate the operation.

Markets

Feira da Ladra, Campo de Santa Clara, Alfama. Flea market. Tues & Sat 7am–6pm.

Mercado 31 de Janeiro Rua Eng. Vera da Silva; metro Picoas or Saldanha. Once an outdoor affair, this is now housed in a smart new block on two floors, featuring everything from fresh fish and flowers to arts and crafts. Mon–Sat 7am–2pm.

Mercado da Ribeira, Avda. 24 de Julho. Just up from Cais do Sodré, one of Lisbon's most atmospheric covered markets; the fish hall is fascinating (see p.68). Mon–Sat 6am–2pm.

Numismatists' market, Praça do Comércio, Baixa. Old coins and notes from Portugal and its former colonies. Sun morning.

Praça do Chile, off Avda. Almirante Reis; metro Arroios. An interesting general market set in a large circular building. Mon–Sat 7am–2pm.

Rotunda do Aeroporto, The main rag-trade market, with complete wardrobes of clothing for a few thousand *escudos*. Take an airport bus to get there and follow the crowds. Sun morning.

Supermarkets and shopping centres

Libersil, Avda. da Liberdade 38. Large shopping centre catering to most consumer needs.

Lojas de Conveniência Extra. Central branches of this supermarket chain include those at Campo das Cebolas 25, Alfama; Praça da Alegria, off Avda. da Liberdade; and Rua Joaquim António de Aguiar 35 near Rotunda. Good for late-night shopping, open 7am–2am.

Monumental, by metro Saldanha. Modern shopping centre with international chain stores.

Pão d'Açúcar. Branches of this Brazilian supermarket chain can be found in the Amoreiras centre, at Rua Luís de Camões 133, Bairro Alto, and throughout the city. Most stay open daily until 8pm; the huge branch in the Amoreiras centre stays open until 11pm.

Wine and food

Instituto do Vinho do Porto, Rua de São Pedro de Alcântara 45. Over 300 types of port, so you should find something to your taste (see p.95 for further details).

Londrina, Rua das Portas de Santo Andrão 55. One of several shops on this street that are crammed with ancient ports, cheeses, *bacalhau* and hams.

Manuel Tavares, Rua da Betesga 1A, Baixa. On the edge of Rossio, this small, century-old shop has a decent selection of wine, chocolate and national cheeses.

Napoleão, Rua dos Fanqueiros 70, Baixa, at the junction with Rua da Conceição. Great range of port and wine, with knowledgeable, English-speaking staff.

Casa Pereira da Conceição, Rua Augusta 102. Fine Art Deco 1930s shop selling tempting coffee beans and teas.

Listings

Airlines Air France, Avda. 5 de Outubro 206 (☎356 21 71); Alitalia, Avda. da Liberdade 225 (☎790 02 02); British Airways, Avda. da Liberdade 36-2° (☎346 43 53); Iberia, Rua Rosa Araújo 2 (☎355 81 19); KLM, Campo Grande 220B (☎795 50 18); Lufthansa, Avda. da Liberdade 192 (☎357 37 22); Sabena, Avda. da Liberdade 144 (☎346 55 72); Swissair, Avda. da Liberdade 38 (☎347 12 00); TAP, Praça Marquês de Pombal 3 (☎357 50 20); Varig, Praça Marquês de Pombal 1 (☎356 38 41).

Airport For flight information call ☎80 20 60.

American Express The local agent is Top Tours, Avda. Duque de Loulé 108 (Mon–Fri 9.30am–1pm & 2.30–6.30pm; ☎315 58 77).

Banks Most main branches are in the Baixa and surrounding streets. Standard banking hours are Mon–Fri 8.30am–3pm, though Banco Borges & Irmão, Avda. da Liberdade 9a, is open until 7.30pm. There's a currency exchange office at the airport (open 24hr) and at Santa Apolónia station (daily 8.30am–8.30pm).

Bicycle rental You'd have to be insane to do it, but you can hire bicycles for the day from Velocipédica do Alto do Pina, Rua Carrilho Videira 7 (☎813 01 77; Arroios metro) and Biocicio-Apoios a Actividade turística, Rua Prof. Egas Moniz, Lt1-Anexo A, Parede (☎435 15 03). For short-term hire, the kiosk by the ferry terminal at Belém hires out bikes for 700$00 per hour (Tues–Fri 10am–5.30pm, Sat & Sun 10am–7.30pm).

Buses Terminals at: Avda. Casal Ribeiro 18 (metro Saldanha; ☎54 54 39) for international and most domestic departures, including express services to the Algarve; Praça de Espanha (metro Palhavã) and Avda. 5 de Outubro 75 (metro Saldanha ☎726 2740) for Rodoviária Sul do Tejo departures; Campo Pequeno for AVIC services to the northwest coast and SolexPresso to the Alentejo and Algarve; Campo das Cebolas, at the end of Rua dos Bacalheiros, east of Praça do Comércio, for Renex destinations in the Minho and Algarve; and Campo Grande by the metro of the same name, for Empresa Mafrense services to Mafra and Ericeira. You can buy advance bus tickets at most major travel agents; try Marcus & Harting, Rossio 45–50 (☎346 92 71).

Car rental If you're not picking up a car at the airport, ask at the main tourist office, who can arrange car rental for you and have the car delivered to your hotel. The main agencies in Lisbon are: Auto Jardim, airport (☎846 31 87); Avis, airport (☎849 99 47), and Avda. Praia da Vitória 12c (☎356 11 76); Budget, airport (☎847 88 03), and Avda. Fontes Pereira de Melo 6 (☎353 77 17); Europcar, airport (☎847 31 81), Santa Apolónia station (☎886 15 73), and Avda. António Augusto Aguiar 24 (☎942 23 06); Hertz, airport (☎849 27 22), and Rua Castilho 72 (☎381 24 30).

Car trouble Automóvel Clube de Portugal, Rua Rosa Araújo 24–26 (☎942 50 95).

Embassies Australia, Avda. da Liberdade 244-4° (☎52 33 50); Canada, Avda. da Liberdade 144-3° (☎347 48 92); Ireland, Rua da Imprensa à Estrêla 1-4° (☎396 15 69); Netherlands, Rua do Sacramento à Lapa 4-1° (☎396 23 06); South Africa, Avda. Luís Bivar 10 (☎352 56 18); Spain, Rua do Salitre 1 (☎347 23 81); UK, Rua São Domingos à Lapa 37 (☎396 11 91); USA, Avda. das Forças Armadas (☎726 66 00).

Email You can send email (but not receive it) from Quiosque Internet (*email@telepac.pt*) inside the Forum Picoas (metro Picoas, Mon–Fri 9am–5pm).

Emergencies The general emergency number is ☎115. For police, see below.

Hospital The British Hospital, Rua Saraiva de Carvalho 49 (☎395 50 67 or 397 63 29) has English-speaking staff. For an ambulance, call ☎301 77 77.

Language courses: Portuguese lessons are given by the Cambridge School, Avda. da Liberdade 173 (☎352 74 74), or the Centro Europeu de Línguas, Rua Joaquim A. Aguiar 43 (☎386 37 82).

Laundry Lava Neve, Rua de Alegria 37, Bairro Alto; or try the one at Rua Saraiva de Carvalho 117, a little west of Rato (bus #9 from Rossio). Lavandaria Sous Ana, in the Centro Comércial da Mouraria, Largo Martim Moniz, does service washes for around 2000$00 (Mon–Sat 9.30am–8pm).

Left luggage There are lockers at the airport, at Rossio, Cais do Sodré and Santa Apolónia stations, and a left-luggage office at the bus terminal on Avda. Casal Ribeiro.

Lost property The police lost property office is at Rua dos Anjos 56a. The metro office is at Restauradores metro (☎342 77 07); the Carris office is at Rua de Santa Justa 11 (☎342 79 44).

Newspapers There are newsstands around Rossio, several of which sell foreign-language papers. Among various other outlets around the city, try the lobbies of five-star hotels or Amoreiras Shopping in the Amoreiras centre and the Centro Cultural in Belém.

Pharmacies Open Mon–Fri 9am–1pm & 3–7pm, Sat 9am–1pm. Local papers carry information about 24hr-duty pharmacies and the details are also posted on every pharmacy door.

Police If you need help, or have something stolen, go to the 24hr office at Rua Capelo 13 (☎346 61 41), west of the Baixa near the Teatro de São Carlos. You need to report here in order to make a claim on your travel insurance. Ask for extension 279 for English-speaking assistance.

Post offices The main post office is on Praça do Comércio (Mon–Fri 8.30am–6.30pm); its *poste restante* section has a separate entrance at Rua do Arsenal 27 (closes at 2pm). More convenient is the post office at Praça dos Restauradores 58 (east side; Mon–Fri 8am–10pm, Sat & Sun 9am–6pm), from where you can send Airmail and *Correio Azul* (Express Mail – the fastest service). There's a 24hr post office at the airport.

River cruises Two-hour return trips up the Tejo depart from the Estação Fluvial (daily April–Oct 11am & 3pm; 3000$00) and go as far as the Ponte 25 de Abril. Prices include a drink and commentary, though the views are little different to the standard ferry crossings.

Students The Instituto da Juventude, Avda. da Liberdade 194, 1000 Lisboa (9.30am–7pm; ☎315 19 55), offers practical advice and a library; or try Turismo Juvenil at Praça de Londres 9 (☎848 53 63, metro Alameda).

Swimming pools The most central option is the pool in the Atheneum club on Rua das Portas de Santo Antão, next to the Coliseu (Mon–Fri 1–4.30pm & 9–10pm, 500$00; Sat 3–7.30pm, 650$00).

Telephones For international calls, you can use the telephone office next to the post office in Praça dos Restauradores (see above). There's a second office on the corner of Rossio (no. 65; 8am–11pm). You can also make international calls from any phone booth; phonecards are available in denominations of 825$00 or 2100$00 from any post office.

Tickets for football matches, films and other spectacles can be bought from ABEP, the kiosk at the corner of Praça dos Restauradores (☎347 58 23/25 94).

Tram and bus tours The Circuito Colinas ("Hills tour"; March–June & Oct, two daily; July, four daily; Aug, five daily; Sept, three daily; 2800$00, children under 10, 1500$00) takes you on a 90min tram ride from Praça do Comércio round the Alfama, Chiado and S. Bento. The Circuito Tejo (May–Sept hourly 11am–4pm; 2000$00, children under 10, 1000$00) is an open-top bus tour around Lisbon's principal sites; a day ticket allows you to get on and off whenever you want. Tickets can be bought on board. For more information call ☎363 93 43.

Trains See "Arrival and information", p.52, for details of Lisbon's various stations. Timetables and train information are available at Rossio station information office (daily 10am–1pm & 2–6pm). For information about departures from any Lisbon station call ☎888 40 25 (daily 8am–11pm). Always check departure times and stations in advance: many intercity services require a seat reservation (particularly to Coimbra/Porto), which you can do prior to departure, though allow yourself plenty of time.

Travel agencies Specialists include: Turismo Juvenil, Praça de Londres 9B, for youth details (Mon–Sat 9am–1pm & 2.30–5.30pm; ☎848 53 63; metro Alameda); Intercentro, Rua Eng. Vieira da Silva 8 (☎54 73 00), the main international bus agents; Transalpino, Avda. Guerra Junqueiro 28 (☎848 22 79); and well-established charter agents Abreu, Avda. da Liberdade 160 (☎347 64 41).

Walks The tourist office in Praça dos Restauradores is the starting point for three-hour guided walks through Lisbon's historical and cultural areas. Tours begin at 9am and cost 2500$00. There are additional walks round the Alfama and Castle areas, beginning from Casa dos Bicos on Praça da Ribeira (Mon, Wed & Fri). For information call ☎340 45 39.

Women's Movement The best contact points are: the Movimento Democrático das Mulheres, Avda. Duque de Loulé 111–4°, 1110 Lisboa (☎352 78 53); Editora das Mulheres bookshop, Rua da Conceição 17, Baixa; and IDM (Informação e Documentação das Mulheres) at Rua Filipe da Mata 115a (metro Palhavã or bus #31 from Rossio or Praça de Espanha) – a women's centre incorporating a small library and café and very eager to welcome foreign travellers.

AROUND LISBON

The most straightforward way to escape the city is to head for the string of beach resorts west along the coast from Belém, which can be reached by train from Cais do Sodré. At places like **Oeiras** and **Carcavelos**, and above all at **Estoril** and **Cascais**, the beaches are good even if the water quality isn't. For better sands and a cleaner ocean you'll have to head north to **Guincho**; or cross the Tejo by ferry to reach the **Costa da Caparica**, a thirty-kilometre expanse of dunes to the south of the capital. There's reasonably priced accommodation at all these places, as well as a youth hostel at Oeiras and campsites at Guincho and Caparica. But as you might imagine, all the beach resorts in the Lisbon area get very crowded at weekends and throughout August.

Basing yourself in Lisbon, you also could take in a fair part of the provinces of Estremadura (Chapter Two) and Alentejo (Chapter Eight) on day-trips. Indeed, some of those regions' greatest attractions lie within a fifty-kilometre or so radius of the capital – such as the palaces of **Queluz** or **Mafra** – and are best seen on a day-trip. The beautiful town of **Sintra**, the most popular excursion from Lisbon, demands a longer look, and reveals a different side if you stay overnight. However you decide to see them, bear in mind that most of the Sintra palaces are closed on Mondays, and those at Queluz and Mafra on Tuesdays. Further afield, south of the Tejo, the large town of **Setúbal** is noted for its Igreja de Jesus, the earliest of all Manueline buildings, while the coast to the southwest sports a succession of small resorts and beaches of varying degrees of popularity.

West to Estoril and Cascais

Stretching for over 30km west of Lisbon, the **Estoril coast** – from Oeiras to Cascais – makes for an enjoyable day out, drifting from beach to bar and strolling along the lively seafront promenades. Sadly, the water itself has suffered badly from pollution and though steps are being taken to clean it up, it remains something of a health hazard. Nonetheless, the coast retains its attractions and **Cascais**, in particular, makes a pleasant alternative to staying in Lisbon, and is well placed for trips to Sintra or the wild Guincho beach.

Access to the resorts could hardly be easier. The Linha de Cascais train leaves every twenty minutes or so between 5.30am and 2.30am (185$00 one way) from **Cais do Sodré** station, stopping at Belém en route to Cascais. Beware, though, that some trains stop only at Alcântara, Oeiras and stations beyond. By road, the **N6** is the coastal highway, passing through most of the centres along the seafront, often as the Avenida Marginal; the faster **A5 motorway** (Auto-Estrada da Oeste) is an (inexpensive) toll road running from Lisbon to Estoril – drive west past Amoreiras and follow the signs.

Oeiras to São João

The first suburb of any size after Belém is **OEIRAS**, where the River Tejo officially turns into the sea. The **beach** here has recently been cleaned up, though most people swim in the Ocean Pool alongside the sands. Riverside walkways are also being improved, though unless you're staying at the youth hostel (see p.63), the only reason for a stop would be to see the **Palácio do Marquês de Pombal**, erstwhile home of the rebuilder of Lisbon. The house is now an adult education centre and the park is not technically open to visitors. However, if there's nothing special going on, the guard should be able to show you the gardens, or at least let you peer over the walls at its massive grotto.

Carcavelos
Next stop along the coast is **CARCAVELOS**, popular for its kilometre of beach and plethora of bars and cafés. The main motivation for a visit is the huge **market** that sprawls between the train station and town centre every Thursday – a great place to pick up cheap clothing. For food, try *Tricana da Barra* on the beach. *Pub*, right by the station in an old train carriage, is the one late-night haunt, open till 2am.

São Pedro and São João
Along the last stretch of the Linha de Cascais, the beaches improve rapidly and you reach the beginning of an esplanade that stretches virtually uninterrupted to Cascais. **SÃO PEDRO** has a superb beach, just down from the station, and **SÃO JOÃO** is flanked by two lovely stretches of sand. The whole seafront here is pretty animated in the summer months, swarming with young surfers and Portuguese holidaymakers frequenting the numerous cafés and restaurants: *A Choupana* on the Estrada Marginal is a good choice.

Estoril

ESTORIL gained a postwar reputation as a haunt of exiled royalty and the idle rich, and it continues to maintain its pretensions towards being a "Portuguese Riviera", with grandiose villas and luxury hotels. It is little surprise, then, that the town's touristic life revolves around an exclusive **golf course** (golf passes are available from the tourist office) and **casino**. The latter – located within the attractive gardens of the **Parque do Estoril** – requires a passport and some semblance of formal attire to get in (daily 3pm–3am, nightly shows at 11pm); you'll have to cough up a few hundred just to get through the door and the minimum bet is 1000$00.

Estoril also holds a yearly **Grand Prix**, which unfortunately had to be cancelled in 1997 because the course was considered too pot-holed; it usually takes place in September and should be repaired in time for the 1998 event. At other times, unless you can afford one of the splendid sea-view hotels, the best move in Estoril is out – following the **seafront promenade** through **Monte Estoril** to Cascais, a lovely walk that takes about an hour.

Practicalities

The **train station** is on Estoril's through-road, with the beach accessible by underpass. Across the main road from the station, at the bottom of the park, you'll find the very helpful **turismo** (Mon–Sat 9am–8pm, Sun 10am–6pm; ☎01/468 01 13), which can give advice on private rooms and details of the area's various golf clubs. In summer, hourly **buses to Sintra** leave from outside the train station.

Upmarket hotels aside, there are just a few **pensões**, of which *Pensão-Residencial Smart*, Rua José Viana 3 (☎01/468 21 64; ④), is perhaps the best, with pleasant rooms and breakfast included. It's east of the park – turn right out of the station, turning left when you reach Avenida Bombeiros Voluntarios, which runs up behind the *Hotel Paris*. If this is full, the *Pensão Maryluz*, Rua Maestro Lacerda 13 (☎01/468 27 40; ④), is just one block south, also off Avenida Bombeiros Voluntarios – breakfast is included here, too, and room prices drop considerably in winter.

For coffee and cake, a meal or just a late **drink**, it's nice to sit at the outdoor tables at *Frolic* (open till 2am), on Avda. Clotilde, overlooking the eastern side of the park. There are plenty of other **cafés and restaurants** around, none particularly worth singling out though the *English Bar*, Avda. Sabóia 9 (just over the main road from Monte Estoril train station), is a bar-restaurant with sea views and a good local reputation, if on the pricey side. For **nightlife**, *Absurdo* on Praia do Tamaris is the current "in" place, or try *Bafureira* on the Avenida Marginal (11pm–4am).

Cascais

At the end of the train line, and with three fairly good beaches along its esplanade, **CASCAIS** is now a major resort, earmarked for substantial "improvements", which may see it in possession of a new marina by the millennium. It is positively bursting at the seams in summer, especially at weekends, but despite its commercialism, it's not too large or difficult to get around and has a much younger, less exclusive, feel than Estoril, even retaining a few elements of its previous existence as a fishing village. There's a lively **market** every Wednesday on Rua do Mercado, to the right of Avda. 25 de Abril, and Sunday evening **bullfights** during summer in the Praça de Touros that draw a largely local crowd.

You'll find the main concentration of **bars and nightlife** – and consequently most of what makes Cascais tick as a town – on Rua Frederico Arouca, the main pedestrian thoroughfare on the east side of the Avenida Combatantes da Grande Guerra, which splits the town. Also in this area and worth a look is the **fish market** that takes place around 8pm (Mon–Sat) between the Ribeira and Rainha beaches. For a wander away from the crowds, cross over Avenida Com. Grande Guerra, and stroll up beyond Largo 5 de Outubro into the old, and surprisingly pretty, west side of town, at its most delightful in the streets around the graceful **Igreja da Assunção**.

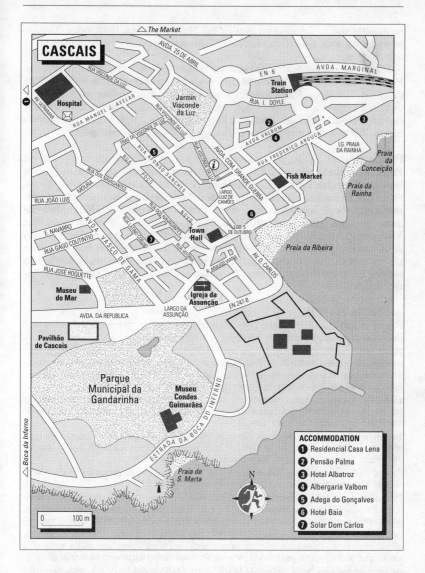

CASCAIS

△ The Market

AVDA. 25 DE ABRIL

EN 6 — AVDA. MARGINAL

Train Station

RUA VISCONDE DA LUZ

Hospital

AV ULTRAMAR

RUA MANUEL J. AVELAR

Jarmin Visconde da Luz

RUA VISCONDE DA LUZ

RUA I. DOYLE

❷

AVDA VALBOM

❹

❸

LG. PRAIA DA RAINHA

Praia da Conceição

TRAV. DO VISCONDE DE LUZ

RUA VISCONDE DA LUZ

RUA AFONSO SANCHES

❺

BELA

RUA DOS NAVEGANTES

POÇO

RUA COM. GRANDE GUERRA

RUA FREDERICO AROUCA

ⓘ

Fish Market

Praia da Rainha

RUA JOÃO LUIS

MOURA

AVDA VASCO DE GAMA

RUA DOS NAVEGANTES

RUA AFONSO SANCHES

NOVA

LARGO LUIZ DE CAMÕES

❻

E. NAVARRO

RUA GAGO COUTINTIO

RUA VITÓRIA

Town Hall

LGO 5 DE OUTUBRO

Praia da Ribeira

RUA JOSÉ ROQUETTE

❼

R. ARAUJO VIANNA

AV D. CARLOS

Museu do Mar

Igreja da Assunção

EN 247-8

AVDA. DA REPUBLICA

LARGO DA ASSUNÇÃO

Pavilhão de Cascais

Parque Municipal da Gandarinha

Museu Condes Guimarães

ESTRADA DA BOCA DO INFERNO

△ Boca do Inferno

Praia de S. Marta

N

0   100 m

ACCOMMODATION

❶ Residencial Casa Lena
❷ Pensão Palma
❸ Hotel Albatroz
❹ Albergaria Valbom
❺ Adega do Gonçalves
❻ Hotel Baia
❼ Solar Dom Carlos

Cascais' other attractions are all to the west of the centre. Beyond the church lies the pleasant **Parque da Gandarinha** (daily 10am–5pm), in whose southern reaches stands the mansion of the counts of Guimarães, preserved complete with its nineteenth-century fittings as the **Museu Biblioteca Conde Castro Guimarães** (Tues–Sun 10am–5pm; 250$00); most days, there's someone around to give you a guided tour of the furniture, paintings and archeological finds housed here. On the north side of the park, opposite the Pavilhão de Cascais, signs point you to the modern **Museu do Mar** (Tues–Sun 10am–5pm; 200$00), an engaging little collection of model boats, sea-related artefacts, old costumes and pictures.

Taking the coastal road, it's about twenty minutes' walk west of the park to the **Boca do Inferno** – the "Mouth of Hell" – where waves crash against caves in the cliff face. The viewpoints above are always packed with tourists (as is the very tacky market on the roadside) but, frankly, the whole affair is rather unimpressive except in stormy weather. En route, however, there's a little beach at **Praia de Santa Marta** with a nice café (see "Eating" below) on a terrace above.

Practicalities

From the **train station** it's just a short walk across to Rua Frederico Arouca; **buses** to Guincho, Cabo da Roca and Sintra leave from the stands outside the station. Walk down Rua Frederico Arouca and cross the main avenue for the **turismo** (June–Sept Mon–Sat 9am–8pm, Sun 10am–6pm; Oct–May Mon–Sat 9am–7pm, Sun 10am–6pm; ☎01/486 82 04), set in an old mansion on Rua Visconde da Luz, where the staff can provide you with a map and will usually phone around on your behalf for private rooms. There are local bus timetables posted in here, too. They can also advise you on the best place to hop on the free **tourist toy train** that rattles from the station to Parque da Gandarinha from May to October.

ACCOMMODATION

Prices in July and August are very high but most of the places listed below will drop room rates by up to forty percent out of season.

Hotel Albatroz, Rua Frederica Arouca 100 (☎483 28 21, fax 484 48 27). Seaside hotels don't come much grander than this – one of the best in the region, with glorious views from rooms and restaurant, and top-of-the-range facilities. Around 40,000$00 in the height of the summer, half that in winter, but even more if you want a sea view. ⑦.

Hotel Baia, Avda. Marginal (☎483 10 95). Modern seafront hotel overlooking the beach and harbour. Rooms are very good value out of season, and not bad in summer; it's worth booking ahead for a room with a sea view. ⑥.

Residencial Casa Lena, Avda. do Ultramar 389 (☎486 87 43). From the station, turn right at the roundabout up Avda. 25 de Abril and keep walking until you see Avda. do Ultramar on your right. Cheaper than many, but a fair walk from the beach. ④.

Adega do Gonçalves, Rua Afonso Sanches 54 (☎483 15 19). Basic rooms above the restaurant; in a handy location but guaranteed to be noisy. ③.

Pensão Palma, Avda. Valbom 15 (☎483 77 97). Highly recommended, beautifully kept *pensão* just a few minutes from the station; ring at the gate. Has a pretty front garden with seating and, inside, airy, pleasant rooms with or without shower. The two cheapest are the attic rooms. ④.

Solar Dom Carlos, Rua Latina Coelho 8 (☎482 81 15, fax 486 51 55). A very attractive sixteenth-century mansion on a quiet backstreet with cool tiling throughout and a welcoming air. Bright, pretty rooms, garden and even an old royal chapel. Breakfast included. ⑤.

Albergaria Valbom, Avda. Valbom 14 (☎486 58 01). Modern, comfortable hotel between the station and the centre, furnished in the 1970s so now fashionably retro. Rooms with bath. Breakast included. ⑥.

EATING

Dom Manolo's, Avda. Marginal 13. Busy grill house just down from the turismo, where the alley runs through to Largo Luís de Camões. Superb chicken and chips; add a salad, local wine and homemade dessert and you'll still pay only around 2000$00.

Esplanada Santa Marta, Praia de Santa Marta. Charcoal-grilled fish served on a tiny terrace overlooking the sea and little beach on the road out to the Boca do Inferno.

Adega do Gonçalves, Rua Afonso Sanches 54. Traditional *adega* not yet overwhelmed by tourists, serving huge portions of good food at moderate prices; the grilled fish is recommended.

Jardim dos Frangos, Avda. Com. Grande Guerra 66. Permanently buzzing with people and sizzling with the speciality, grilled chicken, which is devoured by the plateload at indoor and outdoor tables.

Os Navegantes, Rua do Poço Novo 171. Splendid local *churrasqueria*; stick to the daily specials and you won't go far wrong. Closed Sun.

O Pescador, Rua das Flores 18. One of several close to the fish market, this offers superior fish meals. Good food and service but pricey. Closed Sun.

A Tasca, Rua Afonso Sanches 61. Basic little tavern with friendly, English-speaking owner who turns out decent, budget-priced meals (including *arroz de marisco*) to locals and tourists. If you can manage dessert, try the bizarrely named *baba de camelo* (camel drool) – drinkable caramel.

DRINKING AND NIGHTLIFE

At night, Cascais shows itself off in the smart pubs, bars and cafés along **Rua Frederico Arouca**. More boisterous behaviour goes on in **Largo Luís de Camões**, down the steps on the west side of the main avenue. By day this is a suntrap, none of whose café-bar-restaurants serve particularly memorable meals but are pleasant (if expensive) places to sit and drink. However, on summer nights, the bars throw open their doors, turn up the music and, come closing time at 2am, the square is full of bleary-eyed drinkers dancing and shouting the words to tunes they never realized they knew.

Belbuerguer, Trav. do Visconde de Luz 20. American rock music and burgers, though on Friday and Saturday nights it does good business as a lively bar. Open till 2am.

Chequers, Largo Luís de Camões. Not quite as "legendary" as it would have you believe, but lively enough English-style pub, especially once the pumping rock music strengthens its grip.

Coconuts, Avda. Rei Humberto II de Itália 126. Disco on the road to Boca do Inferno, attracting an odd mix of the trendiest locals and raving tourists. Theme nights include karaoke and male strippers on Wednesday nights.

John Bull, Praça Costa Pinto 32. Backing onto the largo, another English-style pub which fills up early with a good-time crowd; serves meals, too.

Music Bar, Largo da Praia da Rainha. One of the few bars in town with decent sea views, which you can take in sitting at outside tables on the patio above the beach. Open till midnight. Closed Mon.

News, Estrada da Malveira. One of the "in" discos in the area, with a terrace and a lively night guaranteed, especially on Fridays. Open till 4am.

Van Gogo, Trav. da Alfarrubeira 9. Small, friendly and unpretentious disco. Open till 4am.

Praia do Guincho

There are hourly buses (Mon–Sat 7.45am–7.45pm, Sun 9am–7.15pm; 250$00 one way) from outside Cascais train station that run the 6km west to **PRAIA DO GUINCHO**, a great sweeping field of **beach** with body-crashing Atlantic rollers. It's a superb place for **surfing and windsurfing** – World Championships have been held here – but also a dangerous one. The undertow is notoriously strong and people are drowned almost every year. To add to that, there's absolutely no shade and on breezy days the wind cuts across the sands. Even if you can't feel the sun, you'll still burn to pieces unless you're careful.

The beach has become increasingly popular over the years and the coastal approach road is flanked by half a dozen large **terrace-restaurants**, and a couple of **hotels**, all with standard, fish-dominated menus and varying views of the breaking rollers. As nearly everyone comes here on day trips, there's nowhere cheap to stay, except the campsite (see below). At the de luxe-class *Hotel de Guincho* (☎487 04 91; ⑦), rooms are around 30,000$00 a night. Slightly more moderate is *Estalagem O Muchaxo* (☎487 02 21; ⑥), showing signs of shabbiness but remaining a highly attractive place, with stone-flagged bar and picture windows looking out across the beach from the restaurant, which is rated as one of the best in the Lisbon area. Pop in for just a coffee or a beer if you don't want to spend around 4000$00 a head on a meal. Just below is a **public pool** (summer only), handy if the waves are too perilous. The local **campsite** (☎285 10 14) is about 1km back from the main part of the beach; follow the signs from the coast road.

Sintra and around

As the summer residence of the kings of Portugal, and the Moorish lords of Lisbon before them, Sintra's verdant charms have long been celebrated. British travellers of the eighteenth and nineteenth centuries found a new Arcadia in its cool, wooded heights, recording with satisfaction the old Spanish proverb: "To see the world and leave out Sintra is to go blind about". Byron stayed here in 1809 and began *Childe Harold*, his great mock-epic travel poem, in which the "horrid crags" of "Cintra's glorious Eden" form a first location. Writing home, in a letter to his mother, he proclaimed the village:

> *perhaps in every aspect the most delightful in Europe; it contains beauties of every description natural and artificial. Palaces and gardens rising in the midst of rocks, cataracts and precipices; convents on stupendous heights, a distant view of the sea and the Tagus . . . it unites in itself all the wildness of the Western Highlands with the verdure of the South of France.*

That the young Byron had seen neither of these is irrelevant: his description of Sintra's romantic appeal is exact – and still telling two centuries later. Move mountains and give yourself the best part of two full days here.

The Town

SINTRA loops around a series of green and wooded ravines making it a confusing place in which to get your bearings. Basically, though, it consists of three distinct and separate villages: the drab **Estefânia** (around the train station), **Sintra-Vila** (the attractive main town) and, 2km to the east, the functional but pleasant **São Pedro de Sintra**. It's a ten- to fifteen-minute walk from the station to Sintra-Vila and around twenty minutes from Sintra-Vila to São Pedro.

Before you head into the town centre, it's worth making a small detour 300m northeast of the station to visit the new **Museu de Arte Moderna** on Avenida Heliodoro Salgado (Wed–Sun 10am–6pm, Tues 2–6pm, 600$00; free on Thurs for under-18s), which is housed in a 1920s building formerly occupied by Sintra's casino. Among its highlights are works by Jackson Pollock, Hockney, Lichtenstein, and Warhol, including his Campbell's soup tin and a wonderful portrait of Judy Garland. Lovers of kitsch will enjoy Jeff Koons's sculpture of a poo-

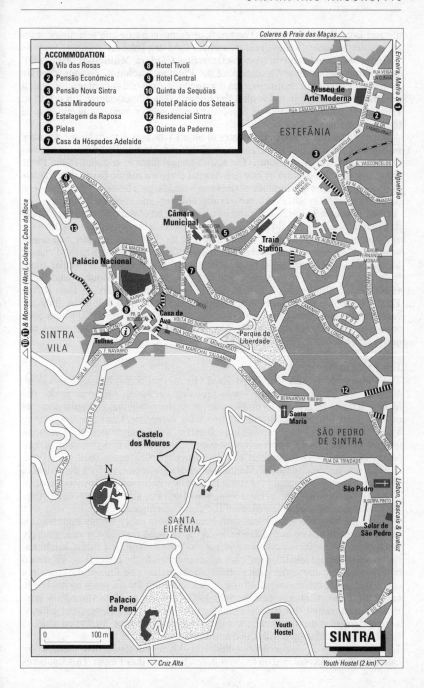

ACCOMMODATION

1. Vila das Rosas
2. Pensão Económica
3. Pensão Nova Sintra
4. Casa Miradouro
5. Estalagem da Raposa
6. Pielas
7. Casa da Hóspedes Adelaide
8. Hotel Tivoli
9. Hotel Central
10. Quinta da Sequóias
11. Hotel Palácio dos Seteais
12. Residencial Sintra
13. Quinta da Paderna

Colares & Praia das Maças △

Ericeira, Mafra & ▷

Museu de Arte Moderna

ESTEFÂNIA

Alguerião ▷

Câmara Municipal

Train Station

Palácio Nacional

Casa da Avo

SINTRA VILA

Tulhas

Parque de Liberdade

Santa Maria

SÃO PEDRO DE SINTRA

Lisbon, Cascais & Queluz ▷

Castelo dos Mouros

São Pedro

Solar de São Pedro

N

SANTA EUFÉMIA

Palacio da Pena

Youth Hostel

0   100 m

SINTRA

△ Cruz Alta

Youth Hostel (2 km) ▽

◁ Monserrate (4km), Colares, Cabo da Roca

dle and Bobtail the sheepdog. The top floor contains a café and restaurant, with an outdoor terrace offering great views over the Pena Palace.

On the way into town you pass the fantastical **Câmara Municipal** (town hall), but it is the extraordinary landmark of the **Palácio Nacional**, distinguished by its vast pair of conical chimneys, that dominates the central square around which the town is gathered. Just downhill the turismo (see "Practicalities" on p.119) in Praça da República can help with accommodation and provides a useful map of the surroundings.

There's a daily **market** in the centre of Sintra-Vila, and a much larger **country market** – with antiques and crafts, as well as food – in São Pedro on the second and last Sunday of every month. The town's annual **festa** in honour of Saint Peter is held on June 28–29, and in July and August there's a **music festival**, with classical performances in a number of the town's buildings. The end of July also sees the Feira Grande in São Pedro, with crafts, antiques and cheeses on sale.

Getting around Sintra's environs involves a fair bit of walking, with the Palácio da Pena an hour or so's climb above the town, Seteais twenty minutes to the west and Monserrate another forty minutes further on. With this in mind, you might want to make use of **taxis**, which cost roughly 1500$00 one way to Pena or Monserrate. The most useful **bus** service is #434, which takes a circular route from Sintra station to Sintra-Vila and the Castelo dos Mouros and back (Tues–Sun; 500$00 return); tickets can be purchased on board. A **Day Rover Ticket** (1200$00) may also be worthwhile if you want to pack it all in; they are valid for one day on any Stagecoach bus; a good option is the #403, which goes from Sintra to Cascais via Cabo da Roca. For full details of buses and times, ask in the turismo.

The Palácio Nacional

The **Palácio Nacional** – or **Paço Real** (10am–1pm & 2–4.30pm; closed Wed; 400$00, free Sunday morning) – was probably already in existence under the Moors. It takes its present form, however, from the rebuilding and enlargements of Dom João I (1385–1433) and his fortunate successor, Dom Manuel, heir to Vasco da Gama's inspired explorations. Its style, as you might expect, is an amalgam of Gothic – with impressive roofline battlements – and the latter king's Manueline additions, with their characteristically extravagant twisted and animate forms. Inside, the Gothic-Manueline modes are tempered by a good deal of Moorish influence, adapted over the centuries by a succession of royal occupants. The last royal to live here, in the 1880s, was Maria Pia, grandmother of the country's last reigning monarch – Manuel II, "The Unfortunate".

Today the palace is a museum, with informal tours every twenty minutes (it's best to go early or late in the day to avoid the crowds) that allow you a leisurely stroll through the various rooms and patios. You're taken first to the **kitchens**, their roofs tapering into the giant chimneys, and then to the upper floor. First stop here is a gallery above the palace chapel, built perhaps on the old mosque. In a room alongside, the deranged Afonso VI was confined for six years by his brother Pedro II; he eventually died here in 1683, listening to Mass through a grid, Pedro having seized "his throne, his liberty and his queen". Beyond the gallery, a succession of state rooms climaxes in the **Sala das Armas**, its domed and coffered ceiling emblazoned with the coats-of-arms of 72 noble families.

Highlights on the lower floor include the Manueline **Sala dos Cisnes**, so-called for the swans painted on its ceiling, and the **Sala das Pegas**. This last takes its name from the flock of magpies (*pegas*) painted on the frieze and ceiling, holding in their beaks the legend *por bem* (in honour) – reputedly the response of João I, caught by his queen, Philippa (of Lancaster), in the act of kissing a lady-in-waiting. He had the room decorated with as many magpies as there were women at court in order to satirize and put a stop to their gossiping.

The Castelo dos Mouros and Palácio da Pena

From near the church of **Santa Maria**, towards São Pedro, a stone pathway leads up to the ruined ramparts of the **Castelo dos Mouros** (daily: June–Sept 10am–7pm; Oct–May 10am–5pm; free). Alternatively you can catch bus #434 from Sintra station. Captured with the aid of Scandinavian Crusaders by Afonso Henriques, the Moorish castle spans two rocky pinnacles, with the remains of a mosque spread midway between the fortifications. **Views** from here are extraordinary: south beyond Lisbon's bridge to the Serra de Arrábida, west to Cascais and Cabo da Roca (the westernmost point of mainland Europe), and north to Peniche and the Berlenga Islands.

The upper gate of the castle gives onto the road up to Pena, opposite the lower entrance to **Pena park** (daily: June–Sept 9am–7pm; Oct–May 10am–5pm), a stretch of rambling woodland, with a scattering of lakes and follies – ideal for a picnic. At the top of the park, about twenty minutes' walk, rears the fabulous **Palácio da Pena** (daily: July–Oct 10am–6.30pm; Sept–June 10am–5pm; 400$00, free Sunday morning), a wild fantasy of domes, towers, ramparts and walkways, approached through mock-Manueline gateways and a drawbridge that doesn't draw. A compelling riot of kitsch, it was built in the 1840s to the specifications of Ferdinand of Saxe-Coburg-Gotha, husband of Queen Maria II, and it bears comparison with the mock-medieval castles of Ludwig of Bavaria. The architect, the German **Baron Eschwege**, immortalized himself in the guise of a warrior-knight on a huge statue that guards the palace from a neighbouring crag. Inside, Pena is no less bizarre, preserved exactly as it was left by the royal family on their flight from Portugal in 1910. The result is fascinating: rooms of concrete decorated to look like wood, statues of turbanned Moors nonchalantly holding electric chandeliers – it's all here. Of an original convent, founded to celebrate the first sight of Vasco da Gama's returning fleet, a chapel and genuine Manueline cloister have been retained.

Above Pena, past the statue of Eschwege, a marked footpath climbs to the **Cruz Alta**, highest point of the Serra de Sintra. Another footpath (unmarked) winds down to the left from Pena, coming out near Seteais (see below).

Seteais, Monserrate and the Convento dos Capuchos

After the castle and Pena, a visit to the palace of **Seteais** and luxuriant gardens of **Monserrate** are the other obvious goals of a Sintra walk. Enthusiastic hikers can make a circuit of these, via the **Convento dos Capuchos** "Cork Convent"; otherwise, to see everything, you're looking at a taxi-ride at least one way.

The Palácio de Seteais

The **Palácio de Seteais** ("Seven Sighs") stands just to the right of the upper Colares road, fifteen minutes' walk west from the centre of town. It is one of the most elegant palaces in Portugal, completed in the last years of the eighteenth century and entered through a majestic Neoclassical arch. Maintained today as an immensely luxurious **hotel** (see "Accommodation", below), it is one of the most expensive places to stay in Portugal. With more modest money to blow, make for the bar and terrace downstairs to the left, past a distinctly unwelcoming reception; its teas are also worth splashing out on.

Monserrate

Beyond Seteais, the road leads past a series of beautiful private *quintas* (manors or estates) until you come upon **Monserrate** – about another forty minutes' walk away.

With its Victorian folly-like mansion and vast botanical park of exotic trees and subtropical shrubs and plants, Monserrate is one of the most romantic sights in Portugal. It would be easy to spend the whole day wandering around the paths laid out through the woods and the charm of the place is immeasurably enhanced by the fact that it's only partially maintained. The name most associated with Monserrate is that of **William Beckford**, author of the Gothic novel *Vathek* and the wealthiest untitled Englishman of his age. He hired the *quinta* here from 1793 to 1799, having been forced to flee Britain because of homosexual scandal – buggery then being a hanging offence. Setting about improving this "beautiful Claude-like place", he landscaped a waterfall and even imported a flock of sheep from his estate at Fonthill. In this Xanadu-like dreamland, he whiled away his days in summer pavilions, entertaining with "bevys of delicate warblers and musicians" posted around the grounds.

Half a century later, a second immensely rich Englishman, **Sir Francis Cook**, bought the estate. His fantasies were scarcely less ambitious, involving the construction of a great Victorian house inspired by Brighton Pavilion. Cook also spared no expense in developing the grounds and imported the head gardener from Kew to lay out succulents and water plants, tropical ferns and palms, and just about every conifer known. Fernando II, who was building the Pena Palace at the time, was suitably impressed, conferring a viscountcy on Cook for his efforts.

The **gardens** are open daily except on public holidays (June–Sept 10am–6pm; Oct–May 10am–5pm; 200$00). **Cook's house** is closed but you can still admire the exterior, with its mix of Moorish and Italian decoration (the dome is modelled on Brunelleschi's Duomo in Florence), and peer into a splendid series of empty salons.

The Convento dos Capuchos

One of the best long walks in the Sintra area is to the **Convento dos Capuchos** (daily: June–Sept 10am–6pm; Oct–May 10am–5pm; 200$00), an extraordinary hermitage with tiny, dwarf-like cells cut from the rock and lined in cork – hence its popular name of the "Cork Convent". Philip II, King of Spain and Portugal, pronounced it the poorest convent of his kingdom, and Byron, visiting a cave where one monk had spent 36 years in seclusion, mocked in *Childe Harold*:

> *Deep in yon cave Honorius long did dwell,*
> *In hope to merit Heaven by making earth a Hell.*

Coming upon the place after a walk through the woods, however, it's hard not to be moved by the simplicity and seclusion of the place. It was occupied for three hundred years and finally abandoned in 1834 by its seven remaining monks, who must have found the gloomy warren of rooms and corridors too much to maintain. Some rooms – **penitents' cells** – can be entered only by crawling through 70cmhigh doors; here, and on every other ceiling, doorframe and lintel, are attached panels of cork, taken from the surrounding woods. Elsewhere, you'll come across a washroom, kitchen, refectory, tiny chapels, even a bread oven set apart from the main complex. The caretaker speaks broken English and may give you a little guided tour if it's not too busy; he sells his own homemade honey at the entrance.

To get there, the most straightforward approach is by the ridge **road from Pena** – a distance of 9km. There are other indistinct paths through the woods from Monserrate and elsewhere in the region, but without local advice and a good map, you'll be hard pushed to find your way. Whichever route you take, the surroundings, too, beg a startled reaction: the minor road between Sintra, the convent and Cabo da Roca sports some of the country's most alarming natural rock formations, with boulders as big as houses looming out of the trees.

Practicalities

Trains depart regularly for Sintra from Lisbon's Rossio station (185$00 one way). The **train station** in Sintra itself is fifteen minutes' walk from the centre of Sintra-Vila; **buses** stop across the street from the station, with services to and from Cascais, Colares, Cabo da Roca, the Sintra beaches, Estoril and Mafra. There are **taxis** outside the train station and in Praça da República, near the palace; check the price first for every journey since the meters aren't always used. You'll find a **post office** and **bank** on Praça da República, too.

Sintra is a popular resort and you should book ahead or turn up early in the day if you intend to stay, especially if you're here during one of the town's festivals (see p.103) when accommodation will definitely be scarce. On the spot, accommodation is best arranged through the efficient and helpful **turismo** (daily: June–Sept 9am–8pm; Oct–May 9am–7pm; ☎923 39 19 or 923 11 57), just off the central Praça da República. There is also a small turismo desk at Sintra station.

Accommodation

There's a fair range of available **accommodation**: a network of private rooms (best booked through the turismo; usually ②), half a dozen **pensões** and **hotels**, and upmarket bed and breakfast in several local *quintas*, or manor houses – the best choices are reviewed below. In addition, there's an attractive **youth hostel** located in the hills above São Pedro de Sintra, while the nearest **campsite** is at Praia Grande (see p.120).

PENSÕES, QUINTAS AND HOTELS

Casa de Hóspedes Adelaide, Rua Guilherme Gomes Fernandes 11 (☎923 08 73). Welcoming and inexpensive place, midway between the train station and Sintra-Vila. ③.

Hotel Central, Largo Rainha D. Amélia 35 (☎923 09 63). Characterful and comfortable nineteenth-century hotel, opposite the Palácio Nacional – polished wood and tiles throughout. Triple rooms available, too, and good off-season discounts. Breakfast included. ⑥.

Pensão Económica, Patio de Olivença 6, off Avda. Heliodoro Salgado (☎923 02 29). Interesting old building and handy for the station; clean, basic and friendly. ②.

Casa Miradouro, Rua Sotto Mayor 55 (☎923 59 00, fax 924 18 36). Renovated turn-of-the-century mansion 500m beyond the Palácio Nacional, with terrific views of coast and castle. Six rooms with bath, terraced garden and good breakfast included. ⑥.

Pensão Nova Sintra, Largo Afonso de Albuquerque 25 (☎923 02 20). Decent rooms and a convenient location on the square by the train station. Some rooms have fine views. ④.

Quinta da Paderna, Rua da Paderna 4 (☎923 50 53). Highly attractive accommodation in a lovely old house, just north of Sintra-Vila. ④.

Hotel Palácio dos Seteais, Rua Barbosa do Bocage 8 (☎923 32 00, fax 923 42 77). One of the most luxurious and expensive hotels in Portugal. Rooms at over 43,000$00 a night in a superb eighteenth-century building, surrounded by elegant gardens. Antique furnishings abound at every turn and there's a terrific restaurant too. ⑦.

Piela's, Rua João de Deus 70–72 (☎924 16 91). On the street behind the train station, this café-*pastelaria* has six simple but spotless double rooms available, presided over by a welcoming and informative proprietor. Serves food and there's a games room. ④.

Quinta das Sequóias (☎923 03 42, fax 923 03 42). Immaculate manor house with six rooms, out in the Sintra hills beyond Seteais – continue past the Palácio de Seteais for 1km and follow the signposted private road on your left. A lovely, antique-furnished place with superb views, gardens, sauna, Jacuzzi and pool. Excellent buffet breakfast included. Recommended. ⑥.

Residencial Sintra, Trav. dos Alvares, São Pedro (☎923 07 38, fax 923 07 38). Big, rambling old *residencial* with a garden and swimming pool, and friendly, multilingual owners. You'll need to book ahead in summer. ⑤.

Hotel Tivoli, Praça da República (☎923 35 05, fax 923 15 72). Sintra's largest, most central hotel – bang next to the palace – with fine views and comfortable rooms with bath. Rates drop in winter. ⑦.

Villa das Rosas, Rua António Cunha 4 (☎923 42 16, fax 923 42 16). Villa set in a large garden, complete with tennis courts. Only has four rooms, all of which feature antique furniture. ⑥.

YOUTH HOSTEL AND CAMPSITES

Pousada de Juventude de Sintra, Santa Eufémia, São Pedro de Sintra (☎924 12 10, fax 924 12 10). The hostel is a 5km walk from the train station, less if you first catch a local bus to São Pedro. Meals served if you can't face the hike down into town and back. Closed noon–6pm.

Camping Praia Grande (☎929 05 81). Properly equipped site on the beach at Praia Grande, west of Sintra. Bus #441 runs from the train station.

Eating and drinking

There are some fine **restaurants** scattered about the various quarters of Sintra. With a couple of honourable exceptions the most mundane are in the centre, near the palace or around the train station; the best concentration is at São Pedro, a twenty-minute walk from town.

Local specialities include *queijadas da Sintra* – sweet cheese pastry-cakes. If you're out for the day, take a **picnic**: the only refreshments out of town are cold drinks from a stall below Pena park (summer only), or exorbitantly priced meals at Palácio dos Seteais.

SINTRA-VILA

Alcobaça, Rua das Padarias 7–11. The best central choice for a decent, straightforward Portuguese meal. Plain tiled dining room with friendly service and large servings of grilled chicken, *arroz de marisco*, clams and steak for around 3000$00 a head.

Augusto, Rua da Pendôa 9. The Esplanade-bar is good for a late-night drink, though the food is fairly forgettable. Head down the hill to the side of the *Café Paris*. Closed Tues.

Casa da Avo, Rua Visconde de Monserrate 46 (☎923 12 80). Basic eating house with few pretensions but the house wine is cheap enough and it's hard to fault dishes like the *caldeirada* (fish stew). There's a decent bar attached, too. Closed Mon.

O Chico, Rua Arco do Teixeira. Standard Sintra prices (ie, fairly high) and food, but come on Thursdays in summer for the fado. It's off Rua das Padarias and has outdoor tables on the cobbles. Bar open till 2am.

Café Paris, Largo Rainha D. Amélia (☎923 23 75). Highly attractive and highest-profile café in town, opposite the Palácio Nacional, which means steep prices for underwhelming food. Great place to sit and nurse a drink in the sun, though.

Casa da Piriquita, Rua das Padarias 1. On the uphill alley across from the *Café Paris*. Quality tearoom and bakery, busy with locals queueing to buy *queijadas da Sintra* and the similarly sticky *travesseiros*. Closed Wed.

Sala de Cha, Rua Consiglieri Pedroso 20. Handicraft shop with a back room offering set teas of scones, cakes, etc for around 800$00.

Tulhas, Rua Gil Vicente 4, behind the turismo (☎923 23 78). Imaginative cooking in a fine building, converted from old grain silos. The speciality is veal with Madeira at a reasonable 1500$00 or so. Closed Wed.

NEAR THE STATION

Cintrália, Largo Afonso de Albuquerque 1 (☎924 22 00). Attractively renovated *marisqueira* where you can try the specialities of *arroz de lagosta* (lobster rice) and the like under sparkling chandeliers. Moderate–expensive.

Piela's, Rua João de Deus 70–72. Budget meals and late-night drinks, as well as rooms (see above). Inexpensive. Closed Tues.

SÃO PEDRO DE SINTRA

Adega do Saloio, Trav. Chão de Meninos (☎923 14 22). A fine grill-restaurant with a standard Portuguese menu and notably hospitable owners. Does a good *arroz de marisco*. Closed Tues.

Solar de São Pedro, Praça Dom Fernando II 12 (☎923 18 60). Locally renowned French-Portuguese dishes served in an azulejo-covered vault. On the main market square. Closed Wed.

Toca do Javali, Rua 1º Dezembro 18 (☎923 35 03). Outdoor tables in summer in a lovely terraced garden and superb cooking at any time of year. Wild boar (*javali*) is the house speciality. Prices are fairly steep, though the set lunch is a great deal at around 2000$00. Closed Wed.

Further west: Colares, the beaches and Cabo da Roca

About 6km further west of Monserrate is **COLARES**, a hill village famed for its wine and boasting several much-prized vintages. It's easily reached on the Sintra–Cascais bus route (#403), with **buses** leaving from outside the train station in both towns, and has a couple of mid-range hotels and country inns, such as the *Estalagem de Colares* (☎928 29 42, fax 928 29 83; ⑤), making it an attractive alternative base to Sintra. For food, there is a smart restaurant and teashop, *Colares Velho* on Largo Dr. Carlos Franca 1–4 (Tues–Sun 11am–11pm) or, if you have your own transport, it is worth making a detour to the excellent *Toca do Júlio* (Tues–Sun; ☎929 08 15) – take the Praia Grande road from the nearby village of Almoçageme.

Continuing west of Colares, the road winds around through the hills to the beach-resort of **PRAIA DAS MAÇÃS**. You can take bus #441 from Sintra train station or, in summer, there's a **tramline** running from just outside Colares – renovation work will eventually extend this all the way to Sintra. Praia das Maçãs has two good *pensões*: *Oceano* (☎929 23 99, fax 929 21 23; ④) and *Real* (☎929 20 02; ④), and a scattering of restaurants. Nearby **AZENHAS DO MAR**, to the north, with a picture-book clifftop town and small beach, makes a pleasant day-trip, as does **PRAIA GRANDE**, to the south. Both can be reached on bus #441 from Sintra; Praia Grande is perhaps the best beach and also has a large **campsite** (see "Accommodation" below).

Cabo da Roca

A major destination in this region is **CABO DA ROCA**, 14km southwest of Colares; regular buses (#403) from Sintra or Cascais train stations make the run throughout the year. It's an enjoyable trip, though the cape itself comprises little more than a lighthouse – below which foamy breakers slam the cliffs – a couple of stalls selling shells, a café and a **tourist office**. In here, you can buy a certificate recording that you've visited the "Most Westerly Point in Europe" – which indeed you have. A **cross** at the cape carries an inscription by Luís Camões ("Here . . . where the land ends, and the sea begins"), whose Muse, for once it seems, deserted him. The bleak, blustery, scrub-covered headland deserves more of a salute.

Palácio de Queluz

The **Palácio de Queluz** (10am–1pm & 2–5pm; closed Tues; 400$00, free Sunday morning) lies on the Sintra train line, making it easy to see either on the way out (it's just twenty minutes from Lisbon's Rossio station; 155$00 one way) or on the way back from Sintra. The station is called Queluz-Belas: turn left out of the station and walk down the main road for fifteen minutes, following the signs through the unremarkable town until you reach a vast cobbled square, with the palace walls reaching out around one side.

The Palace

The building is as perfect a counterpoint to Mafra (see p.123) as you could imagine: an elegant, restrained structure regarded as the country's finest example of Rococo architecture. Its low, pink-washed wings enclose a series of public and private rooms and suites, as well as rambling eighteenth-century formal gardens. Although preserved as a museum, it doesn't quite feel like one – retaining instead a strong sense of its past royal owners. In fact, the palace is still pressed into service for accommodating state guests and dignitaries, and hosts classical concerts in the summer months.

It was built by Dom Pedro III, husband and regent to his niece, **Queen Maria I**, who lived here throughout her 39-year reign (1777–1816), quite mad for the last 27, following the death of her eldest son, José. William Beckford visited when the Queen's wits were dwindling, and ran races in the gardens with the Princess of Brazil's ladies-in-waiting; at other times firework displays were held above the ornamental canal and bullfights in the courtyards.

Visitors first enter the **Throne Room**, lined with mirrors surmounted by paintings and golden flourishes. Beyond is the more restrained **Music Chamber** with its portrait of Queen Maria above the French grand piano. Smaller quarters include bed- and sitting rooms; a tiny oratory overwhelmed with red velvet; and a **Sculpture Room**, whose only exhibit is an earthenware bust of Maria. Another wing comprises an elegant suite of **public rooms** – smoking, coffee and dining rooms – all intimate in scale and surprisingly tastefully decorated. The **Ambassador's Chamber**, where diplomats and foreign ministers were received during the nineteenth century, echoes the Throne Room in style, with one side lined with porcelain chinoiserie. In the end, though, perhaps one of the most pleasing rooms is the simple **Dressing Room** with its geometric inlaid wooden floor and spider's web ceiling of radial gilt bands.

The formal **gardens** are included in the ticket price. Low box hedges and elaborate (if weatherworn) statues spread out from the protection of the palace wings, while small pools and fountains, steps and terracing form a harmonious background to the building.

THE KITCHEN
Visits can be greatly enhanced by a meal in the original kitchen, the **Cozinha Velha** (☎435 02 32), which retains its stone chimney, arches and wooden vaulted ceiling, and sports copper pots, pans and utensils in every niche and alcove. The food – classic French-Portuguese – is superb, but you're looking at around 5000$00 a head for a full meal (though there is a cheaper café in the main body of the palace). The kitchens are now part of the *Pousada Dona Maria I* (☎435 61 58; ⑦), a **hotel** that gives you the chance to stay in an annexe of the palace itself. Its 28 rooms come equipped with satellite TV, but as you would expect, it isn't cheap.

Mafra

Moving on from Lisbon or Sintra, **MAFRA** makes an interesting approach to Estremadura. It is distinguished – and utterly dominated – by just one building: the vast **Palace-Convent** (10am–1pm & 2–5pm; closed Tues; 400$00), which João V – the wealthiest and most extravagant of all Portuguese monarchs – built in emulation of El Escorial in Madrid. Arrive at least an hour before closing time to be sure of getting on a guided **tour** (which lasts for one hour).

The palace-convent
Begun in 1717 to honour a vow made on the birth of a royal heir, **Mafra Convent** was initially intended for just thirteen Franciscan friars. But as wealth poured in from the gold and diamonds of Brazil, João V and his German court architect, Frederico Ludovice, amplified their plans to include a massive basilica, two royal wings and monastic quarters for 300 monks and 150 novices. The result, completed in thirteen years, is quite extraordinary and, on its own bizarre terms, extremely impressive.

In style the building is a fusion of Baroque and Italianate Neoclassicism, but it is the sheer magnitude and logistics that stand out. In the last stages of construction more than 45,000 labourers were employed, while throughout the years of building there was a daily average of nearly 15,000. There are 5200 doorways, 2500 windows and two immense bell towers each containing over 50 bells. An apocryphal story records the astonishment of the Flemish bellmakers at the size of the order: on their querying it, and asking for payment in advance, Dom João retorted by doubling their price and his original requirement.

Parts of the convent are used by the military but an ingenious cadre of guides marches you around a sizeable enough portion. The **royal apartments** are a mix of the tedious and the shocking: the latter most obviously in the **Sala dos Troféus**, with its furniture (even chandeliers) constructed of antlers and upholstered in deerskin. Beyond are the **monastic quarters**, including cells, a pharmacy and a curious infirmary with beds positioned so the ailing monks could see Mass performed. The highlight, however, is the magnificent Rococo **library** – brilliantly lit and rivalling Coimbra's in grandeur. Byron, shown the 35,000 volumes by one of the monks, was asked if "the English had any books in their

country?" The **basilica** itself, which can be seen outside the tour, is no less imposing, with the multicoloured marble designs of its floor mirrored in the ceiling
decoration.

The **Tapada de Mafra**, the palace's extensive hunting grounds, are also open
for ninety-minute tours (summer Fri & Sat 10am, 11am, 3pm & 4pm; winter Sat &
Sun 10am & 3pm; 950$00). For details, ask at the turismo (see below).

Practicalities

Hourly **buses** run from Largo Martim Moniz (metro Socorro) or Centro Alvalade
(by Alvalade stadium, metro Campo Grande) in Lisbon, stopping near the convent. The **town** of Mafra itself is dull, and with frequent buses heading on to the
lively resort of Ericeira, 12km away (see p.136), there seems no point in linger-
ing. Alternatively, you can see the palace as a day-trip **from Sintra**: there are
hourly services from outside Sintra station.

If you need to stay, the **turismo** on Avda. 25 de Abril (daily: July–Sept
9.30am–7.30pm; Oct–June 9.30am–6pm; Sat & Sun closed 1–2.30pm; ☎ 061/81 20
23) can give details of rooms; or try the modern *Hotel Castelão*, also on Avda. 25
de Abril (☎061/81 20 50; ③). For an inexpensive **restaurant** with good food try
the *Solar d'El Rei*, Rua Detras dos Quintas, five minutes' walk from the palace.

Sobreiro

The small village of **SOBREIRO**, around 5km northwest of Mafra on the road to
Ericeira (see p.136), is home to a **craft village** (daily 8am–8pm) – the Aldeia
Típica – established by José Franco. As well as Franco's own work, the show-
room sells other reasonably priced ceramics from all over the country, while
elsewhere in the craft village you'll find a bakery, smithy, clockmaker, cobbler,
schoolroom, distillery, wind- and water-mills and several other small museum
shops, all displaying various tools, furniture and artefacts collected over many
years. The place is perfect for children, while there is an *adega* that makes a
splendid stop for lunch, serving local wine, bread and meals; at weekends, there
is also a restaurant.

The Lisbon–Mafra–Ericeira **bus** passes by every hour or so, and it's definitely
worth a stop if you're driving on to Ericeira from Mafra. There is also a pleasant
campsite should you wish to stay (☎061/525 25).

South of the Tejo: Costa da Caparica, Setúbal and its coast

As late as the nineteenth century, the southern bank of the Tejo estuary was an
underpopulated area used as a quarantine station for foreign visitors; the village
of Trafaria here was so lawless that the police visited it only when accompanied
by members of the army. The huge **Ponte 25 de Abril**, a suspension bridge
inaugurated as the "Salazar Bridge" in 1966 and renamed after the 1974
Revolution, finally ended what remained of this separation between "town and
country". Since then, Lisbon has spilled over the river in a string of tatty industrial suburbs that spread east of the bridge, while to the west the **Costa da
Caparica** has become a major holiday resort. **Setúbal**, 50km south of the capital,
sustains one remarkable church, but little else to delay you. That said, it's not a

bad first stop on your way further south and its **coastal** surroundings are particularly attractive.

Across the river: Cacilhas and the Cristo-Rei

The most enjoyable approach to the Setúbal peninsula is to take a **ferry** (90$00 one way) from Lisbon's Fluvial (Cais de Alfândega) station, by Praça do Comércio, to the suburb of **CACILHAS**. The ferries run every ten minutes, the last returning at around 10.30pm (slightly earlier at weekends); the crossing takes around ten minutes. The blustery ride itself is fun, though the **seafood** is as good a reason as any to go over for an evening; Cacilhas's main street – Rua Candido dos Reis – is one long line of reasonably priced **fish restaurants**, popular with Lisbon locals. *Arroz de marisco* is a speciality in most, particularly good in the *Escondidinho de Cacilhas* (closed Thurs), immediately on the right as you leave the ferry. More upmarket, but with better views, is the riverside *Cervejaria Farol* (closed Wed). **Late-night ferries** back to the capital go to **Cais do Sodré**; these run every 20 to 30 minutes during the day, every 40 to 50 minutes throughout the night (90$00 one way).

The ferry ride over grants you wonderful views of the city, as well as of the enormous **Ponte 25 de Abril** and – on the south bank above Cacilhas at Almada – the **Cristo-Rei**, built in 1959, is a relatively modest version of Rio's Christ-statue landmark. A lift at the statue (summer daily 9am–7pm; 250$00) shuttles you up the plinth above its church, via a souvenir shop, to a highly dramatic viewing platform, 80m up in the air. On a good day, Lisbon stretches like a map below you and you can catch the glistening roof of the Pena Palace at Sintra in the distance. Back at ground level, there is also a new **visitor centre** next to the Cristo-Rei, showing occasional art exhibits and with a handy bar should you need a pick-me-up.

There's a large **bus station** opposite the ferry terminal in Cacilhas. Bus #9 runs **to the statue** (2–3 per hour; daily 8am–8pm), or you can come direct from Lisbon centre on the #52 or #53 (to "Almada"; every 20–30min) from Praça de Espanha (metro Palhavã). Get off at the first stop over Ponte 25 de Abril, cross the motorway bridge and take the first left – Rua Fernão Mendes Pinto – from where it's a ten-minute walk. If you're driving, cross the bridge (there's a toll of 180$00) and take the first exit off the highway, following signs for Almada and Cristo-Rei.

From the Cacilhas bus station, you can also catch regular **buses** to Costa da Caparica, Setúbal, Sesimbra and Vila Fresca de Azeitão, for all of which see the relevant sections that follow.

Costa da Caparica

Regular buses from Cacilhas (every 15–30min, express buses every 30 min; daily 7am–9pm), or from Praça de Espanha (every 30min; daily 7am–12.45am), run on to **Costa da Caparica**, half an hour from Cacilhas, around forty minutes (or 1hr in rush hour) from Praça de Espanha. Though anything but a pretty place, this is a thoroughly lively Portuguese resort, crammed with restaurants and summer bars and discos and it's here that most locals come if they want to swim or laze around on the sand: there are foreign tourists, too, but they're in a minority. In Caparica town itself, **Rua dos Pescadores** leads up from the central Praça da Liberdade (where you'll find the market, supermarkets and banks) to the beach and is lined on both sides by café-restaurants with outdoor seating.

The **beach** stretches north towards Lisbon and away south into the distance, its initial stretch backed by apartments and more cafés. A promenade with wooden shacks at intervals offering grilled sardines, fresh fish, ice cream and drinks lies alongside the **mini-railway** which runs along the 8km or so of dunes to Fonte da Telha (June–Sept; 500$00 to the end of the line) – if you're after solitude you need only take it this far and walk. However, it's useful to know that each of the twenty mini-train stops, based around one or two beach-cafés, has a very particular scene or feel. Earlier stops tend to be family oriented, later ones are on the whole younger and more trendy, with nudity (though officially illegal) more or less obligatory, especially around Stop 18–19, which is also something of a gay area.

As far as sea and sand go the beaches are excellent, taking in coves and lagoons as they spread southwards. The water is of good quality, though watch out for dangerous undertows – if the sea gets too wild to swim in, there's **Onda Parque** (June–Sept daily 10am–8pm), a water park full of slides and pools, just outside Caparica on the road to Lisbon.

Practicalities

Buses in summer stop at the bus park in town near the beginning of the sands. In winter, buses go to the station in Praça Padre Manuel Bernades, in which case it is best to get off at the first stop in Caparica, on the edge of the leafy square, Praça da Liberdade, five minutes back from the beach. If you arrive here, walk diagonally across the square, turn right and at Avda. da Liberdade 18 you'll find the **turismo** (Mon–Sat 9.30am–1pm & 2.30–6pm; ☎290 00 71).

There are a growing number of **hotels** in Caparica, though they are relatively pricey and full in summer; *Pensão Real* on Rua Mestre Manuel 18 (☎290 17 13; ③) is one of the more reasonable central options. Accommodation is hardly a problem though, given the frequency of the buses and ferries back to Lisbon. If you really want to stay, talk first to the turismo or aim for one of the string of **campsites**, all of which, again, are pricier than average and crowded in summer. Your best bet is also the nearest, the well-equipped *Orbitur* (☎290 06 61), complete with café and tennis courts – it's one of the only ones where camping club membership is not required.

Among the dozens of fish and seafood places, a couple of recommended **restaurants** are: *O Borbas*, Praia da Costa (☎290 01 63) at the northern end of the beach with window seats looking out over the sands and bubbling fish tanks inside; and *Primoroso*, further round the seafront towards Lisbon, which has excellent *cataplanas* and outdoor tables facing the beach.

Setúbal and around

Some 50km south from Lisbon, **SETÚBAL** is Portugal's third port and a major industrial centre. It was once described by Hans Christian Andersen as a "terrestrial paradise", and although most of its visual charm is long gone, it's a friendly, enjoyable enough place. If you're heading south and have time to break the journey, it's worth stopping at least for a look at the remarkable Igreja de Jesus. On a more prolonged visit, you could take in some fine views from local vantage points such as the town of Palmela, and the series of excellent **beaches** nearby.

The Town

Setúbal's greatest monument is the **Igreja de Jesus**, designed by Diogo de Boitaca and possibly the first of all Manueline buildings. Essentially a late-Gothic structure, with a huge, flamboyant doorway, Boitaca transformed its interior design by introducing fantastically twisted pillars to support the vault. The rough granite surfaces of the pillars contrast with the delicacy of the blue and white azulejos around the high altar, which were added in the seventeenth century.

The rest of town has little to detain you, though the pedestrianized shopping streets in the **old town** around Rua A. Castelões are handsome enough, and there are gardens, a market and port to poke around. There's a certain amount of interest, too, in the central **Museu Arqueológico**, at Avda. Luísa Todi 162 (Tues–Sat 9am–12.30pm & 2–5.30pm, Sun 9.30am–12.30pm; closed Sat in Aug; free) where finds from the city's Roman age are displayed; if you nip into the nearby turismo, too (see below), you can see the foundations of a Roman warehouse underneath the glass floor.

You might also climb up to the **Castelo São Felipe**, half an hour's walk to the west of the town; head along Avenida Luísa Todi and keep following the signs. Built on the orders of Felipe II in 1590, it's a grand military structure, harbouring an azulejo-lined chapel and protected by sheer walls of overpowering height. It's now a *pousada* (see below) but the ramparts and bar are open to non-guests and there are fine views over the mouth of the Sado estuary and the Tróia peninsula.

A half-hour walk along the coast road, further west out of Setúbal, takes you to **Albarquel**, where a magnificently located **café-restaurant** sits on an outcrop of rock above the sea (reasonably priced café, expensive and highly renowned restaurant).

Practicalities

You can reach Setúbal by **train**, though since it involves crossing to Barreiro and changing (see p.52), it's quicker to take the half-hourly **bus** from Lisbon's Praça de Espanha, which takes around an hour. There are buses, too, from Cacilhas (every 30min; 50min–1hr). By **car**, the fast A2 from Ponte 25 de Abril whisks you to Setúbal in around forty minutes. Trains from Lisbon drop you at Praça do Brasil, north of the centre; local trains use Setúbal's more central station at the eastern end of Avenida 5 de Outubro, along which the city turismo and bus station can also be found.

There are two **tourist offices** in Setúbal, the city one across from the local train station in the Casa do Corpo Santo, on Praça do Quebedo (Mon–Fri 9am–12.30pm & 2–7pm, Sun 9am–12.30pm; closed Sat; ☎065/53 42 22) and the regional one, just off Avenida Luísa Todi at Travessa Frei Gaspar (Mon–Sat 9am–12.30pm & 2–7pm, Sun 9am–12.30pm; ☎065/52 42 84), worth a visit for the remains of the Roman "fish condiments" factory under its glass floor. Both hand out maps and can help with finding rooms; the regional office also offers a useful *Walking Guide to Arrábida* should you wish to explore the region on foot (see p.129).

ACCOMMODATION

Accommodation is rarely a problem. Among **pensões** worth trying are: *Residencial Boa Regresso*, Praça de Bocage (☎065/298 12; ②), with simple rooms, some of which overlook the square; *Residencial Bocage*, Rua de São Cristovão 14 (☎065/215 98; ④), offering small rooms with private bathrooms and TVs; or *Residencial Setubalense*, Rua Major Afonso Pala 17 (☎065/525 790, fax 525 789; ③), a good choice with smartish rooms and a friendly welcome in a quiet part of town. The extremely attractive **pousada**, the *São Filipe* (☎065/52 38 44; ⑦), occupies the castle, high above the river; and there's a muncipal **campsite**, too, the *Toca do Pai Lopes* (☎065/52 24 75), on Rua da Praia Saúde, to the west of town on the shore beneath the castle.

EATING, DRINKING AND NIGHTLIFE

Good-value fish and seafood **restaurants** abound in the dock area and around the western end of Avenida Luísa Todi. A good option is *A Roda,* on the Travessa Postigo do Cais, which serves up tasty Portuguese dishes and has a lovely courtyard. *O Escondidinho*, Rua José António Januário da Silva 6, is another inexpensive option with outdoor tables. There are also plenty of places around the **market**; in midsummer, the surrounding area is considerably expanded with clothes and touristy bric-a-brac.

Nightlife in Setúbal is reasonably promising. You could start drinking at the *Cactus* on Praça de Bocage and finish at *Torib's,* which stays open till about 3am. Between bars you might visit the music bar and club *Absurdo* (usually no entrance charge) at the end of Avenida Luísa Todi, or the *Teatro Luísa Todi,* which stages shows at weekends and often runs art-house movies during the week. The best **clubs** are out of town: *TGV,* at Estrada da Rasca 23 (Thurs–Sat); the *Seagull,* a ten-minute drive along the coast road at Praia de Galapos; or the less pretentious *Leo Taurus,* 3km east along the N10 road.

Tróia

Setúbal's traditional **beaches**, reached by frequent ferries from the town, are on the **PENÍNSULA DE TRÓIA**, a large sand spit hemming in the Sado estuary. The peninsula was settled by the Phoenicians and subsequently by the Romans, whose town of Cetobriga appears to have been overwhelmed by a tidal wave in the fifth century. There are some desultory remains, including tanks for salting fish, opposite the marina on the landward shore. Originally a wilderness of sand and wild flowers, Tróia must once have been magnificent, but it's now a heavily developed high-rise resort. To avoid the worst, and the crowds, be prepared to walk for twenty minutes or so south along the beach. The **ferries** depart daily from Setúbal (every 15–30min, 5am–11pm; hourly during the night; 150$00, cars 600$00); be prepared for long queues for cars in summer.

Palmela

The small town of **PALMELA**, around 10km north of Setúbal, is worth a quick visit for the views from its medieval **castle**, which on a clear day encompass Lisbon, Setúbal, the Sado estuary and Tróia. Like that of Setúbal, the castle incorporates a church and has been restored and extended as a *pousada*, the *Castelo de Palmela* (☎01/235 12 26; ⑦) – a fine place to stay. There are also a couple of less exalted country *quintas* in Palmela, as well as a nearby mill that you can hire: details from Palmela's **turismo** (Mon–Sat 9am–12.30pm & 2–6pm; ☎01/235 00 89), very near the **bus station** in Largo do Chafariz D. Maria I – the square is noticeable for its fine eighteenth-century fountain (*chafariz*).

The Parque Natural da Arrábida

Between Setúbal and Sesimbra lies the **PARQUE NATURAL DA ARRÁBIDA**, whose main feature is the 500-metre granite ridge known as the Serra da Arrábida, visible for miles around and popular for its wild mountain scenery. The twisted pillars of Setúbal's Igreja de Jesus were hewn from here. If you want to explore the area on foot, a useful publication is the *Walking Guide to Arrábida*, available from the regional tourist office in Setúbal (see p.128).

The **bus** from Setúbal to Sesimbra takes the main road, well back from the coast, passing through the town of **VILA FRESCA DE AZEITÃO**, where the José Maria da Fonseca **wine vaults** can be visited. The free tour lasting 45 minutes (Mon–Thurs 9am–noon & 2–7pm, Fri 9am–1pm; ☎065/218 02 27) is interesting and a good introduction to the local Setúbal Moscatel. Vila Fresca de Azeitão can also be reached by bus from Lisbon's Praça de Espanha (hourly; 45min). There is a **campsite**, *Picheleiros* (☎065/218 13 22), just outside town, which is the only site in the park area.

If you have your own transport, a better route, and one not covered by buses, is the twisting coast road, the N10-4. Nestling in the cliffs – and signposted above this road – is the sixteenth-century **Convento da Arrábida,** whose crumbling white buildings with their stunning ocean views are the home of a silent Franciscan order. Nearby is the tiny harbour village of **PORTINHO DA ARRÁBIDA**, which has a couple of excellent, clean beaches – wonderful out of season and always quieter than Tróia. There are prehistoric cave sites nearby and a good **restaurant** by the water's edge. Next along is **GALAPOS**, arguably the best beach along this whole coast.

Sesimbra

If you get up early enough in **SESIMBRA**, you'll still see the fishermen mending their nets on the town's beach, but that's about the limit of this fishing town's tradition now that it's a full-blown resort, with apartment buildings and hotels mushrooming in the low, bare hills beyond the steep narrow streets of the old centre. It's largely a day-trip destination for residents of Lisbon, though the wealthier ones have bought second homes here for the summer, during which time Sesimbra is extremely busy. Nonetheless, it's still an admirable spot, with excellent swimming from the long **beach** and an endless row of **café-restaurants** along the beach road, each with an outdoor charcoal-grill wafting fine smells across the town. The beach splits into two, with a strand either side of the waterfront seventeenth-century **Forte do Santiago** (now a police office) – offshore, jet skis and little ketches zip up and down the clear blue sea.

A **Moorish castle** sits above Sesimbra, a stiff half-hour climb from the centre. Within the walls are a church and various ruins, while a circuit of battlements gives amazing panoramas over the surrounding countryside and coastline. Back in the town, just off Avenida da Liberdade (take the steps by *Restaurante Xurrex*), the **Museu Municipal** (Mon–Sat 10am–12.30pm & 2–5.30pm; free) features archeological and historical finds from the area, while the best of the churches, the Manueline **Igreja da Mai**, is on nearby Rua João de Deus.

Give yourself time, too, to see the original fishing port, **Porto de Abrigo**, with its brightly painted boats, daily fish auctions, and stalls selling a superb variety of shellfish. It's a pleasant walk from the centre, along Avenida dos Náufragos – follow the signs towards the **Forte do Cavalo**, where the local anglers try their hand at sea fishing.

Practicalities

There are six **buses** a day from Lisbon's Praça de Espanha; and half-hourly services from Cacilhas and Setúbal. Coming from Lisbon in summer, it's usually much quicker to take the ferry across to Cacilhas (p.125) and pick up a bus there, as the main bridge road is often jammed solid with traffic.

In Sesimbra, you're dropped at the **bus station**, halfway up Avenida da Liberdade, a five-minute walk from the seafront. Walk down to the water, turn right past the fort, and the **turismo** (daily: June–Sept 9am–8pm; Oct–May 9am–12.30pm & 2–5.30pm; ☎01/223 57 43) is underneath the terrace, a step back from the seafront Avenida dos Náufragos.

ACCOMMODATION

Accommodation is sparse at any time of year, with just a handful of *pensões* and pricey hotels. If you haven't booked in advance, your best bet is to try for private rooms through the turismo. Otherwise, head for the very central *Residencial Chic*, Trav. Xavier da Silva 2–6 (☎01/223 31 10; ③), just back from the sea on a corner with Rua Candido dos Reis. It has bright rooms, some with restricted sea views; ask in the pizza restaurant below. *Pensão Náutico*, off Rua General Humberto Delgado (☎01/223 32 33; ④), is another comfortable place and a little more secluded. The *Hotel Do Mar* (☎01/223 33 26, fax 223 38 88; ⑦) is an upmarket choice, high above the beach with its own swimming pool. There's also a well-located **campsite** at Forte do Cavalo (☎01/223 39 05), just past the fishing port.

Houses in Alfama, Lisbon

Torre de Belém, Lisbon

Tram #28 Alfama, Lisbon

Pensão in Restauradores, Lisbon

Chiado's famous café, Lisbon

Looking down from the Monumento dos Descobrimentos, Belém

Food shop in the Baixa, Lisbon

Elevador da Bica, Bairro Alto, Lisbon

Coastline, Cabo Espichel

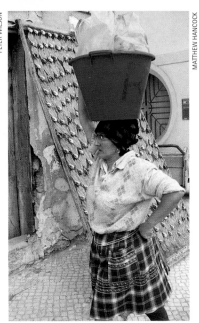

Convento de Cristo, Tomar

Nazaré fisherwoman

Óbidos

If you have your own transport, consider staying out of town at the *Casa da Terrina* (☎01/268 02 64; ⑤), 3km inland at Quintola de Santana; a white, nine-teenth-century farmhouse with garden, pool and breakfast served on the terrace. There are only five rooms, so ring ahead. The bus to Cabo Espichel (see below) passes through Santana.

EATING, DRINKING AND NIGHTLIFE
At night, families crowd the line of **restaurants** east of the fort, along Avenida 25 de Abril. For a quality fish meal, the *Tony Bar* (☎01/223 31 99) in the little square, Largo dos Bombaldes, is hard to beat but expensive. The *Nova Fortaleza*, also on the square is another good option as is the extremely popular *Café Filipe* (closed Wed), further along. It's one of the more expensive places – 4000$00 and upwards – but serves great grilled fish, a bumper *arroz de marisco* and some decent wines. The attractive *O Farol*, opposite, is possibly even better, though if you choose from the fish slab outside make sure you know what you're spending; it can be outrageously expensive here. *Santiago*, at Avda. dos Náufragos 22, has some of the best sea views. Cheaper places (meals under 2000$00) abound in the backstreets on either side of the central spine, Avenida da Liberdade, though you'll sacrifice the outdoor seating and the views; one that doesn't is the budget grill house on the west side of the fort at Avenida dos Náufragos 1.

West of the fort along the avenue is also where most of the **music bars** and **cafés** are found. At some point in the evening, dip into *De Facto*, Avda. dos Náufragos 26; the *Sereia* at no. 22, more of a hippy rock bar; *Bote Douro* at no. 10, a *cervejaria*-café; or the sleek and booming *Mareante* at no. 13, which sometimes has live music. *A Galé*, Rua Capitão Leitão 5, on a raised terrace overlooking the sea, next to the Safari surf shop, is that rare thing in Sesimbra, a proper local bar with no frills and extremely rough house wine.

Clubs with a bit of a summer reputation include *Belle Epoch*, off Largo do Calvario, and *Virzal,* Rua Prof. Fernandes Marques; both stay open till 4am.

Cabo Espichel and Aldeia do Meco

Twice a day (both in the afternoon, making a day trip by bus feasible if brief), buses make the eleven-kilometre journey west from Sesimbra to the **CABO ESPICHEL**, a desolate end-of-the-world plateau where the road winds up at a wide church square. This is enclosed on three sides by ramshackle eighteenth-century pilgrimage lodgings, now hardly used. Beyond, wild and windswept cliffs drop almost vertically several hundred feet into the Atlantic.

A few kilometres to the north and up the surprisingly verdant and undeveloped coast from here is the village of **ALDEIA DO MECO** with four buses a day from Sesimbra, providing easy access to the southern beaches of the **Costa da Caparica** (see p.125 for the northern section). Again these are prone to over-crowding in July and August, but they can be almost deserted and extremely warm and pleasant in May or October. Several villages have **rooms** for rent and there are a growing number of official **campsites** – including a particularly good one at Fetais (☎01/268 29 78), between Aldeia and Praia do Penedo. The best strip of beach is by the lagoon at **Lagoa de Albufeira**: it is extremely clean and excellent for windsurfing.

travel details

Trains

Cais do Sodré to: Belém (every 15–30min; 7min); Cascais (every 15–30min; 30–40min); Estoril (every 15–30min; 25–30min).

Fluvial, via Barreiro, to: Albufeira (2 daily; 5hr–5hr 30min); Beja (4 daily; 2hr 15min); Évora (2 daily; 2hr); Faro (2 daily; 4hr 30min–6hr); Palmela (hourly; 40min); Setúbal (every 30min–1hr; 1hr); Tavira (2 daily; 5–7hr); Vila Real de Santo António (2 daily; 5hr 30min–8hr).

Rossio to: Caldas da Rainha (11 daily, change at Cacém; 1hr 30min–2hr); Leiria (6 daily, change at Cacém; 2–3hr); Óbidos (11 daily, change at Cacém; 2hr); Queluz (every 15–20min; 20min); Sintra (every 15–20min; 50min); Torres Vedras (16 daily; 1hr 10min).

Santa Apolónia to: Abrantes (4 daily; 1hr 30min–2hr 30min); Aveiro (11 daily; 2hr 30min–3hr 15min); Braga (2 daily; 4hr 40min); Castelo Branco (6 daily; 3hr 30min–4hr); Coimbra (13 daily; 2hr–2hr 30min); Covilhã (4 daily; 4hr 30min–5hr); Elvas (4 daily; 5hr 30min); Figueira da Foz (2 daily; 4hr 40min); Guarda (5 daily; 5hr 30min–6hr); Porto, for connections to Spain (13 daily; 3–4hr); Santarém (2–4 daily; 45min–1hr 15 min); Tomar (hourly, 2hr 15 min).

Buses

Express buses run daily to all main towns throughout the country; see entries at the end of relevant chapters. Information from the main bus terminal at Avenida Casal Ribeiro (see p.53). Other services depart from a variety of termini. Local services include:

Lisbon to: Costa da Caparica (every 15–30min; 30min–1hr); Mafra (10 daily; 1hr 30min); Ericeira (10 daily; 1hr 50min); Évora (6 daily; 2hr); Nazaré (6 daily; 2hr); Peniche (9 daily; 1hr 45min); Sesimbra (7–10 daily; 1hr 30min–2hr); Setúbal (every 30min; 45min–1hr); Tomar (2-4 daily; 1hr 45min–2hr); Torres Vedras (12 daily; 2hr); Vila Fresca Azeitão (hourly; 45min).

Domestic flights

There are **internal flights** of varying regularity from Lisbon to: Bragança, Chaves, Covilhã, Faro, Porto, Vila Real, Viseu and to Madeira and the Azores. Check current schedules at any travel agency.

International Trains

Santa Apolónia to: Bordeaux (1 daily; 19hr 30min); Madrid (1 night train; 10hr 30min); Paris (1 daily; 23–25hr); San Sebastián (1 daily; 16hr 30min).

ESTREMADURA AND RIBATEJO

T he **Estremadura** and **Ribatejo** regions have played a crucial role in each phase of the nation's history, and have the monuments to prove it. They are also comparatively wealthy regions, both having received substantial EU grants to help restructure agriculture. Although they encompass a comparatively small area, the provinces boast an extraordinary concentration of vivid architecture and engaging towns: **Alcobaça**, **Batalha**, and **Tomar** – comprising the most exciting buildings in Portugal – all lie within a ninety-minute bus ride of each other. Other attractions are equally compelling: ferries sail from Peniche to the remote **Ilha Berlenga**; **Óbidos** is a completely walled medieval village; spectacular underground caverns can be visited at **Mira d'Aire**; and there are tremendous castles at **Porto de Mós**, **Leiria** (itself an elegant town), and on **Almourol**, an islet in the middle of the Rio Tejo.

The Estremaduran coast – the lower half of the Costa de Prata – provides an excellent complement to all this, and if you're simply seeking sun and sand it's not a bad alternative to the Algarve. **Nazaré** and **Ericeira** are justifiably the most popular resorts but there are scores of less developed beaches. For more isolation, try the area around **São Martinho do Porto** or the coastline west of **Leiria**, backed most of the way by the pine forest of **Pinhal de Leiria**.

Virtually all of these highlights fall within the boundaries of Estremadura, which, with its fertile rolling hills, is perhaps second in beauty only to the Minho. Although the flat, bull-breeding lands of **Ribatejo** (literally "banks-of-the-Tejo") fade into the dull expanses of northwestern Alentejo, the Tejo river valley itself boasts some of Portugal's richest **vineyards**, while many of its towns host lively traditional **festivals**. The wildest and most famous of these is the Festa do Colete Encarnado of **Vila Franca de Xira,** with Pamplona-style bull-running through the streets.

ACCOMMODATION PRICE CODES

All the accommodation prices in this book have been coded using the symbols below. The symbols represent the lowest prices you can expect to pay for a **double room in high season**; for a full explanation, see p.29.

① Under 3000$00   ② 3000$00–4000$00   ③ 4000$00–5500$00
④ 5500$00–8500$00   ⑤ 8500$00–12,500$00   ⑥ 12,500$00–20,000$00
⑦ Over 20,000$00

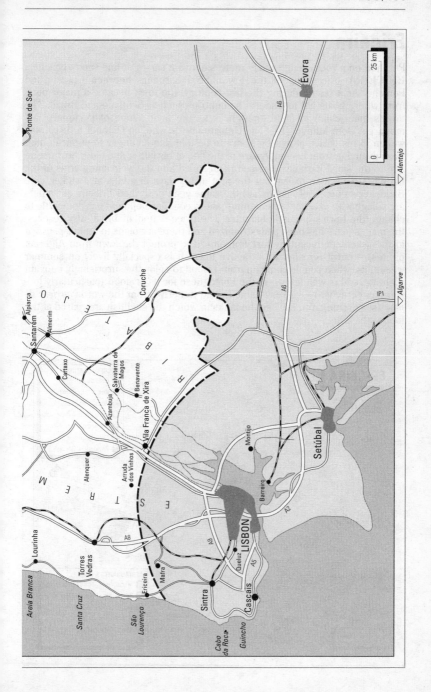

Ericeira

Perched on a rocky ledge thirty metres above a series of fine sandy beaches, **ERICEIRA** offers one of the few natural harbours between Cascais and Peniche. As a result, during the last century, the town became a major port, from where boats left to trade with countries such as Scotland and Brazil. The town's main claim to fame, though, is as the final refuge of Portugal's last monarch, Dom Manuel II – "The Unfortunate" – who, on October 5, 1910, was woken in his palace at nearby Mafra to be told that an angry Republican mob was advancing from Lisbon. Aware of the fate of his father and elder brother, he fled to the small harbour at Ericeira and sailed into the welcoming arms of the British at Gibraltar, to live out the rest of his days in a villa at Twickenham. Baedeker's guidebook, published the same year, described Ericeira as "a fishing village with excellent sea bathing" and recent development has done little to change the town's original character. The place is undeniably a busy resort – the main square has been pedestrianized and there are plans to build a *pousada* in the seventeenth-century fort (once used to protect the town from Algerian pirates) – but it remains an attractive town. It is especially lively on summer weekends, when people come up from Lisbon to enjoy the surprisingly buoyant nightlife, and is well known to the Portuguese for its seafood (particularly lobsters and crayfish) – its very name is said to derive from the words *ouriços do mar* (sea urchin). You can see the tanks in which the shellfish are reared at the foot of the cliffs.

At the centre of town **Praça da República**, the small main square, is busy with sidewalk cafés and wonderful *pastelarias*, while bars and restaurants are concentrated on Rua Dr. Eduardo Burnay, which leads from the southwestern corner of the praça towards the town's main beach, **Praia do Sul**. The most central of the beaches is the tempting one in the Porto de Pesca, but it's a working fishermen's beach and you're not allowed to swim there. To the north of town you'll find the **Praia do Norte** and the prettier, less crowded, **Praia do São Sebastião**, a fifteen-minute walk past the next headland and popular with surfers. Another option is to take the bus from Praça dos Navigantes to reach the series of untouched local beaches further to the north – if you're here in September, you can catch the World Surfing Championships, held 3km out of town at Praia da Ribeira d'Ilhas. The best local beach, however, is perhaps the one at **São Lourenço**, a peaceful hamlet just 5km north of Ericeira.

Back in town, if the sea is too rough, you can use the pool in the *Hotel de Turismo* (1000$00) just beyond the pretty Parque Santa Marta, which has tennis courts. If you want to try surfing, equipment can be hired in town from *Ultimar* at Rua 5 de Outubro 37 (closed Sun).

Practicalities

Buses run virtually every hour to and from Mafra (see p.123) and Lisbon, making Ericeira a useful first or last stop in Estremadura, and there are also services to Sintra. If you arrive by bus, you will be dropped in town at the top of Rua Prudêncio Franco da Trindade, which leads down to the main square. The **turismo**, at Rua Dr. Eduardo Burnay 33a (daily: July–Aug 9am–midnight; Sept–June 9am–10pm; ☎061/631 22), may help with finding **private rooms**, which are advertised throughout town above bars and restaurants.

Accommodation

Pensões and hotels are generally good value and pleasant (there's a list of the best below), though most are not open all year round; those that are should be a good deal cheaper in winter. There's an excellent, well-equipped **campsite** at Parque Mil Regos, just beyond Praia do São Sebastião (☎061/627 06), and a second at Sobreiro (see p.124).

Hospedaria Bernado, Rua Prudêncio Franco da Trindade 17 (☎061/623 78). Spotless and attractive *pensão*, fairly close to the main square. ③.

Casa do Sol, Rua Prudêncio Franco da Trindade 1 (☎061/86 44 00). A small, but grand, house with shady gardens at the top end of the steep street into town. Rooms are small but some have attached bathrooms. ④.

Hospedaria Fortunato, Rua Dr. Eduardo Burnay 7 (☎061/628 29). Good views of Praia do Sul from the rooms, but a little noisy. There's a range of accommodation and prices; an annexe copes with the overflow. Breakfast included. ③.

Residencial Gomes, Rua Mendes Leal 11 (☎061/636 19). An old, rambling building with faded decor, but clean and fresh with friendly, if somewhat eccentric, staff. ②.

Hotel Pedro o Pescador, Rua Dr. Eduardo Burnay 22 (☎061/86 43 02). Traditional, elegant and friendly establishment with its own patio, but the lively bar and club downstairs may disturb early-nighters. Closed Jan. ④.

Hotel Vilazul, Calçada da Baleia 10 (☎061/86 41 01). Just off Rua Dr. Eduardo Burnay, this plush, good-value hotel is popular with upmarket British tour operators. The rooms have private bathrooms and good views from the balconies. Serves great breakfasts. ④.

Pensão Vinnu's, Rua Prudêncio Franco da Trindade 25 (☎061/638 30). Close to the main square, this is clean, modern and airy with a lively bar to boot. Some rooms have small balconies. ③.

Eating

The lively *pastelarias* around Praça da República are recommended for lunch – or tea-time indulgences. In the **restaurants**, seafood is obviously the thing to go for; the local speciality is *açorda de mariscos*, a sort of shellfish stew with bread.

O Barco, Rua Capitão João Lopes 14 (☎061/627 59). Upmarket and expensive seafood restaurant overlooking the harbour; the *ementa turística* is around 3000$00 a head. Closed Thurs & Nov.

Marisqueira Jogo da Bola, on the corner of Rua Provedor Jorge Fialho and Rua Fonte do Cabo. Try the *açorda* at this moderately priced seafood restaurant.

Mar a Vista, Largo das Ribas. This popular place for locals has some tables with sea views; a full meal with wine will set you back 2500$00 a head. Closed Wed.

O Miradouro do Baleia, Praia do Sul. Great sea views and a wide range of reasonably priced seafood.

Restaurante Patio dos Marialvas, Rua Dr. Eduardo Burnay 29. A friendly place with outdoor tables, serving excellent *arroz de marisco* at moderate prices. Closed Mon.

Nightlife

Ericeira after dark is surprisingly animated – its bars, clubs and proximity to the beaches attract an influx of young Lisboetas. In Ericeira itself, the bars are on or around Rua Dr. Eduardo Burnay, but most of the "in" places are to be found out of town. The following are recommended:

Big Surprise, Seixal, 8km south of Ericeira. A large and brash out-of-town venue which can be great fun on summer weekends but a big let-down at other times.

Bar Big Waves, Praça dos Navigantes 22. One of the happening bars on the square near Praia do Sul. The place where locals start off the evening.

Cadillac Bar, Praça dos Navigantes 21. Next door to *Big Waves* and easily recognized by the model Cadillac sticking out of the front. Lively rock and pop.

Limpicos, Foz do Lizandro. This is one of the best of a group of trendy bars in this small beach resort 8km south of Ericeira – part of the night-time circuit for those with their own transport.

Bar Neptuno, Trav. J. Mola. A good-time bar with a two-for-one Happy Hour and frequent live music.

Disco Ouriço, Rua Capitao João Lopes 10, next to *O Barco* restaurant. Currently the in-place for the trendies of Ericeira.

Hotel Pedro o Pescador, Rua Dr. Eduardo Burnay 22. The club below the hotel is a popular young hang-out.

Disco-Bar Pirata, attached to the *Hotel de Turismo*, Rua Porto de Revez, at the top of Praia do Sul. Biggest disco in town, slightly pricey and mainly frequented by tourists but always has a hectic buzz.

Torres Vedras

TORRES VEDRAS, 27km to the north and inland from Ericeira, took its name from the Duke of Wellington's famous defence lines (Linhas de Torres) in the **Peninsular War** against Napoleonic France. The "Lines" consisted of a chain of 150 hilltop fortresses, stretching some 40km from the mouth of the Rio Sizandro, directly west of Torres Vedras, to Alhandra, southeast of Torres Vedras, where the Tejo widens out into a huge lake. Astonishingly, they were built in a matter of months and without any apparent reaction from the French. Here, in 1810, Wellington and his forces retired, comfortably supplied by sea and completely unassailable. The French, frustrated by impossibly long lines of communication and by British scorching of the land north of the Lines, eventually retreated back to Spain in despair. Thus from a last line of defence, Wellington completely reversed the progress of the campaign – storming after the disconsolate enemy to effect a series of swift and devastating victories.

The Town

In view of this historical glory, modern Torres Vedras is somewhat disappointing. There are a few ruins of the old fortresses and a couple of imposing sixteenth-century churches, but all this is swamped by a dull sprawl of recent buildings. Yet, from the thirteenth to the sixteenth century, the **castle** (daily 9am–7pm; free) at Torres Vedras was a popular royal residence. It was here, in 1414, that Dom João I confirmed the decision to take Ceuta – the first overseas venture leading towards the future Portuguese maritime empire. The castle was eventually abandoned and then reduced to rubble by the earthquake of 1755.

Booklets and old maps can be read at the **turismo**, Rua 9 de Abril, off Praça 25 de Abril (summer daily 10am–7pm; winter Mon–Sat 10am–1pm & 2–6pm; ☎061/31 40 94); while across Praça 25 de Abril, in the old Convento da Graça, is the **Museu Municipal** (Tues–Sun 10am–noon & 2–6pm; 150$00), with a room devoted to the Peninsular War. Unless you get hooked on the local wine, there's not much else to keep you in the town.

However, if you decide **to stay**, try the clean but basic *Pensão-Restaurante 1° de Maio*, Rua 1° de Dezembro 3 (☎061/228 75; ②), or *Residencial Moderna*, opposite the cinema on Avda. Tenente Valadim (☎061/31 41 46; ③). For a **meal**, *Gordo* in Rua Almirante Gado Coutinho 15 (☎061/230 79; closed Tues) and *Patio*, Rua José Eduardo Cesar 16 (☎061/32 14 96; closed Sun), are good options.

In general, however, you'd probably be better off taking one of the many buses on to Peniche, Óbidos, or the popular local resort of Praia de Santa Cruz. The **bus station** is just uphill from the **train station** which is located at the end of the central Avenida 5 Outubro.

Praia de Santa Cruz and other beaches

Most people at the modern resort of **PRAIA DE SANTA CRUZ** are locals from Torres Vedras, 13km to the east, and the place has a friendly, easy-going feel, as well as some excellent places to eat. There are two sandy beaches, **Praia Guincho** below the town, and the more secluded **Praia Formosa**, beneath cliffs to the south. In between is a "screaming rock" – partly covered by the tide – where air and water is forced through a hole in the rock at certain times to produce the distinctive sound. **Rooms** are available at the *Pensão-Restaurante Mar Lindo*, Trav. Jorge Cardoso (☎061/93 72 97; ④), some with sea views, and at the modern *Hotel de Santa Cruz*, Rua José Pedro Lopes (☎061/93 71 48; ④). There's a shady **campsite** north of the village, five minutes' walk from the sea but it fills up quickly in summer.

Quieter resorts – uncrowded outside public holidays or summer weekends – are to be found to the north of here and are easily reached on buses heading to Lourinhã or Peniche.

Praia de Porto Novo

Five kilometres north of Santa Cruz, **PRAIA DE PORTO NOVO** is just beginning to show signs of development, but the beach is still relatively unspoilt and there are good walking possibilities inland. In August 1808, British reinforcements were landed here, at the mouth of the River Maceira. They enabled Wellington, in his first serious encounter with the French, to defeat General Junot at the battle of Vimeiro, following which the French sued for peace. Should you want **to stay**, the reliable *Residencial Promar* (☎061/98 42 20; ④) is the best bet among the cluster of *pensões* and restaurants opposite the beach.

Areia Branca and Consolação

Further north on the Peniche road, 21km from Torres Vedras, lies **AREIA BRANCA** ("White Sand"), a small resort with a congenial campsite (☎061/41 21 99) and a good beachside **youth hostel** (☎061/42 21 27). Other **accommodation** options include *Estalagem Areia Branca*, Praia da Areia Branca (☎061/41 24 91; ⑤), near the beach, and *Residencial Restaurante D. Lourenço*, on the way out of town (☎061/42 28 09; ④); alternatively, ask at the **turismo** (summer Mon–Fri 9am–5.30pm, Sat & Sun 10am–noon & 3–7pm; winter Mon–Fri 9am–5.30pm; ☎061/42 21 67) for a list of private **rooms**. The *Restaurante Dom Lourenço* is the best place for **food**.

Despite the attractive sands here, the sea at Areia Branca is not too clean and it's better to go north to **CONSOLAÇÃO**, just south of Peniche, with its great swathe of beach. There's a rash of development behind the sand dunes, but it's relatively hidden. There are few places to stay the night but you're probably better off moving on to Peniche or Baleal for accommodation. For snacks and drinks, try *Bar Forte Club* in the old fort in the attractive old part of town.

Peniche and the Ilha Berlenga

PENICHE, impressively enclosed by ramparts and one of Portugal's most active fishing ports, is the embarkation point for the **Ilha Berlenga**. As late as the fifteenth century the town was an island but the area has silted up and is now joined to the mainland by a narrow isthmus with gently sloping beaches on either side. Unfortunately, Peniche has burst out of its natural confines and unsightly development now stretches along the coast, but inside the walled town there is more to appreciate. The main attraction is the fortress which dominates the south side of town, and there's also an enjoyable market on the *campo*, held on the last Thursday of the month.

The sixteenth-century **Fortaleza** (summer Tues–Sun 10am–12.30pm & 2–7pm; winter Tues–Sun 10am–noon & 2–5pm; 100$00) was one of the dictator Salazar's most notorious jails. Greatly expanded in the 1950s and 1960s to accommodate the growing crowds of political prisoners, it later served as a temporary refugee camp for *retornados* from the colonies. Today it houses a **museum** (100$00 extra), with the familiar mix of local archeology, natural history and craft displays, among which you can still see the old cells (on the top floor), the solitary confinement pens (*segredos*) and the visitors' grille (*parlatório*).

Just outside the city walls, off the fine **north beach** of the peninsula, there's a traditional boat yard. It's fascinating to watch the shipwrights here manoeuvring

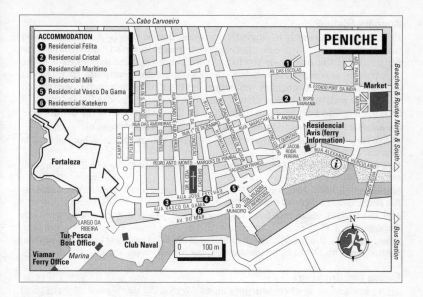

huge timbers into position to form the skeletal framework of a new fishing vessel. If you've got more time to spare, you can take a ninety-minute walk (though if you have a car it's a good idea to drive clear of the suburbs first) beyond the fortress – out to the tip of **Cabo Carvoeiro**, the rugged, rock-pillared and lighthouse-topped peninsula, where there's a smart restaurant, the *Nau dos Corvos*, with a superb view and a tourist menu for around 2000$00. Another rewarding walk, a few kilometres to the north of Peniche, is to **BALEAL**, an islet-village, joined to the mainland by a narrow strip of fine sand. This would make a good base in its own right, with a fine beach, not too much development and a few **rooms** for rent. It has a small, but reasonably equipped **campsite** (☎062/76 93 33) or you could try *Hospedaria Mar-a-Vista* on the main Peniche road (☎062/76 94 67; ③), or the wonderful *A Casa das Marés* (☎062/76 93 71; ⑥).

If you are in Peniche over the first weekend in August, you'll see the **festival** of Nossa Senhora da Boa Viagem (Our Lady of Good Journeys), during which the statue of the Virgin is brought to the harbour by boat to be greeted by candle-bearing locals. After the village priest has blessed the fleet, there are fireworks, bands and dancing in the street.

Practicalities

Buses arriving in Peniche pull in at the station on the isthmus just outside the town walls. It's a ten-minute walk into the centre across the Ponte Velha, which takes you to Rua Alexandre Herculano, where you turn left for the **turismo** (daily: summer 9am–8pm; winter 10am–12.30pm & 2–5pm; ☎062/78 95 71). Nearly all of Peniche's hotels, bars and restaurants are on or just back from Rua Alexandre Herculano and Avenida do Mar, which leads down to the harbour by Largo da Ribeira.

Accommodation

In summer (particularly in August), **accommodation** can be hard to find; you may be approached by people offering private rooms, but it's best to head for the turismo who can usually help you to find something. Out of season, or early in the day, try one of **residenciais** below. There's a municipal **campsite** (☎062/78 95 29) on the way into town, after you've crossed the Rio Lagôa, which is well placed for the bus station, and a fine private campsite, *Camping Peniche Praia* (☎062/78 34 60), complete with pool and restaurant, on the north shore of the peninsula.

Cristal, Rua 1° de Dezembro (☎062/78 27 24). Smallish but clean rooms. ④.

Félita, Largo Prof. Francisco Freire (☎062/78 21 90). Fairly characterless but comfortable rooms in a modern building. ④.

Katekero, Avda. do Mar 70 (☎062/78 71 07). Good-value, airy rooms with TVs, some with sea views. ③.

Marítimo, Rua José Estêvão (☎062/78 28 50). Set just back from the harbour, this *residencial* has simple rooms with private bathrooms. ②.

Mili, Rua José Estêvão 45 (☎062/78 71 07). Comfortable, well-located and efficient place with friendly owners. ④.

Vasco da Gama, Rua José Estêvão 23 (☎062/78 19 02). Good value and in a central position. Rooms come with TV and bathrooms and the price includes breakfast. ④.

Eating and drinking

There is a fine array of **restaurants** along Avenida do Mar – most of them good value, and serving huge portions. *Restaurante Gaivota* and *Restaurante Onda Azul*, both by the harbour on Largo da Ribeira, are good value for seafood and often set up outdoor barbecues. The wonderful **market snack bar** just off Arq. Paulino Montez is just the place for breakfast or picnic provisions; it's usually full of fishwives in knitted capes and socks, swinging plastic bags of fish as they sip *bicas* and exchange news. Your best bet for a lively drink and a view of the world going by is one of the harbourside **bars**.

Ilha Berlenga

The **ILHA BERLENGA**, 10km offshore and just visible from the cape, is a dreamlike place – rather like a Scottish isle transported to warmer climes. Just two-and-a-half square kilometres in extent, it is the largest island of a tiny archipelago, with a jagged coastline of grottoes, miniature fjords, and extraordinary rock formations. In summer the sea is calm, crystal clear, and perfect for snorkelling and diving – rare in the Atlantic.

The only people permitted to live here are a couple of dozen fishermen, as the whole island has been declared a **Natural Reserve**, the home of thousands upon thousands of seabirds, including gulls, puffins and cormorants, perched in every conceivable cranny and clearly plotting to leave their mark on every possible victim. Makeshift paths are marked out with stones, and guardians watch out for visitors straying into the prohibited areas and disturbing the birds.

The island

Human life revolves around the main **landing dock** with its colour-washed fishing boats and small sandy **beach**. It can get crowded and noisy down here at the height of the season – it takes very few people to make the place seem packed – though the only buildings are a cluster of huts, a rather basic shop and a lighthouse. If you want **to stay**, it's a choice between the nearby bar-restaurant *Pavilhão Mar e Sol* (☎062/75 03 31; ⑤) which offers somewhat pricey **rooms** or, for the tighter budget, the rudimentary **hostel** (☎062/785 263; ①) in the seventeenth-century Forte de São João Baptista, a short walk beyond the lighthouse, on an islet joined by the narrowest of causeways. You have to reserve in advance and bookings are for a minimum of one week – you'll need to bring your own food (the hostel has a kitchen) and sleeping stuff. There's also a free **campsite**, which clings to a strictly limited site on the rocky slopes above the harbour. If you want to stay here, you have to book at the turismo in Peniche – it's best to write in advance.

Rowing boats can be hired at the jetty to explore the intricacies of the coastline, though you may prefer to go in something with a motor if there's any motion on the sea (you can get a guided trip for a few hundred *escudos*). Don't miss the **Furado Grande**, a fantastic tunnel 75m long which culminates in the aptly named **Cova do Sonho** (Dream Cove) with its precipitous cliffs.

Getting there

The **ferry** from Peniche to Berlenga is operated by Viamar and takes one hour – longer if the sea is rough. Information and tickets are available from *Residencial Avis* on Largo Jacob Pereira (☎062/78 21 53), near the turismo. The service operates from May 15 to September 20; currently, there are three ferries daily in July and August (9am, 11am and 5pm; return at 10am, 4pm & 6pm) and one daily in May, June and September (10am; return at 6pm in June, 4pm in May and Sept). A return **ticket** costs 2500$00 and there's a limit of 300 tickets sold each day; one person can buy up to five at a time. In July and August the ticket office opens at 8pm to take bookings for the next day's ferry; if you want to be sure of a place, get there in good time. Outside these months, it's not usually a problem getting a ticket on the day of travel.

Another company, Tur-Pesca, operates boat trips all year round except December (minimum four people) and takes bookings at the pyramid building in Largo da Ribeira (9am–5pm; ☎062/78 99 60 or 78 30 13). Tickets are 3500$00 return and the price includes a visit to the caves along the coastline. They can also arrange four-hour fishing or diving trips, for which equipment can be hired from the Clube Naval near the old harbour in Peniche (☎062/78 25 68 or 78 25 50). Note that you can use Tur-Pesca for overnight stays on the island only between June and September; the rest of the year it will take only day-trippers.

However, bear in mind that if the weather is difficult, times will change and boats may be cancelled. In any case, be sure to go without breakfast – it's a rough ride, as evinced by the grim collection of buckets under the seats!

Óbidos

ÓBIDOS, "The Wedding City", was the traditional bridal gift of the kings of Portugal to their queens. The custom was begun in 1282 by Dom Dinis and Dona Isabel, and the town can hardly have changed much in appearance since then. It is very small and completely enclosed by lofty medieval walls: streets are cobbled, houses whitewashed with bright blue and yellow borders, and at all points steep staircases wind up to the ramparts, where you can gaze across a ludicrously fable-like countryside of windmills and vineyards.

It wasn't always like this. Five hundred years ago, when Peniche was an island, the sea also reached the foot of the ridge on which Óbidos stands and boats were moored below its walls. However, by the fifteenth century the sea had retreated, leaving a fertile green plain and the distant Lagoa de Óbidos with its narrow, shallow entrance to the sea.

The town is touristy, of course, and the area around it is becoming somewhat built up. However, you can walk right around the town along its perimeter **walls** – a narrow and at times hair-raising walkway with no handrails, and from this vantage point the town still seems to have a private life of its own. If you stay the night, the feeling is reinforced, as the town slowly empties to regain its charm.

The Town

The most striking building in town is Dom Dinis's massively-towered **Castelo**, which has been converted to a very splendid *pousada* (see "Accommodation" on p.145). Below the castle, the principal focus of the streets is the parish church, the **Igreja de Santa Maria**, in the central praça – chosen for the wedding of the ten-year-old child king, Afonso V, and his eight-year-old cousin, Isabel, in 1444. It dates mainly from the Renaissance period, though the interior is lined with seventeenth-century blue azulejos in a homely manner typical of Portuguese churches. On the left-hand wall is an elaborate tomb designed by Nicolas Chanterene, an influential French sculptor active in Portugal in the first half of the sixteenth century. The retábulo to the right of the main altar was painted by **Josefa de Óbidos**, one of the finest of all Portuguese painters – and one of the few women artists afforded any reputation by art historians. Born at Seville in 1634, Josefa spent most of her life in a convent at Óbidos. She began her career as an etcher and miniaturist and a remarkable handling of detail is a feature of her later full-scale religious works. Another of her paintings, a portrait, can be seen in the adjacent **museum** in the old town hall (daily 10am–12.30pm & 2–6pm; 250$00).

There's an annual **festival of ancient music** in October, held in various venues around the town, including the purpose-built **Casa da Música**, just inside Porta da Vila, the principal town gate at the far end of Rua Direita. The town is also busy on August 20 – Tourist Day – when free wine is on offer. If you're on the lookout for things to buy, there's a range of **shops** on the main Rua Direita, from the Casa Mourisco (ceramics, paintings and carvings) to the worthy old people's **handicrafts centre**, which has a good variety of nicely made items.

Practicalities

Buses from Caldas da Rainha (6km to the north) and Peniche (24km west) stop outside the Porta da Vila. From here **Rua Direita** leads straight through the town to the **turismo** (Mon–Fri 9.30am–7pm, Sat & Sun 9.30am–1pm & 2–7pm; ☎062/95 92 31). The **train station** is at the foot of the ridge; there is no ticket office here, so pay once you are on the train. If you are not too heavily laden, you can cross the tracks and climb the steps, which will bring you to the gate by the Castelo *pousada* – at the opposite end of Rua Direita. Otherwise, follow the road and the easier gradients to reach the Porta da Vila.

Accommodation

Accommodation is on the expensive side, unless you get one of the handful of private **rooms** (usually ③), advertised in the windows of a few houses and sometimes touted at the bus station. Try those at Rua Direita 40 (☎062/95 91 88). Of the **pensões and hotels** the following represent a good selection:

Casa do Poço, Trav. da Rua Nova (☎062/95 93 58). Downhill from the castle, this renovated house retains its Moorish foundations and a well in the courtyard. There are only four double rooms, all en suite, and there's fado in the bar at weekends. ④.

Casa da Relógio, Rua da Graça (☎062/95 92 82). Outside the walls, a former eighteenth-century mansion whose "clock" is in fact a stone sundial. Six double rooms available, all with bath. Real value for money. ④.

Pousada do Castelo (☎062/95 91 05). Relatively small but nevertheless one of the country's finest and priciest *pousadas* – visit for morning coffee or afternoon tea at the very least. Its size means it fills up quickly. ⑦.

Estalagem do Convento, Rua Dr. João de Ornelas (☎062/95 92 17). A minor convent, converted rather tastelessly into a hotel. Expensive patio dining in summer is the best feature. ⑥.

Albergaria Josefa de Óbidos, Rua Dr. João de Ornelas (☎062/95 92 28). A modern air-conditioned hotel, outside the walls. Rooms all have TVs and breakfast is included. ⑤.

Residencial Martim de Freitas, Estrada Nacional 8 (☎062/95 91 85). On the road to Caldas da Rainha, this has huge, simply furnished rooms, and is generally friendly. Breakfast is included. ④.

Albergaria Rainha Santa Isabel, Rua Direita (☎062/95 91 15). The carefully preserved facade hides a modern hotel with lounge and bar. Hearty breakfasts included. Some of the rooms have balconies overlooking the main street. ⑤.

Eating

Restaurants are geared towards day-trippers and are not generally high on atmosphere, but the quality of the cuisine is good as long as you don't mind paying above-average prices.

Restaurante Alcaide, Rua Direita, opposite the *Albergaria Rainha Santa Isabel* (☎062/95 92 20). Arrive early – or book – particularly if you want to eat on the balcony; pricey. Closed Mon & Nov.

Casa de Ramiro, Rua Porta do Vale. Just outside the walls in an old house, redesigned in Arabic style. It's noted for its aromatic grills and is moderately priced. Closed Thurs & Jan–Feb.

Restaurante O Conquistador, Rua Josefa de Óbidos, off Rua Direita. Near the Porta da Vila; try the soup and the duck, or eat from the *ementa turística* for around 1500$00.

Estalagem do Convento, Rua Dr. João de Ornelas. Excellent but expensive patio dining, though the *ementa turística* isn't outrageously priced at 2800$00.

Café-Restaurante 1° de Dezembro, Largo Sao Pedro, next to the church. The best bet for a cheap meal, although service can be slack.

Caldas da Rainha

Six kilometres north of Óbidos, **CALDAS DA RAINHA** ("Queen's Spa") was put firmly on the map by Dona Leonor. Passing by in her carriage, she was so impressed by the strong sulphuric waters that she founded a hospital here, initiating four centuries of noble and royal patronage. That was in 1484 but the town was to reach the peak of its popularity in the nineteenth century when, all over Europe, spas became as much social as medical institutions. The English Gothic novelist, William Beckford, stopping off on his journey to Batalha and Alcobaça (recorded in his *Travels in Spain and Portugal*), found it a lively if depressing place – "every tenth or twelfth person a rheumatic or palsied invalid, with his limbs all atwist, and his mouth all awry, being conveyed to the baths in a chair".

Disappointingly little remains of all the royal wealth poured into the spa, though it is still a pleasant stop on your way to Nazaré or Alcobaça. From the central **Praça da República**, which hosts a fruit market every morning, the **royal spa hospital**, still very much in use, is a short walk downhill, but you can bathe in the warm, sulphurous swimming pools only under doctor's orders. Protruding from the back of the spa is the striking Manueline belfry of **Nossa Senhora do Pópulo**, the hospital church. There's a *Virgin and Child* by Josefa de Óbidos in the sacristry.

In the leafy Parque Dom Carlos I, the **Museu de José Malhoa** (Tues–Sun 10am–12.30pm & 2–5pm; 250$00, free Sunday morning) displays Malhoa's work and that of other late-nineteenth-century Portuguese painters. There are two other museums at the far edge of the park: the **Atelier Museu António Duarte** (Mon–Fri 9am–1pm & 2–6pm, Sat & Sun 10am–1pm & 2–6pm; 250$00), devoted to the eminent sculptor; and, alongside, the much better **Museu da Cerâmica** (Tues–Sun 10am–12.30pm & 2–5pm; 250$00), which contains some of the original work of local potter and caricaturist Rafael Bordalo Pinheiro – look for his series of life-sized ceramic figures representing the Passion. Indeed, Caldas remains famed for its traditional ceramics (including peculiar phallus-shaped objects) and the **Feira Nacional da Cerâmica** is held here during July or October in the *Expooeste*, an industrial part of town, northwest of the railway tracks.

Practicalities

It's a short walk from either the **bus** or **train station** to **Praça da República**, where you'll find the summer **turismo** (Mon–Fri 9am–7pm, Sat & Sun 10am–1pm & 3–7pm; ☎062/83 10 03); the main turismo (same hours & ☎) is open all year and is situated next to the town hall in Praça 25 de Abril.

Accommodation

Due to the presence of the spa, there's a fair amount of **accommodation** around town, most of it reasonably priced. There's also an *Orbitur* **campsite** (☎062/83 23 67; closed Dec), centrally located by the park – a lovely place with a boating lake.

Caldas Internacional Hotel, Rua Dr. Figueirõa Rêgo 45 (☎062/83 23 07). The smartest option in town, if unexciting. ⑤.

Pensão Central, Largo Dr. José Barbosa (☎062/83 19 14). A pleasant choice and the birthplace of painter José Malhoa. Breakfast included. ③.

Pensão Residencial Estremadura, Largo Dr. José Barbosa 23 (☎062/83 23 13). Central, but somewhat rundown for the price. ③.

Residencial Europeia, Rua Almirante Cândido dos Reis 64 (☎062/83 15 08). Another central, smart choice with heavy wooden furniture, TVs and a bar. ④.

Pensão Portugal, Rua Almirante Cândido dos Reis 24 (☎062/83 27 87). A long-standing favourite on a busy pedestrianized shopping street. ④.

Residencial Rainha D. Leonor, Hermicício João Paulo II, 9 (☎062/84 21 71). A big, modern, soulless block but with satellite TV, private parking and all mod cons. ④.

Eating and drinking

For **food**, it's hard to beat the spit-roasts and grills at the *Zé do Barrete,* at Trav. da Cova da Onça 16–18 (☎062/83 27 87; closed Sun), midway down Rua Almirante Cândido dos Reis. There are several other good restaurants along this street, as well as the *Pensão Portugal* which serves pretty substantial meals. *Populus* (closed Mon), on the edge of the park at Rua de Camões, has lovely outdoor seating and serves up good salads and beef dishes at moderate prices. You may also be tempted to visit *Supatra* (☎062/84 29 20; closed Mon), 1km out on Rua General Amílcar Mota (the Óbidos road) – an unlikely setting for one of the country's most respected Thai restaurants. The cafés around Largo Rainha D. Leonor are a good bet for an evening **drink**, and also for sampling the local, rather sickly, sweets, such as *trouxas de ovos.*

North to Nazaré

Heading **north from Caldas**, buses and trains loop inland, touching the coast only at São Martinho do Porto, 13km south of Nazaré. However, if you have your own transport, you can bear northwest from Caldas along the N360, which takes you past the tranquil **Lagoa de Óbidos**, and then out along the coast via Foz do Arelho on a beautiful clifftop route – a much better option than the busy N8.

Foz do Arelho

At **FOZ DO ARELHO**, 9km from Caldas and the first resort you come to, there's a fine beach and a lagoon where you can swim. There are a few decent **places to stay**: the modern *Penedo Furado* (☎062/97 96 10; ④); the upmarket but not always welcoming *Foz Praia* (☎062/97 94 13; ⑤), complete with pool, tennis courts and restaurant; and, 1km before the village and only 500m from the lake, the *Quinta da Foz* (☎062/97 93 69; ⑥) – a lovely sixteenth-century country house hotel with just five rooms. Good seafood **restaurants** can be found behind the beach, while *Dreamer's* nightclub, at the northern end of the beach, is the place to head for after dark.

São Martinho do Porto

SÃO MARTINHO DO PORTO is the main resort between Peniche and Nazaré, and one of the more developed spots along the Estremaduran coast, though at least most of the new building is relatively low-rise. In high season, it's probably not worth the struggle to find a room – or even a place in the campsite.

The reason for São Martinho's tourist success is its **beach**: a vast sweep of sand which curls around a landlocked bay to form a natural swimming pool. This shelter makes it one of the warmest places to swim on the west coast, with the sands sloping down into calm, shallow, solar-heated water. For something more bracing – or less crowded – there's a good northern beach, beyond the bay. Beware of the Atlantic beaches beyond the bay; they can be dangerous.

Check with the **turismo**, at the far end of Avenida 25 de Abril (summer Mon–Fri 9am–7pm, Sat & Sun 9am–1pm & 3–6pm; winter Mon–Fri 10am–1pm & 3–6pm; ☎062/98 91 10), about the possibility of accommodation in **private rooms**. Alternatively, try one of the following: *Pensão Americana,* Rua D. José Saldanha 2 (☎062/98 91 70; ④), a popular place two blocks from the seafront, which also rents out mountain bikes; *Pensão Carvalho,* Rua Miguel Bombarda 6

(☎062/98 96 05; ⑤), slightly nearer to the beach and with a good restaurant; or *Residencial Concha*, Largo Vitorino Froís (☎062/98 92 20; ⑥), a comfortable place some of whose rooms have satellite TV and balconies. There's also a **campsite**, *Colina do Sol* (☎062/98 97 64), 2km to the north, off the Nazaré road (N242), and a **youth hostel** (☎062/99 95 06), 4km away and further inland at Alfeizerão, off the Caldas da Rainha/Alcobaça road (N8).

Eating is best done at the restaurants attached to the *Americana* or *Carvalho pensões*. Other good options include: *A Cave*, Rua Conde de Avalar (closed Wed); *O Largo* at Largo Vitorino Froís 21; or the *Café Baia*, Rua Vasco da Gama, behind the turismo. After that, look into the *Discoteca Bonnie*, near the *Residencial Concha*, open every night from midnight and with a disco at weekends open until 6am.

Nazaré

After years of advertising itself as the most picturesque seaside village in Portugal, **NAZARÉ** has finally more or less destroyed itself in the process. In summer, the crowds are way too much for the place to cope with, and the enduring characteristics are not so much "gentle traditions" as trinket stalls and high prices. That said, local traditions are still just about managing to coexist with tourism – you'll see women weaving barefoot through the town bearing immense trays of fish on their heads, and a few fishermen sitting unperturbed on the beach, mending their nets beside brilliantly painted sardine boats. However, most of the boats have disappeared to a new harbour, fifteen minutes' walk from the village, where cranes have replaced the oxen once used to haul them in.

The village and beaches

The original settlement was not at Nazaré but at Sítio, 110m up the rock face above the present sprawl of holiday apartment buildings, a location that was, by most accounts, the legacy of pirate raids which continued well into the nineteenth century. However, legend has a different explanation, telling of a twelfth-century knight, Dom Fuas Roupinho, who, while out hunting, was led up the cliff by a deer. The deer dived off into the void and Dom Fuas was saved from following by the timely vision of **Nossa Senhora da Nazaré**, in whose name a church was subsequently built.

You can reach this church, and the surrounding Sítio district, by a **funicular**, which rumbles up and down almost continuously from 7am to midnight (85$00). There is an enjoyable *miradouro* at the top, though the shrine itself is unimpressive, despite an icon carved by Saint Joseph and painted by Saint Luke (a handy partnership active throughout Europe). The church does, however, host a well-attended **romaria** (Sept 8–10) with processions, folk dancing, and bullfights. The Sítio bullring also stages Saturday night *touradas* in summer.

Back down below, the area between the funicular and Praça Dr. Manuel de Arriaga retains an old-world charm which the seafront has all but lost. But the main disadvantage of staying in Nazaré is that its **beaches** – grand, tent-studded sweeps of clean sand, stretching out to the north beyond the headland of Sítio, and south across the narrow Alcôa estuary – are dangerous for swimming. The Atlantic can be fierce along the Estremaduran coast, so, for safety's sake, stick to the patrolled main beach where the bathers are packed in as tightly as the sardine boats. Alternatively, tramp southwards towards the village of Gralha, where you'll find a number of small coves and one sheltered beach isolated enough to be a popular spot for nude bathing.

Practicalities

Using public transport, it's simplest to arrive at Nazaré by bus. There are regular connections with most towns in the region, and the **bus station** is centrally located, halfway down Avenida Vieira Guimarães, which meets the main drag, Avenida da República, at right angles at the foot of the hill. The nearest **train station** is at Valado, 6km inland, on the Alcobaça road; buses from Alcobaça call there on the way into town.

Avenida da República runs the length of the beach and is where you'll find most of the hotels and restaurants, as well as the **turismo** (daily: July & Aug 10am–10pm; Sept–June 10am–1pm & 3–7pm; ☎062/56 11 94), near the funicular. There's a second office on Rua Mouzinho de Albuquerque, up the hill and near the town hall, but neither is particularly enterprising.

Accommodation

Pensões in Nazaré are heavily booked throughout the summer but **rooms** are plentiful and you'll be accosted by their owners at the bus station – expect to pay around 4500$00 in high season. If you have problems finding a place, consult one of the turismos, which hold lists of available rooms. The more promising *pensão* and hotel possibilities are listed below. There's a **campsite** at Valado (☎062/56 11 11; closed mid-Nov to mid-Jan), near the train station, and another – the well-equipped *Vale Paraíso* (☎062/56 18 00) – nestling in pine woods 2km out of town on the road to Marinha Grande (N242), complete with pool and bikes for rent.

Residencial Beira-Mar, Avda. da República 40 (☎062/56 13 58). Right on the beachfront and very pleasant, with large breezy rooms (some with sea views) and private bathrooms; the price includes breakfast. Closed Nov–Feb. ⑤.

Quinta do Campo, Valado dos Frades (☎062/57 71 35, fax 57 75 55). Situated in a tranquil setting 6km inland, this *quinta* was founded as an agricultural college by monks in the fourteenth century and makes an excellent base if you have your own transport. The building is set in extensive grounds and offers various sports facilities including a pool and tennis courts. ⑥.

Pensão Central, Rua Mouzinho de Albuquerque 85 (☎062/55 15 10). Old and well-managed; book in advance if you can. The rooms facing the courtyard are best. Breakfast included. ④.

Residencial Cubata, Avda. da República 6 (☎062/56 17 06). A great position and good value if you can get a sea view. It's between the turismo and the foot of the funicular. ④.

Pensão Europa, Praça Dr. Manuel de Arriaga 24 (☎062/55 15 36). Bright but cramped rooms (which can be noisy) in the smaller of the two squares opening on to Avenida da República. There's a restaurant at street level. ③.

Residencial Marina, Rua Mouzinho de Albuquerque 6 (☎062/55 15 41). Down the street from the *Central*, this is a good-value, cheerful choice. ④.

Hotel de Nazaré, Largo Afonso Zuquete (☎062/56 13 11). Upmarket choice with small rooms, simply furnished. The views from the upper floors are splendid, and even better from the rooftop terrace. Closed Jan. ⑥.

Pensão Restaurante Ribamar, Rua Gomes Freire 9 (☎062/551 58). Across the road from the turismo, with some rooms overlooking the beach. The bathrooms are tiled with azulejos and breakfast is included in the price. ⑤.

Eating and drinking

The main concentration of **restaurants and cafés** is along Avenida da República and the several squares off the avenue. Places worth trying include:

Aquário, Largo das Caldeiras 13. Moderately priced and one of the best of a cluster of places in this pretty square with outdoor tables.

Carlota e Catarina, Rua Adrião Batalha 162. Good seafood served in an agreeable setting and at reasonable prices, but it's quite a climb to get there.

Casa do Largo, Avda. da República. A pretty café and the perfect seafront spot for tea, breakfast or just a beer.

Casa Lazaro, Rua Adrião Batalho. Good-value seafood and excellent house wine in tiled surroundings by the seafront.

O Casalinho, Praça Sousa Oliveira 6. Popular with locals which is recommendation enough for its fish and meat dishes. Service is with a smile and prices are moderate.

Pôr do Sol, Avda. da República 54. Expensive but top-quality seafood overlooking the beach.

Alcobaça

The Cistercian monastery at **ALCOBAÇA** was founded in 1153 by Dom Henrique to celebrate his victory over the Moors at Santarém six years earlier. Building started soon after, and by the end of the thirteenth century it was the most powerful monastery in the country. Owning vast tracts of farmland, orchards and vineyards, it was immensely rich and held jurisdiction over a dozen towns and three seaports. Its church and cloister are the purest and the most inspired creation of all Portuguese Gothic architecture and, alongside Belém and Batalha, are the most impressive monuments in the country. The church is also the burial place of those romantic figures of Portuguese history, Dom Pedro and Dona Inês de Castro.

Aside from the monastery, the only other point of interest in Alcobaça is the **Museu do Vinho** (daily 8.30am–12.30pm & 2–5.30pm; free), ten minutes' walk from the bus station out on the Leiria road, which gives a fascinating glimpse into the area's wine-making and agricultural past. There are free guided tours, which last about an hour, and you get the chance to purchase some of the local produce.

The Mosteiro de Alcobaça

The **Mosteiro de Alcobaça** (daily: April–Sept 9am–7pm; Oct–March 9am–5pm; 400$00), although empty since its dissolution in 1834, still seems to assert power, magnificence and opulence. And it takes little imagination to people it again with the monks, said once to have numbered 999. Mass was once celebrated here without interruption, but it was the residents' legendary extravagant and aristocratic lifestyles that formed the common ingredients of the awed anecdotes of eighteenth-century travellers.

Even William Beckford, no stranger to high living, found their decadence unsettling, growing weary of "perpetual gormandising . . . the fumes of banquets and incense . . . the fat waddling monks and sleek friars with wanton eyes, twanging away on the Jew's harp". Another contemporary observer, Richard Twiss, for his part found "the bottle went as briskly about as ever I saw it do in Scotland" – a tribute indeed. For all the "high romps" and luxuriance, though, it has to be added that the monks enjoyed a reputation for hospitality, generosity and charity, while the surrounding countryside is to this day one of the most productive areas in Portugal, thanks to their agricultural expertise.

The abbey church

The main **Abbey Church**, modelled on the original Cistercian abbey at Citeaux in France, is the largest in Portugal. External impressions are disappointing, as the Gothic facade has been superseded by unexceptional Baroque additions of the seventeenth and eighteenth centuries. Inside, however, all later adornments have been swept away, restoring the narrow soaring aisles to their original vertical simplicity. The only exception to this Gothic purity is the frothy Manueline doorway to the sacristy, hidden directly behind the high altar, and, as at Tomar and Batalha, encrusted with intricate, swirling motifs of coral and seaweed.

The church's most precious treasures are the fourteenth-century **tombs of Dom Pedro and Dona Inês de Castro**, each occupying one of the transepts and sculpted with phenomenal wealth of detail. Animals, heraldic emblems, musicians and biblical scenes are all portrayed in an architectural setting of miniature windows, canopies, domes and towers; most graphic of all is a dragon-shaped Hell's mouth at Inês's feet, consuming the damned. The tombs are inscribed with the motto "Até ao Fim do Mundo" (Until the End of the World) and in accordance with Dom Pedro's orders have been placed foot to foot so that on the Day of Judgement the pair may rise and immediately feast their eyes on one another.

Pedro's earthly love for Inês de Castro, the great theme of epic Portuguese poetry, was cruelly stifled by high politics. Inês, as the daughter of a Galician nobleman, was a potential source of Spanish influence over the Portuguese throne and Pedro's father, Afonso IV, forbade their marriage. The ceremony took place nevertheless – secretly at Bragança in remote Trás-os-Montes – and eventually Afonso was persuaded to sanction his daughter-in-law's murder. When Pedro succeeded to the throne in 1357 he brought the murderers to justice, personally ripping out their hearts and gorging his love-crazed appetite for blood upon them. More poignantly, he also exhumed and crowned the corpse of his lover, forcing the entire royal circle to acknowledge her as queen by kissing her decomposing hand.

The kitchen

From one highlight to another. Beckford – Romantic dilettante that he was – stood bewildered by the charms of these tombs when "in came the Grand Priors hand in hand, all three together. 'To the *kitchen*,' said they in unison, 'to the kitchen and that immediately.' " They led him past the fourteenth-century Chapter House to a cavernous room in the corner of the cloisters – a route that you can follow.

Alcobaça's feasting has already been mentioned but this **kitchen** – with its cellars and gargantuan conical chimney, supported by eight trunk-like iron columns – sets it in real perspective. A stream tapped from the River Alcôa still runs straight through the room: it was not used only for cooking and washing but also to provide a constant supply of fresh fish, which plopped out into a stone basin. At the centre of the room, on the vast wooden tables, Beckford continued to marvel at:

pastry in vast abundance which a numerous tribe of lay brothers and their attendants were rolling out and puffing up into a hundred different shapes, singing all the while as blithely as larks in a cornfield. "There," said the Lord Abbot, "we shall not starve. God's bounties are great, it is fit we should enjoy them."

And enjoy them they did, with a majestic feast of "rarities and delicacies, potted lampreys, strange Brazilian messes, edible birds' nests and sharks' fins dressed after the mode of Macau by a Chinese lay brother"! As a practical test for obesity the monks had to file through a narrow door on their way to the **refectory**; those who failed were forced to fast until they could squeeze through.

The cloisters and Sala dos Reis

The **Claustro do Silencio** (Cloisters of Silence), notable for their traceried stone windows, were built in the reign of Dom Dinis, the "poet-king" who established an enduring literary and artistic tradition at the abbey. An upper storey of twisted columns and Manueline arches was added in the sixteenth century, along with, in its standard position opposite the refectory, a beautiful hexagonal lavatory.

The **Sala dos Reis** (Kings' Room), off the cloister, displays statues of virtually every king of Portugal up until Dom José, who died in 1777. Blue eighteenth-century azulejos depict the siege of Santarém, Dom Afonso's vow, and the founding of the monastery. Also on show here is a piece of war booty which must have warmed the souls of the brothers – the huge metal cauldron in which soup was heated up for the Spanish army before the battle of Aljubarrota in 1385 (for more of which, see "Batalha" on p.157).

The rest of the monastery, including four other cloisters, seven dormitories and endless corridors, is closed to the public; parts of it are currently occupied by an old people's home. For the best overall view of the monastery, make your way to the ruined hilltop **castle**, about five minutes' walk away.

Practicalities

Though Alcobaça itself is not a hive of activity, it's not a bad place to stay. A useful first stop is the **turismo** (daily: summer 10am–6pm; winter 10am–1pm & 3–6pm; ☎062/423 77) on the central Praça 25 de Abril, opposite the monastery. It can supply maps of the town and advise on accommodation and transport. The **bus station** is five minutes' walk from the centre of town, across the bridge; coming into town, bear right and head towards the abbey towers. There are reasonably frequent connections to Nazaré and Leiria.

Accommodation

Alcobaça has a scattering of inexpensive **pensões and hotels**, just off Praça 25 de Abril. The local **campsite** (☎062/422 65) is some ten minutes' walk north of the bus station, on Avda. Manuel da Silva Carolina, near the covered market; there are some trees for shade, but the ground here is hard and barren.

Challet Fonte Nova Palacete, Estrada da Fonte Nova (☎062/59 83 00). This upmarket option is located in a restored palace built in 1861. ⑤.

Pensão Corações Unidos, Rua Frei António Brandão 39, just off the main square (☎062/421 42). Big but rather dark rooms, some overlooking an internal courtyard. The restaurant below is well thought of. ③.

Residencial Mosteiro, Avda. João de Deus 1 (☎062/421 83). On the corner of Rua Frei Estevão Martins and just up from the turismo, this has airy rooms, some with bathrooms and pleasant balconies. Price includes breakfast. It also has two restaurants – the one in the basement is a noisy *taberna típica* seating 180, which, nevertheless, fills up at weekends. ②.

Hotel Santa Maria, Rua Dr. Francisco Zagalo (☎062/59 73 95). A modern hotel facing the monastery and with all mod cons. Rooms at the front have good views. ④.

Eating

In addition to the **restaurants** at the various *pensões*, you could consider eating at the *Celeiro dos Frades* ("monks' barn"), on Arco de Cister under the arches alongside the abbey, where you can dine well for around 2000$00, or just enjoy a coffee in its atmospheric café. *Restaurante O Telheiro*, Rua da Levadinha (closed Sat), up the road beyond the *Hotel Santa Maria*, is more expensive but has great views over the abbey. Also worth a try is the huge *Frie Bernardo* on Rua D. Pedro V 17–19, which seats 180 and serves the sort of meals you need to fast after, and at moderate prices – albeit geared to tourists.

Leiria

A royal castle hangs almost vertically above the large town of **LEIRIA**, whose graceful old town is a place of cobbled streets, attractive gardens, and fine old squares, once you penetrate its drab modern outskirts. If you are travelling around on public transport, you will probably want to make it your base for a couple of nights, as the three big sites of northern Estremadura – Alcobaça, Batalha and

Fátima – all make easy day excursions by bus. Not so easy, but still quite feasible, are day-trips to Porto de Mós and the caves of Mira de Aire, Alvados and Santo António (see p.162); or to São Pedro de Muel and the coast (see p.156). Leiria also has enough restaurants, bars and nightlife to keep the evenings occupied, with most of the bars being concentrated around the lively Largo Cândido dos Reis.

Leiria's **Castelo** (daily: April–Sept 9am–6.30pm; Oct–March 9am–5.30pm; 135$00) was one of the most important strongholds in Moorish Portugal, reconquered by Afonso Henriques as he fought his way south in 1135. The actual building you see today dates mostly from the fourteenth and eighteenth centuries. Within its walls stands a royal palace, with a magnificent balcony high above the Rio Lis. Leiria was the main residence of Dom Dinis, who gave the town to his beloved Queen Isabel along with Óbidos, Abrantes, Porto de Mós and Trancoso. The walls also contain the **Church of Nossa Senhora da Penha**, erected by João I in about 1400 and now reduced to an eerie, roofless shell. If you have small children with you, beware: there are several precipitous, unguarded points among the buildings and staircases. Nearby, on Largo de Sé, is the town's sixteenth-century **Cathedral**, which was built under the reign of Dom João III and has three naves. It was designed by Afonso Alvares, who worked on the São Roque in Lisbon.

At the heart of the old town is **Praça Rodrigues Lobo**, surrounded by beautiful arcaded buildings and dominated by a splendidly pompous statue of the eponymous seventeenth-century local poet. In fact, Leiria's literary connections go back much further than this – in 1480, the town had one of Portugal's first printing presses, which was run by Jews who printed in Hebrew.

Practicalities

Arriving by **bus**, you'll be dropped at a modern terminal at the near end of Avenida Heróis de Angola, but with another entrance on Praça Paulo VI. Across the Jardim Luís de Camões, on Praça Goa Damão e Dio, is the very helpful **turismo** (May–Sept Mon–Fri 9am–7pm, Sat & Sun 10am–1pm & 3–7pm; closes at 6pm in winter; ☎044/81 47 48), which dispenses maps. The **train station** is 4km north of town – a cheap taxi ride away.

Accommodation

For **accommodation**, make your way to Praça Rodrigues Lobo and look around the restaurants and *pensões* both here and on the narrow side streets: try Rua Mestre de Aviz and Rua Miguel Bombarda. Other cheap rooms are to be found in Largo Paio Guterres and Largo Cónego Maia, both near the cathedral. There's also a very well-appointed **youth hostel** – one of the most enjoyable in the country – at Largo Cândido dos Reis 7 (☎044/318 68).

Pensão Alcôa, Rua Rodrigues Cordeiro 24–26 (☎044/326 90). Smallish but good-value rooms with TVs. Price includes breakfast. There's a good restaurant, too. ④.

Pensão Berlinga, Rua Miguel Bombarda 3 (☎044/82 38 46). Just off Praça Rodrigues Lobo; look for the sign in the corner of the square. A big, rambling, friendly place. ③.

Residencial Dom Dinis, Trav. de Tomar 2 (☎044/81 53 42). Across the bridge from the turismo and up a steep side road. A modern, popular place with a pleasant roof-terrace and parking. ④.

Pensão Residencial Leirense, Rua Afonso de Albuquerque 6 (☎044/320 61). A firm favourite for some years that offers good value for money. It's very central and breakfast is included. ④.

Pensão Lis, Largo Alexandre Herculano 10–13 (☎044/81 40 17). Fairly central, near the bridge by the turismo. Good value, with breakfast included. ④.

Residencial Ramalhete, Rua Dr. Correia Mateus 30 (☎044/81 28 02). An efficiently run place; the rooms at the rear are quieter. ④.

Hotel São Luís, Rua Henrique Sommer (☎044/81 31 97). Good value and a good location, albeit out of the centre. Breakfast included. ④.

Eating and drinking

September is the best time to sample the region's cuisine, when the **Festival of Gastronomy** fills up the Mercado Santana with row upon row of food stalls. The best place for a **drink** and a snack is at one of the **cafés** or **bars** around Largo Cândido dos Reis which also give you the chance to take in Leiria's lively streetlife – try *Bar Estrebaria* at no. 23, or *Bar Santo Estevão* at Trav. da Paz 9. Alternatively, the *Galeria Bar*, Quinta de Santo António 43, is worth a visit. **Eating** options include:

Restaurante Aquário, Rua Mouzinho de Albuquerque 17, on a side street running off Jardim Luís de Camões. There's a good *ementa turística* here for around 2000$00 but you could eat for less, especially if you sit at the bar. Closed Thurs.

Pastelaria Arcadia, Praça Rodrigues Lobo. Under the arches in the main square and a good place to enjoy breakfast or a tea stop at the outdoor tables.

Jardim, Jardim Luís de Camões. Nice position overlooking the river and the park, serving inexpensive seafood and other specialities; popular with students. Closed Mon.

Restaurante Montecarlo, Rua Dr. Correia Mateus 32–34. The best on this street – you can eat for under 1000$00 if you have a *meia dose*, which should be sufficient.

Tromba Rija, Rua Professores Portelas 22 (☎044/85 64 21). Real Portuguese cuisine – expensive, but worth every penny – can be found out of town on the Marrazes road; go under the N1 and take a left turning after the *Casa da Palmeira*. Closed Sun, Mon lunch & Aug.

The Pinhal de Leiria and its beaches

Some of the most idyllic spots on the stretch of coast west of Leiria are in the **Pinhal de Leiria** (or Pinhal do Rei), a vast 700-year-old pine forest stretching from São Pedro de Muel to Pedrógão. Although there were always trees here, the "Royal Pine Forest" was planned by Dom Dinis, a king renowned for his agrarian reforms, to protect fertile arable land from the menacing inward march of sand dunes. It has since grown into an area of great natural beauty, with sunlight filtering through endless miles of trees and the air perfumed with the scent of resin. The turismo at Marinha Grande, halfway between Leiria and the coast, can supply maps of the forest if you want to make your way through its grid-like tracks on foot.

The **beaches**, for the most part, are superb, and currently the sea is free of pollution from Paredes da Vitória, 12km south of São Pedro de Muel, to Leirosa, 11km south of Figueira da Foz.

São Pedro de Muel

The nearest beach to Leiria is at **SÃO PEDRO DE MUEL**, 22km to the west, where development has remained low-key. Many buildings have been renovated or built in the old style with attractive wooden balconies, making it a pleasant place to stay, though the town gets very busy in high season. If the sea is too fierce to swim in you can try one of the swimming pools situated surreally above the beach.

Buses from Leiria involve a change at Marinha Grande, about halfway, but even out of season there's a bus each way every two hours or so. If you wish to stay, **accommodation** – even in high season – should be no problem, since there are more than a dozen *pensões* and hotels. The seasonal **turismo** (☎044/59 91 52), at the top of the village by the post office, should be able to help. Otherwise, try *Residencial Perola do Oceano* (☎044/59 91 57; ③) in Trav. Antigos Armazens, which is virtually on the seafront; it has a large annexe up the hill, too. Next door, *A Fonte* restaurant (☎044/59 94 79; ③) also has good-value rooms. There are two **campsites**, north of the village. The nearer is the *Orbitur* site (☎044/59 91 68), which can get packed; further out but less expensive is the *Inatel* (☎044/59 92 89; closed mid-Dec to mid-Jan).

Excellent **restaurants** abound, among them the *Brisamar*, Rua Dr. Nicolau Bettencourt, and *A Forte*, on Praçeta Afonso Lopes Vieira, both of which specialize in seafood, and the upmarket *A Concha*, Rua Duquesa de Caminha 16 (closed Thurs). However, for sunsets and sea views *Estrela do Mar* (closed Thurs in winter) is hard to beat, situated right above the town beach. For breakfast, try *Café Central* on Rua Dr. Alfonso Leitão, where you can relax on wicker chairs outside.

South of São Pedro, too, you can find sheltered stretches of beach – especially around **PAREDES DA VITÓRIA**, 6km to the south and popular with the Portuguese for camping wild – though here you're no longer in the forest. Another quiet spot is **AGUA DE MADEIROS**, 3km south, where the smart *Residencial Água de Madeiros* sits above the wild, often deserted beach (☎ 044/59 93 24; ⑤).

Praia Velha, Praia da Vieira and Pedrógoã

A couple of kilometres north of the lighthouse at São Pedro, **PRAIA VELHA** is a popular local resort, mainly because of the chance to swim in its small lake, though it can get littered in summer. There's no accommodation but some great restaurants; *O Pai dos Frangos* has won awards – try its amazing mixed kebabs.

Ten kilometres to the north of Velha, **PRAIA DA VIEIRA** and the main town of **VIEIRA DE LEIRIA** (the latter 3km inland) are on the estuary of the Rio Liz and are notable for their fish restaurants. Praia de Vieira is served by a patchy bus service from Marinha Grande and has grown into quite an unattractive modern resort, though it does have a great beach. Of the several *residenciais*, try first the *Ouro Verde* (☎044/69 59 31; ④) or the *Estrela do Mar* (☎044/69 57 62; ④). Alternatively, the seasonal **turismo** (☎044/69 52 30) can recommend places to stay. Among the resort's several **restaurants** is the excellent *Solemar,* on Rua José Botas (☎044/69 54 04).

PEDRÓGOÃ, 6km further to the north, also has a rash of modern development spread around another fantastic expanse of beach, which is still used by fishermen to launch their high-prowed boats. There's a great **campsite** (☎044/69 54 03; closed mid-Dec to Jan) in the woods, while in town there are several restaurants and a seasonal **turismo** (July & Aug Tues–Sun 10am–1pm & 3–7pm; ☎044/69 54 11), which can give information about private **rooms**.

Batalha and around

Eleven kilometres south of Leiria, the Mosteiro de Santa Maria da Vitória, better known as **BATALHA** (Battle Abbey), is the supreme achievement of Portuguese architecture – the dazzling richness and originality of its Manueline decoration rivalled only by the Mosteiro dos Jerónimos at Belém, with which it shares UNESCO world monument status. An exuberant symbol of national pride, it was built to commemorate the battle that sealed Portugal's independence after decades of Spanish intrigue.

With the death of Dom Fernando in 1383, the royal house of Burgundy died out, and in its wake there followed a period of feverish factional plotting over the Portuguese throne. Fernando's widow, Leonor Teles, had a Spanish lover even during her husband's lifetime, and when Fernando died she betrothed her daughter, Beatriz, to Juan I of Castile, encouraging his claim to the Portuguese throne. João, Mestre de Aviz, Fernando's illegitimate stepbrother, also claimed the throne. He assassinated Leonor's lover and braced himself for the inevitable invasion from Spain. The two armies clashed on August 14, 1385, at the **Battle of Aljubarrota**, which despite its name was actually fought at São Jorge, 10km northeast of Aljubarrota and just 4km south of present-day Batalha (see p.160). Faced with seemingly impossible odds, João struck a deal with the Virgin Mary, promising to build a magnificent abbey in return for her military assistance. It worked: Nuno Álvares Pereira led the Portuguese forces to a memorable victory and the new king duly summoned the finest architects of the day.

Today, however, the abbey is rattled by the N1 highway from Lisbon to Coimbra which runs across an embankment perilously close to the abbey and is gradually altering the structure as vibrations and fumes take their toll. There is talk of "moving" the road, though no plans have yet been forthcoming. Furthermore, the abbey is showing its age: built largely of limestone, it's being increasingly affected by acid rain.

The Abbey

The honey-coloured **Abbey** (daily: April–Sept 9am–6pm; Oct–March 9am–5pm; 400$00; free on Sunday morning) was transformed by the uniquely Portuguese Manueline additions of the late fifteenth and early sixteenth centuries, but the bulk of the building was completed between 1388 and 1434 in a profusely ornate version of French Gothic. Pinnacles, parapets, windows and flying buttresses are all lavishly and intricately sculpted. Within this flamboyant framework there are also strong elements of the English Perpendicular style. Huge pilasters and prominent vertical decorations divide the main facade; the nave, with its narrow soaring dimensions, and the chapter house, are reminiscent of church architecture in the English cathedral cities of Winchester and York.

The Capela do Fundador

Medieval architects were frequently attracted by lucrative foreign commissions, but there is a special explanation for the English influence at Batalha. This is revealed in the **Capela do Fundador** (Founder's Chapel), directly to the right upon entering the church. Beneath the octagonal lantern rests the joint tomb of Dom João I and Philippa of Lancaster, their hands clasped in the ultimate expression of harmonious relations between Portugal and England.

In 1373, Dom Fernando had entered into an alliance with John of Gaunt, Duke of Lancaster, who claimed the Spanish throne by virtue of his marriage to a daughter of Pedro the Cruel, king of Castile. A crack contingent of English longbowmen had played a significant role in the victory at Aljubarrota, and in 1386 both countries willingly signed the **Treaty of Windsor**, "an inviolable, eternal, solid, perpetual, and true league of friendship". As part of the same political package Dom João married Philippa, John of Gaunt's daughter, and with her came English architects to assist at Batalha. The alliance between the two countries, reconfirmed by the marriage of Charles II to Catherine of Bragança in 1661 and the Methuen Commercial Treaty of 1703, has become the longest-standing international friendship of modern times – it was invoked by the Allies in World War II to establish bases on the Azores, and the facilities of those islands were offered to the British Navy during the 1982 Falklands war.

The four younger sons of João and Philippa are buried along the south wall of the Capela do Fundador in a row of recessed arches. Second from the right is the **tomb of Prince Henry the Navigator**, who guided the discovery of Madeira, the Azores and the African coast as far as Sierra Leone. Henry himself never ventured further than Tangiers but it was a measure of his personal importance, drive and expertise that the growth of the empire was temporarily shelved after his death in 1460.

Concerted maritime exploration resumed under João II (1481–95) and accelerated with the accession of Manuel I (1495–1521). Vasco da Gama opened up the trade route to India in 1498, Cabral reached Brazil two years later and Newfoundland was discovered in 1501. The momentous era of burgeoning self-confidence, wealth and widening horizons is reflected in the peculiarly Portuguese style of architecture known (after the king) as Manueline. As befitted the great national shrine, Batalha was adapted to incorporate two masterpieces of the new order: the Royal Cloister and the so-called Unfinished Chapels.

The Claustro Real and Sala do Capítulo

In the **Claustro Real** (Royal Cloister), stone grilles of ineffable beauty and intricacy were added to the original Gothic windows by Diogo de Boitaca, architect of the cloister at Belém and the prime genius of Manueline art. Crosses of the Order of Christ and armillary spheres – symbols of overseas exploration – are entwined in a network of lotus blossom, briar branches and exotic vegetation.

Off the east side opens the early fifteenth-century **Sala do Capítulo** (Chapter House), remarkable for the audacious unsupported span of its ceiling – so daring, in fact, that the Church authorities were convinced that the whole chamber would come crashing down and employed criminals already condemned to death to build it. The architect, Afonso Domingues, could finally silence his critics only by sleeping in the chamber night after night. Soldiers now stand guard here over Portugal's **Tomb of the Unknown Warriors**, one killed in France during World War I, the other in the country's colonial wars in Africa. The **refectory**, on the opposite side of the cloister, houses a military museum in their honour. From here, a short passage leads into the **Claustro de Dom Afonso V**, built in a conventional Gothic style which provides a yardstick against which to measure the Manueline flamboyance of the Royal Cloister.

The Capelas Imperfeitas

The **Capelas Imperfeitas** (Unfinished Chapels) form a separate structure tacked on to the east end of the church and accessible only from outside the main complex. Dom Duarte, eldest son of João and Philippa, commissioned them in 1437 as a royal mausoleum but, as with the cloister, the original design was transformed beyond all recognition by Dom Manuel's architects. The portal rises to a towering fifteen metres and every centimetre is carved with a honeycomb of mouldings: florid projections, clover-shaped arches, strange vegetables; there are even stone snails. The place is unique among Christian architecture and evocative of the great shrines of Islam and Hinduism: perhaps it was inspired by the tales of Indian monuments that filtered back along the eastern trade routes. Although conveniently referred to as Manueline, it is really in a class by itself and illustrates the variety and uninhibited excitement of Portuguese art during the Age of Discovery.

The architect of this masterpiece was Mateus Fernandes, whose tomb lies directly outside the entrance to the Capela do Fundador. Within the portal, a large octagonal space is surrounded by seven hexagonal chapels, two of which contain the sepulchres of Dom Duarte and his queen, Leonor of Aragon. An ambitious upper storey – equal in magnificence to the portal – was designed by Diogo de Boitaca, but the huge buttresses were subsequently abandoned after a few years.

Practicalities

The Batalha stands alone, the huddle of cottages that once surrounded it swept away and replaced by a bare concrete expanse. There's a **turismo** (May–Sept Mon–Fri 10am–1pm & 3–7pm, Sat & Sun 10am–1pm & 3–6pm; ☎044/961 80), but not much else here except a sprinkling of tourist shops, bars and restaurants, which all do brisk business during the Fátima weekend in early October, when the place is packed. **Buses** stop on central Largo da Misericórdia.

Accommodation is limited and the best idea is to see Batalha on a day-trip from Leiria. If you do want to stay, try: *Casa do Outeiro*, Largo Carvalho 4 (☎044/968 06; ④), near the town hall, a charmingly converted small house with a swimming pool; *Residencial Batalha* on Largo da Misericórdia (☎044/76 75 00; ④), a modern, comfortable option; or, for leisured luxury, the *Pousada do Mestre Afonso Domingues*, Largo Mestre Afonso Domingues (☎044/962 61; ⑥), is impossible to better. For **food**, the meat and fish dishes are of good quality and moderate in price at *Boutaca* on Rua António Cândido da Encarnação (closed Sat & Sun evening).

Around Batalha

The busy N1 highway carries heavy traffic from Batalha to the small town of **São Jorge**, 4km to the south and site of one of Portugal's most important battles. Just beyond here the quieter N243 branches off to **Porto de Mós**, with its distinctive castle and the added attraction of being the nearest base from which to visit the fabulous **underground caves** at Mira de Aire, Alvados and Santo António – all of which lie within the wild and craggy Parque Natural das Serras de Aire e Candeeiros. The N362 provides an alternative scenic route through the park, running from Porto de Mós in the north all the way to Santarém, though the caves themselves are all located in the more wooded eastern half of the park

São Jorge: the battle site
The Battle of Aljubarrota was fought on a plain 10km northeast of Aljubarrota itself, at the small hamlet of **SÃO JORGE**, just 4km south of Batalha. When the fighting was over a **chapel** was built and it still stands today. The battle lasted only one hour, but it was a hot day and the commander of the victorious Portuguese

forces, Nuno Álvares Pereira, complained loudly of thirst; even today, a jug of fresh water is placed daily in the porch of the chapel in his memory. Legend has it that Aljubarrota itself was defended by its baker, Brites de Almeida, who fended off the Castilian army with her baking spoon. This fearsome weapon dispensed with seven soldiers, whom Brites then proceeded to bake in her oven.

Also in São Jorge, the **Museu Militar** (Tues–Fri 2–5pm, Sat & Sun 10am–noon & 2–5pm) deals with the battle itself and the contemporary political intrigue, while nearby there's a frieze commemorating the battle with carved blocks of stone representing, it is said, the archers and foot soldiers.

None of this is particularly any reason to come, though you can always break your journey here on the way to or from Porto de Mós (see below), 5km to the south; indeed, you may have to change buses in São Jorge anyway.

Porto de Mós

High above the expanding and uninspiring village of **PORTO DE MÓS**, 8km south of Batalha, a grandiose thirteenth-century **castle** stands guard. It was given to Nuno Álvares Pereira in 1385 by the grateful Dom João I in recognition of his victory at Aljubarrota – significantly, the Portuguese army had rested here on the eve of the battle – and was later turned into a fortified palace reminiscent in scale of that at Leiria. Severely damaged in the earthquake of 1755, the castle (Tues–Sun 8am–5pm; free) has been renovated piecemeal since then; four of its original five electric-green conical towers have been restored so far. Just below the castle is the town's small **archeology and geology museum**, (Tues–Sun 10am–12.30pm & 2–5.30pm), which boasts locally collected dinosaur bones amongst its displays.

The town's bus terminal is on Avenida Dr. Francisco Sá Carneiro. On weekdays, there are around three **buses to Porto de Mós** from Leiria, via Batalha, and others from Alcobaça, Santarém or from Batalha itself. At other times, you could catch one of the long-distance buses from Leiria or Batalha to Alcobaça or Caldas da Rainha and ask to be set down at São Jorge, just off the main N1, and take a local bus from there to Porto de Mós. The **turismo** (summer daily 10am–1pm & 3–7pm; winter Mon–Sat 10am–1pm & 3–6pm; ☎044/49 13 23) is in the Jardim Público, adjacent to the main Largo do Rossio. If you plan to stay, there are two **overnight** possibilities: the *Residencial O Filipe*, Largo do Rossio 41 (☎044/40 14 55; ③); and the *Quinta do Rio Alcaide* (☎044/40 21 24; ⑤), a converted mill around 1km out of the village on the road to the caves (the N243). Cafés and **restaurants** are grouped around the bus terminal.

The caves

The largest, most spectacular and most accessible caves in Portugal are the **GRUTAS DE MIRA DE AIRE** (daily: April–June & Sept 9.30am–6.30pm; July & Aug 9am–8pm; Oct–March 9.30am–6pm; 500$00; ☎044/44 03 22), ten minutes' walk from the bus stop in the drab textile town from which they take their name. There are three daily **buses** to Mira de Aire from Porto de Mós, at 12.05pm, 2.30pm and 5.20pm (2 daily on Sat & Sun at 8.05am & 9.35am), but note that the last one back from Mira de Aire is at around 5pm.

Known locally for years but only open to the public since 1974, the caves comprise a fantasy land of spaghetti-like stalactites and stalagmites and bizarre rock formations with names like "Hell's Door", "Jelly Fish" and "Church Organ". Rough steps take you down and the excellent 45-minute guided tour (in French or Portuguese, or even English on occasion) culminates in an extravagant fountain display in a natural lake 110m underground. You might have to wait some time for a group of acceptable size to gather. At the end of the tour, you emerge beside an aquatic park (summer only; use of its pools and slides is included in the entry fee for the caves), a great place to cool off and admire the views.

There are similar caves in open country near the hamlets of **ALVADOS** and **SANTO ANTÓNIO** (both daily: April–May 9.30am–6pm; June & Sept 9.30am–7pm; July & Aug 9.30am–8.30pm; Oct–March 9.30am–5.30pm; 500$00; ☎044/84 18 76). The three daily buses between Porto de Mós and Mira de Aire pass within 3km of Alvados and 7km of Santo António. Hitching along the main road is not too difficult but there's a good chance you'll have to walk part of the way.

Fátima and around

FÁTIMA is the fountainhead of religious devotion in Portugal and one of the most important centres of pilgrimage in the Roman Catholic world. Its cult is founded on a series of six **Apparitions of the Virgin Mary**, in the first of which, on May 13, 1917, three peasant children from the village were confronted, while tending their parents' flock, with a flash of lightning and "a lady brighter than the sun" sitting in the branches of a tree. According to the memoirs of Lúcia, who was the only one who could hear what was said – and the only one of the children to survive into her teens – the Lady announced, "I am from Heaven. I have come to ask you to return here six times, at this same hour, on the thirteenth of every month. Then, in October, I will tell you who I am and what I want."

News of the miracle was greeted with scepticism, and only a few casual onlookers attended the second appearance, but for the third, July 13, apparition, the crowd had swollen to a few thousand. Although only the three children could see the heavenly visitor, Fátima became a *cause célèbre*, with the anticlerical government accusing the Church of fabricating a miracle to revive its flagging influence, and Church authorities afraid to acknowledge what they feared was a hoax. The children were arrested and interrogated but refused to change their story.

By the date of the final appearance, October 13, as many as 70,000 people had converged on Fátima where they witnessed the so-called **Miracle of the Sun**. Eyewitnesses described the skies clearing and the sun, intensified to a blinding, swirling ball of fire, shooting beams of multicoloured light to earth. Lifelong illnesses, supposedly, were cured; the blind could see again and the dumb were able to speak. It was enough to convince most of the terrified witnesses. Nevertheless, the three children remained the only ones actually to see the Virgin, and only Lúcia could communicate with her.

To her were revealed the three **Secrets of Fátima**. The first was a message of peace (this was during World War I) and a vision of Hell, with anguished, charred souls plunged into an ocean of fire. The second was more prophetic and controversial: "If you pay heed to my request," the vision declared, "Russia will be converted and there will be peace. If not, Russia will spread her errors through the world, causing wars and persecution against the Church" – all this just a few weeks before the Bolshevik takeover in St Petersburg, though not, perhaps, before it could have been predicted. The **third secret** has never been divulged – it lies in a drawer of the pope's desk in the Vatican, read by successive popes on their accession but supposedly too horrible to be revealed, though the present incumbent has hinted that the day may not be far off when he will announce its contents. In 1984, an Irish priest tried to hijack an Aer Lingus plane in an attempt to persuade the Pope to reveal the secret, but the crisis was defused with no one any the wiser.

The Basilica and the Town

To commemorate the extraordinary events and to accommodate the hordes of pilgrims who flock here, a shrine has been built, which has little to recommend it but its size. The vast white **Basilica**, completed in 1953, and its gigantic esplanade are capable of holding more than a million devotees. In the church the **tombs of Jacinta and Francisco** – Lúcia's fellow witnesses, both of whom died in the European flu epidemic of 1919–20 – are the subject of constant attention in their chapels. Long Neoclassical colonnades flank the basilica and enclose part of the sloping esplanade in front. This huge area, reminiscent of an airport runway, is twice the size of the piazza of Saint Peter's in Rome. On its left-hand side the original oak tree in which the Virgin appeared was long ago consumed by souvenir-hunting pilgrims; the small **Chapel of the Apparitions** now stands in its place, with a new tree a few yards away.

Whatever your feelings about the place, there is an undeniable atmosphere of mystery around it, perhaps created by nothing more than the obvious faith of the vast majority of its visitors. It's all at its most intense during the great **annual pilgrimages** on May 12–13 and October 12–13. Crowds of up to 100,000 congregate, most arriving on foot, some even walking on their knees in penance. Open-air Mass is celebrated at 5am and an image of the Virgin is paraded by candlelight as priests move among the pilgrims hearing confessions. The fiftieth anniversary of the apparitions attracted one-and-a-half million worshippers, including Pope Paul VI and Lúcia – who is still alive, a Carmelite nun in the Convent of Santa Teresa near Coimbra. Lúcia was again part of the vast crowds that greeted John Paul II here in 1982 and 1991.

A multitude of hotels, car parks, hospices and convents have sprung up in the shadow of the basilica. Inevitably the fame of Fátima has resulted in its commercialization and some of the town's last surviving old houses and mansions are under threat of demolition to make way for further developments. (The latest plan is to build a covered area to shelter up to ten thousand people during open-air Mass.) As each year goes by, the grotesquely kitsch souvenirs on sale move into hitherto unexplored territories of taste – look out for the Fátima ballpoint pens, which tilt to reveal the Virgin in Glory. Business is particularly brisk on Sunday, when thousands of local families converge by bus, car, lorry and cart, often just for a family picnic – yet the shrine itself is not yet swamped. Make sure you catch the daily torchlit procession at dusk, which can be uplifting whatever your religious feelings; the procession is largest on the twelfth day of each month.

The town's other attractions include the **Museu de Cera** (Wax Museum) on Rua Jacinto Marto (April–Oct Mon–Sat 9.30am–6.30pm, Sun 9am–6.30pm; Nov–March Mon–Fri 10am–5pm, Sat & Sun 9am–5.30pm; 600$00), which relates the story of the miracle in 28 scenes filled with somewhat grotesque wax figures. There is also a pleasant walk from the Rotunda de Santa Teresa de Ourém, on the outskirts of town, up to the place of the "**Apparitions of the Angel**", along which pilgrims follow the Stations of the Cross.

Practicalities

There are regular **bus services** to Fátima from Leiria (25km to the northwest) and Tomar (35km east) making it an easy day-trip. Coming **from Batalha** (20km west) on the N356, you'll pass Reguengo do Fétal, another pilgrimage site that's host to a torchlit procession (lit by burning oil carried in shells) up to a hilltop sanctuary around October 3. If you arrive **by train**, you'll need to get a local bus (there's not always an immediate connection) from Estação de Fátima, a hefty 25km east of town; the station is on the main Lisbon–Porto line. The **turismo** (May–Oct Mon–Fri 9am–7pm, Sat & Sun 10am–1pm & 3–7pm; closes at 6pm in winter; ☎049/531 11 39) is just off the main esplanade on Avenida D. José Alves Correia da Silva.

Pensões and restaurants abound in Fátima, but during the pilgrimages (when most accommodation is booked up months in advance), people camp all around the back and sides of the basilica. However, outside the major pilgrimages – and weekends – there's enough **accommodation** to go round, since many of the older boarding houses are built on monastic lines, with over a hundred rooms and private chapels; the huge modern hotels which abound can be bargains in low season. Otherwise, try *Residencial Santo Amaro,* Rua Francisco Marto 59 (☎049/53 14 55; ②), with modern, comfortable rooms but away from the main area of restaurants and bars; *Residencial São Paulo*, Rua de São Paulo 10 (☎049/43 15 72; ②), another modern giant, but friendly and welcoming; or, best of all, *Irmãs Dominicanos*, Rua Francisco Monto 50 (☎049/53 33 17; ④), one of the few remaining attractive old buildings.

One of the best **restaurants** is *Santa Cruz*, on the corner of Rua Jacinto Mauro and Rua de São José, with a pleasant outlook and reasonably priced dishes. Other possibilities are *O Zé Grande*, Rua Jacinto Mauro 32, or *Restaurante O Truão*, 4km out of Fátima at Boleiros but worth the trip.

Grutas da Moeda

Six kilometres west of Fátima, the labyrinthine **Grutas da Moeda** (daily: April–Sept 9am–8pm; Oct–March 9am–6pm; 500$00; ☎044/903 02) at **SÃO MAMEDE** are well worth seeing, not least because one of the chambers has been converted into a bar with rock music, subtle lighting and stalactites nose-diving into your glass of beer. With haggling, you should be able to arrange a reasonably priced taxi, though you may have to wait for a group to form before you can enter the caves.

Ourém

If you have your own transport, you may prefer to visit Fátima from a base at **OURÉM**, 12km east, staying at *Pensão Ouriense*, Avda. D. Nuno Álvares Pereira (☎049/422 02; ②); plans are afoot to build a *pousada*. Although the new town, Vila Nova de Ourém, is nothing special, Ourém **castle** (Mon–Fri 8am–5pm, Sat & Sun 8am–noon & 1–5pm), is just 2km above it, sitting on a hilltop within an impressive medieval walled town. The town's heyday was in the fifteenth century, when the the fourth count of Ourém, Don Afonso, built several grand monuments and converted the castle into a palace. The castle was virtually destroyed by Napoleon's forces, but is now largely restored; walk around its parapet, and you'll get stunning views, with the basilica in Fátima to the west. The well-signed history trail round the old town will lead you to the **cisterns** (daily 3–6pm), which, according to local legend, have never run dry. Look out also for the fifteenth-century **fountain** by the town gates. The **turismo** in Praça do Município (daily 10am–1pm & 3–7pm; ☎049/421 94) can provide maps and point out the small **archeological museum** (Tues 1–6pm, Wed–Sun 10am–noon & 1–6pm; free).

Tomar

The Convento de Cristo at **TOMAR**, 34km east of Fátima, is an artistic *tour de force* which entwines the most outstanding military, religious and imperial strands in the history of Portugal. The Order of the Knights Templar and their successors, the Order of Christ, established their headquarters here and successive Grand Masters employed experts in Romanesque, Manueline and Renaissance architecture to embellish and expand the convent in a manner worthy of their power, prestige and wealth.

In addition, Tomar is an attractive town in its own right, well worth a couple of days of slow exploration. Built on a simple grid plan, it is split in two by the Rio Nabão, with almost everything of interest on the west bank. Here, Tomar's old quarters preserve all their traditional charm, with whitewashed, terraced cottages lining narrow cobbled streets. This pleasing backdrop is seen to best effect during Tomar's famous **Festa dos Tabuleiros**, held at intermittent intervals (see box on p.167), when the entire town takes to the streets.

The Town

On the central Praça da República stands an elegant seventeenth-century town hall, a ring of houses of the same period, and the Manueline church of **São João Baptista**, remarkable for its octagonal belfry, elaborate doorway, and six panels attributed to Gregório Lopes (c.1490–1550), one of Portugal's finest artists. Nearby at Rua Joaquim Jacinto 73 is an excellently preserved fifteenth-century synagogue, now the **Museu Luso-Hebraico Abraham Zacuto** (summer 9.30am–12.30pm & 2–6pm; winter 9.30am–12.30pm & 2–5pm; closed Wed; free), named after the Spanish astronomer, Abraham Zacuto, who prepared navigational aids for Vasco da Gama. The museum is particularly interesting in a town dominated for so long by crusading Defenders of the Faith, and its stark interior, with plain vaults supported by four slender columns, houses a collection of thirteenth- to fourteenth-century Hebraic inscriptions. In 1496 Dom Manuel followed the example of the Reis Católicos (Catholic Kings) of Spain and ordered the conversion or expulsion of all Portuguese Jews. The synagogue at Tomar was one of the very few to survive so far south – there's another at Castelo de Vide in the Alentejo (see p.417). Many Jews fled northwards, especially to Trás-os-Montes where Inquisitional supervision was less hawk-eyed.

Midway between the town and the Convento de Cristo, it's worth taking the time for a look around the unassumingly beautiful Renaissance church of **Nossa Senhora da Conceição** (daily 11am–noon). It is attributed to Diogo de Torralva, architect of the Convento's Great Cloisters. Also of interest is the town **market**, held on Fridays, just off Rua de Santa Iria, and the impressive seventeenth-century Pegões **aqueduct**, built to supply the convent with water; the best place

△ *Coimbra*

Bull Ring

ACCOMMODATION
- ❶ Estalagem de Santa Iria
- ❷ Residencial Luanda
- ❸ Pensão Bonjardim
- ❹ Residencial Sinagoga
- ❺ Residencial Luz
- ❻ Residencial União
- ❼ Pensão Tomarense
- ❽ Pensão Nun'Álvares
- ❾ Residencial Trovador

RESTAURANTS
- Ⓐ Parque das Merendas
- Ⓑ Restaurante Nabão
- Ⓒ Bela Vista
- Ⓓ Restaurante Piri-Piri
- Ⓔ Chez Nous

Campsite

Estadio Municipal

△ *Fatima, Leiria & Aquaduct (2 km)*

Disco Pim-Pim

Parque do Mouchão

Market

Rio Nabão

▽ *Santarém*

N.S. da Conceição

Castelo dos Templários

Câmara Municipal

São João Baptista

Museu Luso-Hebraico

S. Francisco (Match Museum)

Train Station

Bus Station

VARZEA GRANDE

TOMAR

Convento de Cristo

0 ___ 200 m

N

THE FESTA DOS TABULEIROS

Tomar is renowned throughout the country for its **Festa dos Tabuleiros** (literally, the Festival of the Trays). Its origins can be traced back to the saintly Queen Isabel who founded the Brotherhood of the Holy Spirit in the fourteenth century, though some believe it to derive from an ancient fertility rite dedicated to Ceres. Whatever its origins, it's now a largely secular event, held at three- or four-yearly intervals. The next one is likely to be in 1998 to coincide with Lisbon's Expo, but check with the local turismo as it could be held over to 1999. It's a five-day affair, at the beginning of July, with the highlight – the parade of "trays" – on the final Sunday.

The **procession** (Procissão dos Tabuleiros) consists of four hundred or so young women wearing white, each escorted by a young man in a white shirt, red tie and black trousers. She carries on her head a tray with thirty loaves threaded on vertical canes, intertwined with leaves and colourful paper flowers, and crowned with a white dove – the symbol of the Holy Spirit. The resulting headdress weighs 15kg, and is roughly person-height – hence the need for an escort to lift and help balance it. As with other festivals, there's music and dancing in the streets, fireworks at dawn and dusk, and a bullfight the night before the procession. The day after the procession, bread, wine and beef are distributed to the local needy, following Isabel's injunction to "give bread to the poor" – needless to say, the bulls providing the beef have their own procession, three days before that of the *tabuleiros*.

to see it – or walk along it – is 2km out on the Leiria road. A touch of eccentricity is provided by the **Aguiles Lima Matchstick Museum** (2–5.30pm, closed Sat), inside the Convento de São Francisco, which claims to have the largest match collection in Europe.

The Convento de Cristo

The **Convento de Cristo** (Tues–Sun: May–Sept 9.15am–12.30pm & 2–5.30pm; Oct–April 9.15am–12.30pm & 2–5.15pm; 400$00) is set among pleasant gardens with splendid views, about a quarter of an hour's walk uphill from the centre of town. Founded in 1162 by Gualdim Pais, first and grandest Master of the **Knights Templar**, it was the headquarters of the Order, and, as such, both a religious and a military centre.

One of the main objectives of the Templars was to expel the Moors from Spain and Portugal, a reconquest seen always as a crusade against the Dark Forces – the defence of Christianity against the Infidel. Spiritual strength was an integral part of the military effort and, despite magnificent additions, the sacred heart of the whole complex remains the **Charola** (also known as the Rotunda or Templars' Apse), the twelfth-century temple from which the Knights drew their moral conviction. It is a strange place, more suggestive of the occult than of Christianity. At the centre of the sixteen-sided, almost circular, chapel stands the high altar, surrounded by a two-storeyed octagon. Deep alcoves, decorated with sixteenth-century paintings, are cut into the outside walls. The Templars are said to have attended mass on horseback. Like almost every circular church, it is ultimately based on the Church of the Holy Sepulchre in Jerusalem, for whose protection the Knights Templar were originally founded. The Charola has been closed for restoration for years, with no indication as to when it will re-open; until it does, you can see it only from a distance.

Dom Manuel's additions

By 1249 the reconquest in Portugal was completed and the Templars reaped enormous rewards for their services. Tracts of land were turned over to them and they controlled a network of castles throughout the Iberian peninsula. But as the Moorish threat receded, the Knights became a powerful political challenge to the stability and authority of European monarchs.

Philippe-le-Bel, King of France, took the lead by confiscating all Templar property in his country, and there followed a formal papal suppression of the Order in 1314. In Spain this prompted a vicious witch-hunt and many of the Knights sought refuge in Portugal, where Dom Dinis coolly reconstituted them in 1320 under a different title: the **Order of Christ**. They inherited all the Portuguese property of the Templars, including the headquarters at Tomar, but their power was now subject to that of the throne.

In the fifteenth and sixteenth centuries, the Order of Christ played a leading role in extending Portugal's overseas empire and was granted spiritual jurisdiction over all conquests. Prince Henry the Navigator was Grand Master from 1417 to 1460, and the remains of his **Palace** in the Convento de Cristo can be seen immediately to the right upon entering the castle walls. Henry ordered two new cloisters, the **Claustro do Cemitério** and the **Claustro da Lavagem**, both reached via a short corridor from the Charola and attractively lined with azulejos.

Dom Manuel succeeded to the Grand Mastership in 1492, three years before he became king. Flush with imperial wealth, he decided to expand the convent by adding a rectangular **nave** to the west side of the Charola. This new structure was divided into two storeys: the lower serving as a chapter house, the upper as a choir. The **main doorway**, which leads directly into the nave, was built by João de Castilho in 1515, two years before Dom Manuel appointed him Master of Works at Belém. Characteristically unconcerned with structural matters, the architect profusely adorned the doorway with appliqué decoration. There are strong similarities in this respect with contemporary Isabeline and Plateresque architecture in Spain.

The crowning highlight of Tomar, though, is the sculptural ornamentation of the windows on the main facade of the **Chapter House**. The richness and self-confidence of Manueline art always suggests the Age of Discovery, but here the connection is crystal clear. A wide range of maritime motifs is jumbled up in two tumultuous window frames, as eternal memorials to the sailors who established the Portuguese Empire. Everything is here: anchors, buoys, sails, coral, seaweed and especially ropes, knotted over and over again into an escapologist's nightmare.

The windows can only be fully appreciated from the roof of the **Claustro de Santa Bárbara**, adjacent to the Great Cloisters, which unfortunately almost completely obscure a similar window on the south wall of the Chapter House.

A new style: João III

João III (1521–57) transformed the convent from the general political headquarters of the Order into a thoroughgoing monastic community, and he endowed it with the necessary conventual buildings: dormitories, kitchens and no fewer than four new cloisters (making a grand total of seven). Yet another, much more classical, style was introduced into the architectural mélange of Tomar. So meteoric was the rise and fall of Manueline art within the reign of Dom Manuel that, to some extent, it must have reflected his personal tastes. João III on the other hand had an entirely different view of art. He is known to have sent schools of architects and sculptors to study in Italy, and his reign finally marked the much-delayed advent of the Renaissance in Portugal.

The two-tiered **Great Cloisters**, abutting the Chapter House, are one of the purest examples of this new style. Begun in 1557, they present a textbook illustration of the principals of Renaissance neoclassicism. Greek columns, gentle arches and simple rectangular bays produce a wonderfully restrained rhythm. At the southwest corner a balcony looks out on to the skeletal remains of a second Chapter House, begun by João III but never completed.

Practicalities

The **train** and **bus stations**, on Avenida Combatentes da Grande Guerra, are within easy walking distance of the centre. Head directly north and you'll soon hit Avenida Dr. Cândido Madureira, at the top end of which there's a **turismo** (Mon–Fri 9.30am–12.30pm & 2–6pm, Sat & Sun 10am–1pm & 3–6pm; ☎049/32 26 03), which can give details of local walks round the Sete Montes National Forest. The turismo faces a fierce statue of Infante Dom Henrique and the gates of a park, which once formed the gardens of the Convento de Cristo. There's also a **regional tourist office** at the bottom of Rua Serpa Pinto (Mon–Fri 9.30am–12.30pm & 2–6pm; ☎049/32 20 15).

Accommodation

Tomar has a good range of **accommodation** and finding a room should be pretty straightforward. The only time when rooms will be hard to come by is during the Festa dos Tabuleiros (see box on p.167 for details). There's a pleasant municipal **campsite** (☎049/32 26 07), out towards the football stadium, and an even nicer site 14km out of town at Castelo do Bode (☎049/99 22 62), served by four buses daily from Tomar. It's set amid pine woods by the reservoir and you can rent out boats to visit the islands in the lake. The pleasant campsite *Campismo Rural* (☎049/30 18 14), in the small village of Pelinos, 7km out of town on the road to Coimbra, rents out mountain bikes and can arrange canoeing trips; but beware that the sporadic buses here from Tomar can take up to two hours.

Pensão Bonjardim, Praçeta de Santo André (☎049/31 31 95). Basic but adequate, though some way out, across the river. ③.

Residencial Luanda, Avda. Marqûes de Tomar 15 (☎049/31 51 53). Modern and comfortable *pensão* facing the river. All the rooms come with bath. ④.

Residencial Luz, Rua Serpa Pinto 144 (☎049/31 23 17). Simple rooms but can be good value, especially those for four to six people. ④.

Pensão Nun'Álvares, Avda. Nuno Álvares Pereira 3 (☎049/31 28 73). Book ahead for one of their eleven large, clean rooms (noisy at the front). Breakfast included. ②.

Estalagem de Santa Iria, Parque do Mouchão (☎049/31 33 26). In the park, by the river, Somerset Maugham once stayed here – but then he was rich. Its restaurant, however, is good value. ⑤.

Pousada São Pedro, Castelo do Bode (☎049/38 11 59). Overlooking the reservoir, 13km from Tomar, this is a great place to unwind if you have the funds. ⑥.

Residencial Sinagoga, Rua Gil Avô 31 (☎049/32 30 83). Near the town hall, this smart place has air-conditioning and satellite TV in all rooms. ④.

Pensão Tomarense, Avda. Torres Pinheiro 13 (☎049/31 29 48). Not a first choice, but cheap. Rooms are spartan and, at the front, noisy, but there are fine views of the convent from the rear rooms. Breakfast included. ②.

Residencial Trovador, Rua de Agosto de 1385 (☎049/32 25 67). Light and airy modern *residencial* facing the bus station. ④.

Residencial União, Rua Serpa Pinto 94 (☎049/32 31 61). Central and very popular; in July and August advance booking is essential. Nice rooms around a courtyard, all with private bath or shower. ③.

Eating, drinking and nightlife

Many of the *pensões* in Tomar have **restaurants** attached. Midday, the busiest **cafés and bars** are on Avenida Dr. Cândido Madureira and around the Varzea Grande; on a summer's evening there's more action on the riverside. The "in" **dance venue** is *Pim-pim* on Estrada do Prado 2.

Bela Vista, Trav. Fonte Choupo 6. Justifiably the town's most renowned restaurant, by the river, with full meals for around 2000$00; try the chicken curry. Closed Mon evening, Tues & Nov.

Chez Nous, Rua do Dr. Joaquim Jacinto 31. Upmarket with decidedly tasty Portuguese and French-influenced dishes such as *bacalhão com natas*. Closed Sun & Mon lunch.

Restaurante Nabão, Trav. Fonte Choupo 3. Standard Portuguese favourites at moderate prices and with a river view. Closed Wed.

Nun'Álvares, Avda. Nuno Álvares Pereira 3. Inexpensive and with the edge on its *pensão* rivals, offering a fine house wine and tasty local dishes.

Restaurante Parque das Merendas. Situated by the river, this has a somewhat limited menu, but it's cheap and in a lovely position, with a lively café attached.

Restaurante Piri-Piri, Rua dos Moinhos 54. Large portions of occasionally bland but reasonably priced food; the grilled trout is good. Closed Tues.

East along the Tejo to Abrantes

Eighteen kilometres south of Tomar, the N110 road and the railway both divide at the dull town of Entroncamento. From here one branch of the railway swings east to follow the Rio Tejo past **Tancos** and the remarkable castle at **Almourol** to meet the Rio Zêzere at **Constância**, one of the most attractive towns on the Tejo. By road, an alternative route to Constância is via Castelo do Bode, which will also take you across the dam (Barragem do Castelo do Bode). From Constância, the Tejo retains its rural hue for the 12km east to **Abrantes**, a town with a historic centre and the last significant stop on the river, beyond which road and rail routes branch out for Spain or north and south for the rest of the country.

Almourol and Tancos

As if conjured up by some medieval-minded magician, the **castle of Almourol** stands deserted on a tiny island in the middle of the Tejo. Built by the Knights Templar in 1171, it never saw military action – except in sixteenth-century romantic literature – and its double perimeter walls and ten small towers are perfectly preserved. It's military property but there's no objection to visitors, and once inside you'll be granted a beautiful rural panorama from the tall central keep.

The train line hugs the northern banks of the Tejo at this point and there are two convenient stations, Tancos and Almourol, thirty and fifteen minutes' walk respectively from the island. The latter is stuck in the middle of nowhere but **TANCOS** is actually a small village with a couple of bars catering for a nearby army barracks. To reach the castle from Tancos, take a taxi or strike out east along the railway tracks; the river banks are an impassable forest of eucalyptus trees, cacti and assorted bushes. For around 200$00 per person, a ferryman will row you around the island and deposit you on a miniature beach to explore the castle at leisure.

Constância

CONSTÂNCIA, 3km upstream from Almourol, is a useful place to stay the night after a visit to the castle. A sleepy, incredibly picturesque, whitewashed town, arranged like an amphitheatre around the Tejo and the mouth of the Rio Zêzere, it is best known in Portugal for its association with **Luís de Camões**, Portugal's national poet. In fact, Camões was here for only three years (1547–50), taking refuge from the court of Dom João III, whom he had managed to offend by the injudicious dedication of a love sonnet to a woman on whom the king himself had designs. Constância, however, is said to have remained dear to the poet's heart until the end of his life. In more troubled times, the town served the Duke of Wellington in 1809: he amassed his forces here and prepared for the Battle of Talavera in Spain. Nowadays, Constância is at its liveliest during the **Festa dos Barqueiros**, on Easter Monday, with parades and traditional boats on the Tejo.

For Constância, get off the **train** at Praia do Ribatejo-Constância, the stop after Almourol. If you want **to stay**, ask for *dormidas* in the central cafés or try one of the following: *Residencial Casa João Chagas*, Rua João Chagas (☎049/994 03; ④); the fantastic Privetur property, *Casa O Palácio* (☎049/992 24; ⑥), by the water's edge; or the *Quinta de Santa Bárbara* (☎049/992 14; ⑤), 1km out of town, off the road to Abrantes. You can **camp** by the river beach, next to the Horto de Camões gardens, which are based on the gardens described in Camões' epic poem, *Os Lusiadas*. The nearest official **campsite** is in an attractive lakeside setting at Castelo do Bode 9km to the north, up the Rio Zêzere (see p.169).

Abrantes

ABRANTES is perched strategically above the Tejo, 15km upstream of Almourol. The streets and praças here are pretty, especially when the spring and summer flowers on Rua da Barca and in the Jardim da República are in bloom; the views are also impressive. Additionally, the town has useful train connections linking up with the lower Beiras and the Alto Alentejo.

The highpoint – in all respects – is the town's battered **Castelo** (Tues–Sun 10am–12.30pm & 2–5pm), constructed in the early fourteenth century. As at Santarém (see p.174), Romans and Moors established strongholds here, and the citadel was again sharply contested during the Peninsular War. The chapel of **Santa Maria do Castelo**, within the fort, houses a motley archeological museum, its prize exhibits being three tombs of the Almeidas, Counts of Abrantes. From the battlements there's a terrific view of the countryside and the rooftops of Abrantes and the gardens around its old town walls. The two large, whitewashed churches visible from here were both rebuilt in the six-teenth century.

Practicalities

The **turismo** (Mon & Fri 9am–6.30pm, Tues–Thurs 8.30am–8pm, Sat & Sun 9.30am–12.30pm & 2–5.30pm; ☎041/225 55) is on Largo da Feira, with the **bus station** nearby on Rua Nossa Senhora da Conceição. There are two local **train stations**, both out of town. The main one is 2km south, across the Tejo, and all trains stop there; you could walk into the centre from here, but it's uphill all the way – shared taxis aren't too expensive.

Accommodation is generally easy enough to find: first choice for atmosphere is the old and very pleasant *Pensão Central*, Praça Raimundo Soares 15 (☎041/224 22; ②); the *Pensão Aliança*, Largo do Chafariz 50 (☎041/223 48; ③), owned by the same proprietor, is slightly less characterful but has better facilities, with showers in some rooms. *Pensão Lírios*, Praça Barao da Batalha 31 (☎041/221 42; ④), is another reliable choice, as is *Pensão Tabuci*, Avda. 25 de Abril 49 (☎041/213 76; ④), around 2km out of town, but with the advantage of being near the swimming pool. Further out still, some 10km from Abrantes, is the *Quinta dos Vales* (☎041/973 63; ⑤), which sits on the southern bank of the Tejo at Tramagal (a 10min walk from Tramagal train station); horses are available for a hack along the river banks. Abrantes' nearest **campsite** is in Rossio ao Sul do Tejo (☎041/315 50), over the bridge on the south side of the Tejo.

There are a number of reasonable **restaurants** in Abrantes: one of the best in town is the *Pelicano* (☎041/223 17; closed Thurs) on Rua Nossa Senhora de Conceição 1, near the bus station, where a meal still shouldn't cost more than 2500$00. *Fumeiro* at Rua do Pisco 9 (closed Sun) serves good Portuguese staples, while *Nova Grelha*, Rua Montéiro de Lima, is the place for good-quality, chunky, grilled food. The locals' favourite is *Cascata* (closed Mon), 3km out of town, at Alferrarede, near the second train station. *Tasquinha Américo e Vera Cruz*, at Rossio ao Sul do Tejo, is highly recommended for those with transport, or if you're staying at the campsite.

Ribatejo: along the east bank

Seven kilometres south of Entroncamento, the attractive town of **Golegã** is one of the main crossing points to the east bank of the Rio Tejo – bull-breeding territory, full of rich plains and riverside marshes. This side of the river isn't as accessible by bus or train but, with your own transport, the N118 from here marks the most attractive route along the river, taking in several small historic towns, villages and *quintas* worth passing by en route to Lisbon or the Alentejo coast. Accommodation isn't particularly plentiful, but then you're unlikely to want to stop for any great length of time, except during their energetic annual **festivals**, when what accommodation there is may be fully booked in any case.

Golegã

GOLEGÃ, on the west bank of the Tejo, midway between Tomar and Santarém, is a very pleasant town, best known for its **Feira Nacional do Cavalo** (National Horse Fair), held during the first two weeks in November. The fair incorporates celebrations for St Martin's Day on November 11, when there's a a running of the bulls and a grand parade in which red-waistcoated grooms mingle with gypsies. Culinary diversions include roasted chestnuts and barbecued chickens, accompanied by *água-pé* (literally "foot water") – a light wine made by adding water to the crushed grape husks left after the initial wine production. During the evening, people crowd into the *Restaurante Central*, on Largo da Imaculada Conceição, both to eat and to mingle with haughty *cavaleiros* who have survived the bull-fighting.

Golegã also boasts two museums: the **Museu Municipal de Pintura e Escultura Martins Correia** (Tues–Sun: June–Sept 11am–12.30pm & 3–5pm; Oct–May 10am–12.30pm & 3–6pm; free), opposite the Igreja Matriz, which hous-es an impressive collection of contemporary art and sculpture; and the amazing **Casa-Museu de Fotografia Carlos Relvas**, at the top of Rua José F. Relvas (same hours; free). Carlos Relvas was father of the Republican José Relvas (see below) and, ironically, godfather to King Carlos, who was assassinated by Republicans in 1908. The museum is an archive of Relvas's interest in the newly discovered art of photography and contains some thirteen thousand glass nega-tives. The house itself is worthy of being a museum piece; it's a fantastic fairy-tale building designed by Henrique Carlos Afonso and set in landscaped gardens. Other attractions in Golegã include the sixteenth-century **Igreja Matriz**, with its Manueline door, and the nearby Reserva Natural Parque do Paúl do Boquilobo, 5km out of Golegã off the road to Azinhaga, where you may be lucky enough to spot some otters.

If you want **to stay** in Golegã, *Restaurante Central* is your best bet, with a few rooms to rent, though they'll almost certainly be occupied during the fair. There's also a lovely **campsite** (☎049/942 22) on the edge of the town, on the N365 road south. Otherwise, if you're continuing south along the west bank, you could stay at the *Casa de Santo António da Azinhaga*, Rua Nova de Santo António (☎049/951 62; ⑥), in the attractive stream-side village of Azinhaga, 12km southwest from Golegã.

Chamusca

Across the Tejo from Golegã and 9km by road, **CHAMUSCA** is the most norther-ly of the east bank's bullfighting towns. Its **Festa da Ascensão** – six days of bull-running and bullfighting – is held during the week incorporating Ascension Day (ie, forty days after Easter) and also features a craft fair. Outside these times, the town remains attractive enough for a brief stopover: the 1930s-style **Casa Rural Tradicional** – a country house reconstructed with traditional furnishings – and the municipal swimming pool, both in the park alongside Largo 25 de Abril, are the main attractions.

Alpiarça

ALPIARÇA, on the east bank 18km south of Chamusca (and just 10km east of Santarém), boasts the **Casa Museu dos Patudos** (Wed–Sun 10am–noon & 2–5.30pm; 300$00), on Rua José Relvas south of town, which was originally the home of José Relvas (1858–1929). Musician, art collector, landowner, bullfighter, diplomat and politician, José is best known as the man who proclaimed the Portuguese Republic in Lisbon in 1910. The exterior of the house, designed by Raul Lino, is striking, with a colonnade and outdoor staircases to the first floor. Inside, you'll find priceless collections of Portuguese paintings, porcelain, furni-ture, tapestries and over forty carpets from Arraiolos, including one embroidered in silk and dating from 1701. The **turismo** in the town hall may be able to help with renting **rooms**; otherwise, there's a **campsite** (☎043/543 99) beyond the museum and off the Almeirim road.

Almeirim and Salvaterra de Magos

Seven kilometres south of Alpiarça lies **ALMEIRIM**, whose golden days were during the reign of the House of Avis (1383–1580), when the royal family – ensconced at Santarém, just 7km to the northwest – hunted from a summer palace on the riverside here. Nothing remains of the palace today but the town does boast an **ethnographical museum** (Mon–Fri 9am–12.30pm & 2–4pm; free) with moderately interesting insights into local traditions. *Restaurante Tonçinho*, on Rua de Timor 2 (closed Thurs) is a good place both for lunch – the brick oven and open kitchen add a certain interest to mealtimes – and to sample the local wines, considered some of the best in the region. If you want to visit the **vineyards**, the eighteenth-century *Quinta da Alorna*, 1km from Almeirim on the Lisbon road, offers tours and tastings on Fridays and Sundays (call ☎043/521 05 for details).

SALVATERRA DE MAGOS, 29km south of Almeirim, retains rather more of its historical relics and has a fine, sandy river beach nearby. A palace built for the Bragança monarchs is long gone, but the palace **chapel** with its outstanding golden altarpiece still survives, as does the **Palácio da Falcoaria** (Falconry Palace), whose 305 niches once housed the royal falcons. In its eighteenth-century heyday, the palace contained a theatre and a bullring, though after the noble Count of Arcos was killed during a bullfight here, Pombal banned the sport – it was only legally reinstated in 1920.

Santarém

SANTARÉM, capital of the Ribatejo, rears high above the Rio Tejo, commanding a tremendous view over the rich pasturelands to the south and east. It ranks among the most historic cities in Portugal: under Julius Caesar it became an important administrative centre for the Roman province of Lusitania; Moorish Santarém was regarded as impregnable (until Afonso Henriques captured it by enlisting the aid of foreign Crusaders in 1147); and it was here that the royal *Cortes* (parliament) was convened throughout the fourteenth and fifteenth centuries. All evidence of Roman and Moorish occupation has vanished but, with its two exquisite churches, modern Santarém remains a pleasant place to stay and a visit will also be rewarded by the famous view from the *miradouro* known as the **Portas do Sol.**

If you can, it's worth planning your stay to coincide with one of the many **festivals** held in the town. The thinly populated agricultural plain above which Santarém stands is the home of Portuguese **bullfighting**: here, the very best horses and bulls graze in lush fields under the watchful eyes of *campinos*, mounted guardians dressed in the traditional bright costume. Agricultural traditions, folk dancing (especially the fandango), and bullfighting all come together in the great annual **Feira Nacional da Agricultura**, held at Santarém for ten days starting on the first Friday in June, while dishes from every region in Portugal are sampled at the **Festival de Gastronomia** (10–12 days, ending on Nov 1). For a fixed price you can eat as much as you like during this event. There are also **street markets** on the second and fourth Sunday of every month.

Around the town

At the heart of the old town is **Praça Sá da Bandeira**, overlooked by the many-windowed Baroque facade of the Jesuit **Seminário** (1676), which serves as the town's cathedral. Rua Serpa Pinto or Rua Capelo e Ivens lead from here towards the signposted Portas do Sol, about fifteen minutes' walk, with the best of the churches conveniently en route.

First of these is the Manueline **Igreja de Marvila** (Tues–Fri 9.30am–12.30pm & 2–6pm, Sat & Sun open till 6.30pm) at the end of Rua Serpa Pinto, with its brilliant seventeenth-century azulejos and lovely stone pulpit comprising eleven

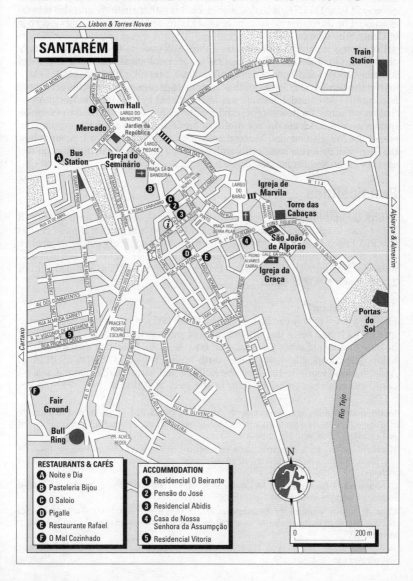

△ Lisbon & Torres Novas

SANTARÉM

Train Station

Town Hall

Mercado

Bus Station

Igreja do Seminário

Igreja de Marvila

Torre das Cabaças

São João de Alporão

Igreja da Graça

Portas do Sol

Fair Ground

Bull Ring

Rio Tejo

N

0   200 m

RESTAURANTS & CAFÉS
- Ⓐ Noite e Dia
- Ⓑ Pasteleria Bijou
- Ⓒ O Saloio
- Ⓓ Pigalle
- Ⓔ Restaurante Rafael
- Ⓕ O Mal Cozinhado

ACCOMMODATION
- ❶ Residencial O Beirante
- ❷ Pensão do José
- ❸ Residencial Abidis
- ❹ Casa de Nossa Senhora da Assumpção
- ❺ Residencial Vitoria

miniature Corinthian columns. From here, Rua J. Araújo, at right angles to the side of the church, descends a few yards to the architectural highlight of Santarém: the early fifteenth-century **Igreja da Graça** (Tues–Sun 9.30am–12.30pm & 2.30–5.30pm). A spectacular rose window dominates the church and overlapping blind arcades above the portal are heavily influenced by the vertical decorations on the main facade at Batalha. Pedro Álvares Cabral, discoverer of Brazil in 1500, is buried within, but his rather austere tomb-slab is overshadowed by the elaborate sarcophagus of Pedro de Menezes, the first Governor of Ceuta, who died in 1437.

Continuing toward the *miradouro*, a third sidetrack is to the twelfth-century church of **São João de Alporão**, now an **archeological museum** (Tues–Fri 9.30am–12.30pm & 2–6pm, Sat open till 6.30pm, Sun till 5.30pm; 200$00). Take a look at the flamboyant Gothic tomb of Duarte de Menezes who met his gruesome fate in 1464 – so comprehensively was he butchered by the Moors in North Africa that only a single tooth was recovered for burial. Avenida 5 de Outubro eventually finishes at the **Portas do Sol** (Gates of the Sun), a large garden occupying the site of the Moorish citadel. Modern battlements look down on a long stretch of the Tejo with its fertile sandbanks and, beyond, a vast swathe of the Ribatejo disappears green and flat into the distance.

Practicalities

The **train station** lies a couple of hundred metres below the town and you'll either have to take a taxi or walk into the centre. The **bus station** is more central and Rua Pedro Canavarro, across the gardens opposite, leads into Rua Capelo e Ivens, the main pedestrian street of the old town. Excellent maps are available from the **turismo** at no. 63 (Mon–Fri 9am–7pm, Sat & Sun 9am–12.30pm & 2.30–5.30pm; ☎043/39 15 12).

Accommodation
Finding a place to stay can be hard during festival times, when your best bet is to turn up early and see if the turismo can find you a **private room**. There should be little problem at other times of year; try one of the **hotels or pensões** listed below. The cheapest beds are at the **youth hostel** (☎043/33 32 92 or 39 19 14) at Avda. Afonso Henrique 109, near the bullring and fairground; while the nearest **campsite** is across the river, 9km to the east, at Alpiarça (☎043/543 99; see p.173).

Residencial Abidis, Rua Guilherme de Azevedo 4 (☎043/220 17). A slice of nineteenth-century style with close on thirty rooms, though only six have a bath. Highly recommended and excellent value, with big breakfasts. ③.

Hotel Alfageme, Avda. Bernardo Santaremo 38, just off the Torres Novas road (☎043/37 08 70). Modern hotel whose rooms are all en suite, air-conditioned and double-glazed. Breakfast included. ⑤.

Residencial O Beirante, Rua Alexandre Herculano 5 (☎043/33 38 45). Moderately priced rooms, all with private bath. ④.

Casa de Nossa Senhora da Assumpção, Rua 1° Dezembro 55 (☎043/250 48). A beautiful old building right in the centre of town, but as it has only two rooms you'll need to book in advance. ⑤.

Pensão do José, Trav. do Frois 14 (☎043/230 88). A clean, basic *pensão*, on a quiet alleyway just off Rua Capelo e Ivens. ②.

Quinta de Vale de Lobo, Azóia de Baixo, 6km north of town (☎043/42 92 64). This pleasant house (where the historian Alexandre Herculano spent the last years of his life) is surrounded by gardens and has a pool. ⑤.

Residencial Vitoria, Rua 2° Visconde de Santarém 21 (☎043/225 73). Fifteen minutes' walk from the centre, with decent, if small, rooms – all with bath. Breakfast included. ④.

Eating

Santarém has a range of **restaurants**, mainly on – or just off – Rua Capelo e Ivens and in the area around the bullring, out on the road to Cartaxo. Among local fish specialities look out for *fataça na telha*, mullet cooked on a tile.

Pastelaria Bijou, Praça Sa da Bandeira. Perfect croissant-and-coffee spot opposite the Seminário, with outdoor tables from where you can watch the world go by.

O Mal Cozinhado, Campo de Feiras (☎043/235 84). Small place where you may need to reserve a table, particularly on Friday, which is fado night. Some of the meat comes from bulls recently on duty in the nearby bullring – and, despite the odd restaurant name ("badly cooked"), dishes are good, if expensive.

Noite e Dia, Rua António José de Almeida 9. Reliable Portuguese cooking at moderate prices.

Pigalle, Rua Capelo e Ivens. Busy restaurant-cum-snack bar. Closed Sun.

Restaurante Rafael, Rua 1° Dezembro 3. Good tourist menu in a friendly, family-run place.

O Saloio, Trav. do Montalvo 11, off Rua Capelo e Ivens (☎043/276 56). Popular with local families, this cheap *tasca* is very good value for money.

The west bank: wine towns and Vila Franca de Xira

The western bank of the Rio Tejo is highly developed south of Santarém, though away from the river it doesn't take long to get into the rolling hills and vineyards. It's around an hour's journey on the fast A1 motorway from Santarém to Lisbon, but if you have a passing interest in **wines**, there are several worthy detours on your way west including *quintas* and museums where you can sample the stuff. In addition, the west bank hosts two of Portugal's most distinctive festivals in the city of **Vila Franca de Xira**, which sits at the edge of the important wetlands of the **Reserva Natural do Estuario do Tejo**.

Wine towns

Some of the Ribatejo's finest vineyards are found on the west bank (see box on p.178) and a good place to start exploring the wine trade is **CARTAXO**, 14km south of Santarém. The town is uninspiring but it has a fine **Museu Rural e do Vinho** (Tues–Fri 10.30am–12.30pm & 3–5.30pm, Sat & Sun 9.30am–12.30pm & 3–5.30pm; 110$00), in a *quinta* on Rua José Ribeiro da Costa, with a couple of traditional houses where you can taste and buy the local, full-bodied, fruity wine.

AZAMBUJA, 13km to the south, is known for its great reds made from the Periquita grape, but the town itself only really comes alive with the bull-running during its Feira do Maio, held during the last weekend in May. The Marquês de Pombal built a 26-kilometre-long canal – the Vala de Azambuja – parallel to the river here, to drain the land when the Tejo was in flood – at its mouth are the ruins

---

RIBATEJO WINES

Wine has been produced on the banks of the Tejo for around 2000 years, but it is only recently that modern wine-making techniques have ensured that the result is appreciated not only in local *tascas* but throughout Europe. The highly respected wines from the five denominations in the Ribatejo region – Almeirim, Cartaxo, Chamusca, Coruche and Santarém – can now be found in supermarkets outside Portugal, marketed under labels such as Ribatejo, Arruda and Liziria. Ribatejan **whites** are typically from the Fernão Pires or Trincadeira-das-Pratas grapes, which give rise to a dry, lemon-coloured and fruity wine. **Reds** tend to be from the Periquita, Tincadeira Preta and Castelão Nacional grapes, though Cabernet Sauvignon produces some of the best-tasting wines.

---

of the **Palácio das Obras Novas**, used as a staging post for the steamers plying from Lisbon north to Constância (see p.171) in the nineteenth century.

Perched on a hillside 17km to the southwest, **ALENQUER** sits in a major wine area; its refreshing and lemony-flavoured whites are particularly worth tasting. There is little else to delay you apart from the attractive upper town spreading up a steep hillside and boasting a **Franciscan convent** as its most prominent building. Founded in 1222 by Dona Sancha, daughter of Dom Sancho I, the convent is the oldest Franciscan house in Portugal and was built during the lifetime of St Francis of Assisi. It features a fine thirteenth-century doorway and Manueline cloisters, the latter added in 1557. Sadly it is open only on the first Sunday of the month between morning and evening Mass.

However, it is in the valleys below the windmill-topped hills around **ARRUDA DOS VINHOS**, 16km south of Alenquer, that the region's vineyards are at their most attractive. The fresh, beaujolais-style Arruda (also known as Arruta) red wines produced here are known throughout Europe, and are one of the reasons why Lisboans come to the village in their droves on Sundays. Many have lunch at the *adega-restaurante O Fuso* (☎063/951 21), where vast slabs of meat and *bacalhao* are grilled over crackling open fires – if you can't get in there, *Restaurante Nazareth* opposite is a good alternative.

Vila Franca de Xira

VILA FRANCA DE XIRA, 45km downriver from Santarém, makes a rival claim to be the capital of the Ribatejo, but it's largely a drab, industrial city – a poor second when it comes to cultural attractions. Its riverside location made it the favoured home for English Crusaders, who named it Cornogoa after Cornwall. Now Vila Franca is the central point of interest for aficionados of the Portuguese bullfight: the rearing of bulls and horses dominates the local economy. The two great annual events are the **Festa do Colete Encarnado** ("Red Waistcoat Festival", a reference to the costume of the *campinos*) held over several days in the first two weeks of July; and the **Feira de Outubro** (October Fair), in the first two weeks of the month. On both occasions there are bullfights and a Pamplona-style running of the bulls through the streets – leading to the usual casualties among the bold (and drunk). The town's other claim to fame is being home to **Imax** – Portugal's only 360-degree cinema screen – in the shopping centre opposite the railway station.

Accommodation is difficult to find during festivals and you're advised to book well in advance or visit on a day-trip from Santarém or Lisbon; the **turismo**, Rua Dr. Manuel Arriaga 24 (☎063/260 43), may be able to help. Places to stay in town include the *Residencial Ribatejana*, Rua da Praia 2 (☎063/229 91; ③), next to the station, and the *Residencial Flora*, Rua Noel Perdigão 12 (☎063/27 12 72; ④), one block from the station and with a good restaurant. There's a shaded **campsite** (☎063/260 31) on the outskirts, near the municipal swimming pool.

For **eating**, *O Copote* in the station square, on the first floor above a bar, is inexpensive; *Restaurante O Redondel*, Praça de Touros (near the bullring on the Lisbon side of town; closed Mon), is also recommended, though the full works here can cost around 3500$00 per person.

The Reserva Natural de Estuario del Tejo

South and southeast from Vila Franca de Xira, the banks of the Tejo are classified as the **Reserva Natural de Estuario del Tejo**, providing protection for the thousands of wild birds that gather in the estuary. It is Portugal's most important wetland, but has been somewhat disrupted by the construction of the enormous Vasco da Gama bridge (see p.86). The reserve's headquarters are in **ALCO-CHETE**, 35km south of Vila Franca and on the south side of the bridge at Avda. Combatentes 1 (☎01/234 17 42), from where information and advice are dispensed. With your own transport, the best approach to the reserve is from Alcamé, south of the N10 Vila Franca–Porto Alto road, or – better still – from Pancas, west of the N118.

Alternatively, you can see the reserve from the Tejo estuary itself by **renting a boat** (or a place in a boat). Without your own transport, you could take the ferry from Lisbon (hourly from Praça do Comércio) to Montijo, a fifty-minute journey, and once there it's a five-kilometre bus or taxi ride to Alcochete. Contact Domingos Chefe, the boat owner (☎01/236 02 78), a day in advance to agree on the timing; you'll also need to obtain permission to visit from the reserve headquarters. The boat can take up to nine people.

The birds on view depend on the time of year of your visit. September to February is best, when you'll be certain to see migrating species such as flamingoes, teal and avocet. Later in the year, you'll catch nesting species: black-winged stilt, purple heron and marsh harriers.

travel details

Trains

Abrantes to: Castelo Branco (8 daily; 1hr 30min–2hr); Covilhã (6 daily; 3hr); Elvas (3 daily; 2hr 45min); Lisbon (9 daily; 1hr 40min–2hr); Portalegre (3 daily; 1hr 45min).

Caldas da Rainha to: Figueira da Foz (6 daily; 1hr 30min–2hr 20min); Leiria (11 daily; 45min–1hr); Lisbon (11 daily; 1hr 30min–2hr); São Martinho do Porto (7 daily; 25 min); Torres Vedras (9 daily; 35–50min).

Leiria to: Caldas da Rainha (11 daily; 45min–1hr); Figueira da Foz (9 daily; 1hr 20min); Lisbon (6 daily; 2–3hr); São Martinho do Porto (10 daily; 50min); Torres Vedras (8 daily; 1hr 40min–2hr).

Lisbon to: Caldas da Rainha (11 daily; 1hr 30min–2hr); Leiria (6 daily; 2hr–3hr); Torres Vedras (16 daily; 1hr 10min–1hr 30min).

Santarém to: Castelo Branco (7 daily; 2hr 30min–3hr); Covilhã (5 daily; 3hr 45min–4hr); Lisbon (24 daily; 50min–1hr); Tomar (hourly; 1hr).

Tomar to: Lisbon (hourly; 2hr 5min); Santarém (hourly; 1hr).

Torres Vedras to: Caldas da Rainha (9 daily; 35–50min); Figueira da Foz (3 daily; 2hr 20min); Leiria (8 daily; 1hr 40min–2hr); Lisbon (16 daily; 1hr 10min–1hr 30min).

Vila Franca de Xira to: Lisbon (hourly; 30–40min); Santarém (hourly; 40min); Tomar (hourly; 1hr 40min).

Buses

Abrantes to: Coimbra (1 daily; 2hr 45min); Fátima (3–4 daily; 1hr 30min); Leiria (1 daily; 2hr); Lisbon (10 daily, 1hr 45min–2hr 50min); Santarém (4 daily; 1hr 25min); Tomar (2–4 daily; 1hr 10min).

Alcobaça to: Batalha (10 daily; 30min); Leiria (4 daily; 45min); Lisbon (3–4 daily; 2hr); Nazaré (hourly; 35 min).

Batalha to: Fátima (4 daily; 25min); Leiria (5 daily; 15min); Lisbon (6 daily; 2hr).

Caldas da Rainha to: Foz do Arelho (9–10 daily, 25min); Leiria (4 daily; 1hr 55min); Lisbon (6 daily; 1hr 45 min); Nazaré (7 daily; 40min); Óbidos (6–12 daily; 20min).

Ericeira to: Lisbon (6–8 daily; 1hr 30min); Sintra (15 daily; 45min).

Fátima to Coimbra (5 daily; 1hr–1hr 30min); Leiria (9 daily; 25 min); Lisbon (7–8 daily; 1hr 45min–2hr 15min); Porto (4–5 daily; 2hr 30min–3hr 30min).

Leiria to: Abrantes (1 daily; 1hr 50min); Alcobaça (4 daily; 50min); Batalha (5 daily; 15min); Coimbra (10 daily; 50min); Fátima (9 daily; 25min); Lisbon (9 daily; 1hr –2hr 10min); Porto de Mós (3 daily; 35min); São Pedro de Muel (4 daily, change at Marinha Grande; 1hr 10min); Tomar (2 daily; 1hr 10 min–2hr).

Nazaré to: Alcobaça (12 daily; 35min); Caldas da Rainha (7 daily; 40min); Leiria (10 daily; 1hr 10min); Lisbon (6 daily; 2hr); Obidos (6–7 daily; 1 hr); São Martinho do Porto (6 daily; 20 min).

Óbidos to: Caldas da Rainha (6–12 daily; 20min); Nazaré (6–7 daily; 1hr); Peniche (7–8 daily; 25–40min).

Peniche to: Areia Branca (6 daily; 30min); Caldas da Rainha (7 daily; 45min); Consolação (hourly; 15min); Lisbon (9 daily; 1 hr 45min); Óbidos (7–8 daily; 25–40min); São Martinho do Porto (3 daily; 1hr); Torre Vedras (9 daily; 50min).

Santarém to: Abrantes (4 daily; 1hr 25min); Fátima (9 daily, 1 hr 10min); Lisbon (12 daily; 1hr–1hr 15min); Ourem (1 daily; 1hr 10min); Tomar (2–4 daily; 1hr 5min); Vila Franca (2–5 daily; 1hr 35min–2hr 20min).

Tomar to: Abrantes (2–4 daily; 1hr 10min); Coimbra (2 daily; 2hr); Fátima (2–5 daily; 45min); Leiria (2 daily; 1hr 10min–2hr); Lisbon (2–4 daily; 1hr 15min–2hr 30min); Porto (1 daily; 3hr 55min); Santarém (2–4 daily; 1hr 5min).

Vila Franca de Xira to: Évora (1 daily; 2hr); Lisbon (15 daily; 50min); Santarém (2–5 daily; 40min–1hr 35min).

COIMBRA AND THE BEIRA LITORAL

The province of **Beira Litoral** is dominated by the city of **Coimbra**, which, with Guimarães, Lisbon and Porto, forms the quartet of Portugal's historic capitals. Sited on a hill above the Rio Mondego, it's a wonderfully moody place, full of ancient alleys and lanes, spreading around the country's oldest university. As a base for exploring the region, the city can't be beaten, with Portugal's most extensive Roman site, **Conímbriga**, 16km to the southwest, the castle at **Montemor-o-Velho** 32km west on the road to Figueira da Foz, and the delightful spa town of **Luso** and ancient **forest of Buçaco** under an hour's journey to the north.

Beira's endlessly sandy coastline, from Figueira da Foz north as far as Porto, has been dubbed the **Costa de Prata** ("Silver Coast"). Although slowly succumbing to development, most noticeably around **Praia de Mira**, it remains one of the least spoiled coasts in Portugal, backed by rolling dunes and pine forests. The only resort of any real size is **Figueira da Foz** and even this remains thoroughly and enjoyably local in character. Inland, the villages and towns of the fertile plain have long been conditioned by the twin threats of floodwaters coming down from Portugal's highest mountains, and silting caused by the restless Atlantic. Drainage channels have had to be cut to make cultivation possible and houses everywhere are built on high ground. At **Aveiro**, positioned on a complex estuary site, a whole network of canals was developed to cope with the currents, and to facilitate salt production and the harvesting of seaweed – still the staple activities of the local economy.

The Beira region also hints at the river valley delights to come, in the Douro and Minho, further north. Following the delightful **Rio Mondego** upstream from

---

ACCOMMODATION PRICE CODES

All the accommodation prices in this book have been coded using the symbols below. The symbols represent the lowest prices you can expect to pay for a **double room in high season**; for a full explanation, see p.29.

① Under 3000$00   ② 3000$00–4000$00   ③ 4000$00–5500$00
④ 5500$00–8500$00   ⑤ 8500$00–12,500$00   ⑥ 12,500$00–20,000$00
                             ⑦ Over 20,000$00

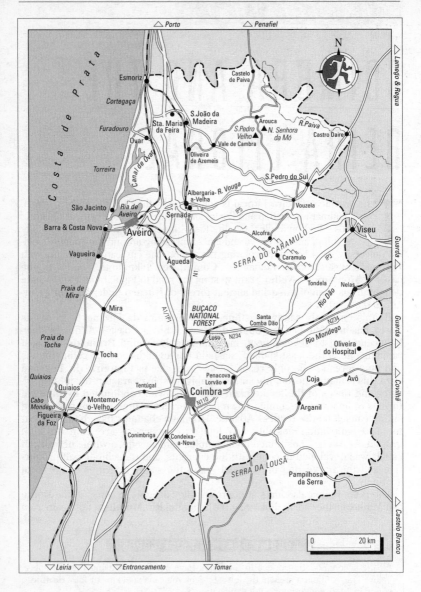

Coimbra, you'll come to see why it has been celebrated so often in Portuguese poetry as the "Rio das Musas" – River of the Muses. An equally beautiful road journey trails the **Rio Vouga**, from Aveiro, up to the town of **Vouzela** and the spa of **São Pedro do Sul**.

Coimbra

COIMBRA was Portugal's capital for over a century (1143–1255) and its famous **university** – founded in 1290 and permanently established here in 1537 after a series of moves back and forth to Lisbon – was the only one in Portugal until the beginning of this century. It remains highly prestigious (though Lisbon has far more students nowadays) and provides the greatest of Coimbra's monuments and buildings, most notably the renowned Baroque library. In addition, there are a remarkable number of other riches: two cathedrals, dozens of lesser churches, and scores of ancient mansions, one housing the superb **Museu Machado de Castro**.

This roll-call of splendours is promoted zealously by the inhabitants of what – when all is said and done – is little more than a small, provincial town. There's an air of self-importance that whistles through city and citizens, bolstered by Coimbra's long academic tradition and fed by shops, galleries and cafés that would sit easily in Lisbon. For visitors, this means that Coimbra can be a lot of fun: it's a very manageable size, with a population of under eighty thousand, its streets packed with bars and taverns, at their liveliest when the students are in town. The best time to be here is in May, when the end of the academic year is celebrated in the **Queima das Fitas**, with graduates ceremoniously tearing or burning their gowns and faculty ribbons. This is also when you're most likely to hear the genuine **Coimbra fado**, distinguished from the Lisbon version by its mournful pace and romantic or intellectual lyrics.

Arrival, information and transport

There are three **train stations** – Coimbra A, Coimbra B and Coimbra Parque. Riverside **Coimbra A** (often just "Coimbra" on timetables) is right at the heart of things; express through-trains call only at **Coimbra B**, 3km to the north, from where you pick up a local train into Coimbra A – just follow eveyone else across the platform (you don't need another ticket). **Coimbra Parque**, southeast of the centre, is for services to and from Lousã, to the south (see p.197).

The **telephone code** for Coimbra is ☎039.

The main **bus station** is on Avenida Fernão de Magalhães, about fifteen minutes' walk northwest of the centre. Almost all long-distance buses operate from here, as do international services to Spain, France and Germany. AVIC buses, operating along the Costa de Prata to and from Praia da Mira, stop at the station at Rua João de Ruão 18, on the way in from the main bus station. AVIC also runs buses to and from Condeixa-a-Nova (for Conímbriga), which also make a stop at the top of Avenida Emídio Navarro, just before Coimbra A station.

Drivers should beware that driving into Coimbra can be a nightmare, since most of the central streets are closed to cars. It's best to use one of the signposted car parks (also marked on the map on pp.184–185) or stay at a hotel with car parking and then walk into town.

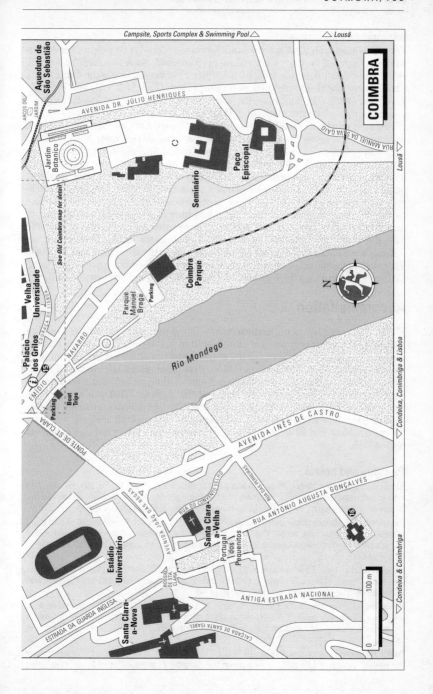

COIMBRA

Campsite, Sports Complex & Swimming Pool △

△ Lousã

Aqueduto de São Sebastião

ARCOS DO JARDIM

AVENIDA DR. JÚLIO HENRIQUES

RUA MANUEL DA SILVA GAIO

Lousã ▷

Jardim Botânico

Seminário

Paço Episcopal

See Old Coimbra map for detail

Velha Universidade

PRAÇA DE LISBOA

Coimbra Parque

Parque Manuel Braga

Parking

Palácio dos Grilos

NAVARRO

EMÍDIO

Rio Mondego

N

Parking

Boat Trips

PONTE DE ST CLARA

AVENIDA INÊS DE CASTRO

Condeixa, Conimbriga & Lisboa ▷

Estádio Universitário

RUA DO CONVENTEVELHO

AVENIDA JOÃO DAS REGAS

Santa Clara-a-Velha

RUA DAS FIGUEIRAS

Portugal dos Pequenitos

RUA ANTÓNIO AUGUSTA GONÇALVES

Condeixa & Conimbriga ▷

Santa Clara-a-Nova

ROSSIO DE STA. CLARA

CAIÇADA DE SANTA ISABEL

ESTRADA DA GUARDA INGLESA

ANTIGA ESTRADA NACIONAL

0   100 m

Information and transport

For a free map, call in at the **turismo** (summer Mon–Fri 9am–8pm, Sat & Sun 9am–12.30pm & 2–5.30pm; winter Mon–Fri 9am–6pm, Sat & Sun 9am–12.30pm & 2–5.30pm; ☎330 19), on the triangular Largo da Portagem, facing the Ponte Santa Clara. There are also tourist offices on Praça Dom Dinis (☎325 91) and Praça da República (☎332 02), both open the same hours as the main office, and a small information kiosk on the platform of Coimbra B.

You'll get most out of **walking** around the old quarter of Coimbra; indeed, you'll have no choice given the complexity and inaccessibility of most of the hillside alleys and streets. Tickets for **town buses** (which include services out to the campsite and youth hostel; see p.187) are sold on board or more cheaply from kiosks in Largo da Portagem, Praça 8 de Maio and Praça da República. Buying a ticket from the driver for a single journey costs 190$00, while a ten-journey ticket-strip (a *senha*), bought from a kiosk, costs just 550$00: cancel it in the machine by the driver as you board. For a cheap bus **tour** of the city, #3 and #26 take in most of the sights. Further information on bus routes and timetables is available from the riverside café in front of the *Hotel Astória*, or the kiosk a little further up.

Taxis are a cheap way of getting around, too, given the short distances involved. There are ranks outside Coimbra A station, at Praça 8 de Maio, opposite the *Santa Cruz* café, and in Praça da República. To call a cab, ring Politaxis (☎48 40 45).

Accommodation

Much of the city's **accommodation** is to be found within a short walk of Coimbra A station. The cheaper *pensões* are concentrated in the rather sleazy Rua da Sota (left and immediately right out of the station) and the little streets between here and the central Praça do Comércio. More expensive places line Avenida Fernão de Magalhães (left and immediately left out of the station) and the riverside Avenida Emídio Navarro (directly ahead of the station). What you won't find is much choice in the hilly streets of the old town. Budget alternatives to the *pensões* and hotels include a **youth hostel** and **campsite**, though both are a fair way from the centre. Note that all accommodation reviewed below is marked on the map on pp.184–185.

Pensões and hotels

Almedina Coimbra Hotel, Avda. Fernão de Magalhães 203 (☎291 61, fax 299 06). Situated next to a fire station on a race-track main road. Double-glazing keeps the noise down, but the rooms here lack charm. Nearby parking, though, and breakfast is included. ⑤.

Residencial Antunes, Rua Castro Matoso 8 (☎230 48, fax 383 73). Quiet, polished and good value – some rooms look across the river, and most are decently sized with bathrooms and TV. It's near Praça da República, a fair walk from the old town, though close to a couple of excellent bars. ④.

Hotel Astória, Avda. Emídio Navarro 21 (☎220 55, fax 220 57). Perfectly placed (look for the landmark dome), classically upmarket choice exhibiting a strange blend of Art Nouveau and 1930s decor. The best rooms overlook the river. ⑥.

Residencial Avenida, Avda. Emídio Navarro 37 (☎221 56, fax 221 55). On the riverside, a gorgeous (if slightly musty) Art Nouveau place with palatial rooms complete with broken chandeliers, sturdy old furniture and small, clean bathrooms. Bar, restaurant and TV lounge, too. ④.

Hotel Bragança, Largo das Ameias 10 (☎221 71, fax 361 35). If you were staying any nearer the train station, you'd be in it – which given the *Bragança*'s pseudo-Soviet brutalist exterior might be no bad thing. Things pick up inside, where rooms are inoffensively modern and spacious, with marble bathrooms; breakfast included. ⑤.

Casa Pombal, Rua dos Flores 18 (☎351 75). Higgledy-piggledy Dutch-run town house near the university with lashings of atmosphere, a tiled dining room and small patio-garden. Breakfast is splendid and you can order good vegetarian meals, too. Thoroughly recommended. ④.

Residencial Dómus, Rua Adelino Veiga 62 (☎285 84). On the nicest of the narrow streets across from the train station, this homely place (entrance hidden next to a rug store) has a wide variety of rooms and friendly owners keen to show them off. The best rooms have shower and TV. ③.

Residencial Internacional, Avda. Emídio Navarro 4 (☎255 03). Facing the river, this once-grand hotel has divided up its rooms, making them a bit on the small side. But it's a friendly place, with a bit of character, though rooms at the front can be rather noisy. ③.

Residencial Kanimambo, Avda. Fernão de Magalhães 484 (☎271 51, fax 284 08). Upstairs in a modern apartment block, this is the best choice near the bus station, with nicely furnished rooms (with and without shower) spread across two cool, dark, quiet floors and accessed by lift. ③.

Quinta das Lágrimas, off Rua António Augusta Gonçalves (☎44 16 15, fax 44 16 95). Situated across the river, this is possibly the most atmospheric choice in Coimbra. A plush stately house set in the infamous gardens and counting Wellington amongst its former guests. ⑥.

Residencial Larbelo, Largo da Portagem 33 (☎290 92, fax 290 94). Close to the main turismo; you can't miss the lime green facade. It's simply furnished and has new bathrooms, but it's also rather gloomy and – for single travellers at least – rather overpriced. You'll pay more for a room with bath or shower. Rooms facing the Largo are noisy. ③.

Residencial Lusa Atenas, Avda. Fernão de Magalhães 68 (☎264 12). Clean, spacious rooms, with private bath and TV, in a once-grand building on the busy main road. Enthusiastic staff keep things running smoothly; try and avoid being put in the annexe at no. 191, which is not as good, or the balconied room on the street corner – it may look tempting but the pedestrian crossing, not four metres from your head, bleeps every thirty seconds. ④.

Hotel Oslo, Avda. Fernão de Magalhães 25 (☎290 71, fax 260 14). Pleasant, modern hotel with a restaurant and bar on the top floor. Despite the Scandinavian style, the rooms facing the street feature traditional Portuguese late-night noise. ⑤.

Pensão Rivoli, Praça do Comércio 27 (☎255 50). Excellent-value rooms (some with en-suite showers) in a splendid central, pedestrianized location. The quiet rooms are tucked away at the back of the building, approached along a plant-filled corridor. ③.

Hospedaria Simões, Rua Fernandes Tomás 69 (☎346 38). Cheapest choice in the old town, with simple, clean monastic lodgings on a cobbled street that climbs from the Arco de Almedina. The ground-floor rooms are noisy but cheaper than in the rest of the building. ①.

Pensão Vitória, Rua da Sota 9 & 19 (☎240 49). Much the best of the two or three cheap *pensões* on this street, closest to the train station and with a good restaurant downstairs. The creaky floorboards may disrupt light sleepers though. ③.

OUTSIDE THE CITY

Casa dos Quintais, at Assarfage, 6km south of Coimbra (☎039/43 83 05). Small private house with a delightful garden and fine views of Coimbra; follow signs to Carvalhais de Cima and then signs for "Casa Rurale". There are just three double rooms with a common lounge area, and an excellent breakfast is served; call ahead to reserve a room. ⑤.

Hostel and campsite

Pousada de Juventude, Rua Henrique Seco 14 (☎ & fax 229 55). Above the Parque Santa Cruz, this is a decent modern hostel with nice rooms, patio, kitchen and TV room: reception is open 9am–noon and 6pm–midnight. It's about twenty minutes' walk, or take buses #7, #8, #29 or #46 from Coimbra A.

Parque de Campismo Municipal, Praça 25 de Abril (☎70 14 97). The well-shaded camp-site is at the municipal sports complex (open all year), and has the added attraction of the adjacent town swimming pool. Bus #5 runs there from Largo da Portagem, or, if you're com-ing from Lousã, get off at São José station, 250m from the campsite entrance. Reception open daily 9am–10pm (winter 6pm).

The City

Old Coimbra straddles a hilly site, with the university crowning its summit, on the north bank of the Rio Mondego. Its slopes are a convoluted mass of ancient alleys around which the modern town has spread, and most of interest is con-centrated on the hill itself or in the largely pedestrianized commercial centre at its foot. Chances are you'll get lost as soon as you start to climb past the remains of the city walls, but that's half the fun. It's probably best to start your exploration of Coimbra with the **Velha Universidade**, not least because it's the easiest place to find, and from its balcony the city is laid out below you like a map. You can see right across the river to the twin **Santa Clara** convents, a visit to which is the only time you need leave the confines of the old city. If you don't feel like walking, bus #1 takes you up to the Museo Machado de Castro and the university buildings.

Into the old town

The old town is bounded on its western side by the pedestrianized main street which runs north from Largo da Portagem and the turismo to the Igreja de Santa Cruz. Here, in the **Baixa**, along **Rua Ferreira Borges** and its continuation **Rua Visconde da Luz**, are most of the fashionable shops and cafés; off to the west, the narrow rat-runs and alleys that cut down to the train station contain budget restaurants, canteens, grocery stores, workshops, butchers and bakers.

Heading up into the old town involves a steep climb, with perhaps the nicest approach being halfway along the main street, through the **Arco de Almedina**, an arch cut through the old city wall; the *Café-Galeria Almedina* bar here on the right (see p.193) actually burrows its way into the medieval wall. Stepped streets climb beyond into the heart of old Coimbra, with attractive alleys off to either side. Down Rua Sub Ripas, to the left, is the **Palácio de Sub Ripas**, sporting a fine Manueline doorway – the Renaissance windows and stone medallions are from the workshop of the French sculptor Jean de Rouen (João de Ruão), which used to be nearby. Almost any other turn you care to make reveals more interest: hidden courtyards, flower-decked balconies, cobbled dead-ends and glimpses of sky and lower town through unexpected gaps in the crumbling walls.

The Sé Velha

The **Sé Velha** (daily 9.30am–12.30pm & 2–5.30pm), an unmistakable fortress-like bulk, squats about halfway up the hill in its own steeply shelving square. Begun in 1162, it's one of the most important Romanesque buildings in Portugal, little altered and seemingly unbowed by the weight of the years. The one significant later addition – the Renaissance Porta Especiosa in the north wall – has, in con-trast to the main structure, almost entirely crumbled away. Solid and square on the outside, the cathedral is also stolid and simple within, the decoration confined to a few giant conch shells holding holy water and some unobtrusive azulejos from Seville around the walls. The Gothic tombs of early bishops and the low-arched cloister (100$00) are equally restrained.

The Velha Universidade

The main buildings of the **Velha Universidade** (daily 10am–noon & 2–5pm; 250$00 for university and library; another 250$00 for Sala dos Capelos) lie further up the hill, and date from the sixteenth century when João III declared its establishment at Coimbra permanent. The buildings are set around the **Pátio das Escolas**, a courtyard dominated by the Baroque clock tower nicknamed "A Cabra" – the goat – and a statue of the portly João III.

The elaborate stairway to the right of the main court leads into the administrative quarters and the **Sala dos Capelos**; tickets are sold here for visits to each of the main sections of the university. The hall itself – hung with portraits of Portugal's kings – is used for conferring degrees and has a fine wood-panelled ceiling with gilded decoration in the Manueline style. The highlight of this part of the building, though, is the narrow catwalk around the outside walls. The central

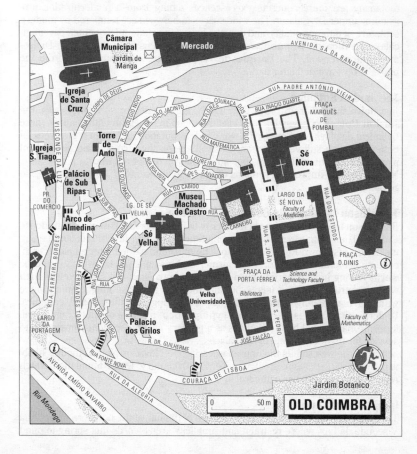

door off the courtyard leads past the **Capela**, not the finest of Coimbra's religious foundations but one of the most elaborate – covered with azulejos and intricate decoration including twisted, rope-like pillars, a frescoed ceiling, and a gaudy Baroque organ.

To the left is the famous library, the **Biblioteca Joanina**, a Baroque fantasy presented to the faculty by João V in the early eighteenth century. Its rooms telescope into each other, focusing on the founder's portrait in a disconcertingly effective use of *trompe l'oeil*. The richness of it all is impressive, such as the expanse of cleverly marbled wood, gold leaf, tables inlaid with ebony, rosewood and jacaranda, Chinese-style lacquer work and carefully calculated frescoed ceilings. The most prized valuables, the rare and ancient books, are locked away out of sight and, despite their impressive multilingual titles, the volumes on the shelves seem largely chosen for their aesthetic value; no one seems likely to disturb the careful arrangement by actually reading anything.

Sadly, the other faculty buildings of the university are almost completely devoid of interest. Their lofty position atop the narrow, cobbled streets notwithstanding, too many are mere concrete excrescences dating from a modernization programme under Dr. Salazar. The wide spaces in between are tempered by modern sculpture of dubious quality, and only the lure of the student-frequented pavement cafés on **Praça da República** – down the steep steps from Praça Dom Dinis – merit the diversion. The **Parque de Santa Cruz**, stretching uphill from the praça, is best avoided after dark.

The Jardim Botânico

Just down the hill from Praça Dom Dinis, ten minutes or so to the south, the **Jardim Botânico** is worth a brief visit. Founded in the eighteenth century, these botanical displays once enjoyed a worldwide reputation and, even if they've seen better days, it's still very pleasant to stroll among the formally laid out beds of plants from around the world, but note that you're not allowed to picnic here. Nearby are the impressive remains of the sixteenth-century **Aqueduto de São Sebastião**.

The Museu Machado de Castro and Sé Nova

Back up on the hill, after the old university buildings, is the **Museu Machado de Castro** (Tues–Sun 9.30am–5.30pm; sometimes closed for lunch; 250$00; free Sun morning), just down Rua de São João. The museum, named after an eighteenth-century sculptor, is housed in the former archbishop's palace, which would be worth visiting in its own right even if it were empty. As it is, it's positively stuffed with treasures: sculpture (see especially the little medieval knight riding home with his mace slung over his shoulder), paintings, furniture, and ceramics. Underneath all this is the Roman **Cryptoportico**, a series of subterranean galleries probably used by the Romans as a granary and subsequently pressed into service for the foundations of the palace.

Across the way stands the unprepossessing **Sé Nova**, or New Cathedral (daily 9am–noon & 2–6.30pm; free), a seventeenth-century Jesuit foundation which replaced the Sé Velha as cathedral in 1772.

Igreja de Santa Cruz

The last old-town stop is right at the bottom of the hill, at the northern end of Rua Visconde da Luz, where restraint and simplicity aren't words that spring to mind when considering the **Igreja de Santa Cruz** (daily 9.30am–noon & 2–6pm; cloister 200$00), the church of the monastery that was founded on the site by São Teotónio. The church predates even the Sé Velha, but nothing remains that has not been substantially remodelled – its exuberant facade and strange double doorway setting the tone. In the early sixteenth century Coimbra was the base of a major sculptural school that included the French artists Nicolas Chanterene and Jean de Rouen (João de Ruão), as well as the two Manueline masters João de Castilho and Diogo de Boitaca, all of whom had a hand in rebuilding Santa Cruz.

These artists designed a variety of projects: **tombs** to house Portugal's first kings, Afonso Henriques and Sancho I; an elaborate **pulpit**; and, most famously, the **Cloister of Silence**. It is here that the Manueline theme is at its clearest, with a series of airy arches decorated with bas-relief scenes from the life of Christ. From the cloister a staircase leads to the raised *coro*, above whose wooden benches is a frieze celebrating the nation's flourishing empire.

Around the back of the church, the small **Jardim da Manga** faces the main road. More cloister than garden, it was at one time surrounded by orange trees, and today still retains a cupola and fountain; there's a handy café at the rear of the garden.

The Santa Clara convents

It was in Santa Cruz that the romantic history of Dom Pedro and Inês de Castro (see "Alcobaça", p.150) came to its ghoulish climax. Pedro, finally proclaimed king, had his lover exhumed and set up on a throne in the church, where his courtiers were forced to pay homage to the decomposing body.

Inês had originally lain in the **Convento de Santa Clara-a-Velha**, a twenty-minute walk away from the main town across the river, her tomb placed alongside the convent's founder and Coimbra's patron, the saint-queen Isabel. Isabel was married to Dom Dinis, whom she infuriated by constantly giving away his wealth to the poor. She performed one of her many miracles when, confronted by her irate husband as she smuggled out yet another cargo of gold, she claimed to be carrying only roses: when her bag was opened that was exactly its contents. The Gothic hall church she built, over time, became almost entirely covered by silt from the River Mondego, but the ruin is slowly being restored.

The two tombs have long since been moved away, Inês's to Alcobaça and Isabel's to the **Convento de Santa Clara-a-Nova** (daily 8.30am–12.30pm & 2–6.30pm), higher up the hill and safe from the shifting river. The new convent, built in 1650, doesn't have much of the charm of the old and the fact that the nuns' quarters now house a Portuguese army barracks doesn't help. Its two saving graces, which make the climb worthwhile, are **Isabel's tomb** – made of solid silver collected by the citizens of Coimbra – and the vast **cloister** (100$00), heady with honeysuckle, which was financed by João V, a king whose devotion to nuns went beyond the normal bounds of spiritual comfort. The army's presence exerts itself in a small **military museum** (daily 10am–noon & 2–5pm; 100$00), displaying bits and bombs retrieved intact from World War II.

Portugal dos Pequenitos

Between the two convents extends the parkland site of **Portugal dos Pequenitos** (daily: summer 9am–7pm; winter 9am–5.30pm; 500$00, under-10s 200$00), a 1950s' theme park where scale models of many of the country's great buildings are interspersed with "typical" farmhouses and sections on the overseas territories, heavy with the White Man's Burden. Historically and architecturally accurate it's not, but the place is great fun for kids who can clamber in and out of the miniature houses.

A short distance beyond is a somewhat more sombre little park, the **Quinta das Lágrimas** (Garden of Tears), in which, so legend has it, Inês de Castro was finally tracked down and murdered.

Eating

The city's **cheapest meals** are to be found in the dives along Rua Direita in the Baixa, where if you're not too bothered about your surroundings – basement saloons and rough tables – or your fellow diners (even rougher old men) you can eat full meals for well under 1000$00. For a tad more sophistication, search out the atmospheric little cafés and restaurants tucked into the tiny alleys between Largo da Portagem, Rua da Sota and Praça do Comércio – Rua das Azeiteiras, in particular, has several good possibilities. Local specialities to try out are *chanfana* – kid goat roasted in wine, a little fatty for some tastes – and Santa Clara pastries. For **breakfast**, the cafés and coffee houses in the Baixa are best; see p.193 for more details.

Américo Machado Pessoa, Rua dos Coutinhos 14. Distinctly unpretentious café up a side street from the Sé Velha, where waist-expanding beef, pork and fish meals are served at zinc-topped tables. Good cheap house wine, too. It's open late, but there's no sign above the door. Closed Tues.

Restaurante Aviz, Rua do Brasil 185. Bustling good-time local eating place, a five-minute taxi ride east of the centre and serving later than most in town. Best-known for its seafood, though it also does great (and cheaper) steaks – try the *bifé Aviz*, cooked in cream and coffee. Around 2000–3000$00.

Dom Pedro, Avda. Emídio Navarro 58. On the main road by the river, the decor (including a fountain) is attractive and the waiters attentive, but the food can sometimes disappoint. Around 3000$00.

5 Vilas, Rua Direita 53. One of the more salubrious of the places on this street, with a clientele that looks as though it might eat the food rather than fight with it. Best at lunchtime, where around 1000$00 gets you the works including the brutal home-made wine.

Adega Funchal, Rua das Azeiteiras 18. Just off Praça do Comércio, this reasonably priced place serves generous helpings of chicken or mutton stew and the like in agreeable rustic surroundings. Under 2000$00.

A Lanterna, Largo da Sota 6. Bar and disco on the ground floor open until 2am, and a more subdued, tasteful restaurant on the first floor. A wide-ranging menu with dishes a cut above the usual – roast duck for instance; up to 2500$00.

Adega Paço do Conde, Rua Paço do Conde 1. Great, locally renowned *churrasqueiria* of cavernous proportions, with a dining room either side of a covered terrace. Under 1500$00 for grilled meat or fish, salad, wine and coffee. Closed Sun.

Restaurante Romano, Rua João Jacinto 18–20. Excellent pizzeria where everything is fresh and the chef is happy to conjure up special requests; you'll pay around 1000–1500$00. Open till 11pm.

Sereia, Rua Henriques Seco 1. Café-bar close to the youth hostel with a popular range of grills, egg dishes and stews at middling prices. Open till midnight.

O Trovador, Largo da Sé Velha 17. Next to the old cathedral, this lovely wood-panelled and ceramic-tiled restaurant is surprisingly good value – around 2500–3500$00 – if rather limited in choice. There are regular fado sessions here, too. Closed Mon.

Viela, Rua das Azeiteiras 35. Gloomy tiled dining room with good food, overseen by a friendly proprietor. The *carne de porco* is delicious and a gluttonous bargain at 900$00 – splitting the enormous full portions means a meal shouldn't top 1200$00 or so.

Restaurante Vitória, Rua da Sota 9 & 19. Under the *pensão* of the same name, this does good lunchtime business with groups of workers who are in no hurry to get back. Daily specials include fried fish platters with rice and salad for under 1000$00.

Zé Neto, Rua das Azeiteiras 8–12. This provides a similar list of Portuguese grills and fries to that served up at *Adega Funchal* but at budget prices, washed down with some of the cheapest house wine in town. Last orders around 9.45pm.

Drinking and nightlife

At some stage of the day, you should visit one of the traditional **cafés** and **coffee houses** along Rua Ferreira Borges and Rua Visconde da Luz, filled with package-laden shoppers. Praça da República, across town by the Parque de Santa Cruz, is also surrounded by cafés, this time popular with students and staying open until 2am. Other trendy **bars** are scattered across old and new parts of town, and the best are reviewed below; all stay open until 2am unless otherwise stated. Coimbra's **clubs** remain open much later; in some, you can expect the music to keep going until 6am. As a rule, you'll pay a minimum entrance fee of around 500–800$00 in the clubs, and in bars where there's a DJ or live music.

You're most likely to catch **fado** during the student celebrations in May, though there are year-round performances in bars like *Diligência* (see below) and even in some restaurants; those around the Sé Velha are good bets. For up-to-the-minute news on **concerts** and events, watch for flyposters stuck up all over university buildings.

Cafés

Pastelaria Arcadia, Rua Ferreira Borges 144. A favourite old-time cake-shop just off Largo do Portagem.

Café Montanha, Largo da Portagem. Best-sited of the square's cafés with a good view of the passing parade and bridge traffic.There's live music or poetry some evenings.

Praça Velha, Praça do Comércio. Tables outside in a veritable suntrap of a square, just down the steps from the main street.

Café Santa Cruz, Praça 8 de Maio. Occupying part of the monastery buildings, it's hard to say which is more attractive – the vaulted stone interior or the tables outside on the busiest downtown shopping stretch.

Café Sé Velha, Rua Joaquim António d'Aguiar 132. At the top of a particularly exhausting flight of steps a stone's throw from the cathedral, with outdoor terrace seating.

Bars

Café-Galeria Almedina, Arco de Almedina 10. A sweeping vault-bar-cum-art gallery in the bowels of the old city walls with live music at weekends. Open 8pm–4am.

Aqui Há Rato, Largo da Sé Velha 20. Bar with dance floor and DJ spinning pop-dance hits from 10pm until 4am.

Boémia Bar, Rua do Cabido 6. Upmarket wood-and-tile jazz/blues bar, which packs in the students at weekends; just off Largo da Sé Velha. Has fado on some Friday and Saturday nights. Closed Sun.

Califa, Rua de Matemática 4. Sparse, youthful, arty, old-town bar with inhospitable seating and a full range of designer beards and sculpted haircuts. Music is rap to rock.

Cartola Esplanada Bar, Praça da República. Student favourite, next to the turismo, with esplanade seats, interior chrome fittings and boombox acoustics.

Diligência Bar, Rua Nova 30, between Rua Direita and Rua da Sofia. There's food, drink and fado every night in this atmospheric joint with cobblestone walls and candles, though the feelings of *saudade* (loss and longing), from which the music draws its spirit, will also be felt in your wallet.

A Noite Tem Mil Olhos, Avda. João das Regras 68, Santa Clara. Just along from *Scotch* (see below); techno bar with a mixed clientele (gay and straight). Open till 3am.

Sing Sing Bar, Rua Castro Matoso 11. More peaceful than most of the late-night bars, with the chance of a seat and some conversation – provided you're not unlucky enough to coincide with karaoke night. Other nights it's a diet of alternative and underground sounds.

De Sjoelbak, Rua do Brasil 93. Out-of-town Dutch bar with lashings of lager and a boisterous crowd swinging to R&B and Sixties' classics; eat at the *Aviz* (see p.152) and pop in here afterwards. Closed Sun.

Tropical, Praça da República, corner of Rua Alexandre Herculano. Split-level bar packed with students at the weekends. The pavement tables soon get swamped, while the barman roves around with trays of ice-cold SuperBocks.

Clubs

Scotch, Quinta da Ínsua, Santa Clara. Lively disco-bar across the river, behind the Galp and Mobil stations. Predominantly dance and techno, with live music on Friday and Saturday nights; there's a café-snack bar here, too. Open till 6am.

States, Praça Machado de Assis 22a. Indie, rock and grunge; don't turn up until after midnight. Open till 4am; closed Sun.

Via Latina, Rua Almeida Garrett 1. Youthful, disco hi-jinks near Praça da República. Smaller than *Scotch*, but with a similar crowd. Open till 4am; closed Sun.

Listings

Banks and exchange Banks are grouped along the avenidas west and east of Coimbra A station, Avenida Emídio Navarro and Avenida Fernão de Magalhães. The *Hotel Astória,* Avda. Emídio Navarro 21 (close to Largo da Portagem), will change currency outside bank hours, as will *Hotel Tivoli*, Rua João Machado.

Boat trips Basófias (☎40 41 35 or 71 44 37) run 75min trips up the Rio Mondego (departing from beside Parque Dr. Manuel Braga), giving you a duck's-eye view of the old city. In summer, trips depart at 3pm, 4.30pm & 6pm, with additional 11.30am & 7.30pm services at weekends; in winter, 3pm & 4.30pm, additional 6pm service at weekends. There are no trips on Monday.

Buses Most services use the main bus station at the top end of Avda. Fernão de Magalhães (information on ☎270 81). AVIC, Rua João de Ruão 18 (☎237 69), runs to the Costa de Prata resorts, Figueira da Foz, Aveiro and Condeixa-a-Nova (for Conímbriga); Moisés Correia de Oliveira, Rua João Machado 23 (☎692 38 or 691 14), runs to Montemor-o-Velho and other villages on or close to the Coimbra–Figueira da Foz road (N11) and direct to Figueira itself.

Car breakdowns Automóvel Club de Portugal (ACP), Avda. Emídio Navarro 6 (☎268 13).

Car rental Hertz, Rua João de Ruão 16 (☎374 91); Hervis, Rua João Machado 94 (☎240 62); Salitur, Rua da Sota 42 (☎205 94).

Cinema Cine Avenida, Avda. Sá da Bandeira (☎263 42); also has a rooftop bar and great city views. Teatro Academico Gil Vicente, Praça da República (☎294 74), has an arts cinema as well as a gallery, café and occasional classical and jazz concerts.

Hospital Hospital da Universidade de Coimbra, Praça Professor Mota Pinto (☎40 04 00).

Markets The main food market is on Rua Nicolau Rui Fernandes, above the post office. On Saturday mornings, there's an open-air antiques market in Praça do Comércio.

Police Main HQ at Rua Nicolau Rui Fernandes, across from the post office (☎220 22).

Post office The main post office is at Avda. Fernão de Magalhães 223, in Largo do Amado (Mon–Fri 8.30am–6.30pm, Sat 9am–12.30pm); other central offices are on Rua Nicolau Rui Fernandes, across from the market, and on Praça da República (both same hours as main post office).

Swimming pool The Piscina Municipal (summer only 10am–1pm & 2–7pm) is at the Estádo Municipal São José sports complex, east of the centre: take bus #5 from Largo da Portagem.

Telephones It's easiest to make international calls from the main post office or the branch across from the market.

Train information Coimbra A (☎349 98); Coimbra B (☎341 27).

Travel agencies Abreu, Rua da Sota 2 (☎270 11), and Intervisa, Avda. Fernão de Magalhães 11 (☎238 73), both sell international bus and flight tickets. Or try Viagens Mondego, Rua João de Ruão 16 (☎220 25).

Conímbriga

The ancient city of **CONÍMBRIGA** (daily: March 16–Sept 30 10am–1pm & 2–6pm; rest of year 8am–1pm & 2–5pm; 350$00), 16km southwest of Coimbra, is by far the most important Roman site in Portugal. It was almost certainly preceded by a substantial Celto-Iberian settlement, dating back to the Iron Age, but the excavated buildings nearly all belong to the latter days of the Roman Empire, from the second to the fourth century AD. Throughout this period Conímbriga was a major stopping point on the road from Olisipo (Lisbon) to Bracara Augusta (Braga). Although by no means the largest town in Roman Portugal, it has survived better than any other – principally because its inhabitants abandoned Conímbriga, apparently for the comparative safety of Coimbra, and never resettled it. That the city came to a violent end is clear from the powerful wall thrown up right through its heart; a wall thrown up so hurriedly and determinedly that it even cut houses in two.

The site

It is the **wall**, with the **Roman road** leading up to and through it, that first strikes you. Little else, indeed, remains above ground level. In the urgency of its construction anything that came to hand was used and a close inspection of the wall reveals pillars, inscribed plaques and bricks thrown in among the rough stonework. Most of what has been excavated is in the immediate environs of the wall; the bulk of the city, still only part-excavated, lies in the ground beyond it.

What you can see is impressive enough, though. **Houses** with excellent mosaic floors (now covered to protect them from the elements), **pools** whose original fountains and water-ducts have been restored to working order, and a complex series of **baths** with their elaborate under-floor heating systems, have been revealed. In one part of the grounds, two skeletons lie partly exposed beneath the dust covering a Visigothic burial site. Beyond the wall, less work has been undertaken, but here, too, are evocative remains, particularly of the **aqueduct**, which fed the city with water, and the **forum**, with its shop entrances, and nearby **temple**. At the edge of the site, on a bluff above the steep valley below – for many years Conímbriga's main defence – the **public baths** enjoy a stupendous view.

There are some explanatory notes in English posted across the site, but to make sense of it all, it's worth investing in the official guidebook at the entrance. In the summer you may find students on site to explain the finer points.

The museum

Hang onto your ticket which includes entry to the excellent **Museo Monográfico de Conímbriga** (closed Mon), opposite the site entrance This displays fascinating finds from the dig, presented thematically in cabinets detailing various trades (glass-making, ironmongery, weaving, even house-building) and aspects of daily life: in the section on health and hygiene, scalpels and needles wink wickedly in the light, while nearby is a lovely collection of carved jade rings. The other side of the museum shows how the finds relate to the site itself, by means of photographs and diagrams. Here, too, are displayed the larger spoils – statues of torsos, carved lintels, gargoyles from temples, monochromatic mosaics, remarkably bright mural fragments, and slabs, pillars and tombstones from the necropolis. The only drawback to this fascinating museum is that there's no English-language labelling whatsoever. Make sure you end up with a visit round the back, to the **café** with terrific views from its terrace down into the valley.

Practicalities

There are two **buses** direct to the site in the morning (9.05am & 9.35am) from the AVIC bus station in Coimbra (see p.183), returning from the site at 12.55pm and 5.55pm. Alternatively, take one of the half-hourly buses (reduced service Sat & Sun) from the AVIC station to the small market town of **CONDEIXA-A-NOVA**, half an hour's walk north of Conímbriga. The bus drops you by the church at the edge of the main square, with the market directly opposite. It's a pleasant little place, with several cafés and bars around the square – try *O Joaquim*, next to the Banco Pinto & Sotto Mayor, a local diner with decent budget meals. For something more upmarket there's the restaurant in the elegant *Pousada de Santa Cristina*. Condeixa is also the centre of the Beira's **hand-painted ceramics** industry and eight local factories are open for visits – you'll pass a couple on the walk out along the main road to the site.

Montemor-o-Velho

Thirty-two kilometres west of Coimbra, the **castle** (10am–12.30pm & 2–5pm; closed Mon; free) at **MONTEMOR-O-VELHO** broods over the flood plain of the Mondego. From the train, or driving along the N111, to Figueira da Foz (see p.206), its keep and crenellated silhouette rival that of Óbidos, as does its early history. First the Romans, then the Moors, fortified this conspicuous rocky bluff; finally taken from the Moors at the end of the eleventh century, it became a favoured royal residence. It was here in 1355 that Dom Afonso IV met with his council to decide on the fate of Inês de Castro, and here, thirty years later, that João of Avis received the homage of the townspeople on his way to Coimbra to be acclaimed king Dom João I.

Despite this royal attention, the town itself never prospered, and today there's little enough to see inside the castle walls either, though the views from the walkways, naturally enough, are stunning. The main attraction within the walls is the Manueline **Igreja de Santa Maria de Alcáçova**, said to have been designed by Diogo de Boitaca of Belém fame; it has a beautiful wooden ceiling, fine twisted columns and Moorish-style azulejo decoration.

If you can, aim to visit on the second or fourth Wednesday of the month, when Montemor's vast **market** spills across the plain in the lee of the castle. Families swarm in from the surrounding countryside, some still by donkey and cart, though most by car and scooter, which soon clog up the congested central streets.

Practicalities

The **train station** is a long, long walk from town and castle; **buses** from Coimbra drop you much more centrally. There's no particular reason to stay, given the proximity of Coimbra or indeed Figueira da Foz, just 13km further west. That said, the *Residencial Abade João*, Rua Combatentes da Grande Guerra 15 (☎039/68 94 58; ④), a beautiful, converted period town house, may persuade you to stop; it's just up the street to the left as you face the large, pink town hall in the central Praça da República. The **turismo**, on the first floor of the town hall (Mon–Fri 9am–12.30pm & 2–5.30pm; ☎039/68 91 14), could doubtless drum up more reasons to hang around, though there's no better excuse than a **meal** at the *Restaurante Ramalhão*, Rua Tenente Valadim 24 (closed Sun evening, Mon, and Oct), where all the dishes – eel stew, chicken with rice, duck or rabbit – use ingredients grown, reared or caught around the town. You'll get away with spending 2000–3000$00 depending on your appetite.

Lousã and the Serra da Lousã

Another popular day-trip from Coimbra is to the small village of **LOUSÃ**, 25km to the southeast, with its ruined castle and surrounding *serra* countryside. You can get there by train (Coimbra Parque station) or by bus (Mon–Fri). There are two train stations at Lousã: get off at the first, **Lousã A**. From here, take the road at right angles to the rail line and walk uphill to the centre. To reach the castle, you'll need to continue on past the church until you see a sign for "C.P. Prado", which you follow until reaching the *Café Lousanese* – at the fork here, it's left for the castle ("Castelo e Ermidas"), right for *A Cave* restaurant (see p.198).

The village

Wandering around Lousã's streets, you pass a succession of intricately decorated **chapels** and **casas brasonadas** (heraldic mansions), while in the handsome town hall, a little museum doubles as the **turismo** (daily 9am–12.30pm & 2–5.30pm; ☎039/99 35 02). Customarily helpful, this can supply you with a sketch map of the Serra da Lousã, vital if you want to explore the range, and useful, too, for the walk up to the castle.

Follow the path up from the village through the pine trees, and you pass springs midway, bubbling beautifully clear water that locals drive up to collect. After around 2km (30min), you emerge at a spot where a tributary of the Mondego curls around a narrow gorge between two splendid wooded hills. On one sits a miniature **castle**, whose stone keep provides views across the valley; on the other is a small hermitage dedicated to **Nossa Senhora da Piedade**. Pilgrims mingle with swimmers, who come to bathe in the chilly river pool between the two; picnickers abound, and there's a **café-restaurant** (Easter–Sept only), with a dining room overlooking the river.

Practicalities

The village has two central **pensões**, both pleasant and moderately priced: the *Residencial Martinho*, Rua Forças Armadas (☎039/99 13 97; ③), whose rooms all have bathrooms; and *Pensão Bem Estar* at Avda. Coelho da Gama 11 (☎039/99 14 45, fax 99 39 15; ②), whose back dining room serves typical country dishes at reasonable prices – all rooms come with TV and telephone, though only some have bathrooms. There is also a **campsite** (☎039/99 10 52, fax 99 35 16; officially open March–Sept, ring to check at other times), ten minutes' east of the centre and signposted from the town hall.

The village's best **restaurant** is a fifteen-minute walk from the centre, in Bairro do Penedo, on the way to the local paper factory. The unlikely-looking *A Cave*, a modern building set among new housing, has a basement dining room dishing up huge portions of local cooking – the *leitão* (suckling pig) is excellent, though there's also lamb, *chanfana* and even *coq au vin*. During your stay, try the shockingly alcoholic **Licor Beirão** – herb-flavoured "firewater" – which is made locally from a secret recipe developed by a pharmacist from Lousã.

The Serra da Lousã

A hike to the top of the **Serra da Lousã** will reward you with stunning views and a sequence of eerie sights, in the range's abandoned villages. The most direct path runs through the woods above Lousã's **castle** and is marked, rather intermittently, with paint blazes on the trees – the map from the turismo is of some help (though not a great deal). You'd need to get an early start out of Lousã to see much of the range, though you could happily spend a couple of hours pottering around the castle's environs, on paths that climb down to river pools and up through the woods to viewpoints and lesser peaks.

There are six villages on the range, all of them deserted in the 1950s as a result of rural emigration. It's quite an unsettling experience to wander through the empty streets and into the open houses. In the first village you come to, **Casal Novo**, a few of the houses are being renovated as holiday homes and it's possible that you may be able to stay the night; check first with the turismo in Lousã. Beyond Casal Novo is **Talasnal**, where more houses are available to rent.

Upriver: Penacova and Lorvão

Northeast of Coimbra, the hilly, wooded valley of the **Rio Mondego** is a delight. The river is trailed by the minor N110 road, along which run regular buses from Coimbra, while for six months of the year it's possible to rent a **kayak** to travel downriver from Penacova to Coimbra. You must book in advance to do this; all the details are given below.

The drive is lovely, the **N110 road** keeping high above the river for the most part, affording the occasional sweeping view of glistening water and improbably perched hamlets. At Penacova, the road forks and drivers can make the most of the scenic surroundings by heading up the equally attractive **N235 to Luso** (see p.202). The **IP3**, meanwhile, sticks intially with the Mondego and forges on for Viseu, via Tondela (p.203), a roller coaster of a main road with some very fast sections and more fine views.

Penacova

PENACOVA, 22km northeast of Coimbra, is a small town of some antiquity set high above the river, with stunning views of the valley – spoiled only by the sweep of the motorway which cuts through on the opposite hillside. There is little enough to the place itself – a pint-sized square, a couple of cafés and restaurants, and the surrounding river and woods – though an oddity is the highly elaborate **toothpicks** (*palitos*) on sale. These are hand-carved from willow by local women and are beautiful artefacts; the more delicate ones are like feathered darts. You can inspect these – buy them, too, if you wish – at the **turismo** (Mon–Sat 9am–5.30pm, Sun 9am–12.30pm & 2–5.30pm; ☎039/47 71 14) in the town hall, in the main square.

If you fancy a night in these quiet surroundings, there are two **places to stay**: the friendly, traditional *Pensão Avenida*, Avda. Abel Rodrigues da Costa (☎039/47 71 42; ③), on a bluff as you drive up into town, with a polished wood interior, sun-terrace and restaurant; and the newer *Residencial São João* (☎039/47 75 45; ③), a modern building across the road from the *Avenida*. For meals, the *O Panorâmico* **restaurant** – next to the town hall and turismo – has a glorious view down the valley; full meals cost around 2500–3300$00. The adjacent *Café Turismo*, behind the turismo at the back of the square, has a terrace with the same views and yet more carved toothpicks on display.

The **campsite** (☎039/47 74 64; closed Jan) is on the opposite bank of the river, below the town, and it's from here that *O Pioneiro do Mondego* arranges the down-river **kayak trips** to Coimbra (April to mid-Oct daily; 2500$00 per person), leaving Penacova at 11am. It's a 25km (3–4hr) trip back to Coimbra. You'll need to book in advance (English-speaking: call ☎039/47 83 85, 1–3pm & 8–10pm), and if you've reserved there's a free minibus **from Coimbra** at 10am to get you to Penacova in time for departure; more information is available from the turismo in Coimbra. *O Pioneiro* also rents out canoes and bicycles for the day (3000$00).

Lorvão

A side-trip from Penacova, or Coimbra, could also be made to the **Convento de Lorvão**, at the village of **LORVÃO**, accessible up a side road off the N110. By public transport, the best you can do is to take the RBL bus to Rebordosa, 3km before Penacova, and then walk the remaining 5km to the convent. This very ancient complex was founded by Benedictines in the ninth century, predating the arrival of the Arabs, and later taken over by Cistercian nuns. The abbesses are buried horizontally in the graveyard; the lesser sisters are buried vertically, in twos and threes.

Most of what remains of the convent is the product of heavy restoration in the eighteenth century. If you ring for admission, you can visit the **church**, which displays the skull of an Arab king in its treasury, and with luck climb up to the *zimbório*, or domed roof, with its splendid views over the village. The visit, however, is a disturbing one, as the convent still serves as a distressingly old-fashioned mental institution.

The Buçaco Forest and Luso

The **Buçaco Forest** is something of a Portuguese icon. The country's most famous and most revered woods were a monastic domain throughout the Middle Ages, and the site in the Peninsular War of a battle that saw Napoleon's first significant defeat. Today, they are a little uncared for and overvisited, but remain an enjoyable spot for rambling.

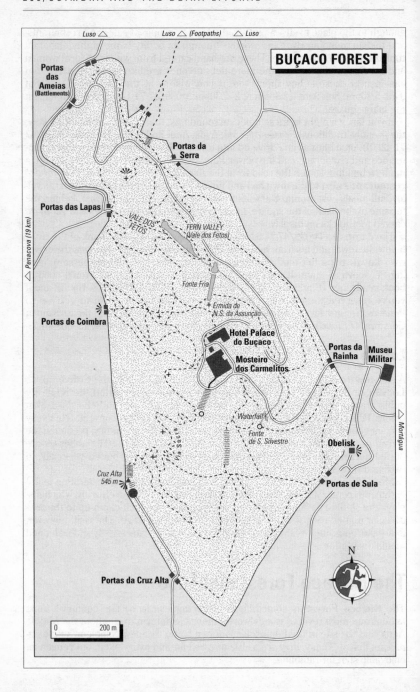

BUÇACO FOREST

Luso △   Luso △ (Footpaths)   △ Luso

Portas das Ameias (Battlements)

Portas da Serra

Portas das Lapas

VALE DOS FETOS

FERN VALLEY (Vale dos Fetos)

Fonte Fria

+ *Ermida de N.S. da Assunção*

Portas de Coimbra

△ Penacova (19 km)

Hotel Palace do Buçaco

Mosteiro dos Carmelitos

Portas da Rainha

Museu Militar

△ Mortágua

Via Sacra

Waterfall

Fonte de S. Silvestre

Obelisk

Cruz Alta 545 m

Portas de Sula

N

Portas da Cruz Alta

0   200 m

Benedictine monks established a hermitage in the midst of Buçaco Forest as early as the sixth century, and the area remained in religious hands right up to the dissolution of the monasteries in 1834. The forest's great fame and beauty, though, came with the **Carmelite monks** who settled here in the seventeenth century, building the walls which still mark its boundary.

In 1643 Pope Urban VIII issued a papal bull threatening anyone who damaged the trees with excommunication; an earlier decree had already protected the monks' virtue by banning women from entering. The monks, meanwhile, were propagating the forest, introducing varieties new to Portugal from all over the world. Nowadays there are estimated to be more than seven hundred different types of tree, but the most impressive remain some of the earliest – particularly the mighty Mexican cedars.

From Coimbra it is easy enough to visit the forest as a day-trip (cars 500$00), or en route to Viseu. All non-express buses from Coimbra to Viseu take a short detour from the spa town of **Luso** (40min from Coimbra), through the forest, stopping at the old royal forest lodge, now the swanky **Hotel Palace do Buçaco**, and again by the **Portas da Rainha**. Alternatively, if you have money to burn, you could stay overnight in the *Hotel Palace* itself (☎031/93 01 01, fax 93 05 09; ⑦), which was built on the site of the old Carmelite monastery as a summer retreat for the Portuguese monarchy. However, as it was completed only in 1907, three years before the declaration of the Republic, it saw little royal use. An enormous imitation Manueline construction, it charges upwards of 20,000$00 for a double room in low season and 30,000$00 in high season, but anyone can stroll in and have a drink (their wine cellar is superb) or a meal. You can also view what remains of the **Mosteiro dos Carmelítas** (June–Sept 10am–noon & 2–6pm; Oct–May 9am–noon & 1–5pm; closed Sat; 100$00), and admire the Afonso Mucha prints or the sequence of azulejos depicting the Portuguese conquest of Ceuta and the Battle of Buçaco (see below). If your budget won't stretch to the *Hotel Palace*, you can find less expensive accommodation in Luso itself (see below).

The Battle of Buçaco and the Museu Militar

The **Battle of Buçaco** (1810) was fought largely on the ridge just above the forest, and it marked the first serious reverse suffered by Napoleon in his campaigns on the Peninsula. The French under Massena launched a frontal assault up the hill on virtually impregnable Anglo-Portuguese positions, sustaining massive losses in what for the Duke of Wellington amounted to little more than a delaying tactic, which he exploited in order to give himself time to retreat to his lines at Torres Vedras. A small **Museu Militar** (Tues–Sun 10am–5pm; 75$00), outside the forest near the Portas da Rainha, contains maps, uniforms and weapons from the campaign. Just above it, a narrow road climbs to the **obelisk** raised as a memorial to the battle, with vistas inland right across to the distant Serra da Estrêla, from where the **Portas de Sula** leads back into the forest.

Walks around the forest

Walks are laid out everywhere in Buçaco: along the **Vale dos Fetos** (Valley of Ferns) to the lake and cascading **Fonte Fria**, for example, or up Avenida dos Cedros to the **Portas de Coimbra**. But you can wander freely anywhere in the forest, and in many ways it's at its most attractive where it's wildest, away from the formal pathways.

The **Via Sacra**, lined with seventeenth-century chapels in which terracotta figures depict the stages of Christ's journey carrying the cross to Calvary, leads from the *Hotel Palace* to the **Cruz Alta**, a giant cross at the summit of the hill. From here, as from the Portas de Coimbra, there are magnificent panoramas of the surrounding country. It's a lovely place, if not always the haven of peace the monks strove to create – at weekends and holidays the woods are packed with picnicking Portuguese.

Luso

LUSO lies just 3km downhill from the forest. A spa town for the past hundred years or so, it still draws crowds of Portuguese, taking the waters as a cure for rheumatism and other complaints. As such places go, it's pretty enjoyable, with a series of elegant spa buildings, a wonderful nineteenth-century *salão do chá* – all white wicker, potted palms and Art Nouveau decor – and a casino.

Taking the waters can be fun, too. You pay an initial 5000$00 and then extra for whichever treatment you choose, with a full session of massage, electrolysis and other therapies from 600$00 to 2500$00 a go; the only serious expenditure is incurred if you see one of the spa's consultants. There's also a fine, Olympic-sized **swimming pool**, attached to the central *Grande Hotel das Termas* (see below), whose somewhat stiff admission fee (Mon–Fri 1000$00; Sat & Sun 1500$00) is more than recompensed by a few hours' basking. Most locals, though, are here to picnic in the surroundings, taking the opportunity to fill bottles and plastic containers for free with spa water from the outdoor **Fonte de São João** (which also has its own *casa do chá*).

PRACTICALITIES

There are regular **buses** to Luso from the bus station in Coimbra, which is much the easiest way to arrive; the bus drops passengers at the bottom of the central avenida. By **train** (on the Coimbra–Guarda line), there's currently only one morning departure suitable for a day-trip – the 10.36am from Coimbra B, returning at 6.18pm (6.29pm in winter). Trains stop on the northern outskirts of Luso – walk down past the *Cesteiro* restaurant and into the centre along Rua Dr. António Granjo.

The **turismo** (Aug Mon–Fri 9.30am–1pm & 2–8pm, Sat & Sun 10am–1pm & 3–5pm; rest of year Mon–Fri 10am–1pm & 2–6pm, Sat 10am–1pm; ☎031/93 91 33) is just up from the bus stop on Avenida Emídio Navarro, near the post office, and can help you find a **room** or provide a list of local accommodation.

The best of the budget **places to stay** is the friendly *Pensão Luso* (☎031/93 92 07; ②) on Rua Dr. Costa Simões above the town centre – from the bus stop, walk up and head right, along Rua Dr. Francisco Diniz. Alternatively, there's the *Pensão Portugal*, Rua Marinha Pimenta (☎031/93 91 58; ③), quite a climb from the town centre – on the way to the turismo, turn left off Avda. Emídio Navarro along Rua Alvaro Castelões – it's fairly unprepossessing but undeniably value for money. More expensive but still good-value are: *Pensão Astória*, Avda. Emídio Navarro (☎031/93 91 82; ④), which has a certain faded charm and is located beyond the turismo, almost opposite the *Grande Hotel*; and *Pensão Alegre*, also on the avenida (☎031/93 02 56; ④), up past the *Hotel Eden*, an impressive building full of nineteenth-century style which was once the residence of the Conde Graciosa. Top-of-the-range is, of course, the *Grande Hotel das Termas de Luso*, Rua dos Banhos (May–mid-Oct; ☎031/93 04 50, fax 93 03 50; ⑥), in need of a lick of paint, though still splendidly furnished inside and with a heated indoor pool.

Most of the *pensões* and hotels have **restaurants** attached, one of the best being that of the *Pensão Central* on Avda. Emídio Navarro (between the *Eden* and the *Alegre*), which has a rooftop terrace. The restaurant at the *Pensão Luso* is good, too, while at the plain and popular *Cesteiro* on Rua Lúcio Pais Abranches, on the way out towards the train station, you can eat well for around 2500$00.

The Dão Valley and the Serra do Caramulo

The route northeast from Coimbra to Caramulo leads through the **valley of the Rio Dão**, heart of the region where **Dão wines** – some of the country's finest and richest reds – are produced. Where they're not covered with vineyards, the slopes are thickly wooded with pine and eucalyptus trees, though all too often there are bare tracts where forest fires have raged. It's a fine ride and though there's no overwhelming point of interest en route, you might stop for coffee at least in the small market town of **SANTA COMBA DÃO**, a little over 50km from Coimbra.

Beyond here, the views from the main IP3 are of the spectacular **Serra do Caramulo**, breaking to the northwest. Tondela (see below) marks the eastern turn-off point for the mountains, accessed along the minor **N230** which winds tortuously through a succession of tiny villages at the heart of the mountain range, before descending to Águeda, from where the fast main road runs due south to Coimbra. With your own transport, you could describe the circle from Coimbra, seeing Luso and Buçaco Forest on the way. By **bus**, the same circuit is possible, though it's a much more complex affair and one which will entail a night in the mountains, at the pretty village of Caramulo – no great hardship.

The Serra do Caramulo

Most of the *serra* villages are little more than hamlets, of interest principally for their environs, full of rhododendrons, brightly coloured azaleas and thick green shrubs growing wild on the hillside. If you feel like staying off the beaten track, places like **Cambarinho** and **Alcofra** have **rooms** to rent, but perhaps the best base is the main village, Caramulo, a twisting 19km from Tondela and the highway. Coming **from Coimbra**, there are three daily buses to Caramulo, via Águeda. **From Luso**, you need first to take the Viseu bus as far as **TONDELA**, where you should be able to pick up one of the two daily buses on to Caramulo/Águeda, a majestic if rather bumpy drive straight across the centre of the Serra do Caramulo. If you're detained by choice or necessity in Tondela, the *Pensão Ferrador* (☎032/82 25 59; ②), in the main square, is excellent value, as is the *Residencial Tondela de Severino Gonçalves* (☎032/82 24 11; ③), also in the main square. For **eating**, there's a good restaurant, *O Solar*, opposite.

An alternative approach to Caramulo, from the north, is **from Vouzela** (see below) in the Vouga valley. On weekdays, two buses daily run between Vouzela and Varzielas, 4km north of Caramulo; from there you can either walk or, with luck, pick up a local bus connection. If you are approaching from the south, Vouzela is an obvious next destination after Caramulo.

Caramulo

Tucked beneath the peaks of the high Beiras *serra*, **CARAMULO** is a great walking base – the loftiest Serra de Caramulo peak, **Caramulinho** at 1075m, is less than an hour's hike away. It's also a very striking village, a diminutive, rather ghostlike place, which makes an almost surreal setting for a couple of very fine museums.

At the **Museu do Caramulo** (daily 10am–1pm & 2–6pm; 600$00), the principal display is the **Museu de Arte**, a wonderfully jumbled art collection, with everything from primitive religious sculpture to sketches by the greatest modern masters – minor works by Picasso and Dalí among them. There's an exquisite series of sixteenth-century Tournai tapestries depicting the earliest Portuguese explorers in India, full of weird animals and natives based on obviously very garbled reports. A painting by British portraitist Graham Sutherland, donated to Portugal by the Queen, and symbolizing the long alliance with Britain, is accompanied by its letter of authenticity from Buckingham Palace. Elsewhere there's a large *John the Baptist*, painted by Grão Vasco, and quantities of beautiful furniture and jewellery. Next door, and even more incongruous, is the **Museu do Automóvel**, a collection of vintage cars and motorcycles, including a pack of chrome-plated American dream machines.

The **turismo** (☎032/86 14 37) is on the Tondela road, past the post office. Caramulo has a fine **pensão**, the *São Cristovão* (☎032/86 13 94; ③), though call first to check it's open; it closes over winter. With more money to spend, first choice is the excellent *Quality Hotel*, Avda. Dr. Abel Lacerda (☎032/86 01 00, fax 86 12 00; ⑤), with superb amenities (including Jacuzzi, hydrotherapy and Internet access in the rooms), and unbeatable views over the plains towards the Serra da Estrela. The six-bedroom **pousada**, *São Jerónimo* (☎032/86 12 91, fax 86 16 40; ⑤), a kilometre along the Tondela road, pales in comparison but is cheaper than most in the chain and has a swimming pool and great views. The *Café-Restaurante Marte*, on the main road through the village, has affordable **meals**; just up the hill, locals while away the hours under the trees at the *Café Avenida*.

Along the Rio Vouga

The **Rio Vouga** is one of the most beautiful, somnolent rivers in the country and a fine route to follow if you feel like taking in a little of backwater Portugal. The old Vouga train line along the river has been replaced by a bus service which stops at various rural spots en route. You probably won't want to get off until **Vouzela** (see below), though drivers will feel compelled to pause now and again to take in the views. Coming from Coimbra or Aveiro, you can get a train as far as **Albergaria-a-Velha**, where you change to a CP bus. Alternatively, you can approach from the south, from Caramulo, or from Viseu, to the east, from where the minor N337 makes a particularly memorable approach.

Vouzela

VOUZELA is one of the most immediately attractive of Beira towns, a small place with an almost palpable sense of civic pride. The locals boast of the peculiar sweet cakes, or *pasteis de Vouzela* (only for the most sweet-toothed), richly flavoured traditional dishes such as *vitela de Lafões*, and the heady local *vinho Lafões* (similar to *vinho verde*). Vouzela also has its own local paper, which is quite a feat for a town with little over two thousand inhabitants.

The old centre is built around a sluggish stream, bordered by lilies and overhung with weeping willows, which serves as the backdrop to the main morning activity – washing clothes. Beneath a low **Romanesque bridge**, garments are spread to dry on the tall grass and soap suds run blue in the clear water. Houses clustered around the bridge are all of the small-town manor type, with granite steps and balconies and whitewashed plaster work. Topping this scene, a viaduct gracefully loops its way across the rooftops, while beyond it the *serras* of Arada and Caramulo rise up, dark and green, to north and south.

Just off the main through-road, at the top of the lane down to the river, the **turismo** (daily 9am–12.30pm & 2–5pm; ☎032/77 15 15) is housed in a former prison in the Largo Morais de Carvalho. On the floor above, there's a **museum** (free) offering insights into local preoccupations such as weaving, photography and painting. It contains a small, rather odd collection, ranging through anthropological and historical exhibits, traditional craftwork and Romanesque fragments, to an array of old dolls. Nearby, up in Praça da República, is the thirteenth-century **parish church** and the town **Pelourinho**, popularly referred to as the *forca* or scaffold, from its days as a site of executions during the Inquisition.

There's a **feira** on May 14 when flowers are strewn in the streets in honour of **São Frei Gil**, and everyone drives up into the hills to witness the blossoming of the rare *loendros*, a type of rhododendron peculiar to this area and which is now protected by law. Otherwise, note that there's a **street market** every first Wednesday in the month, a good time to be in town.

Practicalities

Buses drop you right in the centre, with the town square and turismo down the main road and off to the left. Finding a **room** shouldn't be much of a problem, either at *Casa Ferreira*, Rua Barão da Costeiro (☎032/77 16 50; ②), just off the main road, a little way up from the turismo, or more attractively at the *Pensão Marquês*, Rua Aires de Gouveia 76 (☎032/77 20 29; ③), which is signposted up a side street one minute from the turismo. The *Marquês* also has a very good **restaurant**, popular with local families. Otherwise, try the *Restaurante Chafariz* or *Restaurante Paulo*, both on Rua Mousinho de Albuquerque, off Praça da República.

There is a municipal **campsite** with fine views (☎032/77 18 47, fax 77 15 13), 4km up the road towards Mortágua and **Senhora do Castelo**, a low hill which is the location for much merrymaking and picnicking on the first Sunday after August 5. There's a signpost pointing the way from Praça da República.

Termas de São Pedro do Sul

Four kilometres northeast of Vouzela is the thermal resort area of **TERMAS DE SÃO PEDRO DO SUL**, possibly the oldest spa in Portugal. It was a great favourite with the Romans, a popular haunt of Portuguese royalty – Dom Afonso Henriques is said to have bathed his wounded leg here after the battle at Badajoz – and remains among the grandest and most attractive in the country. Its position beside the Vouga, and the pine trees all around, certainly lend it charm, and the resort makes for a pleasant stop between buses or an afternoon trip from Vouzela. Under the central span of the bridge, a small island teems with swans and ducks, while downstream, fishermen and young boys fool around on and in the water. The **spa** itself is open all year for those who want to sluice themselves in its foul-smelling waters and avail themselves of the usual range of treatments.

You can get here by **bus** from Viseu (Mon–Fri 4–5 daily, weekends 1–2) or Vouzela (Mon–Fri 2 daily); for information on onward bus travel ask at the

Quiosque das Termas facing the spa. The **turismo** (Mon–Sat 9am–noon & 2–5.30pm; ☎032/71 13 20), on Largo dos Correios, by the bridge, has a list of *pensões* and can help with **rooms** in private houses. If you plan to stay, you'd be wise to book ahead since the **hotels** and **pensões** stacked up above the river are frequently full. Among the best options – all easily found – are the modern, family-run *Pensão Romana* (☎032/71 15 24; ③; closed Dec & Jan), *Pensão Ultramarina* (☎032/72 30 11; ④), the *Hotel Vouga* (☎032/72 30 63, fax 72 35 00; ④), and the modern *Hotel do Parque* (☎032/72 34 61, fax 72 30 47; ⑤). In high season, these and the other places may insist on your paying for full board. The resort's brand-new **youth hostel** is situated in a big high-rise overlooking the centre (☎ & fax 032/72 30 48); it also has double rooms available (③). There's a **campsite** (☎032/71 17 93; June–Sept) on the eastern outskirts of town, signposted from the stone bridge.

The town of **SÃO PEDRO DO SUL** itself is another 3km to the northeast, an unremarkable spread of buildings either side of a busy main road, at the confluence of the Sul and Vouga rivers. You can pick up more bus connections here to Viseu and Lamego, if you're unlucky in Termas. For details of the extraordinary driving route between here and **Arouca** to the northwest, see p.220.

Figueira da Foz

FIGUEIRA DA FOZ is one of the liveliest towns on the west coast, a major resort and deep-sea fishing port. Sited at the mouth of the Mondego, roughly equidistant from Lisbon and Porto and just over an hour by train from Coimbra, it attracts people from all over the country to its superb beaches and surf. That said, it's not the most initially alluring of beach resorts: there's a somewhat industrial approach from the south, and the town itself is resolutely modern with its long promenade backed by a line of anonymous apartment blocks. But it's as close to a typical Portuguese resort as you'll find. Most of the action, in fact, takes place away from the sands in the atmospheric backstreets, where a bubbling good humour prevails, even when the town's packed to the gills.

Arrival, information and accommodation

The **train station** is a long 20- to 25-minute walk from the centre and beach. Keep walking along the river until you see the ocean and then cut into the town – a useful beachfront landmark is the concrete clock tower, close to the tourist office. AVIC **buses to Buarcos** – a fishing village at the northern end of the bay, which has become more or less part of Figueira – leave from directly outside the train station (Mon–Sat every 30min until 11pm; hourly on Sun). The **bus station** is slightly closer in, though it's still a fair walk down to São Julião church and the municipal gardens, from where the streets run straight to the beach.

If you need help with anything, the **main turismo** (summer daily 9am–11pm; winter Mon–Fri 10am–12.30pm & 2–5.30pm; ☎033/229 35) is in Edifício Atlântico on Avenida 25 de Abril and is even more helpful than most; there's another in Buarcos at Largo Tomás de Aquino (summer daily 9am–8pm; ☎033/226 10), which is served by regular buses along the seafront. If you stay some way out of

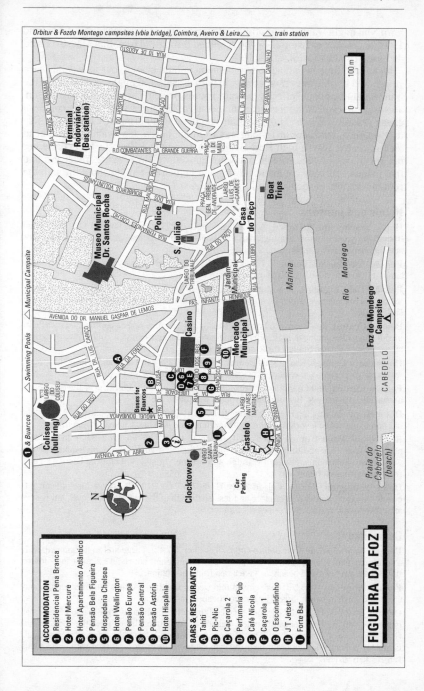

Orbitur & Fozdo Montego campsites (vbia bridge), Coimbra, Aveiro & Leira △   △ train station

FIGUEIRA DA FOZ

ACCOMMODATION
1 Residencial Pena Branca
2 Hotel Mercure
3 Hotel Apartamento Atlântico
4 Pensão Bella Figueira
5 Hospedaria Chelsea
6 Hotel Wellington
7 Pensão Europa
8 Pensão Central
9 Pensão Astória
10 Hotel Hispânia

BARS & RESTAURANTS
A Tahiti
B Pic-Nic
C Caçarola 2
D Perfumaria Pub
E Café Nicola
F Caçarola 1
G O Escondidinho
H J T Jetset
I Forte Bar

town, you might want to **rent a bike** from the municipal campsite; it costs around 1500$00 per day; **car rental** can be arranged through Marco, Rua Maestro David de Sousa (☎033/251 13).

It can take time to find a room in Figueira in high season, but with persistence you should be able to get something. In high season, you might well be met at the train station by people offering **private rooms**, which – provided they're reasonably central – will be the best bargains in town. Otherwise, there are a couple of cheap *pensões* just in front of the train station on Rua Fernandes Tomás and Rua da República, but these are a long way from the beach. It's much better to head for the centre, where both **Rua Bernardo Lopes** and **Rua da Liberdade** are lined with possibilities, though many are booked well in advance. You'll also find that **prices** – already comparatively high in Figueira – tend to shoot through the roof in summer, particularly in July and August.

Hotels and *pensões*

Hotel Apartmento Atlântico, Avda. 25 de Abril (☎033/221 46, fax 224 20). Very good upmarket option in a modern high-rise with pool. En-suite rooms with all mod cons. Prices are higher on Fri & Sat. ⑥.

Pensão Astória, Rua Bernardo Lopes 45 (☎033/222 56). Not as nice as the *Central*, opposite, but a decent fall-back. It's above a restaurant. ③.

Pensão Bela Figueira, Rua Miguel Bombarda 13 (☎ & fax 033/227 28). Near the main beach and town centre. It can be noisy; many of the unremarkable rooms come with shower and TV. ③.

Pensão Central, Rua Bernardo Lopes 36 (☎033/223 08). Airy *pensão* approached up a flight of side-steps. Rooms have high ceilings and nice old furniture, and a couple share a grand street-facing balcony, though these are noisy. ④.

Hospedaria Chelsea, Rua Miguel Bombarda 8 (☎033/232 44). Good and reasonably priced with a range of rooms, the more expensive ones with bath or shower. ③.

Pensão Europa, Rua Cândido dos Reis 40 (☎033/222 65). Very central, near the casino and above a fish restaurant. Bare, adequate rooms with basin. ④.

Hotel Hispânia, Rua Dr. Francisco António Dinis 61 (☎033/221 64, fax 296 64). A rambling old hotel, one of the few right in the centre with private parking. Closed Nov–Feb. ④.

Residencial Pena Branca, Rua 5° de Outubro 42 (☎033/326 65, fax 218 92). In Buarcos, near the post office and turismo, and just outside the city wall. Splendid, high-quality set-up with private bathrooms, phone, TV, fridge and balcony; breakfast included. There's a good regional restaurant below. ④.

Hotel Wellington, Rua Dr. Calado 23 (☎033/267 67, fax 275 93). Three blocks from the beach, this is a genteel sort of place and less shabby than the exterior suggests, but rooms are rather small and it's overpriced in summer. ⑤.

Campsites

Parque Municipal de Campismo (☎033/330 33 or 327 42). Large and well-equipped, with a swimming pool (though you have to pay to use it) and tennis courts. It's 2km inland – follow the signs from town and beach, or take a taxi from the station.

Foz do Mondego (☎033/314 96; closed mid-Dec to mid-Jan). Across the river mouth, and close to Cabadelo beach, this is by far the cheapest in the area.

Orbitur (☎033/314 92), Mata de Lavos, Gala, 4km to the south, across the estuary. The most expensive – though the ocean is much cleaner for swimming here. Take the AVIC "Cova Gala" bus (every 30min till 10.15pm, fewer at weekends) from the Mercado Municipal. *Carrossel*, at Largo da Beira-Mar near the campsite, serves great *tasquinha* with snacks and *petiscos* (savouries).

The Town and beaches

The town doesn't offer much in the way of sightseeing – the most impressive sights are the beaches – but there are a couple of places to scout around once you tire of the sands. On the edge of the town park, Parque Abadias, the **Museu Municipal Dr. Santos Rocha** (Tues–Sun 9am–12.30pm & 2–5.30pm; free), Rua Calouste Gulbenkian, has an impressive archeological section, as well as a large number of photographs of nineteenth-century bathing belles. Meanwhile, the inside walls of the **Casa do Paço** (Mon–Fri 9.30am–12.30pm & 2–5pm; 200$00), on the waterfront by the marina, are covered with thousands of Delft tiles, part of a ship's cargo which somehow got stranded in Figueira.

Apart from this, you can check out Figueira's central streets which form a tight little grid set back from the eastern end of the beach. Many are pedestrianized, brimming with pavement cafés and strolling holidaymakers, while back along the river, on Rua 5° de Outubro, is the **market** (summer Mon–Sat 7am–7pm; winter Mon–Fri 8am–5pm, Sat 8am–1pm), good for food and just about anything else you might need.

The beaches

Figueira's **town beach** is enormous, not so much in length as in width: it's a good five-minute walk across the sand to the sea and unless you wear shoes or stay on the wooden walkways provided, the soles of your feet will have been burned long before you get there. There are cafés along the whole length of the beach, but since the busy main road and promenade are set well back from the water, there's no great sense of place. Best spot is probably at the **Buarcos** end of the beach, 2km away, where a huddle of pastel-coloured fishermen's houses sit amidst a rash of new concrete high-rises behind what remains of the old defensive wall.

If it's **surfing** you're after, then just step around the promontory at Buarcos, where fans gather to admire the breakers. By contrast, **Cabadelo beach**, behind the mole on the Mondego river mouth's south bank, is small, sheltered and good for families – though to reach it you have to go right out through the town and over the bridge by bus.

The only problem in recent years has been that of pollution; the EU blue flag, denoting water acceptable to swim in, does not always fly over all of Figueira's beaches. If this concerns you, an up-to-date appraisal of the water quality at each of the beaches is posted outside the turismo – tests are carried out weekly in summer and monthly during the winter.

You can always have a dip instead in the fee-paying **swimming pools** on the north side of town: the nearest is Piscina de Santa Catarina, a fifteen-minute walk along Rua Joaquim Sotto Mayor, in a park on the right. Further along, there's another pool in the Ginásio Club next to the municipal stadium.

Eating

The centre of town is packed with **places to eat**, with any number of snack bars, cafés and seafood restaurants offering *ementas turísticas* at reasonable prices.

Aquário, Alto do Forno, Buarcos. One of several good seafood places in Buarcos, with a great *cataplana*, and fado on Fridays.

Bela Figueira, Rua Miguel Bombarda 13. The *pensão*'s restaurant serves fine Indian and Portuguese food. Try the shrimp and rice curry – and eat on the terrace (where prices are slightly higher). Around 2000$00.

Caçarola I, Rua Cândido dos Reis 65. Basement shellfish restaurant with daily specials chalked on the board. To keep costs down, you could just sit at the bar and have a plate of prawns and a beer.

Caçarola II, Rua Bernardo Lopes 85–87. Sister restaurant to *Caçarola I* and just as good, if not better. Open till 4am.

Dory Negro, Largo Caras Direitas 16, Buarcos. On the edge of Buarcos, this is a good place to come for fish, with dishes around the 1600$00 mark. It's hidden out of sight from the sea, but has a little covered patio. Closed Tues in winter.

O Escondidinho, Rua Dr. Francisco António Dinis 62. Hidden away (as the name suggests), this is worth seeking out for superb and inexpensive Goan food. Under 2000$00 if you pick and choose. Closed Mon.

Café Nicola, Rua Bernardo Lopes. At the corner with Rua Cândido dos Reis. A busy, modern, two-tier affair with reasonable snacks.

Pena Branca, Rua 5° de Outubro 42, Buarcos. With windows overlooking the beach at Buarcos, this is the best place for an *arroz de sardinha* and *caldeirada*. Other fish and meat specials, too, and full meals for 2500–3000$00.

Pic-Nic, Rua de São Lourenço, at junction with Rua David de Sousa. Well-priced menu (under 2500$00 for a full meal), with plenty of fish and a lovely roof-terrace to eat it on.

Tahiti, Rua da Fonte 86. Nice little backstreet restaurant, away from the central bustle, with friendly English-speaking staff, great prices and decent food – which extends to English breakfasts and fish and chips for the criminally unadventurous.

Nightlife, entertainment and events

Nightlife centres on the **casino** at Rua Bernardo Lopes 1 (3pm–3am; take your passport for entry), for which semi-formal dress and an initial outlay on chips are compulsory. The casino also houses a couple of **cinemas**, which generally have up-to-date releases. In the first couple of weeks of September the casino hosts an **International Film Festival** – a little uneven in its organization, but always with a good selection of new films shown in their original language; ask at the turismo for more information.

Alternatively, there are several central **pubs** and **bars**, like *Perfumaria*, Rua Dr. Calado 37; *Dom Copo*, Rua São Lourenço 13; *J T Jet Set*, at the south end of Avda. 25 de Abril; and *Dona Bárbara*, Rua A. Zagalo, all of which play the same kind of rock and pop until around 4am. However, for sheer location, *Forte Bar*, set in the castle's crumbling ramparts, is hard to match. Of the **discos**, long-standing favourites include *Disco Bergantim*, Rua Dr. Lopes Guimarães 28, and *Parlamento*, Avda. de Tavanede, near the train station and the bridge over the Mondego. If you have transport you could make a late-night trip out to *Flashen,* hidden in pine trees outside the village of Quiaios, 8km north of Figueira. None of these gets going till around midnight but they don't close till 4am and all-nighters are not unheard of in summer.

One of the best of the year's parties is **Saint John's Eve** (June 23/24) with bonfires on the beach and a "Holy Bathe" in the sea at dawn; while **bullfights** are often held during the summer season.

North of Figueira: to Praia de Mira

The coastline immediately **north of Figueira** is remarkable only for its air of total desertion. Beyond Buarcos, there's very little, and for long stretches hardly even a road. Off the main north–south road (N109) you can get to the coast at just three points before Aveiro: at **Quiaios**, **Tocha** and **Mira**, each with their respective beaches, all of them flying EU blue flags declaring them clean enough to swim in. If you're driving **on to Aveiro** (see p.212), stick with the minor coastal route beyond Praia de Mira, a pleasant run through farmland with dunes to one side and river to the other; this way, you'll pass through probably the nicest of this coast's small resorts, **Costa Nova** (see p.215).

Praia de Quiaios and Praia da Tocha

With a car you can find virtually empty beaches around either **QUIAIOS** or **TOCHA**, though the low-lying coastal plain offers no protection against the Atlantic winds. For more sheltered leisure pusuits, aim for the inland lakes between the two beaches, particularly the large, pine-fringed **Lagoa da Vela**, where there are scores of picnic areas, and windsurfing and sailing schools.

Buses run every hour or so from Figueira bus station up the N109, stopping at both Praia de Quiaios (25min) and Praia da Tocha (40min). There isn't any accommodation once you get to either beach other than the excellent **campsites**, *Praia de Quiaios* (☎033/91 04 99; June–Sept), which has its own swimming pool, and *Praia da Tocha* (☎031/44 11 43; mid-June to Sept).

Praia de Mira

Set on a small lagoon – the southernmost point of a system of waterways and canals centered around Aveiro – **PRAIA DE MIRA** is the focus of increasing development. Seven kilometres west of the inland town of Mira, it is rather more accessible than the beaches at Quiaios or Tocha, with half a dozen buses a day from either Figueira, Coimbra, or Aveiro. There's a lot more accommodation, too, the downside being that you may not want to stay. You couldn't exactly describe Praia de Mira as a beautiful place – its one extremely long main street, Avenida Cidade de Coimbra, spears towards the sea, lined by new apartments and dusty building sites. But the beach that stretches around it is seemingly endless and backed by dunes: ideal if your aims extend no further than beach-lounging and walks.

Any number of places offer cheap, basic *dormidas* along the main street – look out for the signs, or ask in any bar. The **turismo**, on Avda. 25 de Abril (☎031/45 85 06) may be able to help with rooms, but is itself often closed out of season. **Pensões** aren't cheap and if you're going to stay in one, it might as well be one with a sea view from its balconies: immediately on the left at the end of the main street, the modern *Arco Íris* on Avda. do Mar (☎034/47 12 02; ④) is a decent spot; a few hundred metres further along the seafront is the similarly pleasant but more expensive *Residencial do Mar* (☎ & fax 031/47 11 44; ⑤).

There are two official **campsites** a short way from the village – the municipal site (☎031/47 21 73; May–Sept) is closer and considerably cheaper, though less well-equipped, than the *Orbitur* site (☎031/47 12 34, fax 47 20 47; closed Dec to mid-Jan), for which you go up the main street, turn right at the roundabout, and continue for two and a half kilometres. There is also a **youth hostel** and campsite in the same direction and a little closer to the village (☎ & fax 031/47 12 75; hostel open all year; campsite June–Sept). The *A Cozinha* **restaurant**, one of several on Avenida Barrinha – the road backing the lagoon – has windows overlooking the lagoon and, among other dishes, serves a buttery grilled squid and tasty *porco à alentejana*.

Aveiro and around

Most visitors to **AVEIRO** are intent on getting straight out again, to the series of excellent **beaches** to north and south and into what a tourist brochure describes as the "virile, iodine-bearing sea". However, Aveiro itself is also a place of some antiquity and interest. It was a thriving port throughout the Middle Ages, up until the 1570s, when the mouth of the Vouga silted up, closing its harbour and creating vast, fever-ridden marshes. Recovery began only in 1808 when a canal was cut through to the sea, re-opening the port and draining much of the water; only the shallow lagoons you see today were left. These form the backbone of a modern economy based on vast **saltpans**, fishing, and the collection of seaweed (*molico*) for fertilizer. The occasional pungent odour wafting across town, seemingly from the lagoon, is actually from the large paper factory nearby.

The town's big annual event is the **Festa da Ria**, celebrated in the last two weeks of August with boat races, folk dances, and competitions for the best decorated *barcos moliceiro*, the flat-bottomed lagoon boats used to collect seaweed.

△ Porto, Viseu & Guarda

AVEIRO

0   200 m

N

ACCOMMODATION
1 Residencial Pomba Branca
2 Residencial Palmeira
3 Residencial Beira
4 Pensão Residencial Estrela
5 A Brasileira
6 Hotel Arcada
7 Hospedagem Rossió
8 Hotel Imperial

▽ Figueira da Foz & Coimbra   ▽ Figueira da Foz & Coimbra

The other major celebration is the **Festa de São Gonçalinho**, held in honour of the patron saint of fishermen and single women in the second week of January. Those who have made vows during the year, either for the safe return of a fisherman or for the finding of a husband, climb to the top of a chapel and throw down loaves of bread to the crowd below; the aim is to catch as much as possible.

The Town

Aveiro casts off its rather dowdy first appearances as soon as you reach the central praça and bridge over the main canal. The traditional industries here are celebrated by imposing statues of the local workers on the bridge – the *marnoto* and the *salineira*, the latter with her salt tray. Handsome, pastel-coloured houses (of which the turismo is one) line Rua João Mendonça, and in the narrow little streets behind the **fish market** tiled houses face each other across arms of the canal. Lagoon boats with raised prows lie tied up along the quaysides.

True, there's only one sight of real note, the fifteenth-century **Convento de Jesus**, across the central canal and five minutes' walk up on the right. This now houses the **town museum** (Tues–Sun 10am–12.30pm & 2–5pm; 250$00), whose finest exhibits all relate to Santa Joana, a daughter of Afonso V who lived in the convent from 1475 until her death in 1489. She was barred from becoming a nun because of her royal station and her father's opposition, and was later beatified for her determination to escape from the material world (or perhaps simply from an unwelcome arranged marriage). Her tomb and chapel are strikingly beautiful, as is the convent itself, and there's a fine collection of art and sculpture – notably a series of naive seventeenth-century paintings depicting the saint's life.

Once you've seen this you may as well cross the road to the **cathedral**, whose exterior concrete loggia and interior breeze-block walls make it resemble a municipal swimming pool. Infinitely more pleasing is the **Misericórdia** church, back down towards the canal, whose seventeenth-century facade features blue snowflake-design tiles. The **town hall**, a century older, stands opposite, both buildings facing a declamatory **statue** of Aveiro's famous son, the nineteenth-century politician José Estevão Coelho de Magalhães.

Beyond these few attractions, the main local interest is in the surrounding beaches and lagoons, for which see p.215. There's a certain fascination, too, in hanging around in the **cafés**, watching life on the Ria: try some of the celebrated local sweets, especially *ovos moles*, candied egg yolks.

Practicalities

Aveiro is on the main Lisbon–Porto rail line, with the **train station** at the northeastern end of town; most **buses** (including services to and from Praia de Mira) use the train station forecourt and adjacent streets as their terminus. From the station, walk straight down the broad main street in front of you – Avenida Dr. Lourenço Peixinho – and you'll eventually hit Praça Humberto Delgado and the bridge, a fifteen-minute walk.

The **turismo** is just up from the bridge on the right in a beautiful Art Nouveau building at Rua João Mendonça 8 (June–Sept daily 9am–8pm; Oct–May Mon–Sat 9am–7pm; ☎034/207 60). It supplies free maps, local bus timetables, books boat trips and can help with finding accommodation. **Bicycles** are an ideal way to explore the lagoon area – once you've negotiated the first few kilometres of fast road – and can be rented from Agência de Viagems Culturália, near to the turismo at Rua João Mendonça 31, 1st Floor (☎034/231 42).

Accommodation

You shouldn't have much trouble finding a **room in Aveiro**, except perhaps during the Festa da Ria in August, when you'd be wise to book ahead. There are several places immediately down from the train station, but they're a little far from things; in the centre, try the backstreets around the fish market, particularly Rua das Marnotos, for inexpensive *dormidas*. Those with transport have the option of staying **out of town** at one of the lagoon- or beach-resorts (see pp.215–217) – although the beaches themselves are accessible by public transport, the nicer places to stay tend to be more off the beaten track.

The local **campsites** are also way out of town, at São Jacinto to the north (see p.216). or to the south at Praia da Barra, Costa Nova and Praia da Vagueira (see pp.215–216).

Hotel Arcada, Rua de Viana do Castelo 4 (☎034/230 01, fax 218 86). Small, unexciting rooms, though pleasant enough staff and a central location in a grand building by the bridge with views over the canal. All rooms with either shower or bath, breakfast and TV. ④.

Residencial Beira, Rua José Estevão 18 (☎034/242 97). Clean, welcoming place just off the praça, with breakfast included. It's often full – call ahead. ③.

A Brasileira, Rua Tenente Resende 47 (☎034/286 34). One of a handful of *dormidas* places near the fish market, this is a good bet for solo travellers, with small, clean rooms charged per person. English spoken. ②.

Pensão Residencial Estrela, Rua José Estevão 4 (☎034/238 18). An old, converted house whose plant-filled staircase and polished wooden corridor are rather grander than the smallish, but cool and comfortable, rooms. Friendly, English-speaking owners, and big discounts out of season. ④.

Hotel Imperial, Rua Dr. Nascimento Leitão (☎034/221 41, fax 223 59). Modern building, not far from the Convento, with fine views of the lagoon from the top-floor bar; breakfast included. At the top of its price range. ⑤.

Quinta do Paço da Ermida, 3km from Ilhavo, south and off the N109 to Vagos and Mira (☎034/32 24 96). A short distance from one of the lagoon arms, this magificent Solares de Portugal manor house (with just four rooms) belongs to the family of the founder of the Vista Alegre porcelain company – one of the oldest in Europe. ⑥.

Residencial Palmeira, Rua da Palmeira 7–11 (☎034/225 21). Pretty, modern, tiled town house with attached dining room, in the old quarter between the praça and the Canal de São Roque. Bright rooms, some with shower or bath, and most with TV. ④.

Residencial Pomba Branca (also known as *Paloma Branca*), Rua Luís Gomes de Carvalho 23 (☎034/225 29, fax 38 18 44). Very comfortable rooms (with bath and TV) in a gracious, quiet town house, near the station and with its own parking. There are traditional features throughout, including a wood-panelled bar. ⑤.

Hospedagem Rossío, Rua Dr. Barbosa de Magalhães 24 (☎034/298 57). Good central location off the canalside park, and about as cheap as you'll find, though the fairly spartan rooms are as gloomy as the proprietor; separate bathrooms. ②.

Eating

There are some excellent restaurants in Aveiro, with **local specialities** including eels and shellfish from the lagoons and powerful *Bairrada* wine. The cheapest eats are in the little *casas de pasto* in the old town streets around the fish market, though there are also several regular restaurants in this area, too.

Alexandre, Cais do Alboi 14, on the corner with Rua 16 de Maio. A short walk along the canal, this is a well-regarded snack bar and adjacent restaurant with good meals for around 2000$00. Closed July.

Neptuno, Rua Mendes Leite 1. Good little grill house serving huge portions of chicken, home-made sausage, chops or fish. Around 1000$00 for a *dose* – you may only need to order half. Closed Sun.

Salpoente, Canal São Roque 83. Ten minutes' walk north along the canal, this superior fish restaurant is set inside a renovated salt barn. Crabs, fish and eels at medium-to-high prices, served Mon–Sat noon–2.30pm & 7.30–10.30pm.

Sonatura, Rua Clube dos Galitos 6. Vegetarian wholefood self-service restaurant serving daily specials of varying size – the food isn't particularly good, but at least it offers veggies a change from omelette and chips. Mon–Fri closes 8.30pm; 3pm on Sat.

O Telheiro, Largo da Praça do Peixe 20–21. Excellent *adega* with wooden benches and tiled tables, and food cooked any way you like as long as it's chargrilled. *Lulas grelhados* (grilled squid) is superb; add a fish soup, wine and coffee and you'll pay around 2500$00. Closed Sat.

O Terraço, Edifício 15, 7th Floor. Mediocre food but stunning views over the Aveiro and the Ria; get the lift to the sixth floor and walk the last flight.

Zé da Parreirinha, Trav. do Lavadouro 10. Rough-and-ready *casa de pasto* with full meals for under 1000$00. Just off Largo do Praça da Peixe. Closed Wed.

Zico, Rua José Estevão 52. Very popular local spot, with most dishes around 1400$00. Menu changes daily, but there are always grills, local fish and good wine. Closed Sun.

Drinking

Estrondo, Canal São Roque 73. Polynesian-style bar, just down from *Salpoente*, on the canal, open till 2–3am for cocktails and drinks. Closed Mon.

Cervejaria Rossio, Largo da Rossio 8a. Central *cervejaria* serving beer and good steak sandwiches until 2am. Closed Mon.

Salpoente, Canal São Roque 83. The restaurant has an enjoyable late-opening bar with occasional live music (500$00 admission) at the weekends. Open till 2am.

Around Aveiro: the lagoon and beaches

There's no beach in Aveiro itself but the coast to north and south is a more or less continuous line of sand, cut off from the mainland for much of the way by the meandering **lagoon**. Although developers have long caught on, the whole sand bar is still little spoilt, and offers ample opportunity for beach lounging as well as fascinating walks along the lagoon's swampy edge, which boasts abundant birdlife. Note that the pine forests shelter several military bases, so stick to the roads and don't camp outside official sites.

From July to September, the turismo organizes two-hour **boat trips** by *moliceiro* along the lagoon (daily: July–Sept 15 at 10am, 1pm & 4pm; Sept 15–30 at 3pm; 1700$00). There's also a motorboat trip to Torreira (daily June 15–Sept 15 at 10am; 2340$00 return). At any time of year a group of people can rent a boat to tour the river; information, again, from the turismo.

Praia da Barra and Costa Nova

The most easily accessible coastal points from Aveiro are **PRAIA DA BARRA**, at the mouth of the Vouga, and **COSTA NOVA**, a little further on; but be warned that both are enormously crowded on summer weekends. Local **buses** from Aveiro (hourly 8am–8pm) depart from outside the train station, also stopping on Rua Clube dos Galitos, across the bridge from the turismo and about 150m down the canal on the right. They call at Barra first, then Costa Nova.

Praia da Barra, though less charming than Costa Nova, has a greater choice of **accommodation**, as well as more restaurants and nightclubs, but prices in all three can be steep. The pick of the cheaper accommodation options is: *Residencial Farol* (☎034/36 92 47; ⑤), situated above a cool and pleasant café and billiards room at the end of the main road and overlooked by Portugal's tallest lighthouse; *Residencial Marisqueira*, Avda. João Corte Real (☎034/36 92 62; ⑤); and the *Hotel Barra*, Avda. Fernandes Lavrador 18 (☎034/36 91 56, fax 36 00 07; ⑤), which has a pool. There's also a municipal **campsite** (☎034/36 94 25; June–Sept). For **nightlife**, head for *EDP*, Rua Vasco da Gama 66 (closed Sun), popular with the locals in summer. It's about 9km east towards Aveiro.

Costa Nova is a highly attractive ensemble of candy-stripe wooden buildings, stuffed into the strip between beach and lagoon. There are two places **to stay**: the excellent *Residencial Azevedo*, Rua Arrais Ança (☎034/39 01 70, fax 39 01 71; ⑤), and the huge **campsite** 1km to the south (☎034/36 98 22, fax 36 00 08), complete with supermarket and disco.

Vagueira

Around 15km south of Aveiro but still accessible by bus, **VAGUEIRA** faces the lagoon, though it is actually situated on the mainland, just 1km from the ocean beaches. The summer **turismo**, on Largo Parracho Branco at the north end of the beach where the bus drops you, can help with **rooms**. Alternatively, there are bungalows for rent, 1500m to the south on the Mira road (☎034/79 77 32 or 79 77 54; ④) next to the entertaining Vaga Splash aqua. There's also an excellent **campsite** here (☎034/79 75 26, fax 79 70 93) where you can rent bikes.

São Jacinto

If you want more than just a beach, then you need to head **north of Aveiro**, though the transport connections are a little more complex. Take the bus from Rua Clube dos Galitos to **Forte de Barra** (7–10 daily), a four-kilometre run through the saltpans and docks, from where a connecting boat (100$00; no cars) chugs the fifteen minutes across the lagoon to **SÃO JACINTO**. With a military base at one end and a forest of cranes cluttering the skyline, beautiful it's not, but it's a thriving little port with a handful of dockside café-restaurants. There's also an enormous dune-fringed **beach** twenty minutes' walk away: off the boat, walk to the right past the post office and, at *Restaurant Ferraz* (the best place to eat), turn left. The beach is straight up the improbably long road ahead, where you'll also find the *Restaurante Marluci*, which has a few **rooms**. Alternatively, good accommodation can be found out of town on the road to Torreira at *Pensão Moliceiro*, Avda. Hintze Ribeiro (☎034/482 35; ③), or, with more money to spend, the *Pousada da Ria*, Bico do Muranzel (☎034/483 32; ⑥) – a mid-priced *pousada* with swimming pool, tennis courts and lagoon-view balconies. There's a municipal campsite (☎034/33 12 20) 2.5km out on the Torreira road and a substantial *Orbitur* **campsite** (☎031/47 12 34, fax 47 20 47; Feb–Nov) with good facilities a further 2.5km on.

São Jacinto backs onto an extensive **bird reserve**, where you can join a five-kilometre (two-hour) guided tour (summer: Mon–Wed, Fri & Sat 9am & 2pm; winter hours erratic; 200$00), though this may depend on numbers; for more information and for times of tours in winter, consult Aveiro's turismo or the reserve itself (☎034/297 52). It's 1km out of town, along the main road to Torreira: turn left at the post office, walk up to the main road and head right. At the reserve there's a small scrap of beach overlooked by the *Portelas* bar-restaurant.

Torreira

In summer, buses run the 13km north from São Jacinto to **TORREIRA**, a lively little resort with several small *pensões*. The best hotel is the four-star *Estalagem Riabela* (☎034/481 37, fax 481 47; ⑤); if you can't quite stretch to that there's the slightly cheaper *Residencial Albertina*, Trav. Arraias Faustino (☎034/483 06; ④), a popular, modern hotel by the beach with air-conditioned rooms and a bar. You can rent bikes from them too. Out of town but well worth the effort to get there is *Albergue A. Mansão* (☎034/460 00; ⑤); continue 5km to the north, cross the lagoon and head for Murtosa – it's signposted on your left. The proprietor and chef conjure up a friendly atmosphere and the price includes breakfast and evening meal; book ahead, though, as there are only six rooms.

For **eating**, the restaurant *Casa Passoiera*, on the main road, is highly recommended. The *Copacabana* piano-bar also has a decent grill-restaurant and live music. The buses at this point loop back round to Aveiro; to head onwards to Furadouro (see below) means making a detour through Ovar.

Ovar, Furadouro and Santa Maria da Feira

The distinctive Ria countryside comes to an end around Ovar, 25km to the north of Aveiro, and there's no great reason to delay the drive or train ride straight to Porto. But Ovar itself is worth at least a coffee break, while the beach to the west is as good as anything that's gone before.

Ovar and Furadouro

OVAR is on the main train line to Porto. If you're lucky, there'll be a bus waiting to take you into the centre of Ovar; failing that, it's a fifteen-minute walk. There are direct buses, too, from São Jacinto and Torreira.

The place is an attractive market town, with the asset of a fine beach 5km away at Furadouro, to which there's a regular bus. The **turismo** (daily: July–Sept 9am–9pm; Oct–June 9.30am–12.30pm & 2.30–5.30pm; ☎056/57 22 15) is off the main square, on Rua Dr. Manuel Arala. In the square itself you'll find the surprisingly good **Museu Etnografica** (daily 10am–noon & 2–6pm), with an international collection of pottery, plus traditional clothing and the usual folklore displays. Perhaps more compellingly, while you're here try some of the local *pão-de-ló* sponge cake – every bit as good as it looks. The nicest **accommodation** in town is provided by the modern *Hotel Meia-Lua*, Quinta das Luzes (☎056/57 50 31, fax 57 52 32; ⑤), and the large, four-star *Albergaria São Cristóvão*, at Rua Aquilino Ribeiro 1 (☎056/57 51 05, fax 57 51 07; ⑥). At the budget end of the scale, the flash new **youth hostel** (☎ & fax 056/59 18 32) is on Avda. Dom Manuel I (the N327 towards Furadouro).

FURADOURO marks pretty much the northern extent of the system of waterways, and like its neighbours to the south boasts a long stretch of pine-backed dunes. There may be a few **rooms** available at *Pensão Avenida* above the *Café Amadeu* on the waterfront at the end of the pedestrianized Avenida Central, and there's a **campsite** (☎056/59 14 71), too.

Santa Maria da Feira

At **SANTA MARIA DA FEIRA** (or, more simply, Feira), easily reached by bus from Aveiro or Espinho (see p.278), one of the most spectacular castles in Portugal – the **Castelo da Feira** (April–Sept Mon 8.30am–noon & 1.30–6pm, Tues–Sun 8.30am–7.30pm; reduced hours in winter; 200$00)–towers above the town, its skyline a fanciful array of domes. A sunken gateway leads into the castle's interior, which has been rather zealously over-restored but provides a handsome indication of its erstwhile grandeur. Its principal room is the **Great Hall**, a magnificent Moorish structure, while, beyond the keep, a tunnel links the two parts of the castle in such a way that no direct or easy access can ever have been offered to intruders – arrow slits and hidden entrances emphasize the point. In some of the walls you may notice a few stones marked with Roman inscriptions, and you can make out the familiar straight Roman road through the wooded hills above. It's a fifteen-minute climb up the hill to the castle; outside, a little café dispenses drinks and sandwiches.

On the way down from the castle, you pass the grand **Convento de Loios** (now a conference centre), at the back of which you'll find an incredibly tacky cement grotto and garden of fake bridges and pebble-lined paths. This apart, there's not much else to the place, which sprawls out from the foot of the hill in a welter of new development.

Best time to visit is undoubtedly during the annual **Festa das Fogaceiras** (Jan 20), when files of little girls parade through the town carrying castle-shaped *fogaça* cakes. It's a custom – much revived in recent years – which dates back to the plague of 1750 when the Infante Pedro made a *vota* to Santa Maria that cakes in the shape of his castle would be baked in thanksgiving for those who survived.

Practicalities

If you want **to stay**, try *Residencial Tony*, Rua Jornal Corrio da Feira 22 (☎056/37 25 93; ②), five minutes' walk from the bus station, which offers clean rooms with toilet and shower. With more money to spend, though, the best place to stay is the outstanding *Casa das Ribas* (⑤), a lovely eighteenth-century manor house with gorgeous gardens, right next to the castle. Decent and inexpensive **meals** are to be had at the *Restaurante Churrasqueira Parque*, which also has rooms. It's on the street at the bottom of the road up to the castle, where there are several other little cafés, too.

Arouca and the Serra da Arada

Picking up the N224, it's a splendid drive from Feira to **Arouca**, 20km to the east, a winding route through forested hills and small terraced slopes of tumbling vineyards, the air heady with the scent of pine resin. There are regular buses from Feira, and although there are no public transport links south from Arouca, through the magnificent **Serra da Arada** (see below), buses do run on north to Porto.

Arouca

AROUCA is a small town entirely overshadowed by the vast **Convento da Arouca** (Tues–Sun 9am–noon & 2–5pm; 200$00), whose imposing walls loom across the busy main road that cuts through town. It was founded as early as 1091,

though most surviving parts are from rather later medieval times. In the kitchen
there are huge fireplaces along Alcobaça lines; the vast Baroque church (which
you can see without buying a ticket; enter from the main road) holds richly
carved choir stalls and a great organ with 1352 notes, played on rare occasions by
one of the country's few experts; while off the central courtyard there's an airy
Sala Capítula, where the abbesses once held court, lined with azulejos.

The convent peaked in importance when Queen Mafalda, of whose dowry it
had formed a part, found her marriage to Dom Henriques I of Castille annulled
and retired here to a life of religious contemplation. In the extensive **museum**
upstairs, you can see some of Mafalda's most prized treasures, including an
exquisite thirteenth-century silver diptych, along with a series of paintings by
Josefa de Óbidos (see p.144) and Diogo Teixeira. In 1792, four centuries after
Mafalda's death, villagers claimed to have witnessed her saving the convent from
the ravages of a terrible fire. She was promptly exhumed and beatified.

The rest of town struggles to make a mark in the face of its prize exhibit, but
it's a handsome little place away from the main road. The central square holds a
couple of cafés with pavement seats, while in the medieval backstreets there are
some beautiful old houses decked with wisteria. Stay for the night if you can:
Arouca is at its quietest and best during the somnolent evenings or in the early
morning when shrouded in rising mist from the surrounding hills.

Local heart rates increase slightly during the annual **Festa de Nossa Senhora
da Mó**, when the whole town turns out for a picnic on the crown of the hill 8km
east of the town. **Holy Week** processions are a big deal here, too, starting on the
Wednesday and culminating on the Saturday night, when most of the inhabitants
parade behind the local saints' statues to the Misericórdia church, with candles lit
in all the town's windows.

Practicalities

Buses (from Porto and Feira) pull up on the main road, opposite the convent.
The road heads straight uphill where, on the left, is the little main square, Praça
Brandão de Vasconcelas, with the **turismo** (Mon–Fri 9.30am–12.30pm &
2–5.30pm; Sat 10am–12.30pm; ☎056/94 35 75).

There are only two **places to stay**: *O Tranca*, Rua Alexandre Herculano
(☎056/94 39 16, fax 94 30 54; ②), a little further up the road from the square and
on the right, has simple, modern rooms above a restaurant; otherwise, keep right
on to the top of the main road and take the left fork (there's a "residencial" sign)
to the *Residencial São Pedro*, Avda. Reinaldo de Noronha (☎056/94 45 80; ④), five
minutes' from the square. This has very smart rooms with bath, the front ones
with balconies overlooking town and convent.

For a **meal**, your best bet is *O Tranco*, which serves marvellous and mountainous *churrasqueiria* dishes for around 2500$00 a head. There are a couple of
casas de pasto around town, too; the *Casa Cernada* in the bottom corner of the
main square is worth a try.

The Serra da Arada

If you have your own transport, consult the turismo for details about places to visit
in the nearby **Serra da Arada**, whose beautiful countryside is terraced like the
Minho and abundantly littered with dolmens, crumbling villages and waterfalls
with ancient bridges.

Perhaps the most extraordinary route is the drive **south**, over the peaks, heading for São Pedro do Sul and Vouzela (see pp.204–205). Initially, you need to follow the minor road out of Arouca which climbs to the radio mast on the heights of **São Pedro Velho** (1100m), from where views of the valley are tremendous. On the way, tiny hamlets cling to the hillside, vines grow on precipitous terraces, while the road snakes first through pine forest and then high across the heather-dotted moorland. At **MANHOUCE**, a mean, medieval hamlet, the road disappears altogether for an instant and degenerates into cart-rutted cobbles worn by centuries of use. After another 12km of incredible bends and views, you emerge onto the N227 – a 43-kilometre journey that takes ninety minutes to negotiate. It's a spectacular drive but be prepared to take evasive action along the whole route, against other drivers or, occasionally, against wandering cattle.

There is – incredibly – a bus service along this route, though it's geared towards market and school times and consequently isn't conducive to day-trips or connections to anywhere reasonable. However, if you fancied extensive **hiking** and camping in the forests, you could just strike out from Arouca, providing you were properly equipped: there are endless paths and tracks connecting all the hamlets along the way.

travel details

Trains

Aveiro to: Coimbra (at least hourly; 45min–1hr); Espinho (every 30min; 35–50min); Lisbon (11–13 daily; 2hr 40min–4hr 50min); Ovar (every 30min; 25–40min); Porto (every 30min; 50min–1hr 30min).

Coimbra to: Aveiro (at least hourly; 45min–1hr); Figueira da Foz (17 daily; 1hr–1hr 20min); Guarda (6 daily; 3hr–3hr 20min); Lisbon (15–16 daily; 2hr–3hr 20min); Lousã (Mon–Fri 17 daily, Sat 12, Sun 8; 50min); Luso-Buçaco (5 daily; 45min); Ovar (5 daily; 50min–1hr 30min); Porto (12 daily; 1hr 20min–2hr).

Figueira da Foz to: Caldas da Rainha (4 daily; 1hr 25min–2hr 25min); Coimbra (17 daily; 1hr–1hr 20min); Leiria (3–6 daily; 1hr 15min); Lisbon (3 daily; 3hr 30min); Torres Vedras (3–5 daily; 2hr–3hr 25min).

Buses

Arouca to: Porto (Mon–Fri 10 daily, Sat & Sun 2; 1hr 30min); Santa Maria de Feira (Mon–Fri 10 daily, Sat & Sun 2; 40min).

Aveiro to: Arouca (Mon–Fri 6 daily; 2hr 50min); Figueira da Foz (6 daily; 1hr 15min); Ilhavo (8–10 daily; 30min); Lisbon (4–6 daily; 4hr); Porto (Mon–Fri 8 daily; 2hr 45min); Praia da Barra (every 30min; 30min); Praia de Mira (6 daily; 45min); Praia da Tocha (4–6 daily; 50min).

Coimbra to: Braga (6–7 daily; 2hr 40min–3hr); Caramulo (3 daily; 2hr); Condeixa-a-Nova (Mon–Fri 7am–11.30pm every 30min; reduced service weekends; 30min); Covilhã (4 daily; 3hr 25min); Fátima (4 daily; 1hr–1hr 25min); Figueira da Foz (10 daily; 1hr–1hr 45min); Guarda (4 daily; 2hr 40min); Leiria (4 daily; 1hr); Lisbon (16 daily; 2hr 20min); Luso (Mon–Fri 5 daily, Sat & Sun 2 daily; 45min); Mira (6 daily; 1hr); Montemor-o-Velho (3–9 daily; 1hr 10min); Penacova (3–5 daily; 45min); Peso da Régua (2–4 daily; 2hr 30min); Porto (7–10 daily; 1hr 30min–2hr 45min); Santa Maria de Feira (2 daily; 2hr 45min); Tondela (2–4 daily; 1hr 40min); Vila Real (2–4 daily; 3hr 20min); Viseu (2–5 daily; 1hr 20min–2hr 20min).

Figueira da Foz to: Aveiro (6 daily; 1hr 30min); Coimbra (Mon–Fri 10 daily, Sat & Sun 4–6 daily; 1hr–1hr 45min); Leiria (9 daily; 1hr 15min); Lisbon (3 daily; 2hr 45min); Mira (6 daily; 1hr); Montemor-o-Velho (Mon–Fri every 30min, Sat & Sun 4–8 daily; 30min); Tocha (6 daily; 40min).

Luso to: Coimbra (Mon–Fri 5 daily, Sat & Sun 2 daily; 45min); Viseu (Mon–Fri 5 daily, Sat & Sun 2 daily; 1hr 50min).

Penacova to: Coimbra (3–5 daily; 45min).

Praia de Mira to: Aveiro (6 daily; 45min); Coimbra (6 daily; 1hr); Figueira da Foz (6 daily; 1hr).

Santa Maria de Feira to: Arouca (Mon–Fri 10 daily, Sat & Sun 2; 40min); Coimbra (2 daily; 2hr 45min); Porto (every 30min; 35min).

São Pedro do Sul to: Sernada do Vouga (9–10 daily; 1hr 45min) for trains to Aveiro and Espinho; Viseu (9–10 daily; 1hr).

Termas de São Pedro do Sul to: Viseu (Mon–Fri 4–5 daily, Sat & Sun 1–2 daily; 1hr); Vouzela (Mon–Fri 2 daily; 10min).

Vouzela to: Sernada do Vouga (9–10 daily; 1hr 35min) for trains to Aveiro and Espinho; Varzielas (Mon–Fri 2 daily; 30min); Viseu (9–10 daily; 1hr 10min).

MOUNTAIN BEIRAS

Composed of two provinces, the **Beira Alta** (Upper) and **Beira Baixa** (Lower), the **Mountain Beiras** region features some of the least explored country in the Iberian peninsula, as well as some of the most spectacular: the enormous boulders which are strewn across much of the region limit

---

ACCOMMODATION PRICE CODES

All the accommodation prices in this book have been coded using the symbols below. The symbols represent the lowest prices you can expect to pay for a **double room in high season**; for a full explanation, see p.29.

① Under 3000$00   ② 3000$00–4000$00   ③ 4000$00–5500$00
④ 5500$00–8500$00   ⑤ 8500$00–12,500$00   ⑥ 12,500$00–20,000$00
⑦ Over 20,000$00

---

agriculture and have instead favoured a pastoral culture of rugged hamlets (*aldeias*). Arguably, it is also the most quintessentially Portuguese part of the country. Little touched by outside influence, it is historically the heart of **ancient Lusitânia**, where Viriatus the Iberian rebel (a symbol of the spirit of independence in Neoclassical literature) made his last stand against the Romans. You'll see many signs of this patriotism in the fine old town of **Viseu**, in Beira Alta, where every other café or hotel is called the *Viriato* or *Lusitânia*. Here, too, in the heights of the stunningly beautiful **Parque Natural da Serra da Estrela**, lies the source of the **Rio Mondego**, that most Portuguese of rivers: the only one (bar the insignificant Zêzere) to run right to the sea without having its origins in Spain. The whole region in and around the park is excellent walking country, especially if you strike off from one of the two main routes which cross the range.

Guarda is perhaps the most fascinating of the Beira Alta towns. Though diminutive in size for somewhere of such renown, it has one of the highest locations of any provincial capital in the country and it bristles with life, especially on *feira* days. To the north and east stretch a whole series of high-sited castle-towns and some of the country's most remote villages. Over to the south lies the more sombre plain of the **Beira Baixa** with its capital at **Castelo Branco** and, its most obvious highlight, the ancient hilltop town of **Monsanto**.

The whole Mountain Beiras region is very little visited by tourists and travellers: if you've spent some days in the fleshpots of Lisbon, Porto, or the Algarve, you'll find a very different **atmosphere** here – and almost exclusively Portuguese company.

Viseu

From its high plateau, **VISEU** surveys the country around with the air of a feudal overlord; and indeed, this dignified little city is capital of all it can see. It's also a place of great antiquity. There was a Roman town here, and on the northern outskirts you can still make out the remains of an encampment claimed to be the site where Viriatus (Viriato in Portuguese) fought his final battle. In fact, it was almost certainly a Roman fortification and, aside from a statue of Viriatus, there's not much there. The heart of the medieval city has changed little, though it's now approached through the broad avenues of a prosperous provincial centre. Parts of the walls survive and it is within their circuit, breached by two doughty gateways, that almost everything of interest lies.

The liveliest event in Viseu's calendar is the **Feira de São Mateus** which takes place from mid-August until its climax on September 21 (Dia do São Mateus) – it's largely an agricultural show, but is enlivened by occasional bullfights and folk-dance festivals. The showground is at the top end of Avenida António José de Almeida, beyond the bus station and across the Rio Paiva.

The Old City

A good place to start exploring the town is the old quarter around the **Praça da Sé**. The approach, from the central **Praça da República** (also known as Rossio), up through the Porta do Soar, or along the shop-lined Rua Dr. Luís Ferreira, exhibits a certain amount of pedestrianization and "beautification", but the jumble of alleys immediately behind the cathedral remains virtually untouched. You suddenly come upon sixteenth-century stone mansions proudly displaying their coats-of-arms in the middle of a street of rundown houses.

The cathedral square itself is lined with noble stone buildings, most striking of which is the **Igreja da Misericórdia** with its white Baroque facade. Silhouetted against a deep blue sky it looks like a film set without substance – you expect to walk around the back and find wooden props holding it up. There's some truth to that feeling: behind the symmetry of the facade, it's a very ordinary, rather dull church.

There's nothing two-dimensional, however, about the **Sé** (daily 7.30am–12.30pm & 2–7pm), a weighty, twin-towered Romanesque base on which a succession of later generations have made their mark. The granite frontage, remodelled in the seventeenth century, is stern and makes the church look smaller than it actually is – inside it opens out into a great hall with intricate vaulting, twisted and knotted to represent ropes. The cathedral's Renaissance **cloister**, of which you get no intimation from outside, is one of the most graceful in the country. The rooms of its upper level look out over the tangled roofs of the oldest part of the town and house the treasures of the cathedral's art collection, including naive sculptures, two thirteenth-century Limoges enamel coffers and a twelfth-century Bible.

Museu de Grão Vasco

The greatest treasure of Viseu is the **Museu de Grão Vasco** (Tues–Sun 9.30am–12.30pm & 2–5.30pm; 250$00; free Sunday mornings), right next door to the cathedral, in the Paço dos Três Escalões – once the Bishop's palace. **Vasco Fernandes** (known always as Grão Vasco, The Great Vasco) was born in Viseu and became the key figure in a school of painting which flourished here in the first half of the sixteenth century. The style of these "Portuguese primitives" was influenced heavily by Flemish masters and in particular by van Eyck, but certain aspects – the realism of portraiture and richness of colour – are distinctively their own. Vasco and his chief rival Gaspar Vaz have a fair claim to being two of the greatest artists Portugal has produced.

The museum is spread over three floors. The lower floor contains evocative historical paintings of Viseu and other Portuguese localities, while the works of the Viseu School are on the uppermost floor. The centrepiece of the collection is the masterly *Saint Peter on His Throne*, one of Grão Vasco's last works and painted, it is said, to rival Gaspar Vaz's treatment of the same theme for the church at São João de Tarouca (see p.298). It shows considerably more Renaissance influence than some of the earlier paintings but its Flemish roots are still evident, particularly in the intricately – and sometimes bizarrely – detailed background. Other works attributed to Vasco include a *Calvary* and a *Pentecost*, but there's consider-

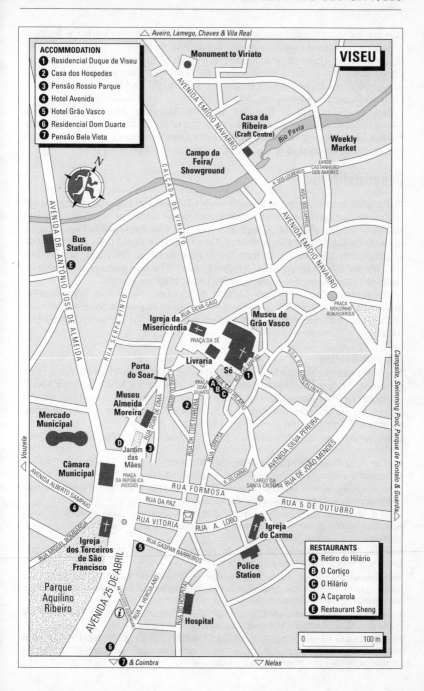

△ Aveiro, Lamego, Chaves & Vila Real

Monument to Viriato

VISEU

ACCOMMODATION
1 Residencial Duque de Viseu
2 Casa dos Hospedes
3 Pensão Rossio Parque
4 Hotel Avenida
5 Hotel Grão Vasco
6 Residencial Dom Duarte
7 Pensão Bela Vista

AVENIDA EMIDIO NAVARRO

Casa da Ribeira (Craft Centre)

Rio Pavia

Weekly Market

LARGO CASTANHEIRO DOS AMORES

Campo da Feira/ Showground

CALÇADA DE VIRIATO

R. DOS LOUREIROS

AVENIDA DOS CAPITÃES

N

AVENIDA DR. ANTÓNIO JOSÉ DE ALMEIDA

Bus Station E

AVENIDA EMIDIO NAVARRO

RUA SERPA PINTO

RUA SILVA GAIO

PRAÇA MOUZINHO ALBUQUERQUE

Igreja da Misericórdia

Museu de Grão Vasco

RUA DO GONÇALINHO

PRAÇA DA SÉ

Livraria

Sé

R. GAMBAS

Porta do Soar

RUA SOAR DE CIMA

PRAÇA DOM DUARTE

A B C

RUA SÃO HILÁRIO

Museu Almeida Moreira

2

RUA DR. LUIS FERREIRA

RUA DIREITA

AVENIDA SILVA PEREIRA

RUA DE JOÃO MENDES

Mercado Municipal

D

Jardim das Mães

3

R. DO CARMO

Campsite, Swimming Pool, Parque de Fontelo & Guarda △

Câmara Municipal

PRAÇA DA REPÚBLICA (ROSSIO)

RUA FORMOSA

LARGO DA SANTA CRISTINA

RUA 5 DE OUTUBRO

4

AVENIDA ALBERTO SAMPAIO

RUA DA PAZ

RUA VITORIA

RUA A. LOBO

Igreja do Carmo

Vouzela △

RUA MIGUEL BOMBARDA

Igreja dos Terceiros de São Francisco

5

RUA GASPAR BARREIROS

AVENIDA 25 DE ABRIL

Police Station

RESTAURANTS
A Retiro do Hilário
B O Cortiço
C O Hilário
D A Caçarola
E Restaurant Sheng

Parque Aquilino Ribeiro

RUA A. HERCULANO

RUA DO HOSPITAL

i

Hospital

0   100 m

6

▽ 7 & Coimbra

▽ Nelas

able argument over what is actually his. Several pictures are clearly the fruits of collaboration – most obviously many of the fourteen panels of the former cathedral altarpiece. These, now exhibited in a room of their own, depict the life of Christ and some sections are clearly better executed than others – notice *The Adoration of the Magi* in which Balthazar, traditionally an African king, is depicted as an Indian from newly discovered Brazil.

Also worth a visit is the tiny **Museu Almeida Moreira** (Tues–Sun 10am–12.30pm & 2–5pm; 100$00) on the edge of the Jardim das Mães. This traditional house displays furniture and pottery from the seventeenth to nineteenth century, and is named after the founder of the Grão Vasco museum.

Practicalities

Viseu is no longer on the rail line, though CP **buses** still operate along the old routes, linking the town with Guarda, Coimbra and Lisbon on the Beira Alta line at Nelas (30min south of Viseu) and with the Coimbra–Aveiro–Porto line at Sernada do Vouga (2hr 45min west of Viseu). Coming from Porto, an alternative approach is to take the Douro train line to Peso da Régua (2hr) and then the bus via Lamego, Castro Daire and Carvalhal (2–3hr). The **bus station** in Viseu is on Avenida António José de Almeida, a short walk from the centre.

The **turismo** (Mon–Fri 9am–12.30pm & 2.30–6pm, Sat & Sun 10am–noon & 3–5.30pm; ☎032/42 20 14) is situated just south of Rossio on Avenida Calouste Gulbenkian, and can provide maps and information on the Beira Alta region as a whole.

Accommodation

The best places to stay are in the old quarter, but Viseu is short on budget accommodation. Among **hotels and pensões**, pick from the list below. There's a well-equipped *Orbitur* **campsite** (☎032/261 46; closed mid-Nov to mid-Jan) in the Parque do Fontelo, ten minutes' walk east from Rossio, and a municipal swimming pool 500m away, on Avenida José Relvas.

Hotel Avenida, Rua Miguel Bombarda 1 (☎ & fax 032/42 34 32). A fairly pleasant hotel near the Parque Aquilino Ribeiro, with a few cheaper rooms. ⑤.

Pensão Bela Vista, Rua Alexandre Herculano 510 (☎032/42 20 26). Functional *pensão* in a street near the turismo; has some cheaper rooms without baths. ③.

Casa dos Hospedes, Rua Dr. Luís Ferreira 65 (☎032/272 05). Basic, but the least expensive option in town, and in a good location. Book ahead. ②.

Casa de Rebordinho, Rebordinho (☎032/46 12 58). Situated 6km south on the N231 Nelas road, this ANTER property is in a converted seventeenth-century manor house on a farm estate. ⑤.

Residencial Dom Duarte, Rua Alexandre Herculano 214 (☎032/42 19 80, fax 42 48 25). Pleasant *residencial*; all rooms with bath and TV. ④.

Residencial Duque de Viseu, Rua das Ameias 22 (☎032/42 12 86). A converted town house right by the cathedral. Somewhat lacking in character and expensive for what you get but it does have air-conditioning. ④.

Hotel Grão Vasco, Rua Gaspar Barreiros (☎032/42 35 11, fax 42 64 44). Viseu's finest – a grand central hotel with bar and swimming pool, but overpriced. ⑥.

Pensão Rossio Parque, Praça da República 55 (☎032/42 20 85). An old hotel that has seen better days but it's in an excellent location. Some rooms are small and cramped; others have no window or shower – prices vary accordingly. ④.

Moliceiro and lagoon, Aveiro

Dressed up for the Festa da Ria, Aveiro

PETER WILSON

The university buildings, Coimbra

MATTHEW HANCOCK

View of Monsanto from the castle

MATTHEW HANCOCK

Mountain Beiras

PETER WILSON

Bom Jesus, Braga

Bacalhau shop, Porto

Cais da Ribeira, Porto

Azulejos, São Bento station, Porto

PETER WILSON

Espigueiro (grain house), the Minho

PETER WILSON

Farming in the Parque Nacional da Peneda-Gerês

PETER WILSON

Azulejo covered church, Porto

Eating and drinking

Viseu is well known for its gastronomic delights, and wherever you eat, or drink, bear in mind that locally produced **Dão wines**, especially the reds, are some of the best you'll find in the country. For provisions, there's a **weekly market** on Tuesday, on the ring road by Largo Castanheiro dos Amores, and a weekday market in the **Mercado Municipal**, just west of Rossio. Most of Viseu's **nightlife** is to be found in the old town around Rua Augusto Hilário, Rua Dom Duarte and the Sé. The **restaurants** listed below are all very popular locally; you may have to wait for a table.

A Caçarola, Trav. Major Teles 3, just off Rossio. This place serves big and cheap portions of traditional fare and gets packed at lunchtimes.

O Cortiço, Rua São Hilário 43. In the old town, just down from the statue of Dom Duarte, this is popular enough for tables to be at a premium. Food and decor are *típicos*, but the service can be a bit sullen. Around 2500$00 a head.

O Hilário, Rua São Hilário 35. Cheaper than *O Cortiço* and not bad for the money; try the *morcela casiera frita* (fried blood-pudding).

Restaurante Kalunga, Rua Miguel Bombarda 76. A cheerful place specializing in African dishes at low prices.

Rodízio Real, Bairro Santa Eulália (☎032/42 22 32). Out in the suburbs in Repeses, on the N2 (Coimbra direction). Diners come from far and wide to sample its Brazilian cooking; up to 3500$00.

Restaurante Sheng, Avda. António José de Almeida. A cheap and tasty Chinese option opposite the bus station.

East to Guarda

East of Viseu, the high and austere territory of the **Serra da Estrela** spreads itself as far as the eye can see: a landscape of great jagged boulders and rough, dry grass – often singed in patches by summer fires. The wilderness of the area, as so often in mountain regions, belies its inhabitants, who, though a little abrupt, have none of the suspicion of outsiders often encountered in Portuguese cities and coastal regions.

The fast IP5 highway from Aveiro cuts east through this region, skirting Viseu and running on to **Guarda**. Train travellers first have to backtrack south to Nelas from Viseu in order to follow the **Beira Alta rail line** from Santa Comba Dão to Guarda. By road or rail, the only realistic stop before Guarda is at **Celorico da Beira**, which lies at a nexus of routes, with bus connections to Linhares (p.240), perhaps the most attractive of the *serra* villages.

Celorico da Beira

CELORICO DA BEIRA, 50km east of Viseu, is an unprepossessing town; its one claim to fame is as the birthplace of the aviator Sacadura Cabral. It is certainly not the most attractive *serra* base, split as it is by heavy traffic along the east–west road from Spain and the north–south route to Lisbon. It does, however, have a pretty enough old town hugging the slopes around the fine castle and, if you're passing through at the right time, it's the best place to pick up a pungent *queijo da serra*, the famed round cheese of the Serra da Estrela district.

The **Castelo** is open intermittently but if it's closed you can get the key from the turismo (see p.228) or the Câmara Municipal. Put your trust in the rickety construction strung up outside the large keep and you can climb to impressive views from the roof. On a clear day the Sé and single tower of the castle at Guarda are both visible, while all around stretches the extraordinary wasteland of the mountains, split only by a small river and a couple of Portuguese highways. The castle has a long military history, forming, together with Trancoso and Guarda, a triangle of defensive fortifications against Spain. In its day, a garrison of three hundred, well equipped with arms and an ample supply of food, were able to hold out with relative ease against border skirmishes. Only on one occasion, in 1198, did they have to call for assistance, which was provided by the stout men of nearby Linhares.

Feiras – held on alternate Fridays for cheese, and on Tuesdays for the ordinary covered market – are the times to catch the town's cheery provinciality. You'll see some of the more rugged mountain types coming in to sell their *queijo da serra*, market-going being the only source of income to support their impoverished hilltop farms. If you miss the cheese market, visit the excellent old cheese shop on the main road through town, just down from the post office. A visit on June 13 will give you the chance to join in the Santo António **festivals** when the whole village enjoys a riverside picnic; ask at the turismo for details of other summer festivals, when locals indulge in the traditional game of climbing a greased pole to try and retrieve a flask of wine and some *bacalhau*.

Practicalities

Celorico's **train station** is 6km north of town at Celorico Gare; bus connections are erratic, so you'll probably need to take a taxi (if you can find one) or walk. If you find yourself walking from the station, look out for the forked rocks near Espinho – 1km west of the road – which were once used to hang criminals, and the megalithic stone necropolis at nearby São Gens. It's more convenient to arrive in Celorico by **bus** as many long-distance services pass through: there are bus stops outside the *Residencial Parque* and the *Café Central* on the town's main road where you can also consult timetables for onward transport. There is a small, helpful **turismo** (Tues–Sat 9.30am–noon & 2–6pm; ☎071/721 09), on the edge of town on the Coimbra road.

The town's best and most central **pensão** is the *Residencial Parque*, Rua Andrade Corvo 48 (☎071/721 97, fax 737 98; ③), located slightly south of the centre. There's also a hotel on the road to the turismo, the *Hotel Mira Serra*, Bairro de Santa Eufémia (☎071/726 04, fax 74 13 82; ⑤), with magnificent views from some of the bedrooms. Just beyond the turismo, on the same road, there are rooms above the *Nova Estrela* (☎071/722 42; ①), whose **restaurant** is excellent, as is the nearby *Boa-Hora*. There is a possible freelance **campsite** by the Rio Mondego, near the station. Seven kilometres further upstream, off the Guarda road, there's an official site, *Parque Ponte do Ladrão* (☎071/726 45; open April–Sept), at Lajeosa do Mondego.

Guarda

Twenty-two kilometres southeast of Celorico da Beira, **GUARDA**, at an altitude of over 1000m, is claimed by its inhabitants to be the highest city in Europe – an assertion to be taken with a pinch of salt. It is high enough, though, to be chilly and windswept all year round and to offer endless views, especially to the east into Spain. The city was founded in 1197 by Dom Sancho I, to guard (as the name

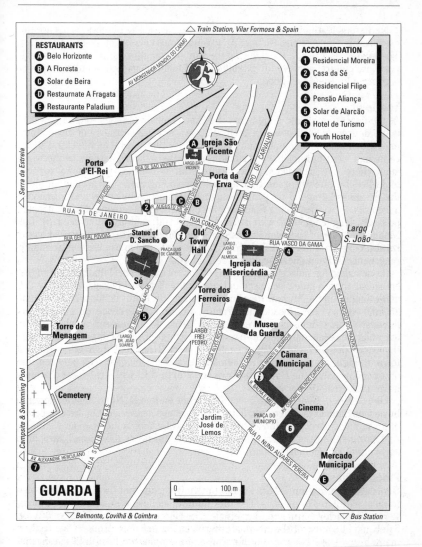

RESTAURANTS
A Belo Horizonte
B A Floresta
C Solar de Beira
D Restaurnate A Fragata
E Restaurante Paladium

ACCOMMODATION
1 Residencial Moreira
2 Casa da Sé
3 Residencial Filipe
4 Pensão Aliança
5 Solar de Alarcão
6 Hotel de Turismo
7 Youth Hostel

implies) the borders against both Moors and Spaniards. It was a heftily fortified place and, despite the fact that castle and walls have all but disappeared, it still has something of the grim air of a city permanently on a war footing. Fortunately, nowadays, the presence of a polytechnic injects a fair amount of life into the town. Guarda is known in Portugal as the city of the four Fs: *Fria, Farta, Forte e Feia* – cold, rich, strong and ugly. However, in recent times, the city fathers – unhappy with the last of these – have launched a "five Fs" campaign to replace *Feia* with *Fiel* (loyal) and *Formosa* (beautiful). Oversensitive perhaps, though it is true to say that the centre of Guarda, with its arcaded streets and little *praças*, can be distinctly picturesque.

Numerous **festivals** take place in the Guarda area. The biggest events are the great **feiras** (June 24 and October 4), extended markets full of life and character. The **Festas da Cidade** (held during the summer months on different dates each year) are cultural affairs with exhibitions and folk-dancing, but a little too highly organized for their own good.

The Town

At the heart of it all and dominating the Praça Luís de Camões (or Praça Velha) is the dour grey **Sé** (Tues–Sun 10am–12.30pm & 2–5.30pm), one of those buildings which took so long to complete (1390–1540) that several architectural styles came and went during its construction, all of them incorporated into the work somewhere. The castellated main facade, with its two heavy octagonal towers, looks like the gateway of some particularly forbidding castle, but around the sides the design is lightened by flying buttresses, fantastic pinnacles, and grimacing gargoyles – the ones facing Spain are particularly mean-looking. Inside, it's surprisingly long and lofty, with twisted pillars and vaulting influenced by the Manueline style of the later stages of its development. The huge carved stone **retábulo** is the work of João de Ruão, a leading figure in the sixteenth-century resurgence of Portuguese sculpture at Coimbra.

It's amazing, for a place of its size and historical importance, that apart from the cathedral, there's little else to see in Guarda: the displays of local archeology, art and sculpture in the **Museu da Guarda** (Tues–Sun 10am–12.30pm & 2–5.30pm; 250$00) on Rua Alves Roçadas are, frankly, dull, and of the castle, on a bleak little hill nearby, only the plain square keep, the **Torre de Menagem**, survives, while the walls are recalled by just three remaining gates – the most impressive of them the **Torre dos Ferreiros** (Blacksmiths' Tower). The cobbled streets of the old town, though, are fascinating in themselves, and the tangled area between the other two portals – the **Porta da Erva** and **Porta d'El-Rei** – can have changed little in the past 400 years.

Like Celorico, Guarda has a covered **market** on Rua D. Nuno Álvares Pereira, busiest on Saturdays, where you'll find delicious *queijo da serra*. On the other side of town, below Avenida Monsenhor Mendes do Carmo, is the open-air Feira Ao Ar Livre, held on the first and third Wednesday of every month and attracting agricultural folk from all around.

Practicalities

Guarda's **train station** is 3km north of the town centre but there's usually a bus to meet all the major arrivals. The **bus station**, alongside Rua D. Nuno Álvares Pereira, is fairly central and ultra-efficient. Services are operated by a variety of companies to most of the neighbouring villages, the only problem being that many buses leave early in the morning and often don't return until late in the afternoon. There are two **turismos**: a central one on Praça Luís de Camões (Mon–Fri 9am–12.30pm & 2–5.30pm; ☎071/22 22 51), where you can pick up a town map; and a more helpful one (Tues–Fri 9.30am–noon & 2–6pm, Sat open till 8pm; ☎071/22 18 17), which doubles as an office for the Parque Natural da Serra da Estrela and is located next to the modern Câmara Municipal.

ACCOMMODATION

You should have no trouble getting a room at one of the **pensões and hotels** detailed below, or try the **youth hostel** on Avenida Alexandre Herculano

(☎071/22 39 38). Guarda's *Orbitur* **campsite** (☎071/21 14 06, fax 22 19 11; closed mid-Nov to mid-Jan) is in a park a short way from the castle; beware that in spring and autumn the nights can get extremely cold. The town's heated swimming pool is 500m further on.

Pensão Aliança, Rua Vasco da Gama 8a (☎071/22 22 35, fax 22 14 51). Just down the hill from the *Filipe*, this welcoming place also has a restaurant. ④.

Casa da Sé, Rua Augusto Gil 17 (☎071/21 25 01). Recently renovated, characterful rooms. Good value and centrally located off the Praça Luís de Camões. ③.

Residencial Filipe, Rua Vasco da Gama 9 (☎071/22 36 58, fax 22 14 02). A more upmarket hotel, opposite the Misericórdia. Some of the rooms are a little cramped, but all have TV and private facilities. Breakfast included. ④.

Residencial Moreira, Rua Mouzinho de Albuquerque 47 (☎071/21 41 31). Central and good-value option; all rooms have bathrooms. ③.

Solar de Alarcão, Rua Dom Miguel de Alarcão 25–27 (☎071/21 43 92). Magnificent granite manor house dating back to the seventeenth century, with wonderful rooms. Highly recommended but you'll need to book ahead. ④.

Hotel de Turismo, Avda. Coronel Orlindo Carvalho (☎071/22 33 66, fax 22 33 99). Guarda's grandest and part of the Best Western chain: big and reasonably well run but without the charm and character of the *Solar de Alarcão*. ⑤.

EATING

Most of the town's **restaurants** are to be found in the area between the Porta da Estrela and the Igreja de São Vicente.

Belo Horizonte, Largo de São Vincente 1. Specializes in local dishes such as rabbit and sausages, and also does an excellent *arroz de tamboril*. Closed first half of July.

Residencial Filipe, Rua Vasco da Gama 9. The first-floor dining room is a shade too florid, but there's no arguing with the generous portions of good food. You'll pay around 1500$00 for a meal.

A Floresta, Rua Franciso dos Passos 40. Reasonably priced and serves enormous portions – grills are the house speciality.

Restaurante A Fragata, Rua 31 de Janeiro 17. Near the cathedral and highly recommended, with an *ementa turística* at around 1300$00; otherwise meals from 1500$00.

Restaurante Paladium, Rua Francisco dos Prezeres 23. On the way to the bus station (and near the *Hotel de Turismo*), this serves daytime snacks and a full menu in the evening. Meals for around 2000$00; the chicken dishes are especially good.

Solar da Beira, Rua Francisco dos Passos 9. Highly recommended option around the corner from Praça Luís de Camões with main courses for around 1000$00. Try the *cabrito de ensopado* (stewed kid goat) or *lombo grelhado* (grilled pork loin). Closed Thurs.

North of Guarda: the planalto of Beira Alta

North and east of Guarda stretches a rough and barren-looking territory known as the **Planalto** – tableland – of the Beira Alta. Villages here are spread far apart, with much of the land between untamed by agriculture, strewn with boulders and great slabs of granite. There is the odd fertile valley, though, and a speciality of the local settlements is roast or dried chestnuts. Once a replacement for potatoes, and now a dessert, they come from vast, shady trees growing beside the roads on almost any approach to a village.

In medieval times, the region's Jewish settlements such as **Trancoso** and **Sernancelhe** prospered, though their merchant trade went into decline from the

Age of Discovery onwards as business moved to the coast. In successive centuries, the *planalto* towns became closely associated with Portuguese independence from Spain, and in particular with Afonso Henriques's march south down the length of the country. Today, their **castles** are the highlight of the region. **Penedono**'s Castelo Roqueiro is especially magnificent, with seventeenth-century reconstructions on top of the original article. Spectacular, too, are the star-shaped fortress at **Almeida**, the site of the penultimate battle in the Peninsular Wars against Napoleon, and, in its own understated way, the town of **Pinhel**, evoking bygone ages in its atmosphere and unspoilt architecture.

If you're travelling in **winter**, take to heart the proverb that *"O frio almoça em Penedono, merenda em Trancoso e ceia na Guarda"* (The cold lunches in Penedono, takes tea in Trancoso and dines in Guarda), and come suitably prepared. You will at least be rewarded by some extraordinary landscapes: the frost (*sincelo*) can have an extraordinary effect on the *planalto*, with massive trees linked by boughs of crystal and metre-long icicles hanging from every house.

Trancoso

Forty-four kilometres north of Guarda, **TRANCOSO**, still largely contained within a circuit of medieval walls, is an atmospheric little town, full of dark alleyways and interesting architectural details. The presence of a large **Jewish community** during the Middle Ages is apparent from the facades of the more ancient homes. Each has two doorways – a broad one for trade and a narrow one (leading to the first floor) for the family – and above the carefully crafted and bevelled stonework, some have clumsy crosses, inscribed by the Inquisition to indicate the family's conversion to Christianity. The most striking is the former **rabbi's house** (known as the Casa do Gato Negro), near the restaurant *São Marcos*, which is decorated with the Lion of Judea, the Gates of Jerusalem, and a figure of *Preguiça,* which some translate as "Sloth".

At the centre of the fortifications is the **castle**, with its squat, almost triangular, tower – a distinctive silhouette visible from many miles away. It's a Moorish design and a reminder of the Saracen domination of the town in the tenth century, following the town's conquest by al-Mansur. The following two centuries saw frequent siege and battle, with the fortress taken by Fernando Magno in 1033, and finally by Afonso Henriques and Egas Moniz in 1139 – an event celebrated by the construction of the monastery at São João de Tarouca (see p.298). Trancoso's later military history includes the usual invasions and billeting during fourteenth-century Castillian troublemaking and the nineteenth-century Peninsular War – look out for the charming corner house with an open stone stairway on the central square, which has the tellingly British name, Quartel do General Beresforde.

An equally historic site is the small **Capela de São Bartolomeu**, on the side of the dusty avenue leading into town, where Dom Dinis married the twelve-year-old Isabel of Aragon in 1282; he later gave her the entire town as a gift. Outside the walls from here, in front of the law courts, **Celtic tombs** attest to very early origins indeed. Here and there a coffin-cover lies askew; the rest of the mound is a carved mass of human-shaped pits of varying sizes – one obviously for a child.

Feiras are held on Fridays, with the big annual bash, the **Feira de São Bartolomeu**, on August 8–14, followed by the **Festa de Nossa Senhora da Fresta** on August 15.

BANDARRA THE COBBLER'S PROPHECY

Trancoso takes its place in Portuguese history through the legend of one **Bandarra**, a shoemaker-prophet who lived in the town in the fifteenth century. The cobbler began his prophetic career with local horoscopes and poems, but after a while moved to more national matters – foretelling, among other things, the end of the Portuguese kingdom. In an age of religious dilemma and disillusionment with monarchical rule his prophecies struck a chord, and attracted the attention of the authorities. Their circulation was banned and Bandarra condemned to death – a sentence commuted after popular outcry to a punishment of walking barefoot around town carrying a massive candle until it burned to the wick.

There the matter might have rested, but twenty years after Bandarra's death, Dom Sebastião did indeed die (along with most of the Portuguese nobility) in the battle of Alcácer-Quibir in Morocco, leaving no heir to the throne. Portugal subsequently lost independence to Spain, and Bandarra was pronounced the Nostradamus of his time.

Practicalities

Buses continue further north from Trancoso to Pinhel and Lamego. Lamego-bound buses, via Sernancelhe, pass by several times a day, though you may have to go out to the main road to catch them; Pinhel-bound buses (1–2 daily) leave from the main square, just outside the town walls. For Guarda and major towns en route to Lisbon there's a daily service (Mon–Fri), also from the main square. The **turismo** (Mon–Sat 9.30am–12.30pm & 2–6pm; ☎071/911 47) is opposite the main gates to the walled town and can point you in the direction of **private rooms** (①).

The town offers a choice of three **pensões**: *Residencial Rico* on the main street, Rua Dr Fernando Vaz (☎071/914 11; ②), a simple but inexpensive option in the old town – if no one is around, ask at the boutique beneath it; the newer *Pensão Vale a Pena* on Largo Senhora da Calçada, outside the walls near the hospital (☎071/919 51; ③; breakfast included), a genial place above a garage; and the *Residencial Dom Dinis* (☎071/915 25; ③) a modern choice above the post office at Campo das Viúvas 2, also outside the walls. For **eating**, the *Café Bandarra*, near the main gateway, serves a wide range of dishes; more expensive, but value for money and very popular with the locals, is *O Brazão* on Rua Adriano Mountinho.

Sernancelhe

Sited 30km northwest from Trancoso, a couple of kilometres off the Guarda–Lamego road, **SERNANCELHE** is not exactly the hub of Beira Alta, but it's a quietly impressive place, in the manner of Trancoso, with further reminders of the area's Jewish past and a fine riverside location. The village is also said to produce the *planalto's* finest chestnuts and its approach is dominated by the broad-boughed trees spreading across the road. Carnivals, love songs, recipes, and folk tales all centre on the fruit, and if you coincide with the **Festa de Nossa Senhora de Ao Pé da Cruz** on May 1 you'll witness a curious mixture of religious devotion, springtime merrymaking, and, above all, folkloric superstition. There's a dance of the chestnuts, a blessing of the trees, and the exchange of handfuls of blossom by local lovers, aside from the religious procession.

Should you want to know more about the town, the local cultural expert, Padre Cândido Azevedo, is more than pleased to welcome a stranger into his majestic, castle-like home overlooking the town. The walk up there takes you through the **old quarter** of town, now only semi-populated and coming alive only for the weekly Thursday market. En route, along the main road, you pass the **Igreja Matriz**, an attractive Romanesque church with a curious facade. Fixed into twin niches on either side of the main doorway are six weathered apostles – said to be the only free-standing sculptures of the period in the whole of Portugal. Inside the church are several sixteenth-century panels, including a magnificent *John the Baptist*.

A wander around the old quarter will also reveal the same features of medieval **Jewish settlement** as in Trancoso – canted lintels, pairs of granite doorways of unequal size, the occasional cross for the converted. Equally noticeable are a number of large **town houses**, dating from the sixteenth and seventeenth centuries. One of these is the supposed birthplace of the Marquês de Pombal, another is the birthplace of Padre João Rodrigues, an eminent and influential missionary who founded a series of mission houses in Japan in the sixteenth century. Japanese tourists often make the pilgrimage here to see the building.

The village has two **pensões**: the *Flora* (☎054/553 04; ②) and *Trasmontana* (☎054/552 44; ②) – both fairly basic and inexpensive. Alternatively, you could put up a tent by the river, just outside Sernancelhe, or at the **Barragem do Tavora**, a man-made barrage 3km to the north. **Buses** on to Lamego (see p.294) leave from the N226, 4km away – there are four a day in the week, fewer at the weekend. There are also buses (Mon–Fri) to Penedono and Trancoso, departing from the same place.

Penedono

Sixteen kilometres to the northeast of Sernancelhe, **PENEDONO** is another one-horse town, but again a likeable place, and with a fantastic **Castelo Roquiero** – visible from miles around. The *roqueiro* ("rock") part of the name is due to the castle's emergence from its granite base, as if the rock and the walls were one and the same. From the top, as you might imagine, there are grand views, with the village's old quarter laid out below. Keys are available from the village shop, who will warn you to rattle the castle doors first in order to get the pigeons in the air – rather than have them flying straight at your face.

The castle, in times of war, and the **Solar dos Freixos** (now the town hall), in times of peace, were supposed to have been home to Álvaro Gonçalves Coutinho, the legendary **King Magriço** ("Lean One"), sung of in Camões's *Os Lusíadas*. It's a claim fought over fiercely with the inhabitants of Trancoso, who likewise are prepared to swear he is their man. According to Camões, the Magriço led eleven men to England to champion the cause of twelve noble English ladies, who found themselves without knights, and fought a joust on their behalf. Such tales of chivalry made them the subjects of numerous allegorical murals and panels of azulejos around the country.

The village has one **pensão**, the *Solneve* (☎054/542 39; ②), on Rua da Lavandeira, with friendly management, though you could also find **rooms** above the *Café Gomes* (☎054/542 35; ②) or the *Café Avenida* (☎054/544 73; ②) on the main road; the latter has excellent food. **Feiras** are held every other Wednesday, and there's a **romaria** on September 15–16. **Buses** continue (Mon–Fri) to Vila Nova de Foz Côa, and to Trancoso.

Pinhel

PINHEL is big enough to run both a wine co-operative (producing an excellent red) and a cake factory (churning out *cavaca* sweetmeats). But, digestibles apart, it's also small enough to have left the old centre of town virtually untouched. You can walk right around the crumbling castle walls, across the top of five intact arch-ways, through vegetable plots and back gardens, and remain almost unaware of the twentieth century. From one corner of the **walls** you look down on the shell of a ruined **Romanesque church**, whose facade alone merits closer inspection. On another stretch you will discover what is left of the original **fortress**, a soar-ing tower with an intricately carved Manueline window.

Down in the town further architectural pleasures are in store, with numerous **manor houses** clustered about magnificent gardens. One of the largest is now the **Câmara Municipal**, its hallway bedecked with a series of excellent pho-tographs of local buildings of interest. An adjacent building houses the town **museum** (Mon–Fri 10am–noon & 2–6pm; free), with a pile of **Celtic tomb-stones** on the ground floor and, upstairs, remnants of a local convent.

Pinhel has two modest-priced **pensões**: the *Residencial Pinhelense* on Trav. do Sepulcro (☎071/423 73; ②), with superb meals, and the *Residencial Falcão*, Avda. Carneiro Gusmão 25 (☎071/430 04; ③). The more upmarket *Hotel Paris* on Rua Pínzio (☎071/941 21; ④) offers all the mod-cons. If you want to **camp**, no one seems to object to tents being pitched around the castle walls. **Buses** leave from the cen-tre of the municipal gardens – ask in the museum or nearby shop for schedules. One useful connection is the daily bus operated by Berrelhas, which you can flag down at about 4.15pm to go to Almeida or on to Figueira de Castelo Rodrigo (see p.294). The local **Festa de Santo António** is held on the Sunday closest to June 13.

Almeida

Perhaps the most attractive of all the fortified border towns, **ALMEIDA** is beau-tifully preserved eighteenth-century stronghold. Its **walls** are in the form of a twelve-pointed star, with six bastions and six curtain walls within ravelins – a Dutch design, influenced by the French military architect Vauban. A four-kilome-tre walk around the walls takes in all the peaks and troughs, and if you stay overnight, there's an irresistible charm in watching the sun go down and the lights come on in a hundred tiny villages across the plateau of the Ribacôa.

This was one of the last stretches of land to be recognized as officially Portuguese in the Treaty of Alcañices with the Spanish in 1297, and it's easy to see why boundaries were not clearly staked out in the broad, flat terrain. Indeed, it was occasionally reoccupied by Spain – the last time was in 1762, after which the present stronghold was completed. The original two double **gates** are among the town's most splendid features – long, shell-proof tunnels with emblazoned entrances and sizeable guardroom. In the outer guard room of the São Francisco gateway there is a small **museum** (daily 9am–noon & 2–5pm), while the larger guardroom houses a **turismo** office. The **Casamatas** (daily 9am–noon & 2–5pm), or barracks, is second in size only to Elvas, with a capacity for five thou-sand men and their supplies. Its layout explains how it withstood lengthy sieges. With its own water supply, rubbish chute, breathing holes, hidden escape routes, munitions chamber (there's a range of cannonballs and gunshot still on view), and dormitory space, the possibilities were limitless.

ALMEIDA IN THE PENINSULAR WAR

Almeida played a key role in the **Peninsular War** (1807–14). In January 1808 it fell to the French General Junot, whom Napoleon subsequently made Governor of Portugal. Later, when the French retreated unscathed following the infamous Convention of Sintra of August 1808, the Portuguese reoccupied the town. The Napoleonic army returned in 1810 and, en route to Buçaco and Torres Vedras, occupied Ciudad Rodrigo in Spain and besieged Almeida. The Luso-Britannic forces held out for seventeen days and then on July 26 the unforeseen happened. A leaky barrel of gunpowder, carried from the cathedral-castle in the centre of town to the Praça Alta (an artillery platform on the northern walls), left a fatal trail of powder. Once ignited, this began a fire which killed hundreds, and the survivors gave themselves up to the French. Wellington, on his victorious return from Torres Vedras, defeated the French on May 11, 1811, at Fuentes d'Onoro and subsequently took the fortress at Almeida with no bloodshed. The French army scuttled away during the night, probably making use of one of three *portas falsas* – narrow slits in the ramparts allowing for a discreet exit.

One other curiosity, opposite the *pousada* gateway in the walls, is an inscription on the side of a small house declaring it to be the dumping ground for illegitimate children. At the **Rodo dos Eispostos** (literally the "Circle of the Deserted"), anyone could come and claim an unwanted child for themselves – a convenient arrangement for both mother and foster parent.

Inevitably, perhaps, tourism has been catching up with Almeida – the number of cafés in town has risen from three to twenty or more within the last decade, while the arrival of the *pousada* in 1987 necessitated the hacking out of a new gateway in Almeida's fortifications, though the result wasn't as outrageous as feared. The locals seem intrigued by the phenomenon of rich tourists turning up in their long-forgotten town to fork out more than a villager's daily earnings to ride in a souped-up pony cart, or to pay through the nose for a coffee on the balcony overlooking the humble dwellings below. If you can possibly do so, try to visit during one of the twice-monthly **feiras** (on the eighth day and last Saturday) or – best of all – come at Pentecost (fifty days after Easter) for the grand picnic in the grounds of the **Convento da Barca**, a former Franciscan monastery with a distinctively Tuscan feel about its domed chapel and setting. It's the only time you can visit the convent grounds, which are now privately owned, but at other times of the year you can sample the excellent red wine, apples, peaches, nuts, and various other produce for which it is famous, at shops in town.

Practicalities

Apart from the luxurious *Pousada Senhora das Neves* (☎071/542 83, fax 543 20; ⑥), **staying** in the old town is a question of talking with the villagers. A good first stop is the *Casa da Amelinha*, where *ginginha* (morello cherry liqueur) has been served since 1883. It's an unofficial gathering place – ask here, or at any of the neighbouring cafés, whether there are any local rooms to let.

Otherwise, there are two modern *residenciais* by the crossroads outside the fort, both comfortable and friendly – *A Muralha* (☎071/543 57; ③) and *Morgado* (☎071/544 12; ③), alongside which, and under the same management, is the *Restaurante A Tertúlia*. A second good **restaurant**, just outside the main gate, is the *Portas de Almeida*. One of the most characterful of the **cafés** within the fort is the *Terreiro Velho*, near the market stalls; it stays open till 2am most nights and, despite fairly modern tastes in music, seems popular with old as well as young. For **camping**, make your way to the Rio Côa, a two-kilometre stroll downhill on the Pinhel road. Just above the old Romanesque bridge (and its present-day equivalent), you'll find some idyllic spots.

Buses for the north come from Vilar Formoso twice daily (Mon–Fri) and go as far as Figueira de Castelo Rodrigo; the Berrelhas-operated bus stops on the main road, 200m from the gates to Almeida at about 5pm every afternoon. Going south there are local services as far as Vilar Formoso, which has trains to Guarda and Spain, and three daily buses to Sabugal and Castelo Branco. There is also one daily bus to Guarda (Mon–Fri) operated by Rodoviária Nacional. At weekends, public transport is virtually non-existent.

The Serra da Estrela

The peaks of the **Serra da Estrela** – the highest mountains in Portugal and the last of the four central Iberian *serras* – rise to the southwest of Guarda. The range is basically a high plateau cut by valleys, from within which emanate two of Portugal's greatest **rivers**: the Rio Mondego, the longest Portuguese river to have its source in Portugal itself, flows north to Celorico da Beira before swinging southwest to Coimbra and the sea at Figueira da Foz; while the Rio Zêzere flows southwest from near Guarda until it joins the Rio Tejo at Constância. Over the last few decades the *serra* landscape has changed. Once, farmers lived in stone houses with straw roofs, dotted across the peaks and valleys, but they have now moved to more modern dwellings on the valley floor. Originally, too, the whole area was heavily forested, but these days the pines are widely cultivated for timber and shepherds now graze their sheep on the higher ground. Rye is grown lower down, where the land is more fertile.

For visitors, most of the interest is in the mountain region known as the **Parque Natural da Serra da Estrela**, established in 1976 to preserve the rural character of the *serra* villages and landscape. In 1990, all land over 1200m was designated "protected countryside", which means in effect that you're not allowed to camp wild, light fires or pick flowers. However, there are three major (and several minor) **trails** through the park, which take in various authorized campsites and villages with accommodation and other facilities. The best time to walk the trails is from May to October; some of them are featured in the box on p.239. If you're interested in staying in rural properties in the park, contact ADRUSE, Largo do Mercado, Gouveia (☎038/49 11 23, fax 402 50), who can provide details and handle reservations.

Park approaches and information

Public transport into the area is erratic at the best of times. **Buses** serve the main towns of Seia, Gouveia, Celorico, Guarda and Covilhã, which form a circle around the highest mountains, but since privatization almost all local services into the more interesting mountain villages have been cut back or axed completely. However, **taxis** are not as prohibitive as you might expect; Covilhã–Penhas costs around 1000$00 and even the longest journey won't set you back more than 2500$00. **Hitching** is another possibility, especially in winter when Penhas de Saúde has Portugal's only skiing facilities.

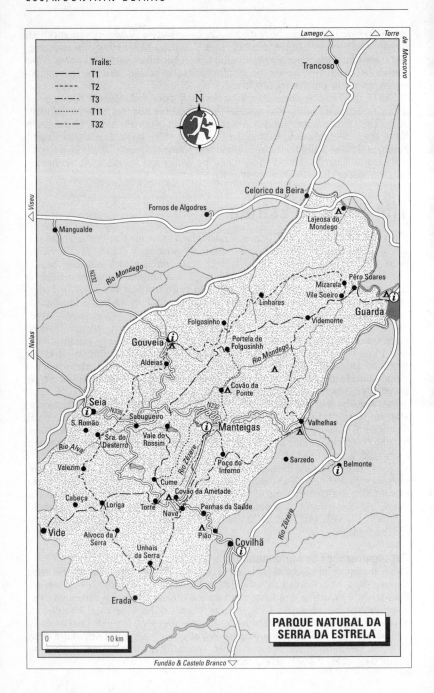

Lamego △   △ Torre

Trancoso

Trails:
— · — — T1
— — — — T2
— · — · — T3
· · · · · · · T11
— · · — T32

N

de Moncorvo

Celorico da Beira

Fornos de Algodres

Lajeosa do Mondego

Mangualde

N232
Rio Mondego

Péro Soares

Mizarela
Vila Soeiro

Linhares

Guarda

Folgosinho

Videmonte

Portela de
Folgosinhh

Gouveia

Rio Mondego

Aldeias

Covão da
Ponte

Seia

N339

Sabugueiro

N232

S. Romão

Manteigas

Sra. do
Desterro

Vale do
Rossim

Rio Zêzere

Valhelhas

Rio Alva

Poço do
Inferno

Sarzedo

Belmonte

Valezim

Cume

Covão da Ametade

Cabeça
Loriga

Torre
Nave

Penhas da Saúde

Rio Zêzere

Vide

Alvoco da
Serra

Pião

Covilhã

Unhais
da Serra

Erada

0   10 km

**PARQUE NATURAL DA
SERRA DA ESTRELA**

Fundão & Castelo Branco ▽

HIKING IN THE PARQUE NATURAL

Several waymarked **hiking trails** cut across the Parque Natural de Serra da Estrela. The map opposite shows the main trails, some of which are detailed here. Those described below would take between three and four days to complete, but shorter, alternative routes spin off from the main trails, while each is broken down into segments which could be tackled as half-day or day hikes. Always check with the park information offices before setting off on hikes; and be properly prepared and equipped for what can be quite tough routes. Further details of **accommodation, campsites and facilities** en route can be found in the relevant town and village accounts.

● T1 (waymarked in red) runs **from Guarda to Vide** (on the N230). The route leads you across high land, first to Videmonte, an inhabited farming area, and then through Portela de Folgosinho on a forest road and to the dammed lake at Rossim. You then reach Torre (see "Penhas da Saúde", p.245), via Cume, after which the route ends either at Loriga (on the N231) or at Vide (N230). You'll need to be self-sufficient after Videmonte; there are no other settlements until you reach Vide.

An alternative route, the T11 (waymarked in red and yellow), leaves the trail at Portela de Folgosinho and cuts through pine woods and farm land to Covoa da Ponte, where there's a campsite. From there you can visit Manteigas (p.246) and return to the T1 at Cume. T14 leaves the trail at Torre instead and runs down to Penhas da Saúde and Covilhã, by way of the Pião campsite.

● T2 (waymarked in yellow) runs from west and then south, **from Vila Soeiro via Gouveia to Loriga**, along the western edge of the Serra da Estrela. Access to Vila Soeira is from Guarda along the T1, after which the route runs to Linhares (p.240) and the atmospheric mountain village of Folgosinho; there's a grocery store, medical centre, and rooms to rent above the restaurant. At Gouveia there's a campsite; then the route runs through Cabeça de Velha and on to Senhora do Desterro (grocery store), Castro de São Romão (superb vantage point), Valezim – a sizeable village on the N231 – and finally to Loriga.

● T3 (waymarked in yellow) runs **from Videmonte via Valhelhas to Loriga**, this time along the eastern slope of the *serra*, crossing the Mondego and Zêzere rivers. As above, you reach Videmonte from Guarda along the T1 and then walk on to Valhelhas (campsite). Next, at Poço do Inferno, there's a spectacular waterfall; the route then follows the Nave de Santo António, a sandy alluvial plain supporting cattle in the summer. Finally, you pass through Alvoco da Serra on the N231 and, from there, to Loriga.

Alternatively, T32 leaves the T3 at Poço do Inferno and takes the forest road to the Rio Zêzere, after which it passes through Manteigas to the Covão da Ametade (summer campsite), before rejoining the T3 at the Nave de Santo António

If you're coming from the west and north **by car**, you can follow the N17 down from Celorico da Beira, branching off on minor roads to enter the park at the quirky village of **Linhares**, or via the larger (and less interesting) towns of **Gouveia** and **Seia** and the traditional settlement of **Sabugeiro**. Alternatively, from the east and south, the railway and N18 road (between Guarda and Castelo Branco) skirt the eastern slopes, with access to the park from **Belmonte** and **Covilhã**. If you're intent on serious hiking, the best base is **Penhas da Saúde**, just northwest of Covilhã. Penhas has the region's only youth hostel and offers easy access to the valleys north to **Manteigas** or south to **Unhais da Serra**.

For specific details about the *parque natural*, there are **information offices** in Manteigas, Covilhã, Guarda, Gouveia, Seia, Belmonte and Fundão; the details are given in the relevant sections below. At each, you'll be able to buy several useful English-language **guidebooks**, invaluable if you intend to delve into the region in any depth: *Discovering the Region of the Serra da Estrela* describes the hiking trails, while the Portuguese-only *Estrela: uma visão natural* ("A Natural Approach"), details all the major habitats and wildlife contained within the park.

Linhares

LINHARES, 20km southwest of Celorico da Beira, perches on a slope overlooking the Rio Mondego valley, and is one of the most accessible of the *serra* villages, with a trio of attractions in its castle, series of troglodyte-like dwellings, and stretch of Roman road. To get here, take the Celorico da Beira–Gouveia **bus** and stop at Carrapichana, from where it's a two-kilometre walk to the village.

The lofty keep of the **Castelo** presides over its surroundings and for good reason: it dates from 1169 when Linhares, then more of a town, was claimed for Portugal. Afonso Henriques realized its potential as a defensive post, and soon the men of Linhares were trained up and equipped to carry out such feats of bravery as the rescue of Celorico da Beira from the Spaniards in 1198. In the walls are traces of the *cisternas* which gave the village a constant supply of water during times of siege. You can still see the course of the spring which now runs along the gully beneath the great slabs of rock on which the castle was constructed.

Although the stone houses of the village have been spruced up with neat, green street signs, Linhares still feels ancient. If you arrive in the early morning the village appears deserted; its only sounds of life are the animals grunting and kicking their stable doors to be let out. Later in the day you'll see the donkeys being brought in from the fields and, depending on the time of year, seeds laid out to dry in the sun, wine casks being washed for the next year's vintage and, whatever the season, village gossips on their doorsteps, keen as ever to meet a stranger.

A little-known secret of the village's **church** is that it contains three paintings almost certainly executed by **Grão Vasco** and belonging to a larger series which is now lost. Propped up behind vulgar wooden statues and, in one case, stuck in one of the side aisles, the panels, depicting the *Adoration of the Magi*, *Descent from the Cross* and *Annunciation*, shine out in the obscurity. They reveal all the qualities of the great painter – his skill as a portraitist and his deft handling of tone and colour, particularly in the depiction of clothing and folds of material.

Near the schoolhouse in Linhares a path branches off towards Figueiró da Serra. Following it, you'll soon realize that you are walking along an old **Roman road** – part of the one which ran to Braga – with heavy slabs of rock for paving stones looking like something out of an Asterix cartoon. The walk is a beauty, the hedgerows lined with flowers in the spring and blackberries in the autumn.

If you want to **stay**, ask at Linhares's only restaurant, *A Taberna* (☎071/763 66; ③), which has airy rooms and an English-speaking owner; to find it, turn left by the town pillory. Alternatively, see if the sporadically open **turismo** (☎071/721 09), attached to the Junta, can advise you where best to pitch your tent – most probably above the village near a football pitch.

Gouveia

Another 20km southwest of Linhares by road, **GOUVEIA** has lost the rural *serra* feel that once constituted its charm, as it has developed into a fair-sized provincial town.

However, it boasts several fine buildings, the most outstanding being the **Câmara Municipal**, on Avenida 25 de Abril. Open-air concerts are held in its courtyard during the summer months, but you are generally free to walk in. Incongruously, the town also has a modern art museum, in the same building as the Câmara Municipal, the **Museu de Abel Manta** (daily 10am–12.30pm & 2–5.30pm), with a broad selection of contemporary Portuguese pictures donated by Gouveia-born artist Abel Manta (1888–1982).

You may have noticed a **statue** of a shepherd with his dog, at the entrance to the town, which is proudly illuminated at night. Though not perhaps the finest piece of sculpture, it is significant for what it represents. The people in the hills around here live a harsh and impoverished existence – there is never a break in the agricultural year, for when the summer is over and the harvest is stored away it is time to begin the cheese-making, an activity which brings in their only serious income. The shepherd's friend in this harsh lifestyle is his dog, the *Cão da Serra da Estrela* – a fearsome looking breed said to be crossbred from wolves.

If you can, it's worth timing your visit to take in Gouveia's Thursday **market** and if you have your own transport or are happy to make the four-kilometre walk, the *Adega Cooperativa de São Pião* (Mon–Fri 9.30am–noon & 2–5pm; free; ☎038/421 01) welcomes visitors to try its Dão wines.

Practicalities

Buses drop you by the bridge; walk up and veer right and you'll reach the centre of town. The **turismo** (Mon–Sat 9am–12pm & 2.30–6pm; ☎038/421 85) is in Jardim Lopes da Costa (if there's no one around try the helpful reception in the Câmara Municipal) and will hand out maps of the town. Walkers may also want to call in at the **information centre** of the *Parque Natural de Serra da Estrela*, around the corner at Rua dos Bombeiros Voluntários 8 (Mon–Sat 9am–12.30pm & 2–5.30pm; ☎038/424 11), which has further maps and leaflets on the area. For a hiking route in the park that passes through Gouveia, see the box on p.239.

Gouveia offers half a dozen **accommodation** possibilities, including *Pensão Estrela do Parque*, Rua da República 36 (☎038/421 71; ③), a dusty old hotel with modern prices, which has a **restaurant** with a good reputation. The town's most upmarket option is the *Hotel de Gouveia*, Avenida 1º de Maio (☎038/49 10 10, fax 413 70; ⑤), with decent if not very characterful rooms and a pool. The local **campsite** (☎038/49 10 08) is at Curral do Negro, around 3km from the centre of town; to get there, turn right immediately after the Câmara Municipal, then right again, before finally forking to the left for 2km.

Seia and Sabugeiro

Cut out **SEIA** (16km southwest of Gouveia) from your itinerary and you would miss very little, but like Gouveia, it can be a useful jumping-off point, providing bus connections to Coimbra and access to the Estrela *parque natural*. If you decide to stay, you could try one of the three rather upmarket **hotels**: the excellent *Hotel Camelo*, Rua 1º de Maio 16 (☎038/255 55; ④); the *Estalagem de Seia*,

Avda. Dr. Afonso Costa (☎038/258 66 or 226 66; ⑤); or the *Albergaria Senhora do Espinheiro*, Rua Senhora do Espinheiro (☎ & fax 038/220 73; ④). Less expensive options are the *Residencial Silva*, Rua 1º de Maio (☎038/223 05; ③), and the *Residência Serra da Estrela*, in the centre of town on Largo Marquês da Silva (☎038/255 73; ③).

With enough time, or transport, however, it's better to press on into the park, after first visiting the **information centre** at Praça da República 28 (Mon–Sat 9am–12.30pm & 2–5.30pm; ☎038/255 06). There's also a **turismo** in Praça da República (Tues–Fri 9am–noon & 2–6pm, Sat 9am–noon & 2–8pm; ☎038/222 72).

If you don't have the time for an extended trip, you can always make a fleeting visit to **SABUGUEIRO**, 10km east of Seia, said to be Portugal's highest village and one of the more interesting in the *serra*. As well as making a good base for walking, Sabugueiro offers the chance to see rye bread, local spice sausage and Estrela cheese being made, and plenty of Serra puppies for sale. There is a string of handicraft shops on the road in from Seia – most of which also rent out **rooms** – but the centre of the village remains essentially agricultural and traditional. Other options should you want to stay are the traditional country houses in the old village: the *Casa do Cruzeiro*, *Casa Nova* and *Casa da Sofia* (all on ☎038/228 25; ⑤). A less expensive option is the *Residencial Altitude* (☎038/258 95; ③), on the Seia road, which has a reasonable restaurant below it.

From Sabugueiro you can continue southeast on the N339 to Penhas da Saúde and Covilhã; or take the minor road northeast to the N232, which runs from Gouveia to Manteigas, Valhelhas and Belmonte – for all of which, see below. There is no regular transport on these routes, but you can usually make do with a mix of walking and hitching. Alternatively, buses cover the southern route to Covilhã, looping around the fringes of the park, via the little spa village of Unhais da Serra on the N230, on Mondays, Wednesdays and Fridays.

Belmonte

Twenty kilometres south of Guarda, the small and rather remote **BELMONTE** has the honour of being the birthplace of Pedro Álvares Cabral, the discoverer of Brazil, and is a village of considerable interest, commanded by a heavily restored thirteenth-century **castle**. Pedro Cabral was actually born in the castle when it was his family's residence; his tomb is next to the thirteenth-century **Igreja de São Tiago**, just below the walls. Inside the newer **Igreja Matriz**, at the foot of Rua 25 de Abril, there's an image of Nossa Senhora da Esperança, said to have accompanied Cabral on his first visit to Brazil. The castle is now equipped with a bar and modern amphitheatre for summer concerts; there are also plans for an archeological museum to display findings from recent excavations.

A little-known fact about Belmonte is that it has one of Portugal's largest Jewish communities, with up to 120 families living in the village. Records show there was a thirteenth-century synagogue in the town, but this fell into ruins after the Inquisition, when many Jews fled the country or were forced to convert to being "New Christians". However, many of the Jews continued to practise their faith in secret, using a town house on Rua Chafariz do Areal as a makeshift synagogue up until the 1970s. Only since the 1974 Revolution have the Jews felt secure enough to "out" their religion, and in the mid-1990s were finally able to build a brand-new synagogue on the site of the old town house.

Practicalities

Belmonte is a pleasant stopping-off point on the route south; for those with transport, it provides access to the *parque natural* as well as to the barren and medieval region of the Beira Baixa (covered later in this chapter). There are **bus** services to the two main Beira Baixa towns of Fundão and Castelo Branco, and a daily Rodoviaria Nacional bus (Mon–Fri) to Sabugal and the fortress-village of Sortelha. Most of the long-distance buses to Lisbon, Coimbra and Porto stop at Gingal junction, 2km below the town, at the foot of the hill. For details of times for onward connections, check in the café by the statue of Cabral, or the helpful **turismo** on Rua 1º de Maio (daily 10am–12.30pm & 2–5pm; ☎075/91 14 88), next to the reconstructed pillory.

If you want **to stay**, try the basic *Pensão Altitude* on Rua Pedro Álvares Cabral (☎075/91 11 70; ②), beyond the park at the western end of the village. For more comfort there's the *Hotel Belsol*, 9km out of town at Quinta do Rio (☎075/91 22 06; ④), which has a swimming pool – it's back down on the main N18 road between the junction and the turn-off for Valhelhas and Manteigas (N232). A few kilometres further, at Valhelhas on the edge of the *parque natural*, there's a **campsite** (☎038/481 60; open mid-May to Sept). Buses for Manteigas, originating in Guarda, pass through at around 6pm daily.

Covilhã

Another 20km beyond Belmonte, **COVILHÃ** lies immediately below the highest peaks of the *serra*, and is the most obvious base for exploring the *parque natural*. In summer, weekend picknickers and campers spread across the hillsides; in winter, ski enthusiasts take over, using Covilhã as a base for trips to the slopes. It's a steeply terraced town with every thoroughfare looking out across the plain below or up to the crags of the Serra da Estrela. A market town since the Middle Ages, it developed a textile industry in the seventeenth century using wool from the local sheep, who also provide the milk for the renowned local *queijo da Serra*. After industrialization, the woollen industry began to harness water power from the mountain streams; factories today, down on the plain below town, are powered by hydroelectricity.

Covilhã's favourite son is **Pêro de Covilhã**, who set out in 1487 on behalf of Dom João II, to search for Prester John (legendary Christian priest and king) in what is now Ethiopia. However, having reached Cairo, de Covilhã sailed instead to India before returning to Cairo and then heading south on his original errand. He never found Prester John and never returned to Portugal, though Vasco da Gama found his report about India useful when he made his own celebrated voyage there, around the Cape of Good Hope, in 1498. In front of the town hall there's a huge, polished granite slab depicting Pêro de Covilhã's voyages and a decidedly queasy-looking statue of the man himself.

Practicalities

The **train station** is 4km from the town, at the foot of the hill; **buses** stop halfway up the hill at Largo São João. From either terminus you'll have to walk up into town or take a taxi to the central Praça do Município, where there's a **turismo** (Mon–Fri & Sun 9am–noon & 2–6pm, Sat 9am–noon & 2–8pm; ☎075/32 21 70) and a bus information office, both on the ground floor of the town hall.

Other than the campsite on the road to Penhas da Saúde (see below), the cheapest **accommodation** is to be found between Largo São João and Praça do Município. Some good options include: *Pensão Central,* Rua Nuno Álvares Pereira 14 (☎075/32 27 27; ②), old, basic and as characterful as the perky old lady who runs it; *Residencial Montalto,* Praça do Município 1 (☎075/32 76 09; ③; rooms with bath ⑤), which has seen better days, but is in a brilliant position; *Pensão Regional,* Rua das Flores 4–6 (☎075/32 25 96 or 32 70 77; ③), a tranquil place tucked away in a side street and with an inexpensive restaurant underneath; the reasonably priced *Hospedaria São Francisco,* Rua Almeida Eusebio 35 (☎075/32 22 63; ②), downhill from the centre in a quiet street; and *Residencial Solneve,* Rua Visconde da Coriscada 126 (☎075/32 30 01, fax 31 54 97; ④), a smart option with its own garage parking.

For **food**, the *pensão* restaurants are usually the best bet. Alternatively, *Restaurante Os Arcos,* next to the *Pensão Regional,* has a good, varied and inexpensive menu, and *Restaurante Solneve,* below the eponymous *residencial,* is another good choice with efficient, friendly service. *Restaurante Sporting,* on Rua Comendador Mendes Veiga, has a limited menu – 1500$00 will buy a full meal –

but its main attraction is its outdoor terrace. If you're sick of Portuguese food, try *Café Ketchup*, Rua Comendador Campos Melo 44, a budget option serving pizza and pasta.

Hikers or skiers intending to move on should contact the Club Nacional de Montanhismo, Rua Pedro Álvares Cabral 5 (office hours; ☎075/32 33 64), for up-to-date details of local conditions. Covilhã also has plenty of shops for stocking up on **provisions**.

Penhas da Saúde and around

PENHAS DA SAÚDE is another good base for hiking, being right at the heart of the *serra* and close to the highest and most spectacular ground. Getting here in the first place, however, is somewhat problematic. You can either hike the 11km up the glacial valley from Covilhã or catch the bus from beside Covilhã's market (August only, daily at 8.30am, the bus back leaves at 8.30pm). If you're hiking, after 4km you'll pass the *Pião* **campsite** (☎075/31 43 12; open all year), followed a couple of kilometres further on by the swanky *Hotel Varanda dos Carqveijas* (☎075/310 11 20, fax 310 11 24; ⑤), which offers breathtaking views over the Beira Baixa far below and has a restaurant (meals under 2000$00) and swimming pool. Further on, you pass the ruins of several large turn-of-the-century sanatoria, before reaching the rather desolate-looking Penhas da Saúde.

If you want to stay at Penhas, try the 112-bed **youth hostel** (☎ & fax 075/253 75), at the crest of a rise as you enter Penhas on the Covilhã road and with superb views across the plain to the Serra de Malcata. For a little more comfort head further up the hill to *Pensão O Pastor* (☎075/32 28 10; ④), which has its own restaurant, or, just below the youth hostel, there's the overpriced *Hotel Serra da Estrela* (☎075/31 38 09, fax 32 37 89; ⑤). In July and August there's also large-scale unofficial **camping** across the hillside, but the site is unpleasant and litter-strewn and you're much better off staying at *Pião* (see above). Bear in mind that, despite the accommodation here, Penhas da Saúde is not really a village and, apart from a few cafés, there are not many facilities.

Torre

From Penhas, you are within striking distance of the chief beauty spots of the *serra*, with the highest peak in Portugal – **Torre** at 1993m – 10km up the road to the northwest. The stone *torre* (tower) here was added in the last century, on the orders of Dom João VI, to raise the height to a more impressive 2000m. You can easily walk up from Penhas, but the road gets busy in summer so you may prefer to drive or hitchhike right to the top where you'll find the rather surprising sight of a small shopping centre and restaurant!

En route you will pass the vast statue of **Nossa Senhora da Boa Estrela**, carved into a niche in the rock, to which there's a massive procession from Covilhã on the second Sunday in August. A little northeast of Torre, on the road to Manteigas, is the narrow rock cone known as the **Cântaro Magro** (Slender Pitcher), which conceals the source of the Rio Zêzere; there's an excellent summer **campsite** below it at Covão d'Ametade. One of the park's hiking routes passes by Torre and through Penhas and Covilhã; see "Hiking in the Parque Natural" on p.239.

Caldas de Manteigas and Manteigas

A few kilometres beyond Penhas, you can strike **north** at Nave de Santo António, between Penhas and Torre, and follow the glacial **valley of the Rio Zêzere** down to the spa of **CALDAS DE MANTEIGAS**. Here the gushing spa waters run past a lovely old water mill (now a hotel training school), and the town spreads along the bottom of the river valley, where you'll find **places to stay**. *Residencial Miralapa* (☎075/98 20 98; ④) has modern comfortable rooms (each with a TV) and a decent restaurant. Further along the same road is the the excellent *Do Manel* restaurant (☎075/98 11 04; ②), which also has rooms; and then, further still, the pine-clad, modern and well-run *Berne Albergaria* (☎075/98 13 51, fax 98 21 14; ④).

Caldas de Manteigas virtually merges with the larger *serra* village of **MANTEIGAS** whose whitewashed houses and red roofs run along the contour above the Rio Zêzere. It is another good option as a base for exploring the *serra* and for hiking, with two of the *parque's* official walks passing through. Joalto run **buses** from Guarda, 45km to the northeast, passing through Belmonte and via the campsite at Valhelhas (see p.243), but check with the turismo in Guarda before setting out as the route has been under threat of closure for some time (in the opposite direction buses for Guarda depart at 12.50pm). The bus stops on the main street, Rua 1º de Maio, setting you down outside the *parque's* **main information office** (Mon–Sat 9am–12.30pm & 2–5.30pm; ☎075/98 23 82), where you can buy books and guides; nearby, next to the small park below the Galp service station, there's a regular **turismo** (Tues–Sat 9.30am–noon & 2–6pm; ☎075/98 11 29), which has a leaflet of circular walks from Manteigas, including the one detailed below.

As for **accommodation**, at the same end of the village as the turismo, high above the main street, is the *Pensão Estrela*, Rua Dr. Sobral 5 (☎075/98 12 88; ④), boasting fine views across the valley but overpriced, and with some poky rooms. A little way along Rua 1º de Maio, *Residencial Serradalto* (☎075/98 11 51; ②) has good simple rooms above a reasonable restaurant, while further on, and up a side street, is the *Casa de São Roque*, Rua de Santo António 51 (☎075/98 11 25; ④), a lovely turn-of-the-century property with a pretty courtyard and the friendliest of owners. Drivers (or energetic hikers) could continue beyond Manteigas, 12km to the west and all uphill, to the marvellous *Pousada de São Lourenço* (☎075/98 24 50, fax 98 24 53; ⑥); it has only 22 rooms, most with spectacular views, so don't turn up without a reservation.

A HIKE FROM MANTEIGAS TO THE POÇO DE INFERNO

There's a lovely round walk from **Manteigas** to the waterfall of **Poço de Inferno** and back via Caldas de Manteigas, which takes around five to six hours. Begin at the Galp petrol station, and take the small road which goes steeply down to the right of the main road, behind the turismo. Follow this road downhill, bearing right, until you cross a small bridge. Bear left and you will start to pick up the yellow marker arrows which head right into the woods. Keep your eyes peeled as these are not always easy to spot, but the arrows will eventually lead you to Poço de Inferno, 'hell's well', which is a great spot for a picnic and has good swimming potential. From here, continue along the paved road and you will arrive back in town at the top of Caldas de Manteigas.

Apart from the hotel **restaurants**, there's the reliable, but less ambitious, *O Olival*, on the way out of town away beyond the turismo; the upmarket but not too expensive *Antiga Casa Anita* near the Santa Maria church on Rua Dr. Sobral; and *A Cascata*, a cheap option with great views below the *Residencial Serradalto*'s craft shop on Rua 1º de Maio.

Sabugal, Sortelha and Serra da Malcata

The area **east of Covilhã**, over towards the Spanish border, is worth exploring for the chance to visit **Sabugal** and, more particularly, **Sortelha**, whose amazing circuit of walls rises amid one of the bleakest locations in all Portugal – undulating highland plateau strewn with giant glacial boulders and desolate but for a few trees and the shepherds who make their living here. If you're dependent on buses, you'll need to pick up connections from Guarda (run by Viuva Monteiro) or Belmonte (Mon–Fri 1 daily at 9am to Sabugal via Sortelha; bus back leaves Sabugal at 1.30pm) but with your own transport, the two towns make an easy side-trip from Covilhã, and you can continue into the **Serra da Malcata** – wild terrain which, believe it or not, harbours a **lynx reserve**.

Sabugal

SABUGAL, like most towns in Beira Alta, has a **castle**. It's a good one, too, with massively high walls, a vast hollow centre, and a pentagonal tower with three arched chambers piled one on top of the other. Trust the rickety staircase and you could be on top of the world; trust the wobbly stonework and you could walk right around the walls. Having explored the castle, there's little reason to hang around Sabugal but, should you need to stay over, the village has a couple of **pensões**: *Restaurante Robalo* (☎071/635 66; ①) by the roundabout 50m from the closed *Hotel Paliz*, with basic rooms; and the modern *Residencial Sol Rio*, down by the bridge (☎071/631 97; ③) which also rents out pedaloes. There's no official camp-site, but nobody should object if you put a tent up by the river, on its out-of-town stretch.

There's a **festa** (June 24) and a grand **feira** (June 29); at other times of year it's all pretty quiet. If you're heading for the Serra da Malcata (see p.249), pay a visit to the *Reserva Natural* office on Largo de São Tiago, near the castle.

Buses will leave from the main square, Largo da Fonte, until the completion of the new bus station behind the defunct *Hotel Paliz*. There are three services daily to Guarda; others buses go north to Vilar Formoso and south to Penamacor and Castelo Branco, though services are few and far between at weekends. Public transport **to Sortelha** is limited to the early-morning bus (Mon–Fri) to Belmonte. Otherwise, there are school buses, which run in the late afternoon (and, obviously, not during the holidays). You may have to walk, though that's no bad thing as the boulder-strewn scenery is as bizarre as it is breathtaking.

Sortelha

SORTELHA is isolated and rather eerie, especially when mist drifts down from the *serra*. It is an ancient town, with Hispano-Arabic origins, and was also the first *castelo roqueiro* ("rock fortress") to be built this side of the Côa. Mystery and legend have grown up with the castle and its fortifications (*sortelha* means "ring"), with stories spun around the figure of an old lady (*a velha*) whose profile you can see on rocks from outside the top gates. At first sight the town seems nothing special. Walk uphill from the new quarters, however, and you arrive at the fantastically walled old town. Within the grid, take a look at the **Igreja Matriz** (keys from the house next door) with its beautiful ceiling, executed by medieval Moors. Arabic script can be seen, too, on several house lintels near the top of town.

It's also worth taking time to browse around the **antique shop** on the road up to the castle, and the **carpet workshop** on the route back down towards Sabugal. Both offer insights into the way life used to be, but above all they show a healthy attitude to present-day tourism. Even if their continuing existence depends entirely on the foreign visitor, you never get the feeling that the show is laid on just for you. The chance to work with the fine materials and coloured wools seems to be enjoyed by all in the workshop, and the antique dealer is as happy to chat about the curious customs and folk tales as strike a bargain.

Sortelha's major event is a **bullfight**, which takes place on August 15, once every two or three years, when the local council has money to stage it. It retains the ancient and peculiar custom of the *forca* – a rudimentary defence against the bull, using branches – which has been handed down from generation to generation. The order of events for the day begins with a *forca* involving all the young boys of the village – at least 25 of whom are needed to carry the device to prevent it from being tipped up by the bull. Later, solo performers strut the stage with their red capes to take the bull's charges. Onlookers are also frequently involved – many a young bull has hopped up onto the terrace of rocks, only to find himself sniffing at discarded hats and bags while nervous laughter rises up from behind the safety of the nearest wall. In non-bullfight years there's still a **festa** on August 15, and a **romaria** in honour of Santo António takes place on June 13.

Practicalities

Sortelha has some superb traditional stone houses to stay in on the outskirts of the village: the *Casa do Vento Que Soa* (☎071/682 60; ④), *Casa do Pátio* (☎071/681 13; ④), *Casa Árabe* (☎071/581 29 or 682 83; ④) and, best of all, the *Casa da Palheiro* (☎071/681 82; ④); advance booking is recommended, especially in summer. Each of the houses is replete with massive walls, wooden furniture, hot baths, cobwebs – all in all, a splendid mix of modern comforts and medieval surroundings. If you want to stay in the old walled town itself, your best bet is to ask at the *Restaurante Alboroque* (see below) which sometimes has rooms to rent in nearby cottages and also acts as a kind of unofficial booking office for the houses mentioned above pending the opening of the village's turismo – probably some time in 1998. They may also be able to point you in the direction of some *dormidas* if you're on a tight budget.

Alternatively, there are any number of promising areas to pitch **camp** above and beyond the old town, where the terrain is rocky and sheep take shelter beneath massive boulders. For meals, the wood-beamed *Restaurante Alboroque*, on Rua da Mesquita (☎071/681 29 or 682 83) is good value, or if your budget can stretch to it there's the classy but expensive *Restaurante Dom Sancho I*, around the corner, which often has *javali* (wild boar) on the menu.

Buses back to Sabugal leave at 7.30am on schooldays, and sometimes at 9am on Tuesdays and Thursdays – check times the day before in one of the restaurants.

The Serra da Malcata

The **Serra da Malcata** has its reserve's headquarters at Penamacor, 33km south of Sabugal. They are full of advice about how to approach the area and where best to go at different times of the year. The **lynx** – a graceful spotted feline with the build of a domestic cat but the dimensions of a labrador – is notoriously difficult to see, especially without the aid of the park keepers, but the countryside is compensation enough if you don't get a sighting. If you're fortunate you might also see a wild boar disappearing into the forests of black oak. The reserve also contains a dam, currently a scar on the landscape, though it will hopefully heal in time; it has good swimming spots.

Penamacor
PENAMACOR's medieval **castle** may not be as impressive as those in Sabugal and Sortelha but it offers great views over the Serra da Malcata towards Spain, and the town itself makes a good base from which to explore the area. You can whet your appetite beforehand in the small municipal **museum** (daily 9.30am–12.30pm & 2.30–5.30pm; free) above *Café Caninhas* – look out for the stuffed lynx here as it's probably the only glimpse you'll get of one. There's also a comprehensive collection of other local fauna, agricultural tools, man-traps and the obligatory Singer sewing machine.

The **reserve's headquarters** can be found on Rua dos Bombeiros Voluntários (☎077/944 67 or 948 54) and there's a **turismo** in the main square at the lower end of town (Tues–Sun 9.30am–noon & 2–6pm, open till 8pm on Sat; ☎077/943 16) which has details of Solares de Portugal properties in the park. If you're making Penamacor your base, a good budget option is to **stay** in one of the rooms at *Café Caninhas*, Rua de São Estevão 20, just beyond the Galp station, or *Cervejaria Karika*, opposite (both ①). The wonderful *Estalagem Vila Rica* (☎077/943 11, fax 943 21; ④), 500m west of the centre on the main road, offers a more sumptuous alternative; the views from this ivy-cloaked eighteenth-century *solar* are marvellous and the rooms comfortable.

Markets are held every first and third Wednesday of the month, and **feiras** on May 10, August 28, September 21, October 15 and November 30.

South from Covilhã: Serra da Gardunha

Fundão and the neighbouring villages of **Alpedrinha** and **Castelo Novo** lie sunk into a ridge, the **Serra da Gardunha**, south of Covilhã. All have magnificent views and are healthy, rural places, with delicious local fruit and, at Castelo Novo, healing waters. Without your own transport, a route through Fundão is an easier approach to Monsanto (see p.253) than cutting across country from Sabugal and Penamacor.

Fundão

FUNDÃO, 17km south of Covilhã by road or rail, is the largest town in the area and a pleasant place to stock up on supplies. As far as sights are concerned, though, even the local tourist pamphlet admits that the town has "no monuments of note". Fundão's rural tranquillity, however, does much to make up for its touristic shortcomings, as does its glorious abundance of fresh fruit and vegetables. The villages around the *serra* are celebrated for their produce and this is the local market centre. In season you'll find cherries, apples, pears, grapes and chestnuts – add to this a visit to the cheese and sausage shops in the Centro Comercial Cidade Nova, at the top of Avenida da Liberdade, and you've got an excellent picnic.

If you want to **stay overnight**, your only budget options are the rather run-down *Pensão 1º de Dezembro*, (☎075/523 84; ①), west of the Praça do Município at Rua da Cale 47, and the equally down-at-heel *Pensão Tarouca* at Rua 25 de Abril 37 (☎075/521 68, fax 521 68; ②) – to find the latter turn left along Rua Jornal do Fundão off Avenida da Liberdade. Alternatively, you could try the five-storey *Hotel Samasa*, Trav. das Oliveiras (☎075/712 99, fax 718 09; ⑤), also off the avenida, or the eighteenth-century ANTER property *Casa dos Maias*, Praça do Município 11 (☎075/521 23; ⑤). The **turismo** on Avenida da Liberdade (Wed–Mon 9.30am–noon & 2–6pm; ☎075/32 21 70) might be able to help with **rooms**; or there's a small all-year **campsite** (☎075/531 18), two kilometres west of town on the N238, with some shade and a swimming pool.

There aren't many **restaurants**, though the *Veneluso*, Trav. das Oliveiras 12, is recommended. The other options are the *Marisqueira* fish restaurant on the same road, or the flash and expensive *Hermínia Restaurante* at Avda. da Liberdade 123. **Bars** are similarly limited: *Praça Velha*, off Rua Jornal do Fundão is open till late, as is the pleasant designer joint *O Alaúde Bar*, on Trav. das Oliveiras.

Most local **bus** services depart from the bus station at the bottom of the avenida; regional services operated by Rodoviária do Beira Interior leave from Rua Conde Idanha-a-Nova, parallel to the avenida and on the same side as the bus station.

Alpedrinha

ALPEDRINHA is set into the side of the *serra*, overlooking fields of olives and fruit trees and is easily reached by any bus from Fundão to Castelo Branco. In spring the hillside flowers, fruit-tree blossoms and springwater oozing from every crack in the road make it as idyllic a spot as you could hope to find – notwithstanding the rumbling lorries crashing through the village on the main road to the south.

A good first stop is at the museum in the former **Paços do Concelho**, which displays a collection of tradesmen's tools – from cobbler to baker to tinsmith – and traditional clothing, including a striking black wedding dress, the customary colour in this part of the world. A short way beyond, the **Capela do Leão**, in the courtyard of the Casa de Misericórdia, provides Alpedrinha with its current talking-point. Something of a mystery surrounds the present whereabouts of a series of valuable sixteenth-century panels that disappeared from the chapel during its renovation and which were last spotted at a Primitivist exhibition in Lisbon.

At the top of the same street, above the plain **Igreja Matriz**, is the elaborate fountain known as the **Chafariz de Dom João V**. When the king passed through in 1714 he found the water so good that he commissioned the *chafariz* as a sign of royal approval. The little village flourished and grand houses such as the now-deserted **Palácio do Picadeiro**, which towers above the fountain, were constructed during the eighteenth century. In front of this spectre of a palace, the old **Roman road** begins to wind its cobbled way up the side of the *serra* toward Fundão.

A further point of interest is the **furniture workshop**, situated below the main road on the way out of town toward Castelo Branco. Ask inside and someone will show you around António Santos Pinto's **sala de arte**, with some of the most consummate single-handed marquetry ever produced. Pinto moulded Louis XV chair legs to Napoleonic dressers and threw the odd carved African pageboy into his structures for good measure. There's even a set of tableaux depicting the first six cantos of Camões's *Lusíadas* – all in the most incredible detail.

Practicalities

Information on **buses** is available from the newspaper kiosk on the side of the main through-road. The Alpedrinha **train station**, on the plain below, is unstaffed but you can buy tickets on the trains.

Perhaps the best **accommodation** in town is the *Casa de Barreiro*, Largo das Escolas (☎075/571 20; ④), a turn-of-the-century house set amid rambling gardens at the north end of town and with magnificent views. Less grand in appearance, but equally luxuriant inside, is the ANTER property *Casa da Comenda* (☎075/571 61; ⑤), on the western edge of town – a seventeenth-century building with lovely gardens. Cheaper options include the recommended *Pensão Clara* (☎075/573 91; ③), run by a sprightly old lady of the same name (there's no sign, but it's on the right as you enter the village on the E802 from the north), and *Pensão Sintra da Beira*, Rua Francisco Dias 14 (☎075/578 58; ②), which is reasonable enough and has a good restaurant. You can unofficially **camp** near the spectacularly situated swimming pool, which has its own bar (open June–Sept), about 1km north of town on the main Fundão road.

The town hosts a tremendous **feira** (market), on the first Sunday in every month, and a full-blown festival, the **Festa do Anjo da Guarda**, each August 3.

Castelo Novo

In northern Portugal **CASTELO NOVO** is best known as the source of *Alardo*, a bottled mineral water reputed to possess healing properties. At the **spa**, marked by just a single café-restaurant, the water gushes from every crack in the earth's surface. The only **accommodation** is the manor house, *Quinta do Ouriço* (☎075/572 36; ⑥), but there's scope for camping – and no shortage of sparkling clear water.

The village proper, like Alpedrinha, has ancient origins, and a few crumbling remains to prove it: a **castle**, an attractive **Paços do Concelho** (above the main square), and a Manueline **pelourinho**. Off to the sides of the square, narrow alleyways and heavy stonework constitute the village's principal charm. Although there is no **bus** to the village, four daily run along the main N18 road (between Fundão and Castelo Branco); you can be dropped or picked up at the crossroads, 4km out.

Into the Beira Baixa

After the surpassing beauty of most of Beira Alta, the flat plain of the lower province, **Beira Baixa**, comes as something of an anticlimax. For the most part it's monotonous, parched country, dotted here and there with cork and carob trees or the occasional orchard. If you are here over Christmas, you may see burning logs outside each church; these are traditionally kept alight until Twelfth Night. From **Castelo Branco**, the capital of the Beira Baixa and its only sizeable town, you can make rewarding and fairly easy excursions to two strange and atmospheric villages – **Monsanto** and **Idanha-a-Velha**.

Castelo Branco

Not much of **CASTELO BRANCO** has survived the successive wars of this frontier area and today it appears as a predominantly modern town. Set out around wide boulevards, large squares, and small parks, it has an air of prosperity and activity in contrast to the somnolent villages round about.

What's left of its **old town** is confined within the narrow cobbled alleyways and stepped side streets leading up to the ruins of the **Castelo**. Around its twelfth-century walls, a garden-viewing point, the **Miradouro de São Gens**, has been laid out. Nearby is the **Palácio Episcopal** (daily 9am–7.30pm; 200$00), the old bishop's palace, with its formal, eighteenth-century garden – a sequence of elaborately shaped hedges, Baroque statues, little pools, fountains and flowerbeds. The balustrades of the two grand staircases are peopled with statues – on one, the Apostles; on the other, the kings of Portugal. Two of the latter are much smaller than the rest: the hated Spanish rulers, Felipe I and II. Elsewhere in the gardens other statues represent months of the year, signs of the zodiac, Christian virtues and the then-known continents.

The palace itself houses the **Museu Tavares Proença Júnior**, a regional museum whose collections roam through the usual local miscellany, save for a large and splendid display of finely embroidered bedspreads, or *colchas*, a craft for which the town is known throughout Portugal. The museum has been closed for a few years for renovations but is due to reopen shortly. The same is true of the elegant sixteenth-century **Câmara Municipal** in the Praça Luís de Camões, though you can still view the exterior and those of the several seventeenth- and eighteenth-century mansions in the streets around it.

Practicalities

There is a **turismo** (Mon–Fri 9am–12.30pm & 2–5.30pm; ☎072/210 02) right in the centre of Castelo Branco, in a little park off the Alameda da Liberdade. The **bus station** is on the corner of Rua Rebelo and Rua do Saibreiro, the latter leading straight up to the Alameda. It's a little further to the **train station**, but equally simple – straight down the broad Avenida de Nuno Álvares.

As the regional capital, the town has a number of **pensões** (ten or more), though less than half of these merit recommendation. *Residencial Lusitânia* (☎072/242 44; ②) at Rua Sidónio Pais 7, the northern extension of the Alameda, is the most central though distinctly tattered, and *Residencial Caravela*, Rua do Sabreiro 24 (☎072/239 39; ③), near the bus station, is adequate. For more comfort, try the well-run *Residencial Arraiana*, Avda. 1º de Maio 18 (☎072/216 34; ④); otherwise, the turismo can point you towards inexpensive *dormidas* behind the Alameda (①). The municipal **campsite** (☎072/216 15; closed mid-Nov to Jan 1) is 3km north of town along the N18.

For somewhere decent to **eat**, head for the *Restaurante Arcadia*, Alameda da Liberdade 19 (near *Residencial Lusitânia*). It's open daily and particularly crowded with locals at the weekend, paying up to 2000$00 for a fine spread. Further up towards the castle (up Rua Sidónio Pais), there's an equally popular Chinese restaurant, *Grande Muralha*, at Rua da Sé 28. Opposite, *Café Beirão* has pleasant outdoor tables facing the cathedral. For your own supplies, there's a large covered **market** on Avenida 1º de Maio.

Monsanto

MONSANTO, 48km northeast of Castelo Branco (buses twice daily bound for Termas de Monfortinho), claims to be the most ancient settlement in Portugal. It is a claim easy enough to believe, for the old village – there's a newer settlement at the bottom of the hill where the bus drops you – looks as if it has barely changed since the Iron Age. The houses cower beneath a huge fortified granite outcrop, the stone from which they are themselves constructed, and from a few hundred yards they disappear almost entirely into the grey, boulder-strewn background bar the odd splash of whitewash, added in these more peaceful times. It is all incredibly basic and beautiful – flowers are everywhere and the streets, barely wide enough even for a mule, are simply carved out of the rock.

The **castle**, too, is impressive, though tumbledown. As you climb up through the village you're quite likely to meet someone who'll insist on guiding you up, showing you the views and expounding some of the legends. A big celebration takes place every May 3, when the village girls throw baskets of flowers off the ramparts. The rite commemorates an ancient siege when, in desperation and close to starvation, the defenders threw their last calf over the walls: their attackers, so disheartened at this evidence of plenty within, gave up and went home.

Practicalities

The only accommodation at present is the new *Pousada de Monsanto* (☎077/344 71, fax 344 81; ⑤) with ten rooms and an excellent restaurant, where you can taste delights such as stewed wild boar or braised kid goat with turnip sprouts for around 2500$00. *Restaurante Jovem*, just below the *pousada*, is cheaper but still good, whilst the *Adega Típica O Cruzeiro*, also near the *pousada* on Rua Fernando Namora 6, is set in a pleasantly converted storehouse and a good place for a drink and snacks. If your budget doesn't stretch to the *pousada*, you could walk or take the twice-daily bus to Penha Garçia, 8km east, where the *Café Isaias* on Rua da Tapada has **rooms** (②) and good **meals**.

Idanha-a-Velha

IDANHA-A-VELHA is another tiny backwater, sited a few kilometres from Monsanto. It sees two buses a day from Idanha-a-Nova, where there are connections to Castelo Branco; however, if you don't have transport, you could try the walk cross-country from Monsanto, but make sure you get good directions before heading off. The village is certainly worth a little effort to reach. It's possibly of a similar age to or even older than Monsanto, but has a considerably more illustrious history. Known as Igaetania, it was once a major Roman city, and subsequently, under Visigothic rule, was the seat of a bishopric – which endured even Moorish occupation. Wamba, the legendary King of the Goths, is said to have been born here. During the reign of Dom Manuel, however, early in the fifteenth century, it is said that a plague of rats forced the occupants to move to Monsanto or nearby Idanha-a-Nova.

The village looks much as it must have done when the rats moved in, and not far different to when the Romans left, either. It still retains a section of massive Roman wall, the **Roman bridge** is still in use, and odd Roman relics lie about everywhere. In the very ancient **Basilica**, which is at least part Visigothic, there's a collection of all the more mobile statues and lumps of inscribed stone found about the place; another small chapel contains an exhibition of coins, pottery, and bones, all found more or less by accident. Ask in the village café for the key to the basilica, if it is locked. Another oddity, whose history nobody seems to know, is a Moorish-inspired balconied mansion.

Termas de Monfortinho

Nestling among pine trees on the banks of the River Erges, **TERMAS DE MON-FORTINHO** is a tranquil wooded spa resort which, with your own transport, makes an attractive base for exploring the surrounding area and nearby Alcántara and Cáceres, over the border in Spain. It has been a popular resort since Roman times, though up until the 1930s it was not connected by road with the rest of Portugal and so was used mostly by the Spanish, who waded across the River Erges and camped among the pine trees. The town has a relaxed atmosphere and pleasant riverside walks, although since the construction of a bridge over the Erges in 1993, connecting the resort to Spain, things have become more lively.

The **thermal baths** (May–Oct daily 8am–12.30pm & 4–7pm) are north of the turismo, hidden away down by the river and surrounded by woods; you may wish to try out one of the treatments or a massage as the waters are among the most mineral-rich in Portugal. The town also boasts three **swimming pools** and several **tennis courts**; **mountain bikes** are also available for hire from the *Hotel Fonte Santa*.

Practicalities

The **turismo** (☎077/442 23) is two blocks down on the main road, next to the municipal swimming pool. There's no shortage of places to **stay** in Monfortinho. In the modern part of town, the *Beira Baixa* (☎077/441 15; ②) on Rua das Fragueiras is comfortable and cheap but not particularly welcoming; while the friendlier *Pensão Boavista* (☎077/442 13; ③) has TV and telephone in all its rooms. In the old town, there's a cluster of inexpensive, attractive but slightly run-down *pensões* in the woods, by the river; take the road towards the thermal baths and turn right at the fork in the road. However, the best place to stay – if you can afford to splash out – is the peaceful *Hotel Fonte Santa* (☎077/441 05, fax 443 43; ⑥), with beautiful rooms and an attractive swimming pool set in landscaped gardens. There are plenty of **restaurants** and **cafés** along the Castelo Branco road, of which *O Garfo* is particularly good.

For onward transport, there are two **buses** daily to Monsanto, Castelo Branco and Penamacor, which arrive at the lot on Rua José Gardete Martins in the modern part of town.

travel details

Trains

Castelo Branco to: Abrantes (5–6 daily; 1hr 20min–2hr); Covilhã (7 daily; 1hr 20min); Lisbon (5–6 daily; 4hr 5min).

Celorico da Beira to: Coimbra (5 daily; 2hr 50min); Guarda (5 daily; 50min); Lisbon (4 daily; 4hr 15min); Vilar Formoso (2 daily; 2hr).

Covilhã to: Abrantes (5 daily; 2hr 25min–3hr 15min); Castelo Branco (7 daily; 1hr–1hr 20min); Guarda (3 daily; 1hr 15min); Lisbon (5 daily; 3hr 20min–5hr 30min).

Fundão to: Castelo Branco (6 daily; 1hr 5min–1hr 30min); Covilhã (7 daily; 25min); Porto (6 daily; 4hr 15min–5hr 15min).

Guarda to: Coimbra (5 daily; 2hr 30min–3hr 40min); Covilhã (3 daily; 1hr 15min); Lisbon (5 daily; 5hr–7hr 50min); Vilar Formoso (4 daily; 50min).

Vilar Formoso (Spanish border) to: Guarda (4 daily; 50min); Lisbon (1 daily; 6hr 30min); Salamanca, Spain (2 onward connections from Portugal daily; 2hr 30min).

Buses

Almeida to: Guarda (1 daily; 2hr).

Alpendrinha to: Castelo Branco (Mon–Fri 5 daily; 30min); Covilhã (2–3 daily; 2hr 35min); Fundão (2–3 daily; 15–25min); Guarda (4 daily; 1hr 20min); Lisbon (5 daily; 4hr 30min).

Belmonte to: Covilhã (3 daily; 1hr); Guarda (3 daily; 45min).

Castelo Branco to: Coimbra (3–4 daily; 3hr); Covilhã (4 daily; 40min–1hr 5min); Guarda (hourly; 1hr 55min); Lisbon (2–6 daily; 3hr 45min–4hr 10min); Termas de Montefortinho (2 daily; 2hr 30min); Viseu (1–2 daily; 3hr 30min).

Celorico da Beira to: Coimbra (4 daily; 2hr 25min); Covilhã (4 daily; 1hr 15min); Guarda (4 daily; 1hr 30min); Lamego (Mon–Fri 3 daily; 3hr 5min); Lisbon (1 daily; 5hr); Viseu (4–6 daily; 50min–1hr).

Covilhã to: Castelo Branco (4 daily; 1hr 5min); Fundão (4 daily; 20min); Guarda (4 daily; 50min); Lisbon (2–4 daily; 5hr 30min); Penhas da Saúde (August only: Sat 2, Sun 3; 35min); Viseu (2 daily, 2hr 10 min).

Guarda to: Almeida (1 daily; 2 hr); Alpedrinha (4 daily; 1hr 20min); Belmonte (3 daily; 45min); Braga (3 daily; 4hr 20min); Castelo Branco (15 daily; 1hr 55min); Covilhã (4 daily; 50min); Fundão (4 daily; 1hr 5min); Lisbon (1–4 daily; 5–6hr); Pinhel (2 daily; 50min); Trancoso (3 daily; 1hr 30min); Viseu (2–5 daily; 2hr 15min).

Seia to: Celorico (4 daily; 45min); Coimbra (3–4 daily; 1hr 40min); Guarda (4 daily; 1hr 15min).

Trancoso to: Braga (1 daily; 4hr 10min); Bragança (2 daily; 3hr); Celorico da Beira (1–2 daily; 1hr 25min); Covilhã (1–2 daily; 1hr 45min); Guarda (1–3 daily; 1hr); Lamego (1–2 daily; 2hr); Lisbon (2 daily; 6hr 10min); Pocinho (2 daily; 1hr 20min); Viseu (2 daily; 1hr 50min).

Vilar Formoso to: Guarda (3 daily; 50min); Lisbon (3 daily; 5hr 40min–6hr).

Viseu to: Belmonte (Ginjal) (2 daily; 1hr 50min); Celorico da Beira (4–6 daily; 50min–1hr); Coimbra (5–10 daily; 1hr 25min); Covilhã (2–6 daily; 2hr 15min); Faro (6 daily; 11hr 35min–12hr 20min); Guarda (2–9 daily; 1hr 20min); Lisbon (5 daily; 4–5hr); Porto (1–3 daily; 1hr 50min); São Pedro do Sul (Mon–Fri 4–5 daily, 1–2 at weekends; 1hr); Trancoso (2–3 daily; 1hr 25min).

PORTO AND THE DOURO

P ortugal's second largest city, **Porto**, is magnificently situated on the great gorge of the Douro River, its old quarters scrambling up the rocky north bank in tangled tiers. It's a massively atmospheric city, almost Dickensian in parts, though the attention of most visitors is focused firmly on the port-producing suburb of **Vila Nova de Gaia**, across the river. The coastal waters

---

ACCOMMODATION PRICE CODES

All the accommodation prices in this book have been coded using the symbols
below. The symbols represent the lowest prices you can expect to pay for a **double
room in high season**; for a full explanation, see p.29.

① Under 3000$00   ② 3000$00–4000$00   ③ 4000$00–5500$00
④ 5500$00–8500$00   ⑤ 8500$00–12,500$00   ⑥ 12,500$00–20,000$00
                         ⑦ Over 20,000$00

---

either side of the city are shockingly polluted these days, but you don't have to
head that far north to find excellent beaches; those at the resorts of **Vila do
Conde** and **Póvoa de Varzim** offer a taste of what's to come as you head into the
Minho.

Above all, though, it's the **Rio Douro** ("river of gold") that dominates every
aspect of this region: a narrow, winding gorge for the major part of its long route
from the Spanish border, with port wine lodges dotted about the hillsides and a
series of tiny villages, visited by few except for the seasonal wine trade workers.
The valleys and tributaries form some of the loveliest and most spectacular landscapes in the whole of Portugal, and even though the wine no longer shoots down
the river's rapids in barges, as it once did, a trip up the valley remains one of the
best scenic routes in the country. The capital of the Alto Douro province is **Peso
da Régua**, a perpetually developing town with more scope for visiting wine
lodges; just 13km south of here is the delightful Baroque town of **Lamego**, the
home of Portugal's champagne-like wine, Raposeira.

If you're driving, you can follow minor roads along the river practically all the
way from Porto to the border crossing at Miranda do Douro (see p.384). Taking
the **train**, though, is probably more fun. The **Douro line** joins the course of the
river about 60km inland from Porto and sticks to it from then on, cutting into the
rock face and criss-crossing the water on a series of rocking bridges: one of those
journeys that needs no justification other than the trip itself. To the north, narrow
gauge rail lines follow the river's tributaries into Minho and Trás-os-Montes: the
Tâmega line runs to the beautiful riverside town of **Amarante**; the **Corgo line**
connects with Vila Real, a useful bus terminal for exploring Trás-os-Montes; while
the **Tua line** goes from Tua to Mirandela in central Trás-os-Montes, from where
you can catch buses to Bragança in the northeast.

Porto

Although the capital of the north, **PORTO** (Oporto) is a very different city from
Lisbon – unpretentious, inward-looking, unashamedly commercial. As the local
saying goes: "Coimbra studies; Braga prays; Lisbon shows off; and Porto works."
The city's greatest sights are its five bridges: three modern, two nineteenth-
century, and all of them spectacular. The older ones are the defunct metalwork
Maria Pia railway link, designed by Eiffel, and the dizzying, two-tiered Ponte Luís
I, which connects the city with **Vila Nova de Gaia**, home of the port wine lodges
– all of which offer tours and tastings to visitors.

In the city proper, there is a handful of buildings around which to direct your
wanderings: the landmark **Torre dos Clérigos** and the **Sé**, the ornate interiors

△ Prelada Campsite, Centro Comercial Brasília, Boavista Stadium & Museu de Arte Moderna

❶❷ △ R. DE ALVARES

❸ △ CABRAL

CENTRAL PORTO

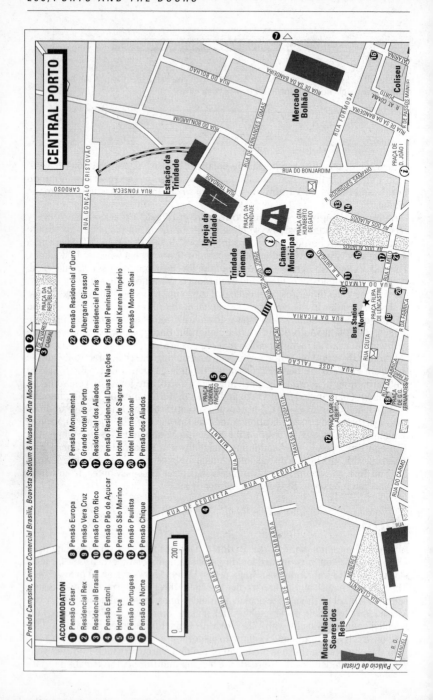

ACCOMMODATION

❶ Pensão César
❷ Residencial Rex
❸ Residencial Brasília
❹ Pensão Estoril
❺ Hotel Inca
❻ Pensão Portuguesa
❼ Pensão do Norte

❽ Pensão Europa
❾ Pensão Vera Cruz
❿ Pensão Porto Rico
⓫ Pensão Pão de Açucar
⓬ Pensão São Marino
⓭ Pensão Paulista
⓮ Pensão Chique

⓯ Pensão Monumental
⓰ Grande Hotel do Porto
⓱ Residencial dos Aliados
⓲ Pensão Residencial Duas Nações
⓳ Hotel Infante de Sagres
⓴ Hotel Internacional
㉑ Pensão dos Aliados

㉒ Pensão Residencial d'Ouro
㉓ Albergaria Girassol
㉔ Residencial Paris
㉕ Hotel Peninsular
㉖ Hotel Karena Império
㉗ Pensão Monte Sinai

PRAÇA DA REPÚBLICA

RUA GONÇALO CRISTOVÃO

RUA CARDOSO

Estação da Trindade

RUA FONSECA

RUA DO BONJARDIM

RUA DO BONJARDIM

RUA DE SÁ DA BANDEIRA

RUA DO BOLHÃO

Mercado Bolhão

RUA FERNANDES TOMÁS

RUA FORMOSA

RUA DE SÁ DA BANDEIRA

Coliseu

RUA DE PASSOS MANUEL

RUA AT COMM

Igreja da Trindade

PRAÇA DA TRINDADE

RUA DA TRINDADE

Trindade Cinema

Câmara Municipal

PRAÇA GEN. HUMBERTO DELGADO

RUA DO BONJARDIM

R RODRIGUES SAMPAIO

PRAÇA DE D. JOÃO I

AV DOS ALIADOS

AV DOS ALIADOS

RUA RICARDO JORGE

RUA DA PICARIA

Bus Station - North ★

PRAÇA FILIPA DE LENCASTRE

RUA CEUTA

RUA DA CONCEIÇÃO

RUA DA FÁBRICA

RUA DE G.G. FERNANDES

PRAÇA DE G.G. FERNANDES

RUA JOSÉ FALCÃO

PRAÇA CORONEL PACHECO

PRAÇA CARLOS ALBERTO

RUA DE MIRANTE

TRAVESSA DE CEDOFEITA

RUA DE CEDOFEITA

RUA DE CEDOFEITA

RUA DO BRENER

RUA DE MIGUEL BOMBARDA

RUA DO CARMO

Museu Nacional Soares dos Reis

RUA D MANUEL II

R D MANUEL

MENERES

0   200 m

△ Palácio de Cristal

Antas Stadium △   🚋 △   △ Alameda das Fontainhas (Fleamarket)

Port Lodges ▽   ▽ Vila Nova de Gaia

Ateneu Comercial

RUA DE SANTA

RUA ALONSO
RUA HERCULANO

Batalha Cinema

Teatro Sá da Bandeira

RUA AUGUSTA ROSA

PRAÇA DA BATALHA

RUA 31 DE JANEIRO

RUA DA MADEIRA

RUA A MENDONÇA

PASSEIO DAS FONTAINHAS

AVENIDA G. EIFFEL

City Wall

Ponte Luis I (Upper Bridge)

RUA SAMPAIO BRUNO

Estação de São Bento

Feira de Vandoma

R. DO LOUREIRO

AV. DE VIMARA PERES

Casa-Museu Guerra Junqueiro

Episcopal Palace

Ponte Luis I (Lower Bridge)

PRAÇA DA LIBERDADE

PRAÇA DE ALMEIDA GARRETT

R. DE D.

Sé

Elevador

CAIS DA RIBEIRA

Igreja dos Clérigos

RUA DOS CLÉRIGOS

RUA DAS FLORES

RUA MOUZINHO DA SILVEIRA

RUA DA BATALHA

Igreja dos Grilos

RUA DOS MERCADORES

TUNNEL

R. DA ESCADA

RUA CONDE DE VIZELA

Igreja da Misericórdia

RUA DA VITÓRIA

RUA DE S. JOAO

Mercado

PRAÇA DA RIBEIRA

PRAÇA DE LISBOA

CAMELITAS

CAMPO DOS MÁRTIRES DA PÁTRIA

LARGO S. DOMINGOS

PRAÇA DO INFANTE D. HENRIQUE

RUA INFANTE D. HENRIQUE

ℹ Casa do Infante

LARGO DO TERREIRO

P. GOMES TEIXEIRA

GALERIA

PRAÇA ARAÚJO LEITÃO

RUA S. BENTO DA VITÓRIA

RUA FERREIRA BORGES

RUA DA PONTE TAURINA

R. REBOLEIRA

Universidade

Jardim da Cordoaria

RUA MIGUEL

RUA DE BELOMONTE

Bolsa

Ig. de S. Francisco

★ Bus to Airport

RUA DAS TAIPAS

JOSÉ CARVALHO

R. DR. B. DE CASTRO

RUA AFONSO ALBUQUERQUE

RUA DAS VIRTUDES

LARGO DE S. JOAO NOVO

Hospital Santo António

Law Courts

Galeria Arvore

Ig. de S. Pedro de Miragaia

RUA NOVA DE ALFANDEGA

RUA DA RESTAURAÇÃO

N

Rio Douro

of the **Bolsa** and church of **São Francisco**, and a clutch of good **museums**. But the fascination of Porto lies very much in the day-to-day life of the place: a bizarre mix of First and Third World, with its prosperous business core surrounded by opulent suburbs and villas, tempered by a heart of cramped streets and ancient alleys, untouched by the planners. This side of Porto comes into focus if you take a walk along the **quayside** between the Luís I and Maria Pia bridges. The improvised sheds and shacks here, clinging to the sides of the gorge, could for all appearances be a Brazilian shanty town.

It's a real shock to discover such poverty in western Europe but it remains hard not to like the city, or to respond to the crowds, tiny bars and antiquated shops. If you can, plan your visit to coincide with **Saint John's Eve** (the night of June 23–24), when the place is at its earthiest and finest for the riotous celebration of São João. On this night, seemingly the entire population takes to the streets, hitting each other over the head with squeaky, plastic hammers, or anything else to hand.

The **telephone code** for the city of Porto is ☎02.

Arrival and information

Buses #56 and #87 shuttle between the **airport**, 13km north of the city, and Jardim da Cordoaria, by the Universidade building, every fifteen to thirty minutes; the journey usually takes forty minutes, but allow an hour at peak times of day. Taxis from the airport into the centre cost 1500–25000$00, depending on your final destination. **Drivers** should try to avoid getting caught up in the downtown grid, whose streets are best negotiated on foot or in a taxi. If you're picking up a rental car, it might be better to wait until the day you leave, then pick one up at the airport.

Coming into Porto by train or bus, you'll find yourself deposited fairly centrally, though the various terminals can cause a little confusion (see p.261). Coming from the south, **trains** drop you at the **Estação de Campanhã**, a few kilometres east of the centre; change here for a local train into **Estação de São Bento**, in the heart of the city – it takes about five minutes and there should never be more than a twenty-minute wait. Most trains from the north run directly to São Bento, though narrow-gauge trains from Guimarães and from the north coast (Vila do Conde/Póvoa de Varzim) use the smaller **Estação da Trindade**, just to the north of Avenida dos Aliados.

Bus companies have no single terminal and a glance at the schedules suggests that each company operates from a different street in a different part of town. Most, though, are fairly central, and a large number operate from a common terminal – Garagem Atlântico – on **Rua Alexandre Herculano** (just east of São Bento). See p.276 for information on Porto's various bus termini.

Information

Porto has three central tourist offices, where you can pick up a large-scale city plan as well as information about train and bus departures. The main **turismo** is at the northern end of the central Avenida dos Aliados, by Praça General Humberto Delgado (Mon–Fri 9am–5.30pm; ☎31 27 40). There's another, partly privatized, tourist office with details on Porto and all of northern Portugal in Praça de Dom João I (Mon–Fri 9am–7.30pm, Sat & Sun 9.30am–3.30pm; open until 7.30pm Sat & Sun during Aug; ☎31 75 14 or 31 31 43), which is closer to São Bento station. The third turismo is near the river at Rua Infante Dom Henrique 63 (Mon–Fri 9am–7pm, Sat & Sun 10am–5pm). There's also a tourist counter (daily 8am–11.30pm; ☎941 25 34) at the airport.

City transport

Although modern Porto sprawls for some miles along the north bank of the Douro, most sights of any interest are within the compact and very hilly centre, and all are within **walking** – or perhaps more accurately climbing – distance. For trips further afield, there's a reliable network of local STCP **buses** which leave from three main terminals: Jardim da Cordoaria, by the Universidade building; the central Praça da Liberdade, at the bottom of Avenida dos Aliados; and Bolhão (stops in front of the theatre on Rua Sá da Bandeira and halfway up at Bolhão itself).

Single **tickets** can be bought for 160$00 on the bus but it works out cheaper to buy them in advance in blocks (10 tickets for 700$00 city centre only, 1030$00 to include the suburbs). If you're intending to use public transport a lot, consider buying a **travel pass**: a one-day city pass costs 360$00 (480$00 to include the suburbs); while a *turístico* pass is 1800$00 (1620$00 with a student card) for four days or 2350$00 (2120$00 with a student card) for seven – the last two are valid outside the city centre, too. They're all available at kiosks around Porto and in the *papelaria* on Praça da Liberdade, next to *McDonald's*.

Central Porto has one surviving **tram route**, #18, which has a flat fare of 85$00 and is worth going on for the ride alone. It leaves (Mon–Sat) from Rua do Carmo by Hospital Santo António and rattles along the river, past the Castelo do Queijo, to the sea at Foz do Douro. You may wish to get off here and catch a tram back in the opposite direction, or you can continue for the full 45-minute ride which winds round to the shopping district at Avenida Boavista, from where it is a 25-minute walk back to the centre. Another option is to take an arranged tram trip or a sightseeing **tour** on a double-decker bus (April–Sept only). You have a choice of a hop-on, hop-off ticket, which gives you the option of spending time at the sights themselves, or a one-and-a-half-hour return trip with commentary in English. Tickets cost 1200$00 and are available from most travel agents, or call Diana Tours on ☎377 12 30.

Accommodation

Porto's **accommodation** is generally good value. The least expensive rooms in the city are in the area south and east of São Bento station; for rather more salubrious places, your best bet is to ignore bargainers at the stations and head for the *pensões* and hotels detailed below, in areas west or east of the central thoroughfare, Avenida dos Aliados. In winter, it's worth investing in more expensive rooms than you might otherwise choose, or you'll freeze, as few budget hotels have any heating.

Hotels and *pensões* west of Avenida dos Aliados

Residencial dos Aliados, Rua Elísio de Melo 27 (☎200 48 53, fax 200 27 10). Just off Avenida dos Aliados, this very comfortable *pensão* fills quickly in summer; book ahead. It can be noisy, though, so try for a room at the back. Breakfast included. ③.

Pensão Residencial Duas Nações, Praça Guilherme Gomes Fernandes 59 (☎208 16 16). Cheap and dependable budget hotel, but often full so it's best to ring ahead. Has a range of rooms and offers a laundry service. English-speaking staff. ②.

Pensão Europa, Rua do Almada 396 (☎200 69 71). All in all a little gloomy, but with a noisy bar and good restaurant. The cheaper rooms come without shower. ①.

Hotel Inca, Praça Coronel Pacheco 52 (☎208 41 51, fax 31 47 56). Modern and ugly hotel but well run, though not as plush as you'd expect for its four-star status. ⑥.

Hotel Infante de Sagres, Praça Filipa de Lencastre 62 (☎200 81 01, fax 31 49 37). This extremely opulent five-star hotel was built in the 1950s and also houses the Peruvian consulate. Has a good restaurant too. Recommended if your budget's up to it. ⑦.

Hotel Internacional, Rua do Almada 131 (☎200 50 32, fax 200 90 63). Upmarket three-star hotel. All rooms have air-conditioning, TV, private bathroom and phone. Breakfast included. ⑤.

Pensão Monumental, Avda. dos Aliados 151 (☎200 39 64, fax 200 57 94). A great, airy, family-run place situated on the fourth and fifth floors of a grand but decrepit building. It can get noisy when school groups are staying. ③.

Pensão Residencial d'Ouro, Praça Parada Leitão 41 (☎208 12 01). Off Praça Gomes Teixeira, by the university. Nothing special and a tad overpriced. ③.

Pensão Pão de Açucar, Rua do Almada 262 (☎200 24 25, fax 31 02 39). Stylish 1930s' hotel with quiet rooms and private bathrooms but it's getting overpriced; book ahead in summer. It's at the junction with Rua Ramalho Ortigão and close to the tourist office. ④.

Residencial Paris, Rua da Fábrica 27–29 (☎207 31 40, fax 207 31 49). Huge rooms with fine ceilings in a place now showing its age – it's always clean, though. Breakfast is included and taken in a restaurant overlooking a small garden. Always a favourite, it's one block up from Rua do Almada. ②.

Pensão Porto Rico, Rua do Almada 237 (☎31 87 85). Small, adequate rooms, quieter at the back (if you prefer the noise of cats to cars). Rooms without facilities are cheaper. ③.

Pensão São Marino, Praça Carlos Alberto 59 (☎332 54 99 or 205 43 80). Efficient and friendly; all rooms with shower and most with a TV; set in a pleasant, garden square 300m from the Torre dos Clérigos. ④.

Pensão Vera Cruz, Rua Ramalho Ortigão 14 (☎32 33 96, fax 32 34 21). Close to the tourist office, this represents a hike in quality, more of a hotel than a *pensão*. It's elegant, if a bit pricey, and breakfast is included. ④.

Hotels and *pensões* east of Avenida dos Aliados

Albergaria Girassol, Rua Sá da Bandeira 133 (☎200 18 91, fax 200 18 92). A good place up the street from the *Peninsular*; all rooms are self-contained and some have TVs. Also has a good restaurant. Breakfast included. ④.

Grande Hotel do Porto, Rua de Santa Catarina 197 (☎200 81 76, fax 208 49 84). Claiming to be the oldest hotel in Porto, this large place still retains a touch of grandeur. It's on the pedestrianized part of the street and less than ten minutes' from São Bento. ⑥.

Hotel Karena Império, Praça da Batalha 130 (☎200 68 61, fax 200 60 09). An old railway hotel, opposite the Batalha cinema complex. Modern and comfortable, despite the dark decor. Good value for money. ⑤.

Pensão Monte Sinai, Rua Alexandre Herculano 146 (☎200 82 18, fax 201 88 61). Fairly big rooms, some with baths and TVs, this is good value – although it can be noisy. ②.

Pensão do Norte, Rua de Fernandes Tomás 579 (☎200 35 03). On the junction with Rua de Santa Catarina (opposite an extravagantly tiled church), this pleasant, rambling old place has masses of rooms, with and without facilities. The best rooms have balconies overlooking the street, though these are undoubtedly noisy. ②.

Pensão Paulista, Avda. dos Aliados 214 (☎31 46 92, fax 600 72 76). Well placed, and with good rooms, but you'll want a room at the back if you're to sleep soundly. Breakfast included. ③.

Hotel Peninsular, Rua Sá da Bandeira 21(☎200 30 12, fax 31 10 61). Central (just uphill from São Bento station) and comfortable two-star hotel with a range of rooms. The azulejos in the entrance reveal it to have once been the outbuilding of the nearby church. Breakfast included. ③.

Hotels and *pensões* north towards Praça da República

Residencial Brasília, Rua Álvares Cabral 221 (☎208 29 81, fax 200 65 10). A really friendly hotel (the best of three in a row), though it's often used by youth groups. ③.

Pensão César, Rua da Boavista 667 (☎31 49 84, fax 202 61 90). Quite a way from the centre (near Praça da República), but worth the effort. The rooms are smallish, but adequate – there's air-conditioning in summer and heating in winter. Breakfast is included. ④.

Pensão Estoril, Rua de Cedofeita 193 (☎200 27 51, fax 208 24 68). Rooms of varying sizes (and sometimes odd shapes) in a friendly and well-maintained *pensão*, with a café on the ground floor for breakfast. Some rooms have balconies, all have TVs. It's on the pedestrianized section of the street, and overlooks a garden. ③.

Pensão Portuguesa, Trav. Coronel Pacheco 11 (☎200 41 74). A converted house, some way out, near Praça da Coronel Pacheco, and consequently quiet. You can pay more for en-suite facilities. ②.

Residencial Rex, Praça da República 117 (☎200 45 48). At the top end of Rua do Almada, facing the garden square. It has the feel of a grand hotel, but was in fact a private house until relatively recently. Rooms are spacious and functional; breakfast is included. Highly recommended, although it can be noisy. ④.

Youth hostel and campsites

Porto's popular **youth hostel**, the *Pousada de Juventude*, is at Rua Paulo da Gama 551, 4km west of the centre in the *bairro* of Pasteleira (☎617 72 57, fax 617 72 47; reception open 9–10am and after 6pm); take bus #35 from Campanhã train station or from Avenida dos Aliados near São Bento train station, or bus #36 from Rua Caldas Xavier by the Rotunda da Boavista. In summer, you'll need to book ahead.

The closest **campsite**, *Parque de Campismo de Prelada*, Rua Monte dos Burgos (☎81 26 16), is 3km northwest of the centre; get there on bus #6 from Praça da Liberdade, #9 from Bolhão until 9pm, or buses #56 and #87 from Cordoaria or the airport until midnight (Mon–Fri & Sat morning only). There's a second local site, the *Parque de Campismo de Salgueiros*, at Rua de Salgueiros, Canidelo (☎781 05 00, fax 781 01 36; May–Sept), across the river near the Salgueiros beach (not a place to swim); take a Santos & Irmãos bus from Rua Augusto Rosa, just off Praça da Batalha. There are also campsites at Medas, near Entre-os-Rios 10km to the east of Porto (☎476 01 61, fax 476 01 62), at Angeiras, near Matosinhos (☎927 05 71, fax 927 11 78; March–Dec), and, in a stunning location on the south side of the river, where it meets the ocean, *Marisol*, at Praia da Madalena (☎711 59 42) – take bus #57 from Praça Almeida Garrett or São Bento train station.

The City

The "centre" is perhaps best regarded as **Avenida dos Aliados**, the commercial hub of the city, fronted by banks and offices. **Praça da Liberdade** marks the bottom end of this sloping avenue and a little further south, across the busy road (or reached via a pedestrian underpass), is the **Estação de São Bento**, the main train station. South of São Bento, a labyrinth of medieval streets and seedy-looking alleyways tumble below the **Sé**, or cathedral, down to the waterfront **Cais da Ribeira**, which is lined with restaurants, bars, clubs and cafés. Here, the two-tier **Ponte Luís I** runs across the river to the port wine suburb of **Vila Nova de Gaia**.

The streets leading off Avenida dos Aliados are the city's major shopping areas: to the west, the busy **Rua da Fábrica** with its stationers and bookshops; to the east, **Rua de Passos Manuel**, which runs into **Praça Dom João I**, and beyond into **Rua de Santa Catarina**, full of clothes and shoe shops. The only other areas of interest are all to the west of the centre: you can walk as far as the **Jardim do Palácio de Cristal** and the Solar do Vinho do Porto, but you'll need to use public transport to reach the shopping complex at **Boavista** or Porto's **Museu de Arte Moderna**, more commonly known as "Serralves".

From Avenida dos Aliados to Cordoaria

The broad **Avenida dos Aliados** is as good a starting point as any for exploration, though other than a quick squint up the avenue to the Câmara Municipal at the very top and a coffee at the pavement tables of one of the cafés at the bottom, there's little reason to linger other than for a visit to the **Ateneu Comercial do Porto**, just east of the avenida at Rua de Passos Manuel 44. This opulent nineteenth century building is the headquarters of Porto's commercial association and houses temporary exhibitions of faience, postage stamps and paintings in its gloriously decorated halls (daily 2–7.30pm; free). If you didn't arrive by train, you may as well cut down briefly to the **Estação de São Bento**, one of the city's grandest buildings in its own right, with magnificent azulejos by Jorge Colaço in the entrance hall. These, somewhat arbitrarily, take on two great themes – the history of transport and the battle of Aljubarrota.

The stifled streets of the old town rarely permit any sort of overall view of the city, so it's a good idea to climb the Baroque **Torre dos Clérigos** (daily: summer 10am–10pm; winter 10am–noon & 2.30–5pm; 100$00), 200m west of São Bento, to get your bearings. This landmark was designed, like the curious oval church beneath it (10am–noon & 2–5pm; closed Wed), by the Italian architect Nicolau Nasoni and was once the tallest structure in Portugal. The dizzying vistas from the top take in the entire city, as well as south across the river to Vila Nova de Gaia and sometimes even to the distant mouth of the Douro and the coast.

The Casa Africana at Rua dos Clérigos 112, is another delight, a combined **bacalhau and port wine shop** that advertises itself by hanging its wares outside. The *bacalhau* (dried, salted codfish) is bundled up in stacks all around the counter, alongside just about every type of port available. Sustenance for the mind can be found in equally wonderful surroundings at the Livraria Lello & Irmão **bookshop**, off Rua dos Clérigos at Rua das Carmelitas 144. Behind the white Gothic Facade, the Art Nouveau interior has been fully restored to its 1906 splendour – Gothic bookcases line the walls and a curved serpentine double staircase leads up to the antiquarian gallery, lit by a stained-glass skylight.

The area immediately below the tower comprises the older sections of the university, and the gardens of the **Cordoaria**. This area is a fairly prestigious quarter of town, housing, for example, most of the city's commercial **art galleries**, which are grouped together on Rua Galeria de Paris, leading off to the north, behind the Cordoaria. At the main dealers here, Galeria Nasoni at nos. 68–80 (closed Aug & Sept), you're free to wander in and take a look at four floors of the best (and priciest) paintings on sale in the country. There is more modern art across the Cordoaria from here, at the **Galeria Árvore** on Passeio das Virtudes.

This is a co-operative of painters, sculptors and designers who run their own art school in close competition with the official Escola das Belas Artes (itself housed in a nearby mansion). They pride themselves on the vitality of the teaching and the freedom they allow their pupils – the results of which are on view in a punchy summer show in June/July.

The Sé and down to the Cais da Ribeira

Set on a rocky outcrop a couple of hundred metres up from São Bento station, Porto's cathedral, the **Sé** (Mon–Sat 9am–12.30pm & 2.30–5.30pm), is a bluff, austere fortress. Despite attempts to beautify it in the eighteenth century, it retains the hard, simple lines of its Romanesque origins – more impressive from a distance than close up. Inside it's depressing, even the vaunted silver altarpiece failing to make any impression in the prevailing gloom. For 200$00, however, you can escape into the neighbouring cloisters, and climb a Nasoni-designed staircase leading up to a dazzling chapterhouse, with more views from the casement windows over the old quarter. There are fine views, too, from the broad flagged courtyard in front of the cathedral.

Beside the Sé stretches the fine facade of the Archbishop's Palace (not open to the public) while around the back, along Rua de Dom Hugo, is the **Casa Museu de Guerra Junqueiro** (currently closed for restoration). This is the former home of the poet and houses his collection of artwork and furniture.

Rua de Dom Hugo curls back around to the Sé to merge with the crumbling, animated old alleys which lead down to the riverside. From the prancing statue of Vimara Peres, **Calçada de Vandoma** plunges downwards, lined with the stalls of an authentic **flea market** (at its best on Saturday mornings). A few of the stalls sell fruit or home-made foods, but most have a spread of unremitting junk – torn clothes, broken transistor radios, used batteries. Nevertheless, this area is the most fascinating and atmospheric part of the city: a medieval ghetto of backstreets that would have been demolished or prettified in most other cities of Europe, although parts are now finally undergoing restoration. Tall, narrow, and rickety, the houses have grown upwards into every available space, adapting as best they can to the steep terrain. There's talk of relocating the market itself to São Lazaro so check at a turismo before you go.

Not much commerce goes on down at the waterfront since the big ships stopped calling here, but along the **Cais da Ribeira** old men still sit around as if they expect to be thrown a line or set to work unloading some urgent cargo, while local children cool off in the summer by leaping into the foul and filthy waters of the Douro. The iron *elevador* (150$00) at the eastern end of the Cais climbs up to a good viewing point achingly close to the top of the Bairro de Sé but as it's fenced in you won't be able to disembark. There's some bustle around the weekday fruit and vegetable market but otherwise it's at night that the riverfront comes alive, with the cafés, clubs and restaurants along the quayside providing some of Porto's best food (see p.272). A post-Modern cube of a fountain adds a slightly surreal air to the quarter.

Following the Cais westward, past the Praça da Ribeira, you reach Rua da Alfândega, which leads away from the water. If you double back along Rua Infante D. Henrique you pass the **Casa do Infante** (Mon–Fri 8.30am–5pm), the house where Prince Henry the Navigator is said to have been born. It's an impressive mansion, which has in its time been the City Customs Hall and a Mint; it currently functions as the headquarters of the city's archives.

The Bolsa and around

Also on Rua Infante de Dom Henrique, Porto's Stock Exchange – the **Bolsa** – faces a statue of the Infante Henry himself, tucked into an eponymously named square. The building is a pompous nineteenth-century edifice with a vast Neoclassical facade and its keepers are inordinately proud of the place. On the **guided tours** (Mon–Fri 9am–1pm & 2–6pm; also Sat & Sun in summer 9am–12.40pm & 2–5.40pm; 550$00) they dwell, with evident glee, on the enormous cost of every item, the exact weight of every piece of precious metal, and the intimate details of anyone with any claim to fame ever to have passed through the doors; President Kennedy, apparently, was one. The tour's nadir is the "Arab" Hall, an oval chamber that misguidedly attempts to copy the Moorish style of the Alhambra; here the guide's superlatives achieve apotheosis. Should you not want to bother with the tour you can see the main courtyard, easily the most elegant part, without having to buy a ticket.

Adjoining the Bolsa is the **Igreja de São Francisco** (summer Mon–Sat 9am–6pm, Sun 9am–5pm; winter Mon–Sat 9am–5pm; 500$00), perhaps the most extraordinary church in Porto. From its entrance on Rua de São Francisco it looks an ordinary enough Gothic construction, but the interior has been transformed by an unbelievably ornate eighteenth-century refurbishment. Altar, pillars, even the ceiling, drip with gilded Rococo carving which reaches its ultimate expression in an interpretation of the *Tree of Jesse* on the north wall. Don't miss the church's small **museum**, housed in the catacombs below, which consists of artefacts salvaged from the former monastery. Beneath the flags of the cellar is an *osseria* – thousands of human bones, cleaned up and stored to await Judgement Day.

Two other churches in this neighbourhood have small museums. Pride of the **Igreja da Misericórdia** (Mon–Fri 10am–noon & 2.30–5pm, Sat 10am–noon; 200$00), a couple of blocks to the north on Rua das Flores, is a remarkable *Fons Vitae*, depicting King Manuel I with his wife Leonor and eight children, richly clothed, kneeling before the crucified Christ. It's an exceptional example of fifteenth-century Portuguese realism – a style which was heavily influenced by Flemish painters like van Eyck and van der Weyden. Over to the west, in the **Igreja de São Pedro de Miragaia**, there's another fine fifteenth-century triptych; the church is kept locked but someone with a key is usually near at hand.

Northwest: to Soares dos Reis and the Jardim do Palácio de Cristal

Northwest of the Cordoaria, on Rua de Dom Manuel II, is the **Museu Nacional Soares dos Reis** (Tues–Sun 10am–12.30pm & 2–5.30pm), Portugal's first designated national museum – dating from 1933. It occupies the former royal Palácio das Carrancas; a building that was the French headquarters in the Peninsular War and from where they fled so hurriedly that the Duke of Wellington, leading his troops across the Douro, was able to sit down and eat the celebratory banquet that had been laid out for Marshal Soult and his officers. The museum contains excellent collections of glass, ceramics and a formidable display of Portuguese art of the eighteenth and nineteenth centuries. Highlights include the paintings by Henrique Pousão and sculptures by Soares dos Reis (*O Desterrado* – "The Exiled" – is probably his best-known work) and his pupil, Teixeira Lopes.

Follow the road for 100m or so past the Museu Soares dos Reis, or take bus #3 from Praça da Liberdade and you soon reach the **Jardim do Palácio de Cristal**, a beautiful stretch of park dominated by a huge domed pavilion; this was built to replace the original "Crystal Palace" and now serves as a sports arena. The park also houses a Quaker animal hospital and, in summer, hosts hockey matches, pop concerts and exhibitions.

Around the back of the park, at no. 220 on the cobbled Rua Entrequintas, stands the **Quinta da Macieirinha**, which houses both the **Museu Romântico** (Tues–Sat 10am–noon & 2–5pm, Sun 2–5.30pm; 100$00), a collection of mid-nineteenth-century furniture and art works, and – on the ground floor – the **Solar do Vinho do Porto** (Mon–Fri 10am–11.45pm, Sat 11am–10.45pm). Here, in a comfortable lounge, whose terrace overlooks the river, you can sample one of hundreds of varieties of **port wine**, starting at around 150$00 a glass. The list is the same as at the *Instituto do Vinho do Porto* in Lisbon but the service is considerably friendlier, the views are better, and the wine, after all, is at home. It's a good prelude to a visit to the port lodges across the river in Vila Nova de Gaia (see p.268).

Boavista and the Igreja de Cedofeita

The road directly west at the top end of Praça da República, Rua da Boavista, leads to Praça Mouzinho de Albuquerque, popularly known as the **Rotunda da Boavista**. This is overlooked by a huge column, with a lion astride a much flattened eagle, erected to celebrate the victory of the Portuguese and British over the French in the Peninsular War. From here you can pick up tram #18 for its roundabout route into town (see p.261). There's also a flash modern shopping centre near here, the **Centro Comercial de Brasília**, on Avenida Boavista. Buses #18 and #19 from here will take you to the Castelo do Queijo on the shore at the end of the Avenida.

A couple of blocks before you reach the Rotunda, you pass the very simple **Igreja de Cedofeita** (Mon–Sat 9am–12.30pm & 4–7pm, Sun 9am–12.30pm), from *cedo feita* meaning "built quickly", and reputed to be the oldest Christian building in the Iberian peninsula. It was supposedly built by the Suevian king Theodomir in 556, though the current building is a twelfth-century Romanesque refashioning.

Museums out of the centre

The best of the museums outside the centre is the highly contemporary **Museu de Arte Moderna** (March–Oct Tues–Fri 2–8pm, Sat & Sun 10am–8pm; Nov–Feb closes at 6pm; 300$00), at Rua de Serralves 977, about half an hour's bus journey to the west; take tram #18 or bus #78 from the Cordoaria or from near the Palácio de Cristal to Rua Dr. Alberto Macedo. Administered by Lisbon's Gulbenkian Foundation, the museum is housed in a 1930s' palace known as the Casa de Serralves and displays the work of a number of Portuguese architects and designers (exhibitions run for a month at a time). No public collection in the country gives you a more accurate picture of Portugal's modern art scene, and the setting manages to be at once majestic and personal. The gardens are worth a visit too – the inventive scarecrows in the farm at the far end are made by schoolchildren and ceremonially burned in October after the harvest period.

Other than the Museu de Arte Moderna, you might want to ask at the tourist office if the **Casa-Museu de Fernando de Castro** has re-opened yet. This extraordinary house is crammed with treasures and in particular with pieces of gilded wood salvaged from the city's convents following the 1910 dissolution of the monasteries. It's maintained by the Soares dos Reis authorities and is at Rua de Costa Cabral 176 (an extension of Rua de Santa Catarina), way to the north of the centre.

Finally, down by the river beyond the Jardim do Palácio de Cristal, you'll find the **Museu do Carro Eléctrico** (Tram Museum; Tues–Sat 9am–noon & 2–5pm;

300$00), housed in an old tram shed on Alameda Basílio Teles. Until recently, trams still ran throughout the city's streets, though these days you have to be content with route #18. Don't bother with the museum's own tram trips – they run exactly the same route as tram #18 (which goes to the museum anyway), but cost considerably more.

Vila Nova de Gaia

The suburb of **Vila Nova de Gaia** is taken over almost entirely by the port trade. As you walk across the **Ponte Luís I** from central Porto, the names of the old **port wine lodges**, spelled out in huge white letters across their roofs, dominate the views. The most direct route to the wine lodges is across the bridge's lower level from Cais da Ribeira, or take buses #32, 57 or 91 from São Bento. However, if you've a head for heights it's an amazing sensation to walk over the upper level some 60m above the river, or take buses #82, 83 or 84 from Avenida dos Aliados. There's a beautiful view of the tiered ranks of Porto's old town from here and an even better one from the terrace of the **Mosteiro da Nossa Serra do Pilar** high above the bridge. From this former convent, Wellington planned his surprise crossing of the Douro in 1809 and it's a barracks again today. The round church is open to the public on Saturday afternoon and Sunday morning, but sadly the unusual circular cloister rests in a sort of no-man's-land between church and army territory; ask at the turismo for details on visiting it.

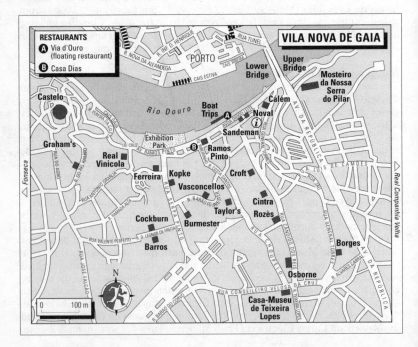

THE ORIGINS OF THE PORT WINE TRADE

The distinction between **port wine** and the other Portuguese wines was first made at the beginning of the eighteenth century. Many British merchants, engaged in importing English cloth and Newfoundland cod to Portugal, were already living in Porto and were familar with Portuguese wines. When Britain prohibited the import of French wines from 1679 to 1685 and later during the War of the Spanish Succession (1702–1714), Portuguese wines became increasingly popular in Britain, with wines from the Douro region being particularly fashionable.

The **Methuen Treaty** of 1703 between Britain and Portugal reduced the duty paid on Portuguese wine in return for the removal of Portuguese restrictions on British woollen goods. As a consequence, the port wine trade became so profitable and competitive that inferior wines, often adulterated and artificially coloured, were passed off as the genuine article – giving port itself a bad name. This led the future Marquês de Pombal to found the Companhia Geral de Agricultura dos Vinhos do Alto Douro in 1756 while, at the same time, **demarcating** the area from which port wine could legitimately come. The monopoly and demarcation were contentious for many years; the area was regularly extended, but only recently was permission granted for port to mature elsewhere than at the lodges at Vila Nova de Gaia. Even now, strictly speaking, the demarcated area lies on either side of the Douro from Barrô, 8km downstream of Peso da Régua, to the Spanish frontier at Barca de Alva and on the Portuguese bank north to Freixo de Espada à Cinta and beyond. Under EU regulations, however, the demarcated port regions are being reshaped in a nine-year conversion and renewal programme.

Touring the lodges

Most of the **port wine lodges** were established in the eighteenth century, in the wake of the Methuen Treaty of 1703 (see box above), and although on the whole they have long since been bought by multinational companies, they still try hard to push a "family" image. Almost without exception, they offer free **tasting and tours**, though not all are open for visits year round. Most are open Monday to Friday (9.30am–12.30pm and 2–5.30pm); in summer, some (like Cálem, Osborne and Graham's) open the same hours at weekends, too (Ferreira opens Saturday mornings only). All the lodges will give you the chance to purchase their produce – worthwhile if you want top-quality stuff but you'll probably find it cheaper to buy the more basic ports in town. Simply stroll along the waterfront and follow the signs to the various lodges: some have tours at specific times, so you may have to pop back later, but many sit you in a waiting room until enough people have arrived. The **turismo** in Vila Nova (Mon–Fri 9am–12.30pm & 2–5.30pm, Sat 10am–12.30 & 2–6pm; ☎370 37 35), which is on the waterfront by Sandeman, has up-to-date details of tours and visiting hours.

It's interesting to contrast one of the large manufacturers, such as **Sandeman** (which has its own museum) or **Real Vinícola** (which operates virtually a production-line process), with the smaller, more traditional lodges such as **Cálem**, **Croft** or **Kopke**. **Taylor's** – a bit of a hike uphill – gives a very informative talk on the processes and is happy to take just a couple of visitors at a time, as is **Fonseca** (whom its owns). There are distinct contrasts, too, between the "British" names and the Portuguese-founded establishments, such as **Ramos Pinto** or **Borges**. It was **Real Companhia Velha** who led the first Portuguese challenge to the British port monopoly in the nineteenth century and their lodge contains numerous warehouses storing casks for the rich and

MAKING PORT WINE

Grapes from vines in the demarcated region are **harvested** from mid-September to mid-October and then crushed – mechanically nowadays and not by foot, whatever the various lodges say. The grape juice ferments for a couple of days and then, when the natural sugar level is sufficiently reduced, the **fermentation** process is arrested by the addition of grape brandy – in a ratio of four parts wine to one part brandy. The wine then stands in casks in the *armazém* (lodge) of the company **quinta** (estate) until the following March, when it's transported downstream to the shippers' lodges at Vila Nova de Gaia, where it matures.

There are four basic **types of port** – *branco* (white), *tinto* (red), *tinto aloirado* (ruby) and *aloirado* (tawny) – which spend varying times maturing. **Vintages** are only declared in certain years, when a *quinta*'s wine is deemed to be of a sufficiently high quality; when this happens, the wine spends only two years in the cask before being bottled and left to mature. A vintage wine is ready to drink between ten and fifteen years after bottling; it's a darker colour than the other wines, because of the time it spends in the bottle, and needs to be decanted to separate it from sediment. The label on the bottle will show the company, the vintage year, the year it was bottled, and sometimes the name of the *quinta*. **Late-bottled vintage wine** (LBV) is wine that's not of vintage quality, but still good enough to mature in bottles, to which it's transferred after five or six years in the cask when it is already good enough to drink. All other ports are made from blends of wines, and most are kept in the cask for much longer – at least seven years for a tawny. Wines designated 20, 30- or 40-year-old port are also blended and spend, on average, that length of time in the cask, after which they lose much of their original red colour, becoming lighter the older they are.

famous (Generalísimo Franco's descendants among them), as well as a 6-kilometre tunnel, which was intended to form part of a rail link but, having turned out to be built at the wrong angle, now serves as a cold storage for Velha's famed sparkling wines and vintage ports.

Casa-Museu de Teixeira Lopes

A more sober visit in Vila Nova de Gaia could be made to the **Casa-Museu de Teixeira Lopes** (Tues–Sat 9am–12.30pm & 2–5.30pm; free) – a very steep hike up Rua Cândido dos Reis from the waterfront. To get there by bus take #33, #82, #83 or #84 from Avenida dos Aliados across the top level of Ponte Luís I, or #57 or #91 from São Bento along the lower level. Lopes was Soares dos Reis's principal pupil and formed the centre of an important artistic and intellectual set that lived in Gaia at the turn of the century. The circle is well represented in the second part of the museum's display, the first being devoted to Lopes's work – much of it preoccupied with the depiction of children. His masterpiece is considered to be the enigmatic portrait of an Englishwoman, *A Inglesa*.

Walks in and around Vila Nova de Gaia

To get a good feel of the town's historical past **walk** up Rua Costa Santos, turn right into Rua do Barão Forrester, then back to the river down Rua Serpa Pinto along cobbled streets and under trailing vines. Another rewarding excursion is the walk 3km **downriver** past the port houses to the small fishing port of **Afurada**, where there's a superb sandbar across much of the rivermouth and strange boulders strewn around its edges. Small ferries, bedecked with Sandeman hoardings and pursuing erratic courses against the currents, cut across the rivermouth between here and the grubby Porto suburb of **Foz do Douro**.

Eating

You may be shocked to discover that the city's speciality is *tripas* (tripe) and that the people are affectionately referred to by the rest of the country as *tripeiros* – tripe eaters. The story goes that the inhabitants gave away all their meat for the expedi-

AROUND THE WATER FRONT: RESTAURANTS, BARS & CAFÉS

RESTAURANTS
- **A** A Tasquinha
- **B** Papagaio
- **C** Restaurante Tipico
- **D** Restaurante Carlos Alberto
- **E** Solar Moinho de Vento
- **F** Café na Praça
- **G** Restaurante O Escondidinho
- **H** Montecarlo
- **I** Churrasqueira de Brasil
- **J** Chabrini
- **K** Casa Meia Lua
- **L** Mar Norte
- **M** O Fado
- **N** Mais Um
- **O** Restaurante Chinês
- **P** Chez Lapin
- **Q** Casa Filha da Mãe Preta & Casa Peza Arroz
- **R** A Canastra
- **S** Taverna do Bebobos
- **T** Dom Tonho
- **U** Café Restaurante Miradouro
- **V** Tripeiro
- **W** Pedro dos Frangos
- **X** O Ginjal
- **Y** Mesa Antiga

BARS & CAFÉS
- **1** Café Guarnay
- **2** Café Majestic
- **3** A Brasileira
- **4** Academia
- **5** Está Se Bem
- **6** Porto Fino
- **7** Aniki Bóbó
- **8** Meia Cave
- **9** Taverna Filha Da Mãe Preta
- **10** Bar Prioridade
- **11** Café do Cais
- **12** Taberna da Ribeira
- **13** Intercyber Café

tions to Cesta in North Africa in the late fourteenth century, leaving themselves only the tripe, and that it's been on the menu ever since. Don't let this put you off – there's always plenty of other choices and the cooking is as good as any in Portugal. You'll be able to eat well and cheaply, though the central shopping areas – on either side of Avenida dos Aliados – are surprisingly short of cafés and restaurants; for the best bargains, you have to be prepared to dig into less salubrious areas. At the basic level, Porto has **workers' cafés** galore, all with wine on tap and often with a cheap set menu for the day. They are mainly lunchtime places, though most serve an evening meal until around 7.30pm and a few stay open later; prime areas are the grid of streets north and south of the Cordoaria: especially Rua do Almada (north) and Rua de São Bento da Vitória (south). Moving more upmarket, into the **restaurant** league, the Cais da Ribeira is hard to beat for atmosphere or for its fish, with any number of café-restaurants installed under the arches of the first tier of dwellings.

If you're **buying your own food**, check the central markets listed on p.277. Also worth seeking out is the **bakery** at Trav. de Cedofeita 20b, one of the oldest in the country, which uses traditional methods such as burning *carqueja* – a variety of broom which reaches high temperatures while producing very little ash. The speciality is *pão-de-ló*, a round sponge cake.

Unless otherwise stated, all the restaurants listed below are open daily; telephone numbers are given for those where it might be necessary to reserve in advance. You'll be able to eat a full meal with drinks for around 3000$00 a head, often much less than this if you're careful.

Central Porto

A Brasileira, Rua do Bonjardim 118. Next door to its café, this is one of the oldest and most elegant of Porto's restaurants, with an Art Deco interior, pavement café, stand-up bar and smallish dining room with attentive waiter service. Around 3000$00. Closed Sun.

Chabrini, Rua do Loureiro 40. Right by São Bento station, this is a rare Indian restaurant with some good vegetarian options (under renovation at time of writing).

Restaurante O Escondidinho, Rua de Passos Manuel 114 (☎200 10 79). Hardly hidden (*escondidinho* means "the little hidden place"), this has a cluttered, country-house interior and excellent French-influenced Portuguese cuisine, but its expensive. Try the hake in Madeira sauce and a kirsch omelette if you have 3500$00 to spend; more like 6000$00 for a feast. Book ahead for evenings. Closed Sun.

Restaurante Ginjal do Porto, Rua do Bonjardim 724 (☎200 06 61). Tripe and other Portuguese specialities served in a no-frills setting. It's cheap – under 1000$00 for the *prato da dia*.

Pedro dos Frangos, Rua do Bonjardim 219–223. Down-to-earth grill house, where you can sit at the bar or in the upstairs restaurant. A *meia frango* (half chicken), fries, salad and wine won't come to more than 1500$00 – leaving change for a night's entertainment. Closed Tues.

Tripeiro, Rua Passos Manuel 195 (☎200 58 86). Despite the name, it gives the tripe a rest and specializes in *bacalhau* instead. Meals for around 2500$00.

Cais da Ribeira and around

Taverna do Bebobos, Cais da Ribeira 24 (☎31 35 65). Established in the nineteenth century, this has a real old *tasca* feel, with its barrels of wine on the walls. Fish and regional specialities – try the pork with wine sauce. Very popular, so book ahead if possible. Full meals will cost up to 3500$00. Closed Mon.

A Canastra, Cais da Ribeira 37. Another homely under-the-arches option, but cheaper and more local than its neighbours.

Casa Peza Arroz, Cais da Ribeira 41–42 (☎31 02 91). Good *ementa turística*, including the usual range of fish dishes. Relaxed and reasonably priced. Closed Wed.

Chez Lapin, Rua Canastreiros 40 (☎200 64 18). Under the arches, this deceptively large place is not too cheap, but very popular locally, particularly on Sundays when many others are closed (reserve in advance then). And, yes, one house speciality is rabbit.

Restaurante Chinês, Avda. Vimara Peres 38 (☎200 89 15). Some of the city's best Chinese food – served in a modern building just at the entrance to the Ponte Luís I. Allow around 2000$00 for the *ementa turística*.

Dom Tonho, Cais da Ribeira 13–15 (☎200 43 07). Typical of the recent move upmarket for the Cais da Ribeira area is this high-class chrome-and-glass restaurant owned by pop star Rui Veloso.

O Fado, Largo de São João Novo 16 (☎202 69 37). The food's OK, but most people come here for the fado, nightly until 3.30am. Closed Sun.

Casa Filha da Mãe Preta, Arcos do Douro 2–3. Built into the arches – the azulejo-decorated upper floor gives you a view over the river. An excellent *ementa turística* features mackerel, sardines and all the business, though it is rather pricey. Closed Mon.

Mais Um, Avda. Vimara Peres 73. More of a café than a restaurant, but good, cheap food and friendly management.

Mar Norte, Rua Mouzinho da Silveira 99. Another good, inexpensive Chinese restaurant.

Café Restaurante Miradouro, Cais da Ribeira, on the arches by the entrance to the bridge. This is a budget option which is always bustling with locals. Serves up great pizzas, *bifanas* and huge salads. Its outdoor tables have as good an outlook as any.

Around Praça da Batalha

Casa Meia Lua, Rua Cimo da Vila 151. Small and friendly place where you can eat well for around 1000$00.

Mesa Antiga, Rua Santo Ildefonso 208 (☎200 64 32). Excellent regional specialities in a family-run restaurant – the most typical dishes are *cabrito assado* (grilled kid) and baked *bacalhau*. Around 2500–3000$00. Closed Sun.

Montecarlo, Rua de Santa Catarina 17. Hidden away up on the second floor, this looks like a badly neglected 1930s' tearoom, has views over Praça da Batalha, a buzzing television, food that veers from good to indifferent and, particularly at Sunday lunchtime, very noisy locals. Not everyone's cup of tea, but very good value for money.

Cordoaria to Praça de Carlos Alberto

Churrasquiera de Brasil, Campo dos Mártires da Pátria 136. Very cheap workers' diner on the square immediately south of the gardens. Open until 10pm.

Restaurante Carlos Alberto, Praça de Carlos Alberto 88. A very friendly, cheap traditional restaurant, with excellent daily specials. Closed Sat.

Churrasqueira Papagaio, Trav. do Carmo 32. Attractive tiled interior, with good grills and an inexpensive *ementa turística*.

Café na Praça, Praça de Lisbon. The outdoor tables are a great place to sit and soak up the surroundings and the *espetada de lulas* (squid kebab) is worth a try.

Solar Moinho de Vento, Largo do Moinho de Vento 81. Largely patronized by locals but not particularly cheap – around 2500$00. It's at the top of end of Rua da Fábrica.

A Tasquinha, Rua do Carmo 24. Attractive, "olde worlde" sort of place with wine barrels, a block north of the gardens. Open only till 10pm and closed Sun.

Restaurante Tipico, Trav. de Cedofeita 56. Fairly authentic Portuguese food at reasonable prices – around 1500$00.

Vila Nova de Gaia

Casa Dias, Avda. Ramos Pinto 242, opposite the exhibition park near the Ramos Pinto port lodge. Has a good value *ementa turística* or you can go à la carte and sample the speciality – tripe.

O Verde, Rua Francisco Alexandre Ferreira 207. One of Porto's few exclusively vegetarian restaurants; meals for around 1400$00.

Via d'Ouro, aboard a Via d'Ouro boat moored at Cais da Estiva (☎938 88 16). The pricey lunches and dinners are just about worth it for the riverside setting. However, the 25 people minimum means that in practice this happens only in high season.

Drinking, nightlife and entertainment

Cafés in Porto rival Lisbon's, with some lovely old Art Deco survivors in the main shopping streets. Trendier, late-night **bars** are found in the streets around the Cais da Ribeira (Rua de Fonte Taurina, Rua de São João and Rua de Belomonte), where establishments run the gamut from unlicensed (and thus illegal) bars selling cheap beer to designer joints aimed squarely at the club crowd. Many of the latter have a minimum charge of around 800$00. Porto's **discos** are highly regarded, too, although most are way outside the centre – you'll need a taxi. As with Lisbon, most of the clubs stay open until 4–5am or so, with a standard 1000–1500$00 admission fee, and at most places you can present the entrance ticket as a voucher for your first couple of drinks.

As for other forms of entertainment, **classical music concerts** are held regularly in the Auditório Nacional Carlos Alberto, Rua das Oliveiras 43 (☎200 45 40) and the Claustros do Convento de São Bento da Vitoria, Rua São Bento da Vitoria (☎200 65 47). **Dance** and other musical events, including major **pop and rock concerts**, usually take place in the Coliseu, Rua de Passos Manuel (☎200 51 96). Since the Revolution, much of the underground dissident tradition of **theatre** has lost its way and musicals have taken over. However, the recent renovation of the Teatro Rivoli on Praça Dom João I, and continued growth of the Teatro Nacional São João on Praça da Batalha, offer some hope. In addition, the smaller Teatro Sá da Bandeira on Rua de Sá da Bandeira occasionally swaps its staple showing of porn films for the latest performances of the Teatro Experimental do Porto. The most central cinemas to catch current **films** are the Cinema Batalha (☎202 24 07), in Praça da Batalha; Cinema Trindade off Praça da Trindade; and Cinema Passos Manuel next to the Coliseu. If you are around in February, look out for

PORTO FESTIVALS

For details of exact dates, times and various venues, check with one of Porto's turismos.

February: Fantasporto international film festival; at the Coliseu and other venues around the city.

May: European Jazz Festival, Puppet Festival; both at the Auditório de Carlos Alberto.

May–June: Book Festival; at the Palácio de Cristal.

June: World Music Festival; at the Palácio de Cristal. São João; all over the city.

August: Rock Festival; at the Palácio de Cristal.

September: Fado Festival; at the Coliseu.

October–December: Contemporary Art Festival; at various venues around the city.

November–December: European Cinema Festival; at various venues around the city.

Fantasporto, Porto's film festival, with films shown at venues around the city. You can pick up monthly cultural and concert **programmes** from the tourist offices; and there are film details and other **listings** in the local edition of *Público*.

Cafés

Aviz, Rua de Almada. A handy place to wait for buses to the north, with marble table tops.

A Brasileira, Rua de Sá da Bandeira 75. A sister branch to the one in Lisbon, with pavement seats and a good stand-up bar for breakfast and refuelling during the day. Open till 8pm, closed Sun.

Guarany, Avda. dos Aliados. Less stylish than *A Brasileira*, but bright and airy, popular with old ladies at tea-time. Open till 10pm.

Intercyber, Praça General Humberto Delgado 291. Pleasant Internet café-bar up Avenida dos Aliados near the Câmara Municipal.

Majestic, Rua de Santa Catarina 112. The nicest and most expensive of the old Art Deco cafés, with perfectly preserved decor, outside tables and excellent coffee. The grand piano features in out-of-season recitals. Closed Sun.

Bars

Academia, Rua de São João 80. Modish disco-bar with pretensions.

Aniki Bóbó, Rua de Fonte Taurina 36. Cool and spacious, sometimes featuring live music – there's a minimum charge. Open till 2am.

Café do Cais, Cais da Ribeira. Currently the trendiest bar in the district, a good blend of modern decor in an old warehouse. Open till 2am.

Está-Se Bem, Rua de Fonte Taurina 70. A nice little *tasca* with a bit of atmosphere as clubbers call in for cheap drinks before moving on.

Taverna Filha Da Mãe Preta, Rua Canestreiros 26. A crusty place where the older locals hang out, with wine straight from the barrel.

Labirintho, Rua Nossa Senhora de Fátima 334. Very pleasant, friendly 1950s-style place, with a shaded back garden and unpretentious gallery space. Occasional live music.

Meia Cave, Praça da Ribeira 6. A prime example of what a bit of prosperity has brought to the area: a smart, well-dressed crowd paying premium prices for drinks served up with loud rock; minimum consumption is 800$00 and prices go up after 2am. Closed Sun & Mon.

Porto Fino, Rua de Fonte Taurina 52. Metallic modernist bar. Its art gallery is open 4–10pm followed by the bar till 2am. Ring the bell for admittance. Closed Sun.

Bar Priordade, Rua da Lada 78. Large but intimate, with chairs outside and generally good music.

Taberna da Ribeira, Praça da Ribeira. In a prime riverside location, this place has outdoor tables, *chouriço assada* (grilled with alcohol at your table) and homemade sangria to wash it down with. Open till 2am.

Ribeira Negra, Rua de Fonte Tavrina 66–68. Proof that Porto has it all: an *upmarket* grunge bar.

Solar do Vinho do Porto, Rua Entre Quintas, Jardim do Palácio de Cristal. Laid-back venue for port-drinking in civilized surroundings; see p.267.

Discos and clubs

Batô, Largo do Castelo 13, Leça da Palmeira. High-camp pirates' galleon interior, just needs Errol Flynn sliding down one of the masts. Trendy clientele, high prices and out of town so you'll have to take a taxi.

Indústria, Avda. do Brasil 853, Centro Comercial da Foz, Foz do Douro. Porto's fashion-conscious at their most vapid but in a great location where the Douro meets the ocean. There is a clutch of other clubs nearby if this doesn't appeal.

K-Max, Rua Ferreira Borges 60. Brand-new club venue with state-of-the-art ambient sound system and lighting. Porto's best DJs and occasional live techno groups, too. Thurs–Sat.

Rocks, 228 Rua Rei Ramiro, Vila Nova de Gaia. Built in old port cellars, this does indeed rock. Fantastic terrace with a view over the Douro, and barbecues in the summer.

Swing, Rua Júlio Dinis. The disco-goers no. 1 choice in the city (Pet Shop Boys, Frankie goes to Hollywood), with a lively clientele bent on enjoying themselves.

Tragaluz, Avda. Menéres 447, Matosinhos. Won't appeal to all but seems proud of its go-go-dancers-on-marble-columns image and comparisons with the *Alcântara* in Lisbon.

Víciado Alcool, Avda. Fontes Pereira de Melo 449. The place for techno, open 11pm–4am. Drinks from 500$00–1200$00.

Via Rápida, Avda. Fontes Pereira de Melo. This is huge but still gets packed; good sounds, always popular and open 10pm–4am.

Listings

Airlines Air France, airport (☎941 33 33); Alitalia, Avda. Boavista 1681-9° (☎600 63 48); British Airways, airport (☎948 63 21); KLM, airport (☎941 07 47); Lufthansa, Avda. Boavista 1681-3° (☎606 70 06); Portugália, airport (☎941 16 63); Sabena, Avda. Boavista 1681-6° (☎600 30 12); Swissair, airport (☎941 38 93); TAP, Praça Mouzinho de Albuquerque 105 (☎600 11 11); TWA, Rua Júlio Dinis 585-7° (☎609 13 35).

Airport information Call ☎948 21 44.

American Express c/o Star Travel, Avda. dos Aliados 202 (☎31 18 20).

Banks and exchange The main branches of the banks are concentrated around Praça da Liberdade (Mon–Fri 8.30am–3pm). When they're closed, Intercontinental (8am–10pm), Rua Ramalho Ortigão 5, next to *Pensão Vera Cruz*, will change money, as will Portocâmbias, Rua Rodrigues Sampaio 193, next to the Câmara Municipal.

Bicycle hire Bicicletas Étiel, Rua Sá da Bandeira 650 (☎200 87 85), operates tours but may have bikes for hire, or try Mad Bike, Rua Anterro de Quental 294 (☎550 57 19).

Books and maps There are English-language bookshops in Rua da Picaria and Rua José Facão. Try also: Livraria Internacional, Rua 31° de Janeiro 43; Livraria Clássica in Clérigos Shopping, next to the tower; or the lovely Livraria Lello & Irmão second-hand shop at Rua dos Carmelitas 144 (see p.264). Maps are available from Porto Editora, Rua da Fábrica.

Boat trips, Short 1hr boat trips along the Douro leave from the Cais da Ribeira (1500$00). Alternatively, on the other side of the river, Via d'Ouro (☎938 88 16) operates a 50min ride (May–Oct daily 10.30am–6.30pm; 1500$00, children under 10 free) which takes you through most of the city, and under four of the bridges; it leaves from the dock next to the Coca-Cola barge. They also run one-day journeys to Peso da Régua and Entre-os-Rios. Longer programmes are offered by Endouro, Rua da Reboleira 49 (☎32 42 36), and Ferreira & Rayford, Rua Sousa Aroso 354, s/n, 4450 Matosinhos (☎938 53 25), whose three luxury boats go up as far as Barca de Alva on the Spanish border.

Buses Porto has many bus companies, most of which operate out of different terminals; check first with the turismo as to the timetable and departure point for your destination. The main companies and their terminals are as follows: Asa Douro, Rua Alexandre Herculano 225; Auto Viação de Espinho, Rua Alexandre Herculano 366; Auto Viação do Minho, Praça D. Filipa de Lencastre 218; Auto Viação do Tâmega, Rua Alexandre Herculano 68; Auto Viação Landim, Rua Gueses de Azevedo 218; Auto Viação Mondinense, Avda. Rodrigues de Freitas 405; Auto Viação Pacense, Praça General Humberto Delgado 329; Caima, Rua Alexandre Herculano 366; EVA, Rua Alexandre Herculano 366; Internorte, Praça da Galiza 96; Joalto, Campo Mártires da Pátria 171; João Ferreira das Neves, Praça D. Filipa de Lencastre 193-195; Linhares, Rua José Falcão 198-204; Marquês, Praça Guilherme Gomes Fernandes 71; Rede Expressos, to the north from Praça D. Filipa de Lencastre, to the south from Rua Alexandre Herculano 366; Renex, Rua das Carmelitas 32; Rodonorte, Central Shopping, Campo 24 de Agosto; Resende, Rua das Carmelitas 183; Santos de Freixo, Central Shopping, Campo 24 de

Agosto; Turilis, Rotunda da Boavista/Rua da Meditação; Valpi, Praça General Humberto Delgado 339.

Car rental Companies include Jumbo Travel, Rua Ceuta 47 (☎38 15 61), and Inter Rent, Rua do Bolhão 182 (☎38 19 64). Most companies maintain offices at the airport, where cars can usually be booked on the spot.

Car repairs Addresses from the Automóvel Clube de Portugal, Rua Gonçalo Cristovão 2 (☎200 92 73), which also operates a breakdown service.

Consulates The Netherlands, Rua Reboleira 7 (☎200 48 67); South Africa, Rua Eugénio de Castro 280 (☎69 89 68); UK, Avda. da Boavista 3072 (☎618 47 89); USA, Rua Júlio Dinis 826-3° (☎630 94).

Hospital Santo António, Rua José de Carvalho (☎200 73 54).

Laundry There's a launderette in Brasília Shopping Centre on Avenida da Boavista.

Left luggage Coin-operated lockers at Estação de São Bento; 400$00 for 48hr.

Markets There's a general daily market in the Mercado Bolhão on Rua Sá da Bandeira, behind the main post office, a must for self-caterers and picnic buyers. On weekdays a fruit and veg market operates along the Cais da Ribeira. Flea markets (best on Saturday mornings) are held along Calçada de Vandoma, below the Sé, and Alameda das Fontaínhas, overlooking the river.

Newspapers English-language papers are available from Tabacaria Senador on Praça da Batalha; the subway kiosk below São Bento station; the kiosk next to *Café A Brasileira*; and Livraria Bertrand in the Centro Comercial de Brasília, Praça Mouzinho de Albuquerque (bus #3 from Praça da Liberdade). Porto's leading paper, the *Jornal de Notícias*, and the local edition of *Público*, are useful sources of information on cinemas, clubs and sports events, etc.

Pharmacies Late-night services are detailed in the *Jornal de Notícias* and *Público*, or call ☎118 for information.

Police ☎200 68 21.

Post office The main post office (daily 8.30am–9pm) is opposite the town hall in Praça General Humberto Delgado (☎208 02 51); *poste restante* mail is held here, and you can also make international phone calls.

Shopping Most shops open Monday to Friday only; those that do open on Saturdays close at lunchtime, except the larger ones which close only on Sundays. However, the Centro Comercial Brasília (at the Praça Mouzinho de Albuquerque end of Avenida Boavista) stays open over the weekend, as does the Shopping Cidade do Porto, near the Brasília, which also has restaurants and cinemas. The pedestrianized streets around Rua de Santa Catarina are where you will find most major international stores as well as the new Via Catarina shopping centre at Rua de Santa Catarina 326, containing the gamut of western brand names from Mothercare to Marks & Spencer. For regional crafts, try O Escano, Rua do Almada 349, Canjirão, Rua Santo Ildefonso 215, or the Centro de Artes Traditionais do Porto, Rua da Reboleria. Late-night shopping and eating options (until 2am) are listed in *Público*.

Sport The city's principal soccer team, F.C. Porto, have in recent years gained the upper hand over Benfica, winning the Portuguese treble – the Tricampeonato – in 1997; they play at the 90,000-capacity Estádio das Antas; take bus #6 or #78 from Praça da Liberdade. If the whole city starts celebrating, you will know the team has just won a major match. First Divison football is on view, too, at Boavista F.C., whose Estádio do Bessa is on Rua Primeiro de Janeiro, while S.C. Salgueiros, who play near Vila Nova de Gaia at the Sport Comércio e Salgueiros, on Rua Álvares Cabral, have also had spells in the top league. Soccer aside, the main swimming pools in Porto are Piscina de Campanhã at Rua Dr. Sousa Avides (☎57 20 41) and Piscina da Constituição at Rua Almirante Leote do Rego (☎59 33 27); each has a gym as well.

Telephones You can make international calls at the post office in Praça General Humberto Delgado and at the Telecom office in Praça da Batalha. There's a further phone office at Praça Liberdade 62. Phonecards are widely available and card-phones can be found on most streets.

Trains See "Arrival and information" for destinations from the various Porto stations. São Bento station information office has timetables for all trains routed from Campanhã; they can tell you the connection you'll need to make from São Bento. If you're leaving Porto on an international connection – Paris especially – in the summer, be sure to reserve a seat several days in advance.

Travel agencies Jumbo Travel, Rua Ceuta 47 (☎38 15 61), is useful for budget/student travel, and Wagon-Lits, Rua Dr. Magalhães Basto 12 (☎31 14 78), is good for long-distance train and bus tickets.

Around Porto: the coast

The coastline immediately **south of Porto** is one of the worst polluted in Europe, with industrial effluent and inadequate sewage facilities constituting a major health hazard. In recent years, there have been several outbreaks of hepatitis in Porto and Vila Nova de Gaia linked with bathing in these waters, and it is currently not safe to swim until you reach Espinho or, better still, Esmoriz, Cortegaça or Furadouro, though Esmoriz has recently had its EU blue flag removed. The coast **to the north** is little better and you should certainly not swim off Matosinhos; indeed, all the Porto beaches from Pastoras to Castelo do Queijo are officially out of bounds to bathers. However, press on a few kilometres further north from Cabo do Mundo to **Vila do Conde** or **Póvoa de Varzim** and you may be tempted to stay; indeed, in summer, you might prefer to visit Porto while based at one of these resorts.

South of Porto

Access to Espinho, Esmoriz and Cortegaça from Porto is either by **train** (hourly from São Bento) or **bus** (Auto Viação do Espinho departing from Rua Alexandre Herculano 366). En route it's well worth stopping at the small settlement of **MIRAMAR**, 10km south of Porto, to see the Capela do Senhor da Pedra, a seventeenth-century chapel bizarrely situated on a rocky, wave-beaten headland jutting out from the beach.

Espinho

ESPINHO, 18km south of Porto, is a major resort – though not a very attractive one. Windswept and overcrowded, it has a feeling of a suburb rather than a town, with a casino, golf course, a few high-rise hotels (more are on the way), hordes of tourist shops, a dull grid of numbered streets and a railway line right through the centre. You'll find the **turismo** at Rua 6, no. 709 (June–Sept Mon–Fri 9am–9pm, Sat & Sun 10am–noon & 3–6pm; Oct–May Mon–Fri 9.30am–12.30pm & 2–5.30pm, Sat 9.30am–noon; ☎02/72 09 11). **Surfing** is possible here – get advice from the surf shop in the Centro Comercial California. **Swimmers** might want to use the pool at the northern end of the esplanade; the Ministry of Health has blacklisted the Silvade beach to the south of town, although it is hoped that the series of breakwaters currently under construction will alleviate the pollution.

    Staying overnight can be expensive since the few remaining old buildings on the seafront, some of which were *pensões*, are being bulldozed to make way for apartments. The cheapest hotel is the *Hotel Mar Azul*, Avda. 8, no. 676 (☎02/72 08 24; ④), with comfortable rooms and reasonable facilities. Under the same management is the older *Residencial Espinho*, Rua 19, no. 326 (☎02/731 26 36; ④), which has a similar range of rooms but at slightly higher prices. More interesting is the nineteenth-century *Vila Maria*, Rua 62, no. 667 (☎02/72 03 53; ④), set in its own grounds. The plushest option is the five-star *Hotel Solverde*, at the northern end of town (☎02/731 31 62, fax 731 32 00; ⑥), which has its own pool and health club. There's a **campsite**, *Lugar dos Mochos* (☎02/72 37 18), inland, on the northern edge of town, not far from the *Vila Maria*.

You'll have no problem finding somewhere to **eat**, the most famous place being *Casa Marreta* on the esplanade at Rua 2, nos. 1355–61, which serves excellent fish and seafood dishes. The *Casa do Pescador* in the fisherman's quarter at the southern end of town, just beyond Rua 2, is more basic but does superlative seafood. There's surprisingly little to do in terms of **nightlife**. Espinho doesn't have any discos, though in summer you'll find a number of shoreline bars trying their best to fill the gap.

Esmoriz and Cortegaça

The beaches at **ESMORIZ** (6km south of Espinho) and **CORTEGAÇA** (a further 2km south) offer a restful contrast to Espinho, primarily because the road and railway start to move inland as they head further south. This leaves you a walk of a couple of kilometres or so to reach either beach, both of which are backed by sand dunes and groves of pine and eucalyptus; both also have all-year **campsites** – *Esmoriz* (☎056/75 27 09, fax 056/75 37 17) and *Cortegaça* (☎056/75 21 99, fax 056/75 51 77). Just to the north of Praia de Esmoriz there's a small lagoon – one of the reasons that the road and railway were forced inland in the first place – and here you can expect to see waders, ducks and, depending on the season, pigeons and doves. From both Esmoriz and Cortegaça, frequent trains continue south to Aveiro (see p.212).

North of Porto

The stretch of coast around the mouth of the Douro is severely polluted, and you need to head beyond Cabo do Mundo to **VILA CHÃ**, 18km north of Porto, for a dip in the ocean. Despite encroaching development, this retains a fishing village identity, and has a fine sandy beach with pools at low tide. There's a **campsite** at Praia de Vila Chã (☎02/927 21 63 or 928 31 63), 3km west of the station and well signposted from the main N13 road. Trains run hourly from Porto's Estação da Trindade, and buses from Praça Filipa de Lencastre, to Vila Chã, before moving on to the larger resorts of Vila do Conde and Póvoa de Varzim.

Vila do Conde

VILA DO CONDE, 27km north of Porto, has become quite a significant resort over the last few years, but it has lost refreshingly little of its character in the process. This is partly because the beaches (and all their attendant development) are a couple of kilometres south of town. Here, long stretches of fine sand, with drinks, kiosks and restaurants to hand, have been steadily developed right up the coast to Póvoa do Varzim. **Guia** and **Cadeira** are the nearest beaches – both a fifteen-minute walk from the centre – with calm waters and a stumpy fortification between the two.

The old part of Vila do Conde itself manages to remain an active fishing port with a bustling Friday **market** and an atmospheric medieval quarter, which juts towards the sea beside the Rio Ave. Dominating the quarter is the white dome of the Capela do Socorro, built in 1603 and renovated in 1989 after a long period of decay. Inside, the azulejos depicting the Adoration of the Magi are notable for the presence of Moorish figures – testament to the fact that here, as well as elsewhere on the Portuguese coast, the Moors chose to stay and convert during the Inquisition. The narrow streets are at their best on saints' days, when the little street corner votive chapels are illuminated by worshippers. On June 23, the whole town descends to the beach to celebrate the night of São João.

Overlooking everything, on a rise behind, is the enormous bulk of the **Convento de Santa Clara** (daily 9am–noon & 2–5.30pm), now a reformatory for boys but still open for visits: just knock on the door. One of the inmates will be designated to show you around its early Gothic church, which contains fine relief carvings, especially on the tombs of the founders. There's an elegant cloister, too, with a fountain fed by the long aqueduct – now partly ruined – which stretches from here into the hills. Below, back in the centre of town, the sixteenth-century **Igreja Matriz** is a beauty, with a soaring, airy interior and – thanks to the Basque workmen who helped with its construction – an unusual but very effective mix of Spanish and Portuguese styles. Like the Capela do Socorro, the church sports a distinctly Moorish dome.

Vila do Conde is also known for its lace – you can visit the **lace-making school and museum** (Tues–Fri 10am–noon & 2–7pm, Sat & Sun 3–6pm; free) at Rua de São Bento 70 and there is work for sale in the turismo at Rua 5 de Outubro. If you're especially interested in Portugal's regional crafts, there's a bonus in the town's annual **Feira Nacional de Artesanato** (crafts fair), held in the last week of July and the first week of August. Vila do Conde also boasts the **Museu Vivo da Comutação Manual** (Telephone Exchange Museum; Tues & Thurs 10am–noon & 2–4pm; free), on Rua Alberto Moreira Soutelo, which claims unsurprisingly to be the only one of its kind in Europe. The **Casa de José Régio**, at Avda. José Régio 132 (Tues–Sat 10am–12.30pm & 2–6pm, Sun 2.30–6pm), is also worth a visit, displaying popular art collected by this famous writer. Another gallery, the **Auditório**, shows temporary exhibitions of photography, local arts and crafts. It's housed in the renovated eighteenth-century Casa dos Vasconcelos on Praça da República (Tues–Fri 3–11pm, Sat & Sun 3pm–midnight) and has a pleasant bar further to recommend it.

PRACTICALITIES

Buses from Porto arrive (and leave from) opposite the smaller turismo (summer Mon–Sat 10am–7pm, Sun 10am–1pm & 3–7pm; winter Mon–Fri 9am–12.30pm & 2–5.30pm, Sat 1.30–5pm, Sun 10am–noon & 1.30–5pm; ☎052/64 27 00) in Rua 5 de Outubro up to six times daily. The **train station** is a five-minute walk from the centre; from the station, follow the river down, past the convent, to the bridge. Just up from the bridge, on the left, is the **main turismo**, an ivy-clad house at Rua 25 de Abril 103 (summer Mon–Fri 9am–noon & 2–5.30pm, Sat & Sun 2–5.30pm; winter Mon–Fri 9am–12.30pm & 2–5.30pm, Sat 1.30–5pm, Sun 10am–noon & 1.30–5pm; ☎052/64 27 00).

Both turismos have a list of private **rooms**, which is likely to be all you'll find in the summer and you're advised to book ahead for any of the following options. On a strictly limited budget, try *Le Villageois*, Praça da República 94 (☎052/63 11 19; ②), with clean, well-furnished rooms, or failing that, the *Residencial Manco D'Areia*, Praça da República (☎ & fax 052/63 17 48; ②) – marked simply "Hospedes" – a rundown place with a mixed bag of rooms, most lacking private bathrooms. Mid-range options include: *Pensão Princesa do Ave*, Rua Dr. António José Sousa Pereira 261 (☎052/64 20 65, fax 63 29 72; ④), a decent, modern place some way from the centre but near the beaches, and with satellite TV in every room; and *Pensão Patarata*, overlooking the waterfront at Cais das Lavandeiras 18 (☎052/63 18 94; ④), with big, pleasant rooms and a reasonable café and restaurant underneath. The nicest hotel in town is the four-star *Estalagem do Brasão*, Avda. Dr. João Canavarro (☎052/64 20 16, fax 64 20 28; ⑤), a seventeenth-century town house with *pousada*-quality furnishings and good breakfasts included. An excellent modern option is the *Motel Sopete Sant'ana* (☎052/64 17 17, fax 64 26 93; ⑤), on the south side of the river by the bridge – its rooms all have en-suite bathrooms and river-view balconies. The nearest **campsite** (☎052/63 32 25) is 3km south of town, near the beach at Árvore.

Of the **restaurants**, the most established is the one at *Le Villageois* (closed Mon), a pretty place serving huge portions and with a few tables outside. Expensive but recommended is *Restaurante São Roque* in Rua do Lidador (closed Mon); more reasonable is the *Restaurante Rendilheira* at no. 48, whose regional specialities are served up within an odd modern-art decor. Also good, with a value-for-money *prato do dia* (1200$00), is *Restaurante Ramon* (closed Tues), near the turismo in Rua 5 de Outubro. The café at Rua de Santo Amaro 6, three doors down from the Casa de José Régio, used to be Régio's (and other artistic dissidents') favourite haunt and is still a good place for food at reasonable prices. There's not much **nightlife** to speak of but live music (anything from grunge to salsa) can be found at *Azenha D. Zameiro Bar* (Thurs–Sat), a three-kilometre taxi ride out of town at Ponte d'Ave, Vilarinho.

Póvoa do Varzim

PÓVOA DO VARZIM is about 4km to the north of Vila do Conde (regular buses) but the two couldn't be more different. Although Póvoa, too, retains a small harbour, along with the ruins of an eighteenth-century fortress, it is very much an out-and-out resort. A casino and a line of concrete hotels open onto the eight-kilometre-long beach, which is crowded throughout the year with Portuguese holidaymakers.

That said, the local council seems well aware of Póvoa's shortcomings and has embarked on a series of projects to prettify the town, such as the state-of-the-art fountains in the Largo do Passeio near the *Grande Hotel*, which "dance" to music during the summer. In any case, the crowds here help to create a lively, enjoyable seaside feel, restaurants are plentiful and excellent value and there usually seems to be enough accommodation to go round. If you feel the need for culture, check out the **Museu Municipal de Etnografia e Historia**, on Rua Visconde de Azevedo (Tues–Sun 10am–12.30pm & 2.30–6pm; 200$00), which displays local archeological finds as well as an exhaustive collection of anything and everything connected to local seafaring through the ages.

There's an international classical music festival in July and a series of **festivals** throughout the summer, the best of which is on August 15 when local fishermen carry life-sized images of Our Lady of Assumption to the quayside to bless those who have perished at sea; the whole event is accompanied by fireworks let off by fishing boats. A similar event occurs at the end of September for Our Lady of Sorrows.

PRACTICALITIES

The helpful **turismo**, at Avda. Mouzinho de Albuquerque 166 (daily: June to mid-Sept 9am–9pm; mid-Sept to May 9am–1pm & 2–7pm; ☎052/61 46 09), has lists of rooms and a leaflet detailing bus and train timetables. **Buses** operate from the central Praça do Almada; the **train station** is a few minutes' walk from here, along Rua Almirante Reis. To reach the beach from the train station (10min), turn right and, on reaching Praça do Almada, turn left and walk straight ahead. You can **rent cars** from Rentaconde on Praça do Almada (☎052/62 28 50) and **bikes** from *Diana Bar* on Avenida dos Banhos.

There are plenty of smart hotels around, while cheaper **pensões** are to be found mostly along Rua Paulo Barreto, which is the main Porto road and runs from Praça do Almada to Praça Marquês de Pombal, next to the market. The best inexpensive option is *Hospedaria Jantarada*, Rua Paulo Barreto 8 (☎052/62 27 89; ③), clean, friendly and above a popular restaurant. *Residencial Gett* (☎052/68 32 06, fax 61 72 95; ④), opposite the turismo on Avda. Mouzinho de Albuquerque, is a pleasant, modern place, with friendly and efficient staff and satellite TV in all rooms, while *Pensão Avô Velino*, Avda. Vasco da Gama (☎052/68 16 28; ④), is a bit out of the way, on the Viana road, but otherwise a good choice. If you can afford it, go for *Hotel Luso-Brasileiro*, Rua dos Cafés 16 (☎052/61 51 61, fax 62 47 13; ⑤), 100m from the beach, or the *Grande Hotel* (☎052/61 54 64, fax 60 74 44; ⑤), the oldest hotel in town housed in the 1930s' powder-pink building next to the casino on Largo do Passeio Alegre.

There is no shortage of **restaurants**, ranging from Chinese to seafood or pizzas – try any along the seafront. Alternatively you can sample the snacks and atmosphere at the *Adega Firmino* on Rua Caetano de Oliveira, two streets closer to the beach from the turismo, which is popular with the locals; the *Restaurante Costa* next door (closed Mon) is less characterful, but serves good food. The liveliest **bars** are *Sector 7* on Esplanade Camalhide, *IT Bar* on Avenida dos Bachos and *Enseada Bar* on Passeio Alegre, in front of the *Grande Hotel*. The best **disco** is at *Hotel Ver a Mar*, 2km north on the seafront, which hots up on Fridays and Saturdays, in particular. No surprises at the **Casino da Póvoa** situated at the southern end of the esplanade – it's the usual concoction of tacky cabaret shows and games (minimum bet 200$00), but for many it remains the main reason to visit the town.

Around Póvoa de Varzim

There are four reasonably accessible sites located in or near villages close to Póvoa, and which, given a spare day and rented bikes, or a car, would make a rewarding circuit. **LAÚNDOS**, 7km to the northeast, is notable for the windmills which stand on São Felix hill. Further on is **RATES** boasting a splendid eleventh-century Romanesque church built in granite by the Benedictines for Henry, Count of Burgundy. The three naves are timber-roofed, while inside, a series of fine pillars with carved capitals are lit by a colourful rose window. **RIO MAU**, 8km east of Póvoa, is the site of a smaller, but even better decorated, Romanesque church, also granite, completed in 1151. The carvings on the capitals are reminiscent of those in Braga cathedral and, in this case, are thought to illustrate the Song of Roland.

The oldest of the settlements on this circuit is **TERROSO**, just 5km northeast of Póvoa de Varzim. A *citânia* similar to the better-known ones at Sanfins (p.283) and Briteiros (p.310) was excavated at the beginning of this century and the double ring of ramparts can still be traced. The spring here once fed the eighteenth-century aqueduct which carried water over 999 arches to the Convento de Santa Clara in Vila do Conde (see p.279).

Santo Tirso and around

Travelling **northeast** by road or rail from Porto towards the southern Minho towns of Guimarães and Braga, you pass through attractive, rolling countryside: a mix of market gardening in the valleys, vines on the gentle slopes, and wooded hill tops. Santo Tirso is the minor capital of this area, a riverside town which serves as a base for visiting the Romanesque church at nearby Roriz and the *citânia* of Sanfins de Ferreira.

Santo Tirso

Just under 30km northeast of Porto, **SANTO TIRSO** lies on the steep southern bank of the River Ave, which flows west to meet the sea at Vila do Conde. At the foot of the slope, by the bridge linking the town to its train station, is the former Benedictine monastery and church of São Bento, which now houses an agricultural college and a small **municipal museum** (Mon–Fri 9am–12.30pm & 2–6pm, Sat 9am–12.30pm). This is less than gripping, fielding the usual motley collection of local archeological finds, but take the opportunity to visit the church, whose cloister features a fine double row of galleries dating from the fourteenth century. On the plateau cresting the slope is the town hall, a charmless, concrete block; the **turismo** (Mon–Fri 9am–12.30pm & 2–5.30pm; ☎052/520 64) occupies an annexe.

Santo Tirso is served by Linhares **buses** from Póvoa, and Mondinense & Landim buses from Porto; both drop you at the station on Rua Infante Dom Henrique. **Trains** (hourly, from Porto's Trindade station) stop on the other side of town, across the river. The train route continues from Santo Tirso to Guimarães. You're unlikely to need to stay – **accommodation**, in any case, is limited and expensive – but if you do, try the homely *Pensão Caroço* at Largo Coronel Batista Coelho 48 (☎052/85 28 23; ③), or the more expensive *Pensão Carvalhais* in the ugly modern block at the top of town on Praça Rodrigues Ferreira (☎052/85 79 10, fax 85 75 81; ⑤).

Roriz

RORIZ, 10km east of Santo Tirso, is much prettier, but ill served by public transport. Any bus on the Santo Tirso–Guimarães route can set you down just after Rebordões, leaving a four-kilometre walk to the church of São Pedro, at the top of the village.

The village itself is a mixture of old, rough granite cottages, whitewashed houses and several fairly kitsch creations built by returned emigrants – one is straight out of Disneyland, a Seven Dwarfs' cottage with brown concrete thatch. The date of the elegant Romanesque **Igreja de São Pedro** is disputed, but it's said to stand on the foundations of a Roman temple, later destroyed by the Moors. It was originally the church of the Benedictine monastery that once stood alongside, of which only one building still stands – and that's in private hands. The fine west door is embellished with an early Gothic rose window, adjacent to the solitary bell tower.

The Citânia de Sanfins de Ferreira

Another 4km beyond the Igreja de of São Pedro, along a track through shady woods and up a gentle slope, is the **Citânia de Sanfins de Ferreira**. Here, on the crest of a hill, you can still trace the outer ramparts and the foundations of circular huts dating from the second century BC, though other than those there's little to see. However, it's a splendidly atmospheric place – the skyline to the south appears infinite and, at the height of summer, the only sound is that of the broom pods popping.

Porto to Penafiel

One of the surviving northern inland train routes – the **Douro railway line** (Linha do Douro) – heads east, out of Porto, although for the initial 40km it runs alongside the Rio Sousa and not the Rio Douro. If you're on one of the slow trains, it will stop at Cête, a dozen stations out of Porto and just a kilometre or so away from the village of **PAÇO DE SOUSA,** which can also be reached by bus from Penafiel (Mon–Fri 6 daily, Sat 2 daily). This was the former headquarters of the Benedictines in Portugal and, set beside the Rio Sousa, is a popular picnic spot for Porto locals.

The principal sight, inevitably, is the old **abbey church**, a dank and dark medieval building in the process of restoration. In one corner is the **tomb of Egas Moniz**, tutor and adviser to the first king of Portugal, Afonso Henriques, and a great figure of loyalty in Portuguese histories. In 1127, shortly after Afonso Henriques had broken away from his grandfather, the king of León, Egas was sent to negotiate a settlement, thus enabling Afonso to concentrate his efforts on the Moors in the south. Within three years, the king of León considered the treaty to be broken on the Portuguese side and threatened all-out war. Egas made his way to León, presented himself and his family, and, as can be seen on the panels around the tomb, offered to receive the punishment due to his master. Mercy was granted and the king sent the loyal minister home unscathed.

There are a couple of **cafés** in the village and an excellent old-fashioned *adega*, *O Moleira*, which serves wine straight from the barrel. You'll find plenty of possible **camping** spots but should you prefer a bed, it's not much further down the line to Penafiel.

Penafiel and around

At Penafiel, 35km from Porto, you enter *vinho verde* country. The wine's origins lie with the Benedictine monks, who were famed in this region for their laborious terracing of the valley slopes. A further legacy of the Benedictine presence is a dozen of the finest **Romanesque churches** in the country, each gorgeously sited in hamlets hidden away in folds of the countryside. South of Penafiel, the Barragem de Torrão offers excellent swimming opportunities, or there's the more relaxing option of a river trip from Torrão itself.

Penafiel

Despite the motorway in the Sousa valley to the west, **PENAFIEL** itself is still split by main-road traffic, and getting to it involves a connecting bus (Mon–Fri only) from the train station, which is 3km down the hill; there are also regular buses from Porto, which stop by the kiosk outside Penafiel's turismo and further along by the Igreja Matriz. The town itself is a pretty place with a laid-back atmosphere and a fabulous local **wine**. You'll find it everywhere in bottles but to get it straight from the *cuba* (barrel) you'll either have to go to the *adega* facing the train station or to the charming Quinta da Aveleda (Mon–Fri 9.15–11.30am & 1–4.30pm; 400$00), where the stuff is made. To get there go 2km down the Porto road, cross the motorway and turn right at the sign – it's 1km further on from this point. Their guided tours include wine and cheese tasting, and the gardens are delightful.

PRACTICALITIES
Accommodation is limited to the good-value *pensão*, the *Casa João da Lixa* (☎055/231 58; ②) in Largo do Padre Américo; *O Cedro*, Rua do Cedro (☎055/235 51; ③); and the *Pena Hotel* (☎055/71 14 20, fax 71 14 25; ④) on Parque do Sameiro, opposite the modern Santuário de Nossa Senhora da Piedade. If you are interested in exploring the area's churches, call in at the **turismo** at Avda. Sacadura Cabral 90 (Mon–Fri 9am–12.30pm & 2–5.30pm; ☎055/71 25 61), and ask them to mark the locations on a map. Beneath it, there's a fine covered **market**. Just downhill from here, at Rua Engenheiro Matos 67, *Restaurante Relógio do Sol* serves good **food** (for around 1500$00 a head) and has a fine view over the Sousa valley. *O Cedro*'s *churrascaria* is a lively place to eat. The most popular **bar** is the *Momentos Bar* at Rua Zeferino de Oliveira 29.

For **onward transport** VALPI runs buses to Amarante and Porto from its garage near the Igreja da Misericórdia; Santos, for services to Boelhe and Termas de São Vicente, has an office at Avda. Egas Moniz 69–71; and Asa Douro at no. 125 operates services to Torrão and Paço de Sousa.

South of Penafiel
Most of the local **churches** are hard to reach without your own transport. The most accessible by bus (Mon–Fri 8 daily, Sat 4 daily, Sun 1 daily) from Penafiel is at **BOELHE**, some 10km southeast along the N312 minor road to Entre-os-Rios. This is reputedly the smallest Romanesque church in the country: a simple building, without much architectural detail, which gains its power from a stunning position on the brow of a hill overlooking the Tâmega valley. If it's closed, ask for the key at the nearest house. Note that the last bus back to Penafiel leaves Boelhe at 2.20pm. With your own transport, a few other diversions to Romanesque churches in the region become possible. At **ABRAGÃO**, 10km southeast along the N320 from Penafiel, all that survives of the Igreja de São Pedro is the vaulted chapel and transept arch with its rose window, while the Igreja de São Salvador or Cabeça Santa (Holy Head) at **GANDRA**, east off the N106 midway between Penafiel and Torrão, gets its name from the holy skull that used to be kept there.

A trip easily made by bus from Penafiel is to the tiny spa town of **TERMAS DE SÃO VICENTE** further along the N312 from Boelhe, where it meets the main N106. En route you'll pass the **Barragem de Torrão** and its reservoir (see below). The turn-of-the-century spa has all the usual treatments but hours vary so check with the turismo in Penafiel before setting out. The last bus back leaves at 5.25pm or you can stay overnight in one of the good self-contained rooms at the *Pensão Regional* (☎055/623 11; ②).

Five kilometres from here, south along the N106, Entre-os-Rios faces **TORRÃO** across the confluence of the Douro and Tâmega. Buses regularly make the journey from Penafiel to Torrão (Mon–Fri 7 daily) and the last one back leaves at 6pm. A good way to see some of the area is to take a **river trip** from Torrão, (daily at 4pm & 5pm; 1hr; 1500$00), operated by the Quinta dos Agros:

cross back over the bridge towards Entre-os-Rios, bear right and then turn right at the war monument – it's at the bottom of the road. Should you want to stay overnight, the best choice is the *Casa Defronte*, a beautiful ANTER town house on the N108 in Entre-os-Rios (☎055/634 84; ④), offering simple but comfortable stone-walled rooms and an ideal base from which to explore the area on foot.

The Tâmega: Amarante and beyond

At **LIVRAÇÃO**, about an hour east from Porto, the Tâmega train line cuts off for Amarante (see below), hugging the ravine of the **Rio Tâmega**, a tributary of the Douro. There is scarcely more than the station at Livração, so if you're intending to change trains, keep your eyes open. The Tâmega line trains terminate at Amarante, from where four buses daily run up into the Serra do Marão – following the course of the Rio Tâmega – to **Celorico de Basto** and on to the next crossroads at Fermil, where a local bus picks up passengers for **Mondim de Basto**. To explore the valley, the best idea is to take a bus to Celorico and walk, following the increasingly overgrown tracks, to Mondim: a pleasant two-hour hike, through woods and over viaducts.

If your time is limited, the half-hour trip from Livração to Amarante is worthwhile in itself. From the start it's an impressive, scenic ride, with pine woods and vines clinging to incredible slopes, and goats scrambling across the steep terrace walls to nibble at haystacks constructed to hang from the branches of trees, although the new motorway running alongside part of the rail line has spoilt it somewhat.

Amarante

AMARANTE is set immaculately along the Tâmega River, the wooden balconies of its old houses leaning over the water. It's a fine place to stop, with any number of bars and cafés along the riverside, mostly on the opposite side from the station. Sadly, the polluted river beaches can no longer be recommended for swimming – though in summer you'll see some brave souls risking it – but *guigas* (pedal boats) or rowing boats can be hired for an hour or two's dawdling and there's a Parque Aquático on the south bank with enough slides and water chutes to keep kids and adults happy for a while.

The church, and former monastery, of **São Gonçalo**, beside the very elegant town bridge, is Amarante's most prominent monument. It forms the heart of an ancient fertility cult – probably with pagan origins – which still persists here at the grand Festa de São Gonçalo, celebrated on the first weekend in June. At this time, traditionally, the local unmarried youth exchange phallic cakes as tokens of their love. In the church, the saint's tomb is said to guarantee a quick marriage to anyone who touches it – his face, hands and feet have been almost worn away by hopeful suitors. Another chapel, devoted to Gonçalo's healing miracles, is offered wax models of every conceivable part of the body along with entire artificial limbs and bottles full of gallstones, although the offerings are removed at the end of each day.

Around the side of the church, in the cloister of the former monastery, is the **Museu Municipal Amadeo de Souza Cardoso** (Tues–Sun 10am–noon & 2–5pm; 200$00). This is a surprising exhibition to find out in the sticks – domi-

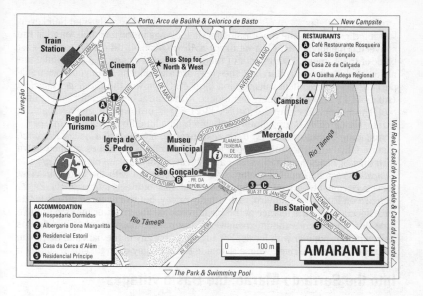

nated by the Cubist works of local boy Amadeo de Souza Cardoso (1887–1918), one of the few Portuguese painters of this century to achieve international renown. Work by modern painters is displayed in the museum's mini-gallery.

If possible, time your visit to coincide with the **Romario de São Gonçalo**, which takes place on the first weekend of June, with a large Sunday procession being the highlight of the festivities. There's also a year-round Wednesday and Saturday morning **market**, held beside the river.

Practicalities

The **train station** is ten minutes' walk northwest of the centre, while **buses** pull up a little closer in, on the other side of the river. When leaving Amarante for the north and west you may find it easier to catch the bus from the stop on Avenida 1º de Maio (see map above) in the north of the town. For information, and help with accommodation during summer when rooms can be hard to come by, head for the **turismo** (summer daily 9am–7pm; winter Mon–Sat 9.30am–12.30pm & 2–5pm, Sun 10am–12.30pm & 2–5pm; ☎055/43 22 59), housed in the Câmara Municipal, next to the art museum. There's also a **regional turismo** at Rua Cândido dos Reis 249 (Mon–Sat: summer 9.30am–noon & 2.30–6pm; winter 9am–noon & 2–5pm; ☎055/43 29 80). Both have details of local Solares de Portugal properties.

First choice for budget **accommodation** in town is the friendly *Residencial Estoril*, Rua 31º de Janeiro 49 (☎055/43 12 91, fax 43 18 92; ③), whose back rooms have superb views of the river. Even cheaper options are the *Residencial Príncipe*, Largo Conselheiro António Cândido dos Reis 53 (☎055/43 29 56; ②), near the bus station – the front rooms here have balconies – and the *Hospedaria Dormidas*, at Rua Cândido dos Reis 288 (☎055/24 33 27; ①) with a range of basic rooms. With more money to spend, the *Albergaria Dona Margaritta*, Rua Cândido dos Reis 53

(☎055/43 21 10, fax 43 79 77; ④), is a comfortable and pleasantly sited hotel over-looking the river but the most atmospheric lodgings in town can be found at the converted manor house, *Casa de Cerca d'Além* (☎055/43 14 49; ⑤), on the east bank of the Tâmega, 200m north of the modern road bridge. It's beautifully fur-nished with antique furniture and the views are magnificent. With your own trans-port there's an excellent-value option 9km east of town, the *Casal de Aboadela* (☎055/44 11 41; ④), a homely farmhouse with central heating and real log fires too. The municipal **campsite** (☎055/43 21 33) is in town, on the riverbank at *Quinta da Cerca de Baixo*; another is being built a little further upstream.

Amarante is quite well served for **restaurants**: try *A Quelha Adega Regional*, Rua de Olivença, where the proprietor serves well-spiced dishes washed down with jugs of heavy local red wine – a meat-eater's dream; the pleasant *Café São Gonçalo*, Praça da República, alongside the church and with the bridge in view, serves reasonably priced evening food and has outdoor tables; *Casa Zé da Calçada* on Rua 31º de Janeiro, is decidedly pricey, but worth every *escudo* for its local specialities – the terrace at the back overlooks the river; or for something a little different, there's the inexpensive *Restaurante Rosqueira,* Rua Cândido dos Reis, which is popular with locals. For **nightlife**, try any of the bars and discos on the south side of the river, whose riverside terraces stay open till late in summer.

Into the Serra do Marão: the Basto villages

Beyond Amarante you really feel the climb into the **Serra do Marão** on the approach to the towns of Celorico and Mondim de Basto, both set astride the Tâmega. To the north – and technically in the Minho region – is the larger, provin-cial town of Cabeceiras de Basto, which provides a useful transport link to Braga and then the Peneda-Gerês national park (see Chapter Six). Together, these three towns and their districts form the **Terras de Basto**, a region of fertile country-side that produces a strong *vinho verde*. The name ("basto" meant "I claim") comes from a group of Celtic statues, symbols of power, which have been found in several local spots.

Celorico to Mondim de Basto

Thirty kilometres northeast of Amarante, **CELORICO DE BASTO** is proud of its neatly laid out lawns and formal flower beds. It has a single **pensão** – the *Progresso* – in Praça Albino Alves Perreira (☎055/32 11 70; ②), and there's an excellent restaurant 1km north of town, the *Quinta do Forno*, set in an old farm-house and specializing in homebred *vitela* (veal). For a brief foray into the woods, there is a labyrinth of paths, heading off from behind the village church, while in the distance lies the prospect of Monte Farinha, the highest peak in the region (see p.289). The mountain is more easily approached from Mondim de Basto, which is accessible from Celorico on frequent Mondinense buses (the station is 200m north of *Pensão Progresso*).

On the main road, halfway between Celorico and Mondim, lies the small, pleasant village of **Fermil**. Buses pass through three to four times daily on their way between Cabeceiras and Amarante. The main attraction in the village is a wonderful Solares de Portugal property, *Casa do Barão de Fermil* (☎055/36 12 11; ⑤), a slightly decay-ing mansion with its own swimming pool and elderly, English-speaking owners.

There's little enough to **MONDIM DE BASTO**, 9km along the main road northeast of Celorico, whose old town has been swamped by modern sprawl, though the views are majestic and there's good river swimming in the Rio Cabril. You might consider making the town a base for exploring the Parque Natural de Alvão (see p.366); there's an information point (☎055/38 12 09) on the Celorico road by the "D" primary school. The **turismo** (summer daily 9am–9pm; winter Mon–Fri 9.30am–12.30pm & 2–5.30pm; ☎055/38 14 79) on Praça 9 de Abril can give details of local Solares de Portugal (and similar organizations') properties. Other **places to stay** include two modern, good-value options: the *Residencial Arcadia*, Avda. Dr. Augusto de Brito (☎055/38 14 10; ③), which can be a touch noisy given that it's above a café and games arcade, and the very friendly *Residencial Carvalho*, by the petrol station on the same road (☎055/38 10 57; ③), whose spotless, self-contained rooms come equipped with TV and minibar. There's also an excellent **campsite** (☎055/38 16 50; closed mid-Dec to mid-Jan) – about 1km from the centre along the EN304 Vila Real road by the Rio Cabril. For **meals**, try the *Churrasqueira Chasselik* on Avenida da Igreja.

Mondim's bus station is by the Mercado Municipal and there are regular **bus connections** to Vila Real (a spectacular ride, skirting the Parque Natural de Alvão; no service on Sun), Guimarães, Coimbra and Lisbon. Alternatively, you could catch a bus to Fermil, and then on to the lively provincial town of Cabeceiras de Basto (see below), from where there are regular buses to Braga.

Monte Farinha and the Cabril Valley

Monte Farinha is surprisingly easy to climb – less than three hours' easy walking – and, if the times coincide, you can get a head start by taking the bus to the foot of the ascent, three-and-a-half kilometres from Mondim. Walking, follow the N312 Cerva road east out of Mondim, then take a path up to the right shortly after Pedra Vedra. Once on the mountain, follow the road which zigzags to the summit. An alternative (but more tiring) route is to take the mountain track towards Carazêdo, turning left after 2km onto the path for Pegodinhas. At the hamlet of Campos, a further 2km on, turn left again and continue north to Pegodinhas, after which you've a good ninety-minute hike up steep terrain to join the zigzags to the top. The panoramic views well repay your efforts, and at the top is the attractive parish church of **Nossa Senhora da Graça**, centre of a major *festa* on the first Sunday in September. This church miraculously survived undamaged when a recent forest fire burned around it for three days, destroying all the trees on the mountain.

Another good hike from Mondim is into the **Cabril valley**. Only about twenty minutes beyond the village campsite, the Cabril – more a stream than a river – is crossed by a Roman bridge; impressive in itself and set near a little waterfall, where there's a good swimming hole. From here, follow the stream upstream to a working watermill or take the stone track (about 200m upriver) along what must have been a Roman road. Follow this, cross a road, and you're at the start of a maze of small paths cutting between the fields and vineyards of the Cabril valley, and leading higher into the slopes.

Cabeceiras de Basto

CABECEIRAS DE BASTO is the most interesting Basto village, at the heart of the Terras de Basto, and proudly displays the finest of the *basto* figures – which has sported a French head since a prank during the Napoleonic Wars – in the gardens across from the bus station. The main local monument is the Baroque **Mosteiro de Refojos** (daily 8am–7pm) – one of the few religious institutions not to have succumbed to the temptation to bludgeon faith into the populace through a quartet of loudspeakers. Ask for the key at the **turismo** next door (daily 9am–12.30pm & 2–6pm; ☎053/66 22 19) and you can visit the treasury (a collection of statues and religious garments) as well as gain access to the clock tower, from which you can view the church's highlight – the *zimbório* (dome). From here, too, you can look down over the peeling houses of the region's old landowners, reminders of the glory and elitism of Portugal's Age of Absolutism; they were hard hit by the Revolution and its aftermath. Another area of town to explore is beyond a patch of ground set aside for the Monday **feira** – a left turn after the school takes you into the Campo do Guinchoso, where there's a *pastelaria* and **swimming** in the river – past the new housing development, signposted *Praia da Ranha*.

There is reasonable **accommodation** to be had at the modern *Residencial-Restaurante A Cafrial* on Avda. General Humberto Delgado (☎053/66 26 90; ④), and at the *Residencial-Restaurante São Miguel*, at Campo do Seco (☎053/66 28 10; ②), further out in the modern quarter of the town, near the post office. A short way up the road, at the back of the Refojos monastery, the *Restaurante Cozinha Real de Basto* serves very good **meals**.

Buses connect Cabeceiras with Celorico and Mondim de Basto, Póvoa de Lanhoso in central Minho, Braga and Porto (Mon–Sat only). Change in Arco de Baúlhe for Chaves.

Along the Douro: to Peso da Régua and on to the Spanish border

Leaving Porto **by road** and heading for Peso da Régua and port wine country, there are two possibilities: either take the motorway eastwards, leaving it at Penafiel or Amarante, or – with more time – follow the N108 southeast. This road hugs the north bank of the Douro River until Entre-os-Rios (where the Tâmega meets the Douro), after which it forks, allowing you to drive along either river bank. The north bank road is quicker; the south bank more attractive. As for the Linha do Douro **train from Porto**, this shadows the motorway, and passes close to Penafiel, but shortly after Livração the line finally turns south to reach the Douro and then heads upstream. At Mesão Frio, the river temporarily leaves its confined channel and broadens into the little plain commanded by the port wine town of **Peso da Régua**. East of here, trains continue as far as **Pocinho**, though to travel any further – and to cross the border into Spain – you'll need to take buses or your own transport. You could always cut north from Régua instead, up the Corgo line, a brief excursion through marvellous vine and granite landscape to Vila Real (see p.362). Régua is also the jumping-off point for buses to the pilgrimage centre of **Lamego**, 13km to the south, at the tip of Beira Alta, and since this is by far the easiest link with the town, Lamego is covered here, along with its immediate region.

Peso da Régua

PESO DA RÉGUA (usually just Régua) is an expanding provincial town that has been known for over two centuries as the "Capital of the Upper Douro" because

RIVER, RAIL AND RIBBON LAKES

In the eighteenth century, when the port-producing area was first demarcated (see p.269), the **Rio Douro** could not be navigated by the traditional *barcos rabelos* (barges) beyond the rapids of Cachão de Valeira. By the end of the century, engineering works had circumnavigated the worst of the rapids and opened up the Douro as far east as Pocinho, but travel was still slow – it took three days to float wine down from Peso da Régua to Porto. The arrival of the **railway** at the end of the nineteenth century accelerated transport up and down the valley: the track reached Régua in 1880 and arrived at the Spanish border in 1887, with the branch lines up the river's tributaries completed by 1910. Later, road transport replaced rail and the river itself became something of a backwater until the 1970s, when dams were planned along the length of the Douro.

With the completion of the fifth dam in 1985, the river was turned into a series of **ribbon lakes** and, thanks to locks along the route, it's now possible to cruise via Régua from Porto to Barca de Alva on the Spanish border, a distance of just over 200km; for details, see Porto "Listings" p.276.

of its role in the port industry. In fact, the centre for quality port wines has shifted to Pinhão, half an hour further east; Régua is simply the junction and the depot through which all the wine must pass on its way to Porto. It's not a pretty place either, sitting next to the almost completed motorway that will eventually link Bragança with Viseu in Beira Alta. Nevertheless, the ornamental *barcos rabelos* anchored on the river, and the sombre Sandeman cutout on the horizon, are a reminder of Régua's previous importance as the first capital of Pombal's demarcated port-producing region.

The small **turismo** (summer daily 9am–12.30pm & 2–6pm; winter Mon–Fri 9am–12.30pm & 2–6pm ☎054/228 46) is on Rua da Ferreirinha, 1km west of the station – turn right and head downhill along the river; it's right at the end of the river road at the junction near the petrol station. They can provide information about the local **port wine lodges** – the easiest to visit is **Quinta de São Domingos** which runs a more personalized and interesting tour than its Vila Nova de Gaia equivalents (Mon–Fri 9am–12.30pm & 2–5pm; free); you'll see signs to it if you turn left from the station. You can also visit the entrance hall of the Casa do Douro on Rua dos Camilos, the headquarters of the port growers' organization, to see the medieval-style stained-glass window by Lino António.

Apart from the alcoholic diversions, there's not much to do in Régua except wander through the upper town. Alternatively, you could take a **river trip** to some of the *quintas* around Régua (summer only). For information and tickets, contact Agência de Viagens Santa Cruz, at Rua dos Camilos 128 (☎054/223 03), facing the post office.

You probably won't want to stay the night in Régua, so be sure of your train connection or next bus out. **Buses** to Lamego run every hour up until 8pm, from in front of the station and there are five trains daily to Vila Real (last one leaves at 6.44pm). If you do need to **stay**, the high-rise *Residencial Império,* Rua José Vasques Osório 8, at the corner of Largo da Estação (☎054/32 23 99, fax 32 14 57; ④), is very close to the station, comfortable and does good breakfasts too; while the *Pensão Borrajo* on Rua dos Camilos (☎054/233 96; ①) is a basic option in an old tiled building above a restaurant, on the same road as the post office. There are plenty of **restaurants** along the riverfront, or try *O Maleiro*, a friendly, bustling place on Rua dos Camilos. The family-run *Restaurante Arco Íris* is an understated place on Avenida Sacadura Cabral, west from the turismo – it offers superlative cooking at good prices (up to 2000$00) and has a number of awards to its name.

East to the border

Just beyond Régua, and past the massive dam of a hydroelectric power station, you begin increasingly to see the terraced slopes where the **port vines** are grown. They're at their best in August, with the grapes ripening, and in September, when the harvest has begun. Quotas for wine production have been in force around here since the mid-eighteenth century, and some terrace walls from that period have withstood the assault of the diggers and dynamite that are used nowadays to clear the way for the vineyard tractors. Grape-treaders and the traditional *barcos rabelos* have also been replaced by machines and cistern lorries, though there's still a demand for large groups of hand-pickers (*rogas*) when there's a bumper crop.

Pinhão to Pocinho

The country continues craggy and beautiful, with the softer hills of the interior fading dark green into the distance, past **PINHÃO**, the main centre for quality ports. There are a couple of very large *pensões* here so **accommodation** shouldn't be a problem. *Pensão Ponto Grande* (☎054/724 56; ③), at Rua Central 103–105, is the better of the two, with TVs and air-conditioning and a good restaurant; *Pensão Douro*, two doors down (☎054/724 04; ③), is more modern and offers much the same. However, if your budget can stretch to it the *Quinta da Rosa*, a working wine estate 2km west of Pinho, has six double rooms for rent (☎054/722 54, fax 054/723 46; ⑤–⑥) and offers wonderful river views and the chance to see at first hand the early processes of port wine making. From Pinhão you could drive (or get a taxi) to the village of **Panascal** and visit the 250-year-old *Quinta de Panascal* (Mon–Fri 10am–7.30pm; ☎054/723 21), a port shipper's property, which offers tours of the grounds and a chance to sample some local port.

The Douro continues on its journey eastwards, through the village of Tua, where buses run up the Tua valley to Mirandela in Trás-os-Montes (see p.367). The train continues on to its terminus, 45km east of Pinhão, at the isolated station of **POCINHO**, where it is met by buses to Torre de Moncorvo, 10km northeast (see p.387).

Vila Nova de Foz Côa

Eight kilometres south of Pocinho, **VILA NOVA DE FOZ CÔA**, is immediately noteworthy in that, although little more than an overgrown village, it has recently been awarded the status of city. A pleasant, functional place, it sits above the Côa river valley and has remained relatively untouched by the modern world, with a tight-knit centre and some fine mansions along the wide, tree-lined Avenida Gago Coutinho. There is not much to see here apart from the **Igreja Matriz**, with its impressive Manueline doorway, bizarrely leaning walls and nearby pillory. However, Foz Côa is known throughout Portugal for its successful battle to save an astonishing collection of **Paleolithic rock art** from submersion under a proposed reservoir (see box opposite).

THE ROCK ART OF FOZ CÔA

The River Côa near Vila Nova de Foz Côa became the centre of one of Portugal's major controversies when plans to construct a massive dam coincided with the discovery in the 1980s of what is now confirmed to be the **most extensive array of Paleolithic art in Europe**. Engravings of horses, deer, goats, and other animals (some extinct, such as the auroch), as well as later, neolithic images of people, were found along 17km of the river's steep, rocky schist valley and subsequent interest gave rise to a flurry of further discoveries in nearby sites. The oldest engravings are estimated to be up to 22,000 years old and are particularly unusual in that they are not in caves but on exposed rock faces. Unfortunately, more precise carbon-dating on paint samples (some of the engravings were also painted) has, for the most part, been made impossible by misguided chemical "cleaning" – intended to relieve the engravings of their moss and lichen covering, it also went a long way to removing most of the traces of paint. The hope is that future discoveries will provide a second chance to date the sites more accurately.

However, the fact that the sites have survived at all is testimony to a remarkable "people's **campaign**" against the proposed dam: if construction had gone ahead, the engravings would have been lost forever under 90m of water. Archeologists and environmental groups joined forces with local people (who also feared the loss of 16,000 hectares of prime-quality vineyards), and schoolchildren and students from across the country in pressurizing EDP, Portugal's then state-owned electricity monopoly, to abandon the project. Success came in 1995 and in place of the dam, the sites were declared a National Monument and will become a UNESCO **World Heritage Site** by 1998; their management is entrusted to the **Parque Arqueológico do Vale do Côa**, created in June 1996.

Of the three major sites, two – Penascosa and Ribeira de Piscos – are open to the public, with the third, Canada do Inferno, open only to researchers. **To arrange a visit**, you must contact the park authorities in advance at Avda. Gago Coutinho 19, Vila Nova de Foz Côa (℡079/76 43 17, fax 079/76 52 57), who will book you on to a guided tour (500$00 for either site). Transport is included in the price but note that you still have to make your own way to the respective "reception centres" of Castelo Melhor (for Penascosa) or Muxagata (for Ribeira de Piscos) – there are no bus services to either, so take a taxi. There's currently a waiting list of three to four days for weekday visits, and one to three weeks for weekends, although you might be lucky and find a place within a day or two.

One daily bus passes through the city on its way from Torre de Moncorvo in Trás-os-Montes (see p.387) to Lisbon. Other buses run by Viação Carneiro and Alfandeguense connect with Pocinho and towns in the Mountain Beiras; ask at Café Luís on Avda. Gago Coutinho for further information. **Accommodation** can be found at *Residencial Avenida*, Avda. Gago Coutinho 8 (℡071/76 21 75; ④), or at the friendly, family-run *Residencial Marina* next door (℡071/76 21 12; ③). If you have your own transport it's well worth staying at the *Residencial Rainha Santa Isabel* (℡079/786 80; ②), Quinta do Montargão, 6km southwest on the road to Freixo de Numão. The rooms are nothing special but the attraction is the isolation, good walks, good food and superlative homemade cheese washed down with a glass of the *quinta*'s own port wine. Good **food** can also be had at *Restaurante A Marisqueira* on Rua Juiz Moutinho André, between Praça da República and Largo Dr. Aguilar.

Onwards to Barca de Alva and the border

Following the last, uppermost reaches of the Portuguese Douro is impossible by road, as on both sides they veer well away from the river. However, the roads converge again over the bridge at Barca de Alva, where the river finally enters Portuguese territory after skirting the border for over 100km. Local Senhor Lopes buses run the two-hour journey to Barca de Alva from Pocinho (Mon–Fri 2pm & 6.30pm, Sat 2pm, Sun 6.30pm) passing through both Vila Nova de Foz Côa and the small, sleepy town of **FIGUEIRA DE CASTELO RODRIGO**, where you'll be dropped in the large Largo Mateus de Castro. There are a couple of basic **pensões** here, the better, but least characterful of which is *Pensão Figueirense* (☎071/325 17; ③; breakfast included), just south of the Largo on Avenida 25 de Abril. But despite a glut of restaurants and a large but simple Romanesque church, the town itself isn't the main draw: nearby, on an isolated hill, is the much older, medieval settlement of **CASTELO RODRIGO** (500$00 by taxi), a site that has been permanently occupied since around 500 BC, when the Turdulos people arrived. It is now inhabited only by a few dozen families settled around the ruins of its castle and is a pleasant place to spend an afternoon – the views are superb and there's a very good restaurant, *O Cantinho dos Avós*, which also has rooms (☎071/326 43; ③). If you're heading south from Figueira de Castelo Rodrigo, there's currently one daily bus at 8.20am (except Sat) to Lisbon via Guarda, Viseu and Coimbra: information and tickets from the kiosk in the southwestern corner of the Largo, in front of the *Café Transmontano*.

Twenty kilometres to the north and less than 2km from the Spanish border is the last Portuguese village along the Douro, **BARCA DE ALVA**. The route is a delight – defiantly unmodernized agricultural land dotted with boulders, storks' nests and conical, stone-roofed houses – and Barca itself is an attractive place, overlooked by mountains on all sides and with a row of whitewashed cottages facing the river. It is the final destination of some of the river cruises from Porto (see p.276), but it's looking a little neglected now since the railway line across the border was discontinued in the 1980s: if you're brave enough you can risk the rickety old metal railway bridge into Spain (beware of rotten sleepers and snakes).

Barca's main appeal is the tranquil atmosphere and attractive countryside, recently declared part of the new Parque Natural do Douro Internacional (see p.386), which also makes it a good local hiking base. A lovely walk along a quiet road starts by crossing the road bridge into Trás-os-Montes; then you can follow the Douro through olive and orange groves, and past the terraced vineyards still providing grapes for the port companies in Porto.

Accommodation in Barca de Alva is at the *Baga d'Ouro* (☎079/351 26; ①), above the restaurant on the main road along the river; the *Casa de Pasto*, a few doors along, also has cheap rooms. The *Baga d'Ouro* is also a good place **to eat**, and does a fine set meal and excellent breakfasts of coffee, fresh bread and local honey. **Onward transport** is restricted as there are no bus services north to Freixo de Espada à Cinta; if you want to continue on to Trás-os-Montes your only option is to catch a Senhor Lopes bus back to Pocinho (Mon–Fri 7.30am & 4.30pm, Sat 7.30am, Sun 4.30pm), from where there are three daily buses to Torre do Moncorvo and beyond.

Lamego and around

Although technically in Beira Alta, **LAMEGO** is isolated at the tip of its mountain province, and much more accessible from Régua and the Douro. The town itself has more in common with the Douro region, too, spreading over gentle slopes of the rich agricultural land fed by the river, a terrain which the locals put to good use in the production of such delights as hams and melons, as well as *Raposeira* – the closest thing to champagne you will find in Portugal.

Lamego is a wealthy place, and long has been, as evidenced by the graceful white *quintas* and villas on the hillsides, and the luxuriant architecture of the centre, where Baroque mansions seem to stand on every corner and lavish decorations are found within the smallest chapel. Lamego also has one of the very greatest Baroque structures in Europe – the shrine of **Nossa Senhora dos Remédios**, which, with its monumental stairway, dominates the west–east axis of the town.

The Town

For all the architectural histrionics of the shrine, it's Lamego's **Sé** that clearly delineates the centre of town. It is basically a Renaissance structure, though with a thirteenth-century tower surviving from a previous building. The mixture works well and the cloister is a beauty. Facing the cathedral, occupying an eighteenth-century palace, is the town's excellent **Museu de Lamego** (Tues–Sun 10am–12.30pm & 2–5pm; 250$00), whose exhibits include five of the remaining panels of a polyptych commissioned from Grão Vasco by the Bishop of Lamego in 1506. Judging by the lack of correlation between the various panels – for instance, the *Creation of the Animals* and the prodigiously executed *Annunciation* – some of the work must be attributed to the great man's school. Also on show are a series of sixteenth-century Flemish tapestries (including a marvellous *Life of Oedipus* sequence), three curious statues of a conspicuously pregnant Virgin Mary (a genre peculiar to this region), a fine assembly of azulejos, piles of ecclesiastical treasure from the Episcopal Palace, and a group of chapels rescued from the decaying Convento das Chagas.

Across the square, Rua da Olaria, a narrow street of tiny shops, leads into Rua de Almacave, which follows the walls of the old inner town. The route takes you past the **Igreja de Almacave**, a very ancient foundation said once to have been a mosque, to Praça do Comércio. From here you can pass through the walls of the **Old Citadel** and climb up to the **Castelo** (summer daily 10am–12 & 2–5pm; free), surrounded by a cluster of ancient stone houses. This has been pressed into service as the local scout headquarters and the boys do have a fairly legitimate claim on the place, having – so they say – cleared eighteen lorryloads of garbage away in the 1970s and saved the building from ruin. You can look around the castle, providing a spare scout is available to show you around – if the wigwams and scout banners inside don't grab you, climb the rickety stairs onto the roof for some stunning views. Nearby, the thirteenth-century **Cisterna** is one of the strangest buildings in the country. The interior of this ancient water source resembles a perfectly preserved Romanesque chapel, its walls still bearing the original stonemasons' marks – sadly, it's closed to the public.

Nossa Senhora dos Remédios

The celebrated shrine of **Nossa Senhora dos Remédios** is a major point of pilgrimage – a reputation for healing miracles draws devotees from all over the country. Standing on a hill overlooking the city, it's approached by a magnificently elaborate eighteenth-century stairway, modelled on the one at Bom Jesus near

△ ①,Campsite, Castro Daire & Serra das Meadas   Peso da Régua & ⑨ △

LAMEGO

ACCOMMODATION
① Motel Turisserra
② Albergaria do Cerrado
③ Residencial São Paulo
④ Café Abrigo
⑤ Residencial Solar da Sé
⑥ Pensão Império
⑦ Pensão Silva
⑧ Hotel do Parque
⑨ Hotel Lamego

RESTAURANTS & BARS
Ⓐ Churrasqueira Londrina
Ⓑ Restaurante Novo
Ⓒ Casa de Filipe & Adega Matos
Ⓓ Bar Doce Bar
Ⓔ Jardim Popular
Ⓕ Discoteca ETDS

N.S. da Esperança

Ig. das Chagas

Ig. da Graça

Chafariz

Porta dos Figi

Palácio Episcopal

Castelo

Old Citadel

Law Courts

Bus Station

Ig. de Almacave

Cisterna

Mercado

Porta do Sol

Museu de Lamego

Sé

Fire Station

Swimming Pool

Recinto da Feira

N.S. dos Remédios

Capela do Desterro

Hospital

0   200 m

Guarda ▽   Balsemão ▽

Braga. Its seven hundred steps – which the most committed pilgrims ascend on their knees – are punctuated by a *via santa* of devotional chapels, azulejos and allegorical fountains and statues. After the approach, and its own facade, the church itself is simply a detail in the architectural ensemble: an assembly hall for the ever-present faithful.

The great **pilgrimage** here takes place on September 6–8, although the accompanying celebrations last several weeks, starting in the last week of August and continuing into mid-September. The main procession, with animals pulling carriages and cavalcades of young children in white, is on September 7. As well as the pilgrimage, there's a traditional "Battle of Flowers", torchlit parades, rock concerts with some of the country's top bands, dances, car races and a fair on the Recinto da Feira, below the sanctuary. The turismo has details of other festivals which take place in May, June and November.

Practicalities

The **bus station** is behind the museum, right in the centre of town. In addition to the Régua connections (hourly until 8.15pm), there are daily services linking Viseu and other points in Beira Alta, as well as Lisbon and Porto. The **turismo** is on Avenida Guedes Visconde Teixeira (July–Sept daily 10am–12.30pm & 2–7pm; Oct–June Mon–Fri 10am–12.30pm & 2–6pm, Sat 10am–12.30pm; ☎054/620 05), just off the main square, Largo de Camões.

Accommodation

Accommodation can be tricky to find and is on the expensive side. Booking ahead is strongly advised, though if you turn up on spec, the turismo may be able to sort you out a **private room**; possibilities include rooms at Rua de Santa Cruz 15 (①) or those above *Café Abrigo* on Rua dos Bancos (☎054/624 32; ②). They can also provide you with details of Solares de Portugal and similar rural properties, though for these you'll need your own transport. The local **campsite** (☎054/620 90) is 4km out in Turisserra, by the *Motel Turisserra* (see below). There are no buses to the campsite; take the road marked to Avões until you see the campsite signs.

Albergaria do Cerrado, on the Régua road, 400m from the Sé (☎ & fax 054/654 64). Lamego's top hotel – modern and well-equipped but a bit characterless. ⑥.

Pensão Império, Trav. dos Loureiros 6, off Avenida Visconde Teixeira (☎054/627 42, fax 632 38). Above the restaurant, pleasant if somewhat fusty rooms which can be noisy. ④.

Hotel Lamego, Quinta da Vista Alegre, about 2km out of town on the Régua road (☎054/65 61 71, fax 65 61 80). Modern, well-run four-star hotel with a pool, sauna and Turkish bath. ⑤.

Hotel do Parque, by the church of Nossa Senhora dos Remédios (☎054/621 05, fax 652 03). An unbeatable location and lovely hotel, set in its own gardens. ⑤.

Residencial São Paulo, Avda. 5 de Outubro (☎054/631 14, fax 623 04). A modern building, but friendly and price includes breakfast. ③.

Pensão Silva, Rua Trás-da-Sé 26 (☎054/629 29). It's next to the Sé so the bells might disturb you but the rooms are decent, the French-speaking owner is friendly, and it's the cheapest in town. ③.

Residencial Solar da Sé, Avda. Visconde Teixeira (☎054/620 60, fax 659 28). Less characterful than *Silva* but smart, and a fraction further from the clock – though still with fine views over the cathedral. ④.

Motel Turisserra, 4km out on the Estrada Florestal (☎054/65 58 82, fax 65 61 52). A modest motel (and very good restaurant), occupying a lofty position on the Serra das Meadas, alongside the campsite. ③.

Eating and drinking

Restaurants in Lamego, like *pensões*, are on the expensive side, especially in the centre of town, so you may prefer to assemble a fine **picnic** from the excellent ham and cheese shops, bakers and nearby grocers on Rua da Olaria. **Nightlife** is limited; there's a saloon-door bar at the top of Rua de Almacave on the way to the castle, or try the *taberna* on Rua do Castelinho 25 – though both close at 9pm. For younger (and female) company, try *Bar Doce Bar* on Avenida Visconde Guedes Teixeira, or *Discoteca ETDS* on Avenida Dr. Alfredo de Sousa, at the foot of the steps to the shrine.

Casa de Filipe and **Adega Matos** on an unnamed side street immediately behind the Sé. Local *casas de pasto*. Very basic but highly recommended.

Pensão Império, Trav. dos Loureiros 6. Serves perhaps the best food in town but watch out for the "hidden" extras – bread and butter can add up to 1200$00. However, worth a visit if your funds will stretch.

Jardim Popular, Rua da Perreira. Around the corner from *Pensão Silva*, this is a rather strange construction in a walled garden but the grills and salads are good. Around 2500$00.

Churrasqueira Londrina, Rua de Fafel. Behind the fire station, an unassuming modern place but with outstanding grills and very reasonably priced.

Restaurante Novo, Largo da Sé. Cheap and cheerful with a few outdoor tables overlooking the Sé.

Around Lamego: Balsemão and the Caves do Raposeira

At the hamlet of **BALSEMÃO**, a three-kilometre hike from the back of the Lamego cathedral, is a seventh-century chapel founded by the Suevi. The route requires three left turns in all: the first is at the Capela do Desterro down into the old quarters of town and across a bridge; the second, a fork on to the hillside road; and the third comes a little while later, taking you down into the valley and above a rushing river. After three large curves, a village school, a collection of outhouses and the chapel appear. The undistinguished facade and dark interior of the **Capelo de São Pedro** (extremely variable hours; check with the turismo in Lamego) give it the air of a family vault, an impression strengthened by the imposing **sarcophagus** of Dom Afonso of Porto. Florid fourteenth-century capitals encircling the tomb make the few remaining Suevi curls on the archway into the choir seem subdued by comparison. Look out for the restored, profoundly pregnant statue of *Nossa Senhora do Ó* (that's Ó as in *Ó! Nossa Senhora, Mãe de Deus . . .*).

The other main attraction of Lamego is a visit to the **Caves do Raposeira** (☎054/65 50 03), 1km out of town on the Castro Daire road. These are open for free guided tours around the cellars and tasting of Portugal's "champagne" (Mon–Fri, usually at 10am, 11am, 2pm, 3pm and 4pm); if in a large group, phone or check with the turismo before setting out.

South from Lamego

Continuing **south from Lamego**, in the direction of Guarda and Viseu, the country of the **Leomil** and **Montemuro** ranges is high, wild and sparsely inhabited. This territory was among the earliest to fall to Afonso Henriques, the first king of Portugal, in his march south against the Moors. It is said that he laid the first stone of the monastery of **São João de Tarouca** after his victories at Trancoso and Sernancelhe in Beira Alta. The region's three other rewarding sights – the monastery of **Salzedas**, the fortified bridge at **Ucanha** and the church at **Tarouca** – were also founded at this time.

São João de Tarouca

The small village of **SÃO JOÃO DE TAROUCA**, off the southeast route from Lamego to Guarda, was the site of the first Cistercian monastery to be founded in Portugal (1124). Only the simple **Romanesque church** is really intact, and even here the greatest treasure – Gaspar Vaz's renowned altarpiece of Saint Peter – is no longer on display. Villagers complain that the authorities in Lisbon removed the painting for cleaning in 1978 and have refused to return it ever since. Being

THE INSTITUTE OF CULTURAL AFFAIRS

The **Montemuro** district, between Lamego and Castro Daire, suffers enormously from unemployment and depopulation, but sports a long tradition of local handicraft industries, including weaving, knitting, basketry, honey and cheese production, pottery and cape-making. There's still a thriving cultural life, too – from theatre and folk dance to religious festivals – which occupies a central place in Montemuro life.

The **Instituto dos Assuntos Culturais** (IAC) is an international development organization with a staff of foreign and Portuguese workers supporting the initiatives of local people. Some twenty villages, with a total population of about 11,000, are currently involved with the IAC's work. It's based at the village of **Mezio**, about 20km southwest of Lamego on the N2 Castro Daire road.

If you're interested in having a look at what the Institute does – and it seems there's not much it doesn't take an interest in – you might like to stop en route between Lamego and the Mountain Beiras and stay for a day or two: visitors are actively encouraged. Facilities are basic, but there are showers and toilets and plenty of organic food. Costs vary from 1,500$00 per person for bed and breakfast or for camping with meals, to around 3000$00 which is pretty much all-inclusive. If you want to make enquiries in advance, write to the IAC at Rua Central 47, Mezio, 3600 Castro Daire or telephone ☎054/68 92 46.

Whether or not you choose to stay, you may find the IAC pamphlet *Hiking Trails in the Montemuro* useful. It describes ten half-day **walks** in the region (though they are pretty strenuous); the IAC can also provide guides and transport for arranged walking circuits for around 3000–4000$00 per person per tour.

less portable, the medieval tomb of Dom Dinis's illegitimate son, the Count of Barcelos, with elaborate hunting scenes carved into the sides, still lies in a side aisle. In summer there are usually students working on the site, who will probably be happy to show you around. There's a pleasant spot for rest and recuperation – and a nice **café** – down by the river, not two minutes' walk from the church. Regular EAVT **buses** (Mon–Fri 9 daily, 3–4 at weekends) make the 25-minute journey here from Lamego's bus station.

Ucanha

In **UCANHA** – north of Tarouca, on the opposite side of the N226 – life revolves around the water. Down below the main road, two ingenious ducts have been made to tap the river upstream in order to provide adequate washing facilities in the centre of the village. The wash houses are practically in ruins, but the system of one tank for suds and another for rinses, common to the Mediterranean, has been preserved. Running below the pools, the river looks so tempting that on a sunny day, regardless of what trash might be floating by, the village children are constantly nipping in and out.

The real beauty of the scene stems from the majestic **tollgate** and single-arched **bridge**. They date from shortly after 1163, when the diocese of Salzedas was awarded to Teresa Afonso, erstwhile nursemaid to Afonso Henriques's five sons and heirs and widow of Egas Moniz, the first king's tutor and closest adviser. Besides marking and protecting the border of her domain, these structures were also, of course, an ostentatious mark of manorial power. Today, clothes are hung out to dry under the arches.

Salzedas

SALZEDAS lies 4km further along the Ucanha road, past Murganheira, another "champagne" co-operative and a rival to Raposeira. The **Monastery** here was once the greatest of its kind, grander even than São João de Tarouca. The complex was rebuilt with money donated by Teresa Afonso in 1168, when the order was Augustinian; it became Cistercian during a later period of administration from Alcobaça.

Unfortunately, eighteenth-century renovation has largely altered its original appearance into a clumsy mixture of Baroque and pseudo-Classical styles. The monastery's main facade presides over the small square of the diminutive village. As at Tarouca, students work here in the summer and, though they may seem surprised to see casual visitors, they will follow you around and open the relevant doors. The smell of decay is strong inside and the two dark and dusty **paintings** of *Saint Peregrine* and *Saint Sebastian* by Grão Vasco, either side of the choir, are easily overlooked. More conspicuous are the fifteenth-century tombs of the Coutinho family – dominant nobles in these parts in the early years of the Portuguese nation – near the entrance. Out through a side door, a succession of courtyards, once fronting formal gardens, bear the scars of a period of extensive pillage and decay, which began in 1834 with the dissolution of the monasteries.

travel details

Amarante to: Livração (7–9 daily; 25min); Porto (8–9 daily; 1hr 40min–2hr).

Espinho to: Coimbra (15–19 daily; 1hr 5min–1hr 40min); Lisbon (9 daily; 3hr 35min–4hr); Porto (15–19 daily; 20–40min).

Penafiel to: Livração (14–17 daily; 25min); Peso da Régua (12–13 daily; 1hr 20min); Pocinho (4 daily; 3hr 15min); Porto (15–18 daily; 45min–1hr 10min); Tua (5 daily; 2hr 10min).

Pocinho to: Penafiel (3–4 daily; 3hr 10min); Peso da Régua (4 daily; 1hr 40min); Porto (4 daily; 4hr 30min); Tua (6–7 daily; 45min).

Peso da Régua to: Pocinho (4 daily; 1hr 40min); Porto (14–15 daily; 2hr 10min–2hr 40min); Tua (6–7 daily; 45min); Vila Real (5 daily; 1hr).

Porto to: Coimbra (15–19 daily; 2hr); Espinho (15–19 daily; 20–40min); Lisbon (12 daily; 3hr–4hr 20min); Livração (15–18 daily; 1hr 15min–1hr 40min); Penafiel (15–18 daily; 45min–1hr 10min); Peso da Régua (14–15 daily; 2hr 10min–2hr 40min); Pocinho (4 daily; 4hr 30min–4hr 50min); Póvoa de Varzim (roughly every 30min; 1hr); Santo Tirso (11–17 daily; 50min); Tua (6–7 daily; 3hr 15min–3hr 35min); Viana do Castelo (9–10 daily; 1hr 45min–2hr 25min); Vila do Conde (roughly every 30min; 50min).

Tua to: Mirandela (5 daily; 1hr 50min).

Buses

NB: Destinations from Porto are followed by an abbreviation of the company who operates the service. Where more than one company is given, the order reflects frequency of service. For departure points of the various companies see "Listings" on p.276. Abbreviations are as follows: Asa Douro (AD); Auto Viação de Espinho (AVE); Auto Viação do Minho (AVMi); Auto Viação do Tâmega (AVT); Auto Viação Mondinese (AVM); Caima (C); EVA; Joalto (J); João Ferreira das Neves (JFN); Linhares (L); Marquês (M); Rede Expressos (RE); Renex (Rx); Resende (Rs); Rodonorte (R); Santos de Freixo (SF); Turilis (T); Valpi (V).

Amarante to: Braga (2–3 daily; 2hr 10min); Cabaceiros de Basto (3–4 daily; 1hr 35min); Celorico de Basto (Mon–Sat 5 daily; 40min); Fermil (3–4 daily; 1hr); Guimarães (Mon–Fri 7 daily; 1hr 15min); Porto (2–3 daily; 1hr 10min); Vila Real (10–12 daily; 2hr 40min).

Lamego to: Braga (1 daily; 2hr 50min); Celorico da Beira (Mon–Fri 3 daily; 3hr); Lisbon (2–4 daily; 6hr); Peso da Régua (16 daily; 25min); Penafiel (3–5 daily; 1hr 40min); Porto (4–6 daily; 4–4hr 30min); Sernancelhe (Mon–Fri 6 daily, Sat & Sun

2 daily; 2hr); Tarouca (Mon–Fri 9 daily, Sat & Sun 3–4 daily; 30min); Trancoso (1–2 daily; 2hr); Viseu (5–7 daily; 1hr 20min–2hr).

Peso da Régua to: Coimbra (1–2 daily; 3hr 40min); Guarda (1 daily; 2hr 30min); Lamego (16 daily; 25min); Vila Real (hourly; 40min); Viseu (Mon–Fri 6 daily, Sat & Sun 1–2; 1hr 30min).

Penafiel to: Amarante (3–6 daily; 30min); Baúlhe (Mon–Fri 8 daily, Sat 4 daily; 1hr 45min); Entre-os-Rios (Mon–Fri 7 daily; 40min–1hr 25min); Lamego (3–5 daily; 1hr 40min); Porto (18 daily; 30min–1hr 20min); Torrão (Mon–Fri 7 daily; 45min–1hr 30min).

Pocinho to: Bragança (2 daily; 1hr 40min); Celerico da Beira (2 daily; 1hr 45min); Coimbra (2 daily; 4hr 55min); Lisbon (2 daily; 7hr 25min); Torre de Moncorvo (3 daily; 30min); Trancoso (Mon–Fri 2 daily; 2hr 30min); Viseu (2 daily; 2hr 45min).

Porto to: Abrantes, R (1 daily; 4hr 35min); Amarante, AD, AVT, R (Mon–Fri 10 daily, Sat & Sun 5 daily; 1hr 10min–1hr 25min); Aveiro, C (4 daily; 2hr 30min); Barcelos, L (Mon–Sat 7 daily; 1hr 45min); Braga, Rx, Rs, C (17 daily; 1hr 10min); Bragança, R (3 daily; 1hr 50min–3hr 50min); Caminha, AVMi (Mon–Fri 5 daily, Sat & Sun 1 daily; 2hr); Chaves, AVT, R (6–12 daily; 3hr 10min–5hr); Coimbra, RE, R, AVT (8–10 daily; 1hr 30min); Fátima, R (6 daily; 3hr 30min); Guarda, M,

J, R (7 daily; 2hr 10min–3hr 20min); Guimarães, JFN (12 daily; 2hr); Lamego, AD (3–5 daily; 4hr–4hr 30min); Leiria, R (6 daily; 1hr 40min–2hr 30min); Lisbon, Rx, RE, EVA (hourly; 3hr–3hr 30min); Melgaço, AVMi (2 daily; 3hr); Mirandela, R, SF (2–4 daily; 2hr 45min); Monção AVMi, T, R (5 daily; 2hr 45min–3hr); Mondim de Basto, AVM (7 daily; 3hr 30min); Penafiel, V, AVT (24 daily; 55min–1hr); Póvoa de Varzim, L, AVMi (16 daily; 40–55min); Tomar, R (1 daily; 4hr); Valença do Minho, AVMi, T, R (5 daily; 2hr 30min–2hr 45min); Viana do Castelo, AVMi, L (12–14 daily; 2hr); Vila do Conde, AVMi, L (16 daily; 35–55min); Vila Real, AVT, R (9 daily; 2hr); Viseu, M, R, & J (8 daily; 2hr).

Póvoa de Varzim to: Barcelos (4–5 daily; 45min); Braga (9 daily; 1hr 15min); Esposende (9–12 daily; 40min); Guimarães (9–11 daily; 1hr 45min); Santo Tirso (Mon–Sat 12 daily, Sun 6 daily; 1hr); Viana do Castelo (Mon–Fri 24 daily, Sat 17 daily, Sun 11 daily; 1hr 5min); Vila do Conde (every 15min; 15min).

Domestic flights

Porto to: Funchal, Madeira (6 weekly; 2hr); Ponta Delgada, Açores (1 daily; 1hr 20min direct, 3hr indirect); Faro (2 daily; 2hr 15min–3hr); Lisbon (19 daily; 45min); Porto Santo, Madeira (2 weekly; 4hr 30min); Terceira, Açores (1 daily; 3hr 15min–4hr).

THE MINHO

With good reason the Portuguese consider the **Minho** – the province north of Porto – to be the most beautiful part of their country. Its river valleys, wooded hills, trailing vines and barely developed coastline are given prominence in every travel brochure, while much is made of the Minho's traditional aspect: you can still see wooden-wheeled ox-carts creak down cobbled lanes, while age-old conventions are maintained at dozens of huge country markets, *festas* and *romarias*. In summer especially, you're likely to happen upon these carnivals, though it's worth trying to plan your trip around the larger events if you're keen to experience Minho life at its most exuberant – the main markets and principal festivals are detailed where appropriate throughout the chapter. As you travel around the region you will see signs of new building in even the smallest and most isolated villages, accounted for by the new-found prosperity of returned emigrants: Minho, more than any other area of Portugal, suffered severe depopulation from the late 1950s onwards as thousands migrated to France, Switzerland, Germany and even as far afield as the United States in search of more lucrative work.

The largest towns are concentrated in the southern Minho and any trip should allow time to examine the competing historic claims of **Guimarães**, first capital of Portugal, and neighbouring **Braga**, the country's ecclesiastical centre. Between them lie the extensive Celtic ruins of the **Citânia de Briteiros**, one of the most impressive archeological sites in Portugal, while from Braga it's also easy to visit **Barcelos**, site of the best-known (and biggest) of the region's weekly markets. It takes place on Thursdays, though for the full experience reserve a room in advance and arrive on Wednesday evening.

At Barcelos, you're only 20km from the **Costa Verde**, the Minho coast, which runs north all the way to the Spanish border. This has some wonderful beaches along the way, though the sea here is cold – and the weather, too, can be uncertain, with cool temperatures even in midsummer. The principal resort is **Viana do Castelo**, an enjoyable and lively town with an elegant historic core, though if you're seeking isolation, there are strands to the north and south that scarcely see visitors. The coast ends at **Caminha**, beyond which the **Rio Minho** runs inland, forming the border with Spanish Galicia. This is a delightful region, featuring a string of compact fortified towns flanking the river on the Portuguese side, their fortresses, in various stages of disrepair, staring across at Spain.

Inland from Viana, the Minho's other major river, the beautiful **Rio Lima**, runs east through a succession of gorgeous small towns where there's little to do but soak up the somnolent scenery. On the whole, much of the Minho is outrageously picturesque and full of quiet charm and interest. In fact it was in the Lima valley, and particularly around the town of **Ponte de Lima**, that Solares de Portugal (formerly Turihab) first exploited the beauty of the countryside to the benefit of

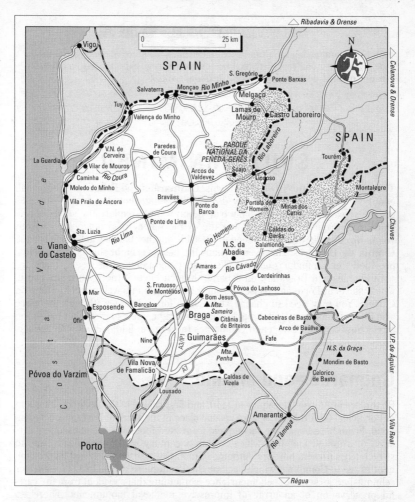

tourists by offering accommodation in local manor houses, old farms and country estates (see p.343). Further east, the gentle Minho scenery eventually gives way to the mountains, waterfalls, river gorges, reservoirs and forests of the protected **Parque Nacional da Peneda-Gerês**, Portugal's only national (as opposed to natural) park. This is superb camping and hiking territory, stretching from the main town and spa of **Caldas do Gerês** north as far as the Rio Minho and the Spanish border and east into Trás-os-Montes. It's possible to dip into the park from a couple of easily accessible towns, but you really need to devote several days if you're going to see the more isolated regions as bus services are limited; even by car the going's slow and on foot you could spend weeks exploring the trails.

SOUTHERN MINHO

The **southern Minho**'s two chief towns, **Guimarães** and **Braga**, are both small enough to walk around in a busy day's sightseeing, though a night's stay has greater rewards. This is especially true if you want to explore the series of religious sites around Braga, including the extraordinary pilgrimage site of **Bom Jesus do Monte**; while you'll need to set aside another half-day at least to see the **Citânia de Briteiros**. However, perhaps the best overnight stop is at **Barcelos**, provided you can find a room on a Wednesday night before the weekly market.

Guimarães and Braga are on separate branch lines of the main **train route**, which starts in Porto and passes through Barcelos on its way north to Viana do Castelo. You may need to change at Lousado for Guimarães (though there are also direct trains from Porto) and at Nine for Braga; but it's far quicker to use the direct **bus** between Braga and Guimarães rather than fiddle about with connections between the train lines.

Guimarães and around

Birthplace of Afonso Henriques in 1110, and first capital of the fledgling kingdom of Portucale, **GUIMARÃES** has a special place in the story of Portuguese nationhood. From here began the reconquest from the Moors and the subsequent creation of a united kingdom which, within a century of Afonso's death, was to stretch to its present borders. Although Guimarães subsequently lost its pre-eminent status to Coimbra – which became the Portuguese capital in 1143 – it never relinquished its sense of self-importance, something that's evident from the careful preservation of an array of impressive medieval monuments. There's a grandeur and a tangible sense of history in the narrow streets, which makes Guimarães one of the most attractive places in the country.

If you can afford to stay at one of the two local *pousadas* – one in the centre, the other in a former monastery at **Penha**, 5km southeast – then the experience is complete. Otherwise, decent budget accommodation is strangely hard to come by, though this matters little since Braga (24km), or even Porto (55km), are close enough to be able to visit Guimarães on a day-trip. And unless you book well in advance, you'll have to see Guimarães this way if you're here during either of the town's festivals.

The major event is the **Festas Gualterianas** (for São Gualter, or Saint Walter), which has taken place on the first weekend in August every year since 1452. If you miss this you can catch most of the same stallholders, and something of the atmosphere, the weekend after in Caldas de Vizela, a spa town 10km south of Guimarães. Next in importance is the long-established *romaria* to **São Torcato**, 6km northeast of town, on the first weekend in July, which, in the curious language of the turismo leaflet, "includes a procession with archaic choirs of virgins". A well-timed visit in winter will enable you to see one or more of the **Nicolinas** (Nov 29–Dec 7), **Nossa Senhora da Conceição** (Dec 8) and **Santa Luzia** (Dec 13).

The Town

The old centre of **Guimarães** is an elongated kernel of small, enclosed squares and cobbled streets. It is bounded at its southern end by the town gardens and overlooked from the north by the imposing castle, an enduring symbol of the emergent Portuguese nation. In between lie a series of medieval churches, convents and buildings that lend an air of dignity to the streets – two of the convents provide an impressive backdrop to a couple of the country's more illuminating museums. The presence of the University of the Minho gives the local cafés and bars a lively, student-orientated feel, particularly in the old town.

Around the Castelo

The imposing **Castelo** (Tues–Sun 10am–12.30pm & 2–5.30pm; free) was built by Henry of Burgundy, though its fame stems from the establishment of the first Portuguese court here, by his son, **Afonso Henriques**. Afonso is reputed to have been born in the great square keep which is surrounded now, as then, by seven castellated towers. A fine structure, its marvellous solidity is enhanced by its juxtaposition with the diminutive Romanesque chapel of **São Miguel** (same hours as the castle), on the grassy slope below, in whose font Afonso was probably baptized.

Just across from the chapel, the **Paço dos Duques** (daily 9am–5.15pm; 400$00) was once the medieval palace of the Dukes of Bragança. Under the Salazar dictatorship, its ruins were "restored" as an official residence for the president, and today, with such memories fading, it looks rather ludicrous – like a mock-Gothic Victorian folly. Inside is an extensive collection of portraits, furniture and porcelain, around which perambulate lengthy guided tours. Free concerts are occasionally held here at weekends; enquire at one of the turismos for details.

Perhaps more appealing are the **children's toys** – hammered out from old tin and no doubt lethal, but beautiful objects nonetheless – on sale in a number of shops opposite the castle; there's a café here, too.

Along Rua de Santa Maria

From the castle, **Rua de Santa Maria** leads down into the heart of the old town, a beautiful thoroughfare featuring iron grilles and granite arches. Many of the town's historic buildings have been superbly restored, and as you descend to the centre you'll pass one of the loveliest – the seventeenth-century convent of Santa Clara, which today does service as the **Câmara Municipal**.

On a much more intimate scale are the buildings ranged around the delightful central squares at the end of the street, **Praça de Santiago** and **Largo de Oliveira**. The latter is dominated by the **Colegíada**, a convent-church built (like the great monastery at Batalha) in honour of a vow made by João I before his deci-

GUIMARÃES

△ Amarante

Hospital

Castelo

ACCOMMODATION
1. Casa de Retiros
2. Residencial das Trinas
3. Albergaria Palmeiras
4. Pousada de NS de Oliveira
5. Hospedaria D. Afonso Henriques
6. Hotel Toural
7. Pensão Imperial
8. Hotel de Guimarães

São Miguel

Monument to Afonso Henriques

Paço dos Duques

Convento do Carmo

Convento de Santa Clara

LARGO DA CONDESSA DE MOMADONA

△ Braga

△ Penha & Fafe

△ Citânia △ de Briteiros

Triangulo Comercial

Market

Museu Martins Sarmento

Bus Station

Museu Arte Primitiva Moderna

Igreja do Oliveira

LARGO JOÃO FRANCO

PRAÇA DE SANTIAGO

LARGO DA OLIVEIRA

São Domingos

Museu Alberto Sampaio

LARGO DO TOURAL

LARGO A.L. DE CARVALHO

LG. DA CONDESSA DO JUNCAL

LARGO DA REPÚBLICA DO BRASIL

△ Teleférico & Penha

Santos Passos

ALAMEDA RESISTÊNCIA AO FASCISMO

São Francisco

△ Penha

RESTAURANTS
A. Churrasqueira
B. El Rei
C. São Domingos
D. Oriental
E. Adega das Caquinhos
F. Café Milenario
G. Vira Bar

0   100 m

▽ 8 , Train Station & Porto

sive victory over Castile. Its unusual dedication is to "Our Lady of the Olive Tree" and before it stands a curious Gothic **canopy-shrine**. This marks the legendary spot where Wamba, unwillingly elected king of the Visigoths, drove a pole into the ground swearing that he would not reign until it blossomed. Naturally it sprouted immediately. João I, feeling this to be a useful indication of divine favour, set out to meet the Castilian forces from this very point.

At the heart of the Colegíada is a simple Romanesque cloister with varied, naively carved capitals. This, and the rooms off it, comprise the **Museu Alberto Sampaio** (Tues–Sun 10am–12.30pm & 2–5.30pm; 200$00), essentially the treasury of the collegiate church and convent but, for once, outstandingly exhibited and containing pieces of real beauty. The highlight is a brilliantly composed silver-gilt *Triptych of the Nativity*, said to have been found in the King of Castile's tent after the Portuguese victory at Aljubarrota in 1385. Close by this is displayed the tunic worn by João I in the battle.

The Museu Martins Sarmento and the Igreja de São Francisco

Across to the west, over the main Largo do Toural, the **Museu Martins Sarmento** (Tues–Sun 9.30am–12pm & 2–5pm; 200$00) is another superb collection, also housed in a former convent. Here, finds from the neighbouring *citânia* of Briteiros (see p.310) are displayed in the fourteenth-century Gothic cloister of the Igreja de São Domingos. They include a remarkable series of bronze votive offerings (among them, a "coach", pulled at each end by men and oxen), and ornately patterned stone lintels and door jambs from the huts; while most spectacular of all are the **Pedras Formosas** ("beautiful stones"). Once taken to be sacrificial altars, these are in fact the portals to funerary monuments. Formerly the museum's prize exhibit, the **Colossus of Pedralva**, a vast granite hulk of a figure with arm raised aloft and an over-sized phallus, now stands nearby in the pedestrian precinct outside the bus station. More enigmatic and considerably more ancient than the Pedras Formosas, it shares the bold, powerfully hewn appearance of the stone pigs found in Trás-os-Montes and, like them, may date from pre-Celtic fertility cults of around 1500 to 1000 BC.

Among the numerous other churches scattered about the centre of Guimarães, the finest is the **Igreja de São Francisco** (Tues–Sat 9.30am–12.30pm & 3–5pm, Sunday Mass at 12.30pm), on the south side of the town gardens. It features a series of huge eighteenth-century azulejos of Saint Francis preaching to the fish, and an elegant Renaissance cloister and fountain. Once again, the church was attached to a monastery of considerable size until the 1834 dissolution.

Penha and Santa Marinha da Costa

Two kilometres southeast of Guimarães on the slopes of **Penha** (617m) stands the region's best-preserved medieval building, the former monastery – and now a *pousada* – of **Santa Marinha da Costa**. It can be reached by taking the São Roque bus (Mon–Sat 6am–10pm, Sun 6am–8pm; every 30min) from the main turismo; get off at "Costa" and follow the signs.

The monastery was founded in 1154 by order of Dona Mafalda, the wife of Afonso Henriques, in honour of a vow to Santa Marinha, patron saint of pregnant women. Originally Augustinian, the foundation passed into the hands of the Order of Saint Jerome in the sixteenth century. In the **chapel** (official hours July–Sept 9am–1pm & 2–7pm but often inexplicably closed), Jerome's twin emblems of the skull and the lion are recurring motifs. They are surrounded by an oddly harmonious mixture of styles – tenth-century doorways on the south wall, sixteenth-century panels in the sacristy (including one depicting Jerome beating his breast with a stone against the temptation of women), and an eighteenth-century organ and stone roof in the choir. Strictly speaking, the rest of the monastic buildings are off limits except to guests of the *pousada* (see p.309 for details), but you can peek into the magnificent **cloister**, with its Mozarabic doorway, while the beautiful **gardens** are open to the public, too. For more of a look around it would be diplomatic to buy a meal, or at least a drink at the bar.

The peak of Penha is crowned by a statue of Nossa Senhora – by far the most fun way to reach it is to take the ingenious **Teleférico da Penha**, whose hi-tech bubbles leave from the end of Rua de Doutor José Sampaio (Mon–Fri 11am–7pm, Sat & Sun 10am–8pm; 300$00 single, 500$00 return).

Practicalities

Arriving by **train**, you'll find yourself ten minutes' walk south of the centre; bear left from the station and take the first right, past the university (occupying the grounds of a former palácio). On the way you'll pass the **main turismo** at Alameda Resistência ao Fascismo (Mon–Fri 9am–12.30pm & 2–5.30pm; ☎053/41 24 50), at the edge of the gardens, opposite Largo do Toural. There's a second turismo above an exhibition room at Praça de Santiago 37 (Mon–Fri 9am–12.30pm & 2–5.30pm; summer also open Sat 10am–1pm & 3–5pm, Sun 10am–1pm; ☎053/51 87 90).

The **bus station** is a fifteen-minute walk from the centre, at the bottom of Avenida Conde de Margaride; it's unmarked, so look out for the *Continente* or *McDonald's* sign above it. To get from the bus station into town, turn right and walk up the avenida until you reach the Museu Martins Sarmento; from here you can either continue along Rua Gil Vicente, or turn right towards Largo do Toural. There are express services from Porto and Lisbon, and regular weekday connections with Braga, Amarante, Cabeceiras and Mondim de Basto, and Póvoa do Lanhoso.

Accommodation

Inexpensive **accommodation** is scarce in town, and even more so during Guimarães' main festivals (see p.304). It's best to book ahead – especially if you're planning a splurge in one of the two *pousadas*. Otherwise, nearby Braga (p.312) has a much better choice of budget accommodation. There are two **campsites** in the locality – the nearest is the *Monte da Penha* (☎053/51 59 12, fax 51 65 69), a pleasant site with a small swimming pool, on the slopes of Penha and accessible by the cable car, while 7km northwest of Guimarães, *Caldas das Taipas* (☎053/57 62 74; June–Sept), by the Rio Ave off the N101, is even more attractive, but pricier with a swimming pool nearby.

Casa dos Pombais, Avda. de Londres (☎053/41 29 17). Opposite the bus station, this Solares de Portugal eighteenth-century manor house is an oasis in a built-up part of town. It's a lovely old building and some of the rooms overlook its attractive gardens. ⑤.

Casa de Retiros, Rua Francisco Agra 163 (☎053/51 15 15, fax 51 15 17). One of the least expensive places in town, this is a hostel, run for pilgrims, which means it's sometimes booked up by groups. There's an 11.30pm curfew, fairly stark surroundings and spartan breakfasts. Price per person is 2500$00.

Hospedaria D. Afonso Henriques, Rua Dom João I 40 (☎053/51 53 33, fax 51 19 34). Tastefully modernized town house near the Igreja de São Domingos, with beautiful rooms (all with TV and telephone) and an excellent restaurant (see p.309). A bargain. ④.

Hotel de Guimarães, Rua Eduardo Almeida (☎053/51 58 88, fax 51 62 34). The top modern choice with four-star comforts, including health club, Jacuzzi, pool, sauna and restaurant. It's 100m from the train station. ⑥.

Pensão Imperial, Alameda Resistência ao Fascismo 111 (☎053/41 51 63). This rundown *pensão* is overpriced by any but Guimarães standards, but offers some of the cheapest beds in town. ③.

Pousada de N.S. de Oliveira, Rua de Santa Maria (☎053/51 41 57, fax 51 42 04). Converted from a row of sixteenth-century houses, right in the medieval centre, this sixteen-room *pousada* is beautifully furnished – and worth every *escudo*. ⑦.

Albergaria Palmeiras, Centro Comercial das Palmeiras, Rua Gil Vicente (☎053/41 03 24, fax 41 72 61). Part of a commercial mall, which can make it difficult to find (and gain entry after shopping hours), but it's modern and good value, with a restaurant and parking facilities. ⑤.

Pensão Penha, at the top of the *teleférico* (☎053/41 42 45). A perfectly good option for those who want to stay in Penha. ④.

Pousada de Santa Marinha da Costa, Penha, 4800 Guimarães (☎053/51 44 53, fax 51 44 59). Occupying a convent, parts of which date from the ninth century, this is reckoned to be one of the top *pousadas* in the country; ask for one of the original rooms, not one of the new additions. ⑦.

Hotel Toural, Largo do Toural (☎053/51 71 84, fax 51 71 49). On the main square (though the entrance is in Largo A.L. de Carvalho, at the back). Once an elegant town house, this has been completely renovated into an ultra-modern four-star establishment – not cheap, but very comfortable. ⑥.

Residencial das Trinas, Rua das Trinas 29 (☎053/51 73 58, fax 51 73 62). Situated in the old town, this has spotless rooms, all with private bathrooms, satellite TV and telephone; very good value. Rooms at the back can be noisy. Breakfast included. ④.

Eating and drinking

Guimarães has no shortage of places to **eat and drink**, most very reasonably priced, although it's difficult to get particularly excited about the options – unless you're destined to eat at the town-centre *pousada*, in which case you're in for a treat.

Adega dos Caquinhos, between Largo A.L. Carvalho and Rua Rainha D. Maria III. A friendly, traditional and no-frills *adega* whose name reflects its decor – walls covered in broken crockery (*caquinhos*). The food is good and reasonably priced, around 1500$00.

Churrasqueira, Rua Francisco Agra 30. Excellent fresh grilled meat served in basic (and smoky) surroundings. Very cheap (under 1000$00).

Restaurante D. Afonso Henriques, Rua Dom João I 40. Under the equally good *hospedaria* and serving excellent and well-presented meals in modern surroundings. Under 2500$00.

Café Milenario, Largo do Toural. A large and airy traditional café serving reasonable snacks; popular with young and old alike.

Oriental, Largo do Toural. Excellent budget option serving very good regional specialities as well as more usual fare: try the *truta grelhada com presunto* (grilled trout stuffed with ham). Offers superb views over the largo. Under 1500$00.

Pousada de N.S. de Oliveira, Rua de Santa Maria. When it's on form it's the best restaurant in town, with traditional Minho dishes served in a wonderful antique dining room or at outside tables in summer. You'll need to reserve a table in advance. From 3000–5000$00 a head.

El Rei, Praça de Santiago 20a. This restaurant is in a prime location and serves good-quality food at moderate prices. Closed Sun.

São Domingos, Rua Dom João I 39–41. Just down the side of the Museu Martins Sarmento, this place serves great dishes in simple surroundings. Prices are reasonable, but it can be lacking in atmosphere.

Vira Bar, Alameda de São Domaso 25. A well-regarded place – church-like in its interior (stained-glass windows, barrel-vaulted ceiling, stone walls) and subdued ambiance – between 2500$00 and 4000$00 for the full works. Closed Mon.

Entertainment and nightlife

Outside festival time, at the beginning of July and August, the only time the town erupts into spontaneous celebration is when the local **soccer** team, FC Guimarães (consistently one of Portugal's better teams), wins at home. The stadium is located to the northwest of the centre, along Rua Dr. A. Pimenta. You'll find a number of **bars** in and around the central Praça de Santiago and the adjacent Largo da Oliveira, all with outdoor tables. As for **clubs**, both the *Crocodile Club*, Rua de São Gonçalo (July–Sept, Fri–Sun 10.30pm–3am) and *Trás Trás*, Rua Gil Vicente (Sat only), attract a young crowd, while *Seculo XIX*, Rua Teixeira de Pascoais (Wed–Sun 10pm–4am) is popular with all ages.

East towards Trás-os-Montes

Heading **east towards Trás-os-Montes**, the minor N206 runs across country towards the Rio Tâmega, a region covered in the previous chapter. **FAFE** is the first place you happen upon, 14km away. Little more than an overgrown bus station (you'll almost certainly need to change here for Trás-os-Montes destinations), it has three *pensões*, a *Comfort Inn* and a large revolutionary statue of a worker violently clubbing his bowler-hatted boss.

Beyond Fafe lies some magnificent countryside, dotted with huge boulders, though you'll really need your own transport to get the most out of the region as bus services are less than regular. Driving, you might want to stop at **GANDARELA**, 17km east of Fafe, which is famed for its topiary, while at **ARCO DE BAÚLHE**, 10km further, a road leads 7km north to Cabeceiras de Basto (see p.289). A dozen kilometres or so further east you finally reach the Tâmega River itself, where you're just 30km from the main Vila Real–Chaves road, one of Trás-os-Montes's finest routes.

The Citânia de Briteiros

Midway between Guimarães and Braga is one of the most impressive and exciting archeological sites in the country, the **Citânia de Briteiros**. *Citânias* – Celtic hill settlements – lie scattered throughout the Minho: remains of twenty-seven have been identified along the coast, plus sixteen more in the region between Braga and Guimarães alone. Most date from the arrival of northern European Celts in the Iron Age (c.600–500 BC), though some are far older, having merged with an existing local culture established since Neolithic times (c.2000 BC). The site at Briteiros was occupied from about 300 BC and seems to have been a last stronghold against the invading Roman forces, resisting colonization until around 20 BC.

The Roman historian Strabo gave a vivid description of the northern Portuguese tribes, who must have occupied these *citânias*, in his *Geographia* (c.20 BC). They organized mass sacrifices, he recorded, and inspected prisoners' entrails without removing them. Otherwise, they liked to:

> *live simply, drink water and sleep on the bare earth . . . two-thirds of the year they live on acorns, which they roast and grind to make bread. They also have beer. They lack wine but when they have it they drink it up, gathering for a family feast. At banquets they sit on a bench against the wall according to age and rank . . . When they assemble to drink they perform round dances to the flute or the horn, leaping in the air and crouching as they fall.*

CITÂNIA DE BRITEIROS

△ Braga

N

0 — 100 m

14

13

11

12

15

10

8

16

9

5

17   18

Parking

1

6   3

19

4

20

Entrance

1

2
Caretaker's
House

Parking

▽ Funerary Monument   Guimarães ▽

1 Area reserved for cattle
2 Early fountain
3 Cross and Christian cemetery
4 Circular house belonging to community
5 Chapel of S.Romão
6 House with helix
7 Houses reconstructed by Martins Sarmento
8 Small paved area
9 Inside wall
10 Second (of four) walls

11 Gateway
12 Gateway
13 Well for water provision
14 Single, isolated house outside inner walls
15 Water source (now defunct)
16 Houses with stone benches
17 Law courts (?), prisons (?)
18 Ingenious method of transporting water
19 House with various rooms
20 Cistern

Entrails aside – and they may have been literary licence – none of this seems far removed from the Minho and Trás-os-Montes of recent memory.

Getting there

The Braga **bus** leaves Guimarães every 30 minutes and stops in the pleasant spa town of Caldas das Taipas, from where you can get a local bus the 5km southwest to the *citânia* or take a taxi (1000$00). Alternatively, you might be able to catch one of the buses that run from Guimarães through Caldas das Taipas to Póvoa do Lanhoso (Mon–Fri 10.45am & 1.30pm, Sat 9am) – which pass through Santo Estevão (Briteiros), just over 1km southeast of the site itself. Leaving the *citânia*, hitching a lift from other visitors, either to Braga or Guimarães, should be fairly easy.

The excavations

The site **excavations** (daily 9am–6pm; 200$00) have revealed foundations of over a hundred and fifty **huts**, a couple of which have been rebuilt to give a sense of their scale and design. Most of them are circular, with porches for their fires, though some are rectangular, among them a larger building which may have been a prison or meeting house – it is labelled the *casa do tribunal*. There's also a clear network of paved streets and paths, two circuits of town walls, plus cisterns, stone guttering and a public fountain (the *fonte*). Most of these features are identifiable as you wander around the place, though the site is more evocative in its layout and extent than for any particular sights.

One feature not to be missed, however, is the **bathhouse** or cistern (a fair walk down the hill to the left of the settlement), with its geometrically patterned stone doorway. This was long believed to be a funerary chamber until recently when it was pointed out that, as much of the hill's runoff flowed into the site, it wouldn't have been the best place to put dead bodies. Similar remnants of construction, along with carved lintels from the huts and other finds from the *citânia*, are displayed at the Museu Martins Sarmento in Guimarães (see p.307). These indicate that the settlement was abandoned as late as 300 AD and – unlike Conímbriga, another Celtic site near Coimbra – show little Roman influence other than the presence of coins.

Braga

BRAGA, the turismo pamphlet claims, is the Portuguese Rome. This is clearly going a bit overboard – the Portuguese Canterbury might be more appropriate –though it neatly illustrates the city's ecclesiastical pretensions. One of the most ancient towns in Portugal, founded by the Romans in 27 BC, Braga was an important Visigothic bishopric before its occupation by the Moors. Reconquered early in the Christian campaigns, by the end of the eleventh century its archbishops were pressing for recognition as "Primate of the Spains", a title they disputed bitterly with archbishops of Toledo over the next six centuries.

The city is still Portugal's religious capital; look around and you'll soon become aware of the weight of church power, embodied by an archbishop's palace built on a truly presidential scale. At **Easter**, Braga is the scene of spectacular celebrations, with torchlit processions and hooded penitents – while its outlying districts boast a selection of important religious buildings and sanctuaries, including that of **Bom Jesus**, one of the country's most extravagant Baroque creations.

BRAGA

Youth Hostel (first left), Bom Jesus, Bracalândia & ⑦ △

Buses to Tibães ★

PR. MOUZINHO DE ALBUQUERQUE

Braga Shopping

Museu Nogueira da Silva

Igr. dos Congregados

PR. A. HERCULANO

AV. GEN. NORTON DE MATAS

RUA DOS CHÃOS

PR. DA REPÚBLICA

Buses to Sameiro

ⓐ Buses to Bom Jesus

AVENIDA DA LIBERDADE

Bus Station

IG. DO S. FRANCISCO

Torre de Menagem

ⓑ

Hospital de S. Marcos

Casa do Raio

LG. DE S. JOAO DO SOUTO

R. DO CASTELO

R. DO RAIO

R. DOS CAPELISTAS

PR. DO COMÉRCIO

Mercado

PRAÇA CONDE DE AGROLONDO

Buses to São Frutuoso ★

Jardim de Santa Bárbara

JUSTINO CRUZ

Capela dos Coimbras

R. F. SANCHES

Ig. de Sta. Cruz

Biblioteca

Sé

R. DO FORNO

Pio XII & Medina Museums

CAMPO DE S. TIAGO

Ig. do Pópulo

PR. DO MUNICÍPIO

LG. DE S. PAULO

Torre de S. Tiago

R. DE S. GONCALO

Palácio dos Biscaínhos

R. DOS BISCAÍNHOS

Câmara Municipal

Torre & Porta Nova

R. DA ROSTA

R. DOM AFONSO HENRIQUES

R. DOM AFONSO ENRIQUES

CAMPO DAS HORTAS

Capela de São Sebastião

RESTAURANTS & CAFÉS
ⓐ A Ceia
ⓑ Café Astória & Café Vianna
ⓒ A Brasileira
ⓓ Casa Pimenta
ⓔ Conde de Agrolongo
ⓕ Café Talisma
ⓖ Campo da Vinha
ⓗ De Bouro
ⓘ Prégão
ⓙ Restaurante Moçambicana
ⓚ Restaurante Inácio & O Alexandre

RUA ANDRADE CORVO

ACCOMMODATION
❶ Hotel Centro Comercial Avenida
❷ Hotel Francfort
❸ Grande Residencial Avenida
❹ Residencial dos Terceiros
❺ Residencial Inácio Filhos
❻ Hotel Largo da Estação
❼ Albergaria da Senhora-a-Branca

Train Station

0   100 m

▽ Barcelos

Braga also has a reputation as a bastion of reactionary politics. It was here, in 1926, that the military coup leading to Salazar's dictatorship was launched, while in the more recent past, after the 1974 Revolution, the Archbishop of Braga personally incited a mob to attack local Communist offices.

The city is an enjoyable place to stay and makes a decent base for touring the southern Minho. It seems recently, under the influence of Braga's mayor,

Mesquita Machado, to have acquired a new energy that reflects less of the church and more of its position as a fast-growing commercial centre. However, the appearance of a network of fast roads, underpasses and big, modern tower blocks in and around the ancient town has angered many residents who feel that the old centre of Braga (the phrase "as old as the Cathedral of Braga" is the Portuguese equivalent of "as old as the hills") should have been better preserved. The uneasy alliance of old and new is never more apparent than when driving – the confused one-way system does its best keep you in the town when you're trying to leave and to keep you out if you're trying to enter. But the most controversial action has been the digging up of the gardens around Praça da República and Avenida Central to make an underground car park. The excavations uncovered, and promptly destroyed, a number of Roman houses though, on the plus side, the new fountain that dominates the Praça seems to have found favour with most locals.

In addition to the **Semana Santa** (Holy Week) celebrations, the whole city is illuminated for the **Festas de São João** (June 23–24), which provides the excuse for ancient folk-dances, a fairground and general partying. The main **pilgrimage to Bom Jesus** (see p.318) takes place over Whitsun (six weeks after Easter). Braga also has a regular **Tuesday market**, held at the exhibition park in Avenida Pires Gonçalves, at the end of Avenida da Liberdade.

Arrival, information and accommodation

Braga is a fair-sized city, though the old town – an oval of streets radiating out from the Sé – is a compact area. From the **train station**, west of the centre, it's a fifteen-minute walk to the old town, reached down Rua Andrade Corvo. The main **bus station** is just over five minutes' walk from the centre; cross the small Praça Alexandre Herculano before following Rua dos Chãos into Praça da República. The **turismo**, at Avda. da Liberdade 1 (Mon–Fri 9am–7pm, Sat 9am–12.30pm & 2–5pm; ☎053/26 25 50), is housed in a wonderful Art Deco building on the corner of the main Praça da República; it offers an impressive large-scale map of the city. Finally, if you're heading for Gerês, it's worth calling in at the **national park headquarters** – a large, white house on Avenida António Macedo in the Quinta das Parretas suburb (Mon–Fri 9am–12.30pm & 2–5.30pm; ☎053/600 34 80, fax 61 31 69), a twenty-minute walk from the centre, where you can buy a useful map and booklet.

Accommodation

Braga has plenty of hotels and *pensões*, though it's unwise to turn up without a reservation during religious events and local festivals (see p.312). There's an excellent **youth hostel** at Rua de Santa Margarida 6 (☎ & fax 053/61 61 63; reception 9am–noon & 6pm–midnight), off Avenida Central, which is very popular in the summer with hikers. The **campsite**, *Camping Parque da Ponte* (☎053/27 33 55), is a two-kilometre walk from the centre, down Avenida da Liberdade and right next to the municipal swimming pool. Alternatively, if none of the Braga options appeals, you can stay at Bom Jesus (see p.318), 4km from the centre.

HOTELS AND PENSÕES

Residencial do Centro Comercial Avenida, Avda. Central 27–37 (☎053/27 57 22). On the second floor of the Centro Comercial. Big, well-furnished rooms with TV and baths. Handy for the cinema below. ④.

Hotel Francfort, Avda. Central 1–7 (☎053/26 26 48). Just across from Praça da República, this charming and friendly place dates from 1879 and is beginning to show its age – though the Art Deco dining room has recently been redecorated. Simple rooms, some with bath, make this one of the best bargains in town, although it can be noisy at the front. ②.

Grande Residencial Avenida, Avda. da Liberdade 738 (☎053/26 29 55). Fine old *pensão* in a great location. Once grand, it too is beginning to fade a little these days, but remains good value for money. Rooms at the rear are quieter than those overlooking the underpass and the Avenida. It fills quickly and reservations are advisable in summer. ④.

Residencial Inácio Filhos, Rua Francisco Sanches 42 (☎053/238 49). Quirky, central, spotless *residencial*, cluttered with antique typewriters, cash registers and telephones. Most rooms come with a bath. It's to the left off Rua do Souto, heading down from the turismo. ③.

Hotel João XXI, Avda. João XXI 849 (☎053/61 66 30, fax 61 66 31). Off Avenida da Liberdade, on the way out of town, this six-storey hotel has a top-floor restaurant and neat, en-suite rooms. Good value. ④.

Hotel Largo da Estaçao, Largo da Estaçao 13 (☎053/21 83 81, fax 768 10). According to the brochure, this modern block next to the train station will give you a "feeling of peace and eternity"; the Jacuzzis in some rooms may go some way to achieving this. ④.

Albergaria da Senhora-a-Branca, Largo da Senhora-a-Branca (☎053/26 99 38, fax 26 99 37). Facing a garden and attractively furnished, this is one of Braga's smarter choices – there's parking space too. It's about a kilometre from the centre; keep going out of town down Avenida Central. ④.

Residencial dos Terceiros, Rua dos Capelistas 85 (☎053/27 04 66, fax 27 57 67). A well situated *residencial*; all rooms have TVs and private bathrooms. ④.

The City

The obvious point from which to start exploring Braga is **Praça da República**, a busy arcaded square at the head of the old town. It's backed by the former town keep, the **Torre de Menagem**, while in the arcade itself you'll find two fine coffee houses which look out down the length of the long central square. From here, almost everything of interest is reached down narrow **Rua do Souto**, the main pedestrianized street which runs past the Sé. The street is also Braga's principal shopping district, though few commercial centres are like this one, where shoe shops rub shoulders with places selling candles, icons and other religious paraphernalia.

The Sé

The old town centre is dominated by the **Sé**, a rambling structure founded on the site of a Moorish mosque in 1070 after the Christian reconquest. The original Romanesque building encompasses Gothic, Renaissance and Baroque additions, though the cathedral's south doorway is a survival from the building's earliest incarnation, carved with rustic scenes from the legend of Reynard the Fox. The most striking element of the cathedral, however, is the intricate ornamentation of the roofline, commissioned by Braga's great Renaissance patron, Archbishop Diogo de Sousa, and executed by João de Castilho, later to become one of the architects of Lisbon's Mosteiro dos Jerónimos – the greatest of all Manueline buildings.

Inside, the cathedral complex is disorientating and, with the exception of the Baroque organs, somewhat disappointing: you enter through a courtyard fronting three Gothic chapels, a cloister and, most prominently, a ticket desk, where you can gain access to the **Museu de Arte Sacra** and Capela dos Reis (daily 8.30am–1pm & 2–6.30pm; 300$00). The museu is essentially the cathedral's treasury and one of the richest of such collections in Portugal, containing representative pieces from the tenth to the eighteenth century, but the items are unlabelled and confusingly arranged and it all manages to look a little dull. Eventually you emerge alongside the magnificent Baroque twin organs in the **Coro Alto**, supported by life-sized figures of satyrs, mermen and monstrous fish. From here you can gaze down into the cathedral proper – unexpectedly small and, when you descend, remarkably uninteresting.

Of the three outer chapels, the fourteenth-century **Capela dos Reis** (King's Chapel) is the most significant, built to house the tombs of the cathedral's founders, Henry of Burgundy, first Count of Portucale, and his wife Teresa – the parents of Afonso Henriques. Exposed beside them is the mummified body of Archbishop Lourenço, found "uncorrupt" when his tomb was opened in the seventeenth century. He had fought in the great victory over the Castilians at Aljubarrota in 1385, riding around bestowing indulgences on the ranks, and there sustained a scar on his cheek – which he himself is said to have carved proudly on his effigy.

The rest of the old town

Opposite the cathedral, across Rua do Souto, you'll find the old **Archbishop's Palace**, a great fortress-like building, which in medieval times actually covered a tenth of the city. Today it easily accommodates the municipal **library** (Mon–Fri 9am–noon & 2–8pm) and various faculties of the university, and inside you can inspect the ornate ceilings of the medieval reading-room and the Sala do Doctor Manuel Monteiro. Unless you have an academic interest, you're unlikely to find Braga's other **churches** very inspiring: most, like the cathedral, were stripped and modernized in the late-seventeenth and eighteenth centuries. Probably the most interesting, architecturally, is the small Renaissance **Capela dos Coimbras**, another of Archbishop de Sousa's commissions, on Largo Carlos Amarante, further east up Rua do Souto and off to the right.

On the whole, more inspiring are the numerous **mansions** from earlier ages, with their extravagant Baroque and Rococo facades. The **Câmara Municipal** and **Casa do Raio** are both by André Soares da Silva, the archbishop's architect, and look out, too, for the apostle-clad roofline of the **Hospital de São Marcos**, adjacent to the Casa do Raio. Best of all, though, is the mid-seventeenth-century **Palácio dos Biscaínhos** (Tues–Sun 9am–12.30pm & 2.30–5.30pm; 250$00), whose flagstoned ground floor was designed to allow carriages through to the stables. Nowadays, it houses a small museum of period furniture; the pretty landscaped gardens out back were again designed by Soares da Silva.

On the eastern side of town, in Campo de São Tiago, a former seminary has been turned into the **Museu Medina e Pio XII** (Tues–Sun 9am–12.30pm & 2.30–5.30pm; 250$00), which consists of two distinct collections: the Pio XII, housing dusty religious regalia, and the Medina, named after the Portuguese painter and donated on the understanding that it would be housed separately from any other exhibits. Save your energy for the collection of fonts and capitals gathered in a courtyard like standing stones, or for the small excavation of a first-century Roman water tank – and try persuading the guide to hold back on a few of the endless locked doors.

Eating, drinking, entertainment and nightlife

The city's most characterful locales are its nineteenth-century **cafés** – busy throughout the day and into the evening. In all of these you can get sandwiches and snacks, and often full meals, though Braga is also well endowed with tempting **restaurants**; a selection of the best is listed below.

For details of local **cultural events**, get hold of a copy of the daily *Correio do Minho* newspaper; the turismo generally has one on the counter and is happy to offer advice. In particular, don't miss out on tickets to anything that's on at the Teatro Circo (☎053/224 03), on Avenida da Liberdade, opposite the Centro Comercial Gold. In addition to theatrical performances, **films** are shown here, as well as at two cinemas in the Centro Comercial Avenida on Avenida Central.

During summer, there's popular entertainment in the **Bracalandia** theme park (10am–midnight; adults 1700$00, free for children under 4), 1km out of town on the Bom Jesus road (any bus to Bom Jesus will stop here), where you'll find the usual assortment of fairground rides, including a ferris wheel and helter-skelter.

There's a fair **club scene** in Braga with most of the action taking place at the bottom end of Avenida da Liberdade, around the *Hotel Turismo*. Venues change hands and names reasonably regularly but the current favourites include *84*, beneath the *Hotel Turismo*, the more fashionable *Pacha* in Praça Mayor, *Sardinha Biba* on Rua Araújo Carandá, and *Populum* on Praça Conde Agrolongo. All play a staple mix of Eighties' disco interspersed with a little salsa.

Cafés

Café Astória, Praça da República. By far the best of the old coffee houses, mahogany-panelled and with cut-glass windows, going very beautifully to seed. Occasional live music and invariably tasty snacks add to its attraction.

A Brasileira, Largo Barão de São Marinha. A superb old-style café, at the top of Rua do Souto, full of crusty old waiters dealing out brandies to a similarly aged clientele. In summer, you can sit in the open window-terrace – virtually on the street.

Café Talisma, Largo do Paço 8. Good for a lunchtime snack, with pleasant outdoor tables.

Café Vianna, Praça da República. One of Braga's best, a gorgeous Art Nouveau turn-of-the-century establishment in a prime location, with outside tables and good beef sandwiches (*pregos*).

Restaurants

De Bouro, Rua Santo António das Travessas 30–32. Tucked away in the old centre, this pleasantly restored Cistercian monastic lodging house claims to continue the monks' tradition of serving food to "enhance spiritual and contemplative heights". All the traditional favourites mixed with a few Minho specialities. Around 2500$00.

A Ceia, Rua do Raio 331 (☎053/26 39 32). This excellent restaurant is always crowded with locals, so arrive early, especially at weekends, or you'll have to eat at the bar. Spit-roast chickens and steaks are served up in enormous portions at moderate prices, and there's a fine wine list. Closed Mon.

Campo da Vinha, Praça Conselheiro Torres e Almeida. Cheap, popular and cheerful: try the *frango*.

Casa Pimenta, Praça Conde de Agrolongo 46. A consistently good bet, especially for the fine set menu at around 2500$00.

Conde de Agrolongo, Praça Conde de Agrolongo 74. Typical Portuguese restaurant serving good rice dishes for under 2000$00. Head for the large, cool basement rather than the deserted ground floor.

Restaurante Inácio, Campo das Hortas 14. Through the town gate at the end of Rua do Souto and off to the left, this is a pricey and rather cosmopolitan restaurant that doesn't limit itself to Portuguese dishes. It's in an old stone house with rustic decor – and costs around 2800$00 a head and upwards. Closed Mon. A close alternative in both food and location is *O Alexandre* at Campo das Hortas 10.

Restaurante Moçambicana, Rua Andrade Corvo 8. Inexpensive option just outside the town gate, at the end of Rua do Souto. As the name suggests, a spattering of African dishes feature on the menu.

Prégão, Largo da Praça Velha 18. Lovely place for a snack and a drink, or for lunch. Chatty barman, good wines and sangria.

Listings

Airline TAP (☎053/61 62 05).

Ambulance ☎053/26 24 70 or 26 40 77.

Books and newspapers There's an English-language bookshop, Bertrand Cruz, at Rua do Souto 133, and international newspapers are available from the Tabacaria, Rua Dr. Justina Cruz 149.

Exchange Caravela Travel on Rua Francisco Sanches (☎053/61 35 00) offers reasonable rates of exchange and doesn't usually charge commission.

Hospital São Marcos, Largo Carlos Amarante (☎053/601 3000).

Laundry 5-à-Sec on Largo da Santa Cruz, is the fastest.

Police ☎053/61 32 50.

Swimming pools Complexo Desportivo de Rodovia, at the junction between the main ring road and Avenida João Paulo II, and the municipal pool (July only) at the far end of Avenida da Liberdade (about 2km from the centre).

Taxis Central Rádio Táxi, ☎053/61 40 19.

Bom Jesus, São Frutuoso and Tibães

Having soaked up the religious atmosphere in Braga itself, there's a number of fascinating sites in its surroundings. The Baroque stairway and pilgrim church of **Bom Jesus do Monte**, 4km east of Braga, is a good enough reason to come in the first place and is within striking distance of the massive, if distinctly oppressive, **Santuário do Sameiro**; while a similar distance to the northwest is the Visigothic church of **São Frutuoso** and a ruined Benedictine monastery at **Tibães**.

Buses to Bom Jesus leave Braga every thirty minutes from Avenida da Liberdade, opposite the Pharmacia Cristal. Those for São Frutuoso leave every thirty minutes from Praça Conde de Agrolongo (they are marked "Sarrido"); get off at the hamlet of São Jerónimo Real, from where it is a five-minute walk. For Tibães, hourly buses, marked "Padim da Graça", leave from Avenida Central. However, for all of these destinations it's worth checking departure points with the turismo first as plans are underway to pedestrianize several streets and reroute traffic on some others. If you want to make things easy you could rent a **taxi** for a few hours (see above).

Bom Jesus do Monte and Santuário do Sameiro

BOM JESUS DO MONTE is one of Portugal's best-known images. Set in the woods high above the city, the glorious ornamental stairway of granite and white plaster is a monumental homage created by Braga's archbishop in the first decades of the eighteenth century. There is no particular reason for its presence – no miracle or vision – yet it remains the object of devoted pilgrimage, with many penitents climbing up on their knees. It is a very pleasant place to spend an afternoon or, best of all, early evening. There are wooded gardens, grottoes and miniature boating pools behind the church and, at the far end, just outside the park up the hill, horse rides.

Buses run the 3km from Braga to the foot of the stairway. At weekends they are packed, as seemingly half the city piles up to picnic in the woods. Most of the local families, armed with immense baskets of food, ride straight to the top in an hydraulic **funicular** (8am–8pm; every 30min and usually timed to coincide with buses; 100$00). If you resist the temptation to ride the funicular and make the climb up the stairway, Bom Jesus's simple allegory unfolds. Each of the **stairway** landings has a fountain: the first symbolizes the wounds of Christ, the next five the Senses, and the final three represent the Virtues. At each corner, too, are chapels with mouldering, larger-than-life wooden tableaux of the Life of Christ, arranged chronologically, leading to the Crucifixion at the altar of the church. As a design it's a triumph – one of the greatest of all Baroque architectural creations – and was later copied at Lamego.

In contrast, the domed **Santuário do Sameiro**, 2km up at the top of the hill, is impressive if only for its size and overtly ugly monumental stairway. It was built in the late nineteenth century but nowadays it bears the heavy mark of Salazar's regime – swathes of concrete and enormous statues. Like it or loathe it, it's a powerful monument to the power and authority of the Roman Catholic Church in Portugal, and the church is the second most venerated shrine in the country after

Fátima (see p.162). There's a very good, if somewhat pricey, restaurant here too, the *Restaurante Sameiro*.

Practicalities

There's a good range of **places to stay** up on the mount, which makes a peaceful and attractive place to spend the night. At the budget end of the scale, the friendly *Pensão Águeda* (☎053/67 65 21; ②), behind the park at the back of the church, has basic rooms (separate bathrooms), but breakfast is included and the downstairs restaurant is good. There are several more expensive options, one of the best being the *Casa dos Lagos* (☎053/67 67 38; ⑤), a lovely old Solares de Portugal house on the road just below the top of the steps, with a very hospitable owner and offering fantastic views. It also has three apartments for rent. The *Hotel do Parque* (☎053/67 65 48, fax 67 66 79; ⑥) is another excellent option – a superb nineteenth-century pile furnished in 1920s style. It's situated next to the church and faces the amusing concrete grotto.

There is a handful of lively **restaurants** on the Monte, which come into their own on Saturdays, when they're filled with parties from a constant stream of weddings. Note, however, that most open only at weekends during winter. A good option is *Restaurante Águeda*, beneath the *pensão* of the same name, which is cheap and serves large portions. *Restaurante Portico*, just beyond the bottom of the steps, is a traditional-style building serving quality food, but at high prices.

São Frutuoso and Tibães

Three and a half kilometres northwest of Braga is another worthwhile church excursion: to **São Frutuoso** (Tues–Sun 9am–noon & 2–5pm; keys are kept in a nearby house), built by the Visigoths in the seventh century, adapted by the Moors, and then restored to Christian worship after the reconquest. It's a gem of a church, flanked by an eighteenth-century chapel but unfortunately its previously tranquil setting has now been engulfed by Braga's ever-expanding suburbs. The approach is from São Jerónimo Real.

Half a kilometre beyond the São Frutuoso turning, to the left of the main road, a paved track leads to the monastery of **Tibães** (Tues–Sun 9am–noon & 2–5pm; free), formerly the grandest Benedictine establishment in the land. A vast and ruined hulk, its abandoned medieval buildings, cloisters and rambling gardens were once occupied by gypsy families. Now, however, it is state-owned, and extensive renovation is currently underway to convert it into a museum and *pousada*. It is an evocative place and you can look around the **church**, which has been maintained. There are guided tours of the monastic buildings (Tues–Sun 10am–12.30pm & 2–6pm; 300$00).

Póvoa do Lanhoso and the road to Gerês

Heading **east from Braga** along the N103 to the Peneda-Gerês park (see p.346), after 16km you come to the turning for **Póvoa do Lanhoso**, which lies 3km south of the main road. If you have transport, and time to spare, this small provincial town is worth a detour for its castle and Romanesque church. Another sight, revered in Portugal though perhaps of more peripheral interest to visitors, is the shrine of **Nossa Senhora da Abadia**, to the north of the Braga–Gerês road, turning off at Santa Maria do Bouro.

Póvoa do Lanhoso

As you walk around **PÓVOA DO LANHOSO** you'll come across the many work-shops (*ourivesarias*) that produce the gold jewellery for which the town is best known, much of it bearing clear traces of Moorish influence especially in the fili-gree work. This point of interest aside, the modern quarters of the town haven't much to offer, but they do lie sandwiched between two ancient sites. At the north-ern end of town (the approach from Braga), a steep mound – the Monte do Pilar – rises up to one of the smallest **castles** in Portugal and a scattering of chapels and picnic tables. In the fourteenth century, the lord of the shire was reported to have locked up his adulterous wife, her lover and their servants in the castle and ordered it to be burned; it was substantially rebuilt in the eighteenth century. The *Panorâmico* **restaurant** nearby keeps a set of keys and offers reasonable food and good views, if you can squeeze in between their regular parties of christen-ing and wedding guests. In the opposite direction, 3km out of town, the small church of **Fonte Areada** is a short walk from the main road (past the white stat-ue). The simple interior, characteristic of the Romanesque style, is in marked con-trast to the complications of the doorway with its centrepiece relief of a large sheep.

The town provides useful transport links to the east into Trás-os-Montes; south to the Douro, via Cabeceiras de Basto; and to Porto, via Famalição. Regular **buses** also connect with Braga, Caldas do Gerês and Guimarães. To pick up a bus to Montalegre and Chaves (5–7 daily), you have to walk the 3km north to Pinheiro, on the main N103.

Nossa Senhora da Abadia

With your own transport, an alternative route into Gerês is the minor N205-4 via Amares, after which the road becomes the N308. Some 13km along you come to **SANTA MARIA DO BOURO** (Bouro to the locals) – which has a shell of a monastery and a large Baroque church. Turning off from here, you arrive at the shrine of **Nossa Senhora da Abadia**. This is said to be the oldest sanctuary in Portugal and, like Bom Jesus, is a centre of pilgrimage: the main festival is on August 15. The focus of devotions is a twelfth-century wooden statue of the Virgin and Child, and while the church itself was largely rebuilt in the eigh-teenth century, outside are two earlier, elegant wings of monks' cells and, usu-ally, some market stalls. There's no accommodation here but you can **eat** well with the pilgrims at the sizeable *Restaurante Abadia*, which can seat up to 500 people.

Back on the main road at Bouro, there are **rooms** available at the *Residencial Santa Maria* (☎053/37 12 31; ②) and **food** can be had next door at the *Restaurante Cruzeiro*.

Barcelos

It's worth making plans to arrive in **BARCELOS**, 20km west of Braga, for the Thursday market, the **Feira de Barcelos** (see p.323). The great weekly event of

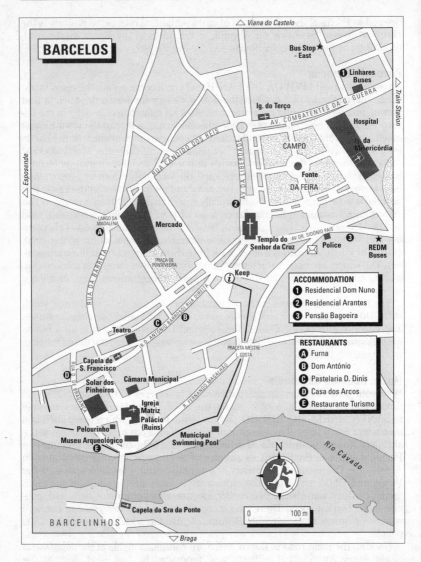

BARCELOS

△ Viana do Castelo

Bus Stop ★
- East

1 Linhares
Buses

△ Train Station

Ig. do Terço

AV. COMBATENTES DA G. GUERRA

Hospital

Ig. da
Misericórdia

RUA CANDIDO DOS REIS

CAMPO

AV. DA LIBERDADE

Fonte

DA FEIRA

△ Esposende

LARGO DA
MADALENA

Ⓐ

Mercado

PRAÇA DE
PONTÉVEDRA

2

Templo do
Senhor da Cruz

AV DR. SIDÓNIO PAIS

Police

3

REDM
Buses ★

RUA DA BARRETA

Keep

ⓘ

ACCOMMODATION

1 Residencial Dom Nuno
2 Residencial Arantes
3 Pensão Bagoeira

Teatro

Ⓒ Ⓑ

R. D. ANTÓNIO BARROSO RUA DIREITA

PRACETA MESTRE
L. COSTA

RESTAURANTS

Ⓐ Furna
Ⓑ Dom António
Ⓒ Pastelaria D. Dinis
Ⓓ Casa dos Arcos
Ⓔ Restaurante Turismo

Capela de
S. Francisco

Ⓓ

RUA D. DE BRAGANÇA

Solar dos
Pinheiros

Câmara Municipal

Igreja
Matriz
Palácio
(Ruins)

R. FERNANDO MAGALHÃO

Pelourinho

Museu Arqueológico

Ⓔ

Municipal
Swimming Pool

Rio Cávado

N

0   100 m

Capela da Sra da Ponte

BARCELINHOS

▽ Braga

southern Minho, it takes place from around dawn until late afternoon on the
Campo da República – also known as the Campo da Feira – a vast open square
that's about the first place you come upon walking into town from the train station. There are traditional events at other times of the year, too: the Festa das
Cruzes (Festival of the Crosses) on May 3, and a renowned **folklore festival**,
with live music, on the last Saturday of July.

The Feira de Barcelos

The Minho's markets are always interesting and the **Feira de Barcelos**, one of the largest in Europe, is both a spectacle and a crash course in the region's economics. There are stalls selling virtually everything – yokes for oxen, sausage skins and superb fresh bread, whole avenues of ducks and rabbits, as well as row upon row of village women squatting behind baskets of their own produce. The Minho is made up of hundreds of tiny, walled smallholdings, rarely more than allotments, and many people here are just selling a few vegetables, some fruit, eggs, and maybe even cheese from the family cow. It all looks unbelievably wholesome.

Apart from produce, clothes and kitchen equipment, the *feira*'s big feature is local **pottery and handicrafts**, for Barcelos is at the centre of Portugal's most active *artesanato* region. The pottery ware – *louça de Barcelos* – is characteristically brown with distinctive yellow dots, and has been highly acclaimed since the 1950s when the imaginative earthenware figurines of Rosa Ramalho (marked RR) began to be collected throughout Europe. In comparison most of today's pieces look as if they fell off a production line (some, indeed, are Far Eastern imports), but there are some good items to be found, sold at around half the price of outlets elsewhere. Look out for Rosa's daughter Julia's work, marked JR. Other crafts, too, are impressive – especially the basketwork, traditionally carved yokes (*cangas*) and wooden toys.

The Town

In addition to its festivities, the town has a few more permanent sights worth visiting. At the southwest corner of the Campo is Barcelos's most striking church, the **Templo do Nosso Senhor da Cruz**, fronted by a Baroque garden of obelisks and box-hedges. Built in 1708, its distinctive exterior, created by a simple contrast of dark granite and white plasterwork, was to be influential in the design of churches throughout the region. It's an odd addition to the old part of town, though, which is essentially Gothic and medieval in character – a small, hillside web of streets spun above the Rio Cávado. Heading south from the Campo, you'll soon end up at the **river**, as beautiful as any in the Minho, overhung by willows, fronted by gardens and spanned by a fifteenth-century bridge. Just above it loom the ruins of the **Paço dos Condes**, the former Palace of the Counts of Barcelos, wrecked by the Great Earthquake of 1755 and now providing a shell for the **Museu Arqueólogico** (daily: summer 9am–7pm; winter 9am–5.30pm; free). This is a miscellaneous outdoor assembly of stone crosses, including a sixteenth-century crucifix locally famed for its connection with the legend of *Senhor do Galo* – the Gentleman of the Cock (see box on p.324); just outside the museum, in the riverside gardens, stands the town's Gothic **pelourinho**. If you wanted to pursue an interest in the local ceramic wares, you could visit the **Museu de Olaria** (Tues–Sun 10am–12.30pm & 2–6pm; 200$00), in the Casa dos Mendanhas on Rua Conego Joaquim, 300m from the archeological museum.

Practicalities

The **train station** is at the drab eastern edge of town; follow the street straight ahead for fifteen minutes and you'll eventually emerge on the Campo da Feira.

THE BARCELOS COCK

A stone cross in Barcelos's archeological museum depicts the legend of the **Galo de Barcelos**, a miraculous roast fowl which rose from the dinner table of a judge to crow the innocence of a Galician pilgrim he had wrongly condemned to the gallows. The pilgrim, having wisely proclaimed "I'll be hanged if that cock don't crow", got his reprieve. It's a story that occurs in different forms in northern Spain, but the Barcelos rooster has taken a special hold on popular folk art, becoming a national symbol of Portugal and now, usually in pottery form, the ubiquitous emblem of Portuguese tourism.

There are two main **bus** companies: Linhares, Avda. dos Combatentes da Grande Guerra 46, for services within Minho and to Vila do Conde and Póvoa do Varzim; and REDM, Avda. Dr. Sidónio Pais, opposite the Campo, for main towns in the region and beyond (also agents for Rede Express, Renex, and Internorte for long-distance services). Both run frequent services to Braga. The **turismo** (Mon–Wed & Fri 9am–12.30pm & 2.30–6pm, Thurs 9am–6pm, Sat & Sun 9.30am–12.30pm & 2.30–4pm; ☎053/81 18 82) is housed in the old castle keep, the Torre da Porta Nova, on Largo da Porta Nova. In addition to its information counter, it features a permanent display and sale of Barcelos handicrafts. The river is too polluted for **swimming** but there are municipal pools just upstream from the bridge.

Accommodation

Residencial Arantes, Avda. da Liberdade 35 (☎053/81 13 26). An eccentric mix of rooms; avoid the cell-like ones overlooking a central well. It's on the west side of the Campo, above a good *pastelaria*. Cheaper rooms without facilities are available. Breakfast included. ③.

Pensão Bagoeira, Avda. Dr Sidónio Pais 57 (☎053/81 12 36, fax 82 45 88). Located on the southeastern corner of Campo da Feira, this is a real old market inn, with a handful of spotless rooms (all with bathrooms); phone ahead if you want to secure one on a Wednesday or Thursday night. ③.

Casa do Monte, Abade de Neiva (☎053/81 15 19). Solares de Portugal country house with large gardens, 3km west of Barcelos on the N103 (Viana do Castelo road). The verandah offers panoramic views of Barcelos and the valley. ⑤.

Residencial Dom Nuno, Avda. Dom Nuno Álvares Pereira 76 (☎053/81 28 10, fax 81 63 36). A fancy but characterless place, off to the right as you approach Campo da Feira from the station. All rooms have bath, telephone and TV. ④.

Eating and drinking

There is a row of three bargain-basement café-restaurants around the corner from the Campo, in the alleyway opposite the Templo; the central one is best value. Other options are:

Bagoeira, Avda. Dr. Sidónio Pais 57. Old market inn full of atmosphere – be sure to have lunch here on market day, when a constant stream of stallholders bring in pots and pans for takeaways. It's open in the evening, too, and meals – mostly stews, steaks and grills – are excellent value.

Casa dos Arcos, Rua Duques de Bragança, just north of the *Solar dos Pinheiros*. In a traditional old stone house, with a menu that often features suckling pig and *arroz de frango*. Closed Mon.

Dom António, Rua Dom António Barroso. Caters for weddings and groups, who enjoy grilled dishes and the odd wild boar.

Pastelaria D. Dinis, Rua Dom António Barroso 100. Pleasant pastry shop with outdoor tables, serving very sweet egg-and-peanut sweets among other goodies.

Furna, Largo da Madalena. You'll see the queues for takeaway chickens stretching out of the door, which gives a good clue as to its best dish. Closed Mon.

Restaurante Turismo, at the foot of Rua Duques de Bragança. This bar (despite its name), overlooking the river, is the perfect place for a beer while catching the last of the day's sun.

THE COSTA VERDE

Spurred by the flow of foreign currency into the Algarve, the Portuguese Tourist Board is energetically trying to promote the Minho's almost continuous line of sandy beaches as the **Costa Verde** – a zone which seems to stretch inland along the north bank of the River Minho itself. So far, the seaside element of the campaign hasn't quite worked, for despite the enticing promises of "unpolluted beaches with a high iodine content . . . health for the whole year", Costa Verde is green for a reason. It can be drizzly and overcast right through summer and the Atlantic here is never too warm. Still, if that doesn't bother you and the weather's looking good there's amazing potential; you can pick almost any road, any village, and find a great **beach** virtually to yourself.

The coast between Póvoa de Varzim and Caminha is virtually one long beach, with the road running, for the most part, 1km or so inland. There are at least four **buses** a day in each direction, most using the resort of **Viana do Castelo** – very much the main event on this coast – as an axis. In addition, there are regular **trains** from Porto, which cut inland to Barcelos before heading back to the coast at Viana do Costelo, from where they run up the coast to Caminha.

North from Porto to Viana

The coast immediately **north of Porto**, as far as Póvoa de Varzim, is accessible by train and covered on pp.279–282. Beyond Póvoa, the train doesn't touch the coast again until Viana do Castelo, but there are local (if slow) **buses**: six daily ones wend from Porto to Viana via Póvoa, Ofir, Esposende and Mar. The route follows the old pilgrim's route to Santiago in Spain. Much of this part of the Costa Verde is protected from development by law: 18km of coastline between Apúlia and the mouth of the River Neiva is designated a protected area.

Esposende and Ofir

The easiest place to reach by public transport is **ESPOSENDE**, 20km north of Póvoa. It's a rather drab sprawl of buildings, with a few modern villas, a modern swimming pool complex and the ruins of an eighteenth-century fort now used as a lighthouse. The town itself is actually sited inland on the estuary of the Rio Cávado, with the nearest beaches 3km west, or else 6km by road across the estuary at **OFIR,** where three ugly high-rise buildings have been built on what was once a beautiful spit of pine-backed sand. If you are driving, Ofir could be a good place to stop and swim. If you want **to stay** your only options are the *Hotel Sopete Ofir* (☎058/98 13 83, fax 98 18 71; ⑤), Avda. Raul de Sousa Martins, and the more characterful *Estalagem Parque do Rio* (☎058/98 15 21, fax 98 15 24; ⑥), Pinhal do Ofir; there is also a decent **campsite** at nearby Fão (☎058/98 17 77).

Mar

North of Ofir, you probably won't see another tourist all the way to the little fishing village of **MAR** (or, more fully, São Bartolomeu do Mar), around 5km inland from one of the best stretches of the Costa Verde. It's just 15km south of Viana do Castelo, but there is still refreshingly little to the place: just a church, shop and café (with a few **rooms** to let), and good unofficial camping amid the pines. As well as fishing, the local economy revolves around gathering **seaweed**. Traditionally, whole families harvest it on the beach using huge shrimping nets, which are then hauled across the sands by beautiful wooden carts pulled by oxen. Although the methods are changing and tractors are supplanting beasts, the seaweed is still stacked at the edge of the village to dry before being spread as fertilizer on the coastal fields.

If you're here on August 24, you'll catch the **romaria** that takes place at the end of the Festas de São Bartolomeu. The festivities draw thousands of people from the area, many of them families with sick children who come in the hope that they will be cured by taking the traditional Banho Santo – a bizarre ritual in which the child circles the church three times with a black cockerel tied to his or her head before being thrown into the ocean three times by an attendant.

Viana do Castelo

VIANA DO CASTELO is the one town in the Minho you could describe as a resort – and it's all the more appealing for it. A lively, attractive place, it has a historic old centre, above-average restaurants and, some distance from the town itself, one of the best beaches in the north. It's also beautifully positioned, spread along the north bank of the Lima estuary and shaped by the thick wooded hill of Monte de Santa Luzia, which is strewn with Celtic remains. If this wasn't enough of an incentive to come, Viana's **romaria** at the end of August (see p.328) is the biggest and most exciting festival in the Minho.

The Town

Viana has long been a prosperous seafaring town. It produced some of the greatest colonists of the "discoveries" under Dom Manuel and, in the eighteenth century, was the first centre for the shipment of port wine to England. Many of the buildings reflect these times – unusually for the north, you'll notice Manueline mouldings around the doors and windows of Viana's mansions.

At the heart of Viana's old town is the distinctive **Praça da República**, a wonderful square enclosed by an elegant ensemble of buildings. You'll see copies of its showpiece Renaissance fountain in towns throughout the Minho, but few structures as curious as the old **Misericórdia** (almshouse) that lines one side of the square. Built in 1589, this is one of the most original and successful buildings of the Portuguese Renaissance, its upper storeys supported by deliberately archaic caryatids. The adjacent sixteenth-century **Câmara Municipal** has been brightly restored, and stands foursquare above a medieval arcade, while just off the square is the **Igreja Matriz**, Viana's parish church, which retains a Gothic door of some interest.

The **Museu Municipal** (Tues–Sun 9am–noon & 2–5pm; 200$00) adds further to these impressions of Viana's sixteenth- to nineteenth-century opulence; it is contained within an eighteenth-century palace and houses a notable collection of

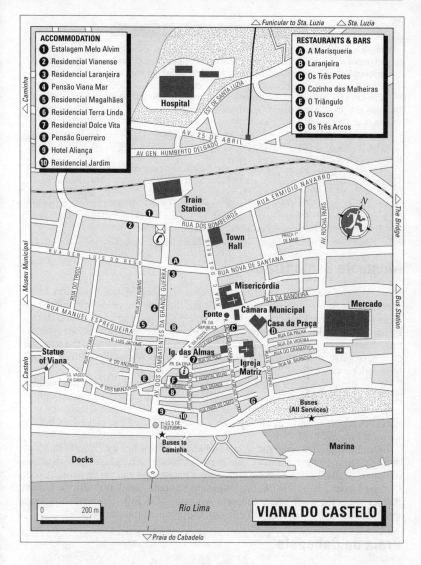

△ Funicular to Sta. Luzia   △ Sta. Luzia

ACCOMMODATION
❶ Estalagem Melo Alvim
❷ Residencial Vianense
❸ Residencial Laranjeira
❹ Pensão Viana Mar
❺ Residencial Magalhães
❻ Residencial Terra Linda
❼ Residencial Dolce Vita
❽ Pensão Guerreiro
❾ Hotel Aliança
❿ Residencial Jardim

RESTAURANTS & BARS
Ⓐ A Marisqueria
Ⓑ Laranjeira
Ⓒ Os Três Potes
Ⓓ Cozinha das Malheiras
Ⓔ O Triângulo
Ⓕ O Vasco
Ⓖ Os Três Arcos

Hospital

Train Station

Town Hall

Misericórdia

Fonte

Câmara Municipal

Casa da Praça

Ig. das Almas

Igreja Matriz

Mercado

Statue of Viana

Buses (All Services)

Buses to Caminha

Docks

Marina

Rio Lima

VIANA DO CASTELO

0   200 m

▽ Praia do Cabadelo

ceramics and furniture. It stands near the end of Rua Manuel Espregueira, ten minutes' walk from the square, on the far side of the main Avenida dos Combatentes da Grande Guerra.

If you continue past the museum, you'll eventually reach the old **Castelo** by the sea, in an area known as the Campo do Castelo. Outside the walls, on Fridays, Viana's **market** takes place; it's much smaller than the famous one at Barcelos but attracts many of the same stallholders.

THE VIANA ROMARIA

Viana's main *romaria*, dedicated to **Nossa Senhora da Agonía** – Our Lady of Sorrows – takes place for three days around the weekend nearest to August 20. A combination of carnival and fair, and fulfilling an important business function for the local communities, it's a great time to be in town.

Events kick off with an impressive **religious parade** on the Friday. But the best day is probably **Saturday**, when there's a massive parade of floats with every village in the region providing an example of a local craft or pursuit: a marvellous display of incongruities, with threshers pounding away in traditional dress while being pulled by a new Lamborghini tractor. If you want a seat in the stands, get a ticket well in advance.

On each of the three days there are lunchtime **processions** with *gigantones* (carnival giants), folk-dancing, remarkably loud drum bands, pipe bands and, needless to say, concerted drinking. The blessing of the fishing boats on Monday morning is quite moving – women in the fishing quarter decorate their streets with pictures in coloured sawdust on religious and quotidian themes. And there are nightly **firework displays** too, of immense brilliance and noise.

Monte de Santa Luzia

Wherever you stand in Viana, the modern basilica atop **Monte de Santa Luzia** makes its presence felt. It's a great walk up, through the pines and eucalyptus trees (take the short cut over the railway tracks), or you can be hauled to the top by an old **funicular** (April–Sept daily; rest of year weekends and public holidays only; hourly 9am–6pm; 100$00). This starts its run from just behind the train station: to reach it, walk through the station and cross the tracks. En route, there are tremendous views down the coast and along the River Lima.

At the summit, there's a café and plenty of wooded walks. While the **basilica** itself is of little interest, look for the side entrance (marked Zimbório), where steps climb right through the building and out on top of the dome itself. It's very narrow, very steep and – at the top – very scary if the wind has picked up, but the views are magnificent.

Behind the basilica, amid the woods and just below the luxury *Pousada do Monte de Santa Luzia*, lie the ruins of a Celto-Iberian **citânia**, which include the foundations of dozens of small, circular stone huts, a thick village wall and partly paved streets. Occupied from around 500 BC, the settlement was only abandoned with the Roman pacification of the north under Emperor Augustus (c.26 BC). The ruins have been fenced off but there should be access from the approach road to the hotel.

Praia do Cabedelo

Viana's town beach, **Praia do Cabedelo**, lies across the river, reached by a **ferry**, which leaves from the harbourside at the southern end of the main avenue (daily 8.45am–around 7pm; every 30min–1hr; 200$00 return); it's a five-minute crossing. Road access from town to beach is over the bridge, east of the centre, a route served by frequent buses (May to mid-Sept).

Given sun, the beach is more or less perfect – a low, curving bay with good (but not wild) breakers and a real horizon-stretching expanse of sand; surfboards, windsurfing equipment and mountain bikes can be rented from Omni Surf Shop, Rua do Poço 38. There's a bar, *Aquarío*, at the windsurf school, and a couple of others close to where the ferry docks, but beyond this there is nowhere to buy food or drink, so take a picnic. From Viana, the beach extends northwards, virtually unbroken, to the Spanish border at Caminha, and south to Póvoa de Varzim. For the energetic, either of these routes makes a memorable and enjoyable hike, and for details of the northern route, see p.332.

Practicalities

The **train station** is at the north end of the main Avenida dos Combatentes da Grande Guerra, which runs right through the town and down to the river at Largo 5 de Outubro. There's a seasonal **turismo** stand at the station (June 20–Aug 20 Mon–Sat 9am–6pm, Sun 9.30am–12.30pm), but the main office (Mon–Sat 9am–12.30pm & 2.30–6pm; Sun 9.30am–12.30pm; ☎058/82 26 20) is in the centre: walk down the avenue and look for the sign pointing to the left; it's in Rua do Hospital Velho, off Praça da Erva. The building dates from 1468 and was first used by pilgrims travelling to Santiago de Compostela in Spain; later it became a hospital.

The **bus station** is at the top end of Rua da Bandeira, twenty minutes' walk northeast of the centre. Outside *festa* time, you might find it easier to catch services from more central bus stops along Avenida Combatentes da Grande Guerra, at the southern end of Largo 5 de Outubro, or further east by the marina.

Accommodation

Pensões – mostly ranged down and off the main avenue – are easy enough to find, although in summer, and particularly during the *romaria*, private **rooms** offer the best deals; ask at the turismo or look for signs in the windows of houses. During the actual festival, you can expect to pay between 5000$00 and 8000$00 for a private room, though they're more like 3000$00 for the rest of the year. You might also ask the turismo about accommodation at **farms** and **manor houses** in the surrounding villages, an ideal way to get to know the countryside, provided you have transport; a couple are listed below.

The town's **campsite** (☎058/32 21 67, fax 32 19 46; closed Jan), run by Orbitur, is overcrowded in summer and overpriced for what you get, but it does at least have the advantage of being at the Praia do Cabedelo, in a location shaded by pine trees. The summer bus (May to mid-Sept) to the beach passes it, or you can take the ferry across the river and walk from there.

Hotel Aliança, Avda. dos Combatentes da Grande Guerra (☎058/82 94 98, fax 252 99). Eighteenth-century building that hasn't entirely lost its period charm. ⑤.

Casa Grande da Bandeira, Largo das Carmelitas 488 (☎058/82 31 69). Off Rua da Bandeira, on a little square on the way out of town, this charming seventeenth-century Solares de Portugal house has a small garden and only three rooms – book ahead. ⑤.

Residencial Dolce Vita, Rua do Poço 44 (☎058/248 60). Excellent value, spacious rooms, with shared bathroom, above a good pizza restaurant; breakfast included. Follow the signs for the turismo. ③.

Pensão Guerreiro, Rua Grande 14 (☎058/82 20 99). Down-at-heel place at the bottom of the main avenue, all rooms with shared bathrooms. It's friendly, though, and the restaurant (see below) is good. ②.

Residencial Jardim, Largo 5 de Outubro 68 (☎058/82 89 15, fax 82 89 17). Overlooking the river, at the bottom of town, this has spotless, well-furnished rooms with bath and TV. Rooms with a balcony have good views; excellent value, especially considering the huge breakfasts. ④.

Residencial Laranjeira, Rua General Luís do Rego 45 (☎058/82 22 61, fax 82 19 02). A reasonable choice, just off the main avenue, with small, but pleasant rooms, all with bath. Friendly, fresh and comfortable, and with breakfast included in the price. ④.

Residencial Magalhães, Rua Manuel Espregueira 62 (☎058/82 32 93). Twin and triple rooms, with or without bath, furnished in the best Minho tradition, with dark, carved headboards on the beds. Avoid the rooms at the back which can be noisy. ③.

Estalagem Melo Alvim, Avda. Conde da Carreira 28 (☎058/810 82 00, fax 810 82 20). Sixteenth-century *solar* superbly renovated in a modern minimalist style. Excellent service and a good restaurant too. ⑥.

Pousada do Monte de Santa Luzia, Monte de Santa Luzia (☎058/82 88 89, fax 79 56 04). Showpiece *pousada* at the top of the hill above town, refurbished in Art Deco style. It's the priciest place in town, and the most comfortable and best equipped, though the restaurant is disappointing. ⑥.

Quinta do Paço d'Anha, Vila Nova de Anha (☎058/32 24 59, fax 32 39 04). A Solares de Portugal property 3km south of town on the N3 road to Esposende. The house is on an estate that produces and bottles its own wine; there are four apartments with kitchenette. ⑥.

Residencial Terra Linda, Rua Luís Jácome 11–15 (☎058/82 89 81). Average and adequate, but tries hard to please. Rooms without bath are cheaper. ②.

Pensão Viana Mar, Avda. dos Combatentes da Grande Guerra 215 (☎ & fax 058/82 89 62). Another reasonably good place, with warm rooms in winter, and a sunken bar. More expensive rooms have baths; the summer overflow of guests is accommodated in two nearby annexes. ②.

Residencial Vianense, Avda. Conde da Carreira 79 (☎058/82 31 18). Comfortable, clean and close to the train station. There's a decent restaurant here, too. Breakfast included. ③.

Eating

There's a wide choice of places to eat in town, as you might expect from a busy resort. Some are lunchtime workers' cafés, while there's also a full range of tourist **restaurants**, many of which serve extremely good food since they cater mostly for demanding Portuguese visitors rather than foreigners, but the service can be surprisingly slow and indifferent. There are a number of cheap **cafés** and restaurants with outdoor tables in Rua Prior do Crato, one road back from the river. Several of the *pensões* also incorporate restaurants, open to non-residents; a couple of them are definitely worth considering. For general provisions, there is a permanent **market** at the eastern end of town, on Rua Martim Velho.

Casa d'Armas, Largo 5 de Outubro. A quality restaurant in a lovely building, but high prices.

Cozinha das Malheiras, Rua Gago Coutinho. Top-quality food, service – and prices.

Pensão Guerreiro, Rua Grande 14. The first-floor restaurant deceives with its unsubtle pictorial tourist menu; the food is actually very good and fairly inexpensive, and features a bumper serving of *porco à alentejana*. The *cabrito* (goat) is good too. Closed Thurs.

Laranjeira, Rua Manuel Espregueira 24. The restaurant here (on a different road from the *residencial*) receives varying reports, partly because it's always busy and sometimes a bit slapdash. It's worth chancing, though, for reasonably priced Portuguese meals.

A Marisqueria, Rua General Luís do Rego 36. Carefully cooked, generous dishes – but service can be shoddy.

Neiva Mar, Largo Infante D. Henriques 1. Great for seafood, off the road on the seafront near the castle.

Os Três Arcos, Largo João Tomás da Costa 25. Facing the Jardim Marginal, this is perhaps the best restaurant in town, with excellent food, a full list of *vinhos verdes*, and a bar where you can eat much more cheaply from the same menu – it's mostly seafood, but the turkey is good. If you want a table, call in earlier to book. Closed Mon.

Os Três Potes, Beco dos Fornos 7. Incredibly popular in high season, with national costumes and music at weekends. Good traditional food, but relatively pricey, with full meals running to at least 3000$00. Again, book ahead in summer. Closed Mon.

O Triângulo, Rua dos Manjovos 14. Quiet, pleasant seafood and snack joint.

O Vasco, Rua Grande. Simple, tasty Portuguese dishes at reasonable prices. Closed Sun.

Viana's Restaurante, Rua Frei Bartolomeu dos Martires 179. The place to pursue an interest in *bacalhau* dishes – simply superb. It's off Avenida Campo do Castelo.

Drinking, nightlife and entertainment

Romaria time aside, there's not an awful lot going on after dark in Viana. But a couple of **cafés** at the bottom of the main avenue are good places for a beer or late-night coffee, and if you're feeling energetic, a number of clubs are worth a try.

For **cultural** events, consult the *Agenda Cultural*, a monthly diary issued by the Câmara Municipal; the turismo should have a copy, and can also provide information on regional events. There is one **cinema** in Viana, the Verde Viana (Praça 1° de Maio); and check the output of the Teatro do Noroeste **theatre company**, based at the Teatro Municipal Sá de Miranda, on Rua Major Xavier da Costa (☎058/82 26 44).

Pastelaria Brasileira, Rua Sacadura Cabral. Nearly 100 years old, this café-cum-pastry shop is good for a stand-up coffee.

Girassol Café, Jardim Marginal. A lovely spot for a *bica*; though it closes at 7pm.

Glamour, Rua da Bandeira 177–183. New, very stylish and trendy with fittingly fashionable soul, blues and salsa.

Pastelaria Paris, Avda. dos Combatentes da Grande Guerra. Great cakes, a pool room and decent toilets for a change!

Disco-Pub-Clube-Viana Sol, Rua dos Manjovos, off Largo Vasco da Gama by *Hotel Viana Sol*. A very youthful crowd packs into this place in summer. Open from the afternoon until 3am; 4am on Saturday nights.

Listings

Banks Main banks are on Praça da República and along the main avenue.

Boat trips Departures from the pier at the bottom of the avenue for trips up the Rio Lima; prices are negotiable but expect to pay around 3000$00 per person.

Books and newspapers English-language books are available at Livraria Bertrand, Rua Sacadura Cabral, and international newspapers are sold in the newsagents on the corner of Praça da República.

Car rental Avis, Rua do Gontim (☎058/818 05 40); Hertz, Avda. Conde da Carreira (☎058/82 22 50).

Hospital Avda. 25 de Abril (☎058/82 90 81).

Pharmacy Nelsina, Praça da República; Central, Rua Manuel Espregueira. The turismo has details of late-night openings.

Police Headquarters at Rua de Aveiro (☎058/82 20 22).

Post office Opposite the train station on Avda. dos Combatentes; you can make international telephone calls from here, too.

Swimming pool The municipal pool is at Avda. 28 de Setembro and you may also be able to use the one at *Hotel do Parque*, Parque da Galiza, east of the waterfront, beyond the train line.

Taxis Available from ranks along Avda. dos Combatentes da Grande Guerra.

Viana to Moledo

North of Viana the train line follows the coast all the way to Caminha. Two trains
a day, in both directions, stop at all the villages en route – notably at Carreço,
Afife, Gelfa, Vila Praia de Âncora and Moledo do Minho – offering easy access to
a sequence of largely deserted beaches. Buses cover the same route with thirteen
services daily (Mon–Fri) and five daily at weekends. It is possible to **walk** the
same route, covering the whole stretch in a couple of days, camping overnight
among the sheltered dunes at Afife, 10km north of Viana. Be warned, though, that
persistent smuggling takes place on these isolated beaches, which can make the
area a dangerous place to be at times, particularly if the local police are pursuing
the villains unloading drugs from Spain on the sands.

Carreço, Afife and Gelfa

The small village of **CARREÇO** lies a couple of kilometres east of its beach,
where there's a café-bar, toilets and showers. **AFIFE**, another 2km further north,
is also a good goal with a fort, several cafés and a casino. The modern *Residencial
Compostela* (☎058/98 15 90, fax 98 12 44; ④) is on the main road just north of the
turning to the beach; it also has a restaurant, although the two on the beach are
preferable. If you're looking for a more dramatic place to stay, *Casa do Penedo*
(☎058/98 14 74; ④) is a typical Minho home, an attractive stone property with a
garden, 1km south of the station, up a hillside with sea views. The dunes – and a
particularly wonderful expanse of beach – are fifteen to twenty minutes' walk
from the village, the least frequented parts being to the south.

At **GELFA**, between Afife and Vila Praia de Âncora, there's a **campsite** in the
pine woods (☎058/91 15 37; mid-March to mid-Oct daily; rest of year weekends
only), but it's on the inland side of the train station and hence some distance from
the beach.

Vila Praia de Âncora

Six kilometres up the coast from Afife, the next major stop on the train line is
VILA PRAIA DE ÂNCORA. This is larger than the previous settlements – a real
resort – and popular with the locals at weekends and in summer. The beach,
which is right alongside the train line, is again superb, sheltered by hills and drifting back into a beautiful river estuary, where you can swim enjoyably even when
the Atlantic breezes are blowing towels around the sands. For good measure
there are two **forts** guarding the bay: the Fortim de Cão, south of the estuary, and
the better-preserved Forte de Lagarteira, recently restored, to the north by the
little fishing harbour.

The **train station** for Vila Praia is called Âncora-Praia, and is the only station
between Viana do Castelo and Caminha at which express trains stop. Finding
accommodation for a few days here shouldn't be hard. **Private rooms** (②–③)
can be arranged through the **turismo** (July–Sept Mon–Sat 9am–7pm &
9.30–11.30pm, Sun 9am–noon; Oct–June Mon–Sat 9.30am–12.30pm & 2.30–6pm,
Sun 9.30am–12.30pm; ☎058/91 13 84), which is located at the southern end of the
seafront. Other choices include *Hotel Meira*, at Rua 5 de Outubro 56 (☎058/91 11
11, fax 91 14 89; ⑥) and the more reasonably priced *Albergaria Quim Barreiros*,
on the seafront behind the train station (☎058/95 12 18, fax 95 12 20; ⑤). There's
a **campsite**, the *Parque de Campismo do Paço* (☎058/91 26 97), on the south bank

of the Rio Âncora, and also unofficial **camping** on the beach, by the Fortim de Cão.

Restaurants are plentiful, as is fresh fish. *Restaurante Fonte Nova*, along Rua Miguel Bombarda from the church, and the *Restaurante Central*, opposite the train station, are both good, serving meals for around 2000$00; while *Restaurante Mar Gelfa* (open July–Sept), twenty minutes' walk south down the beach, is recommended for both food (try the lamprey) and sunsets.

Moledo do Minho

North of Vila Praia de Âncora, **MOLEDO DO MINHO** is the train traveller's last chance to swim in the sea. Very much in the same mould as Vila Praia, it too has a fort – this time half-ruined, guarding the river from a long, sandy spit – and is predominantly a Portuguese family resort, with a reputation for attracting the nouveaux riches. If you're heading for Caminha, Valença, or even Spain, you could easily stop off here, wander down to the beach, and catch the next train. If you want **to stay**, the *Pensão Ideal*, Rua Eng. Sousa Rego 125 (☎058/72 15 05, fax 72 15 18; ④), might tempt you with its convenient location next to the train station and its well-equipped rooms; alternatively, the seafront **turismo** (Mon–Fri 9.30am–12.30pm & 2.30–6pm) might be able to help you find a room. You can **eat** at the good *Restaurante O Lagar* on the seafront, where you'll also find a number of bars serving snacks.

ALONG THE RIO MINHO

At Moledo, the train line finally leaves the coast to follow the south bank of the **Rio Minho**, which meanders northeastwards forming the country's border with Spain. **Caminha** is the first river town, a pleasant stopover, either for a night or for a meal between trains. Beyond here, several small fortified towns guard the Portuguese side of the river, with the Minho train line coming to a halt in perhaps the best of the lot, **Valença do Minho**. This is also the site of a splendid weekly market and a major crossing-point into Spain. However, the best section of the river route is from Valença east to **Monção** and **Melgaço**, which you can reach only by bus. Both towns are also minor border crossings, with buses onwards from the Spanish side.

Caminha

Resembling a smaller version of Viana do Castelo, **CAMINHA** is a quiet river port with a few reminders of better days. These are principally in the main square, Praça Conselheiro Silva Torres (known locally as Largo Terreiro), which sports a battlemented town hall, a Renaissance clock tower and a large fountain. Caminha's most distinguished building, though, is the **Igreja Matriz**, a couple of minutes' walk from the main square towards the river; take the street through the arch by the clock tower, past the **turismo** (Mon–Sat 9.30am–12.30pm & 2.30–6pm; ☎058/92 19 52). The church was built towards the end of the fifteenth century, when the town was reputed to rival Porto in trade, and it still stands within part of the old city walls. Try and find someone with a key, for it has a magnificent inlaid *artesanato* ceiling – a rare burst of Moorish inspiration in the north.

Note also the figures carved on the two Renaissance doorways, one on the north side giving the finger to Spain across the river!

A couple of kilometres south of town, the island of **Fortaleza da Ínsua** makes an enjoyable trip – local fishermen run trips across on Sundays from the spit of sand at Foz do Minho, on the river side of its fine beach. If you want to arrange something during the week (for the next morning), ask in the *Café Valadares* for directions to António Garrafão's house. He will go only if there is a reasonably large – or affluent – group gathered.

Practicalities

The town's best **accommodation** is in the new *Hotel Porta do Sol* (☎058/72 23 40, fax 72 23 47; ⑥), on Avenida Marginal at the southern entrance to town – a four-star resort with pools and tennis courts. Otherwise, there are three **pensões** in the centre of town: the *Residencial Arca Nova* (☎058/72 15 90, fax 72 15 91; ④), near the train station in Largo Sidónio Pais but a little overpriced for what it offers; the older and better-value *Pensão Rio Coura* (☎058/92 11 42; ③), in Avenida Saraiva de Carvalho; and the friendly *Residencial Galo d'Ouro*, Rua da Corredoura 15 (☎058/92 11 60; ③), just off the main square. Alternatives include a few **private rooms** in houses (ask at the turismo or the *Pêro de Caminha* restaurant; see below), and the *Casa do Esteiró* (☎058/92 13 56; ⑤), at the entrance to town, where there is an apartment to rent in a small Solares de Portugal property with lovely gardens.

There are two nearby **campsites**. The better of them is a little inland at Vilar de Mouros (☎058/72 74 72), which is nicely positioned by a small river gorge, and has a swimming pool; there are two buses daily (Mon–Fri) to the site from outside the café, 200m left out of the train station. The other, which tends to be crowded in summer, is an *Orbitur* site (☎058/92 12 95, fax 92 14 73; closed Dec 1–Jan 15), 2km to the south, between the river and the sea, opposite the Fortaleza da Ínsua; three daily buses (Mon–Fri) from the town hall stop close by.

Several of the best **cafés and restaurants** are found in the main square: the *Sporting Clube O Caminhense* has superb regional specialities; the cheerful *Pêro de Caminha* serves pizzas amongst other things; and the *Confeitaria Colmeia* is the place for breakfast. There's good, if more expensive food, too, at the *Adega do Chico* on Rua Visconde de Sousa Rego (head up the right-hand side of the main square, away from the clock tower).

The town has a **ferry** link to La Guardia in Spain, which leaves from beside the bridge over the Rio Coura. There are services daily throughout summer (hourly 8am–7pm; 120$00; cars are free) but winter times are variable

Vila Nova de Cerveira

Up to seven daily trains run along the banks of the Rio Minho to **VILA NOVA DE CERVEIRA**, 11km to the northeast of Caminha. This small walled town has a car-and passenger-ferry – actually little more than a floating platform – which drifts every half-hour across the river to Goyan in Galicia. The **ferry** (summer 8.30am–8.55pm; winter 8.30am–7.25pm; passengers 60$00, cars 280$00) has turned the village into something of a shopping centre for Spaniards, but it remains a pleasant and accessible place and in many respects is more enticing than the bigger and better known Valença further upstream. The town is also home to an art school, hence its surprising prevalence of modern works around town.

The **Solar dos Castros** on Praça da Liberdade was once a manor house and now serves as a cultural centre. At the back, facing a beautifully well-kept garden, is the **turismo** (Mon–Sat 9.30am–12.30pm & 2.30–6pm; ☎051/79 57 87), while alongside, in a small garden, is a striking sculpture of a tripod holding aloft a rock. This has become the symbol of the **arts festival** held here every two years in August/September; the remarkable statue depicting men talking, which won first prize in 1984, is displayed just inside the front door of the Solar dos Castros.

Practicalities

If you want to stay, you'll find accommodation available in all price ranges. For budget travellers, the pleasant **youth hostel** at Largo 16 de Fevereiro 21 (☎ & fax 051/79 61 13) boasts its own kitchen and a terrace, and if you have money to burn, you can do no better than the excellent **pousada** *Dom Dinis* (☎051/79 56 01, fax 79 56 04; ⑦), built within the sixteenth-century fortress walls and overlooking the ramparts. Although not a historic building itself, this would provide a memorable first or last night in Portugal; not surprisingly, it also has the best restaurant in town. In between these two extremes, standard accommodation is offered at the *Residencial Marinel*, on Largo 16 de Fevereiro (☎051/79 51 14; ③), near the hostel, and *Residencial Rainha Santa Isabel*, Rua Herois do Ultramar (☎ & fax 051/79 62 27; ④), some of whose rooms have fine river views. For **food**, the *Café Restaurant Central*, near the *Marinel*, is one of several good places to eat, while the *Barril Bar*, off the main square, is where much of the evening action takes place.

Valença do Minho and around

The border town of **VALENÇA DO MINHO** (usually just referred to as Valença) has become a bustling modern town, surrounding its absurdly quaint old town area clumped amid perfectly preserved, multi-layered seventeenth-century ramparts on a hillock above the river. There are great walks here, both down by the river and along the **ramparts** (watch out for hidden stairwells), the design of which was influenced by the work of the seventeenth-century French military architect, Vauban.

On foot, you're likely to approach the old town from the crossroads at the bottom of the hill, where Avenida Espanha – which runs from the train station – enters the new part of town. Climb the hill to the left and you enter through the **Portas da Coroada**, further along from which a causeway leads over a dry moat to the **Portas do Meio**, the bastion's middle gates. Through here, around Largo de São João, there's a rich diversity of buildings lining the narrow, cobbled streets, with sudden views of the surrounding countryside appearing over the lower reaches of the walls. In the daytime these charms are exploited by a myriad souvenir shops, catering for the day-trippers who cross the border from Spain to pick up Portuguese linen, ceramics and electrical goods. Increasingly, the extent of this commercialism is reducing the appeal of the town – Tuy, across the river in Spain, is probably nicer. By late afternoon, though, the crowds are gone and at night the old part of Valença is almost a ghost town.

The newer part of town, to the south of the ramparts, has nothing of interest but it's here that you'll track down all the basic necessities. Come on Wednesday and you'll encounter the huge weekly **market**, held on the wooded slopes below the walls. Apart from the rows of tourist shops in the old town, the best place for **shopping** is Garrafeira Vasco da Gama on Largo da Esplanada in the new town, to stock up on wines, cheeses, port or chocolate.

Practicalities

Now that European cross-border controls have been relaxed, arriving in Valença **from Tuy in Spain**, over the river, is a simple matter of staying on the train for another few minutes as it rattles over the bridge (there are three daily trains to and from Vigo to Valença), or simply walking over from Tuy. Domestic **trains from Viana do Castelo** end their run in Valença; to head further east or south you'll have to take a local **bus**, which arrives at and departs from in front of the train station. There are no obvious signs to the old town; turn right at the avenue that leads away from the station, then head uphill after the crossroads. You'll see the **turismo** (Mon–Sat 9.30am–12.30pm & 2.30–6pm, Sun 9.30am–12.30pm; ☎051/233 74), in a wooden building opposite a small park; it isn't outstandingly helpful, but can give maps detailing various walking circuits round the old town.

Accommodation

Private rooms are available in the old town, alternatively, you could **camp** below the ramparts at the western end, as numerous summer travellers do. Otherwise try the following:

Casa do Poço, Trav. da Gaviarva 4 (☎051/82 52 35, fax 82 54 69). This former doctor's home has been converted into a luxurious Privetur property and is worth every *escudo*. It's in the old, walled town next to the *pousada*, which it equals for views and surpasses in atmosphere and furnishings. There are only five rooms so it's advisable to book ahead. ⑤.

Lara Hotel, S. Sebastião (☎051/82 43 48, fax 82 43 58). A smart, efficient place in the new town, facing the walls. All rooms have a balcony and TV. ④.

Residencial Ponte Seca, Avda. Tito Fontes (☎051/225 80). To the east on the edge of the new town, this is spotless and good value. Back rooms overlook fields with the mountains beyond. ④.

Residencial Rio Minho, Largo da Estação (☎051/223 31). Opposite the train station, this has simple, airy rooms; a bit rundown but it's probably the cheapest option in town and it does have a pleasant restaurant. ②.

Pousada de São Teotónio (☎051/82 42 42, fax 82 43 97). Located inside the fortress itself, though much of the building is modern. Even if this is out of your price range, a drink in the bar – or lunch in the excellent restaurant (around 3000–4000$00 a head) – is money well spent. ⑦.

Residencial Val Flores, Esplanada (☎051/82 41 06, fax 82 41 29). A friendly place with small, modern and functional rooms, just along from the *Lara Hotel*. ④.

Restaurants

Restaurante Balvarte, Rua S. José. Reasonably priced meals inside the walls, with a fine range of *bacalhau* dishes.

Bom Jesus, Largo Bom Jesus. Popular with the Portuguese and Spanish alike.

Fortaleza, Rua Apolinário da Fonseca 5. Just outside the Portas do Meio, this is not as pricey as it looks. It specializes in goat, among other things, which you can enjoy at its outdoor tables.

A Gruta, just inside the Portas do Meio. Has an outside bar and an indoor restaurant under the vaults, where you can see your food being cooked.

Monumental, built into the walls, just inside the Portas da Coroada. Serves a wonderful, spicy *arroz de marisco* and is reasonably priced.

Pousada Porto, Avenida Miguel Dantas. Opposite the old town by the crossroads, this serves reasonably priced staples and some good salad and egg options.

Crossing to Spain: Tuy

Just a mile from Valença, Spanish **TUY** is an ancient, pyramid-shaped town with a grand battlemented parish church. It, too, is partly walled and it looks far sturdier than Valença, though the first English guidebook to Portugal (*Murray's* in 1855) reported that "the guns of Valença could without difficulty lay Tuy in ruins". If you're not planning to go on to Spain, at least walk across the frontier bridge to explore Tuy's old quarter by the river. There's no longer any passport control post: walking from the centre of one old town to the other takes around 30 minutes.

By **road** (there's a new bridge over the river) and **train** you can go direct from Valença to Vigo, which is within easy reach of Santiago de Compostela, the ancient and beautiful pilgrimage town of Galicia.

Inland: Paredes de Coura

PAREDES DE COURA, 28km south of Valença, claims to be the oldest village in Portugal, a claim that's just about conceivable and, if you are headed for Ponte da Barca or Ponte de Lima, it warrants a detour. You can climb up to the top of the town for views over an almost Swiss landscape, with chalet-style houses and white church spires, or follow the track down beyond the football field to the river for the town's best swimming spot. Every year, over the first whole weekend in August, there's a **festival** featuring the usual Minho mix of dance, costumed procession and music.

On Mondays to Fridays, there is one daily **bus** to the town from Valença, one from Monção, and two to five daily from Ponte de Lima. The best **place to stay** is the *Pensão Paredes de Coura*, Rua Dr. Narciso Alves da Cunha (☎051/78 24 50, fax 78 20 29; ③), not far from the **turismo** (Mon–Sat 9.30am–12.30pm & 2.30–6pm; ☎051/78 21 05), which is housed in an old prison in Largo Visconde Mouzelos.

Monção and around

MONÇÃO, 16km east of Valença, preserves yet another Minho **fortress**, though it doesn't quite make the grade – there being little more than a doorway, a section of walling above the bus station and a high defensive walkway that runs along the northern, river-facing, side of town. Perhaps for this reason, Monção has escaped much of the daytime tourist attention that bedevils the towns to the west; the liveliest day to visit is Thursday, market day. But there's an attractive old centre, which always rewards a stroll, and the town's history, in which two local women played a prominent part, provides a colourful backdrop to the surviving fortifications and buildings.

The principal figure in the town's history is **Deu-la-Deu Martins** (the name means "God gave her"), who is commemorated by a statue and fountain in Largo

Casa de Rodas (☎051/65 21 05). A lovely, low eighteenth-century Solares de Portugal building with four guest rooms, just out of town on Lugar de Rodar. The turismo will find out if there's space and give you directions. ⑤.

Croissanteria Raiano, Praça Deu-la-Deu (☎051/65 35 34). Modern, good-value rooms (some self-contained) above the café; the best ones look out over the square to Spain. ③.

Residencial Esteves, Rua General Pimenta de Castro (☎051/65 23 86). Near the station and reasonably priced, with smart, modern rooms – all have bathrooms and TVs. The entrance is on Rua de Santo António. ②.

Eating and drinking

Minho trout and salmon are always tremendous and between January and March the rich, eel-like **lamprey** are in season. The local **wine**, the finest *vinho verde* in the country, is available on draft in a couple of bars off the main square; the most delicious bottled variety is *Palácio da Brejoeira Alvarinho*, which, as a splendid Monção tourist leaflet one-liner puts it, "someone in France once classified as being the best in the world".

Probably the best bet for **food** in Monção is the *Café Restaurante Central* on Praça Deu-la-Deu – the entrance is in the side street at the back. There's also a good late-night bar at the front. Alternatively, the *Restaurante Terra Nova*, in Praça da República, does good trout and salmon at very reasonable prices.

The spa, Cortes and Lapela

The presence of a **thermal spa** 1500m to the east of Monção (follow the walls) has turned the town into something of a resort for Spanish day-trippers and Portuguese weekenders. Aside from the dubious pleasures of the alkaline water, there's a park and a free campsite by the river. However, it's not exactly the most luxurious of spas, and the Victorian cells – each of which contains a cast-iron bath and assortment of frightening-looking equipment – are rather unsettling, though the new building currently under construction may change all this.

Further afield, to the west of the town, a pleasant walk trails off into the woods from the stop at Senhora da Cabeça to the hamlet of **CORTES**, which was Monção's medieval site. About 3km further west is **LAPELA**, whose river beach is safer for swimmers. The village is dominated by a lofty **tower**, all that remains of a fortress destroyed in 1706 to provide materials for the restoration of the battered walls of Monção.

East to Melgaço

An historic incident in Anglo-Portuguese relations took place on the fragile-looking bridge over the Rio Mouro just before **CEIVÃES**, 10km along the road from Monção to Melgaço. This is the spot where John of Gaunt, the Duke of Lancaster, arranged the marriage of his daughter Philippa to King Dom João I in 1386, an arrangement that resulted in the signing of the **Treaty of Windsor** between the two countries. It gave rise to an alliance lasting over six hundred years and to the naming of numerous public places in honour of "Filipa de Lencastre".

Thermal spa enthusiasts might want to stop at **PESO** (also known as Termas de Melgaço), another 10km to the east (and just 4km short of Melgaço). This is a tiny spa town, spread along the main road and looking down on a magnificent

The Spanish border

The **Spanish border post** is at **PONTE BARXAS**, 1km east of **SÃO GREGÓRIO**, which itself is 10km east of Melgaço. Other than taking one of the buses outlined above in "Practicalities", the only way to get there is by taxi, which is reasonably inexpensive.

Across the frontier, buses leave twice daily (Mon–Fri) for Ribadavia and Orense. Ribadavia (along the Minho and with superb local red wine) and Celanova (on a different route to Orense and dwarfed by a vast medieval monastery) must be two of the most lovely and characteristic towns of Spanish Galicia. The Minho itself – or Miño as it becomes known – is more placid in the further reaches, as it is dammed shortly after the point when both of its banks are within Spain.

THE LIMA VALLEY AND PARQUE NACIONAL DA PENEDA-GERÊS

The **Rio Lima**, whose valley is perhaps the most beautiful in Portugal, was thought by the Romans to be the Lethe, the mythical River of Oblivion. Beyond it, they imagined, lay the Elysian Fields; to cross would mean certain destruction, for its waters possessed the power of the lotus, making the traveller forget country and home. The Roman Consul Decimus Junius Brutus, having led his legions across most of Spain, had to seize the standard and plunge into the water shouting the names of his legionaries from the far bank – to show his memory remained intact – before they could be persuaded to follow.

There are roads along both banks of the Lima from **Viana do Castelo** (see p.326), where the river meets the sea. Travelling from Viana on the main N202, regular bus services pass through two highly attractive towns – **Ponte de Lima** and **Ponte da Barca** – from either of which you could take fine walks into the hilly and wooded surroundings, perhaps exploring one or two of the many Romanesque churches in the region, such as that at **Bravães,** between the two towns.

Further east, the Lima runs into the heart of the **Parque Nacional da Peneda-Gerês**, the largest nature reserve in Portugal. The easiest point of access to the central section of the park is from Ponte da Barca or from **Arcos de Valdevez**, 5km to the north, though there's a possible far northern approach, too, from Melgaço on the Rio Minho.

Ponte de Lima

An hour's ride east of Viana do Castelo, **PONTE DE LIMA** lies at the end of a low stone bridge, Roman in origin and said to mark the path of their first hesitant crossing. It's a delightful small town, whose old centre – as is often the way – has no specific attraction other than its air of sleepy indifference to the wider world. You might disagree if you visit in July or August, when Ponte de Lima begins to show worrying signs of midsummer tourist strain, which the local authorities have capitalized on with a new eighteen-hole golf complex. But at almost any other time of year, the town remains one of Portugal's most pleasing.

WALKS AROUND PONTE DE LIMA

There's beautiful **walking country** all around Ponte de Lima, especially along both banks of the river east of the town. The turismo can provide a set of beautifully illustrated (but somewhat dated) leaflets describing local trails. Keep your wits about you, however, as some of the trails are now very overgrown and directions and left/right details are not all they might be. Even if you get lost, just wandering through some of the cobbled and vine-covered lanes in the villages on the opposite side of the river to Ponte de Lima is a joy. One easy-to-follow walk goes over the bridge and up a winding, dusty road to the TV-mast-topped summit of the hill opposite the town. Here stands the chapel of **Santo Ovidio**, patron saint of ears. If, as is likely, it is closed, you can still peep through the grille and see the walls strung with wax ears and a table covered in them. Each is a model of the afflicted ear of a parishioner, brought here for saintly treatment, or as thanks for relief received. The way back down, as detailed by the leaflet, is harder to follow – either double back along the road or make your own way down through the woods.

The river here offers fine swimming and has wide sandbank beaches where the town's bi-monthly Monday **market**, the oldest in Portugal, has been held since a charter was first granted in 1125. So, too, have the curiously named **"New Fairs"** (second/third weekend of September), a tremendous festival and market, seemingly attended by half the Minho, with fireworks, a fairground, wandering accordionists and *gigantones*, and a large brass band competition. More tradition is on display in early June, with the **Vaca das Cordas** festival, when a tethered bull is dragged through town, round the fountain and down to the river beach; the event dates back 300 years. The more sedate **Corpo do Deus** the following day sees the streets covered with flowers carefully arranged into ornate patterns.

The town's main focus is a long riverside **Alameda** (Passeio 25 de Abril), shaded by magnificent plane trees, leading to the rambling old convent of Santo António, which contains a small museum of treasures within its church. In the town, spare an hour to glance around at the handsome buildings: there are several sixteenth-century **mansions** with stone coats of arms, and interesting remains of the old fourteenth-century **keep**, used up to the 1960s as a prison (the occupants were allowed to hang cups down from the windows for money and cigarettes). It now houses a small craft shop. Should the river not tempt you, there is a municipal **pool** in Rua Francisco Sá Carneiro (Mon–Fri 5pm–10pm, Sat & Sun 9am–noon & 5pm–10pm). Ponte de Lima also has a **cinema** (Fri–Mon) in the Centro Comercial Rio Lima.

Practicalities

The **bus station** is behind the market, just a minute or so from the river, though plans are afoot to move it to the far end of Avenida António Feijó. There are several daily services to Arcos de Valdevez, Viana do Castelo, Barcelos, Ponte da Barca, Paredes de Coura, Braga and Porto. A few minutes' walk away, in Praça da República in the town centre, the **turismo** (Mon–Sat 9am–12.30pm & 2.30–6pm, Sun 9.30am–12.30pm; ☎058/94 23 35) hands out a map of town, though you're hardly likely to need one. The tourist office shares its premises with the headquarters of the Solares de Portugal (see below).

Accommodation

Ponte de Lima is the birthplace of the **Solares de Portugal** organization (formerly Turismo de Habitação or commonly Turihab), founded in 1983 in order to promote and rent out accommodation in local manor houses, farms and country estates around the region (see pp.29–30 for further details). There are now thirty properties in the Ponte de Lima area and ninety in the country as a whole, all offering top-quality accommodation. Bookings can be made through Solares de Portugal, Praça da República, 4990 Ponte de Lima (☎058/74 16 72, fax 058/74 14 44). Privetur, a similar organization, can provide you with details of their properties in the area: phone or fax ☎058/74 14 93, or call in at their office on Largo das Pereiras. Some of the best options from both organizations are given below; note that you will need your own transport to reach them.

At the lower end of the price scale, there are plenty of good *pensões* in town or you could **camp** (unofficially) out of town on the riverbank, but be warned that the police will move you on if you go near the New Fairs site during the festival, when families wash clothes, auction cattle, and let off fireworks throughout the night.

Pensão Beira Rio, on the Alameda (☎058/94 34 71). This lies on the waterfront, with grandstand views of the comings and goings for the Monday market. ②.

Casa de Crasto, 1km out of town on the N203 to Ponte de Barca (☎058/94 11 56). A seventeenth-century Solares de Portugal property, which – legend has it – was partly demolished by the owner in 1896 while looking for hidden treasure. ⑤.

Casa do Outeiro, Arcozelo, 2km from Ponte de Lima. This stately Solares de Portugal manor house dates from the sixteenth century and is surrounded by a garden and woods. Napoleonic forces were suitably impressed, too, when they decided to use it as their headquarters in 1809. Has three twin rooms. ⑨.

Casa das Pereiras, Largo das Pereiras (☎058/94 29 39). Privetur property with a pool and splendid dinners served every Friday evening. The garden contains a 100-year-old camelia. Open June–Oct. ⑤.

Casa da Roseira, 1km out of town on the Darque road (☎058/94 13 54). A lovely nineteenth-century farm, set among vineyards and fruit trees, with its own swimming pool and horses. ⑤.

Moínho de Estorãos, Estorãos, 7km from Ponte de Lima. A Solares de Portugal property occupying a converted seventeenth-century water mill. The location is beautiful – next to a Romanesque bridge and with walking, fishing and swimming all at hand. If you want a double room, book in advance as there's only one. Open mid-May to mid-Oct. ⑤.

Pensão Morais, Rua da Matriz 8 (☎058/94 24 70). Basic, traditional rooms, some with balconies overlooking a quiet street. ②.

Paço de Calheiros, Calheiros, 7km from Ponte de Lima. This elegant seventeenth-century mansion is the country retreat of none other than the Count of Calheiros, original founder of the Turihab scheme (see above). Set in beautifully landscaped gardens with views over the Lima valley, it has nine tastefully decorated bedrooms and six apartments. Has a swimming pool and tennis courts too. ⑥.

Pensão São João, Largo de São João (☎058/94 12 88). Near the bridge, this is excellent value and serves good food downstairs in its restaurant. ④.

Eating and drinking

There are a few inexpensive **cafés** and **restaurants** along the riverfront, especially in Praça de Camões, by the old bridge. *Bar S.A. Galeria* and *Cervejaria Rampinha*, both at the foot of Rua Formosa, are popular evening hang-outs, while the bar next to the *Catrina* on the riverfront is the place to sample *vinho verde* served in china cups straight from the barrel.

Alameda, Largo da Feira, by the bridge on the town side of the river. Highly recommended with splendid views, photographs of Ponte de Lima at New Fairs time, and a good menu that allows you to eat for under 1500$00. Closed Wed.

O Brasão, Rua Formosa 1. Good service in an old stone building. Delicious *arroz de marisco* and a long wine list. Closed Wed.

Restaurante Encanada, on the Alameda. A good place to eat traditional local food such as *sarrabulho* (a pork blood dish), close to the market and with a terrace overlooking the river. The food is good and very modestly priced. Closed Thurs.

Restaurante Parisiense, on the Alameda. This simple restaurant has a limited menu but a good view of the river from its first- and second-floor tables.

Pekim Restaurante Chinês, Avda. General Norton de Matos 166. Cheap Chinese with weekday lunchtime menus between 550$00 and 850$00. Head south from the turismo and follow the avenida as it forks to the left.

São João, Largo de São João. At lunchtime, this place is heaving with locals tucking into the huge, regional dishes, such as *rojões à minhota* – a very tasty mix of pork, sausages and roast potatoes baked in the oven.

East to Ponte da Barca

From Ponte de Lima, the N203 runs 18km east to **Ponte da Barca**, another Minho market town with a bridge so attractive it, too, has been incorporated into the town's name. On the way, call a halt at the small hamlet of **BRAVÃES**, 14km east of Ponte de Lima, home of the fine Romanesque **Church of São Salvador**, just to the left of the road. Its two sculpted doorways are perhaps the best in the country, filled with carvings of doves, griffins, monkeys and two of the local wide-horned oxen. If the church is locked ask at the cottage behind and the doors will be flung open for you, lighting up medieval murals of Saint Sebastian and the Virgin. The church is one of several in the Lima region that is simple and rustic in design but features beautiful, naive carvings on the doorways and columns. Most of these churches were built in the twelfth and thirteenth centuries under the supervision of Cluniac monks, who brought their architecture to Spain and Portugal along the pilgrimage routes to Santiago de Compostela in Galicia; the main Portuguese route ran through Braga and so Minho has the highest concentration.

There's a **bar** in Bravães where local transport-users can debate the chances of getting a bus going on to Ponte da Barca, 4km further east; it's probably quicker to walk.

Ponte da Barca

If you ignore the modern suburbs of **PONTE DA BARCA**, and head for the river, the old town quarters form a quintessential pastoral vision. The Lima is spanned here by a lovely, sixteenth-century bridge; alongside is a splendid market and, on the adjoining corner of Largo de Misericórdia, a seasonal **turismo** (Mon–Fri 9am–12.30pm & 2–6pm, Sat 9am–12.30pm; ☎058/428 99). On alternate Wednesdays there's a superb open-air **market**, which spreads out by the river in an almost medieval atmosphere, drawing hundreds of people from outlying hamlets. Walk down to the other end of the main road and you'll come to the cattle market area. It's also worth noting that the town's annual Feira de São Bartolomeu takes place on August 24; don't expect to get any sleep once the party starts.

A WALK FROM PONTE DA BARCA

The Ponte da Barca turismo publishes details of a fine **local walk** – a seven-hour circuit to São Miguel near Entre-Ambos-os-Rios (8km east of town). The instructions are somewhat out of date, so a compass and a good map would be useful. It's an uphill hike most of the way, but passes through some gorgeous villages – Sobredo, especially – which seem unchanged from centuries past. There's food available at several points along the way (midway at Germil, for example).

One of the nicest places **to stay** is the friendly *Pensão Maria Gomes*, Rua Conselheiro Rocha Peixoto 13 (☎058/422 88; ②), overlooking the river and bridge, where breakfast is served on the balcony. It's worth phoning ahead to book. More upmarket is *Pensão Os Poetas*, Rua Dr. Alberto Cruz (☎058/435 78; ④), which has well-appointed, modern rooms – some with river views. On the north bank of the river, opposite the town, the Solares de Portugal property, *Quinta da Prova* (☎058/421 63; ⑤), has five apartments with kitchen (two doubles and three sleeping up to four people).

For **meals**, you could do far worse than eat upstairs at *Pensão Maria Gomes*, or try the pricier *Restaurante Bar do Rio*, close to the Praia Fluvial – a beach on the left bank of the river – which is an excellent place to dine while watching the sunset. Another good option is *Restaurante Varanda do Lima* (closed Thurs), near the bridge, which specializes in *rodobalho*, a type of flatfish, which you choose from the tank by the door; a meal here will set you back around 2500–3000$00. As for **bars**, top marks for novelty go to *Bar Ruinas*, behind *Restaurante Bar do Rio*, one street back from the river, which is housed in the roofless ruin of a farmhouse and attracts a lively, youthful clientele.

From the **bus stop** by the bridge, near the arches of the town hall, there are connections to Lindoso and Arcos de Valdevez (2–4 daily) and Braga (4 daily).

Arcos de Valdevez

As a diversion from the main Minho river route you might contemplate exploring the Rio Vez, which can be reached just 5km north of Ponte da Barca, at **ARCOS DE VALDEVEZ** (Arches of the Valley of the Vez). Like almost everywhere in this region, it's ordinarily a sleepy little place, though it shows its true Minho colours during the fortnightly Wednesday **market**. And, as at Ponte de Lima and Ponte da Barca, it only really comes alive during its annual festival, in this case the three-day **Festas do Concelho**, held over the first or second week in August, featuring *gigantones* (giant figures), *zés pereiras* (red-caped drummers), horse races and noisy fireworks. Traditionally these celebrations should take place on the last weekend of the holiday month, but they've been shifted to take account of local emigrants who return to work abroad at the end of August; one of the festival days is actually named the Dia do Emigrante.

Practicalities

The **turismo** is by the bridge's western side on Avenida Marginal (Mon–Sat 9.30am–12.30pm & 2.30–6pm; mid-June to mid-Sept also Sun 9.30am–12.30pm; ☎058/660 01) and has maps to give away. For information on the **bus** service to

Lindoso, ask at the depot above Largo da Lapa, from where there are also regular services to Monção, Ponte de Lima and Viana do Castelo. Buses en route to Soajo or Braga (as well as Monção or Lindoso) leave from a stop by the turismo.

Like Ponte da Barca, Arcos de Valvedez is a useful point of departure for the Parque Nacional da Peneda-Gerês and there's a **park information office** beside the river in Arcos on Avenida de Tilias (see box on p.351 for details), where you can buy an English-language map of the park.

The town has several good and reasonably priced **pensões**, including the wonderfully decrepit *Pensão Ribeira* on Largo dos Milagres (☎058/651 74; ②), at the east end of the bridge, which is unfortunately planning wholesale modernization, and the more expensive *Pensão Tavares*, on Rua Padre Manuel José da Cunha Brito (☎058/662 53; ④; breakfast included). A third, attractively sited in the upper part of town, is the small and unpretentious *Pensão Flor do Minho*, at Largo da Valeta 11–15 (☎058/652 16; ①). There are also a couple of cheap *dormidas* (①) up the side road from the turismo.

A cluster of nice **restaurants** can be found in Rua de São João, while other local places that recommend themselves include the *Minho Verde*, Avenida de Tilias, beyond the park office, and *O Lagar*, Rua Dr. Vaz Guedes, in the old quarter. For a real treat, though, visit *Casa Delfim*, a café down the right-hand side of the church in Largo da Lapa, run by an ageing "world-famous" accordionist and stacked with his instruments, any of which are liable, suddenly, to be snatched up for an impromptu jam session.

Parque Nacional da Peneda-Gerês

The magnificent **PARQUE NACIONAL DA PENEDA-GERÊS** is hardly a secret. Caldas do Gerês (known simply as Gerês), the main centre of the park, attracts more tourists than anywhere else in the Minho, with the possible exception of Viana do Castelo, and at weekends, when Portuguese campers arrive in force, parts of it can seem a bit too close to civilization. The park as a whole, though, is large enough to absorb the great numbers of visitors. It's split into two distinct parts, based around the southern **Serra do Gerês** and the wilder northern section containing the **Serra da Peneda**; this latter area, in particular (best approached from Melgaço, on the River Minho), remains largely undiscovered, though the same could be said of the eastern reaches of the former – spectacular and largely impenetrable mountain terrain. Almost all of the park contains vestiges of early human occupation, in the form of *antas* (megaliths), dolmens, stone circles and cave art, the locations of which are marked (approximately) on the park's maps.

Approaches and information

You can see a great deal of the park under your own steam, along a number of roads in varying states of repair, but note that **bus** services are limited (and often nonexistent at weekends). The main connections are: Melgaço to Lamas de Mouro and Castro Laboreiro in the north; Arcos de Valdevez and Ponte da Barca to Soajo and Lindoso in the centre; and Braga to Caldas de Gêres. Alternatively, a taxi ride from Arcos de Valdevez or Ponte da Barca to Soajo is a very reasonable 2000$00.

Once in the park, **walking** is generally the only option for getting around, for which you'll need a good map – available from the **information** centres and park offices (see box on p.351 for details) – and a compass. At many of the hamlets and

THE TRILHO DO LONG CURSO

A long-distance footpath – the **Trilho do Longo Curso** – is planned to run from one side of the Peneda-Gerês park to the other. At present the park office produces detailed leaflets (300$00) covering two sections of the Trilho, from Lamas de Mouro to Soajo in the north of the park, and from Cabril to Paradela in the south. Eventually there should be similar leaflets covering the entire route: from Sezelhe near Montalegre, north to Tourem on the Spanish border, and on through Pitões das Junias, Paradela, Cabril, Caldas de Gerês, Campo do Gerês, Entre-ambos-os-Rios, Lindoso, Soajo, Peneda, Lamas de Mouro campsite and ending in Castro Laboreiro. This takes into account most of the main areas of interest in the park and has been designed so that there is always somewhere to stay or camp at the end of a reasonable day's walk. However, if you are looking for the shortest way from A to B, the *trilho* is not your best bet. It often goes out of its way to take in interesting diversions and to avoid following busy roads. Several sections are also very steep, overgrown or hard-going; although other sections follow minor roads.

At the beginning of each completed section is a large map, showing the route; at every junction along the path, a yellow arrow points the way. On longer stretches, an acorn logo on rocks and trees keeps you on the right track. All the paths the *trilho* follows are old routes, used by generations of villagers; indeed, the *trilho* is particularly good as it passes through villages and hamlets, where it guides you along age-old cobbled paths overhung with trellises and vines.

villages there's access to **accommodation**, campsites and **food**. Trails and paths cover large areas, and there are dozens of hiking opportunities, from short strolls to two- and three-day **hikes** across whole sections of the park. A long-distance, cross-park trail is planned, too; see the box above for more details. If you'd like someone else to take care of the arrangements and plan your walks, contact Trilhos, Rua de Belém 94, 4300 Porto (☎02/48 07 40), which may have vacancies on their small group hiking holidays; they'll provide transport, guides, food and accommodation.

Caldas do Gerês

The national park is centred on the old spa town of **CALDAS DO GERÊS** (commonly known as Gerês), which can be reached easily from Braga by bus – a one and a half hour journey (operated by Empresa Hoteleira do Gêres). Weekends aside, when Portuguese picnickers arrive en masse, it's a relaxed and very elegant base. "The Spa of Gerês" became fashionable in the early years of the last century – an epoch convincingly evoked by a row of grand Victorian hotels (many now sadly run-down and boarded up) along the sedate old main street, Avenida Manuel Francisco da Costa. The spa still functions, attracting the infirm in the summer season, though most visitors nowadays are younger and healthier, up from the northern cities to picnic in the woods or, in the case of eccentric foreigners, to hike. There's been a lot of recent development in town, but it's not all to the bad and you'll probably appreciate the public outdoor swimming pool (reached through the park), tennis courts, boating lake and countless cafés. Pick up information either at the **turismo** (9am–noon & 2–6pm; closed Tues & Sun; ☎053/39 11 33), at the top end of the main avenue, or at the national park office, a little further up (see box on p.351).

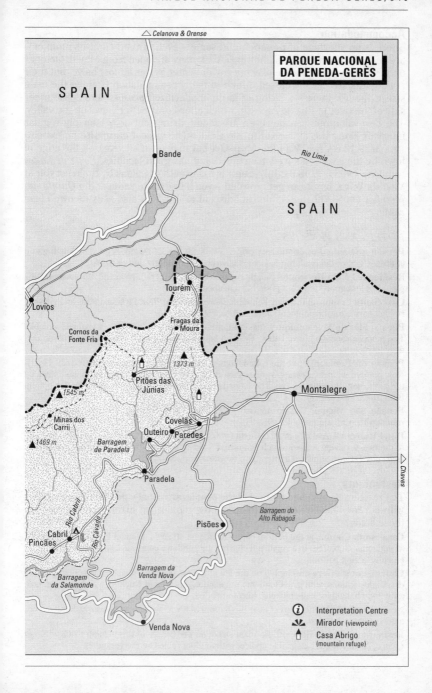

△ Celanova & Orense

**PARQUE NACIONAL
DA PENEDA-GERÊS**

SPAIN

Bande

Rio Limia

SPAIN

Tourém

Lovios

Fragas da
Moura

Cornos da
Fonte Fria

▲ 1373 m

☐ Pitões das
Júnias

Montalegre

▲ 1545 m

Minas dos
Carrii

Covelãs

▲ 1469 m

Barragem
de Paradela

Outeiro • Paredes

△ Chaves

Paradela

Rio Cabril

Barragem do
Alto Rabagoã

Pisões

Cabril
Pincães

Rio Cávado

Barragem da
Venda Nova

Barragem
da Salamonde

ⓘ Interpretation Centre

🔻 Mirador (viewpoint)

⛺ Casa Abrigo
(mountain refuge)

Venda Nova

Accommodation

There is no shortage of **pensões** and some – even in the height of summer – are reasonably priced. Note, however, that many are open from May to October only; while in those that do stay open over winter, prices almost halve, but their restaurants are usually closed. Much of the accommodation is along the main street, though there's a string of large, modernized *pensões* across the other side of the river in Rua do Amasso, which afford ever better views up the valley. The best-value options, however, are found strung out at reasonably regular intervals along the 8km road to Rio Caldo. The closest **campsite** is *Vidoeiro* (☎053/39 12 89, fax 39 14 96; April–Oct but may open all year) on the edge of town by the river – it's well-maintained and has good facilities. *Ponte de Saltos* campsite (☎053/39 13 94; July–Sept) is 3km south of Caldas by the reservoir at Vilar da Veiga, but it can get crowded – you'll find more room at the *Quinta dos Moinhos* (☎053/39 15 81), almost adjacent to it, which also sells its own *vinho verde*.

HOTELS AND PENSÕES

Pensão Adelaide, Rua do Amasso (☎053/390 00 20, fax 390 00 29). A good option, high up at the top end of the road; the balconies have correspondingly fine views. ④.

Residencial Belo Horizonte, Rua do Amasso (☎053/39 12 60). Near the *Moçambique*, this place has less good views but is slightly cheaper. ④.

Casa Santa Comba, in the alley behind *Restaurante Pedra Bela*. Plyboard walls and views of rusting agricultural equipment, but the cheapest in town. ②.

Pensão Flôr de Moçambique, Rua do Amasso (☎ & fax 053/39 11 19). Clean and amiable. The modern rooms all have baths, TVs and balconies and there's a restaurant with an outdoor terrace. ④.

Pensão da Ponte, right at the roundabout at the southern end of town (☎053/39 11 21). Now merged with the *Pensão Príncipe* next door. The former is a long-established place by the river, now showing its age. The latter is less characterful but possibly a better option. Both ③.

Pensão São Miguel, Rua do Amasso (☎053/39 13 60). This has good value, large, airy rooms with stunning outlooks. ④.

Hotel Universal, Avda. Manuel F. Costa (☎053/39 11 35, fax 39 11 02). Gerês finest and one of the two surviving – albeit much renovated – old-style grand hotels (the other is its sister *Hotel das Termas*, similar if a little more downmarket). ⑤.

Restaurants

The restaurants attached to most of the *pensões* are usually good if unmemorable, with portions healthy enough to satisfy the most jaded hiker. Alternatively, try those below.

Casa Santa Comba, at the bottom end of town, just off Avda. Manuel F. Costa, on the right as you enter Gerês. Set in a small and charmingly rundown courtyard, with average food but an entertaining patron.

Churrasqueira Geresino, uphill on the left at the top of town. At last, an excellent place to eat. Unpretentious, with great food and outstanding barbecued chicken, which you can take away too (400$00 for half-chicken). Recommended.

Novo Sol, along the main street near the bottom of town. Service can be surly, but it serves a good *ementa turística*.

Restaurante Pedra Bela, on the main street on the corner of the turning to *Casa Santa Comba*. A limited but reasonable choice, with outdoor tables on the verandah.

Hiking in central Gerês

The main reason, of course, for staying in Caldas de Gerês is to explore the national park. From the spa town, there are several interesting and accessible hikes, though, frustratingly, the **central Gerês** section is not well equipped with footpaths and walking off the tracks can be difficult and painful, with small shrubs slashing the legs.

West: to Campo do Gerês and around the mountain

This is an exhausting and long day's hike (10–12hr; or camp overnight) but a good one, taking you along the Roman road that began at Braga and stretched ultimately to Rome and Byzantium. The route also runs alongside the **Vilarinho das Furnas** reservoir, with obvious swimming potential. In the height of summer you can see the submerged village of Vilarinho das Furnas itself – turn right after crossing the dam.

Setting out from Gerês, follow the road north towards **PORTELA DO HOMEM**, the Spanish/Portuguese border post where there's a café and a collection of Roman milestones. It's 13km from Gerês, and locals often hitch up here to swim in the nearby **river pool** at the bottom of the Minas dos Carris valley. However, to get to Campo de Gerês, you don't need to go as far as Portela de Homen; instead, veer left off the road beyond the defunct campsite at Albergaria following signs to Campo do Gerês and the reservoir. There is a path off to the reservoir, but the main track heads southwest – first along gladed

---

MAPS AND INFORMATION

A **map of the park** is available (420$00), which details altitudes and all roads (but none of the footpaths). You should be able to pick this up, as well as leaflets, hiking information and other advice, from one of four **national park information offices** (listed below) or from one of the park's new **Centros de Interpretação** (10am–12.30pm & 2–6pm, Sun 10am–noon & 2–5.30pm, closed Wed) located at various park entrances: Lamas de Mouro in the north; Mezio, between Arcos and Soajo; and Lindoso on the Spanish border.

Arcos de Valdevez, Avda. de Tilias (Mon–Fri 9am–12.30 & 2–5.30pm; ☎058/653 38, fax 52 27 07).

Braga, Avenida António Macedo, Quinta das Parretas, Rodovia (Mon–Fri 9am–12.30pm & 2–5.30pm; ☎053/600 34 80, fax 61 31 69).

Caldas do Gerês, Avda. Manuel Francisco da Costa (Mon–Fri 9.30am–12.30pm & 2.30–6pm; ☎053/39 11 81, fax 39 14 96). There is a 24-hour telephone service available for emergencies.

Montalegre, Portal Veiga (Mon–Fri 9am–12.30pm & 2–5.30pm; ☎076/522 81).

EQUIPMENT AND DANGERS

Maps aside, if you plan a long hike, take good boots, warm and waterproof clothes, a compass, food and a water bottle (there are plenty of streams). Beware of fog in spring and winter. Picking flowers and – more importantly – **lighting fires** are forbidden in Gerês. The Portuguese have an alarming habit of lighting them whenever and wherever they picnic – no doubt a contributory factor in disastrous fires such as those that destroyed over 800 square kilometres of forest in 1985 alone.

A HIKE FROM CAIDAS DE GERÊS TO ERMIDA

One of the most spectacular and isolated **walks** in the Peneda-Gerês region is a two-day 29km trek round Gerês, passing through craggy scenery, steep gorges and verdant valleys. The paths are easy to follow, yet are seldom used by anyone other than local farmers and shepherds. Take plenty of water as streams may be dry, especially in summer.

Begin by walking north out of Caldas de Gerês on the road leading to the campsite and continue walking until you reach the checkpoint at Portela de Leonte. About 20m before the checkpoint, on the right-hand side of the road, is a path leading up the mountain; it can be quite hard to find so ask at the checkpoint for the path to Borrageiro mountain. Once on the path, there should be no problem finding the way as every turn is marked by a pile of stones left by shepherds. The path is stony at first and climbs steeply, giving way to excellent views north into the Spanish mountains and down the valley to Caldas. On approaching the summit of Borrageiro mountain, the scenery becomes desolate and rocky and the path gives way to open plains and valleys. Keep following the piles of stones for about forty minutes until the path becomes clear once more. On rejoining the path, follow it for about 5km along the course of a stream to the junction of two rivers (about half an hour's walk) – an idyllic spot to spend the night. Although camping is officially banned in the park, it is tolerated in places like this, which throng with locals during the day.

To return to Gerês, take the dusty track along the river for 2km and follow the signs to Ermida. Walk along the cobbled path through the village, then turn right and follow the forestry track uphill. On reaching a T-junction a few kilometres later, take the left-hand path and you're back on the main road between the Miradouro and Caldas de Gerês. Simply head downhill and follow the signs to Gerês.

paths and then suddenly into the open, following stretches of the old Roman road. Fires here have seared the foliage and given the granite crags an almost apocalyptic grandeur. Staying with the road (past an old stone building housing a weaving project run by the park), you veer left into **CAMPO DO GERÊS** (to which there are daily buses from Braga, operated by Empresa Hoteleira do Gerês).

Here, the friendly *Residencial Stop* (☎053/35 12 91; ③) attracts a young and active crowd. The *Cerdeira* **campsite** (☎053/35 18 35; open all year), also lets out bungalows which sleep up to eight people (roughly 2000$00 per person), and hires bicycles; it has its own restaurant, too. Nearby is the *Vilarinho das Furnas* **youth hostel** (☎053/35 13 39), so-called because, until 1972, it provided accommodation for those who built the dam – hence its bungalows, swimming pool, tennis court and disco. Through any of these establishments you can contact Equi Campo, which offers local **horse-trekking** trips.

Soon after Campo do Gerês you come to the crucifix of São João do Campo. Turn off the road here, to the left, on to a dirt track. This will take you around the southern tip of the mountain and, apart from the occasional obsessive car driver, you'll be pretty much alone – eerily so at times, amid the Neolithic boulders. Follow the sign to **Calcedónia**, a Celtic and Roman *citânia* with an impressive cave. This stretch can be hard-going in the midday heat, as there is no shelter, so save it for the late afternoon. At the end of the circuit, the way back to Gerês is signposted (right at the first junction, then right again at the water fountain).

The Miradouro and Ermida

An hour's walk to the southeast of Caldas do Gerês, the **Miradouro do Gerês** is *the* destination for Portuguese weekend picnickers. And small wonder, with its site overlooking the vast reservoir of Caniçada and a good part of the Gerês range. The only catch, if you're intent on following suit, is the extent of local enthusiasm. This is not a road to walk unless you're immune to inhalation of exhaust fumes and dust; it's better to hitch up and then start hiking. The quickest approach to the Miradouro is to follow the road behind the service station at Gerês, where it becomes an uphill path. The most obvious, and probably the most attractive, route to follow beyond the Miradouro is to **Ermida** (see below). Just before arriving here, there's a sign pointing you to the Cascata do Arado, left off the main track; follow this and a brief walk leads to the magnificent **Arado waterfalls**, with its refreshing pools for swimming.

South: to Caniçada reservoir, Rio Caldo and São Bento da Porta Aberta

The best base for the **Caniçada reservoir** is the village of **RIO CALDO**, on its west bank and just 8km south of Caldas do Gerês; change here for buses from Caldas to São Bento. There are numerous **water sports** available locally at the reservoir, with possibilities for both windsurfing and waterskiing; swimming is fine, too. For water-sports equipment, contact the English-run AML (☎053/39 17 40 or 39 15 98), who rent canoes, motorboats, mountain bikes and walking gear. There are plenty of places to stay along the edge of the reservoir, as well as along the road to Caldas de Gerês – a good bet is the *Pensão Pontes de Rio Caldo* (☎053/39 15 40, fax 39 11 95; ④), a stone building with a garden bar at the road junction with the bridges. More modern, but in an unbeatable reservoir location, is *Casa Beira Rio* (☎053/39 11 97; ④), on the north side of the bridge to Gerês. Alternatively, you could catch a bus uphill towards Cerdrinhas to the *Pousada de São Bento* (☎053/64 71 90, fax 64 78 67; ⑦), in a superb position overlooking the reservoir from the east. This timber-beamed former hunting lodge has its own a swimming pool and a superb restaurant, with great views.

Three kilometres beyond Rio Caldo, in the Covide direction, **SÃO BENTO DA PORTA ABERTA** is a small village, high above the reservoir, commanding superb views. Its austere sanctuary is a favourite spot with pilgrims, who gather here at the beginning of July and again a month later (and on most Sundays throughout the year) – at such times the traffic and fumes make it a place best avoided. The former monastery, hidden under an ugly modern facade, is now the *Estalgem de São Bento da Porta Aberta* (☎053/39 11 06, fax 39 11 17; ⑤), still a little severe inside but nevertheless comfortable and with a good restaurant. Cheaper rooms (③) may be available in the *Restaurante Mira Serra* at the western end of the village, and at the charming turn-of-the-century *Pensão São José*, halfway between São Bento and Rio Caldo (☎053/39 11 20; ④).

Ermida and east to Cabril

ERMIDA, despite its proximity to Gerês (90min on foot) and the Miradouro (30min), has an air of isolation about it – be warned that driving there and beyond involves some extremely steep sections, in parts badly pitted by floods. If you're looking for a quiet base for hiking or else just soaking up the mountain atmosphere, this could be a good choice: there's good accommodation and food at *Casa do Criado* (☎053/39 13 90; ②; phone ahead), a scattering of *dormidas*, an orchard to camp in and a couple of cafés, but it is still very much a farming community.

Continuing **east from Ermida**, along a blackberry-lined lane, you'll pass a gorgeous group of small waterfalls – paradise to swim in – and cross a distinctly unsafe-looking (and sounding) bridge before coming to **FAFIÃO**, a tiny farming hamlet. There's a restaurant here, the *Retiro do Gerês*, which also has rooms (②). Past here the countryside becomes more fertile, terraced with vines and maize, the road winding down to another hamlet, **PINCÃES**, and through it (turn right at the end of the houses) to the slightly larger village of Cabril.

A lovely, isolated place, sat on the Rio Cabril and surrounded on all sides by mountains, **CABRIL** flaunts odd attempts at modernity, though its centre is still sauntered through by oxen, goats and flocks of sheep. Parts of the locality have been submerged because of the Salamonde dam near Fafião. Consequently, the old bridge is half under water and makes for great swimming, through the bridge arch. There's a **campsite** here, *Outeiro Alto* (☎053/65 98 60), 1km out on the Pincães road, which is fine provided it's not too busy – there are only two toilets. It also rents out bicycles and canoes and offers horse riding. You can get a good **meal** at the *Restaurante Ponte Novo*, by the bridge, which serves a warming meat stew; the *Café 1º de Maio*, further up the road, also serves food but usually needs advance warning.

On to Montalegre and the Trás-os-Montes: Paradela and Venda Nova

From Cabril, if you're hiking or driving, you could go on to Paradela, Outeiro, Paredes do Rio, Covelães and Pitões das Júnias, the latter with a decaying monastery nearby. There's a *pensão* at Paradela, another at Paredes do Rio and one at Pitões – the *Casa do Preto* (☎076/561 58; ②), which also houses one of Pitões' two excellent restaurants, the other being the *Pitões do Gerês*. Any of these settlements would make an ideal base for a leisurely exploration of this little-known corner of the Minho.

In particular, the signposted path from Cabril to **PARADELA** – around 23km – is stunningly dramatic, winding along the river valley through the handsome villages of Sirvozelo, Lapela and Xertola. At Paradela, a particularly attractive mountain village whose cobbled streets are lined with vines, you're rewarded by fine views over the dam and mountains. The *Pensão Pousadinha* (☎076/561 65; ③) has the feel of an English B&B and, for eating, the nearby *Restaurante Sol Rio*, on the Montalegre road, boasts marvellous views, as does the *Restaurante D. Dinis* (which also rents rooms) on the road to Cabril.

Alternatively, from Cabril or Paradela you can move on to **Montalegre**, via another vast reservoir. Montalegre itself (see p.375) provides a suitably remote and dramatic link with the Trás-os-Montes region, and can be reached by bus from Venda Nova or from Braga. The appeal lies as much in the road there as in the place itself. Bumpy and narrow, it makes for one of those journeys that seem to trigger madness in bus drivers, simultaneously delighting and terrifying unaccustomed passengers.

This route takes you through **VENDA NOVA**, with the smart *Estalagem São Cristóvão* (☎053/65 93 87; ⑤) by the reservoir, or the cheaper *Residencial Africana* (☎059/65 91 98; ③). There are some lovely walks in the vicinity and exceptionally bracing swimming. Buses from from Braga pass through Venda Nova to Montalegre and Chaves, passing the hydroelectric plant of **Pisões** – the largest dam in the country, and an unexpectedly modern development in this otherwise very remote region.

Festa in the Minho

Tending the vineyards, Trás-os-Montes

Bragança castle

Doorway, Castelo de Vide

Vila Nova de Milfontes

Cove in Lagos

Taking a break, Monsaraz

Albufeira rooftops

Olive groves and cacti, the Algarve

PETER WILSON

Fishing boats, Olhão

PETER WILSON

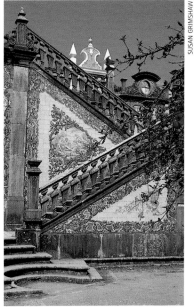
SUSAN GRIMSHAW

Capela dos Ossos, Évora

Palácio do Visconde, Estói

Soajo and Lindoso

The neighbouring villages of **Soajo** and **Lindoso**, midway between the Peneda and the Gerês sections of the park, are reached most easily from (respectively) Arcos de Valdevez and Ponte da Barca. **Buses** to Soajo leave Arcos de Valdevez at 5.40pm (Mon–Fri; also 12.20pm Mon, Wed, Fri & Sat). There are also buses from Arcos, via Ponte da Barca, to Lindoso, leaving at 7.45am and 1.30pm (Mon–Fri; 7.45am only on Sat). The taxi journey to either will set you back 2000$00. Note that if you are approaching from the Rio Minho there is no public transport through the park so you have to catch a bus to either Arcos or Ponte da Barca from Monção or Melgaço. Approaching from Arcos to Soajo, you enter the park at **MEZIO**, which has an interpretation centre (see box on p.351); the staff can give you details on a good half-day excursion to see the prehistoric rock art in the vicinity. A new campsite is due to open in 1998 at Travanca, 3km away.

Both Soajo and Lindoso are fine centres for hiking, and the walk or drive between the two is enjoyable, too, crossing the dam of the Lindoso reservoir.

Soajo

SOAJO is a small village tucked into the folds of a hilly landscape. Its highlight is a collection of eighteenth- and nineteenth-century **espigueiros** (grain houses), over twenty of which are clumped together on a stony platform, their roof-crosses (intended to bless the annual crop) giving them the look of a graveyard. In addition to providing a ready-made, breezy threshing ground, the *espigueiros* site offers a degree of protection from rats, though the tall stone mushrooms that raise the houses from the ground do not appear to keep vermin entirely at bay. Their grouping together is a vestige of the days when the isolated village depended heavily on communal effort for its survival. Even now there are several flocks of sheep and goats that belong to the whole community and are tended by the village shepherds. If you set off on a hike at the crack of dawn you will walk up into the hills to the sound of small brass bells.

Changes are not accepted easily and the village takes its traditions very seriously. Folkloric groups are maintained by those who stay behind, while the emigrants all try to inculcate a sense of *minha terra* (my homeland) into their modern-minded (and in many cases American) offspring. The local **festival** (Aug 13–15) has a special feel, with the fun and games spontaneous. Owing to a lack of horses, the *corrida* is a race on foot – balancing blue plastic urns full of water on their heads, the contestants compete for the honour of being ceremonially drenched by all the others. Large, homemade fireworks are set off all over the place without warning.

Staying in Soajo is no longer a problem since ten private homes joined together in a pioneering Turismo de Aldeia scheme. Each house has its own character and costs 7000$00 for a double room or 13000$00 for the whole house (two rooms). Contact ADERE Soajo (☎ & fax 058/674 27), or enquire at the supermarket. There's also a luxurious Solares de Portugal property, *Casa do Adro* (☎058/67 43 27; ④), offering rooms in a beautiful eighteenth-century house. You'll need to book well ahead at festival time.

Lindoso

Set high above the Rio Lima, **LINDOSO** is one of the most attractive villages in Peneda-Gerês. It is most easily reached from Ponte da Barca. Like Soajo, Lindoso is dominated by a cluster of *espigueiros*, and its life is again very traditional. The rearing of **livestock** is central. Every morning starts with the lowing of cows or the clattering of the communally herded sheep and goats, and the smell of animals lies thick in the air. The traditional method of baking bread in these parts involved removing hot coals from the oven and sealing the door with an ash and dung mixture, and it's a technique still in use in the old part of the village. If you're at all interested, there's one of these ovens still in place in the heavily restored **Castelo** (Tues–Sat 10am–12.30pm & 2–6pm, Sun 10am–noon & 2–5.30pm; 200$00), whose museum details the results of local excavations.

Accommodation is difficult to find in Lindoso and it's a question of enquiring about the availability of private rooms at the *Alto Lindoso* (☎058/674 22; ②), just outside the village on the road to the Spanish border, or the *O Telheiro Restaurante* (☎058/674 03; ②), 1km further along; alternatively, ask around for the local priest, Padre Aladinho, who also rents out rooms. But far and away the best **lodging** prospect in the vicinity is the *Três Cabanas* (☎058/672 18; ②), 3km out of Lindoso on the Soajo road, across the dam. Run by a charming couple who speak some English, the en-suite rooms are pleasant and there are fine views over the valley and River Lima; ring beforehand to check that they are open.

The northern section: Peneda

Peneda, the northern section of the Parque Nacional da Peneda-Gerês, sees far fewer tourists than Gerês to the south, partly because of the difficulty of access. Without your own transport, you have to rely on the infrequent buses which seem to take a perverse delight in seeing how early they can leave the Minho river town of Melgaço (see p.340). However, the route from here is one of the best approaches to this area of staggering scenery and awesome rock formations.

Weekday **buses** leave Melgaço for Lamas de Mouro and Castro Laboreiro at 7.30am (with an additional 12.50pm service on Fridays) and return at around 6.30pm – check times with the parcel depot in Melgaço, just around the corner from the *Pensão Pemba*, or ask at the turismo. If you're **driving**, you will find that the route south of Lamas de Mouro into the park, along the valley of the Peneda, has been much improved – you can drive all the way to Soajo with no difficulty.

Lamas de Mouro, Peneda and walks south

LAMAS DE MOURO, 19km southeast of Melgaço, has a beautifully situated **campsite** (☎051/454 94; ring ahead in winter), one of three owned by the national park; it has hot showers, a bar, a nearby natural pool for swimming and a restaurant. It's just inside the park, past the interpretation centre (see p.351 for details). **Accommodation** may also be available at the *Café Restaurante Paysan* (☎051/452 23; ③), at the road junction just north of the campsite, where the N202 forks off to Castro Laboreiro. The owner is charming and a fount of information on the region. She can also arrange day-trips with guides (on foot or horseback). For **food**, the *Churrasqueiria Vidoeiro* is 1km up the road from the campsite – slightly expensive but with generous portions.

Nine kilometres beyond the campsite, you reach the sanctuary of **Nossa Senhora da Peneda**, a miniature version of Bom Jesus, full of devotees at the beginning of September (especially on the 7th and 8th), but pretty much deserted the rest of the year. You can take a fairly easy two-hour return walk from the southeast corner of the sanctuary up to the peak of **Penameda** (1258m), where there are freshwater lagoons and fine views across the whole of the Parque Nacional.

PENEDA village itself has cafés and religious artefact shops clustered around the main square. The *Hotel de Peneda* has rooms available (②), and a café downstairs. There are slightly pricier rooms at the *Café Star* and nice, modern ones slightly further towards the junction on the right: for the latter contact Isolina Domingues Fernandes at the *Casa de Artigos Religiosos* in the main square (☎051/451 39; ③). If you don't mind roughing it, you'll probably be allowed to stay in one of the many basic local rooms built for the pilgrims who flood the village for the festival in September. A dramatic and attractive walk (about 20km) is to follow the well-signposted and not too busy lane south from Peneda; bear left at the fork in the lane just before the village of Adrão and you'll join the Soajo–Lindoso road by the *Três Cabanas* (see p.356).

Castro Laboreiro

The left-hand fork at Lamas takes you up to the ancient village of **CASTRO LABOREIRO** (9km further), a place that's best known for the breed of mountain dog to which it gives its name. Before the arrival of tourism, the village was practically deserted every summer when the the pastoral community would leave to find greener fields and build *brandas* ("soft" houses) elsewhere for the warmer months, returning in winter to their *inverneiras* (winter houses) in Laboreiro. The best **accommodation** is at *Miradouro do Castelo* (☎051/454 69; ②), at the far end of the village overlooking a magnificent valley and overlooked by the castle. You'll also find good, modern rooms at *Casa S. José* (☎051/451 34; ②), 500m out on the Lamas road. For **eating**, the *Miradouro do Castelo* has a good restaurant, or try the *cabrito serrano* (mountain kid goat) in the *Restaurante da Serra* opposite.

To reach the ruins of the town's **castle**, you have a steep twenty-minute walk: left at the roundabout on the other side of the village, then left up a path where the road drops to the right, past a large rock known as the *Tartaruga* (Tortoise), and through heather and between boulders, with sheer drops to each side and steps hacked out of the rock face.

travel details

Trains

Barcelos to: Porto (10–14 daily; 1hr 5min–1hr 40min); Valença do Minho (5 daily; 1hr); Viana do Castelo (12 daily; 30min).

Braga to: Nine – change for Viana and Valença (hourly; 12–20min); Porto (13–16 daily; 1hr–1hr 45min).

Caminha to: Porto (5–8 daily; 1 hr 30min–3hr 10min); Valença do Minho (6–7 daily; 20–40min); Viana do Castelo (7–9 daily; 20–40min).

Guimarães to: Porto (11–15 daily; 1hr 45min); Santo Tirso (11–15 daily; 45min).

Porto to: Barcelos (9–11 daily; 1hr 10min–1hr 40min); Caminha (4–6 daily; 2hr–3hr 10min);

Guimarães (11–15 daily; 1hr 45min); Santo Tirso (hourly; 1hr); Valença do Minho (5 daily; 2hr 10min–3hr 40min); Viana do Castelo (10–12 daily; 1hr 30min–2hr 15min).

Valença do Minho to: Afife (3–5 daily; 1hr); Barcelos (5–6 daily; 1hr 15min–2hr); Caminha (6–8 daily; 20–45min); Nine – change for Braga (7 daily; 2hr 20min); Porto (5 daily; 2hr 10min–3hr 40min); Vigo, Spain (4 daily; 1hr 10min; connections to Santiago de Compostela and La Coruña); Vila Nova de Cerveira (6–8 daily; 12–18min); Vila Praia de Âncora (6–8 daily; 20min–1hr).

Viana do Castelo to: Afife (4 daily; 20min); Barcelos (12 daily; 25–45min); Caminha (7–9 daily; 20–40min); Porto (10–12 daily; 1hr

30min–2hr 15min); Vila Nova de Cerveira (6–8 daily; 30min–1hr); Vila Praia de Âncora (5–7 daily; 15–25min).

Vila Nova de Cerveira to: Porto (6–7 daily; 2hr 10min–3hr 30min); Valença do Minho (6–8 daily; 12–18min); Viana do Castelo (6–8 daily; 30min–1hr).

Buses

Arcos de Valdevez to: Braga (2–4 daily; 1hr 15min); Lindoso (Mon–Fri 2 daily; 30min–1hr); Ponte de Lima (5–8 daily; 1hr); Soajo (Mon–Fri hourly; fewer at weekends; 30min); Porto (2–4 daily; 2hr); Viana do Castelo (5–8 daily; 1hr 45min).

Barcelos to: Braga (Mon–Fri every 30min, Sat & Sun hourly; 50min); Chaves (Mon–Fri 13 daily, Sat & Sun 3–6 daily; 6hr); Ponte de Lima (Mon–Fri 8 daily, 1–2 at weekends; 40–55min); Porto (Mon–Sat 9–12 daily, Sun 1–2; 1hr 45min).

Braga to: Arcos de Valdevez (2–4 daily; 1hr 30min); Barcelos (Mon–Fri every 30min, Sat & Sun hourly; 50min); Bragança (3–5 daily; 6hr); Cabaceiras de Basto (4–5 daily; 1hr 45min); Caldas do Gerês (Mon–Fri hourly, Sat & Sun 8–10 daily; 1hr 30min); Campo do Gerês (3–7 daily; 1hr 20min); Cerdeirinhas (5–9 daily; 45min); Chaves (5–7 daily; 4hr); Coimbra (1 daily; 3hr 15min); Covide (5 daily; 1hr 10min); Guimarães (every 30 min; 30min–1hr); Leiria (6–9 daily; 4hr 5min); Lisbon (8–11 daily; 5hr 30min); Monção (3–5 daily; 2hr 20min); Montalegre (4–5 daily; 2hr 40min); Pisões (4–5 daily; 2hr 15min); Ponte da Barca (4 daily; 1hr 15min); Ponte de Lima (Mon–Fri 9 daily, Sat 5, Sun 1; 1hr); Porto (hourly; 1hr 10min); Póvoa do Lanhoso (5–7 daily; 35min); Póvoa do Varzim (9 daily; 1hr); Terras do Bouro (7–9 daily; 55min); Venda Nova (5–7 daily; 1hr 50min); Viana do Castelo (9–11 daily; 1hr 30min).

Caldas do Gerês to: Braga (6–10 daily; 1hr 30min).

Campo do Gerês to: Braga (3–6 daily; 1hr 20min).

Guimarães to: Braga (every 30 mins; 30min–1hr); Cabeceiras de Basto (6–8 daily; 1hr 15min);

Lisbon (4–6 daily; 5hr 30min–6hr); Mondim de Basto (2 daily; 1hr 5min); Porto (6–8 daily; 2hr 30min–3hr).

Melgaço to: Castro Laboreiro (Mon–Fri 1 daily; 1hr); Coimbra (1–3 daily; 5hr); Lamas de Mouro (Mon–Fri 1 daily; 40min); Lisbon (1–3 daily; 6hr); Monção (Mon–Fri 5 daily, Sat & Sun 1 daily; 40 min); Porto (1–3 daily; 3hr); São Gregório (Mon–Fri 3 daily; 30min).

Monção to: Braga (3–6 daily; 1hr 45min); Melgaço (Mon–Fri 5 daily, Sat & Sun 1 daily; 40 min); Viana do Castelo (5 daily, 1 hr 20 min).

Ponte de Barca to: Braga (14 daily; 1hr); Lindoso (3–4 daily; 45min); Ponte de Lima (3–4 daily; 20–30min); Viana do Castelo (6–8 daily; 1hr 30min).

Ponte de Lima to: Arcos de Valdevez (5–8 daily; 50min); Barcelos (Mon–Fri 8 daily, 1–2 at weekends; 40–55min); Braga (Mon–Fri 10 daily, Sat 6, Sun 3; 1hr); Paredes de Coura (2–5 daily; 1hr 20min); Ponte de Barca (3–4 daily; 20–30min); Porto (7 daily; 2hr); Valença (1 daily; 1hr); Viana do Castelo (Mon–Fri 21 daily, Sat & Sun 9 daily; 50min).

Valença do Minho to: Lisbon (4 daily; 6hr 30min); Melgaço (8 daily; 40min); Monçao (10 daily; 20min); Ponte de Lima (1 daily; 1hr); Porto (7 daily; 2hr 30min); Viana do Castelo via Caminha (7 daily; 1 hr); Vila Nova de Cerveira (6 daily; 15min); to Spain: Sat to Vigo/Santiago (2hr/4hr 15min); Tues, Thurs, and Fri via Monção and Melgaço for Ponte Barxas.

Viana do Castelo to: Afife (5–13 daily; 15min); Arcos de Valdevez (3–7 daily; 1hr 50min); Braga (8–14 daily; 1hr 30min); Caminha (Mon–Fri 13 daily, Sat & Sun 5 daily; 35min); Esposende (Mon–Fri 10–15 daily, Sun 4; 40min); Lisbon (2 daily; 6hr); Moledo do Minho (Mon–Fri 13 daily, Sat & Sun 5 daily; 30min); Ponte de Lima (Mon–Fri 20 daily, Sat & Sun 9 daily; 50min); Ponte da Barca (6–8 daily; 1hr 30min); Porto (Mon–Sat 10–14 daily, Sun 4; 2hr 5min); Póvoa de Varzim (Mon–Sat 10–15 daily, Sun 4 daily; 1hr 5min); Vila do Conde (Mon–Sat 10–14 daily, Sun 4; 1hr 40min); Vila Praia de Ancora (Mon–Fri 13 daily, Sat & Sun 5 daily; 25min).

TRÁS-OS-MONTES

TRÁS-OS-MONTES – literally "Beyond the Mountains" – is Portugal's Lost Domain. For centuries this remote, rural province has been a place to hide and practise one's beliefs in peace: its peculiar traditions and dialects have been formed by a diversity of populations, from the prehistoric tribes who carved the *porcas* (stone pigs) to Jews who sought refuge here from the Inquisition. The extremity of the climate – "Nine months of winter and three months of hell", as the local proverb puts it – and the aridity of much of its land have kept Trás-os-Montes well apart from the mainstream. Even today, with some industry coming to the major towns, the province has a population half the size of that of the Minho in almost twice the area. But change is approaching rapidly: a recent seven-year World Bank investment project saw over £400 million pumped into the area's agricultural sector and an EU-funded road construction programme is already well on the way to completion, with major new roads providing faster links between the main towns of the region.

A sharp natural divide cuts across the province. In the south is the fertile territory officially entitled the Upper Douro, but known unofficially as the **Terra Quente** (Hot Land), which encompasses the terraced stretches of the rivers Douro, Corgo and Tua, and produces peaches, oranges, melons and wine. By contrast, the bitter winters of the north have earned it the name of **Terra Fria** (Cold Land). Out beyond Mogadouro, the most visible features of this wild and rugged terrain are the countless pony carts and pigeon houses (*pombais*), while the ubiquitous almond trees, whose fleeting blossom time is in late-February and early March, draws weekenders to the border town of Miranda do Douro.

Travelling into and around the province can be a slow business, with few remaining train services and buses between the larger towns generally operating on weekdays only. However, almost any route in Trás-os-Montes has its rewards, and the fortified frontier towns of **Chaves** and **Bragança** should feature on any itinerary of northern Portugal. But, for the most part, Trás-os-Montes' sights are defiantly rural: a succession of hardworking mountain or valley villages, and small, fortified settlements – **Mirando do Douro, Mogadouro, Freixo de Espada à Cinta** – guarding the border with Spain, whose appeal lies above all in their isolation. One of the few towns of any real size in the entire region is **Vila Real** – a good starting point for a tour of the province, especially for hikers, with its access to the dramatic granite scenery of the **Parque Natural de Alvão**. A second natural park hugs the border with Spain in the far north of the province, beyond Bragança, in the **Serra de Montesinho**, where walkers can experience Trás-os-Montes at its most rural and remote; while a third, the **Parque Natural do Douro Internacional**, has recently been designated in the east of the region where the Douro and its tributary, the Rio Águeda, skirt the Spanish border.

Chaves can be reached, a little tortuously, from the Peneda-Gerês park (see p.346), but the most obvious approach to the region is from the Douro, whose

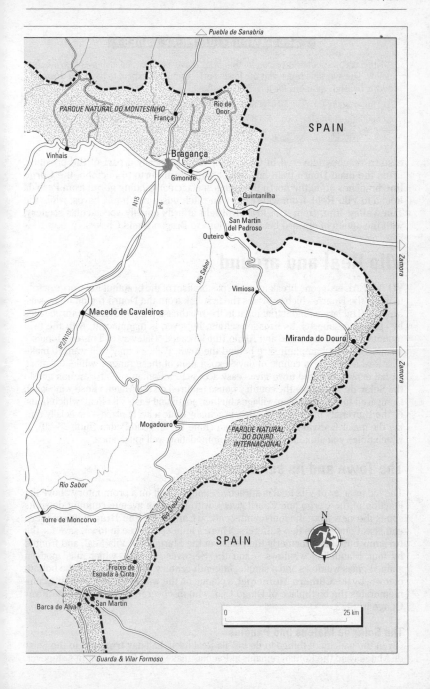

ACCOMMODATION PRICE CODES

All the accommodation prices in this book have been coded using the symbols below. The symbols represent the lowest prices you can expect to pay for a **double room in high season**; for a full explanation, see p.29.

① Under 3000$00   ② 3000$00–4000$00   ③ 4000$00–5500$00
④ 5500$00–8500$00   ⑤ 8500$00–12,500$00   ⑥ 12,500$00–20,000$00
                          ⑦ Over 20,000$00

---

eastern reaches (covered in Chapter 5) are technically a part of the province. From the main Douro train line, which runs from Porto to Pocinho, the **Corgo line** branches off to the north through a spectacular winding gorge from Peso da Régua to **Vila Real**, from where you can catch buses north to Chaves; while the **Tua Valley line**, from Tua to **Mirandela** affords equally spectacular scenery, with the option of onward bus connections to Bragança and Chaves.

Vila Real and around

VILA REAL is the one break from the pastoralism of the beautiful Rio Corgo, a tributary of the Douro which provides the first link from the Douro region to Trás-os-Montes. The largest industrial town in the northeast, it is bordered on three sides by sprawling suburbs. Its broader setting, however, is magnificent, with the twin mountain ranges of **Marão** and **Alvão** (the so-called "Gateway to Trás-os-Montes") forming a natural amphitheatre behind the town. Walkers may well want to make Vila Real a base for a couple of days' exploration of these ranges, while, for more casual exploration, the town gives easy access to a Roman site at **Panóias** and to the **Solar de Mateus** – the country house featured on the Mateus Rosé wine label. Compared to the somnolent villages further north and east, Vila Real, which houses the University of Trás-os-Montes, is actually quite a lively place – especially during the major **festivals** of Santo António (June 13) and São Pedro (June 28–29), at which times you should book your accommodation well in advance.

The Town and its surroundings

The old quarter of Vila Real is attractive enough, built on a promontory above the junction of the Corgo and Cabril rivers, with the main avenue running down its spine; the view from the fourteenth-century **Capela de São Brás** at its southern end is not one for vertigo sufferers. There's little else to see in town, save for the **turismo** building – formerly the palace of the Marquês of Vila Real, and fronted by four Manueline windows – and the **Sé**, over the way, which has modern stained-glass windows and a simple, fifteenth-century interior. Back at the bottom of town, by the **Câmara Municipal**, a plaque on the wall of the café opposite commemorates the birthplace of Diogo Cão, who discovered the mouth of the River Congo in 1482.

The Solar de Mateus and Panóias

Given the paucity of things to do in Vila Real itself, half-day **trips** out to the Solar de Mateus and the Roman remains at Panóias make good use of a night's stopover.

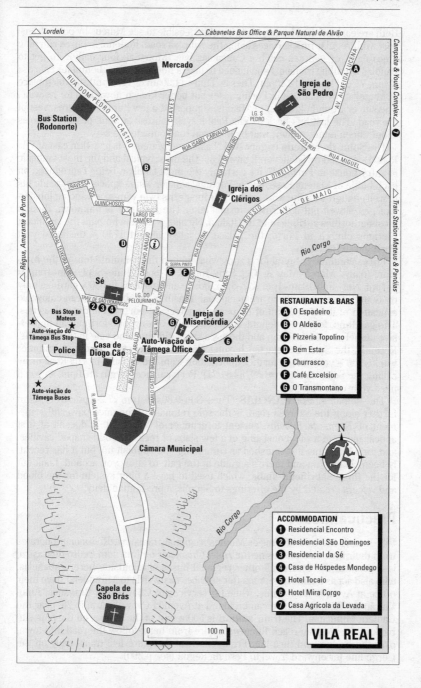

△ Lordelo △ Cabanelas Bus Office & Parque Natural de Alvão Campsite & Youth Complex △▼

RUA DOM PEDRO DE CASTRO

Mercado

Igreja de São Pedro

AV. ALMEIDA LUCENA Ⓐ

Bus Station (Rodonorte)

LG. S PEDRO

R. CANDIDO DOS REIS

RUA D. MARG. CHAVES

RUA ISABEL CARVALHO

RUA 31 DE JANEIRO

RUA MIGUEL

RUA DIREITA

Ⓑ

Igreja dos Clérigos

AV. 1 DE MAIO

△ Régua, Amarante & Porto

RUA MAL. TEIXEIRA REBELO

TRAVESSA DOS QUINCHOSOS

LARGO DE CAMÕES

AV. CARVALHO ARAÚJO

RUA CENTRAL

RUA DO ROSSIO

Rio Corgo

Ⓒ

Ⓘ

Ⓓ

R. SERPA PINTO

Ⓔ Ⓕ

△ Train Station Mateus & Panóias

Sé

RUA NOVA

Ⓐ

LG. DO PELOURINHO

RUA TEIXEIRA DE SOUSA

RESTAURANTS & BARS

Ⓐ O Espadeiro
Ⓑ O Aldeão
Ⓒ Pizzeria Topolino
Ⓓ Bem Estar
Ⓔ Churrasco
Ⓕ Café Excelsior
Ⓖ O Transmontano

Bus Stop to Mateus
★ Auto-viação do Tâmega Bus Stop

TRAV. DE SÃO DOMINGOS

❷❸④⑤

Igreja de Misericórdia

RUA ANTÓNIO DE AZEVEDO

AV. 1 DE MAIO

Police

Casa de Diogo Cão

Ⓖ

Auto-Viação do Tâmega Office

❻

★ Auto-viação do Tâmega Buses

AV. CARVALHO ARAÚJO

RUA CAMILO CASTELO BRANCO

Supermarket

R. IRMÃ VIRTUDES

Câmara Municipal

N

ACCOMMODATION

❶ Residencial Encontro
❷ Residencial São Domingos
❸ Residencial da Sé
④ Casa de Hóspedes Mondego
⑤ Hotel Tocaio
❻ Hotel Mira Corgo
⑦ Casa Agrícola da Levada

Rio Corgo

Capela de São Brás

0 _____ 100 m

VILA REAL

Both are easily visited by car, while it's quite feasible to see Mateus by public transport, with regular **bus** services along the Sabrosa road. Rodonorte buses run nine times daily, or you can catch a Cabanelas bus (Mon–Sat; four daily). To get to Panóias by public transport you'll need to take a Rodonorte bus bound for Sabrosa (Mon, Wed, Fri–Sun 12.10pm; Tues & Thurs 11.30am & 12.10pm), the birthplace of Magellan (Magalhães in Portuguese) but better known nowadays for its wine. The site is around 6km east of Mateus, signposted a few hundred metres west of the road. The last bus back to Vila Real leaves Sabrosa at 3pm, passing Panóias about fifteen minutes later; wait by the main road outside the site.

The **Solar de Mateus** (signposted "Palácio de Mateus") is just 4km east of Vila Real. Described by Sacheverell Sitwell as "the most typical and the most fantastic country house in Portugal", it's certainly the most familiar, being reproduced on each bottle of Mateus Rosé, one of Portugal's major wine exports. The facade fits in well enough with the wine's soft-focus image, its twin wings "advancing lobster-like", as Sitwell put it, across a formal lake. The architect is unknown, though most authorities attribute it to the Italian, Nicolau Nasoni, who built the landmark Clérigos church in Porto; the palace is dated around 1740 – the heyday of Portuguese Baroque.

Prices continue to spiral for a somewhat limited thirty-minute tour of the **interior** (daily: March–May & Oct 9am–1pm & 2–6pm; June–Sept 9am–1pm & 2–7pm; Nov–Feb 10am–1pm & 2–5pm; house and gardens 950$00, gardens only 650$00) but although there are no special treasures, the building is an enjoyable evocation of its period, full of draperies, aristocratic portraits and rural scenes. The **gardens**, too, are a delight, the spectacular box avenue forming an impressive tunnel about 50m long, and there's a small gift shop and café in the grounds. Recently, the Solar has started hosting classical **concerts** (usually on summer weekends) – you can get further information from the turismo in Vila Real, or by calling the Solar directly (☎059/32 31 21). Performances begin at 10pm, so you'll need your own transport.

The Roman site of **PANÓIAS** (Tues–Sun 9.30am–1pm & 2–6pm; free), 6km further along the Sabrosa road, is the sole remnant of the once powerful settlement of *Terras de Panóias*, ancient forerunner of Vila Real. It doesn't at first appear much of a site, consisting of a few slabs of rock with odd-shaped cavities, and for a long time it languished as something of a rubbish tip, but it has recently been cleaned up and there's a guide at the gate to show you around. Look out for the three **sacrificial slabs**, which used to have a filter system for the blood and viscera created by the offerings to Serapis, a pre-Roman deity.

Practicalities

Vila Real is the hub of Trás-os-Montes' regional transport. Rodonorte operates from their **bus station** beside the *Hotel Cabanelas* on Rua dom Pedro de Castro, just north of the centre; all other regional buses stop outside here. Cabanelas, who also act as agents for Santos (for services eastwards to Mirandela) have their office at Avenida Dom Dinis; while for services to Chaves and Bragança, Auto-Viação do Tâmega's office can be found at Avenida Carvallo Araújo 26, near the Camâra Municipal. The **train station** is 500m east of the centre, on the opposite bank of the river; to reach the town centre from here, follow the road into town, over the bridge, and turn left. From Vila Real there are five trains daily on the Corgo line for onward travel to Peso da Régua (see p.290).

The **turismo** (Mon–Sat: April & May 9.30am–12.30pm & 2–7pm; June–Sept 9.30am–7pm; Oct–March 9.30am–12.30pm & 2–5pm; ☎059/32 28 19) is on the central avenue, Avenida Carvalho Araújo, at no. 94. Helpful as ever, it can provide transport and accommodation details, including advice on the various Solares de Portugal properties in the area. If you're heading for the Serra do Marão, it's worth dropping in to the **regional tourist office** at Avda. 1º de Maio 70, first floor (☎059/32 28 19, fax 32 17 12); while for information on the **Parque Natural de Alvão** (see p.366 Cruz das Almas (☎059/32 41 38). The main **post office** is located at the northern end of Avenida Carvalho Araújo.

Accommodation

The pick of the town's **pensões and hotels** is reviewed below but be warned that the more basic places can get distinctly chilly and damp in winter. The cheapest hostel-type accommodation is at the *Instituto da Juventude* youth complex on Avenida Dr. Manuel Cardona (☎059/32 35 51). There is also a pleasant **campsite** with a swimming pool, down by the river (☎059/32 47 24). To get there from the centre, follow Avenida 1º de Maio; if you're coming from the train station, turn right after crossing the bridge. There's adequate shade here, but arrive early if you want a riverside site.

Casa Agrícola da Levada, Timpeira (☎059/32 21 90, fax 34 69 55). Take the Mateus bus or follow Avenida 1º de Maio towards Bragança for 2km until the road descends towards a stone bridge; on the left you'll see this impressive Solares de Portugal farmhouse set in its own grounds and with an attached chapel. It helps to have your own transport, though. ⑥.

Residencial Encontro, Avda. Carvalho Araújo 76–78 (☎059/32 25 32). Family-run place, inexpensive but with a mixed bag of rooms above a restaurant. It's near the turismo, and can be a bit noisy at night. Breakfast included. ③.

Hotel Mira Corgo, Avda. 1º de Maio 76 (☎059/32 50 01, fax 32 50 06). Vila Real's swankiest hotel is an ugly modern block but its rooms overlook the stepped terraces of the Corgo, far below, and there's an indoor swimming pool. ⑤.

Casa de Hóspedes Mondego, Trav. de São Domingos 11 (☎059/32 30 97, fax 32 20 39). Off Avenida Carvalho Araújo and near the Sé, this has some of the cheapest rooms in town, but the plumbing is somewhat archaic. ②.

Residencial São Domingos, Trav. de São Domingos 33 (☎ & fax 059/32 20 39). A nice, run-down but friendly *pensão*, operated by the same family as the *Mondego*, that makes an effort to be modern by putting TVs in all rooms. ③.

Residencial da Sé, Trav. de São Domingos 19–23 (☎059/32 45 75). Next to the *Mondego*, this place has private facilities attached to most of the rooms, and a restaurant below. ③.

Hotel Tocaio, Avda. Carvalho Araújo 55 (☎059/32 31 06, fax 716 75). Large and rather dark 1950s hotel. All rooms come with a private bathroom, and the reception area comes with a stuffed wild pig. ④.

Eating, drinking and nightlife

For inexpensive local **meals**, try any of the cafés in the streets behind the turismo. There's also a timeless (and nameless) *adega* – dark, cave-like and festooned with hams and plastic wine jars – at Trav. de São Domingos 17. If you're planning day-trips out of Vila Real you can stock up on your own supplies at the local **supermarkets** – Mercado Municipal, opposite the bus station, and the Supermercado Mira Corgo on Avenida 1º de Maio – and there's a good **wine shop** on Largo do Pelourinho.

The liveliest **nightspots** in town are the bars along Largo do Pelourinho and Rua Serpa Pinto, notably *Café Excelsior* at nos. 30–36 on the latter, which has a huge pool hall featuring the strangest timing meters for your game you'll ever see.

RESTAURANTS

Restaurante O Aldeão, Rua Dom Pedro de Castro 70, just down from the Rodonorte bus station. This is popular and very reasonably priced, with a changing daily menu of standards: meals cost upwards of 1500$00.

Bem Estar, Avda. Carvalho Araújo, opposite the turismo. Family-run, basic, and inexpensive.

Churrasco, Rua António de Azevedo 24. A simple place that does wonderful grills and spit-roast chicken. Closed Sun.

Restaurante O Espadeiro, Avda. Almeida Lucena. Regional dishes – including stuffed trout and roast kid – are a good bet; meals here cost 2500$00 upwards.

Pizzeria Topolino, Rua António de Azevedo, off the Praça de Camões. A pleasant interior with good options for vegetarians.

Restaurante O Transmontano, Rua da Misericórdia 37. Caters for big groups and can be a bit touristy, but good value nonetheless, specializing in *bacalhao* dishes.

The Parque Natural de Alvão

Portugal's smallest natural park, the **Parque Natural de Alvão**, can be glimpsed when travelling by road between Vila Real and Amarante along the IP4, but you'll see more from the N304, which branches off the IP4 towards Mondim de Basto and goes through the park itself, around Ermelo. This route is served by buses but if you have your own transport, you might prefer to take the minor road to Mondim de Basto (see p.288) that cuts right through the park, via Lamas de Ôlo.

Basically a schist basin formed around the **Rio Ôlo** – a tributary of the Tâmega – the park has some spectacular waterfalls at **FISGAS DE ERMELO** (with a restaurant nearby) and a handful of quiet, rural hamlets, whose houses are constructed from the layered rock of the hillsides. The whole district has dramatic, boulder-strewn scenery reminiscent of the Wild West. Good targets would be **LAMAS DE ÔLO**, on the N313, with its mill and primitive aqueduct; the waterfall (and another mill) at **GALEGOS DA SERRA**; and the western fringe around Ermelo.

Without a car, you're dependent on the sketchy **bus** services to explore the park: the service from Vila Real to Mondim de Basto and Chaves drops you on the park outskirts, a good few hours' hike from the places mentioned above. Still, it's a beautiful walk and at weekends especially you should be able to hitch a lift back with other visitors. Serious walkers intending to cross the whole reserve should obtain maps in advance from Porto or Lisbon and consult the **park headquarters** in Vila Real (see p.365 for details), who can provide information about local **campsites**. The turismo in Vila Real also has a brochure detailing **accommodation** options on the park outskirts.

Northeast: routes to Chaves and Bragança

Beyond Vila Real, Trás-os-Montes begins in earnest, with two main routes heading **northeast**, either to Chaves (64km) or to Bragança (136km). The IP3 (formerly the N2) to Chaves is a particularly fine route, the road constrained by the twists and turns of the **Corgo river valley**, though there's really only one worthwhile overnight stop, at the spa town of **Vidago**. The longer roads to Bragança (the N15 or the new, faster IP4, now nearing completion) have more of interest to delay you, with a possible stopover halfway at medieval **Mirandela** in the **Tua valley** (from where the minor N213 cuts north to Chaves); from here, there are also diversions **south** along the N213/N214 to intriguing towns like Vila Flôr and Carrazeda de Ansiães.

The Corgo Valley and Vidago

From Vila Real, Auto-Viação do Tâmega buses run regularly along the IP3 through the spectacular **Corgo river valley**, where everything from cowsheds to vine posts is made from granite, and where the luscious green of the vines belies the apparent barrenness of the earth. En route, you'll also see the strange *espigueiros* or corn sheds, long and improbably thin granite constructions perched atop stone or wooden stilts. It's a less dramatic ride than that once provided by the old Linha do Corgo train line, long since abandoned to the elements, but it's handsome enough, the road following the valley fairly closely as far as the village of **VILA POUCA DE AGUIAR**, 28km from Vila Real, which is famous in the north for its bread. There's not much reason to stay here, though if you get stuck, there are a handful of *residenciais* along the main road. Beyond here, the road cuts through the edge of the Serra da Padrela, before reaching the upper valley of the Tâmega River at Vidago, which it then traces for the rest of the route to Chaves.

Vidago

The spa town of **VIDAGO** is easily the most interesting stop along the way, with some lovely walks in the vicinity and the opportunity to splash about in the local rivers. It's important to note, however, that the spa closes in winter, as do most of the hotels and *pensões*. Buses drop you by the summer **turismo** (9am–noon & 2–6pm; ☎076/974 70) on the main road and from here it's only a short walk to the spa and hotels – follow the flurry of signs.

The **spa** itself (mid-June to mid-Oct Mon–Sat 8am–noon & 4–7pm) is set in the beautiful grounds of the *Vidago Palace Hotel* (☎076/973 56, fax 973 59; ⑦), an astonishingly opulent Edwardian pile and without doubt one of Portugal's finest hotels. The pump room is magnificent, and there's also a bandstand amid the trees, a boating lake and bikes for rent (for residents only), not to mention the pool, tennis courts and nine-hole golf course. Its restaurant is worth a visit, too, with less scary prices than you may imagine (under 3000$00 per head). *Hotel Parque*, Avda. Teixeira de Sousa (☎076/971 57, fax 996 66; ⑤), is a modern rival to the *Vidago Palace*, with tennis courts and a pool, but lacks its grace and character. The best of the less expensive options include *Pensão Alameda*, Rua Padre Adolfo Magalhães 2 (☎076/972 46; ②), a small, friendly, family-run place, with breakfast thrown in; and *Pensão Primavera*, on Avenida Conde de Caria, facing the *Vidago Palace* (☎076/972 30; ②), a good-value and attractive place with a wide range of rooms and its own restaurant.

Mirandela and the Tua Valley

It's 71km along the N15 (or 65km along the new IP4) from Vila Real to **MIRANDELA**, an odd little town with a few remnants of a medieval centre, a scattering of Baroque mansions and a modern art gallery, as well as some horrible concrete constructions. The town's most striking feature is undoubtedly its **Roman bridge**, renovated in the fifteenth century and stretching a good 200m across seventeen arches. It's now open only to pedestrians, with traffic forced to use the new concrete bridge beside it, or the Ponte Europa upstream. Kayaks and pedaloes splash up and down here, and the riverside gardens and lawns are pleasant places to loaf around.

Parts of the decaying **old town** have recently been renovated or demolished; the chapel near the Câmara Municipal, at the summit of the ancient citadel, simply fell down in 1985. Scavengers pilfered the best of the stonework, and what was left was rebuilt in a four-square style topped with an ugly glass pyramid that contrasts awkwardly with the grandiose **Câmara Municipal** itself. Formerly the Palácio dos Távoras, this was one of several flamboyant town houses associated with the **Távora** family, who controlled the town between the fourteenth and seventeenth centuries. The modern art gallery, the **Museu Armindo Teixeira Lopes** (Mon–Fri 9.30am–12.30pm & 2–6pm; free), is combined with the town's library and displays modern sculptures and paintings, with one section being dedicated to local artist Armindo Teixeira Lopes's images of Mirandela and Lisbon.

The best time to visit Mirandela is during its **festa** – one of the longest in Portugal (July 25 to the first Sunday in August, with the big day on the final Saturday) – or, failing that, for one of the weekday **markets**, held as close as possible to the 3rd, 14th, or 25th of every month. In Portugal, Mirandela is best known for its *alheira* sausages, a legacy of the Jewish community that has since disappeared. Made from chicken and bread and pre-cooked, they're available from the shops along Rua da República, or the *Casa das Alheiras* on Travessa de Praça 5 de Outubro, off the praça itself.

PRACTICALITIES

All **buses** now arrive at the new terminal next to the rail station. To get to the town centre turn right, then right again and with the river on your left it's a five-minute walk to the Roman bridge, from where the road veers right into Rua da República. The **turismo** (Mon–Fri 9.30am–12.30pm & 2–6pm; ☎078/237 46) is located here in the right wing of the new market building.

Somewhat surprisingly, Mirandela has half a dozen **pensões and hotels**, so rooms are pretty easy to find, except during the *festa*. *Pensão Praia*, Largo do 1º Janeiro 6 (☎078/224 97; ①), off Rua da República, has attractive lake views from its upper-floor rooms, which compensate for the rather elementary facilities. The *Pensão Sá Moreno*, also off Rua da República at Rua das Amoreiras 71 (☎078/224 34; ②), is reasonable, though the *Pensão O Lagar*, Rua da República 120 (☎078/227 12; ③), is nicer, furnished in pine and run by friendly people. *Residencial Globo*, Rua Cidade de Ortez 35 (☎078/282 10, fax 288 71; ③), over the old bridge near the hospital, is good value with better facilities and *Hotel Mira Tua*, at Rua da República 42 (☎078/224 03, fax 291 08; ④), is a decent high-rise with well-appointed rooms. The local **campsite** (☎078/231 77) is 3km north of town, on the Bragança road, and has a swimming pool. For **meals**, try the good restaurant at *Pensão Sá Moreno* or *O Pomar* on Avenida Dr. Francisco Sá Carneiro.

On to Bragança: Macedo de Cavaleiros

At Mirandela the Tua valley broadens and the Bragança road veers east along the Rio Azibo, past **MACEDO DE CAVALEIROS**. Unless the shooting and fishing parties at the exclusive *Estalagem do Caçador* on Praça Manuel Pinto de Azevedo (☎078/42 63 56 or 42 63 81; ⑥) are your bag, this is not much of a place to linger. If you want a lunch-stop from driving, or get stranded trying to make a bus connection southeast to Mogadouro, you might sample the delicious **pizzas** at the *Pizzaria d'Itália* at Rua Fonte do Paço 5. There are inexpensive **rooms** available at *Residencial Nova Churrasqueira*, Rua Pereira Charula 8 (☎078/42 17 31; ②); *Residencial Muchacha* opposite (☎078/42 26 58; ②); and the very central *Restaurante Residencial Flórida* (☎078/42 13 42; ①), facing the Câmara Municipal on Rua Dr. Francisco Sá Carneiro. You can buy **bus tickets** from the kiosk outside the *Estalagem do Caçador*.

South to Vila Flôr and Carrezeda de Ansiães

Travelling by road between Mirandela and the Douro, the main route (IP2) runs to the southeast of the Tua valley, through **Vila Flôr** and **Carrezeda de Ansiães**. Both are rewarding halts, and are connected by bus to each other, Tua, Mirandela and Moncorvo.

Vila Flôr

Twenty-four kilometres south of Mirandela, **VILA FLÔR** (Town of Flowers) was given its name in the thirteenth century by Dom Dinis, on his way to meet Isabel of Aragon. His favouritism was short-lived, though, for soon Vila Flôr was forced to contribute a third of its revenue to rebuilding the walls of rival Torre de Moncorvo, 30km to the south. Vila Flôr still has a piece of old wall known as the *Arco Dom Dinis* and a so-called "Roman" fountain.

With its tree-lined squares, attractive location and striking church, the town warrants at least a night's stay, and the eccentric **Museu Municipal**, just south of the main square (10am–12.30pm & 2–5.30pm; closed Tues; free), certainly merits a visit. Three eminent Vilaflôrians donated the contents of their houses to the museum when it was founded in 1946, and the result is an incredible hodge-podge: a much-glued stone *porca* and a few dusty pictures by Manuel Moura being the only items of value. The enveloping clutter includes typewriters, the town's first telephone, sewing machines, snake skins, a set of broken percussion instruments, religious sculptures, teacups, stuffed animals and an ensemble of zebra-hide furniture.

The town **festa** runs from August 22 to 28, with live music and open-air stalls on the last weekend: the main day is on the 24th. There's also an extensive **street market** on the weekday closest to the 15th and 28th of every month and every August 15 (Nossa Senhora da Assunção) an important **romaria** takes place at a hilltop sanctuary at nearby Vilas Boas, 8km northwest.

PRACTICALITIES

The Carrazeda-Vila Flôr **bus station** is on Avenida Marechal Carmuna; there are regular weekday services but weekend services are very restricted with no Saturday service and only one to two buses on Sundays.

There are three **pensões** at the new, upper end of town, of which *Pensão Campos,* on Nova Avenida (☎0789/523 11; ③), is the most pleasant, with big rooms (all with TVs) and breakfast included. The *Casa Rocha*, a little further up at Avda. Marechal Carmuna 4 (no ☎; ①), closer to the bus station, is a cheaper option, but best of all is the *Quinta da Veiguinha* (☎078/527 71; ③), an Agroturismo property

6km northwest on the Mirandela road, close to the Rio Tua and with lovely views over its valley. A stay here will also give you the chance to sample their homemade bread, cheese and sausages. The municipal **campsite** (☎078/523 50), 2km to the southeast along the N215 Torre de Moncorvo road, is one of very few in this area, and comes equipped with a swimming pool. For **meals**, the best bet is the *Pensão Campos*, or *Restaurante Tony* next door. Otherwise, you may find sustenance at one of the cafés down by the museum. The local red **wines**, from the Co-op Vila Flôr, are regarded as among the best in the country.

Carrezeda de Ansiães

CARREZEDA DE ANSIÃES, 16km southwest of Vila Flôr, is a modern town of little intrinsic interest. However, three and a half kilometres to its south (a taxi should cost around 500$00 each way) are the intriguing ruins of a medieval **walled town**, known as Ansiães. Little remains within the perimeter of walls except rocks and boulders, but two chapels stand outside, the better preserved of which – the twelfth-century **São Salvador** – has a Romanesque portal, extravagantly carved with leaves, animals, and human figures. Local myth has it that a tunnel connects Ansiães to another castle beyond the Douro, 12km away; a gaping, fly-ridden hole beneath an impressive slab is the principal piece of supporting evidence. What is undoubtedly true, however, is that the town was a base for five different kings, including the King of Léon and Castile, before Portuguese independence; they're listed by the gateway on a plaque unveiled by Mário Soares in February 1987.

The last inhabitants of old Ansiães left in the mid-eighteenth century. The gradual depopulation resulted from the decision, in 1734, of a gentleman named Francisco de Araújo e Costa, to transfer the official council seat to the new town below (known by then as Carrezeda de Ansiães). In response to local protests at the time he ordered the castle *pelourinho* to be destroyed; with this symbol gone and deprived of a sufficient supply of water, the hill community had no hope of putting up effective resistance. The medieval town went into decline and was soon totally abandoned.

Chaves

CHAVES stands just 12km from the Spanish border and its name, which means "keys", reflects a strategic history of occupation and ownership. Between 1128 and 1160 the town was an Islamic enclave, and in the following seven centuries it was fought over in turn by the French, Spanish and Portuguese. One of its greatest overlords, **Nuno Álvares Pereira**, was awarded the "keys" of the north by João I for his valiant service at the battle of Aljubarrota, and from him the town passed into the steady hands of the House of Bragança. However, as recently as 1912, Chaves bore the brunt of a Royalist attack from Spain – two years after Portugal had become a republic.

Today, Chaves is considerably less significant, though it's still a market centre for the villages of the fertile Tâmega plain – the richest agricultural lands in the province – and regional capital for northern Trás-os-Montes. For visitors, its principal attractions are its **spa**, together with its splendid setting, a modest array of monuments, and its gastronomy: Chaves is famed in Portugal for its smoked hams, delicious meat cakes (*bolas de carne*), sausages and a strong red wine. The

RESTAURANTS & BARS
- Ⓐ Restaurante Dionisyos
- Ⓑ Restaurante Carvalho
- Ⓒ Feng-Hão
- Ⓓ Casa Costa
- Ⓔ Adega Faustino
- Ⓕ Restaurante Cozinha do Convento
- Ⓖ Restaurante Liborio

ACCOMMODATION
- ① Hotel Aquae Flaviae
- ② Pensão Jaime
- ③ Hotel de Chaves
- ④ Hospedaria Flávia
- ⑤ Hotel Trajano
- ⑥ Estalagem Santiago
- ⑦ Forte São Francisco Hotel

CHAVES

town centre also boasts a wonderful medieval jumble of streets, many of whose houses support wooden verandahs on their crumbling facades.

Festivals are another feature of Chaves; the town hosts an important winter fair, held on November 1, as well as the annual ten-day **Feira de Artesanato**, held in the Jardim Público in mid-August, and featuring the crafts, music and food of the Alto Tâmega region and neighbouring Spanish Galicia. The turismo can give details of the **Feira de Velherias**, the antiquities festival that takes place one Saturday a month from May to November. Outside the summer months, check out the fixtures for Chaves FC, which generally puts out a good first-division soccer team.

The Town and spa

The old quarter of Chaves is highly compact, grouped above the river, with the spa just below the old walls to the west. Here, in the centre, the town's military past is still much in evidence. There are two seventeenth-century fortresses, built in the characteristic Vaubanesque style of the north: the **Forte de São Neutel** is closed for visits but occasionally hosts concerts (check with the turismo for details); while the **Forte de São Francisco** has been converted into a luxury hotel (see p.373), worth visiting for its beautiful interior and the magnificent views from the ramparts. The **Castelo**, near the bridge, has a fourteenth-century keep (Torre de Menagem), which houses a small **Museu Militar** (Tues–Sun 9am–12pm & 2–5pm; free). The highlight of the collection is the battle colours of the infantry regiment that repulsed the Royalist attack from Spain in 1912. That said, the castle gardens and the views from the battlements are the main attractions here.

The better town museum is the **Museu da Região Flaviense** (Tues–Sun 9am–12pm & 2–5pm; free) on Praça de Camões, a haphazard assortment of material tracing the history of the town and its customs, including quite an assembly of remains from the old Roman spa settlement. The town was known to the Romans as "Aquae Flaviae", after its spa waters, and was an important point on the imperial road from Astorga, in Spanish León, to Braga. In the first century AD it was the army headquarters under Aulus Flaviensis, who was responsible for developing the thermal stations here and elsewhere in the region – at Vidago, Carvalhelos and Pedras Salgadas.

You can still take the waters at the Chaves **spa** (open all year; ☎076 33 24 45) built around the *nascente* (spring) below the city walls, towards the river, and offering a whole range of treatments. The water emerges at a piping 73°C and is not very tasty (loaded as it is with sodium bicarbonate), though the spa is generally full of old ladies with crocheted mug-holders taking a swig – it's reckoned to be particularly good for gout, obesity, senility and rheumatism. Unfortunately, the river itself is polluted, frustrating any chance of a swim, though the gardens are well kept and attractive, and you can take a pedalo ride up and down its banks to view the traces of the Roman past in the form of the **Ponte Trajano** – the Roman bridge – and its ancient milestones. The two churches in Praça de Camões are worth a look, too: the **Igreja de Matriz**, which is partly Romanesque, and the **Igreja da Misericórdia**, distinguished by vast azulejo panels.

The area around Chaves boasts several **Paleolithic and Roman sites**; if you have your own transport, you may want to pick up the *Circuitos Turísticos* pamphlet from the turismo (see below) in which these sites and and other possible day-trips into the surrounding area are detailed.

Practicalities

Rodonorte **buses** for Vila Real and Braga operate from outside their office on Rua da Familia de Camões. The Auto-Viação do Tâmega bus station (for Vila Real and Bragança) is five minutes' walk north of the centre around the back of the supermarket next to the old train station; if you're coming into town from here, follow the main road directly ahead, bear left at the roundabout, and you'll emerge near the **turismo** (Mon–Fri 9am–12.30pm & 2–7pm, Sat & Sun closes at 6.30pm; ☎076/33 30 29), which is facing the gardens. The regional tourist board – **Região de Turismo do Alto Tâmega e Barroso** – is nearby at Avda. Tenente Valdim 39, 1st Floor (☎076/33 30 29).

Accommodation

Accommodation is plentiful but can be pricey in the summer months, when space is restricted, and intensely cold in winter if you're in an inexpensive, unheated room. At the cheaper end of the budget, *Casa Costa* on Rua do Tabolado (☎076/235 68) can fix you up with rooms in **private houses** (①), or there's the small riverside *São Roque* **campsite** (☎076/227 33; open all year), across the Ponte Trajano, which also rents out canoes.

Hotel Aquae Flaviae, Praça do Brasil (☎076/330 90 00, fax 330 90 10). Adjacent to the spa itself, this is Chaves' largest (and ugliest) hotel. It's four-star with pool and tennis courts. ⑤.

Hotel de Chaves, Rua 25 de Abril (☎076/211 18). Late nineteenth-century hotel which retains a few trappings of grandeur (and, by the looks of it, its towels) from its better days, including a marvellous antiquated lift. Rooms with or without bath, and rather large price differences, depending on what you choose. ②.

Hospedaria Flávia, Trav. Cândido dos Reis 12 (☎076/225 13). Friendly but basic, opposite the *Hotel Trajano*, this has a pleasant, vine-draped courtyard. Same price for single and doubles. ②.

Forte São Francisco Hotel (☎076/33 37 00, fax 33 37 01). Chaves' best luxury option has a superb setting in a seventeenth-century fortress with spectacular views. The conversion is a sensitive blend of the old and new, with all the trappings you'd expect of a four-star hotel – pool, café, excellent restaurant, and even minigolf. Highly recommended. ⑥.

Pensão Jaime, Avda. da Muralha (☎076/212 73). Fifty metres from the spa and not much further from the city walls. It's well placed and good value with countless rooms; some have nice views of the town walls. Baths in some rooms. ②.

Quinta de Santa Isabel, Santo Estêvão (☎076/218 18). A traditional Trás-os-Montes country house, with vineyards, 7km from Chaves, 500m off the N103 to Bragança. Queen Isabel is said to have slept here the night before she married Dom Dinis. ⑤.

Estalagem Santiago, Rua de Olival (☎076/225 45). A 1970s' block facing the Largo do Arrabide, with very good, large, self-contained rooms. Breakfast included. Excellent value. ③.

Hotel Trajano, Trav. Cândido dos Reis (☎076/33 24 15, fax 270 02). Modern, comfortable and a bit dull, though some of the pleasant rooms have traditional local furniture and good views. There's a renowned restaurant in the basement (see below). Breakfast included. ④.

Eating

Some of the *pensões* and hotels have reasonable **restaurants** attached, but wherever you eat you shouldn't have any difficulty finding good Chaves smoked ham, tasty local sausages and fine Trás-os-Montes red wine. For coffee and cakes try *Café Geraldes*, at Rua Santo António at the corner with Largo do Arrabaide.

Restaurante Carvalho, Largo das Caldas. Some of Portugal's best food is served here, as testified by the numerous awards on the walls. Service is excellent – efficient and unobtrusive – and prices are keen: a meal costs 2000$00–2500$00. Highly recommended. Closed Thurs.

Casa Costa, Rua do Tabolado. An excellent and simple place serving huge portions of good homely cooking; the speciality is *bacalhau à Costa*. Has a pleasant, vine-covered rear garden.

Restaurante Cozinha do Convento, *Forte São Francisco Hotel*. Offers the most elegant setting you'll find in Chaves and serves up a variety of unusual dishes including wild boar and partridge. Slick service and (as yet) reasonable prices; under 3000$00 per head.

Restaurante Dionisyos, Praça do Município 2, opposite the Torre de Menagem. Serves huge portions at reasonable prices (with a cheap *prato do dia*). Try the local speciality, *folar*, an interesting and wholesome pork bread. There are tables outside in summer.

Adega Faustino, Trav. Cândido dos Reis. Next to the *Hospedaria Flávia*, this old converted wine cellar, filled with huge wooden barrels, serves great bean salads and a selection of *petiscos*, which you can turn into an inexpensive meal. And, of course, it has terrific wine. There is also an art gallery in one corner.

Restaurante Feng-Hão, Rua do Tabolado. Reasonable Chinese food for around 1800$00.

Restaurante Liborio, Estrada de Outeiro Seco. A good bet for decent Portuguese dishes, but it means trekking out to near the football stadium.

Restaurante Pote. Over the bridge and 1km out on the Bragança road. Serves up generously sized local dishes to an enthusiastic clientele. Closed Mon.

Hotel Trajano, Trav. Cândido dos Reis. A very slick operation in the basement and not too expensive; just the place for Chaves ham and local trout. Open till 9.30pm.

Bars and nightlife

Despite the number of elderly spa-clients in town, there are several trendy **bars** in Chaves. Many of them line the Largo das Caldas, including the *Pórtico Bar*, which plays mainly Latin music until 2am. Local students frequent the cosy *Sá Cristia Bar*, near the Castelo in Rua da Misericórdia, while for a more Stateside experience there's the *Bar Garage* on Travessa Cândido dos Reis, which has bits of cars protruding from the walls. Opposite, the town's only central **nightclub**, *Vanity*, is true to its name, attracting the town's fashion-conscious. *Triunfo*, the main club, is 4km out of town on the road to Valpaços – take a taxi or get a ride with other clubbers from around the Largo dos Caldas at around 10pm.

Routes on from Chaves: Montalegre and Vinhais

Chaves has useful bus connections west to Braga and the Peneda-Gerês national park via **Montalegre** (45km); east to **Vinhais** (65km) and Bragança; and southeast to Mirandela (53km). However, it's worth noting that Saturday services to Bragança are few and far between and that there is no bus from Chaves to Mirandela on Saturday. Heading **into Spain**, you could pick up an express bus to Orense, via Verin, on a Thursday or Sunday (originating in Porto; these pass through Chaves in the afternoon; book ahead at Chaves bus station if possible), or else, catch one of the frequent services (marked "Fronteira" – border), and then a Spanish bus on the other side. There is no currency exchange at the border post.

West to Montalegre

West of Chaves, **MONTALEGRE** – a ten-kilometre detour off the N103 – looms up suddenly, commanding the surrounding plains. Looking at its isolated position on the map, you might expect this frontier town, with a history rooted in past centuries, to be relatively untouched. In fact, there is a fair amount of modern development, caused by the nearby Pisões dam, and it's gradually encroaching on the medieval centre and castle. However, it remains quite an atmospheric place and makes an enjoyable stopover of a night or two, being set amid good walking territory scattered with dolmens and the odd Templar and Romanesque church.

The **turismo** is on the main square, Praça do Município (Mon–Fri 9.30am–12.30pm & 2–6pm; ☎076/522 54) and the best **accommodation** is at the surprisingly fancy *Residencial Fidalgo*, Rua da Corujeira 34 (☎076/524 62; ③), uphill to the left from the main square. There are nice, clean rooms here, with good views over the valley. Another reasonable option is *Residencial Pedreira*, at Rua Dom Afonso III 41 (☎076/525 01; ②). Up the hill from the *Fidalgo* is the *Restaurante Floresta*, where it's worth paying the higher than usual prices for good **food** and views. The *Brasilieira*, on the southwest side of Praça do Município, is also a good bet for an excellent meal, serving large portions. You might ask at the local bars about *Vinhos Mortos* – Wines of the Dead – so called because of the practice of maturing the wine in bottles buried underground at the nearby villages of the Serra do Barroso, notably at Boticas, 27km to the southeast.

There's a minor **border crossing** into Spain north of Montalegre, at Tourém, which is also on the Trilho do Longo Curso (see p.347).

East to Vinhais

Heading eastwards from Chaves, Auto-Viação do Tâmega buses roll through the hills along a superb scenic route to Bragança, 96km away. The route becomes ever more barren as you climb and there are fabulous, if bleak, views from various tortuous bends in the road. Two thirds of the way along is the pleasant village of **VINHAIS**. Its main sight is the Baroque convent of **São Francisco**, a vast building incorporating a pair of churches in its facade. It is situated at the Chaves end of the main street, which runs for 1km or more, and offers staggering views away to the south at every turn.

Should you get stuck in Vinhais, there are three **places to stay**, the best is the *Residencial Ribeirinha*, Rua Nova 34 (☎073/714 90; ①), halfway between the main square and the convent, which has lovely old rooms with balconies overlooking the valley. Otherwise, there are fairly basic rooms at the *Pensão da Calçada*, above the *Restaurante Comercial* at Rua da Corujeira 1 (☎073/717 71; ①), which also takes bookings for its more pleasant branch, *Pensão Leão*, Largo do Arrabalde 20. For **food**, *Restaurante Comercial* has a good menu, and there are several other restaurants as you head out of town on the Chaves road.

For onward travel, the Auto-Viação do Tâmega **bus** office is on the main street, just west of *Restaurante Comercial*. If you have your own transport, you can take the minor road from Vinhais that leads into the Parque Natural de Montesinho (see p.380) – for advice, ask for the *Delegação do Parque* at the Casa do Povo (town hall).

Bragança

On a dark hillock above **BRAGANÇA**, the remote capital of Trás-os-Montes, stands a small circle of perfectly preserved medieval walls, rising to a massive keep and castle, and enclosing a white medieval village. Known as the Cidadela, this is one of the most memorable sights in Portugal, seemingly untouched by the centuries, with a hamlet whose size is wonderfully at odds with the royal connotations of the town's dynastic name. The Braganças were the last line of **Portuguese monarchs**, ruling from 1640, when they replaced the Spaniards, until the fall of the monarchy in 1910. To the British, the name is most readily associated with Catherine, queen to Charles II. For the Portuguese, however, the town represents the defence of the liberty of the people, because the Bragançans were the first to muster a popular revolt against Junot in 1808, and have always defended their power to make their own decisions.

The citadel, along with an excellent museum, provides the principal reason for a visit to the town. However, for anyone interested in a bit of wilderness hiking, the nearby **Parque Natural de Montesinho** provides an additional draw (see p.380), while the **cultural festival** held from August 14 to 22 offers another very good reason to be in town. Bragança is well connected with most major towns by public transport.

The Cidadela

At the heart of the **Cidadela** stands the thirteenth-century council chamber, the **Domus Municipalis**. Very few Romanesque civic buildings have survived, and no other has this pentagonal form. Its meetings – for solving land disputes and the like – took place on the arcaded first floor; below was a cistern. Rising to its side is the **Igreja de Santa Maria**, whose interior is distinguished by an eighteenth-century, barrel-vaulted, painted ceiling – a feature of several churches in Bragança. Keys for the Domus are kept by Dona Emilia at no. 40 nearby.

Facing these buildings is the town keep, the **Torre de Menagem** (9–11.45am & 2–4.45pm; closed Thurs; 100$00, free Sun morning), which the royal family rejected as a residence in favour of their vast estate in the Alentejo. It was one of the first works of restoration by the Society of National Monuments in 1928, and now houses a collection of military odds and ends as well as offering great views from the top. At the side of the keep, a curious **pelourinho** (pillory) rises from the back of a prehistoric granite pig. The town's museum has three more of these crudely sculpted **porcas**, but their most famous representative is to be seen at Murça, halfway between Vila Real and Mirandela. They are thought to have been the fertility idols of a prehistoric cult, and it's easy to understand the beast's prominence in this province of wild boars and chestnut forests, where the staple winter diet is smoked sausage.

Look over the furthest walls of the castle and you'll see the Parque Natural de Montesinho stretching to Spain, a view which seems to stress the town's remoteness. One group who made the most of this isolation were the **Jews**, who escaped over the border in the sixteenth century from the terrors of the Inquisition in Spain. Despite the common rule by Spaniards over the two countries during this period, the Inquisition in Portugal was relatively inefficient – administered in municipalities, the organization spread slowly northwards with ever-decreasing

BRAGANÇA

N

Montesinho, Miranda do Douro & Spain ▷

◁ Campsite & França (Montesinho)

◁ Vinhais, Chaves & Campsite

Mirandela, Vila Real & Porto ▷

Montesinho Park Headquarters

Cemetery

São Francisco

Santa Maria

Torre da Menagen

CIDADELA

Domus Municipalis

São Bento

São Vicente

Museu do Abade de Baçal

Misericórdia

Mercado

Sé

Jardim António José Almeida

Rio Fervença

Footbridge

ESTRADA DE TURISMO

RUA SÃO FRANCISCO
RUA ST CONDESTÁVEL
RUA SERRA PINTO
RUA T. COELHO
RUA MIGUEL TARGA
RUA ABÍLIO BEÇA
RUA DOS COMBATENTES DA GRANDE GUERRA
R. MARQUES DE POMBAL
RUA DA ESTAÇÃO
RUA DR ABÍLIO VAZ DAS NEVES
RUA EMÍDIO NAVARRO
RUA ALMIRANTE REIS
RUA DA PRAÇA
RUA ALEXANDRE HERCULANO
RUA ALEXANDRE HERCULANO
RUA DA FERREIRAL?
AVENIDA CIDADE DE ZAMORA
AVENIDA JOÃO DA CRUZ
AVENIDA DR SÁ CARNEIRO
RUA DR FELGUEIRAS
RUA DR
PRAÇA DA SÉ
PRAÇA CAVALEIRO FERREIRA
RUA ADELINO AMARO DA COSTA

Old Train Station (Museum)
Rodonorte Bus Stop
Cabanelas Turismo
Sanvitur Bus Stop
Auto-Viação do Tâmega Bus Stop
Santos Bus Stop
Cinema

ⓘ

① ② ③ ④ ⑤ ⑥ ⑦

Ⓐ Ⓑ Ⓒ Ⓓ Ⓔ Ⓕ

ACCOMMODATION
① Pensão Transmontano
② Residencial Tulipa
③ Pensão Bragança
④ Residencial Cruzeiro
⑤ Residencial São Roque
⑥ Pensão Rucha
⑦ Residencial Poças
⑧ Pousada de São Bartolomeu

RESTAURANTS & BARS
Ⓐ Lá em Casa
Ⓑ Solar Bragançano
Ⓒ Restaurante Poças
Ⓓ Bó Bar
Ⓔ Rest. Bar D. Fernando
Ⓕ Duque de Bragança

0   100 m

zeal. The Jewish community has left its mark in the names of local families and in the town's cuisine (the *alheira* sausage is made from chicken rather than pork), but the once-thriving synagogue is no more.

You can get a superb **view** of the Cidadela from the bottom of the steps of the church of São Bartolomeu; to get there, follow the signs to the *pousada*, which is next to the church – a half-hour walk from the town centre.

The rest of the town

Modern Bragança, set along the valley below the Cidadela, is a pleasant enough place, despite an eruption of concrete apartment blocks on the outskirts. From the Cidadela, the narrow, stepped Rua Serpa Pinto leads to the **Igreja de São Vicente**, where Dom Pedro I claimed to have secretly married Inês de Castro (see p.151); while a small diversion to the east along Rua São Francisco will bring you to the **Igreja de São Bento**, the town's finest church – a simple Renaissance structure with three contrasting ceilings.

On the way into town, along Rua Abílio Beça, you will find the **Museu do Abade de Baçal**, the town's distinguished museum (Tues–Fri 10am–5pm, Sat & Sun 10am–6pm; 250$00, free Sun morning), installed in the former Bishop's Palace. In its gardens Celtic-inspired medieval tombstones rub shoulders with a menagerie of *porcas*; while inside, the collection of sacred art and the topographical watercolours of Alberto Souza are the highlights, along with displays of local costumes – especially the dress of the *Pauliteiros* ("stick dancers"), who still perform at festivals around Bragança and Miranda do Douro. Further down the street is a fine Renaissance-style **Misericórdia** dating from 1873.

One last, incidental sight, which rail buffs will want to check out, is the tiny **transport museum** at the old train station (variable opening hours, check with the turismo; 250$00). This features the first steam train operative in northern Portugal, and the royal carriage of Portugal's penultimate king, Dom Carlos, both brought here from Arco de Baulhe, following the closure of the upper reaches of the Tâmega train line.

Practicalities

Most **buses** operate from Avenida João da Cruz: Rodonorte, for services to Mirandela, Vila Real, and south of Trás-os-Montes, has a kiosk here next to the old train station; and Santos, which runs to Miranda do Douro and Mirandela, is based at no. 5 (also agents for Alfandeguense buses to Lisbon). Sanvitur – agents for Rede Expressos services further afield – can also be found on the avenida. For onward travel to Vinhais or Chaves, Auto-Viação do Tâmega has an agent, Cabanelas Turismo, at Rua Guerra de Junqueiro 111. For details of travel into the Parque Natural de Monteshino see p.380, and for **crossing the border** into Spain, see p.380.

From the Rodonorte bus stop it's a short walk south along Avenida João da Cruz to Praça da Sé, essentially the centre of town. From here it's a couple of hundred metres north to the very helpful **turismo** (summer Mon–Sat 9am–12.30pm & 2–8pm, Sun 2–8pm; winter Mon–Fri 9am–12.30pm & 2–5pm, Sat 10am–12.30pm; ☎073/38 12 73), on Avenida Cidade de Zamora, a wide boulevard split by gardens. Another 200m down the avenue, in a modern development on the left, is the head office of the **Parque Natural de Montesinho** at Apart. 90,

Lote 5, Bairro Salvador Nunes Teixeira (Mon–Fri 9am–12.30 & 2–5.30pm; also Sat & Sun noon–9pm during summer; ☎073/38 12 34), who can provide you with information about visiting the park.

Accommodation

Pensões and hotels are scattered around town. The nearest **campsite** (☎073/33 15 35; May–Oct) is 6km north of town, on the França road, and has pretty sparse facilities. Eight kilometres out of town on the N103 Vinhais road, there's a private campsite, *Cepo Verde* (☎ 073/993 71), with better facilities, including a pool.

Pensão Bragança, Avda. Dr. Francisco Sá Carneiro (☎073/33 15 79, fax 33 12 42). Box-like concrete structure above the cinema, popular with visiting businessmen. Comfortable and well-run. ⑤.

Residencial Cruzeiro, Trav. do Hospital (☎073/33 16 33). On an alley off Rua Almirante Reis, this central place, opposite a noisy games arcade, was renovating its rooms at the time of writing. ③.

Residencial Poças, Rua Combatentes da Grande Guerra 200 (☎073/33 14 28). As cheap as it gets in the centre, though pick your room with care – some are very bare and in winter this place is freezing. Check in at the restaurant next door. Breakfast included. ②.

Pensão Rucha, Rua Almirante Reis 42 (☎073/33 16 72). More of a family home than a *pensão*, run by an elderly couple and including a hearty breakfast; you'll have to look hard to spot the sign. Some rooms are a bit airless, and it can be noisy. ④.

Pousada de São Bartolomeu, Estrada de Turismo (☎073/33 14 93, fax 234 53). South of the river, about 1km by road from the centre – follow the signs off Rua Alexandre Herculano. Purpose-built in 1959, it's got wood panelling, cork ceilings, great views and a good restaurant. ⑥.

Residencial São Roque, Rua da Estacada 26–27 (☎073/38 14 81). A purpose-built high-rise block with well-furnished rooms and attentive service. Good value. The top floors have great views. ④.

Pensão Transmontano, Avda. João da Cruz l68 (☎073/33 18 99). Opposite the train station, this is one of the cheapest *pensões* in town, but it's brusquely run. ②.

Residencial Tulipa, Rua Dr. Francisco Felgueiras 8–10 (☎073/33 16 75). Clean, simple but overpriced place near the train station with cramped rooms that, nevertheless, is highly sought after in summer; arrive early or book ahead. It also has a reasonable restaurant. ④.

Eating, drinking and nightlife

Bragança has a promising array of **bars** and **restaurants** and the places listed below are all recommended. For the town's rather limited **nightlife**, the places to go are *Bô*, a late-night bar with good music on Rua Combatentes da Grande Guerra, and *Duque de Bragança,* a more upmarket but lively place inside the walled town, which sometimes has live music and is open until 2am.

RESTAURANTS

Restaurante Bar D. Fernando, Cidadela 197. Good-value even without considering its location just inside the walls of the old town. There's a lively bar downstairs, too.

Lá em Casa, Rua Marquês de Pombal 7. A convivial place near the Igreja da Misericórdia. Don't be put off by the over-rustic decor. Full meals from 2500$00.

Restaurante Poças, Rua Combatentes da Grande Guerra 200. Excellent and inexpensive food in the restaurant below the *residencial* – family-run and popular enough to fill a couple of floors.

Solar Bragançano, Praça da Sé. An upmarket but excellent *casa típica*, where you dine in oak-panelled rooms to the accompaniment of classical music. There's a nice bar, too.

Crossing to Spain

The easiest way to get to Spain is on the Internorte **express bus**, which runs to Zamora and Valladolid and on to Madrid, on Mondays, Tuesdays, Thursdays and Fridays; you can get tickets from the Rodonorte bus station. Failing that, take a Rodonorte bus to the Portuguese border post at **QUINTANILHA**, 34km away (1–2 daily). At the Spanish frontier village of San Martin del Pedroso, there's a single, combined *pensão* and restaurant, the *Evaristo*, and an early-morning bus to Zamora.

An alternative crossing is to take the road through the Parque Natural de Montesinho (see below), through the border villages of **PORTELO** (Portugal) and Calabor (Spain) to the Spanish town of Puebla de Sanabria, which has onwards bus and train services and accommodation. Using public transport, you can catch Rodonorte buses to Portelo (1–2 daily during school times only) and then irregular Spanish buses (Mon–Fri) between Calabor and Puebla de Sanabria, but you'll have to walk or hitch the 6km between Portelo and Calabor.

The Parque Natural de Montesinho

Occupying the extreme northeastern tip of Portugal, the **Parque Natural de Montesinho** is the only sector of the Terra Fria where the way of life and the appearance of villages have not yet been changed by the new wealth of the emigrant workers. The Terra Fria's predominantly barren landscape is here disrupted by microclimates which give rise to the Serra de Montesinho's heather-clad hills, wet grass plains and thick forests of oak. Another curious feature of the region is the round *pombal* or pigeon house – a structure which, no matter how well-established its position, invariably seems to have dropped in from another world. The ethnographic museum in Miranda do Douro (see p.384) can fill you in on these and other aspects of traditional village life, such as the black cape and the cloaks of straw – as much a protection against heat as against cold.

For leaflets and advice for walkers, contact the **Montesinho park office** in Bragança (see p.378), which also has brochures on the local flora and fauna and is due to produce maps for walkers by mid-1998. In addition, this is the place to ask about **renting traditional houses** (*Casas Abrigo*), which are scattered throughout the small villages in the park – prices range from around 5000$00 a night, for a studio sleeping two, to 50,000$000 for a property that will hold 21. Note that **camping** in the park is prohibited and the only two official sites are located on the southern boundary of the park (see p.379).

The most useful **bus links from Bragança** are to França/Portelo, due north of Bragança (1–2 Rodonorte buses daily during school times only), and to Rio de Onor, to the northeast (1–2 STUB buses daily; see p.383). It is not too hard to hitch on the França road in summer, and walking beyond here, alongside the **Rio Sabor**, is idyllic, with wonderful and deserted spots for swimming (see below). **Walking to Rio de Onor** is also an option, for more on which see below.

Rio de Onor

RIO DE ONOR, hard by the Spanish border, 25km north of Bragança, provides perhaps the most fascinating insight into the village life of the Serra de Montesinho. There are in fact two Rio de Onors – one in Spain (called Riohonor de Castilla) and one in Portugal – but two stone blocks labelled "E" and "P", and

PARQUE NATURAL
DE MONTESINHO

WALKING IN MONTESINHO

One of the nicest places to base yourself if you want to do some walking is the village of **França**, 10km north of Bragança and in the heart of the park. The village has a small shop, café and a bar, as well as a pony trekking and mountain bike rental centre ; the nearest official campsite is 4km south on the Bragança road (see p.379).

The best **trail** in the area is a moderately easy two-day walk beginning and ending at França. Start by turning left off the main road, just past a small bar, and walk along the track which follows the Rio Sabor. This track is rarely used by vehicles and winds through a steep gorge, where you can spot many species of birds and, in summer, maybe some wild boar. The track passes a hydroelectric power station and a trout farm (on your left), then after about 4km there's a turning off to the left marked Soutelo. If you have only a short time, take this track and follow it through the picturesque villages of **Soutelo** and **Carragosa**; it will lead you back to França within a few hours.

If you're doing the longer walk, ignore the turning and continue for about 6km along the track towards the isolated reservoir, **Barragem de Serra Serrada**, near the Spanish border. There's a mountain hut for spending the night – just past the reservoir take a right-hand path signposted *Lama Grande*. About 2km before the reservoir, there's a turning off to the left, signposted **Montesinho**: it's a worthwhile detour – signs clearly point the way – to see a traditional mountain village. Look out for the inscriptions on the doors of the houses, and the blacksmith's forge, which has been here since the sixteenth century and stopped working only fifteen years ago. There's a good restaurant here – the *Café Montesinho* – as well as two *pensões*, *Maria Rita* (☎073/912 93; ②) and *Constância* (☎073/912 27; ②). To rejoin the track to the reservoir, you can leave Montesinho via the road at the top of the village, next to the bar, and follow any of the narrow paths over the hills until you rejoin the main track; this should take around half an hour. However, many of the smaller paths are quite overgrown and difficult to navigate, so you may find it easier to retrace your steps back to the Montesinho junction and join the track there.

About 2km after the reservoir, the track spilts in two; take the right-hand turning for the mountain hut (see above) and the left-hand turning – signposted França and Soutelo – to start the return journey to França. The track leads over a high plateau covered with expanses of heather and rock formations, and giving spectacular views over to Bragança in the distance. Follow the track, descending steadily for a few kilometres, then take a left-hand turning. A couple of kilometres further on, you'll see a right-hand turning – clearly signposted to França – take this turning and after about 4km you'll rejoin the track in França where the walk started.

a change from cobbles on the Portuguese side to smooth concrete on the Spanish, are all that delineate the frontier. The villagers have come and gone between the two for generations, intermarrying and buying goods; both sides spoke, until recently, a hybrid Portuguese-Spanish dialect known as *Rionorês*. Their extreme isolation encouraged systems of justice and mutual co-operation that are independent of the state and which still exist today, something for which Rio de Onor has become famous in Portugal. The ageing villagers (most of the youth have left for the cities) share land, flocks, winepresses, mills and ovens.

The two villages are set on either side of a stream: the granite steps and wooden balconies of rough schist houses line narrow alleyways, and straw creeps out across the cobbles. The bar in the Portuguese "half" of the village contains a long stick on which locals once marked the number of cattle and sheep they owned. Communal meetings fined troublemakers and miscreants in wine! If you want to **stay**, there's the possibility of basic shelter in the *Casa do Povo* (parish rooms) provided you contact the village *presidente* on arrival, but don't count on it.

STUB **buses**, fluctuating according to local school and market timetables, connect the village with Bragança. Outside school times, a day-trip by bus is not a realistic option; indeed, often the bus goes no further than the village of Varges. But you could always **walk** the 13km here from Varges, with its traditional stone houses. The route indicates very clearly how isolated Rio de Onor is – the road has existed for only twenty years, before which time the locals had to walk across open country to and from Bragança.

Southeast to Miranda do Douro

From Bragança, the N218 southeast to Miranda do Douro runs across the **Planalto Mirandês**, a breathtaking journey in late February and early March, when the sudden blossoming of the almond trees transforms the countryside. Some say that it was the beauty of this vista – and Miranda do Douro itself – that decided Afonso Henriques, the future first king of Portugal, to turn against his Spanish kinsmen, refortify the border and begin his victorious sweep across Lusitânia at the start of the twelfth century. The route offers the chance for stop-offs in some extremely attractive towns and villages on the way; if you don't have your own transport, you can take one of the Rodonorte or Santos buses that make the trip one to three times daily.

Seven kilometres out of Bragança is **GIMONDE**, a rural village of traditional wooden houses beautifully sited on the edge of the Montesinho park and which, in fact, would make a fine base should you want to stay somewhere even quieter than Bragança. The rivers Onor, Sabor and Igrejas all meet here near a Romanesque bridge, a favourite spot for stork-watching in early summer. There are **rooms** above the *Restaurante 4* (☎073/38 16 49; ②), slightly out of town on the Bragança road.

Fifteen kilometres beyond Gimonde, the N218 branches away from the main cross-border road and runs another 10km south to **OUTEIRO**, a once-grand village with a disproportionately huge church, Santo Cristo, built in 1755. Outeiro's erstwhile status as defender of Portugal's eastern tranches is confirmed by the presence of a ruined **castle** on the hill above the village. The small bar on the green by the church contains a sketch of this in its heyday, before it was destroyed in the wars with Spain. The local water hereabouts is believed to cure breathing problems, its miraculous powers supposedly enhanced after a visitation by Nossa Senhora de Fátima on 11 June 1848.

Between Outeiro and **VIMIOSA**, 22km south, the countryside becomes ever more mountainous and dramatic. The town itself is spectacularly set, though despite some pretty, traditional houses on the steep streets around the Igreja Matriz, there's little of interest in Vimiosa, much of which is swamped by *emigrante*-financed development. There are two modern *residenciais* here, the *Central* and more upmarket *Charneca*, signposted off the main Bragança road, but you'd do far better to press on to Miranda do Douro, only another 30km to the southeast.

Miranda do Douro

Facing Spain across the deep gorge of the Douro, **MIRANDA DO DOURO** played a key role in all of the country's wars subsequent to Afonso Henriques' conquest of Lusitânia in the early twelfth century. After valiant service in the Independence, Spanish Succession, and Seven Years wars, it ended its fighting days in 1762 when an explosion during a Spanish attack destroyed the castle and the town, and killed 400 inhabitants.

Today, the old town of Miranda seems scarcely more than a village. In 1762, an unexplained explosion flattened two hundred houses and Miranda remained a neglected outpost for nearly two centuries until the huge Douro dam was built in 1955 breathing some new life into the town. Yet it has the status of a city, and a sturdy sixteenth-century **Sé** overlooks its cobbled streets and low white houses. This cathedral and the city status date from a decision by the Portuguese church authorities to make Miranda the capital of the diocese to counteract the feudal power of the House of Bragança in Trás-os-Montes. At the end of the eighteenth century, however, the see was transferred to the larger of the two towns, leaving Miranda cathedral as a cumbersome memento of past glory. To the bitter comment "The sacristy is in Bragança, but the cathedral is in Miranda", the astute Bragançans reply, "If ever you go to Miranda, see the cathedral and come home."

The cathedral aside, Miranda has a certain neat charm, despite its modern sprawling outskirts and a rather off-putting rash of frontier tourist shops. The tidied-up ruins of its Episcopal Palace, now a café, and the medieval facades along **Rua da Costanilha** set the tone, and there is a small medieval bridge, too, over the diminutive Rio Fresno. Beyond here you reach an eighteenth-century fountain, the Fonte dos Canos.

However, the main focus of interest in town is the **Museu da Terra de Miranda** (Tues–Sun 10am–1pm & 2–6pm; 150$00) on Praça Dom João III, just off Rua da Constanilha. This is literally bursting with curiosities, from pistols to children's balloons made out of sheep's stomachs, and features a couple of reconstructed rooms in traditional Mirandês style – an illustration of local life that's inaccurate only in that the agricultural labourers of the region generally live, sleep and die in a single room.

Apart from the local **festa** periods (Santa Bárbara on the third Sunday in August; Romaria Nossa Senhora do Nazo, Sept 7–8), and the **feira** held on the first weekday of every month, Miranda's main action is supplied by the shopping antics of Spanish day-trippers.

Practicalities

The **turismo**, on Largo do Menino Jesus da Cartolinha (summer Mon–Sat 9am–12.30pm & 2–8pm, Sun 2–8pm; winter Mon–Fri 9am–12.30pm & 2–5pm; ☎073/411 32), can provide details on river trips and will also help with **accommodation**. One of the best options is the *Residencial Flor do Douro*, Rua do Mercado Municipal 7–9 (☎073/421 86; ②), in a modern block in a shopping centre, but with fine views from some of its back rooms. *Residencial Planalto*, Rua 1º de Maio (☎073/43 13 62, fax 427 80; ③), is another good choice, with modern, ensuite rooms, but no views. The only *pensão* in the old town is the characterful

---

TELEPHONE NUMBERS

Note that at the time of writing, some of the older five-digit telephone numbers in Miranda da Douro were being upgraded to six digits. If you are unable to get through to any of the five-digit numbers given here, try inserting a "3" after the first digit.

Santa Cruz, Rua Abade de Baçal 61 (☎073/413 74; ②), near Largo do Castelo, with a family atmosphere and a good restaurant. The local *pousada*, *Santa Catarina* (☎073/410 05, fax 410 63; ⑥), is just off Largo Meninho Jesus da Cartolinha; its twelve balconied rooms overlook the huge Miranda do Douro reservoir but the *pousada* itself is modern and unexceptional, except for its service. There's a **campsite**, *Santa Luzia* (☎073/421 96; June–Sept), on the southern side of town, by the stadium and municipal swimming pools; it's run by the municipality and is free.

In addition to the *pensão* and hotel **restaurants**, you might like to check out the menus at *O Mirandês* (from 1500$00) on Largo do Moagem, or the cheaper *Balbina*; the latter has a collection of grandfather clocks, serves excellent wine and a local *posta assada à mirandesa* (beef) which will feed two or three. The *São Pedro* at Rua Mouzinho de Albuquerque 20 in the old town is also good value, serving excellent *tamboril* and prawn kebabs. For nightlife, try *Bar Black and White* on Rua do Mercado, or *Bar Atalaia* on Largo do Castelo, both lively spots in the old town.

Crossing to Spain

The Spanish border lies just three kilometres to the west of Miranda, across the **Barragem de Miranda**, at 528m the highest hydroelectric dam in the country and the last before the Portuguese Douro becomes the Spanish Duero. If you have your own transport, this crossing is a good point from which to approach Zamora.

Mogadouro, Torre de Moncorvo and Freixo de Espada à Cinta

For much of its journey southwest from Miranda do Douro to the border with Spain the N221 runs along the western fringes of Portugal's newest and largest nature reserve, the **Parque Natural do Douro Internacional** (see box on p.386), visible as tantalizing glimpses of water and forested valleys to the east. It's not until the town of Mogadouro, almost 50km away, that the road finally breaks loose from the plains and olive groves and begins to skirt the forest proper. From Mogadouro there are onward travel options south to Freixo de Espada à Cinta – a good base from which to explore the natural park – or southwest to Torre de Moncorvo and Pocinho (see p.292).

Halfway between Miranda and Mogadouro is the pleasant, functional town of **SENDIM**, but the only real reason to stop off here is to sample some of the country's top cooking, at the *Restaurante Gabriela*. The restaurant is run by Alicia, an award-winning celebrity chef but sadly, if she's not there, the food can be average and overpriced (around 2000–2700$00). Should you strike lucky, and proceed to

THE PARQUE NATURAL DO DOURO INTERNATIONAL

Designated in September 1997, the **Parque Natural do Douro Internacional** covers a vast tract of land along the west bank of the Douro as it flows along the Spanish border from Miranda do Douro in the north (p.384) to Barca de Alva (p.294) – the point at which the river officially enters Portuguese territory – as well as a stretch of the Rio Águeda further south in Beira Alta.

The upper Douro is ecologically important owing to its Mediterranean microclimate, which contrasts markedly with the harsher, mountainous terrain of the Terra Fria which encloses it. The combination of mild winters and its isolation from both large human populations (the mountains saw to that) and the Mediterranean zone proper, has led to the survival of a number of animal and plant species now extinct in the south. To the visitor, this quirk of geology is most visible in the region's famous **almond trees**, explained in a legend of a Moorish prince who married a northern European princess. Though happy in summer, she grew sad and wistful in winter, and ached for the snow-clad hills of her homeland. Unable to fulfil her wish, the prince hurried instead to the Algarve, from where he brought back the almond trees, so that from then on, every February when the trees blossomed, the princess beheld white as far as the eye could see.

Despite some river pollution (mild in comparison with further downstream) and industrial sand extraction on the Spanish side, the area has been left largely untouched by the more damaging aspects of twentieth-century agriculture and industry, and preserves a rich, if endangered, local **flora and fauna**, including rare mammals such as wolves, wild cats and otters, as well as various species of bats and amphibians. The area is also an ornithologist's dream, home to over **170 bird species**, including rare peregrine falcons, black storks and Europe's largest population of Egyptian vultures.

In common with all natural parks, its success depends on achieving a fine balance between the encouragement of much-needed investment in the agricultural infrastructure on its margins, and the development of eco-tourism within the park itself to benefit the local population, which has one of the highest unemployment rates in the country. As the park is still in its infancy, no official park office has yet been set up, and **information** concerning its wildlife, possible walking routes and camping spots is non-existent. For the time being, **visiting the park** is a simple matter of choosing one of the towns in the area – Miranda da Douro, Freixo de Espada à Cinta or Barca de Alva – as a base (see the relevant accounts in the text for details of accommodation). You might also consider staying in Vila Nova de Foz Côa (see p.292), which has the added attraction of the Parque Arqueologico do Vale do Côa. Alternatively, **camping** in the park is permitted at present, although this is likely to be more strictly controlled in future. Enquire locally as to possible walks; only Miranda do Douro has a **turismo** but the Câmara Municipal in other towns may be of some help.

eat and drink your fill, you may be glad of the **rooms** at the restaurant (☎073/731 80; ②), or those around the corner at the *Galego* (☎073/732 02; ②).

Mogadouro

For an unkempt and authentic picture of town life in the Terra Fria, you need look no further than **MOGADOURO**, specifically its **castle**. This is unexceptional as a monument, but the ground in front is common land where children play and farmers sort out their produce. During the harvest period the area is stacked high with dried *tremoços* bushes, whose seeds are consumed as beer-time snacks and used in soups. The castle hill also commands terrific views over a long, low horizon and a patchwork of fields and *pombais*. The **Câmara Municipal** occupies a former convent, but is treated by the townspeople as their own backyard, for herding cows home in the evening, saddling up pony carts, and playing at tossing coins for hours at a time there.

The main tree-lined Avenida Nossa Senhora do Caminho has a sports complex and views over the hills on one side, and a row of shops and cafés on the other. The avenue ends at Praça Engenheiro Duarte Pacheco, where **buses** drop you, with the old town and ruined castle beyond. The Santos ticket office is at Largo Trindade Coelho (☎079/325 37). Should you want to **stay**, there are plenty of places from which to choose, including three *residenciais* on the road to Freixo and a string along the main avenue, including *Residencial A Lareira*, at no. 58 (☎079/34 23 63; ④; closed Jan), with a renowned **restaurant** (closed Mon). In addition, there are reasonable rooms at the *Pensão Russo*, Rua 15 de Outubro 10 (☎079/34 21 34; ②), which also has its own restaurant, and rooms to rent at the otherwise overpriced *Restaurante Estoril* (☎079/34 27 93; ②), on Rua da República, off the praça. *Restaurante Kalifa*, on Rua Santa Marinha, also off the praça, is recommended for its steak and superb red wine.

Be warned that the town is busy (and rooms at a premium) in August, when the emigrants are back home with their families. There is an annual **festa** at this time, in honour of Nossa Senhora do Caminho (Aug 7–23), with a special *emigrante* weekend on the last Saturday and Sunday of August, before they leave the country again.

Onward travel

Twenty-five kilometres south of Mogadouro along the N221 is **LAGOAÇA**, a very old village whose houses feature Manueline stone-arched windows, and whose women still wear traditional dress. Pass through the village, beyond the cemetery, and there's a superb viewing platform, looking over the deep Douro valley into Spain. A further 6km along, the road divides: the N221 continues south to Freixo de Espada à Cinta, while the N220 branches off southwest to Torre de Moncorvo.

Torre de Moncorvo

Aside from its sixteenth-century cathedral there's little to see in **TORRE DE MONCORVO**, 58km southwest of Mogodouro, though its network of handsome, narrow medieval streets make the town a pleasant place to spend the night. The **turismo**, on Rua Manuel Sexas (Mon–Fri 9am–12.30pm & 2–5.30pm; ☎079/222 89), can advise you as to how to track down the remains of the old town walls. The town's other attraction is its almond trees, the blossoming of which draws crowds of Portuguese in February and March. Later, the nuts are gathered and sugared, and sold in local shops.

There are three **bus** connections a day from Mogodouro to Moncorvo (as it's known locally), which then continue on to Pocinho, 10km to the southwest, where they meet the trains running along the Douro line (see p.292). Buses also run from Moncorvo to Freixo de Espada à Cinta (see below) and there's a daily connection south to Vila Nova de Foz Côa, in Beira Alta, which continues to Lisbon. Buses to Porto run on Tuesdays and Thursdays. All these buses arrive in and depart from the bus station on Estrada 220, next to the telecom building near the hospital.

Accommodation should be no problem. The best *pensão*, in fact one of the best in Portugal, is the *Passarinho* at Rua Infante Dom Henrique 23 (☎079/25 23 19; ②), whose large rooms are in a turn-of-the-century town house. Alternatively, try *Campos Monteiro*, Rua Visconde de Vila Maior 55 (☎079/25 40 55, fax 25 42 80; ③) or *Residencial Caçula*, (☎079/25 42 18; ③) just down from the Sé, on Rua das Amoreiras. More upmarket are the *Casa da Avó*, a town house built in 1880 and a member of the Solares de Portugal network – at Rua Manuel Sexas 12 (☎079/224 01; ⑤; Feb–Nov), and the ugly modern *Residencial Brasília* (☎079/25 40 94; ⑤), 1km north on the N220 (the Freixo de Espada à Cinta road), which has the benefit of a swimming pool. The cosy *Quinta do Avelinho*, 300m from the bus station on the Pocinho road (☎079/221 37; ⑤), has three bedrooms in an old farmhouse, each with kitchenettes, and bicycles for rent. For **food**, your best bet is the restaurant attached to *Campos Monteiro*.

Freixo de Espada à Cinta

The southernmost town in Trás-os-Montes, **FREIXO DE ESPADA À CINTA** is served by four daily buses operated by Santos (☎079/65 21 88), from Miranda do Douro and Mogadouro. The town feels end-of-the-worldish as the bus climbs down to its valley, hidden on each side by wild, dark mountains, a backdrop against which you might glimpse the occasional hawk or black kite. You're unlikely to come across any other travellers on the road; in fact the town was once considered so remote that prisoners who had been granted an amnesty were allowed to settle here – it's this sense of isolation that makes the town worth a visit.

Curiously, for such a remote outpost, there is a very rich parish church, the **Igreja Matriz** – part Romanesque, part Manueline – with a *retábulo* of paintings by Grão Vasco (see Viseu, p.223). Across the way from the church is a magnificent heptagonal **keep** (Mon–Fri 9am–12.30pm & 2–5.30pm; free), a landmark for miles around, which affords great views from its bell tower for those who brave the very steep steps. Another, unpublicized, attraction is a mansion in Largo do Outeiro that maintains a garden of mulberry bushes complete with worms for silk production; ask around and you may be taken for a look.

The town has a ring of dull new buildings and, among them, some **places to stay**, such as the modern *Hospedaria Santo António* (☎079/63 31 04; ②), a little distance from Avenida 25 de Abril where the bus drops you and facing the Capela de Santo António. A more comfortable option is the *Quinta da Boa Vista* (☎079/621 45; ⑤), on the outskirts of town as you come in from Moncorvo, which has four bungalows for rent, a pool and pleasant views over the town; call in advance or you might find the place deserted. The *Cinta de Ouro* (☎079/65 25 50; ③), opposite the new municipal market on the way out of town to the south, is very good (if a little bland) with TVs and private bathrooms in each room. Its restaurant has an outdoor patio and is the place for **meals**, though you'll find there's a strong Spanish influence in the cooking. For typical Portuguese dishes try the *Bom Retiro*, 100m further along, which is also cheaper. There's a **campsite**, *Congida*, just over 4km east on the banks of the Douro (☎079/65 33 71); follow the signs or take a taxi. The complex also houses the municipal swimming pools, a couple of cafés and a restaurant.

To the south, the N221 follows a beautiful stretch of the Douro to Barca de Alva, 20km southwest (see p.384), but you'll need your own transport as there are no buses along this route.

travel details

Trains

Peso da Régua to: Livraçao (for Amarante) (7–8 daily; 1hr); Tua (7–8 daily; 1 hr); Vila Real (5 daily; 1hr).

Tua to: Mirandela (5 daily; 1hr 50min).

Vila Real to: Peso da Régua (5 daily; 1hr).

Buses

With ongoing construction of new and faster roads, bus routes, hours of operation and journey times change frequently. It's advisable to check exact timetables with the turismos or relevant bus companies given in the accounts of each destination.

Bragança to: Braga (3–5 daily; 6hr); Chaves (Mon–Fri & Sun 3 daily; Sat 1 daily; 2hr); Coimbra (2–3 daily; 6hr 50min); Lamego (2–3 daily; 4hr); Lisbon (2–4 daily; 9–10hr); Macedo de Cavaleiros (5 daily; 35–45min); Miranda do Douro (1–3 daily; 1hr 30min–2hr 15min); Mirandela (10 daily; 1hr 25min–2hr 45min); Mogadouro (Mon–Fri 1 daily; 1hr 40min); Peso da Régua (2–3 daily; 3hr 45min); Porto (2–6 daily; 5hr–5hr 20min); Sendim (Mon–Fri 1 daily; 2hr 10min); Vila Nova de Foz Côa (2 daily; 2hr); Vila Real (Mon–Fri 7 daily; Sat & Sun 3 daily; 2hr 50min); Vinhais (2–3 daily; 35min); Viseu (2–4 daily; 5hr 15min).

Chaves to: Braga (4–5 daily; 2–4hr); Bragança (Mon–Fri & Sun 3 daily, Sat 1; 2hr); Lamego (3–4 daily; 2hr); Coimbra (4–6 daily; 2hr 40min); Fronteira (3–6 daily; 1hr); Lisbon (4–7 daily; 8–10hr); Mirandela (Mon–Fri & Sun 1–2 daily; 2hr); Montalegre (Mon–Fri 5 daily; 1hr 20min);

Porto (3 daily; 3hr 20min); Vila Real (6–12 daily; 1hr 10min–2hr).

Freixo de Espada à Cinta to: Mogadouro (4 daily; 2–3hr).

Miranda do Douro to: Bragança (1–3 daily; 1hr 30min); Freixo de Espada à Cinta (4 daily; 3hr); Mirandela (1 daily Mon-Fri 2hr–2hr 30min); Mogadouro (3–4 daily; 2hr 20min).

Mirandela to: Bragança (10 daily; 1hr 25min–2hr 45min); Chaves (Mon–Fri & Sun 1–2 daily; 2hr); Miranda (1 daily Mon–Fri; 2hr–2 hr 30min); Vila Flôr (3 weekly; 40min); Vila Real (Mon–Fri 7 daily; Sat & Sun 3 daily; 1hr).

Mogadouro to: Freixo de Espada à Cinta (4 daily; 2–3hr); Miranda do Douro (3–4 daily; 2hr 20min); Pocinho (3 daily; 3hr); Torre de Moncorvo (3 daily; 2hr 40min).

Montalegre to: Braga (4–6 daily; 2hr 40min); Chaves (Mon–Fri 5 daily; 1hr 20min).

Vila Flôr to: Carrazeda (Mon–Fri 4 daily; Sun 2 daily; 1hr); Mirandela (4 weekly; 40min); Moncorvo (Mon–Fri 2 daily; 1hr); Tua (Mon–Fri 4 daily; Sun 1 daily; 1hr)

Vila Real to: Amarante (10–12 daily; 1hr 25min); Braga (2–4 daily; 3hr 10min); Bragança (Mon–Fri 7 daily; Sat & Sun 3 daily; 2hr 50min); Chaves (5–11 daily; 1 hr 20min–2hr); Coimbra (4–6 daily; 3hr 20min); Guimarães (Mon–Fri 7 daily; Sat & Sun 1 daily; 1hr 30min); Lamego (4–6 daily; 1hr 30min); Lisbon (2–4 daily; 7hr); Mirandela (Mon–Fri 7 daily; Sat & Sun 3 daily; 1hr); Peso da Régua (7–9 daily; 45min); Porto (10–12 daily; 2hr); Viseu (4–6 daily; 1hr 45min).

ALENTEJO

The huge, sparsely populated plains of the **Alentejo** are overwhelmingly agricultural, dominated by vast cork plantations – the one crop that is well suited to the low rainfall, sweltering heat and poor soil. This is one of the poorest parts of the country (indeed, one of the poorest parts of Europe), much of whose sparse population still derives a living from the huge agricultural estates, known as *latifúndios*. However, despite the tedium of the interior landscape, there are unexpected surprises throughout the region, from the strong rural traditions still expressed in a variety of local festivals, to the wealth of ornithological interest – the Alentejo is home to hundreds of species of birds, from black storks to great bustards, all finely adapted to the mix of varied agriculture and marginal wilderness.

For most visitors, understandably, the region's major draws are its few towns and cities, with the outstanding attraction being historic **Évora**, whose Roman temple and medieval walls and cathedral have put it very much on the tourist map. Elsewhere in **Alto Alentejo** (Upper Alentejo), few towns see more than a handful of visitors in a day. Yet there is much to see and enjoy: the spectacular fortifications of **Elvas**; the hilltop sites of **Monsaraz**, **Évora Monte** and **Marvão**; and the marble towns of **Estremoz**, **Borba** and **Vila Viçosa**, northeast of Évora, where even the humblest homes are made of fine stone from the local quarries. This region is also scattered with **prehistoric remains**, including over a dozen megalithic sites with dolmens, standing stones and stone circles.

South of Évora, the plains of **Baixo Alentejo** (Lower Alentejo), have rather less appeal, and the towns, with the notable exception of **Beja** – once an important Moorish stronghold – can seem rather dull. But the Alentejo **coastline** is almost as extensive as the Algarve's and more than compensates for the lack of urban pleasures. Whipped by the Atlantic winds, its **beaches** can seem pretty wild, but in summer at least the sea is warm enough for swimming, and very few of the resorts attract more than weekend crowds. Particularly enticing are the lagoons of **Melides** and **Santo André** – between Setúbal and the eminently avoidable industrial port of Sines – and the long beaches further south at **Ilha do Pessegueiro**, **Vila Nova de Milfontes** and **Zambujeira do Mar**. If you want to

---

ACCOMMODATION PRICE CODES

All the accommodation prices in this book have been coded using the symbols below. The symbols represent the lowest prices you can expect to pay for a **double room in high season**; for a full explanation, see p.29.

① Under 3000$00   ② 3000$00–4000$00   ③ 4000$00–5500$00
④ 5500$00–8500$00   ⑤ 8500$00–12,500$00   ⑥ 12,500$00–20,000$00
                           ⑦ Over 20,000$00

LAND REFORM IN ALENTEJO

The Alentejo's structure of **land ownership** has been in place since Roman times, when the new settlers established massive agricultural estates – *latifúndios* – on which they grew imported crops, such as wheat, barley and olives. Handed down from generation to generation, these estates remained feudal in character, employing large numbers of farm labourers with no stake in the land they worked. In the wake of the 1974 Revolution, much of the land in Alentejo – then a Communist stronghold – was collectivized. However, the workers possessed neither the financial means nor the technical know-how to cope with a succession of poor harvests, and increasingly the original *latifúndio* owners have been clawing back their estates at depressed prices. Jobs today are scarcer than ever, as mechanization has done away with much casual farm labour – a move hastened by European Community grants for modernization programmes and the introduction of new agricultural methods. Only the Beja district, known in Portugal as the reddest region of the country, has a government still controlled by the Communists, who have gradually lost sway in the rest of Alentejo.

head straight for these southern resorts, there are express buses in summer from Lisbon. Accommodation is somewhat limited, but there are plenty of campsites strategically positioned along the coast.

ALTO ALENTEJO

Unless you are heading south to the beaches, **Évora** provides the easiest starting point in Alentejo, with frequent and fast buses, or rather slower trains, from Lisbon. From here, you're within striking distance of **Estremoz** and the marble towns, beyond which, to the east, lie the superbly preserved walls of **Elvas**, close to the Spanish frontier. The northern part of Alto Alentejo is characterized by more fortified towns – **Portalegre**, **Castelo de Vide**, **Marvão** – any of which would make a splendid night's stopover on your way to points further north.

Évora

ÉVORA is one of the most impressive and enjoyable cities in Portugal, its relaxed provincial atmosphere forming a perfect setting for a range of memorable monuments. A Roman temple, Moorish alleys, a circuit of medieval walls, and a rather grand sixteenth-century ensemble of palaces and mansions are all in superb condition, spruced up by a long-term restoration programme and placed under UNESCO protection. Inevitably, they attract a great many summer tourists but, despite the crowds, the city is far from spoiled. It still plays its part in the agricultural life of the region, with a morning produce market on the second Tuesday of the month; while the university, re-established here in the 1970s, adds an independent side to city life.

Évora's big annual event is the **Feira de São João**, a folklore, handicraft, gastronomic and musical festival, whose origins date from pre-Christian times and which takes over the city during the last ten days of June.

Arrival and accommodation

Évora's **train station** is 1km southeast of the centre; if you follow Rua da República, straight ahead, you'll reach **Praça do Giraldo**, the city's main square. CP **buses** to and from Estremoz, Vila Viçosa and Reguengos de Monsaraz use the train station as a depot; others operate from a **bus terminal** on Rua da República, at the edge of the historic zone. If you're **driving**, you're in for a hard time amid the maze of one-way and narrow streets; try to park as soon as possible, and then walk into the centre.

The **turismo** (daily: summer 9am–7pm; winter 9am–12.30pm & 2–5.30pm; ☎066/226 71), on Praça do Giraldo, has maps of the city and province, which include some excellent walking routes. It can also provide information about **renting bicycles** (or call ☎066/76 14 53), which cost around 1500$00 per day and are a good way to reach the megalithic sights in the surroundings (see p.399). For the less energetic, there are day trips to the megaliths for 4500$00 per person; ask at the turismo or call ☎066/74 31 34 for details.

Accommodation

Hotel and pensão prices in Évora are higher than in the rest of the Alentejo, and are more or less comparable with Lisbon. In summer you're advised to book at least a day in advance for any of the places listed below; **private rooms** (②) can be arranged through the turismo. Évora's *Orbitur* **campsite** (☎066/251 90, fax 298 30) is 2km southwest of town on the N380 Alcáçovas road. There's no reliable bus service and you're best off taking a taxi (which should cost around $500) if you can't face the 45-minute trudge. The campsite itself is clean and well equipped, with a restaurant and swimming pool.

Casa Palma, Rua Bernardo Matos 29A (☎066/235 60). First-floor rooms in a scrupulously clean family house stuffed with antiques and assorted china. ③.

Residencial Diana, Rua Diogo Cão 2 (☎066/220 08, fax 74 31 01). Adequate rooms in a house between the Sé and Praça do Giraldo; price includes breakfast. ④.

Pensão Giraldo, Rua dos Mercadores 15 (☎066/258 33). Very pleasant rooms, some with bath; also some "overspill" rooms available, which are not as nice but much cheaper. ④.

Pensão Invicta, Rua Romão Ramalho 37A (☎066/220 47). Évora's cheapest, with clean but dingy rooms; some have good views over the Igreja de São Francisco. ②.

Pousada dos Lóios, Largo do Conde de Vila Flor (☎066/240 51, fax 272 48). One of the country's loveliest *pousadas*, housed in the cloistered Convento dos Lóios (see p.395) and with a good open-air restaurant. ⑦.

Pensão Os Manuéis, Rua do Raimundo 35-1° (☎066/228 61). Decent rooms just west of Praça do Giraldo. There's a less preferable annexe across the road. ②.

Solar Monfalim, Largo da Misericórdia 1 (☎066/220 31, fax 74 23 67). A restored summer palace formerly belonging to the Dukes of Monfalim – elegant, spacious and relaxed. Breakfasts are taken on the veranda with superb views. ⑥.

Estalagem Monte das Flores, 2km south of the *Orbitur* campsite on the N380 (☎066/ 250 18, fax 275 64). A modern "activities guest house" in a rural setting offering horse riding as well as tennis courts, pool and a decent restaurant. ⑥.

Hotel Planície, Rua Miguel Bombarda 40 (☎066/240 26, fax 298 80). A modernized old villa run by the Best Western hotel group, and featuring a good restaurant. ⑤.

Residencial Policarpo, Rua do Conde da Serra da Tourega 9 (☎066/224 24, fax 224 64). One of the best places to stay in Évora, this former ducal summer palace has beautiful views, a cosy lounge with a fire in winter, 16th-century azulejos and bags of charm; excellent value and highly recommended. ④.

Pensão Riviera, Rua 5 de Outubro 49 (☎066/233 04, fax 204 67). A reasonable if unexciting *pensão* between the Sé and Praça do Giraldo. ⑤.

Hotel Santa Clara, Trav. da Milheira 19 (☎066/241 41, fax 265 44). A hundred metres from Praça do Giraldo (follow the signs), this modern hotel is bland but functional; all rooms with bath, TV and air-conditioning. ⑤.

The City

Évora was shaped by its **Roman** and **Moorish** occupations: the former is commemorated by a temple, the latter by a characteristic tangle of alleys, rising steeply among the whitewashed houses. Most of the city's other monuments, however, date from the fourteenth to the sixteenth century, when Évora prospered under the patronage of the ruling **House of Avis**. To them are owed the many noble palaces scattered about the city; as are the Jesuit **university**, founded in 1559 by Cardinal Henrique, the future "Cardinal King"; and the wonderful array of Manueline and Renaissance buildings.

That the city's monuments have survived intact is due, in large part, to Évora's decline after the Spanish usurpation of the throne in 1580. Future Portuguese monarchs chose to live nearer Lisbon, and the university was closed down; for the next four hundred years, Évora drifted back into a rural existence as a provincial market centre. Even today, the 45,000-strong population is only half its medieval number.

The Templo Romano and Convento dos Lóios

The graceful **Templo Romano** stands at the very heart of the old city. Dating from the second century AD, it is the best preserved temple in Portugal, despite (or perhaps because of) its use as a slaughterhouse until 1870. The stark remains consist of a small platform supporting fourteen granite columns with Corinthian capitals and a marble entablature. Its popular attribution to Diana is apparently fanciful; Jupiter is a more likely alternative.

Directly opposite the temple, the magnificent fifteenth-century **Convento dos Lóios** has been converted into a top-grade *pousada*. Its cloisters now serve as a dining area in summer, and the hotel staff can be sniffy about allowing in non-residents (or non-diners) to look around. However, dress up as formally as you can – a tie is a help for men – and walk in regardless. The dual horseshoe arches, slender twisted columns and the intricate carvings on the doorway to the chapter house are fine examples of the so-called Luso-Moorish style and have been attributed to Francisco de Arruda, architect of Évora's aqueduct and the Belém tower in Lisbon.

To the left of the *pousada* lies the former conventual church, dedicated to **São João Evangelista**. This is still the private property of the ducal Cadaval family, who occupy a wing or two of their adjacent ancestral palace. Entrance costs 500$00 – just hang around for a few minutes and one of the three guides will let you in to see the floor-to-ceiling azulejos within, the masterpiece of one António Oliveira Bernardes and created early in the eighteenth century. Other highlights include a Moorish cistern (the church and convent were built over an old castle), a grisly ossuary containing the bones of the convent's monks, and a magnificent Manueline altar.

△ Estremoz

ÉVORA

ACCOMMODATION		RESTAURANTS & CAFÉS	
❶ Pousada dos Lóios		Ⓐ Rest. Molhóbico	
❷ Residencial Policarpo		Ⓑ O Portão	
❸ Pensão Riviera		Ⓒ O Fialho	
❹ Residencial Diana		Ⓓ Pasteleria Violeta	
❺ Hotel Santa Clara		Ⓔ Almedina Restaurante	
❻ Solar Monfalim		Ⓕ Adega do Alentejano	
❼ Hotel Planície		Ⓖ O Arcada	
❽ Pensão Giraldo		Ⓗ Burgo Velho	
❾ Pensão Os Manuéis		Ⓘ Pane & Vino	
❿ Pensão Invicta		Ⓙ Cozinha de Santo Humberto	
⓫ Casa Palma		Ⓚ O Focardo	
		Ⓛ Gelateria Zoka	

The Sé and Museu Municipal

Évora's cathedral, the **Sé** (daily 9am–12.30pm & 2–5pm), was begun in 1186, about twenty years after the reconquest of Évora from the Moors. The Romanesque solidity of its original battlemented towers and roofline contrasts sharply with the pointed Gothic arches of subsequent and less militaristic additions, such as the porch and central window. The interior is more straightforwardly Gothic, although the choir and high altar were remodelled in the eighteenth century by the German, Friedrich Ludwig, architect of the Convent at Mafra. For a nominal fee you can clamber onto a terrace above the west entrance and take an unusually close look at the towers and the *zimbório* (the lantern above the crossing of the transepts). Don't miss the cathedral **museum** (Tues–Sun 9–11.45am & 2–4.45pm; 250$00), either: it's stuffed with treasures and relics, the prize exhibits being a reliquary studded with 1426 stones and a carved statue of the Madonna whose midriff opens out to display layered scenes from the Bible.

Immediately adjacent to the Sé is the former archbishop's palace, now the **Museu Municipal** (Tues–Sun 10am–12.30pm & 2–5pm; 250$00), housing important collections of fifteenth- and sixteenth-century Flemish and Portuguese paintings assembled from the city's churches and convents. These provide a good illustration of the significance of Flemish artists in the development of the "Portuguese School", and reflect the strong medieval trade links between the two countries. Frei Carlos, probably the most important Flemish artist known to have worked in Évora, is well represented, but the centrepiece of the museum is a series of thirteen panels by an anonymous fifteenth-century Flemish artist, portraying scenes from the life of the Virgin. This was once the cathedral altarpiece.

Up behind the museum, a quick stroll to the north will take you to the beautiful entrance courtyard of the **Antiga Universidade**, with its brazilwood ceiling and azulejos, which you wander around at will. You can enter the inner courtyard by request (Mon–Fri 9am–12.30pm & 3–5pm). The university was closed down by the Jesuit-hating Marquês de Pombal during the eighteenth century but since its re-opening in the 1970s it is now one of the liveliest corners of the city.

The Igreja de São Francisco and the Capela dos Ossos

Situated on the eastern side of Praça de Maio, the **Igreja de São Francisco** contains perhaps the most memorable monument in Évora – the **Capela dos Ossos** (Chapel of Bones; Mon–Sat 8.30am–1pm & 2.30–5.30pm; Sun 10am–1pm & 2.30–6pm; 100$00, plus another 50$00 for taking photos). A timeless and gruesome memorial to the mortality of man, the walls and pillars of this chilling chamber are entirely covered in the bones of more than 5000 monks. There's a grim humour in the neat, artfully planned arrangement of skulls, tibias and vertibrae around the vaults, and in the rhyming inscription over the door which reads "*Nós ossos que aqui estamos pelos vossos esperamos*" (We bones here are waiting for your bones). Such macabre warnings can be encountered in a couple of other locations in Portugal – at Campo Maior, northeast of Évora, and at Faro in the Algarve.

Another interesting feature of this fifteenth-century church is its large **porch**, which combines pointed, rounded, and horseshoe arches in a manner typical of Manueline architecture. Appropriately enough, the restored **Palácio de Dom Manuel** – the king who gave his name to the style – lies no more than a minute's walk away, in the Jardim Público. Early sixteenth-century, it too incorporates inventive horseshoe arches with strange serrated edges.

Directly opposite São Francisco, on Praça 1º de Maio, the rich craft traditions of the Évora district are well displayed in the **Museu do Artesanato Regional** (daily 10am–noon & 2–5pm). The collections include pottery, weaving, tapestry and carvings in wood, cork and bone; modern pieces are on sale, too.

The rest of the city

As well as artists and writers such as Gil Vicente and Garcia, great Portuguese and European architects also gravitated to Évora, and the **Ermida de São Brás**, just outside the city walls on the road to the train station, has been identified as an early work by Diogo de Boitaca, pioneer of the flamboyant Manueline style. Its tubular, dunce-capped buttresses and crenellated roofline bear scant resemblance to his masterpieces at Lisbon and Setúbal, but they certainly foreshadow the style's uninhibited originality.

No less bizarre is the mid-sixteenth-century facade of the **Igreja Nossa Senhora da Graça**, out behind the bus station. At each of the corners of its Renaissance pediment, grotesque Atlas-giants support two globes – the emblem of Dom Manuel and his burgeoning overseas empire.

Other buildings worth seeing in Évora include the lavish Neoclassical **Theatre of Garcia de Redende** on Praça Aguiar; the **Misericórdia's** baroque bas-reliefs and azulejos, on Largo da Misericórdia; the **Calvario Convent**, built by the Infanta Dona Maria in 1570, at the far end of Rua Candido dos Reis; and **Church and Convent of Santa Clara**, on Rua Serpa de Pinto, for its beautiful gilded altar. Lastly, it's worth following **Rua do Cano**, north of the old centre, behind the Câmara Municipal. Here, you can travel the course of the medieval **Aqueduto do Água Prata** (Silver Water Aqueduct), into whose arches a row of houses has been incorporated.

Eating and drinking

Évora goes to bed pretty early, as if exhausted by the attentions of the tour groups. Finding a place to eat, however, is no problem, with a range of decent **restaurants** to suit most budgets located around the centre; below we've listed some of the best. For **picnic** supplies try the large market on the second Thursday of every month in Rossio São Brás or *Pastelaria Violeta*, Rua José Elias Garcia 47 on the corner of Praça Aguiar, which sells a wide range of mouth-watering cakes and pastries. For a late-evening **drink**, in summer you'll find a couple of outdoor cafés in Praça do Giraldo or, just off the praça on Rua João de Deus, there's the cavernous 1930s' *O Arcada*, and the very pleasant *Gelateria Zoka* at Rua Miguel Bombarda 10.

Adega do Alentejano, Rua Gabriel Vitor do Monte Pereira 21A. Traditional, well-cooked fare served in a delightful old *adega* adorned with giant amphorae. The à la carte menu is a bargain at 1200$00 including wine. Closed Mon.

Almedina Restaurante, Trav. de Santa Martha (off Praça Aguiar). In cosy Moorish-style surroundings, this restaurant serves excellent main courses for around 1300$00, including succulent *migas alentejanas* and *bacalhau almedina* (cod fried with marinaded onions).

Burgo Velho, Rua de Burgos 10. Serves a comprehensive range of the more common Alentejan dishes for under 1000$00, as well as a tasty shark soup.

Restaurante Cozinha de Santo Humberto, Rua da Moeda 39 (☎066/242 51). Top-notch establishment highly recommended by locals, this is on a street which runs downhill from Praça do Giraldo; there's only a small sign. Downstairs, in a converted cellar, you can eat from a fine menu of local dishes for around 4000$00 a head; try the *chispe assado de Santo Humberto* (knuckle of pork). Closed Nov.

O Fialho, Trav. do Mascarenhas 14–16. Up a cobbled alley off Praça Aguiar, this is reckoned to be one of the ten best restaurants in Portugal. Starters, particularly, are superb, the wine list is good and prices, unsurprisingly, are high.

O Focardo, Rua dos Mercadores 26. Best of a quartet of modestly priced restaurants in this central old city street; good prices and solid quality. The set menu costs 1450$00, while à la carte should set you back another 500$00.

Restaurante Molhóbico, 89 Rua de Aviz. Excellent and modestly priced range of regional meat and fish dishes, served in a small square outside. Main courses from 1100$00.

Pane & Vino, Patio do Salema (entrance on Rua Diogo Focardo, visible from Rua 5 Outubro). Once the stables of a town house, this restaurant serves up a wide range of dishes in a brick-walled, vaulted interior. There's a set menu for 1950$00.

O Portão, Rua do Cano. Local haunt next to the aqueduct, popular with students for good, inexpensive food (it does a very decent *porco alentejana*). A full meal with wine will rarely cost more than 1000$00.

Pousada dos Lóios, Largo do Conde de Vila Flor. Elegant, upmarket, classic Portuguese dining in the monastery's cloisters. Meals from 4000$00 upwards.

Around Évora

The administrative district of Évora contains over a dozen **megalithic sites** dating from around 3000 BC. The dolmens, standing stones and stone circles found here have their origins in a culture which flourished in the peninsula before spreading north as far as Brittany and Denmark. Two of the most accessible sites lie to the west and northwest of Évora in the Serra de Monfurado, which makes them possible visits in conjunction with the carpet town of **Arraiolos**. For descriptions of – and directions to – sites other than the couple covered below, ask at the turismo in Évora for the *Guide to the Megalithic Monuments of the Évora Region* (1000$00). An additional attraction in the district, en route to Estremoz from Évora, is Évora Monte, with its superb Renaissance castle.

Os Almendres

One of the sites nearest to Évora is the **stone circle** and three-metre-high **menhir** (upright stone) at a cork plantation called **OS ALMENDRES**. It's located west of the city, about 3km out of Guadalupe, just south of the N114 Évora–Montemor road. Ask for directions in the village and expect a stiff uphill walk through wild country. The legend goes that this stone is the tomb of an enchanted Moorish princess, who appears once a year on the eve of São João and can be seen combing her hair. Those with ornithological interests will have the additional pleasure of seeing the **hoopoes** of the area.

Montemor-o-Novo

Back on the N114, 30km northwest of Évora, lies the white town of **MONTE-MOR-O-NOVO**, birthplace of São João de Deus, patron saint of the sick. This large, sleepy town has a dearth of spectacular monuments though it does boast the **castle** (Mon–Sat 10am–5pm; free) where Vasco da Gama finalized his plans for opening up the sea route to India, and a **convent** founded at the end of the fifteenth century by São João de Deus. In the town's main square stands a statue of him carrying an injured beggar in need of care.

The **turismo** is on Largo Calouste Gulbenkian (Mon–Fri 9am–5.30pm, Sat 9.30am–12.30pm; ☎066/823 45 ext 76). **Accommodation** is plentiful if unexciting. Pleasant and inexpensive **rooms** can be found at Rua do Poço do Paço 34 (☎066/823 57; ②); while the pick of the **pensões** includes the modern *Residencial Monte Alentejano*, Avda. Gago Coutinho (☎066/821 41; ③), the functional *Residencial Sampaio* at no. 12 on the same street (☎066/822 37, fax 801 95; ③), and the rather rundown *Pensão Ribetejo*, Rua do Passo 8 (☎066/823 62; ③). For **restaurants**, try any of the cluster along the Arraiolos road twenty minutes' walk north of town, or the more upmarket *Residencial Sampaio* restaurant, across the road from the *residencial*.

Twelve kilometres to the south of town are the neolithic caves of **Escoural**, their weird leathery stalacmites alone worth the visit, and 6km east of the caves, at **São Brissos**, is another dolmen chapel similar to that of São Dinis at Pavia (see below), and just as impressive.

Arraiolos and Pavia

ARRAIOLOS, 22km north of Évora (and connected to it by bus twice a day), is the birthplace of Dom Nuno Álvares Pereira and home of the "noiva de Arraiolos", a legendary bride who took a fortnight to adorn herself only to appear at her wedding in a shepherd's cloak. But the real source of Arraiolos' fame, and fortune, lies with its superb carpets, which have been handwoven here since the thirteenth century. Based on elaborate Persian imports, the designs tend nowadays to be simpler and more brightly coloured; you can still see some of the originals at the **Casa de Artes e Ofícios** (Mon–Sat 9am–11am & 2–5pm), in the village of Pelegrejinha 10km to the east of Arraiolos, while the most luxuriant eighteenth-century creations hang on the walls of Queluz Palace, near Lisbon (p.122).

Apart from the carpet shops – where the carpets are expensive, but a lot less so than elsewhere – Arraiolos is a typical Alentejo village with its ruined hilltop castle, whitewashed houses and sixteenth-century pillory. While you're here you might as well visit the Quinta dos Lóios **carpet workshop** in Ilhas, just to the east of Arraiolos on the N370; it has an outlet in Évora itself, Castelo das Ilhas, at Rua 5 de Outubro 66, between Praça do Giraldo and the Sé. The **turismo** on Praça Lima e Brito (daily 10am–noon & 2–6pm; ☎066/242 51) can help with **accommodation**. For **food** try the excellent *Arco de Noe* restaurant, on Rua S. Condestavel 23.

In the hamlet of **PAVIA**, 20km north of Arraiolos along the N370, is a massive **dolmen**, within which the tiny sixteenth-century chapel of São Dinis was built. The effect is a bit grotesque and out of keeping with Pavia's traditional Alentejan architecture, but impressive nonetheless.

Évora Monte

Twenty-nine kilometres northeast of Évora, along the N18, the sixteenth-century **castle** at **ÉVORA MONTE** stands on fortifications going back to Roman times and occupies a spectacular position, atop a steep mound. Its keep is constructed in Italian Renaissance style, with four robust round towers, and is adorned with a simple rope-like relief of Manueline stonework. Within are three vaulted chambers, each displaying intricately carved granite capitals. The town – predominantly medieval in appearance – rings the castle mound.

It was here in 1834 that the regent Miguel was finally defeated and the convention signed that put Pedro IV on the Portuguese throne. Legend has it that the signing took so long that there was only stale bread left to eat, causing the invention of the well-known Portuguese dish *açorda* (a soup of bread, water, coriander, garlic and olive oil).

If you want to **stay** overnight, try *Monte da Fazenda*, (☎068/95 91 72; ⑤), an ANTER farmhouse by the castle; it has three apartments and two rooms for rent, all with private baths and use of the swimming pool. For **food**, the *Restaurante A Convento*, Rua de Santa Maria 26–30, is the town's best bet, with specialities including *bacalhau alentejana* and Brazilian-style pork with pineapple; a full meal costs upwards of 2000$00.

Estremoz and the marble towns

Northeast of Évora, quarry trucks and tracks announce your entry into marble country. Around **Estremoz**, 46km from Évora, the area is so rich in marble that it replaces brick or concrete as a building material, giving butchers' stalls and simple cottages the sort of luxurious finish you generally see only in churches and the grandest houses. Estremoz itself, and **Borba** and **Vila Viçosa**, are all distinctive marble towns, and the latter has an additional attraction in its ducal palace – the last residence of the Portuguese monarchy.

Estremoz

ESTREMOZ is the largest and liveliest of the three marble towns, and comes into its own every Saturday when the **market** takes over the Rossio, the main square of the **lower town**. This is a classic marketplace of huge dimensions, surrounded by bars, restaurants and churches, and selling – among other things – what are renowned as some of the best cheeses in Portugal, mainly made from ewe's and goat's milk. Estremoz's annual *feira* takes place in the Rossio on the first weekend in September, with bull-running, concerts and roll-baking contests. At the start of May it sees a cattle and handicraft fair, including displays of the **earthenware pottery** for which the town has been celebrated since the sixteenth century. The pottery is characterized by simple floral and leaf patterns, sometimes inlaid with marble chips, and is on sale at the weekly market; the most distinctive products are the porous water coolers known as *moringues*, globe-shaped jars with narrow bases, two short spouts, and one handle. Although nowadays largely ornamental, the pottery used to play an important role in gypsy weddings: the procession would march into town, whereupon the bride made a sudden dash for freedom across the market place, hotly pursued by the groom. When the groom finally caught up with his bride, a fine Estremoz dish was thrown into the air. The couple were pronounced man and wife at the moment that the dish fell to the ground in pieces.

Arriving b bus, you'll be dropped in the east of town on Avenida 9 de Abril at the old train station. From here, it's a short walk west down Avenida Condessa da Cuba to the Rossio, dominated by the twin-towered marble facade of the eighteenth-century **Câmara Municipal**, which now houses the police station. At no. 62 on the Rossio, the **Museu Rural** (Mon–Sat 10am–12.30pm & 2.30–5pm; 100$00) features a display of earthenware figurines from the town potteries, and has an illuminating ethnographic collection of locally produced artefacts in clay, wood, rush, straw, cork, textile and metal. Nearby, at Rua de Serpa Pinto 87, is a **Museu Agricultura** (Mon–Fri 9am–12.30pm & 2–5.30pm, Sat & Sun 2–5.30pm; 160$00) with a surprisingly fascinating display of old kitchen equipment.

In its heyday, the population of Estremoz was ten times its current size and the town was once one of the most strongly fortified in the country. An army garrison is still stationed here, and the inner star-shaped **ramparts** of the **upper town** are well preserved. On the hill within these fortifications stands a white, prison-like building, easily visible from the Rossio; despite its external austerity, it was once a palace of Dom Dinis, the king famous for his administrative, economic and military reforms. It is now a *pousada*, but you're free to wander in and look around; there's a splendid panoramic view from the thirteenth-century **Torre das Três**

ESTREMOZ

ACCOMMODATION
1 Antiga Ginginha
2 Pensão Restaurante Mateus
3 Residencial Miguel José
4 Pousada Rainha Isabel
5 Café-Pensão Alentejano
6 Residencial Carvalho
7 Josefina Ferro Saruga

RESTAURANTS & BARS
A Café-Restaurante Zona Verde
B O Cantinho
C Restaurante São Rosas
D Café-Restaurante Aguis D'Ouro
E Pastelaria Formosa
F Cervejaria Restaurante O Figo

N

▷ Elvas & Borba

▷ Évoramonte & Lisbon

500 m

0

Bus Station

Theatre

Igreja de São Francisco

Museu Rural

Portas de S. António

Hospital

Portas de S. Catarina

ROSSIO

Misericórdia

Câmara Municipal

Museu Agricultura

Portas dos Currais

Museu Municipal

Torre das Três Coroas

Chapel of Queen Isabel

Coroas (Tower of the Three Crowns), so called because three kings took part in its construction, including Afonso III and Dom Dinis. With its Islamic-style battlements and Gothic balconies, it bears a close resemblance to the great tower of Beja, its exact contemporary. From this part of town the castle of Évora Monte is clearly visible on the horizon, 15km to the southwest. Opposite the tower, in an old almshouse, is a small **Museu Municipal** (Tues–Sun 10am–noon & 3–7pm; 170$00), with more displays of Estremoz pottery and Alentejan life.

Practicalities

The **turismo** (Mon–Fri 9am–12.30pm & 2–6pm, Sat & Sun 10am–1pm & 3–6pm; ☎068/33 35 41) is at Largo da República 26. Unless you're stopping over on Friday night, before the market, **accommodation** should be easy enough to find; for inexpensive rooms try *Josefina Ferro Saruga*, Rua Brito Capelo 27A (☎068/33 24 63; ②), or *Antiga Ginginha*, Rua 31 Janeiro 4 (☎068/226 43; ②), run by an energetic elderly *senhora* who rents out her two spare rooms. In the same price range, there's also the wonderfully decrepit *Residencial Carvalho* at Largo da República 27 (☎068/227 12; ②). Slightly more upmarket but still good value are: *Café-Pensão Alentejano*, Rossio Marquês de Pombal 14–15 (☎068/228 34; ③; breakfast included), with a marble staircase and good views over Rossio; the *Pensão-Restaurante Mateus*, Rua Almeida 39–41 (☎068/222 26; ③) in the old quarter; and the characterful *Residencial Miguel José*, Trav. da Levada 8 (☎068/223 26; ③). Both the *Mateus* and *Miguel José* have good restaurants. The grandest option in town is the *Pousada de Santa Rainha Isabel* (☎068/33 20 75, fax 33 20 79; ⑦), occupying the lavish thirteenth-century palace of Dom Dinis in the old castle. Lastly, there are a couple of upmarket rural hotels just outside town, both with modern facilities: *Monte das Pensamentos* (☎068/223 75, fax 33 24 09; ⑤) is an ANTER property 4km west of Estremoz on Estrada da Estação do Ameixal; the less expensive *Monte Gil* (☎068/33 29 96; ⑤) is at Fonte Nova, 3km north on the Sousel road.

Estremoz's best **restaurant** is the *São Rosas*, Largo de D. Dinis 11, opposite the castle keep (☎068/33 33 45; booking advised). Once a medieval inn, now beautifully restored and run by the Cabaço family, this restaurant serves excellently cooked meals and a bargain *ementa turística* at 2500$00; wines, however, although uniformly good, can be expensive. For good-value budget *ementas turísticas* try the *Café-Restaurante Zona Verde*, Largo Dragões de Olivença 86, or the very basic *O Continho*, Rua do Marmelo 2. The *Cervejaria Restaurante O Figo*, Rua da Restauração 36, is worth visiting for its specialities (all priced at 1000$00), including an excellent *arroz de marisco*, and the *Café-Restaurante Aguias d'Ouro*, Rossio Marquês de Pombal 26–27, serves reasonably priced, hearty food, but is interesting principally for its eccentric mismatch of architectural styles. For **picnic** supplies, the place to go is the Saturday-morning market on the Rossio where a wide array of cheeses, spicy sausages and olives are on sale; for **snacks** and pastries, visit the *Pastelaria Formosa*, just off the Rossio at 16B Largo da República, which sells homemade specialities.

Borba

Eleven kilometres east of Estremoz is **BORBA**, a dazzlingly white little place, where just about anything not whitewashed is made of white marble. The town seems not to have exploited the wider commercial possibilities of its quarries, though, and with the exception of a fine eighteenth-century fountain there are no particular signs of wealth, no extravagant mansions or remarkable churches. All this only serves to make more extraordinary the extensive use of marble in even the most commonplace cottages, shops and streets. Borba is an unassuming town with an unusually high concentration of antique shops where one might easily spend an afternoon's browsing. Its other other main attributes are the magnificent **wines** produced by the local co-operative, which are receiving increasing plaudits from the rest of Europe; phone the *Adega Cooperative de Borba* (☎068/942 64) or contact the **turismo**, Rua Convento das Servas (Aug & Sept 10am–1pm & 2–8pm; rest of year 10am–1pm & 2–6pm; ☎068/941 13), to arrange a tour of the winery. For **accommodation** try the *Residencial Inarmos*, just up from the bus stop, at Avda. do Povo 22 (☎068/945 63; ③), or the spacious *Residencial Vila Borba*, Rua da Cruz 8 (☎ & fax 068/943 76; ③; breakfast included). Alternatively, **rooms** are available at the *Restaurante Lisboeta* at Rua de Mateus Pais 31 (☎068/943 32; ③), which also serves a decent *ementa turística* for 1500$00.

Vila Viçosa

The road from Borba to **VILA VIÇOSA**, 6km to the southeast, is lined on either side with enormous marble quarries, and in town everything from the pavements to the toilets in the bus station are made of the local marble. The town is justly famous, too, for its Paço-Ducal, the last palace-residence of the **Bragança dynasty**. The dukes of Bragança were descended from the illegitimate offspring of João I of Avis, and established their seat here in the fifteenth century. For the next two centuries they were on the edge of the Portuguese ruling circle but their claims to the throne were overridden in 1580 by Philip II of Spain. Sixty years later, while Spanish attention was diverted by a revolt in Catalonia, Portuguese resentment erupted and massive public pressure forced the reluctant João, eighth Duke of Bragança, to seize the throne; his descendants ruled Portugal until the foundation of the Republic in 1910.

The Paço Ducal and palace square
Despite a choice of sumptuous palaces throughout Portugal – Mafra, Sintra and Queluz are the most renowned – the Bragança kings retained a special affection for their residence at Vila Viçosa, a relatively ordinary country home, constructed in various stages during the sixteenth and seventeenth centuries. Dom Carlos spent his last night here before his assassination on the riverfront in Lisbon in 1908, and it was a favourite haven of his successor, Manuel II, the last king of Portugal.

The **Paço Ducal** (Tues–Sun 9am–1pm & 2–6pm; 1hr guided tour; 1000$00, 400$00 extra for the Castelo and coach house) has a simple, rhythmic facade. Inside, the standard regal trappings of the more formal chambers are tedious, but the private apartments and mementoes of Dom Carlos and his wife Marie-Amélia have a *Hello!* magazine fascination. Faded family photographs hang on the walls, changes of clothing are laid out, and the table is set for dinner: the whole scene seems to await the royals' return. In reality, Dom Duarte, heir to the nonexistent throne, spends his days in experimental eco-farming at his estate near Viseu.

On the south side of the palace square stands the **Convento das Chagas**, used as a mausoleum for the duchesses of Bragança. Their husbands were buried opposite the palace in marble tombs in the chapel of the **Mostéiro dos Agostinhos**, adjacent to one of the most attractive of Vila Viçosa's 22 churches,

Nossa Senhora de Conceição, worth a visit for its beautiful eighteenth-century azulejos.

The old town and castle

The **old town**, still enclosed within walls on its hilltop site, was built by Dom Dinis at the end of the thirteenth century and reinforced four centuries later. Originally the population of Vila Viçosa was based within these walls and a few of the cottages are still lived in. The **Castelo** (Tues–Sun 9am–1pm & 2–5.30pm; 45min guided tour; 400$00), in one corner of the town, was the seat of the Braganças before the construction of their palace. Its interior has been renovated beyond recognition and houses an indifferent archeological museum. However, from the roof there's a good view of the Braganças' old **Tapada Real** (Royal Hunting Ground), set within its eighteen-kilometre circuit of walls.

Practicalities

Buses park at the elongated Praça da República, from where the old town is straight ahead of you, and the Paço Ducal beyond. Vila Viçosa is a quiet town and despite its attractions there's very little available **accommodation**. Your best bet is to arrange **private rooms** through the **turismo** (☎068/88 11 01) by the town hall on Praça da República. Try those with Maria da Conceição Paixão at Rua Dr. Couto Jardim 7 (☎068/981 69; ③; breakfast included), just off the square. With more money, your options extend to the seventeenth-century mansion house *Casa dos Peixinhos* (☎068/984 72, fax 88 13 48; ⑤) or, at the top of the price range, the new *Pousada de D. João IV*, on the south side of Terreiro do Paço (☎01/848 12 21, fax 840 58 46; ⑦), which is converted from a former convent dating from 1514. However, when all's said and done, it's probably simpler to make a day-trip from Évora or Estremoz or to stay in nearby Borba. The town has plenty of **restaurants** around the Praça da República and near the football field, the best of which is the *Ouro Branco* at Campo da Restauração 43. Two kilometres out of town on the Borba road is the recommended *Burg Restaurant*, where a meal will set you back around 2000$00 a head.

Southeast to Monsaraz

The road **southeast from Vila Viçosa** provides great insights into the rural nature of the Alentejo, taking you past Moorish Alandroal and Terena, both quite prosperous villages set below a castle, before entering a region of scattered farming communities. A couple of buses cover the route daily, with numerous diversions along crumbling backroads.

Reguengos de Monsaraz

One of the better targets is the town of **REGUENGOS DE MONSARAZ** (which is also connected by the dull N256 with Évora, to its west). It's known for its fine local Terras del Rei white and red wines, and you can visit the *adega* just outside town where the wine is bottled: officially you need written permission, but if you just turn up you may find someone willing to take you around. For more information contact the **turismo** (Mon–Fri 9am–12.30pm & 2–6pm, Sat & Sun 10am–12.30pm & 2–5pm; ☎066/513 15) in the Câmara Municipal on Rua 1º de Maio.

From Reguengos, there are two daily buses 17km further east to the dramatic fortified village of Monsaraz, as well as six daily buses to Évora, leaving from the square off Rua de São Marcos do Campo. Given this, it's unlikely you'd get stranded in Reguengos, but it's not a bad place to spend the night in any case. There are **rooms** at *Pensão Gato* (☎ & fax 066/523 52; ③) on the main Praça da Liberdade, and at the cheaper *Pensão Filhão* (☎066/51 92 66; ②), next door. A better bet might be the rooms advertised in the beautiful old house at Praça de Santo António 1 (☎066/523 62; ②). Good-value **restaurants** include the *Café Central* on Praça da Liberdade, and *A Grelha*, on Rua do Covalinho, behind the church and on the left. The best place to sample the local wine is at the *Adega D'el Rei* **bar** opposite the market (up the road by the cinema); it's filled with huge barrels, from which the barman dispenses 40$00 glasses of wine.

Monsaraz

MONSARAZ – known to the locals as "Ninho das Águias" (Eagles' Nest) – is perched high above the border plains, a tiny village, fortified to the hilt and entirely contained within its walls. From its heights, the landscape of the Alentejo takes on a magical quality, with absolutely nothing stirring amid a sensational panorama of sun-baked fields, neatly cultivated and dotted with cork and olive trees. To the east, you can make out the Rio Guadiana, delineating the frontier with Spain.

There's something peculiarly satisfying, too, about such a small village. From the clock tower of the main gateway, the only real street, Rua Direita, leads past a bar (unmarked, on the left, next to the post office) to the village square. Here you'll find an unusual eighteenth-century pillory topped by a sphere of the universe.

The **Torre das Feiticeiras** (Witches' Tower) looms from the castle at the far end of the village, part of a chain of frontier fortresses continued to the south at Mourão, Moura and Serpa, and to the north at Alandroal, Elvas and Campo Maior. When the Moors were ejected in 1167 the village was handed over to the Knights Templar, and later to their successors, the Order of Christ; their fort has now been converted into a bullring.

Practicalities

The **turismo**, on Largo D. Nuno Álvares (daily 10am–1pm & 2–5.30pm; ☎066/551 36), can help with **accommodation**. Alternatively, try the rooms along the main street with Dona Antonia (☎066/551 42; ③) or at *Casa Dom Nuno*, Rua do Castelo 6 (☎066/551 46, fax 554 00; ④). All these places include breakfast in the price and fill quickly in summer; out of season you can probably negotiate a reduction in the room rate. There's also a rather fancy **hotel**, the *Estalagem de Monsaraz*, with a pool and restaurant, at Largo São Bartolomeu 6 (☎066/551 12, fax 551 01; ⑤), in the settlement below the castle walls; while below the village, heading north towards the tiny village of Barrada, you'll find *Monte Saraz* (☎066/553 85, fax 554 85; ⑥; advance booking recommended) – a very pretty cluster of converted farmhouses with a swimming pool and ornamental gardens. The *Lumumba*, opposite Dona Antonia's house, is the most reasonably priced **restaurant**, with a nice patio and good views; a more upmarket option is the attractive, balconied *Casa do Forno*, on a side road between the lower and main roads.

Buses to Reguengos leave four times daily; to Évora, the once-daily service currently leaves at 8am.

Menhirs around Monsaraz

There are two giant menhirs close by Monsaraz, just off the Reguengos road: at **Outeiro**, and at **Bulhoa**, where the stone is covered with symbolic engravings. Further menhirs lie at **São Pedro do Corval**, 12km west of Monsaraz along the Reguengos road, which is known by locals as the Lovers' Rock, and at **MONTE DO XAREZ**, between Monsaraz and the Guadiana River. This later one is four metres high, surrounded by a square of standing stones, and was probably the site of neolithic fertility rites.

Elvas

The hilltop town of **ELVAS**, 40km east of Estremoz, was long one of Portugal's mightiest frontier posts, a response to the Spanish stronghold of Badajoz, just 15km to the east across the Rio Guadiana. Its star-shaped walls and trio of forts are among the most complex and best-preserved military fortifications surviving in Europe. If you make a special detour to see just one Alentejo castle, Elvas is the natural choice; in addition, the town itself is a delight – all steep cobbled streets and mansions.

Elvas was recaptured from the Moors in 1230 and withstood periodic attacks from Spain through much of the following three centuries. It succumbed just once, however, to Spanish conquest, when the garrison was betrayed by Spanish bribery in 1580, allowing Philip II to enter and, for a period the following year, establish his court. The town subsequently made amends, during the war over the succession of Philip IV to the Portuguese territories. In 1644, the garrison resisted a nine-day siege by Spanish troops, and in 1658, with its numbers reduced by an epidemic to a mere thousand, saw off a fifteen-thousand-strong Spanish army.

During this period, the fortifications underwent intensive rebuilding and expansion, and they were later pressed into service twice more: in 1801, when the town withstood a Spanish siege during the War of the Oranges, and ten years later, during the Peninsular War, when the fort provided the base from which Wellington advanced to launch his bloody but successful assault on Badajoz. Perhaps out of tradition as much as anything, a military garrison is still stationed in the town.

Elvas's fortnightly event is its **Monday market** – a vibrantly chaotic affair attracting people from miles around, held just outside town behind the aqueduct. Otherwise, the town's big annual bash is its **Festa de São Mateus**, which lasts for six days in late September and encompasses a programme of agricultural, cultural and religious events, including the largest procession in southern Portugal. It's well worth coming at this time, although accommodation is at a premium.

The Town

Any exploration of Elvas has to start with its **fortifications**. The earliest stretches of the walls date from the thirteenth century, but most of what you see today is a result of the Wars of Succession with Spain in the seventeenth century. Under the direction of the great French military engineer, Vauban, the old circuit of walls was supplemented by extensive moats and star-shaped ramparts, their bastions jutting out at irregular but carefully judged intervals to maximize the effects of artillery crossfire. Echoes of these designs are to be seen at Estremoz and

ELVAS

ACCOMMODATION
1 Casa Coelho/Mocisso.
2 Senhore Joaquina T. Dias
3 Estalgem Dom Sancho II
4 Pensão O Lidador
5 Residencial Elvense
6 Hotel Dom Luis
7 Pousada de Santa Luzia

RESTAURANTS & BARS
A Discoteca Luigi
B Canal 7
C Centro Artistico Elvense
D Restaurante João Vieira
E Meson Pepe
F A Coluna

0   200 m

throughout Portugal. Further chains in the fortifications were provided by the **Forte da Graça**, a couple of kilometres north of Elvas, and the superb star-shaped **Forte de Santa Luzia**, a few minutes' walk to the south of the town. The Forte de Graça is still used by the military (part of it serves as a prison) and visits can only be arranged in advance by writing to the turismo (see below). Unfortunately, Santa Luzia is closed for repairs until further notice.

The Aqueduto da Amoreira

With its jagged and ungainly course, the **Aqueduto da Amoreira**, at the entrance to the town, looks at first like a bizarre extension of the fortifications. Despite its stark and awkward appearance, it is an imaginative and original feat of engineering: monstrous piles of masonry, distinctive cylindrical buttresses, and up to five tiers of arches support a tiny water channel along its seven-kilometre course, until it is finally discharged at the fountain in Largo da Misericórdia. It was built between 1498 and 1622 to the Manueline designs of Francisco de Arruda.

The town centre

Arruda was also responsible for the **Igreja de Nossa Senhora da Assunção** (9.30am–12.30pm & 2.30–7pm; closes at 5.30pm in winter; closed Tues), dominating Praça da República, which was the cathedral until Elvas lost episcopal status in 1882. Alterations in the seventeenth and eighteenth centuries left a ragged hodge-podge of styles, but its original Manueline inspiration remains evident on the south portal and in the unusual painted conical dome above the belfry.

Behind the church lies **Largo de Santa Clara**, a tiny cobbled square built on a slope around a splendid sixteenth-century **pelourinho**. Criminals were chained from the four metal hooks toward the top but, aside from the grisly technicalities, it's also a work of art, with a typically Manueline twisted column, and rope-like decorations. Directly opposite stands the strange and beautiful church of **Nossa Senhora da Consolação** (Tues–Sun 9.30am–12.30pm & 2.30–7pm; closes at 5.30pm in winter). From the outside, it's nothing more than a whitewashed wall with a mediocre Renaissance porch, but the interior reveals a sumptuous octagonal chapel: richly painted columns support a central cupola and virtually all the surfaces are decorated with magnificent seventeenth-century azulejos. The chapel was built between 1543 and 1557, on the site of a Knights Templar chapel – providing the inspiration for its octagonal design.

Largo de Santa Clara tapers upwards to a restored tenth-century archway flanked by fortified towers and surmounted by a **loggia**, or gallery. Originally part of the old town walls, this was built by the Moors, who occupied Elvas from the early eighth century until 1226. The street beneath the gateway leads to the **Castelo** (daily: summer 9am–1pm & 3–6pm; winter 9am–12.30pm & 2–5.30pm), also constructed by the Moors on an old Roman fortified site, but strengthened by Dom Dinis and João II in the late fifteenth century.

Practicalities

The walls make Elvas a pretty easy place to get your bearings. Arriving by **bus**, you'll find yourself right in the centre of town, in Praça da República; the **turismo** (daily 9am–6pm; closes at 5.30pm in winter; ☎068/62 22 36) is next door. Shuttle buses also run to Praça da República from the local **train station**, 4km down the Campo Maior road at Fontaínhas; the station is on the Lisbon–Badajoz line.

Crossing to the Spanish city of Badajoz, 15km to the east, is in fact easiest by train, with three daily services taking fifteen minutes. Buses to Badajoz leave from Praça da República four times daily, but take at least an hour and you'll have to change onto a Spanish bus when you reach the border.

Accommodation

Most of the mid- to upper-range accommodation tends to be situated on the out-skirts of Elvas, while in the old town budget rooms abound, of varying quality; some (listed below) are excellent value. There's also a **campsite**, *Piedade* (☎068/62 89 97; May–Sept), on the outskirts of town on the N4 to Estremoz.

Casa Coelho/Mocisso, Rua Aires Varela 5 (☎068/62 21 26). Large, well-appointed rooms in the Moorish quarter, well-signposted from Praça da República; highly recommended. ③.

Hotel Dom Luís, Avda. de Badajoz (☎068/62 27 56, fax 62 07 33). One of several modern hotels situated beyond the old walls on the major Spain to Portugal highway. The rooms are good, but the location has absolutely nothing going for it. ⑤.

Estalagem Dom Sancho II, Praça da República 20 (☎068/62 26 86, fax 62 47 17). The best bet for a hotel in the centre, this is a reliable place on the main square. Its restaurant has a beau-tiful inner courtyard for summer dining, though the food is nothing to write home about. ④.

Residencial Elvense/Garçia de Orta, Avda. Garçia de Orta 3A (☎068/62 31 52). A cheap but friendly *quartos*-cum-hotel, by the Portas de Olivença. ③.

Pensão O Lidador, Rua de Alcamim 33 (☎068/62 34 42). Adequate rooms in a family house. ①.

Monte de Amoreira, Estrada de Barbacena (☎068/62 59 12). A small and reasonably priced rural property, 6km northeast of town. ④.

Pousada de Santa Luzia, Avda. de Badajoz (☎068/62 21 94, fax 62 21 27). The country's first *pousada* (established 1942) but one of the more missable. A modern building, outside the town walls, on the fume-filled N4. ⑦.

Senhora Joaquina T. Dias, Rua João d'Olivença 5 (☎068/62 47 22). Three rooms with showers, in a dingy but friendly family house. ③.

Eating

Elvas has a good selection of restaurants, covering all price ranges; those in the old town tend to have the best atmosphere. If you want to put your own **picnic** together, the place to buy supplies is a small, early-morning food market held Monday to Saturday at the bottom of Rua dos Chilões.

Canal 7, Rua dos Sapateiros 16, off the main square. The best of the budget places, always popular; 850$00 for a greasy fill-up.

Centro Artistico Elvense, Praça da República, next to the bus station. Reasonably priced café-restaurant with outdoor tables overlooking the praça; the *arroz de marisco* is very good.

A Coluna, Rua do Cabrito 11. Locally considered Elvas's best restaurant, and deservedly so. It's in an old stables, cavernous, whitewashed but still intimate, and specializes in cod dish-es; the *ementa turística* (which invariably includes *bacalhau*) goes for 1500$00.

Restaurante Chimarrão, 2km west off the Estremoz road. Pricey, but serves excellent-quality Brazilian dishes.

Restaurante João Vieira, Largo Cisterna 5. Very cheap, very friendly, family-run canteen-cum-restaurant. You'll be hard put to spend more than 800$00.

Meson Pepe, Rua da Feira 25. A moderately priced charcoal grill snack bar, serving up deli-cious chicken, lamb and pork loin.

Drinking and nightlife

Elvas is not a late-night town, but if you do want to make a night of it try the unnamed bar (first floor) on Rua São Pedro, on the left-hand side coming from the praça or the cosy *Não Sei* bar at Rua Sa da Bandeira 52a, which is open until 2am and also serves great Portuguese tapas. For something more energetic try *Discoteca Luigi* in the square facing the castle.

Campo Maior

Eighteen kilometres to the north of Elvas lies the fortress town of **CAMPO MAIOR**. The road from Elvas passes through olive groves and sunflower fields and it's a pleasant enough trip, though the town itself would be unremarkable were it not for the presence of its **Capela dos Ossos** (Mon–Sat 9am–7pm), a diminutive version of the Chapel of Bones in Évora. This stands immediately to the right of the large parish church just off Rua 1º de Maio: ask for the key in the church or try the door next to the chapel. Adding to the surreal effect, the entrance is through a neat local government office.

The walls and vaults in the claustrophobic chapel interior are completely covered in human bones, while two skeletons hang from the walls, and three rows of skulls are positioned on the window ledge to inspect passers-by. The chapel is dated 1766 and its purpose is indicated by two verses from the Book of Job traced out in collarbones near the window: "My bone cleaveth to my skin and to my flesh, and I am escaped with the skin of my teeth." Job is complaining of his horrific physical and mental suffering, but takes solace in the knowledge that "though after my skin worms destroy this body, yet in my flesh shall I see God".

The chapel may have been "furnished" following the disaster which devastated Campo Maior in 1732, when a gunpowder magazine in the town's castle was struck by lightning, killing 1500 people and destroying 823 houses. Today the castle is little more than a ruin, though with fine views over the borderlands.

Practicalities

The **bus** journey from Elvas takes just 35 minutes, making it an easy side-trip. There's a **turismo** on Rua Major Talaya (Mon–Fri 9am–12.30pm & 2–5.30pm; ☎068/68 89 36). If you want **to stay**, *Pensão-Restaurante Francisco Carlos* at Largo Barão Barcelinhos 5, off Rua 1º de Maio (☎068/68 73 21; ②), is a good option: owned by a famous fado singer, it's decorated with pictures of the great man, while meals there are often accompanied by some of Francisco's finest renditions. Otherwise, there's the similarly priced *O Ministro*, Trav. da Praça 1 (☎ & fax 068/68 78 69; ②), or the more upmarket *Hotel de Santa Beatrice,* on Avda. Combatentes da Grande Guerra (☎068/6901040, fax 68 81 09; ⑤); both are off Praça da República. There's also a **campsite** (☎068/68 94 92) just west of the town. For **food**, try *O Ministro*'s affiliated restaurant at Rua 13 de Dezembro 41, or the pleasant *O Fa são*, opposite the parish church.

Portalegre

PORTALEGRE is the capital, market centre and transport hub of Alto Alentejo. It is an attractive town, crouched at the foot of the Serra de São Mamede where there are good hiking possibilities (see box on p.412), and is endowed with the province's usual contingent of whitewashed and walled old quarters, along with some interesting reminders of its industrial history. These include a cork factory, whose great twin chimneys greet you on the way into town, and the **Fábrica Real**

HIKING INTO THE SERRA DE SÃO MAMEDE: FROM PORTALEGRE TO MARVÃO

The sixteen-kilometre walk begins from the *Quinta da Saúde* campsite, 3km outside **Portalegre** on the N246-2. Turn right out of the campsite and follow the road for a few kilometres until you see a signpost to the left marked São Julião. Turn left here, then left again shortly afterwards, following signs to Porto Espada. You'll pass a reservoir on the left-hand side of the road after about 3 or 4km; you'll also see plenty of abandoned farmhouses and buildings, as a result of the flooding caused by the construction of the reservoir. On reaching the small village of **Rasa**, turn right, then shortly afterwards, as the road bends sharply to the left, take the dirt track that leads straight ahead. This track emerges at a whitewashed stone bridge – turn right to go over this, then after about 50m turn left. Continue along here for about five minutes until you reach a main road; there are several cafés and restaurants here, where you can rest before tackling the long slog uphill to Marvão. If you're not up to the strenuous climb, which is best done early in the morning or late in the day, you can catch a bus from here up to Marvão. If you want to continue the walk, turn left onto the main road, then right straight after the bridge and right immediately afterwards. Follow this road for a few hundred metres, then turn left up a cobbled track soon after a group of houses. Follow the track upwards through the olive groves for roughly an hour and you will arrive just outside the walls of Marvão.

---

de Tapeçarias on Rua Gomes Fernandes – the town's single surviving tapestry factory and the last remnant of a great textile industry that peaked in the seventeenth and eighteenth centuries. In its studios and weaving hall over five thousand shades of wool are used in the reproduction of centuries-old patterns.

The wealth produced in the town's boom years, in particular from the silk workshops, has a further legacy in the collection of grand mercantile mansions and town houses, which give the town an air of faded affluence. It is especially apparent as you walk up Rua 19 de Junho – the main thoroughfare of the old town – which is lined by a spectacular concentration of late Renaissance and Baroque mansions. At the southern end of the street, and dominating the quarter, is the **Sé**, an austere building save for a flash of fancy in the pyramidal pinnacles of its towers. To one side of this an eighteenth-century palace houses the **Museu Municipal** (9.30am–12.30pm & 2–6pm; closed Tues; 250$00). It's not exactly a compelling visit, with much routine furniture and fittings on display, though there are some lovely ceramics and ivories a well as some early Arraiolos carpets.

If you have some time to kill in town, you may also consider a visit to the **Museu José Régio**, by the cemetery on Rua Poeta José Régio (Tues–Sun 9.30am–12.30pm & 2–6pm; 250$00), where you can see the poet's collection of over three hundred antique crucifixes, altarpieces and powder horns.

Practicalities

All the main roads converge on the **Rossio**, a large square at the centre of the new town. Uphill from here, the Rua 5º de Outubro runs into the walled **old town**. The **bus station** is just a few blocks from the Rossio on Rua Nuno Álvarez Pereira. Shuttle buses to and from here meet **trains** at the Estação de Portalegre, 10km out of town to the south, on the Lisbon–Badajoz line. The **turismo** (daily

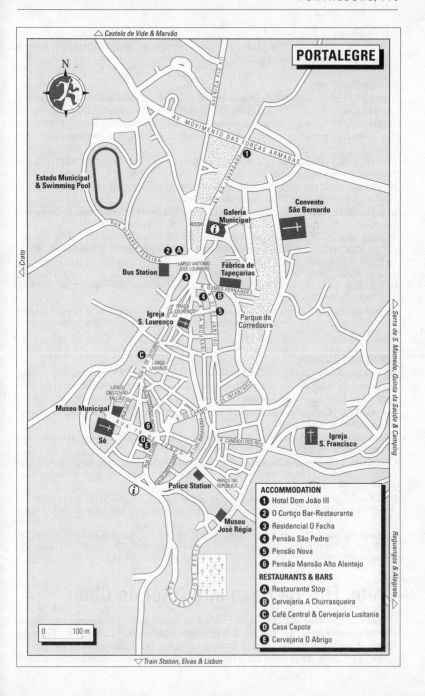

PORTALEGRE

N

△ Castelo de Vide & Marvão

AV. DA PIO XII

AV. MOVIMENTO DAS FORÇAS ARMADAS

RUA ALVARES PEREIRA

AV. DA LIBERDADE

△ Crato

Estado Municipal & Swimming Pool

ROSSIO

Galeria Municipal *i*

Convento São Bernardo

Bus Station

LARGO ANTÓNIO JOSÉ LOURINHO

Fábrica de Tapeçarias

R. GOMES FERNANDES

31 DE JANEIRO

DA MOURARIA

PRAÇA S. LOURENÇO

Igreja S. Lourenço

Parque da Corredoura

RUA 5 DE OUTUBRO

LARGO LARANJO

LARGO CRISTOVÃO FALCÃO

R. DE INFANTARIA

R. DO CARMO

Museu Municipal

RUA 19 DE

RUA DE ELVAS

RUA LUIZ MOUZINHO

R. CANDIDO DOS REIS

Sé

Igreja S. Francisco

i

Police Station

PRAÇA DA REPÚBLICA

Museu José Régio

RUA POETA JOSÉ RÉGIO

△ Serra de S. Mamede, Quinta da Saúde & Camping

△ Reguengos & Alegrete

ACCOMMODATION
- **1** Hotel Dom João III
- **2** O Cortiço Bar-Restaurante
- **3** Residencial O Facha
- **4** Pensão São Pedro
- **5** Pensão Nova
- **6** Pensão Mansão Alto Alentejo

RESTAURANTS & BARS
- **A** Restaurante Stop
- **B** Cervejaria A Churrasqueira
- **C** Café Central & Cervejaria Lusitania
- **D** Casa Capote
- **E** Cervejaria O Abrigo

0 _____ 100 m

▽ Train Station, Elvas & Lisbon

9am–12.30pm & 2–5pm; ☎045/228 15) is at the far end of Rua de Elvas by the old town walls, and the Galerie Municipal (summer 10am–7pm; winter 10am–1pm & 3–6pm) also dispenses information.

Accommodation

There is limited **accommodation** available, and it's advisable to book a day ahead to be sure of a bed. **Camping** is an attractive option; the *Orbitur* site (☎045/228 48; mid-Jan to mid-Nov) at Quinta da Saúde, 3km into the hills, on the N246-2, is well equipped, with electricity, showers and a few bungalows for rent.

O Cortiço Bar-Restaurant, Rua Dom Nuno Álvares Pereira 17 (☎045/221 76). Has a few reasonable rooms upstairs. ③.

Hotel Dom João III, Avda. da Liberdade (☎045/33 01 92, fax 33 04 44). A dull, functional hotel, opposite the Jardim Municipal in the new town. ⑤.

Residencial O Facha, Largo António José Lourinho 3–5 (☎045/231 61). Close to the Rossio, this place is rather rundown and should be tried only as a last resort. ③.

Pensão Mansão Alto Alentejo, Rua 19 de Junho 59 (☎045/222 90, fax 33 06 17). Comfortable *pensão* in the old town, near the Sé, with reasonably priced rooms with private bath, and heating. ④.

Pensão Nova, Rua 31 de Janeiro 28–30 (☎045/33 12 12, fax 33 04 93; ④). Newly renovated, friendly hostel, with the same management as the nearby *Pensão São Pedro* (☎045/33 12 12; ④), at Rua da Mouraria 14.

Quinta da Saúde, Estrada de São Mamede, 3km out of Portalegre next to the campsite (☎045/223 24). An attractive property with a great view over the surrounding hills and a good rooftop restuarant. ④.

Eating and drinking

By day the Rossio is the liveliest place for a drink, but in the evening the action, such as it is, switches to the old town; try the *Café Central* on Largo Frederico Laranjo or the *Cervejaria Lusitania*, close by at Rua Luís de Camões 43.

Cervejaria O Abrigo, Rua de Elvas 74. Serves inexpensive Alentejan dishes; the *ementa turística* costs around 1500$00.

Casa Capote, Rua 19 de Junho 56. Friendly restaurant whose walls are hung with tapestries and paintings; a full meal will set you back around 2000$00.

Cervejaria A Churrasqueira, Rua Guilherme Gomes Fernandes 29, just off the Rossio. The cheapest option in town serves an excellent set menu for 800$00, with most main dishes between 250$00 and 650$00.

Residencial O Facha, Largo António José Lourinho 3–5. Wide choice of expensive dishes (more international than regional) served in glorious glass and brass Art Deco surroundings.

Restaurante Stop, 11–15 Rua Dom Nuno Álvares Pereira. One of the better options, just off the Rossio, serving typical Alentejan cuisine in pleasant surroundings; a slap-up meal will cost under 2000$00.

Crato, Flôr da Rosa and Alter do Chão

Directly to the west of Portalegre, **Crato** has small-town charms and, nearby, an impressive **dolmen**, as well as the beautiful honey-stone convent of **Flôr da Rosa**. Horse enthusiasts may also want to make the thirteen-kilometre detour south of Crato to **Alter do Chão**, home of a prestigious *coudelaria* (stud farm).

Buses run intermittently from Portalegre to both Crato and Alter do Chão, while the **Estação de Crato** gives access to the Lisbon–Badajoz train line, with connections west to Abrantes and east to Elvas.

Crato

CRATO – 21km west of Portalegre – is an ancient agricultural town which has clearly seen better days and larger populations. A trio of imposing, ornate churches and the elegant **Varanda do Grão Prior** in the main square attest, like Portalegre's monuments, to the textile boom years of the sixteenth century. The *varanda* is the most interesting of the structures – built for the outdoor celebration of Mass. Also worth a look is a town mansion a couple of streets away, by the public gardens, which houses a small **museum** (erratic hours) of Alto Alentejo handicrafts and domestic traditions. Well into this century, alms were handed out to the local poor from a balcony-chapel upstairs.

The town **castle** was once among the mightiest in the Alentejo, but today it's a pastoral ruin, overrun by farm animals, fig trees and oregano plants. It is normally locked, but keys are generally kept beneath an abandoned blue cart in the field in front; if they're not there, ask at one of the nearby farm dwellings. From the ramparts, there is a splendid view over the town and across the countless rows of olive trees to the hills of Portalegre.

For a good rural walk from Crato, follow the N363 northwest towards Aldeia da Mata. On the left-hand side of the road, about 5km from town, is what is reckoned to be the best-preserved **dolmen** in Portugal. On the corner of the road leading out of town, you'll find an excellent **adega**, with delicious home-cooking and a crowded bar where everyone plays *belho* – a kind of miniature version of *boules*.

The town has just one small **pensão**, above the *Café Parque* on Avenida Dom Nuno Álvares Pereira (☎045/972 23; ③), though the **turismo** in the Câmara Municipal may be able to fix you up with rooms in private houses. **Campers** can pick their own spots by the old Roman bridge near the train station, or up by the castle. If you arrive at the **train station**, 3km south of town, the station master will telephone for a taxi, which is not expensive.

Flôr da Rosa

Two kilometres north of Crato lies the village of **FLÔR DA ROSA**, traditionally a centre for **pottery**, with as many as seventy families engaged in the trade in the early part of this century. Today the distinctive *olaria* of the region is made in only two workshops, whose shared kiln is near the convent, high above the broad streets and low houses. Their methods of manufacture haven't changed in centuries, though the clay – yellow for waterproofing, grey for ovenware – has to be sought further and further afield. Purchases break easily, but it's nice to know that these functional (and inexpensive) pieces aren't designed for the tourist trade.

The **Convento de Flôr da Rosa**, founded in the fourteenth century and much endowed over the next two hundred years, was abandoned in 1897, due to leaking roofs and a decaying structure. After extensive state restoration (begun in 1940), the fortress monastery finally re-opened in 1995 as one of Portugal's most lavish *pousadas* (☎045/99 72 10, fax 99 72 12; ⑦). It is still possible to see inside, though, and to look round the adjoining church. Around the main building you can trace the plan of the gardens (still being restored), laid out in the insignia of the Order of Malta, in honour of the warlord **Nuno Álvares Pereira**, whose father founded the monastery.

Father Pereira's tomb (dated 1382) is prominent in the narrow, soaring convent church. Adjoining it, on the ground floor, is the sixteenth-century **Sala do Capítulo**, distinguished by fine brickwork, fan-vaulting and a Gothic cloister. On the first floor are the monks' **dormitories**, whose open casements offer sweeping views across acres of olive trees.

If you need to stay in the village and can't afford the luxury of the *pousada*, the more cosy *Palacete Florida Rosa*, on Rua da Cruz (☎045/974 51, fax 975 91; ⑤), is a cheaper option.

Alter do Chão

ALTER DO CHÃO, 13km to the south of Crato, is another town that did well from textiles, particularly during the sixteenth century, as indicated by its attractive Renaissance marble fountain and an array of handsome town houses. There is a **castle**, too, whose central tower can be climbed for an overview of the region, but the chief reason for a visit is the Coudelaria de Alter-Real stud farm, 3km out of town.

The **Coudelaria de Alter-Real** was founded in 1748 by Dom João V of the House of Bragança, and remained in the family until 1910 when the War Office took it over. Today, maintained by the state, it is open for public visits (daily 9am–5pm), though to see the horses in action it's best to arrive in the morning: between 10am and noon you can watch them filing in from the fields to feed, accompanied by the ringing of forty bells. In the town itself you may be lucky enough to see the Coudelaria coach and horses when they come to collect the mail.

The tours of the stud are also interesting with a museum display of carriages and horse regalia, through which you are conducted at a stately pace by a cavalry officer. Alter-Real horses have been sought after since the stud's foundation – one is depicted in the equestrian statue of Dom José in Lisbon's Praça do Comércio, for example – and they remain the favoured breed of the Portuguese mounted police and the Lisbon Riding School at Queluz.

If you can time a visit, April 25 is the best day to be at the Coudelaria, when the **annual sale** takes place. The town's main festival – the **Festa de Nossa Senhora da Alegria** – occurs on the following day.

Practicalities

Several **pensões** are clustered in the road opposite the castle in Alter do Chão, including the *Pensão Ferreira* (☎045/622 54; ②) and *Pensão Restaurante Avenida* (☎045/622 59; ②), both worth a try. Alternatively, ask for rooms above the *Snack Bar Avenida* on Avenida Dr. João Pestana (☎045/623 01; ②).

For **meals**, the *Café/Restaurante Lareira Alentejana*, Estrada Nacional 369, serves good local cuisine and has an *ementa turística* for 1750$00. *Café Oasis* is pretty good, and there are tasty cakes at the nearby *Pastelaria Ateneia*. **Buses** connect the town with Portalegre and Crato.

Castelo de Vide and Marvão

The upland district **north of Portalegre** is a bucolic landscape, with tree-clad mountain ranges and a series of gorgeous hilltop villages. Among these, the best targets are **Castelo de Vide** and **Marvão**, both with castles, and the former with a spa. Castelo de Vide is the most easily accessible, connected by bus five times daily with Portalegre; Marvão has three daily services, Monday to Friday only. Getting between the two, one morning and one late afternoon bus from Castelo de Vide to Portalegre connects with buses to Marvão at the main road junction of Portagem.

Castelo de Vide

CASTELO DE VIDE covers the slopes around a fourteenth-century castle, its blindingly white cottages delineated in brilliant contrast to the greenery around. Arriving by bus, you'll be dropped at the *pelourinho* outside the **turismo** (daily: summer Mon–Fri 9am–12.30pm & 2–7pm; winter 9am–12.30pm & 2–3.30pm; ☎045/913 61) in the centre of town. From here, half a dozen parallel streets make a sharp climb up to the aptly named **Praça Alta** on the edge of town. The main road, meanwhile, peters out into a narrow path, descending past a tranquil Renaissance fountain to the twisting alleyways of the **Judairia** – the old Jewish quarter. Amid the cottages, most of which still have Gothic doorways and windows, is a thirteenth-century **synagogue** (daily 9am–7pm), the oldest surviving in Portugal. From the outside it doesn't look very different from the cottages, so you will probably need to ask for directions.

On a hill above the Judairia, the **Castelo** (daily: summer 8am–7pm; winter 9am–12.30pm & 2–5.30pm) squats within the wider fortifications of the original medieval village. While there, chat to the man at the castle door and he'll probably show you the elaborate moving wooden toys that he produces; his neighbour is a lacemaker who trains young women in the art.

Practicalities

Given its size, the town has a surprising amount of **accommodation**. Of the budget options, the best value is provided by the friendly, English-speaking *Casa de Hóspedes Melanie*, Largo do Paço Novo 3 (☎045/916 32; ③). Other options in the same price range include the *Pensão Cantinho Particular*, Rua Miguel Bombarda 9 (☎045/911 51; ③) – friendly if a bit on the basic side – and the *Residencial Xinxel* by the castle (☎045/914 06; ③); both include breakfast in the price. With more money, your best bet is one of the elegant rooms in the *Albergaria El Rei Dom Miguel*, Rua Bartolomeu Álvares da Santa (☎045/91 91 91, fax 915 92; ④; breakfast included) as the town's only hotel, *Hotel Sol e Serra*, Estrada de São Vincente (☎045/913 01, fax 913 73; ⑤) is rather dated and soulless. The **restaurant** at the *Cantinho Particular* is basic but good, but for an expensive splurge (around 3000–4000$00) try the excellent *Restaurante Marino's* on Praça Dom Pedro (☎045/91 92 07), which specializes in Italian and regional dishes. The *Restaurante São João*, on the road to Portalegre, and *Don Pedro V*, Praça Dom Pedro V, are also very good. The perfect place for **snacks** is the *Pastelaria Sol Nascente* at Rua de Olivença 31, which has a wonderful selection of pastries.

Marvão

Beautiful as Castelo de Vide is, **MARVÃO** surpasses it. The panoramas from its remote eyrie site are unrivalled and the atmosphere even quieter than a population of less than a thousand would suggest. No more than a handful of houses –

each as scrupulously whitewashed as the rest – lies outside the seventeenth-century walls. Originally the village seems to have been an outlying suburb of Medobriga, a mysterious Roman city which vanished almost without trace. Its inhabitants fled before the Moorish advance in around 715 but later returned to live under Muslim rule, when the place was renamed after Marvan, the Moorish Lord of Coimbra. It fell to the Christians in 1166 and the **castle** was rebuilt by Dom Dinis around 1229 as another important link in the chain of outposts along the Spanish border. The castle stands at the far end of the village, its walls blending into the sharp slopes of the *serra*. It's dauntingly impenetrable and was indeed captured only once, in 1833, when the attackers entered through a secret gate. Also worth a visit is the **municipal museum** in the Church of Santa Maria, if only for its disturbing display of medieval medical equipment.

The village makes a superb night's stop, as several houses within the walls are rented out under a scheme organized by the **turismo**, on Rua Dr. António Matos Magalhães (☎045/931 04). In some of these you can get just a room, while others are rented out as a unit; prices, consequently, are extremely varied. Additional **accommodation** is provided by *Restaurante Varanda do Alentejo* in Praça do Pelourinho, which rents out pleasant rooms (☎045/932 72; ④); *Pensão Dom Dinis* on Rua Dr. António Matos Magalhães (☎ & fax 045/932 36; ⑤; breakfast included); and the attractively converted *Pousada de Santa Maria* (☎045/932 01, fax 934 40; ⑦) on Rua 24 de Janeiro.

For **meals**, the *Restaurante Varanda do Alentejo* is good (see above) and you can also eat and drink at *Bar da Casa do Povo* or *Bar Marcelino*, both just off the square. The *pousada*'s restaurant serves meals at 3500–5000$00 per head which, even allowing for the grand views, is expensive.

Marvão-Beirã: on into Spain

Lisbon–Madrid trains stop at the station of **MARVÃO-BEIRÃ**, 9km north of Marvão village. Heading for Spain by public transport, this is the easiest way to go, although services, especially outside summer, can be infrequent; check with the turismo for current times. The road border at **GALEGOS**, 14km east of Marvão, is open to traffic but very few cars use it. In addition, there's one daily **bus** from Portalegre direct to the Spanish border town of Valencia de Alcántara.

Belver Castle

Travelling northwest from Portalegre, the N18/N118 roads take you up to the Tejo valley, and, of course, the Alentejo border. The most interesting targets on this route are the castles of Abrantes and Almourol in Ribatejo (see pp.170–171), and **Belver**, which, although sited with its town on the north bank of the Tejo, is technically a part of Alentejo. If you are dependent on public transport, it is easiest to take a train or bus to Abrantes, and approach Belver from there.

BELVER CASTLE is one of the most famous in the country, its fanciful position, name and tiny size having ensured it a place in dozens of Portuguese legends. The name comes from *belo ver* (beautiful to see), the supposed exclamation of some medieval princess, waking up to look out from its keep at the river valley below. It dates from the twelfth century, when the Portuguese frontier stood at the Tejo, the Moors having reclaimed all the territories to the south, save Évora, that Afonso Henriques had conquered for his kingdom. Its founder was Dom

Sancho I, who entrusted its construction and care to the knight-monks of the Order of Saint John.

The walls form an irregular pentagon, tracing the crown of a hill, with a narrow access path to limit attackers to virtual single file. If you find the castle locked, search out the guard who lives at no. 1 on the main square in Belver village. For a small fee, he will unlock the **chapel** to show you its formidable fifteenth-century reliquary. All the pieces of bone were stolen during the French invasions in the nineteenth century, but fortunately for the villagers there was a casket of "spares" hidden away by the priest, and these substitutes are today paraded at the **Festa de Santa Reliquária**, held around August 18.

You're very likely to track down the castle guard sharing a few jokes over a glass of *bagaceira* (Portugal's cheapest hangover) in Belver's single **café-restau-rant-pension**. Rooms (②) are usually available, outside the August festival times.

Buses leave from the praça or from the street above the **train station**, which is directly below the village beside the river. If you take the train north along the valley towards Castelo Branco, look out for the striking rock faces before Vila Velha de Ródão known as the **Portas do Ródão** (Gates of Ródão).

BAIXO ALENTEJO

The hot, dry inland routes of Baixo Alentejo have little to offer beyond a stop at **Beja** – the most interesting southern Alentejo town – en route to the Algarve, or, if you're heading for Spain, at the frontier towns of **Serpa** or **Mértola**. The coastline, however, is another matter, with resorts like **Vila Nova de Milfontes**, **Almograve** and **Zambujeira do Mar** providing an attractive alternative to the summer crowds on the Algarve. Their only disadvantage – and the reason for a very patchy tourist development – is their exposure to the Atlantic winds, which at times create huge breakers and dangerous swimming conditions. But as long as you're prepared to spend occasional days out of the water, they are enjoyable places to take it easy for a few days by the sea.

All the beaches are situated along minor roads, but there are local **bus services** from Santiago do Cacém and Odemira. Alternatively, coming from Lisbon, you can take the express bus direct to Vila Nova de Milfontes, Almograve and Zambujeira do Mar; it leaves Lisbon twice a day from the Casal Ribeiro terminal (p.53) and, as with all *expressos*, it's wise to buy tickets in advance.

Southeast from Lisbon

Heading southeast into the Alentejo from Lisbon or Setúbal, the main road (and bus) loops around the **Rio Sado estuary**, through **Alcácer do Sal**, at the mouth of the river, and on through the agricultural town of **Grândola**. Heading **towards Beja**, drivers could head instead directly east from Alcácer do Sal, cutting across a succession of country roads and past a couple of huge reservoirs before meeting the main Évora–Beja road.

Alcácer do Sal

Fifty-two kilometres from Setúbal, **ALCÁCER DO SAL** is one of Portugal's oldest ports, founded by the Phoenicians and made a regional capital under the

Moors – whence its name (*al-Ksar*, the town) derives. The other part of its name, *do Sal*, "of salt", reflects the dominance of the salt industry in these parts; the Sado estuary is still fringed with salt marshes. Alcácer today is slightly seedy-looking, but quite attractively so, particularly along its waterfront promenade. A couple of roads back from the promenade at its western end is a charming quarter of mainly medieval houses, centred around Rua Rui Salem. Further uphill, above the town, stands the part-ruined Moorish **castle** (daily 10am–noon & 2–5pm), from where there are striking views of the lush green paddy-fields which almost surround the town, and of the storks' nests on the church rooftops.

The *Café-Restaurant Sado* is at the eastern end of the promenade, past the bus depot at Largo Luís de Camões – try the house speciality of prawns, beer and buttered toast. Here, too, or at one of the town's bakeries, you can sample *pinhoadas,* a honey and pine-seed toffee, or for a more substantial meal try *Restaurant O Campinho* on Avenida dos Aviadores. If you decide to **stay the night**, there are *dormidas* at Rua Periera 2 (☎065/62 23 55; ②), near the post office, but for a little more you can get a room at *Residencial Silvano*, Rua 1º de Maio 15 (☎065/62 25 90; ②).

At the beginning of October, for around three days, the town hosts a **regional fair** featuring an assembly of agricultural machinery, a couple of bullfights and acres of stalls. It's one of the most enjoyable fairs in the south.

Grândola

At **GRÂNDOLA**, 24km south of Alcácer do Sal, the roads diverge: southwest to the coast; east to Beja, Serpa and, ultimately, Spanish Andalucía. As well as the main road through Alcácer to Grândola, there's an enjoyable alternative approach for drivers from Setúbal who can take the ferry to Tróia and make their way down the long, sand-fringed **Pensinsula de Tróia** along the N253. The town was made legendary through the song *Grândola vila morena*, the broadcasting of which was the pre-arranged signal for the start of the 1974 Revolution. There's precious little reason to stop in town, though it has a few decent restaurants – the pricey *Picapu* on Rua Dom Nuno Álvares Pereira has the best reputation – and a couple of average hotels, should you be stuck.

East towards Beja: Viana do Alentejo

Heading **east** instead from Alcácer do Sal, the minor N5 runs to Torrão, curving around the Rio Sado, past the **Barragem de Vale do Gaio**. Sited on the edge of the reservoir is the *Pousada de Vale do Gaio* (☎065/66 96 10, fax 66 95 45; ⑥), a fairly simple conversion of the lodge used by the dam engineers.

Continuing east, along the N383, you pass through **VIANA DO ALENTEJO**, a sleepy and typically southern Alentejan village which preserves a highly decorative **castle**, full of Mudejar and Manueline features (Tues–Sun 10am–12.30pm & 2–5pm; closed Aug). The castle walls were built on a pentagonal plan by Dom Dinis in 1313, and the interior ensemble of buildings was expanded under Dom João II and Dom Manuel I in the late fifteenth century. To this latter period belong a sequence of elaborate battlements and the beautiful parish church, part of a striking group of buildings within the walls, encompassing a Misericórdia, town hall, cistern and *pelourinho*. Viana also boasts a very good restaurant, the expensive *Bernadino Santos Banha* at Rua António I Sousa 36 (☎066/931 16). **From Viana**, the N384 runs 30km east, past another huge reservoir, to meet the main Évora–Beja road.

Beja

On the inland route through southern Alentejo, **BEJA** appears as a welcome oasis amid the sweltering, featureless wheat fields. Commanding this strategic position in the centre of the plains, it has long been an important and prosperous city. Founded by Julius Caesar in 48BC it was named Pax Julia, in honour of the peace accord signed here between Rome and the Lusitanians, but later became Pax Augusta and then just Pax, from which it gradually corrupted to Paca, Baca, Baju, and finally Beja.

South of Évora, it's the most interesting stop on the way to the Algarve, and once past the modern suburbs Beja reveals an unhurried old quarter with a cluster of peculiar churches, a beautiful convent and a thirteenth-century castle. You can take in most of the sights in this compact historic centre in half a day, though in summer the heat will probably turn you towards a bar within an hour or so.

If you visit the town during May, you'll witness the town celebrating the **Festas da Cidade** – a month-long jamboree of music, dance, gastronomy and bullfighting.

The Town

In Portugal Beja is best known for the love affair of a seventeenth-century nun who lived in the **Convento de Nossa Senhora da Conceição**, just off Largo dos Duques de Beja. Sister Mariana Alcoforado is believed to have fallen in love with Count Chamilly, a French cavalry officer, and is credited with the notorious (in Portugal anyway) *Five Love Letters of a Portuguese Nun*, first published in Paris in 1669. The originals have never been discovered, and a scholarly debate has raged over the authenticity of the French "translation". Nonetheless, English and Portuguese editions soon appeared and the letters became internationally famous as a classic of romantic literature.

Sentimental associations aside, the convent is quite a building. Founded in the fifteenth century, it has a panoply of Manueline fripperies, with elaborate portals and a rhythmic roofline decorated with balustrades and pinnacles. The walls of the cloisters and chapter house are completely covered with multicoloured six-teenth- and seventeenth-century azulejos, and present one of the finest examples of this art form. The other highlight is a magnificent Rococo chapel, sumptuous-ly gilded and embellished with flying cherubs. The convent was dissolved in 1834 and today houses the **Museu Regional** (daily 9.45am–12.30pm & 2–5.30pm; 100$00, free on Sun). Compared to the architecture of the building, the museum pieces are comparatively lacklustre, though they include a wide-ranging display on the town's past eras – including items as diverse as Roman and Visigothic stone, fifteenth- to eighteenth-century Dutch and Portuguese painting, and the grille through which the errant nun first glimpsed her lover.

Beja's **Castelo** (Tues–Sun: summer 10am–1pm & 2–6pm; winter 9am–noon & 1–4pm) rises decoratively on the edge of the old quarter. It was built – yet again – by Dom Dinis and is remarkable for the playful battlements of its Torre de

BEJA

Ermida de Santo André

RESTAURANTS
- Ⓐ Restaurante A Esquina
- Ⓑ O Portão
- Ⓒ Restaurante Alentejano
- Ⓓ Restaurante Pena
- Ⓔ Luis da Rocha

Train Station

Santo Amaro

Castelo

Sé

Misericórdia

Santa Maria

Salvador

Convento de N. S. da Conceição

Jardim Publico

Market

ACCOMMODATION
- ❶ Casa de Hospedes Pax Julia
- ❷ Residencial Coelho
- ❸ Residencial Bejense
- ❹ Pousada de São Francisco
- ❺ Residencial Santa Bárbara
- ❻ Casa de Hospedes Rocha
- ❼ Residencial Cristina
- ❽ Hotel Melius

AV. DO BRASIL

Bus Station

Stadium

Campsite

0   200 m

▽ Mertola & Castro Verde

Menagem, which costs 200$00 to climb up. Similarly, an exaggerated horseshoe window halfway up hints at the architect's artistic intent. In the shadow of the keep stands the Visigothic basilica of **Santo Amaro**, today a small archeological museum. The building is a rare survival from pre-Moorish Portugal; the interior columns are carved with seventh-century geometric motifs.

Among other churches in Beja, the most distinctive is the mid-sixteenth-century **Misericórdia** in Praça da República; its huge projecting porch served originally as a meat market and the stonework is deliberately chiselled to give a coarse, "rustic" appearance. Earlier, fortress-inclined Gothic elements are to be seen on the church of **Santa Maria**, in the heart of the old quarter, and on the fifteenth-century **Ermida de Santo André**, on the road out to Lisbon, which is endowed with gigantic tubular buttresses.

Practicalities

The old quarter is a circular tangle of streets, enclosed within a ring road which has replaced the town walls. At its heart is a pair of interlocking squares – Largo de Santa Maria and Largo dos Duques de Beja. The **bus station** lies five minutes' walk southeast of this quarter; the **train station** five minutes northeast. A very helpful **turismo** (June–Sept Mon–Fri 10am–8pm, Sat 10am–12.30pm & 2.30–6pm; Oct–May Mon–Sat 10am–6pm; ☎084/236 93) is located just south of the central squares at Rua Capitão J.F. de Sousa 25.

Beja has good **transport connections** to the rest of central and southern Portugal, as well as a bus link to Seville in Spain. In most cases you have a choice of bus or train: for Lisbon and the western Algarve take the train, while for Évora, Vila Real de Santo António (for the eastern Algarve) and Santiago do Cacém (for the western Algarve) it's quicker to go by bus.

Accommodation

Most of the town's **accommodation** is to be found within a few blocks of the turismo. In summer and during the Festas da Cidade (see p.421) it is well worth booking ahead. The municipal **campsite** (☎084/243 28, fax 084/32 72 25) is located on the south side of town, past the stadium on Avenida Vasco da Gama. It's fairly pleasant and shaded, and adjoins the local swimming pool.

Residencial Bejense, Rua do Capitão J.F. de Sousa 57 (☎084/32 50 01, fax 32 50 02). Situated close to the turismo, this newly renovated *residencial* has doubles (all with bath) and cheaper singles (without bath). ④.

Residencial Coelho, Praça da República 15 (☎084/32 40 31, fax 32 89 39). Decent-value pension, with a few rooms overlooking the square; all rooms have private showers. ④.

Residencial Cristina, Rua de Mértola 71 (☎084/32 30 35, fax 32 98 74). A rather soulless, modern hotel, but Beja's most comfortable, if it's comfort you're after. ⑤.

Hotel Melius, Avda. Fialho de Almeida (☎084/32 18 22, fax 32 18 25). Modern hotel on the edge of town, complete with gym and sauna. ⑤.

Casa de Hóspedes Pax Julia, Rua Pedro Victor 8 (☎084/225 75). One of the least expensive options in town, with clean, comfortable rooms. ③.

Casa de Hóspedes Rocha, Largo Dom Nuno Álvares Pereira 12 (☎084/32 42 71). Friendly, decrepit old hotel facing the *pousada*. ②.

Residencial Santa Bárbara, Rua de Mértola 56 (☎084/32 20 28, fax 32 12 31). Reasonably priced modern rooms, with breakfast included. ④.

Pousada de São Francisco, Largo Dom Nuno Álvares Pereira (☎084/32 84 41, fax 32 91 43). Imposing *pousada* inside the convent of São Francisco, where rooms are in former monastic cells. Even if you can't afford to stay, you can wander in and have a look around anyway. ⑦.

Eating and drinking

Restaurante Alentejano, Largo dos Duques de Beja. A popular, local restaurant. where most main courses come in at around 800$00.

Restaurante A Esquina, Rua Infante D. Henrique 26. Located in the west of town and serving up good-quality, traditional food.

Luís da Rocha, Rua do Capitão J.F. de Sousa 63. An immensely popular café serving a wide range of Alentejan fare and a great selection of inexpensive wines. Specials include grilled squid and rack of lamb. There's an *ementa turística* for around 1250$00.

Restaurante Pena, Praça de Diogo Fernandes de Beja 19a. Modest prices and dependable cooking, with fish a speciality. It's between the pedestrian shopping district and the castle.

Restaurante O Portão, Trav. da Audiença 1 (off Rua dos Infantes). Not an enormous choice, but excellent quality and great value – the *ementa turística* is 1500$00 – served in an old *adega*.

Serpa and around

Thirty kilometres east of Beja, the small market town of **SERPA** offers the classic Alentejan attractions – a walled centre, a castle and narrow, whitewashed streets – and makes an enjoyable stop if you are heading towards Spain, or feel like a roundabout but scenic approach to the Algarve, via Mértola. The town has at various times been occupied by Celts, Romans, Moors and Spaniards, and inevitably is dominated by its **Castle** (Tues–Sun 9am–12.30pm & 2–5.30pm), predominantly Moorish, and with spectacular vistas of the plain to the north and the hills to the south. There is a tiny archeological museum in the keep and, close by, the thirteenth-century church of **Santa Maria**, containing an altarpiece of intricate woodcarving, surrounded by seventeenth-century azulejos.

From the castle, you can track the course of the well-preserved eleventh-century **aqueduct**. It is worth a look from close up, too, with the remnants of a chain-pump at one end. If you have time to fill, you might also wander down to the **Museu Etnográfico** (Tues–Sun 9am–noon & 2–5pm; free), near the hospital, which offers an interesting account of the changing economic activity of the area.

Practicalities

Serpa's **turismo** is at Largo Dom Jorge de Melo 2 and the **bus station** is on the Avenida de Paz in the southwest of town; there are six connections a day to Beja. The rail bus also connects with Beja (and Moura) three times a day, but drops you on the main road, well outside Serpa. You may well find private rooms advertised around the largo but official **places to stay** in town are limited. There's the smart *Residencial Beatriz*, at Largo do Salvador 10 (☎ & fax 084/534 23; ④), near São Salvador church; the *Residencial Serpinia*, in the northwest of town on Rua de Santo António (☎084/530 55; ④), though the disco below may put you off; or the centrally located *Casa da Muralha*, Rua das Portas de Beja 43 (☎ & fax 084/54 31 50; ⑤), a country house furnished with antiques. A good out-of-town option is the modern *pousada*, the *São Gens* (☎084/537 24, fax 533 37; ⑥), 2km to the south, on a hill known as Alto de São Gens; it has a swimming pool and wonderful views. Serpa's well-equipped **campsite** (☎084/532 90, fax 534 94) is at the southwest corner of town near the swimming pool complex.

Among Serpa's **restaurants**, the *Cervejaria Vila Branca*, Avda. da Paz 4, is highly recommended for its excellent *cataplanas* amd seafood, while *O Zé* at Praça da República 10 serves a decent *gaspacho* and delicious local cheese. Opposite, the Art Deco *Café Alentejano* has a very good, if slightly pricey, restaurant above it; alternatively there's a more reasonable, unnamed restaurant at the top of Rua Quente.

Around Serpa

Situated 15km and 30km to the north of Serpa respectively, the wine-producing village of Pias and the spa town of Moura make for interesting destinations in the area, with Moura offering the best options for an overnight stay. If you have your own transport, it's also an easy half-day trip to the Pulo do Lobo waterfall, sited amid stark, rocky scenery 18km south of Serpa.

Pias

The village of **PIAS** is well known hereabouts for its red wine, Margaça and Encostas – the Sociedade Agrícola de Pias, Rua Santo António 8 (☎085/852 22), can arrange tours of the vineyards and winery. There are no particular sights, and the local train station has closed down, but if you're driving it makes a worthwhile detour for anyone who wants to examine what is still a very traditional Alentejan village. Pias also has a surprisingly good **restaurant**, the *Arroz Doce* in Rua Luís de Camões – try the *migas*. If you just want a **drink**, head for the wonderful *Pias Bar* on Rua de João Tiágo Coelho, or the next door *Taverna*. For a **room**, ask for Manuel Baião at the shop on the main street at no. 79, or for Senhor José Carvalho Godinho on the road past the Caixa de Credito Agricular bank, who has rooms (①) in a lovely old house.

Moura

A further 15km north, the thermal spa town of **MOURA** is an opulent place full of grand mansions, houses and pretty squares. The Moors occupied the town from the eighth century until 1233 – an Arabic well still survives in the old town – and the town is named after a Moorish maiden, Moura Saluquia, who ostensibly threw herself from the castle tower in despair when Christians murdered her betrothed and overran the town. But it was the discovery of the **thermal springs** that prompted Moura's later wealth; located beside the Jardim Doutora Santiago, they are still in use (Mon–Sat 10am–5pm; 60$00 a bath). The key to the adjacent **castle**, built by Dom Dinis over a Moorish castle and largely destroyed by the Duke of Osuna in 1701 (though one Moorish tower survives), is at the Câmara Municipal. Outside the gardens stands the sixteenth-century Manueline **Igreja de São João Batista**, its chapel decorated with Sevillian azulejos. Behind the castle lies the ruined Renaissance **Convento do Carmo**, where you can still see statues and beautiful frescoes.

Moura is connected to Beja three times a day by **bus**, via Serpa, which drops you at the southern end of town, and daily to Évora, arriving at the central Praça Cabral. The **turismo** is on Largo Santa Clara (Mon–Fri 9am–1pm & 2–6pm) and may be able to help with private **rooms**. Alternatively, try the *Pensão Alentejana* at Largo José Maria dos Santos 40 (☎085/225 29; ①), which has large and rambling rooms but is often full, or *Residencial Mourense*, Largo Dr. Rodrigues Acabado (☎ & fax 085/25 72 64; ④), offering very pleasant, modern rooms. The town's upmarket option is the *Hotel de Moura*, on the peaceful Praça Gago Coutinho (☎085/25 10 90, fax 246 10; ⑤), a superbly ornate building complete with azulejos, patios, mirrored doors and a rambling garden. There are plenty of **restaurants** in town; *O Trilho*, Rua 5 de Outubro 5 (closed Mon), serves good regional dishes. In the upper town, try *O Arco* by Porta Nova, with its huge range of *aguardiente* liquors. For **nightlife**, there's *Discoteca Shahazade* by the ruined convent, and the pub *Caprixus* at 14 Rua da Mollejas (just off Praça Cabral).

The Pulo do Lobo waterfall

The **Pulo do Lobo** (Wolf's Leap) waterfall lies in a deep gorge carved through the hills by the river and the valley has some strikingly eerie rock formations. You'll probably have the falls all to yourself; to get there from Serpa, follow the road which is signposted behind the Jardim Botanico. It's well surfaced as far as the village of **São Brás** (6km) but as it climbs into the mountainous countryside, it deteriorates suddenly to a rough track, which becomes narrow and vertiginous as it leads down, around the 16km mark, to a stream – a tributary of the Guadiana. Following the track, after a couple of kilometres you can turn left to arrive very close to the Pulo do Lobo.

South to the Algarve

There are three main routes **south from Beja to the Algarve**. The most interesting and enjoyable is the **N122** to Vila Real de Santo António (2 buses daily), on the eastern border of the province with Spain; this passes through the old Moorish fortress town of **Mértola** and a scenic stretch of the Guadiana river valley. Alternatives, more convenient if you are heading for western or central Algarve, are to take the N391 across the plains to **Castro Verde**, then the fast E1 to **Albufeira**, or the more mountainous N2 to **Faro** (three buses daily).

Via Castro Verde
If you're a bird fancier, you may consider the route from Beja to **CASTRO VERDE** (46km south) a must, for the chance to see **great bustards** winging across the plains. This apart, the road has few attractions, with a handful of small agricultural towns set amid interminable parched tracts of wheat fields. Following the N2, directly south of Castro Verde, the route continues in similar vein until you hit the lush greenery of the **Serra do Malhão** and the **Serra do Caldeirão** around Ameixial – just across the border in the Algarve.

To the west, the N264 provides faster access to the Algarve, as well as an interesting detour in the **Castro da Cola**, the remains of a small, Romano-Celtic village, similar to the *citânias* of the north. This is located to the west of the road, a few kilometres beyond the village of Aldeia dos Palheiros. There is a pilgrimage to the site on September 7–8.

Via Mértola
The N122 gets a green edge on the *Michelin* map as it approaches **MÉRTOLA** – a sure sign of rising gradients and an escape from the plains. The town is as beautifully sited as any in the south, set high above the Rio Guadiana, around the extensive ruins of a Moorish frontier castle. It's a quiet, isolated place, certainly worth a night's stopover – more if you feel like a walking or bird-watching base. The region is home to the rare black stork.

The obvious focus for a visit is the **Castelo** (Tues–Sun 9am–12.30pm & 2–5.30pm; free), views from whose keep sweep across the Guadiana valley. To the north, you may be able to make out the copper mines a few kilometres down the Serpa road at Mina de São Domingos. Until recent decades, these were the principal source of the town's employment, and until World War II they were owned by a British company, which employed a private police force and treated the workers with appalling brutality. Back in town, take time to look around the **Igreja Matriz**, which started life as a Moorish mosque and retains its *mihrab* (prayer niche) behind the altar on the eastern wall. Also worth searching out is the little **Museu Arqueológico** (Mon–Sat 9am–12.30pm & 2–5.30pm; 500$00), a well-presented collection of recoveries from local digs, notably Roman pottery, jewellery and needles, plus a set of strange-looking religious figures retrieved from the castle.

PRACTICALITIES
Orientation is straightforward, with **buses** (to and from Beja and Vila Real de Santo António) stopping by the bridge, close to the **turismo**, on Rua da República (Mon–Fri 9am–12.30pm & 2–5.30pm, Sat & Sun 10am–12.30pm & 2–5.30pm; ☎086/625 73). **Accommodation** options include the *Pensão Beira Rio*, Rua Dr. Afonso Costa 18 (☎086/623 40; ③), which has the edge on *Residencial San Remo*, Avda. Aureliano Mira Fernandes (☎086/621 33; ③), in character and situation. For a little more, you could stay at the *Casa das Janelas Verdes*, Rua Dr. Manuel Francisco Gomes 38–40 (☎086/621 45; ④; breakfast included) – a traditional Alentejan house. The *Restaurante Boa Viagem*, opposite the bus stop, offers a good and inexpensive selection of **meals**.

Santiago do Cacém and around

Heading south on the main route from Lisbon or Setúbal, **Santiago do Cacém** is the first place that might, realistically, tempt you to stop. A pleasant little provincial town, it is overlooked by a castle, and has on its outskirts – half an hour's walk away – the fascinating Roman ruins of **Miróbriga**. In addition, it's only a short bus journey from the **Santo André** and **Melides lagoons**, forming two of the Alentejo's finest beaches.

Santiago do Cacém

The Moorish **Castle** (Mon–Fri 8.30am–4.30pm, Sat 8.30am–1pm) in **SANTIAGO DO CACÉM** was later rebuilt by the Knights Templar but now serves as a cemetery. There are splendid views over to the sea from the battlements, whose crumbling masonry provides the habitat for a curious species of large golden beetle. It's also worth making your way to the **Museu Municipal**, facing the municipal gardens off Avenida Pereira (Tues–Fri 10am–noon & 2–5pm, Sat & Sun 2.30–5pm; free), one of the most interesting of its kind and housed in one of Salazar's more notorious prisons in a small park just northeast of the centre. A suitably political strain pervades its display: one of the spartan prison cells has been preserved while two others have been converted into a "typical country bedroom" and "a rich bourgeois bedroom". Even a drawing in the section devoted to the local primary school shows a child's impression of the "Great Revolution" of 1974.

The archeological section in Santiago's museum should whet your appetite for a visit to Roman **Miróbriga** (Tues–Sun 9am–12.30pm & 2–5.30pm; closes at 4.30pm in winter; 300$00). From the centre, follow Rua de Lisboa (N120) for about 1km up the hill, then take the marked turning to the right, and, after another ten-minute walk, turn left at a sign marking the entrance to the site, which lies isolated amid arcadian green hills. At the highest point of the site a **Temple of Jupiter** has been partly reconstructed, overlooking a small forum with a row of shops built into its supporting wall. A paved street descends to a **villa and bath complex** whose underground central heating system is still intact.

Practicalities

Staying in Santiago is not a problem, but be warned that out of season, bus services to the coast can be annoyingly irregular. The **turismo** in Largo do Mercado (Mon–Sat 9am–6.30pm; ☎069/82 66 96) might be able to help with **rooms**, otherwise try *Porto das Covas* (☎069/227 66, fax 82 69 02; ②), a newsagent just off Largo 25 Abril. **Pensões and hotels** include: *Pensão/Restaurante Covas*, by the bus station, at Rua Cidade de Setúbal 8–10 (☎069/226 75; ③); *Residencial Hotelagoa*, Lagoa de Santo André (☎069/791 17; ④); *Residencial Gabriel*, Rua Professor Egas Moniz 24 (☎069/222 45, fax 82 61 02; ④), with modern, comfortable rooms and helpful staff; and *Albergaria D. Nuno*, Avda. D. Nuno Álvares Pereira (☎069/233 25, fax 233 28; ⑤), with swimming pool and parking. Best of all, however, is the *Pousada de São Tiago*, Estrada Nacional (☎ & fax 069/224 59; ⑥), 1km out of town on the Lisbon road – a simple but pleasant *pousada*, with a pool and a decent restaurant.

However, the best **restaurant** in Santiago is the *Pensão/Restaurante Covas*, which specializes in seafood and has a great-value *ementa turística* for 1300$00. Alternatively, try *O Retiro*, Rua Machado dos Santos 8 (off Avda. Pereira), a cosy little place serving regional cuisine, or the friendly, modestly priced *Restaurante Praceta*, Largo Zeca Afonso (behind the bus station), serving fish and chicken cooked on coals outside. If you really want to push the boat out, the regional specialities at the *Pousada de São Tiago* will set you back around 3500$00 a head. There's also a fine covered **market** in the centre of town, next to the turismo, useful for stocking up for a stay at one of the beaches.

The Santo André and Melides lagoons

In summer there are five buses a day from Santiago do Cacém to **LAGOA DE SANTO ANDRÉ**, and it's a short walk from there along the shore to **LAGOA DE MELIDES**. These two **lagoon beaches**, separated from the sea by a narrow strip of sand, are named after the nearest inland towns, but each has its own small, laid-back community entirely devoted to having a good time on the beach. The **campsites** at both places are of a high standard and there are masses of signs offering rooms, chalets and houses to let. Space is at a premium in July and August, but at other times accommodation should be no problem at all.

At either place, the social scene centres around the beach-cafés and ice-cream stalls. Beyond these is the sand – miles and miles of it, stretching all the way to Comporta in the north and to Sines in the south. The sea is very enticing with high waves and good surf, but be warned and take local advice on water conditions: the undertow can be fierce and people drown here every year.

Sines and south to Pessegueiro

SINES – the cape just south of Santiago do Cacém – is the one place not to go to on this stretch of coast. Vasco da Gama was born here, but he'd probably turn in his grave if he could see the massive oil refinery and the sacrifice of the environment to new roads, railways, pipelines and wells. It's an ugly industrial town, with only a highly rated **seafood restaurant** to recommend it: *Varanda do Oceano* on Largo Nossa Senhora Salvas in the old town, serving fresh shellfish in 1930s-style surroundings. Should you need the **turismo** (summer Mon–Sat 10am–6pm; winter Mon–Fri 9am–1pm & 2–6pm; ☎069/63 44 72), it's in the Discovery Gardens near the disused train station. In the unlikely event that you need to **stay the night** here, try the *Residencial Carvalho*, Rua Gago Coutinho 13 (☎069/63 20 19; ②)), or the friendly *Pensão Fredemar*, Rua Cândido dos Reis 31–35 (☎069/63 21 22; ③)).

The ugliness around Sines is short-lived and just south of here there's a whole set of untouched little beach settlements. The best of all of them is the furthest south, the area around Ilha do Pessegueiro, reached from the road heading down to Porto Côvo – which is served by three buses daily from Sines.

Porto Côvo

The centre of **PORTO CÔVO** is a simple, unassuming, whitewashed place with a small cove harbour, a few *pensões*, some rooms to let, a camping site . . . and a sewage plant right on the oceanfront. However, developers have discovered Porto Côvo with a vengeance over the last decade or so and the land behind the village has been engulfed into one large building site. Despite this, it remains a lively and pleasant place to base yourself, not least for the series of beautiful coves stretching along the coast and the Ilha do Pessegueiro within easy walking distance.

The summer-only **turismo** (10am–1pm & 2–5pm; ☎069/954 60) is on the main square. Buses connect Porto Côvo at least twice daily with Almograve, Vila Nova de Milfontes and Praia Zambujeira, and once or twice daily with Odemira and Santiago do Cacém. There are several services daily to and from Sines. **Accommodation** isn't a problem, except at the height of summer when advance booking is recommended – the *Pensão Boa Esperança*, Rua Conde Bandeira (☎069/951 09; ③), is the best and longest-established option. Apartments are for rent at nos. 6 and 7 Rua da Farmacía, with no. 6 (☎069/951 25; 9000$00 for four people) having the edge owing to its congenial owner. Outside town is the bland, three-star *Porto Côvo Hotel* (☎069/950 95, fax 950 58; ⑤). There's not much to choose between the village's **restaurants**, though the *Herminio*, on Rua Vasco da Gama, distinguishes itself by also selling local honey. On the same road is *Restaurante Cácome*, popular with locals for its seafood: *arroz de marisco*, grilled squid and an excellent *cataplana royal*. For a good selection of **snacks** and pastries, you need look no further than the popular *Gelateria/Caféteria Marques* at the opposite end of the square to the turismo.

Ilha do Pessegueiro

ILHA DO PESSEGUEIRO (Peach Tree Island) can be reached from the Porto Côvo–Vila Nova de Milfontes road, but the nicest approach is to walk, following the coastal path south from Porto Côvo. It's only a couple of kilometres and en route you'll pass the remains of a Bronze Age burial site.

The resort's name actually applies to the mainland beach; the island itself is less than a kilometre offshore and reachable on local fishing boats. On the mainland, there's the wonderful *Restaurante A Ilha* (☎069/951 13), a small seaside **fort**, a rural hotel *Herdade Agro Turística do Pessegueiro* (apartments 10,000$00 for four people; bookings through *A Ilha*), and a **campsite** (☎069/951 78). Quite a few people – a good mix of Portuguese and foreign travellers – camp out on the island itself, and although there are no facilities here, it makes an excellent place to hole up for a while if the very simple life appeals. If you're feeling energetic you could even walk the 20km or so south from here to Vila Nova de Milfontes, a good half-day's walk along the beach and cliffs – take enough water for the whole journey.

The south Alentejo resorts and Odemira

On the southern half of the Alentejo coast, **Vila Nova de Milfontes** is the main beach resort, with **Almograve** and **Zambujeira do Mar**, further south, being quieter, less developed seaside villages. **Odemira** – about 15km from the coast – makes a good inland base, and offers local bus connections to the coast.

Vila Nova de Milfontes

VILA NOVA DE MILFONTES lies on the estuary of the Rio Mira, whose sandy banks gradually merge into the coastline. It has an advantage of geography for sailors (the port is reputed to have harboured Hannibal and his Carthaginians during a storm) and swimmers: if the waves of the Atlantic are too fierce you can always swim in the estuary, though beware of very strong currents.

The resort is not exactly undiscovered – the Germans, especially, built villas here through the 1980s – and it is perhaps the most crowded and popular resort in the Alentejo. The old town, however, huddled around a striking, ivy-wreathed castle, remains a pretty enough place; while Portuguese families on holiday from the big cities of the north give it a homely atmosphere quite distinct from the cosmopolitan trendiness of the Algarve. If you want to escape some of the crowds, take the ferry from the little jetty to the far side of the estuary to beaches nearby.

Practicalities

Arriving by **bus**, you'll be dropped off in a small lot near the **turismo** on Rua António Mantas (summer daily 10am–1pm & 2.30–7pm; ☎083/965 99). Buses run four times daily (Mon–Fri) and once daily at weekends to Odemira, Alcácer do Sal, Porto Côvo and Zambujeira do Mar. If you're Algarve-bound, forget the direct service to Odemira; instead, catch the 10am bus to Cercal and transfer onto the Portimão express from Lisbon – the **ticket office** is on Largo Almada. A range of activities can be arranged through the turismo. Alternatively, **horse riding** is offered by the Sociedade Turística Cerca dos Árvores (☎083/961 23; 2000$00 per hour); **bike rental** is available from *Corpo Vivo*, in Eira de Pedro (☎083/968 93), opposite the *Quinta das Varandas*; details of **river trips** to Casa Branca and Odemira can be obtained on ☎083/993 93; and for **jeep tours** ring ☎083/968 93.

ACCOMMODATION

Finding a place to stay should pose no problems out of season but it's advisable to book ahead in summer. If you turn up without a reservation ask at the turismo for a list of available **rooms** or look for others advertised in windows around town. Most of the newer **hotels** are situated in modern developments to the west of town – they usually have excellent facilities and can be very good value if you don't mind staying on a building site. Many of the new streets do not yet have names, but the hotels are well signposted. There are two **campsites** just north of town: the massive *Parque de Milfontes* (☎ & fax 083/961 04) has excellent

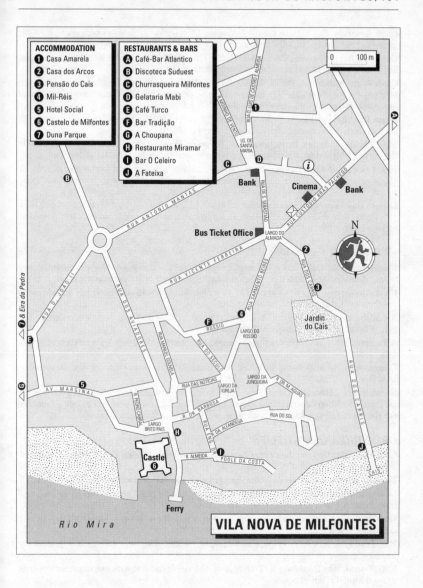

ACCOMMODATION
1. Casa Amarela
2. Casa dos Arcos
3. Pensão do Cais
4. Mil-Réis
5. Hotel Social
6. Castelo de Milfontes
7. Duna Parque

RESTAURANTS & BARS
A. Café-Bar Atlantico
B. Discoteca Suduest
C. Churrasqueira Milfontes
D. Gelataria Mabi
E. Café Turco
F. Bar Tradição
G. A Choupana
H. Restaurante Miramar
I. Bar O Celeiro
J. A Fateixa

VILA NOVA DE MILFONTES

facilites; more modest is the nearby *Campiférias* (☎083/964 09, fax 965 81; closed Dec).

Pensão do Cais, Rua dos Carris 9 (☎083/962 68). Very friendly hotel, full of Portuguese in summer (advance booking advised). Modern, spacious rooms, some with beautiful views over the estuary. ④.

Casa Amarela, Rua D. Luís Castro e Almeida (☎083/966 32). A small pension with rooms for up to four people (10,500$00 for four). ④.

Casa dos Arcos, Rua dos Carris (☎083/962 64, fax 99 71 56). A large 1960s' functional building; rooms are clean and breakfast is included. ⑤.

Castelo de Milfontes, (☎083/961 08, fax 99 71 22). Vila Nova's best lodgings, inside the fortress – cross the drawbridge to enter. The owner offers full board and is very picky about her guests, so dress well. Breakfast included. ⑥, full board ⑦.

Duna Parque, Rua Eira da Pedra (☎083/964 51, fax 964 59). Milfontes' largest complex, with very well-equipped rooms; all rooms sleep four people. ⑤.

Mil-Réis Actividades Hosteleiras Ltd, Largo do Rossio 2 (☎083/992 33, fax 993 28). On the corner with Rossio, an old-fashioned pension with kindly owners. ⑤.

Hotel Social, Avda. Marginal (☎083/965 17, fax 965 17). Attached to the *Misericórdia de Odemira* and with a rather muted atmosphere. Friendly management, however, and good rooms, some with verandas overlooking the estuary. ⑤.

Quinta das Varandas, Eira da Pedra (☎083/961 55, fax 991 02). Part of an uninspiring complex by the dunes. Good value, though, in family-run apartments, all mod-cons with breakfast included. ④.

EATING

Restaurante do Cais, Rua dos Carris. Below the *pensão*, this good-value restaurant serves hearty Alentejan fare, with the *grelhados* (anything grilled) being particularly good.

Casa dos Arcos, Rua dos Carris. The airy restaurant beneath the hotel has a basic menu but the view is excellent.

A Choupana, Avda. Marginal. At far western end on Praia do Farol. Serves excellent grilled fish, is good value and popular with the locals.

A Fateixa, Rua dos Carris. On the riverbank; moderately priced and serves excellent grilled fish.

Churrasqueira Milfontes, Rua António Mantas. Popular takeaway serving inexpensive, local fare.

Restaurante Miramar, Largo Brito Pais (facing the castle). Modestly priced, attracting a local crowd with good music and decent food; grilled fish, roast beef and *açorda de marisco* are the specialities. A full meal, with wine, will set you back around 2000$00.

DRINKING AND NIGHTLIFE

Café-Bar Atlantico, on the Porto Côvo road (follow Rua Custódio Brás Pachego). A friendly late-night drinking den.

Bar O Celeiro, Rua Poole da Costa. An upmarket bar, full of black marble and chrome.

Gelataria Mabi, opposite the bus depot. A combined ice-cream parlour and bar, attracting a mixed clientele.

Discoteca Suduest, on northern continuation of Rua dos Aviadores. Plays the latest in rave and dance music.

Bar Tradição, Rossio. A weird, traditional-cum-cocktail dive next door to *Bar Azul* on the Rossio.

Café Turco, Rua Dom João II. Trendy, mock-Moorish café-bar with live music at weekend (closed Mon–Fri out of season).

Almograve

The coast south of Vila Nova de Milfontes becomes ever more rugged and spectacular. At the tiny resort of **ALMOGRAVE**, 5km west of the Odemira–Vila Nova de Milfontes road, huge waves come crashing down on the rocks and for most of the day swimming is impossible. It can get very crowded at high tide, too, when the beaches are reduced to thin strips with occasional waves drenching everybody's belongings; but, for all that, it's an exhilarating place.

You could **camp** virtually anywhere back from the beach at Almograve, and there are a few cafés and bars, but the bus service from Odemira is just right for a day-trip. Should you need to stay overnight, however, the *Restaurante Torralta*, Avda. da Praia (☎083/641 20; ①) has **rooms** available, or there's the *Pensão Paulo Campos*, Rua Antónia Pachecho 9 (☎083/641 18; ②; May–Oct). If you can stretch to it, though, the best option is the pleasant new *residencial*, *Duna Praia* (☎083/641 15, fax 641 12; ④), conveniently situated on the way to the beach and with a restaurant grill.

Odemira

In summer, the southern Alentejo resorts can get quite crowded, so you may prefer to stay in **ODEMIRA** and take day-trips to the seaside – be warned, though, that the bus services can be erratic. The town is pretty enough, set around the River Mira, and has several **pensões**, best of which are the very good *Casa Rita*, Largo do Poço Novo (☎083/225 31; ④), and *Residencial Idálio*, Rua Eng. Arantes Oliveira 28 (☎083/221 56; ③), both off to the left when you come out of the bus station. Alternatively, try the **rooms** above the *Restaurant Esperança*, Estrada de Circunvalação (☎083/224 24; ①), run by the same management. The **campsite** (☎082/941 45) is out of town at São Miguel, but has good facilities including tennis and a pool. Among **restaurants**, try *O Tarro*, near the main road junction, where 1500$00 will get you a hearty meal, and for a drink head to *O Cais*, a terrace-bar down by the river, with live music at weekends (turn left over the bridge, then left again).

Zambujeira do Mar and on to the Algarve

At the village of **ZAMBUJEIRA DO MAR**, south of Odemira and 7km west of the main road, a large cliff provides a dramatic backdrop to the beach, which, like that of Vila Nova de Milfontes, can get very crowded in July and August. The scenery more than compensates for the winds and the sea – which can get positively chilly, even in summer – but can't disguise the rundown state of the village and the encircling villas. If you need to **stay** – and the bus schedule from Odemira makes a day-trip impossible – try the *Residencial Mira Mar* (☎ & fax 083/613 52; ④), the modern *Residencial Ondazul* (☎083/614 50; ⑤), currently located in a building site, or the *Residencial Mar-e-Sol* (☎083/611 71; ⑤). A reasonable **campsite** (☎083/611 72, fax 613 20), about 1km from the cliffs, has showers and a café-bar. The best **restaurants** are the *Taverna Ti Vítório*, on Largo Mira Mar, which serves wonderful grilled fish, and the *Cervejaria A Marisqueira da Praia*, on Rua Mira Mar, which does a good *arroz de marisco* among other dishes. The popular and tacky late-night joint is the *Bar/Discoteca Clube da Praia*, on the beach.

Zambujeira is the southernmost Alentejo beach, and an attractive road twists its way into the hills of the Algarve from the river crossing at Odeceixe. For the most dramatic approach, however, take the road from Odemira through the **Serra de Monchique**, descending to the Algarve coast at Portimão.

travel details

Trains

Alcácer do Sal to: Lisbon (3 daily; 2hr–2hr 40min).

Beja to: Évora (2 daily; 1hr 30min–2hr); Faro (1 daily; 4hr 10min); Lisbon (4 daily; 2hr 45min–3hr 30min); Moura (2 daily; 1hr 20min).

Belver to: Lisbon (4 daily; 2hr 25min–3hr).

Crato to: Lisbon (2 daily; 3–4hr).

Elvas to: Lisbon (2 daily; 4hr 25min–5hr); Portalegre (3 daily; 50min).

Évora to: Beja (3–4 daily; 1hr 30min–2hr 10min); Faro (1 daily; 6hr); Lisbon (5 daily; 2hr 45min–5hr 50min).

Portalegre to: Crato (3 daily; 20min); Elvas (2 daily; 50min); Lisbon (3 daily; 3hr 25min–4hr 40min).

Buses

Alcácer do Sal to: Lisbon (3 daily; 1hr 30min).

Almograve to: Lisbon (3 daily; 4hr 10min); Porto Côvo (3–4 daily; 1hr); Vila Nova de Milfontes (2 daily; 35min).

Alter do Chão to: Lisbon (1 daily; 3hr 35min); Portalegre (1 daily; 35min).

Beja to: Albufeira (3–4 daily; 2hr 15min); Elvas (1 daily; 3hr 25min); Évora (5 daily; 1hr 20min); Faro (1 daily; 3hr 10min–4hr 30min); Lisbon (4–6 daily; 3hr 20min); Moura (3–7 daily; 1hr 25min); Portalegre (2 daily; 4hr); Serpa (5–11 daily; 45min).

Borba to: Elvas (4 daily; 30min); Estremoz (2 daily; 15min); Évora (2 daily; 1hr); Lisbon (3 daily; 3hr–3hr 30min).

Castelo de Vide to: Portalegre (2 daily; 20min).

Crato to: Lisbon (1 daily; 3hr 50min); Portalegre (1 daily; 20min).

Elvas to: Elvas train station (5 daily; 20min); Beja (1 daily; 3hr 25min); Borba (1 daily; 30min); Campo Maior (Mon–Fri 3 daily; 30min); Évora (4–7 daily; 1hr 35min–2hr 10min); Lisbon (5–6 daily; 3hr 30min–4hr 20min); Portalegre (Mon–Fri 2 daily; 1hr 30min).

Estremoz to: Borba (2 daily; 15min); Évora (2–3 daily; 45min); Lisbon (2 daily; 3hr 20min); Portalegre (2 daily; 1hr).

Évora to: Albufeira (4 daily; 3hr 40min); Beja (5–7 daily; 1hr–1hr 20min); Borba (2 daily; 1hr); Coimbra (2 daily; 4hr 35min); Elvas (2 daily; 1hr 35min); Estremoz (2 daily; 45min); Faro (4 daily; 4hr 35min); Lisbon (Mon–Fri 11 daily, Sat & Sun 6–7 daily; 1hr 45min); Monsaraz (2 daily; 55min); Moura (1 daily; 1hr 30min); Portalegre (2 daily; 1hr 45min); Santarém (3 daily; 2hr).

Mértola to: Lisbon (2 daily; 4hr 15min).

Moura to: Évora (1 daily; 1hr 30min); Lisbon (1 daily; 4hr).

Odemira to: Lisbon (4 daily; 3hr 50min–4hr 20min); Vila Nova de Milfontes (2 daily; 20min).

Portalegre to: Portalegre train station (3 daily; 15min); Alter do Chão (1 daily; 35min); Beja (2 daily; 3hr 50min); Castelo do Vide (2 daily; 20min); Crato (1 daily; 20min); Estremoz (2 daily; 1hr); Évora (2–3 daily; 1hr 45min); Lisbon (3 daily; 4hr 10min–4hr 25min); Viseu (2 daily; 5hr).

Porto Côvo to: Almograve (4 daily; 40min); Lisbon (6 daily; 3hr 35min); Santiago do Cacém (4 daily; 1hr); Vila Nova de Milfontes (7 daily; 30min).

Santiago do Cacém to: Lisbon (9 daily; 2hr 25min); Porto Côvo (5 daily; 1hr); Sines (5 daily; 35–45min); Vila Nova de Milfontes (6 daily; 1hr 25min).

Serpa to: Beja (2–3 daily; 35min); Lisbon (2–3 daily; 4hr).

Sines to: Beja (2 daily; 2hr 50min); Lisbon (6–8 daily; 3hr–3hr 20min); Odemira (1 daily; 1hr 10min); Porto Côvo (5 daily; 25min); Santiago do Cacém (5 daily; 35min); Zambujeira do Mar (3 daily; 1hr 30min).

Vila Nova de Milfontes to: Almograve (2 daily; 15min); Lisbon (3–7 daily; 3hr 35min–4hr 10min); Porto Côvo (2 daily; 25min); Zambujeira do Mar (2 daily; 40min).

Vila Viçosa to: Borba (3–4 daily; 10min); Elvas (2 daily; 35min); Estremoz (3 daily; 25min); Évora (3 daily; 1hr); Lisbon (2 daily; 3hr–3hr 50min).

Zambujeira do Mar to: Almograve (2 daily; 25min); Lisbon (1 daily; 4hr 45min); Porto Côvo (2 daily; 1hr 5min–1hr 15min); Santiago do Cacém (1 daily; 2hr 15min); Sines (3 daily; 1hr 40min); Vila Nova de Milfontes (2 daily; 40–45min).

THE ALGARVE

With its long, sandy beaches and picturesque rocky coves, the **Algarve** has attracted more tourist development than the rest of the country put together. In parts, this has all but destroyed the charms that it was intended to exploit. The strip of coast from Faro west to Lagos has suffered most, with its endless villa complexes creating a rather depressing Mediterranean-style suburbia. On the fringes, though, especially around Sagres and Tavira, things are far better, with small-scale and relaxed resorts and the odd undeveloped beach or island sandbank.

The coastline in fact has two quite distinct characters. To the **west of Faro** you'll find the classic postcard images of the province – a series of tiny bays and coves, broken up by weird rocky outcrops and fantastic grottoes. They're at their most exotic around the major resort towns of **Lagos** and **Albufeira**. For fewer crowds, alternative bases include the beach village of **Salema**, the historic cape of **Sagres** – site of Henry the Navigator's naval school – or one of the string of villages along the rougher west coast as far as **Odeceixe**.

East of Faro, there's a complete change as you encounter the first of a series of sandy offshore islets, the *ilhas*, which front the coastline virtually all the way to the Spanish border. Overall, this is the quieter section of the coast and it has the bonus of much warmer waters than those further west. First-choice bases along this stretch would be Faro itself, **Olhão** and **Tavira**, all of which offer access to sandbank-islands.

Inland, there are scattered attractions in the Roman ruins of **Estói** and the market town of **Loulé**, both north of Faro; and the old Moorish town of **Silves**, easily reached from Portimão. The outstanding area, however, is the **Serra de Monchique**, the highest mountain range in the south, with cork and chestnut woods, remote little villages and a beautiful old spa in **Caldas de Monchique**.

The Algarve is an all-year-round destination, with sunny and relatively mild winters. In many respects the region is at its best in **spring** or **winter**. Most *pensões* and restaurants stay open, so rooms are easy to find. Indeed, **off-season travel** in the Algarve will get you some of the best deals in the country, with luxury hotels offering all-in packages at discounts of up to seventy percent; check out the latest deals at the local tourist offices. May has the added attraction of the Algarve's **International Music Festival**, sponsored by the Gulbenkian Foundation and hosting major classical artists. If you come in the **summer**, without a booking, finding accommodation can be a real struggle, though you'll usually find something. Be prepared for very high summer prices relative to the rest of the country.

Transport

Getting around by **public transport** is easier here than anywhere else in Portugal, and since the coastline is only 240km long from east to west, you can see an awful lot in just a few days. The **Algarve rail line** runs from Lagos in the west to Vila Real de Santo António on the Spanish border, calling at most major towns en route; **buses** link all the resorts and main inland villages. The two main bus companies running services are EVA and Frota Azul, which link together in the western Algarve to offer a *Passe Turístico* (3 days 2500$00; 7 days 3750$00), giving unlimited bus travel between Lagos and Loulé, covering all the main resorts in between (though not Faro). You can buy a pass from any bus station in the region.

ACCOMMODATION PRICE CODES

All the accommodation prices in this book have been coded using the symbols below. The symbols represent the lowest prices you can expect to pay for a **double room in high season**; for a full explanation, see p.29.

① Under 3000$00
② 3000$00–4000$00
③ 4000$00–5500$00
④ 5500$00–8500$00
⑤ 8500$00–12,500$00
⑥ 12,500$00–20,000$00
⑦ Over 20,000$00

Driving is often more trouble than it's worth. It's undeniably useful if you want to reach the more out-of-the-way inland villages and inaccesssible cove beaches (or head further into Portugal) but driving the main east–west N125 can be a pain since it's constantly being upgraded to cope with increasing traffic: expect road works, diversions and traffic jams.

THE EASTERN ALGARVE

All flights to the Algarve land at **Faro**, the administrative capital of the region and by far the largest town along the coast. Although no great holiday destination in itself, the centre of the town is considerably more attractive than the concrete suburbs might suggest; and there are some fine beaches and interesting local villages within easy reach. It's also not a bad place to start or finish a tour of the rest of the Algarve: Faro is connected with Lisbon by fast express coaches and offers efficient access to most Algarve towns by bus and – a little slower – on the Algarve rail line.

Faro marks a geographical boundary on the Algarve. The **coastline** east from here to Manta Rota, near the Spanish border, is protected by thin stretches of mud flats, fringed in turn by a chain of long and magnificent sandbanks, or *ilhas*. Often accessible only by boat, they're usually far less crowded than the small rocky resorts of the western Algarve. The towns of **Olhão**, **Tavira** and **Vila Real de Santo António** preserve a fair bit of character, while most of the resorts – with the exception of **Monte Gordo** – are fairly small-scale. Ornithologists should take binoculars, as the shores are thick with various types of wading bird in winter and spring.

Inland, the eastern Algarve offers few diversions, though a couple of day-trips provide some distraction: from Faro to the Roman remains at **Estói** and the small country town of **São Brás de Alportel**; and along the Spanish border from Vila Real de Santo António to **Castro Marim** and **Alcoutim**. With longer detours in mind, you might find equal rewards in travelling across the frontier **into Spain**, with Seville only a couple of hours from Vila Real.

Faro and around

FARO has been transformed from a sleepy provincial town into a centre of tourism, trade and commerce within three decades. However, although the international airport delivers visitors right to its door, the town has a job holding on to them, since most are whisked immediately away to the out-and-out resorts on either side of Faro. This is a little unfair: there's an attractive harbour, backed by a bustling, pedestrianized shopping area, and boats and buses run out to a couple of excellent local **beaches**. In summer, too, there's quite a **nightlife** scene, as thousands of travellers pass through on their way to and from the airport. There are certainly better places to spend a holiday on the Algarve, but for a night or two's stay at either end, it can be an enjoyable enough base.

Faro's Roman predecessor was 8km to the north, at Ossonoba (see p.444); the present city was founded by the Moors, under whom it was a thriving commercial port, supplying the regional capital at Silves. Following its conquest by the Christians, under Afonso III in 1249, the city experienced a chequered few centuries, surviving a series of conquests and disasters. Sacked and burned by the Earl of Essex in 1596, and devastated by the Great Earthquake of 1755, it is no surprise that the modern city has so few historic buildings. What interest it does retain is contained within the **Cidade Velha** (Old Town), which lies behind a series of defensive walls, across the harbour from the main part of town.

Arrival and information

In the summer months, flights land at Faro's international **airport**, 6km west of the town centre, 24 hours a day. Here, you'll find a police and first-aid post, bank, post office and tourist office (daily 10am–midnight; ☎089/81 85 82), but nothing much in the provisions line apart from a poor airport restaurant. A number of **car rental** companies (see "Listings", pp.443–444) also have offices at the airport.

The quickest way to get into the centre is by **taxi**, which should cost about 1100$00, plus 300$00 for any luggage that goes in the boot; there's also a twenty percent surcharge between 10pm and 6am, and at weekends. Two **buses** run from the airport to the centre, a twenty-minute ride costing 160$00: the #16

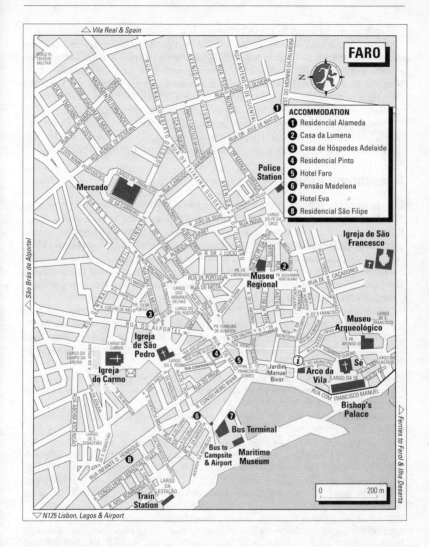

(roughly hourly 8am–9pm; July to mid-Sept until 11pm) and the rather less frequent #14 both stop outside the bus terminal in town (see below) and further on, at the Jardim Manuel Bivar (*Jardim* on the timetables) by the harbour. In the other direction, bus #16 runs to the beach and campsite at Praia de Faro, just 3km from the airport (see below). There are timetables posted at the airport bus stop; buy tickets on board.

The **bus terminal** is located on Avenida da República, behind the *Hotel Eva*, just across the harbour from the old part of town. The **train station** is a few minutes' walk further north up the avenue, facing Largo da Estação.

Faro's main **turismo** is close to the harbour front at Rua da Misericórdia 8 (summer daily 9.30am–7pm; winter Mon–Fri 9.30am–7pm, Sat & Sun 9.30am–12.30pm & 2–5.30pm; ☎089/80 36 04); they can provide a map of the town and their noticeboards deal comprehensively with local and long-distance bus, boat and train timetables, too. The regional tourist office – **Região de Turismo do Algarve** – at Avda. 5º Outubro (Mon–Fri 9.30am–12.30pm & 2–5.30pm; ☎089/80 04 00) is another source of information on the area as a whole.

The compact town centre is simple to negotiate **on foot**, and all the *pensões* and hotels are extremely central. There is a **town bus service**, but you'll need it only to get to the beach and campsite (for which, see below) and the airport.

Accommodation

Like most of the Algarve, Faro's accommodation is stretched to the limit in summer. If you fly in without a reservation, it's worth asking the airport tourist office to try and book you a place; otherwise the main turismo and regional tourist office in town (see above) can give you an idea of where to look for **rooms**. Most of the city's **pensões** and **hotels** – the best of which are picked out below – are concentrated in the area just north of the harbour. You might want to note that if sleep is a priority, you should avoid street-facing rooms on Rua Conselheiro Bivar – the bars (and street) are full until 3.30am at weekends.

In summer, Faro's **campsite** at Praia de Faro is always full and very cramped; if you want to stay, phone or fax ahead (reception 8am–9.30pm; ☎089/81 78 76, fax 80 23 26). Take bus #16, either direct from the airport, or from the stop opposite the bus terminal in town; the site is a ten-minute walk from the bus stop at Praia de Faro.

Casa de Hóspedes Adelaide, Rua Cruz das Mestras 7–9 (☎089/80 23 83, fax 82 68 70). Clean, basic rooms, though only a few have their own bathroom. Very friendly owner and several communal areas, including kitchen and lounge. ③.

Residencial Alameda, Rua José de Matos 31 (☎089/80 19 62, fax 80 42 18). Excellent rooms for the price and better value than the *Faro*. Breakfast included. ④.

Casa da Lumena, Praça Alexandre Herculano 27 (☎089/80 19 90, fax 80 40 19). Highly attractive town house with a courtyard bar and pleasant, individually furnished rooms with bath. There's a Mexican restaurant in the building, too. Advance bookings recommended. ④.

Hotel Eva, Avda. da República 1 (☎089/80 33 54, fax 80 23 04). The town's best hotel, with a superb harbourfront position and rooms whose balconies look across to the old town or the marina. There's a pool, too, and a courtesy bus to the local beach. Breakfast included. ⑦.

Hotel Faro, Praça Dom Francisco Gomes 2 (☎089/80 32 76, fax 80 35 46). The only other hotel on the waterfront, this is cheaper (though far less well appointed) than the *Eva*, with harbour views from the front rooms (for which you'll pay another 1000–1500$00) and from the first-floor bar. All rooms have shower and TV; breakfast included. ⑤.

Pensão Madalena, Rua Conselheiro Bivar 109 (☎ & fax 089/80 58 06). One of the better budget places to stay – cool marble-and-tile decor, with mostly good, clean rooms, some overlooking the (noisy) street, and a friendly reception. Check first, though, as some of the rooms are a bit gloomy. ③.

Residencial Pinto, Rua 1º de Maio 27 (☎089/82 28 20). Small place with a few rooms sharing a common bathroom. It's a little past its sell-by date, but is cheap and friendly enough. ③.

Pensão São Filipe, Rua Infante Dom Henrique 55a (☎089/82 41 82). Clean, reasonable rooms and about as cheap as things get in town. ②.

The Town

The only part of town to have survived the various violent historic upheavals is the **Cidade Velha**, across the harbour, an oval of cobbled streets and brightly painted restored buildings set within a run of sturdy walls. It is entered through the eighteenth-century town gate, the **Arco da Vila**, next to the turismo. From here, Rua do Município leads up to the majestic Largo da Sé, flanked by the cathedral and a group of palaces – including the former bishop's palace – and lined with orange trees. The **Sé** itself (Mon–Sat 10am–noon & 2.30pm–5.30pm, Sun open for Mass at 10am & noon) is a squat, white mismatch of Gothic, Renaissance and Baroque styles, all heavily remodelled after the 1755 earthquake. It's worth looking inside, though, mainly for the fine eighteenth-century azulejo tiling.

More impressive is the **Museu Arqueológico** (Mon–Fri 9am–noon & 2–5pm; 110$00) installed in a sixteenth-century convent in nearby Praça Afonso III; in front of the building stands a forthright, crucifix-carrying statue of the conqueror Afonso himself, king between 1249 and 1279. The most striking of the museum's exhibits is a superb third-century AD Roman mosaic of Neptune surrounded by the four winds, unearthed near the train station. Other items include a collection of Roman statues from the excavations at Estói (see p.444), and a selection of local paintings, military artefacts and naive sixteenth-century multicoloured tiles, upstairs in the art gallery. In the rest of the old town, the streets have mostly been scrubbed clean of interest. However, it's well worth wandering around some of the cobbled side streets, whose houses are fronted by decorative balconies and tiling – the odd one serving as an antique shop or art gallery.

The **harbour** is the next most interesting area. The town gardens and a cluster of outdoor cafés overlook the moored yachts, while in the backstreets around **Rua de Santo António** shops, bars and restaurants do their best to keep you off the local beach. At the end of Rua de Santo António, on Praça de Liberdade, is the most intriguing of Faro's museums, the **Museu Regional** (Mon–Fri 9am–5pm; 300$00), which has a display of local crafts and industries, including reconstructions of typical cottage interiors, and models of the net systems still used in fishing for tuna.

By far the most curious sight in town, however, is the twin-towered, Baroque **Igreja do Carmo** (Mon–Sat 10am–1pm & 3–5pm, Sun during services), near the central post office on the Largo do Carmo. A door to the right of its altar leads to the sacristy where you buy a ticket (120$00) to view the macabre **Capela dos Ossos** (Chapel of the Bones), set in an overgrown garden out back. Like the one at Évora (see p.391), its walls are decorated with human bones – in this case disinterred from the adjacent monks' cemetery. Nearby, in Largo de São Pedro, the sixteenth-century **Igreja de São Pedro** is infinitely more attractive as a church, its finest decorative work an altar (to the left of the main altar) whose central image is a gilded, wooden *Last Supper* in relief.

The beaches

Faro's "town beach" – **Praia de Faro** – is typical of the sand-spit *ilha* beaches of the eastern Algarve; a long sweep of beautiful sand with both a sea-facing and a more sheltered land-facing side. It's less characteristic in being both overcrowded and overdeveloped, with bars, restaurants, villas and a campsite jammed onto a sandy island far too narrow to cope in the height of summer. Still, if you just want a few hours away from the centre of Faro, it's more than adequate; out of season you'll probably have the sands to yourself. The beach is situated on the Ilha de Faro, southwest of the town; bus #16 runs hourly (8am–8.40pm; until 9.40pm in summer) from the harbour gardens, or from the stop opposite the bus terminal, on a rather circuitous nine-kilometre trip that calls in at the airport first.

Alternatively, **ferries** shuttle through narrow marshy channels to a couple of other local sandbar beaches, between Faro and Olhão. They depart from the jetty below the old town, either to **Farol** on the Ilha da Culatra (June–Sept 4 daily; 500$00 return; 45min), which is described on p.447; or to the nearby **Ilha Deserta** (June–Sept 4 daily; 1000$00 return), part of the Parque Natural da Ria Formosa, where there's a bar-restaurant – *O Estaminé* – to cater for your needs.

Eating, drinking and nightlife

The heart of the town is a modern, pedestrianized shopping area on either side of Rua de Santo António, where you can find innumerable **restaurants, cafés and bakeries** – the latter stocked with almond delicacies, the regional speciality. Most of the pavement restaurants have similar menus (and similar prices); if you're prepared to scout around the backstreets, you can often find cheaper, better food, though without the accompanying streetlife that makes central Faro so attractive. As you'd expect, the cuisine is predominantly seafood-based, including the ubiquitous and often expensive *arroz de marisco* (a stew of shellfish and rice).

Cafés and restaurants

Café Aliança, Rua F. Gomes 6–11. A down-at-heel coffee house – faded but rather appealing in its way – with seats outside in summer, and a full menu of breakfasts, burgers, salads, omelettes, pastries and ice cream.

Cidade Velha, Rua Domingos Guieiro 19 (☎089/271 45). Situated by the Sé, this is the only restaurant in the old town. It serves elegant French and Portuguese cooking in a fine eighteenth-century building. At least 4000$00 a head; booking essential. Closed Sat lunch & Sun.

Dois Irmãos, Largo Terreiro do Bispo 13–15. Next to Praça Ferreira de Almeida, this is one of the oldest of the city's fish and seafood restaurants, a moderately priced place which specializes in tasty *cataplanas* (served for two only). Try the sardines, too. Upwards of 2500$00 a head.

Esplanada Parreiras, Rua Rebelo da Silva 22. An outdoor patio shaded by grape-bearing vines, where you can choose from a shortish menu of meat or fish grills – the *frango no churrasco* is good. You'll get away with spending around 1750$00 a head.

Fim do Mundo, Rua Vasco da Gama 53. Poorly lit, barely welcoming *frango* joint. Don't go if you don't want chicken – if you do, you'll get half a bird, fries and wine for 1000$00. It's actually very good – ask for the *piri-piri* (hot chilli and olive oil seasoning) only if you have health insurance.

Gardy, Rua de Santo António 16. Popular local *pastelaria* where seats are always at a premium – excellent cakes, pastries and coffee.

Adega Nova, Rua Francisco Barreto 24. Near the train station, this is an old-fashioned *adega* with classic Portuguese food and jugs of wine. An inexpensive choice – under 2000$00.

Adega Rocha, Rua da Misericórdia 50. Up the road from the turismo, this checked-table-clothed *adega* is just out of the central bustle and reassuringly good value – around 2000$00 for meat and fish grills.

Sol e Jardim, Praça Ferreira de Almeida 22–23. Associated with (and virtually next door to) the *Dois Irmãos*, this is a junk shop turned restaurant – flags of the world, football jerseys, old agricultural equipment, baskets and pots and pans suspended from the ceiling of a barn-like "garden" dining room. From 1750$00 a head, though more like double that if you stray into the shellfish and specialities.

Taska, Rua do Aportel 38. Friendly place serving traditional Algarve fare to a mostly Portuguese crowd. House specialities include corn mash and peanut mousse.

Bars and discos

The best of Faro's **nightlife** is concentrated along two or three central pedestrianized and cobbled streets – in particular **Rua Conselheiro Bivar** with its café-bars with outdoor seating, and the parallel **Rua do Prior**, where many of the bars and clubs feature DJs, live bands and video screens. Things get going around midnight; soon afterwards, as the bars fill up, drinkers tumble out onto the cobbled alleys to party. Faro also occasionally hosts big-name rock and pop **gigs** at the football stadium – check posters around town, or ask at the turismo.

Barracuda, Praia de Faro. The beach's most popular disco, with an outdoor first-floor bar. It's close to the campsite.

Binómio, Rua Conselheiro Bivar 40–44. One of the most raucous along the strip – you'll have to come early to get an outdoor seat. Otherwise, it's a free-for-all in the inside crush, with videos to jolly things along.

O Cofre, Rua Conselheiro Bivar 54. Café-*pastelaria* by day, youth hang-out by night with the tables hogged by locals fortifying themselves before a night spent shouting in the street.

Conselheiro, Rua Conselheiro Bivar 72–78. A bit more relaxed than most along here, with indoor tables, palms and some attempt at proper conversation by the patrons.

Emporium D, Rua do Prior 21. Large club with industrial-warehouse feel, good DJs and regular performances by local bands. One of the better venues.

Kingburger Bar, Rua do Prior 40. A small and relaxed bar, one of the first to open up along here, and one of the last to close. There are other branches on Praia da Faro and on Conselheiro Bivar.

Kream, Rua do Prior 38. Glitzy disco open until 4am; live bands on occasion, too.

Rochas, Rua do Prior 26. Typically loud and typically packed – a properly enforced ID check (no one under 16) at the door would turn away around 95 percent of the clientele.

Universidade, Rua de São Pedro 19–23. At the end of Rua do Prior – regular live bands and a post-11pm Happy Hour for cheap beer make this a popular student hang-out.

Versailles, Rua Ivens 7–9. Restaurant-bar that's good for a drink post-restaurant/pre-club, with outdoor seating and – later on at least – a youthful, local crowd. Open till midnight.

Listings

Airlines British Airways, no Faro office (☎089/80 07 73); Lufthansa, no Faro office (☎089/80 07 51); TAP, Francisco Gomes 8 (☎0808/21 31 41); airport switchboard (☎089/80 08 00).

Airport Flight information on ☎089/80 08 01.

Bus terminal There's an English-speaking information office inside the terminal; bus information on ☎089/89 97 00.

Car rental Auto Algarve, Rua do Aportel 150 (☎089/82 46 72); Auto Jardim (airport; ☎089/81 84 91); Avis (airport; ☎089/81 86 24); Eurodollar (airport; ☎089/81 82 94); Europcar (airport; ☎089/81 87 77); Hertz (Rua 1º de Maio 9; ☎089/82 48 77); I Per Rent, Avda. da República 100 (☎089/80 36 12).

Cinema In the Galerias Santo António shopping centre at Rua de Santo António 25.

Consulate The only British consulate in the Algarve is in Portimão (p.465), at Largo Francisco A. Maurício 7-1º (Mon–Fri 10am–noon & 3–4.30pm; ☎082/41 78 00). In Faro itself, there's a Canadian consulate (Rua Frei Lourenço de Santa Maria 1-1º; ☎089/80 37 57); a Dutch consulate (Rua Frei Lourenço de Santa Maria 2-1º; ☎089/20 903); and a German consulate (Avda. da República 166-4º; ☎089/80 31 48).

Hospital Hospital Distrital (☎089/80 34 11).

Left luggage At the bus terminal (Mon 9am–1pm & 2–6pm, Tues–Thurs 9am–1pm & 2–6pm, Fri 8.30am–1pm & 2–6pm).

Police Rua da Policia de Segurança Pública 32 (☎089/82 20 22).

Post office Largo do Carmo (Mon–Fri 8.30am–6.30pm, Sat 9am–12.30pm); also has *poste restante* facilities.

Taxis There's a rank in front of the *Hotel Faro*, by the town gardens.

Telephones You can make international calls from the post office.

Travel agencies Abreu, Avda. da República 124; Marcus & Harting, Rua Conselheiro Bivar 69; Space Travel, Rua Conselheiro Bivar 36.

North of Faro: Estói and São Brás de Alportel

Apart from the beach, other worthwhile day-trips from Faro are to the couple of villages in the gentle hills to the north. At Estói, you can divide your time between a delightful eighteenth-century country estate and the remains of a Roman settlement at Milreu, just below the village. Further north, the hilltop town of São Brás de Alportel also makes a pleasant excursion. Travelling by bus, unless you make a fairly early start, it's difficult to see both villages on the same day. However, if you feel reasonably energetic it's perfectly feasible to take the bus to São Brás and walk the 7km down to Estói, catching the late-afternoon bus back to Faro from there.

Estói

Regular buses make the twenty-minute journey 11km north of Faro to **ESTÓI,** which basically consists of a main street, a little square and a small white church. Buses drop you in the square, just off which is the delightful peach-coloured **Palácio do Visconde de Estói**, a diminutive version of the Rococo palace of Queluz near Lisbon (see p.122). At present, only the attractive grounds are open to the public (Mon–Sat 9.30am–12.30pm & 2–5.30pm; free); long-term renovations of the palace itself are still in progress.

The main reason for a visit to Estói, however, is the Roman site at **Milreu** (Tues–Sun 10am–12.30pm & 2.30–6pm; free), a ten-minute walk downhill from the square. Known to the Romans as Ossonoba, the town that once stood here predated Faro and was inhabited from the second to the sixth century AD. The surviving ruins are associated with a peristyle villa – one with a gallery of columns surrounding a courtyard – and dominated by the apse of a temple, which was converted into a Christian basilica in the third century AD, making it one of the earliest of all known churches. The other recognizable remains are of a bathing complex with fragments of mosaic; the *apodyterium*, or changing room, with its stone benches and arched niches below for clothes is clearly visible. The site was finally abandoned in the eighth century AD, after which date the Moors founded Faro to the south.

Back in the village, there's good **food** at *Victor's*, just off the square, where you'd be hard pushed to spend more than 1500$00 a head. There's also no fewer than eleven **bars** along and around the main street.

São Brás de Alportel

Seven kilometres north of Estói, **SÃO BRÁS DE ALPORTEL**, in a valley of the Serra do Caldeirão, also makes an appealing detour for those with a couple of hours to spare. Buses pull up in the main square, where, from its little circular booth, the **turismo** (Mon–Fri 9.30am–12.30pm & 2–5.30pm, Sat 9.30am–noon; ☎089/84 22 11) will provide you with a map – though it's rather unnecessary given that everything lies within a three-minute walk.

Checking out the sights, therefore, doesn't take long: walk to the bottom of town to the church of **Senhor dos Passos** (signposted Igreja Matriz), for its views of the surrounding valleys. There's a fine open-air **swimming pool** (*piscina*) a couple of minutes along from here, from where you can cut up Rua Nova de Fonte to the main street, Rua Dr. José Dias Sancho. Here, the **Museu Etnográfico do Trajo Algarvio**, at no. 61 (Tues–Fri 10am–1pm & 2–5pm; Sat & Sun 2–5pm; 100$00), housed in an old mansion, is quite the best reason to come to São Brás, its alcoves and corridors full of traditional costumes and farming and domestic equipment. If you're the only person there (which is quite likely), you'll be given a personal tour, which consists of the ticket seller walking behind you saying "meat" and "cork" as you stare at various agricultural implements.

PRACTICALITIES

The quiet surroundings entice a few visitors to make the village their Algarve base. **Accommodation** isn't the good value it might be, but try for rooms (all with showers) at the *Residencial São Brás*, Rua Luís Bivar 27 (☎& fax 089/84 22 13; ④), which runs off the main square, or at the slightly more expensive *Estalagem Sequeira* at Rua Dr. Evaristo Gago 9 (☎ & fax 089/84 34 44; ④), which provides modern en-suite rooms; both include breakfast in the price. Big spenders might want to stay at the very comfortable *Pousada de São Brás* (☎089/84 23 05, fax 84 17 26; ⑦), 2km north of town. The views from here are splendid, and there's an (expensive) restaurant, too; advance booking is essential in summer.

Bars and **restaurants** are sparse but try the excellent *Luís dos Frangos*, a five-minute walk up the Tavira road, or the *Savoy* (closed Sun lunch), on Rua Luís Bivar, past the *Residencial São Brás*. However, the best restaurant in the immediate area is the *Adega Nunes* (☎089/84 25 06; closed Sun), about 4km along the Faro road at Machados. It has a menu to suit most budgets and counts the President of Portugal among its customers.

Olhão and its ilhas

OLHÃO, eight kilometres east of Faro, is the largest fishing port on the Algarve and an excellent base for visiting the surrounding sandbank *ilhas*. It's an otherwise uneventful place, notwithstanding the rather surreal prose of a local brochure, which proclaimed Olhão home of the "amazing poodle of the Algarve . . . muscular and strong. . . [and] of valuable assistance to the fishermen for whom it dives into the water. . . to a depth of over four metres, to guide the fish into the nets". Unfortunately, the aquatic poodles were abandoned for more modern methods in the 1950s, though some are kept at the **Parque Natural** (daily 9am–12.30pm & 2–5.30pm; 200$00) around 3km east of town, signposted off the N125.

Once past the built-up outskirts, Olhão is quite an attractive town. There are no sights as such, but the flat roofs, outdoor stairways and white terraces of the old town are striking and give a North African look to the place. No surprise, then, that Olhão has centuries-old trading links with Morocco, as well as a small place in history for its uprising against the French garrison in 1808. Following the

French departure, the local fishermen sent a small boat across the Atlantic to Brazil to transmit the news to the exiled king, João VI. The journey, completed without navigational aids, was rewarded after the king's restoration to the throne by the granting of a town charter.

The best view of the whitewashed cube-houses is from the bell tower of the seventeenth-century parish church of **Nossa Senhora do Rosário** (Tues–Sun 9.30am–noon & 3–6pm), right in the middle of town. Outside, at the back of the church, an iron grille protects the chapel of **Nossa Senhora dos Aflitos**, where traditionally townswomen gather when there's a storm at sea to pray for their sailors amid candles and curious wax models of children and limbs.

The other obvious focus of the town is the **market**, held in the two large buildings on the harbourside at the bottom of town. Open from the crack of dawn (Mon–Sat), there's meat, fruit and vegetables on one side, fish on the other, the latter hall full of such delights as swordfish heads propped up on the marble counters and squid ink running off the tables into the gutter.

Practicalities

The **train station** is at the northeastern edge of town, off Avenida dos Combatentes da Grande Guerra; the **bus terminal** is a few minutes away on Rua General Humberto Delgado. From either, it's a quick walk down to the main Avenida da República, a wide boulevard which leads into the city centre, a further five minutes' walk away. At the parish church, the avenue forks into two: follow Rua do Comércio, the main (pedestrianized) shopping street, and when it rounds the corner you'll find the **turismo** (summer Mon–Fri 9.30am–7pm, Sat & Sun 9.30am–12.30pm & 2–5.30pm; winter Mon–Fri 9.30am–5.30pm; ☎089/71 39 36), which can provide a town map, advice on accommodation and sailing times of boats to the *ilhas*.

Accommodation

Accommodation can be hard to find in the height of summer, despite a fair scattering of **pensões**. Of these, first choice should be the *Pensão Bela Vista*, Rua Teófilo Braga 65–67 (☎089/70 25 38; ③), which has a range of bright rooms arranged around a tiled, flower-filled courtyard; from the turismo, turn left, then left again, and its sign is directly opposite. Second choice is the *Pensão Boémia*, slightly further out of the centre at Rua da Cerca 20, off Rua 18 de Junho (☎ & fax 089/71 45 13; ③): rooms come with shower and balcony. Back in the centre, other options include two on Rua Vasco da Gama, the other fork off Avda. da República: the *Pensão Bicuar* at no. 5 (☎089/71 48 16; ③), cheerful enough for the price and with smart communal areas; and the *Pensão Vasco de Gama* opposite, at no. 6 (☎089/70 27 85; ②). If all else fails, you should find room at the *Hotel Ria Sol*, Rua General Humberto Delgado 37 (☎089/70 52 67, fax 70 52 68; ⑤), an anonymous concrete hotel, by the bus station. The local **campsite** (☎089/700 13 00, fax 700 13 90) is at Marim, 3km east of town, and has a pool and good views of Armona. Buses from the Palace of Justice and Avda. 5 Outubro run hourly to Marim until around 7pm during the week and on Saturday mornings.

Eating and drinking

Rua do Comércio has its share of **cafés** with outdoor seating, and streets on either side harbour a few **restaurants**. For cheaper eating, there are two simple *casas de pasto* in the small square in front of the market, open for lunch and dinner, while the best places for local **fish** dishes are the nearby restaurants on Avda. 5 de Outubro, past the market towards the harbourside gardens. Here, *Papy's* is terrific – its *arroz de marisco* being a mammoth serving of prawns, crabs and clams – as is *Flamingo* (closed Mon).

The ilhas: Armona and Culatra

Separate **ferries** leave for the *ilhas* of Armona and Culatra from the jetty at the eastern end of Olhão's municipal gardens, five minutes' walk from the market. There's a timetable posted at the kiosk; if it isn't open, you can buy tickets on the ferries. The **Ilha da Armona**, a fifteen-minute ride away, is reasonably accessible all year round (June to mid-Sept 14 daily; rest of year 3 daily; 150$00 one way), as are Culatra (35min) and Farol (45min), on the **Ilha da Culatra** (June & Sept 7 daily; rest of year 4 daily; 160$00 to Culatra, 210$00 to Farol one way), though in summer you may prefer to get the boat to Farol from Faro; see p.442.

Ilha da Armona
Ferries drop their passengers at the southern end of the single settlement on **Ilha da Armona** – a long, crowded strip of holiday chalets and huts that stretches right across the island on either side of the main path. It's a fifteen-minute walk to the ocean, where the beach disappears into the distance; a short walk will take you to attractive stretches of sand and dune – the further you go, the greater the privacy.

There are a few **bar-restaurants** by the jetty, while at the other end, the self-service *Santo António* has a terrace overlooking the beach where you can tuck into sardines, salad and beer. There are no *pensões* or hotels on Armona, but *Orbitur* (☎089/71 41 73) operates a series of holiday **chalets** on the island – though you'll be lucky to find anywhere in high season. Camping on the beach is frowned upon, but there is a **campsite** (☎089/71 41 73) on the island.

Ilha da Culatra
The **Ilha da Culatra** is another huge sand spit, though very different in character from Armona, its northern shore dotted with a series of fishing settlements, mixed with an incongruous sprinkling of holiday chalets. The ferry's first port of call, **Culatra**, is the largest settlement, though **Farol**, the second stop, is far more agreeable. It's a rather commonplace, untidy village of holiday homes, but is edged by beautiful tracts of beach on the ocean side, though the mainland-facing beach is grubby. Once again, **camping** on the island is not encouraged, and in any case tends to be conspicuous among the fishing villages. In Farol, basic **rooms** and **food** at not-so-basic prices can be found at *À do João Restaurant* (☎089/70 20 01).

Tavira and around

Situated 30km east of Faro, **TAVIRA** is one of the most beautiful towns on the Algarve and a clear winner if you are looking for a base on the eastern stretch. It's sited on both sides of the broad Rio Gilão, which is overlooked by ancient balconied houses and straddled by two low bridges, one of Roman origin. This is an eminently attractive ensemble, which persuades many to stay longer than planned – particularly those intent on lounging around on the superb island beach of the **Ilha de Tavira**, which lies within easy reach of the town. Ferries to the island operate only from May to mid-October, but you can reach other local beaches, like that at **Pedras d'el Rei**, all year round. In any case, Tavira itself is certainly worth visiting, at any time of the year. Despite ever-increasing numbers of visitors and encroaching development, it continues to make its principal living as a tuna-fishing port, and fish dinners at restaurants along the palm-lined river are in themselves a powerful incentive to stop.

The Town

Founded as long ago as 400 BC, Tavira's greatest period of prosperity came in the sixteenth to eighteenth century, the age that produced most of its graceful array of churches and mansions. In the old town streets on both sides of the river, numerous houses retain fine old doorways and coats-of-arms.

From the arcaded **Praça da República**, by the river, it's a short climb up into the old town following Rua da Galeria. Ahead of you stands the **Igreja da Misericórdia** with its once fine (now badly worn), carved stone doorway from 1541 depicting, among other decorative twirls, a couple of lute-playing figures. Inside there's a fine tiled interior and gilt altar, but unfortunately the church is almost always locked. Turn left here and a couple of hundred metres up the cobbled street are the ruins of the **Castelo** (Mon–Fri 9.30am–5.30pm; free), half hidden amid landscaped gardens on a low hill in the centre of town. From the walls you can look down over the peculiarly Oriental rooftops and the town's twenty other churches (most of which too, sadly, are kept locked). Adjacent to the castle, the whitewashed **Santa Maria do Castelo** contains the tomb of Dom Paio Peres Correia, who reconquered much of the Algarve, including Tavira in 1242, from the Moors. Fittingly, the church stands on the site of the former mosque.

The best part of Tavira is the **river**. Gardens lined with cafés run as far as the lively harbourside **market** (Mon–Sat mornings only), beyond which are moored the fishing boats that still operate out of the river port. This is a great place to wander, among the nets and marine clutter, stopping at one of the restaurants or more basic fishermen's bars, most of which serve up memorable meals, generally involving big tuna steaks.

Practicalities

Tavira's **bus terminal** is by the river, from where it's a two-minute walk to the old bridge and Praça da República. The **train station** is 1km from the centre of town, straight up the Rua da Liberdade and at the end of Avda. Dr. Mateus Teixeira de Azevedo. There's a **turismo** at Rua da Galeria 9 (Mon–Fri 9.30am–7pm, Sat & Sun 9.30am–5.30pm; ☎081/32 25 11), up the steps just off Praça da República. **Bikes** and mopeds can be rented from *Das Neves*, Rua Dr. Parreira 135 (☎081/32 12 82) and, on the other side of the river, *Calhambeque*, Rua Dr. Augusto da Silva Carvalho 3 (☎081/32 33 23) – you'll pay from around 1000$00 a day (1300$00 for mountain bikes), slightly less for longer periods. **Taxis** line up in the praça.

Accommodation

As throughout the Algarve, be warned that places are at a premium during the summer season; if a tout offers you a room, take it, at least for the first night, and look around on your own later on. The tourist office can help with **private rooms** if you have no luck at any of the *pensões* listed below. There are also informal rooms (all ①) at Rua José Pires Padinha 44, opposite the market; Rua da Liberdade 75, opposite the post office; and Trav. M. Bombarda 4, closer to the train station, these ones with access to a kitchen. The nearest **campsite** is on the Ilha de Tavira, for which see p.451.

Pensão do Castelo, Rua da Liberdade 4 (☎081/32 39 42). Very centrally located, with views of the castle and river. Clean rooms with separate bathroom; rates drop out of season. ③.

Convento de Santo António, Atalaia (☎ & fax 081/32 56 32). Very elegant rooms in an old, converted convent with swimming pool and roof-terrace, located 1km out of Tavira on the Faro road. Breakfast is served in the arched courtyard. Minimum stay four nights in summer; three in winter. Booking essential. ⑥.

Residencial Imperial, Rua José Pires Padinha 24 (☎081/32 22 34). Small *residencial* next to the restaurant (see below); avoid the noisy street-facing rooms and go for one of those overlooking the gardens and river. Breakfast included. ④.

Residencial Lagôas, Rua Almirante Cândido dos Reis 24 (☎081/32 22 52). Situated on the north side of the river, this has attractive rooms and rooftop views. There's an added bonus in the top-notch budget restaurant, *Bica*, below – though the rooms above the kitchen can get uncomfortably hot. ④.

Residencial Marés, Rua José Pires Padinha 134–140 (☎081/32 58 15, fax 32 58 19). Extremely pleasant rooms with tiled floors, azulejos in the bathrooms, balconies over the river and a decent restaurant below. Breakfast included. Rates drop in the winter. ⑤.

Residencial Mirante, Rua da Liberdade 83 (☎081/32 22 55). Opposite the post office, and sporting a faded tiled facade, this place is all right, but some of the rooms overlooking the street are a bit noisy. ④.

Residencial Princesa do Gilão, Rua Borda de Água de Aguiar 10–12 (☎ & fax 081/32 51 71). A modern, white building with azulejo-decorated interior, this friendly *residencial* stands right on the quayside. Go for a room at the front, with a balcony overlooking the river. Breakfast included. ④.

Eating, drinking and nightlife

A succession of **cafés** and **restaurants** front the gardens along the riverbank, while further down, on Rua José Pires Padinha, tables edge out on to the riverside. For some of the best cakes in town, try *Tavirense*, an old-fashioned *pastelaria* on Rua Marcelino Franco 19, opposite the cinema. As for **drinking**, there are a couple of cafés in the main square, plenty of nameless backstreet **bars** with matchstick-chewing old-timers for company, and a couple of trendier spots north of the river, including the *Arco Bar* on Rua Almirante Cândido dos Reis 67 – a friendly place attracting a laid-back crowd. A more cultured spot for a drink is the courtyard of the *Galeria Spatium,* Rua Jacques Pessoa 17, which is the favoured watering hole of local artists, some of whose work you can see in the gallery beside it. The small bar specializes in cocktails – try the Cuban "Mogito".

Tavira's best **disco**, *UBI*, is reached by following Rua Almirante Cândido dos Reis to the outskirts of town; it's housed in the huge shiny, metallic warehouse on the right. The locals warm up with a few pre-clubbing drinks in the *Bubi Bar* in the same building.

RESTAURANTS

Anazu, Rua Jacques Pessoa 11–13. Large bar-restaurant on the riverfront – a good place to sit and watch the sun set.

Aquasul, Rua Dr. Augusto da Silva Carvalho 11–13. Pizza restaurant on the north side that makes a pleasant change. It also has French-influenced main dishes and amenable staff. Around 2000$00 for pizza and drinks.

A Barquinha, Rua José Pires Padinha 142. This unpretentious bar-restaurant, along the riverfront from the market, has seats outside and serves a good tuna steak, with stewed onions and fries. A plateful, wine and coffee comes to 1500$00.

Beira Rio, Rua Borda d'Água de Assêca 46–48. This riverside bar-restaurant with tree-shaded tables is a nice venue for a drink but the food's pricey. Situated on the west side of the bridge, opposite the bus station.

Bica, Rua Almirante Cândido dos Reis 22–24. Inexpensive, excellent Portuguese meals on the north side of the river, under the *Residencial Lagôas*. From around 1500$00 a head.

Cad'Oro, Rua José Pires Padinha 150. Upmarket riverfront fish restaurant with live music on certain summer evenings. Around 3000$00 and up or there's an *ementa turística* for 1885$00.

Imperial, Rua José Pires Padinha 22. Just back from the riverside gardens, the *Imperial* is well known for its seafood, including clams and tuna. A decent meal here will cost around 3000$00.

Churrasqueira Grill "O Manel", Rua Almirante Cândido dos Reis 6. Reliable Portuguese grill restaurant near the *Bica* with most meals around 1500–2000$00.

O Patio, Rua Dr. António Cabreira 30. Pricey fish restaurant with French-influenced dishes and attractive summer roof-terrace. From 3000$00 and upwards.

Patrick's, Rua Dr. António Cabreira 25–27. Welcoming *adega*-style, English-run bar-restaurant with food to match and even mugs of English tea! Breakfasts (890$00) served until 3pm; otherwise sandwiches, curries, burgers, salads. There's satellite TV too.

Ilha de Tavira

The **Ilha de Tavira** stretches southwest from Tavira almost as far as Fuzeta, some fourteen kilometres away. For most of its length the landward side of the island is a dank morass of mud flat, but at the eastern tip the mud disappears and the *ilha* ends in an expanse of sand and sea. The beach is enormous, backed by tufted dunes, and over the years its growing popularity has led to a certain amount of development: at the end of the main path, which runs from the jetty through a small chalet settlement, there are water-sports facilities, beach umbrellas and loungers, and half a dozen bar-restaurants facing the sea. But, rather than spoiling things, this has fostered something of a good-time feel at the beach. The **campsite** (☎081/32 44 55; May to mid-Oct), a minute from the sands and with a well-stocked mini-market, shelters a youthful crowd, and the bars pump out music into the night. The *Sunshine Bar* serves a tasty tuna steak, and has a full breakfast menu and vegetarian options, too.

Buses (July to mid-Sept hourly 8am–8pm; June Mon–Fri 5 daily, Sat & Sun hourly) leave from the bus station in Tavira, stopping outside the cinema, for the ten-minute trip to the jetty at **Quatro Águas**, 2km east of town. Out of season, you've the choice of a half-hour walk from the town (along the river, past the market, and just keep going) or a taxi. The **boats** to the island (May to mid-Oct; 100$00 return) run every thirty minutes in July and August, hourly during the other months, with the first departure at around 7.30am. Last boats **back from the island** are at 9pm in May and mid-September to mid-October, 10pm in June, and at 11.45pm from July to mid-September.

Less frequent boats to the island depart from the quayside just downstream from the fish market in town; up to six daily departures in summer, four to five during winter (200$00 return).

Pedras d'el Rei and Barril

If you're after a little more space in summer, it's better to head 4km west from Tavira to **PEDRAS D'EL REI**, a holiday village, which, while a bit sterile, is not too big. Chalets can be hired on a short-term basis at reasonable prices for small groups, though the complex is usually full in July and August. Fairly regular **buses** (Mon–Sat only) connect the resort with Tavira, or you can walk from the main coastal highway to Pedras in about fifteen minutes.

From Pedras, you cross a causeway and then catch a miniature train (200$00) which shuttles backwards and forwards across the mud flats to the beach of **BARRIL** on the Ilha de Tavira. It's a few minutes' walk right or left to escape the tourist facilities at the terminus, and there you are: miles of beautiful, peaceful, dune-fringed beach. Take your own food and drink, though, since the relative isolation means high prices in the couple of café-bars here. This whole area constitutes the **Parque Natural da Ria Formosa**, a nature reserve where you can watch tens of thousands of fiddler crabs, scuttling about and waving their claws at the sky.

East of Tavira: to Vila Real

Just to the east of Tavira, the sand spit that protects much of the eastern Algarve from the developers starts to thin out, merging with the shoreline beach at Manta Rota, 12km away. The result is predictable: **Cabanas**, **Manta Rota** and **Alagoa** have all been intensively developed, although the beaches at all three resorts are splendid, if crowded in summer; there are more alluring sandy stops at **Praia Verde** and **Monte Gordo**. However, there is one surprise on this part of the coast: for some reason, the small hamlet of **Cacela Velha** (not to be confused with Vila Nova de Cacela, 2km inland) is barely touched by tourism.

You can reach Cabanas and Monte Gordo by **bus** from Tavira; for Manta Rota, the only services are from Vila Real (or Monte Gordo); and for Praia Verde, the best you can do is get off any bus to Vila Real on the highway and walk down the side road. You can of course always **walk** along the beach: from Manta Rota it's around thirty minutes to Alagoa, another twenty minutes to Praia Verde, and forty more to Monte Gordo.

Cacela Velha

Ten kilometres from Tavira, **CACELA VELHA** is perched on a rocky bluff over-looking the sea, surrounded by olive groves, and home to an old church and the remains of a fort. It is spectacularly pretty – a reminder of how the Algarve must have looked half a century ago. Naturally enough, the hamlet is short on facilities, but it has a little restaurant, a tapas bar, a couple of cafés and a handful of **rooms** that are snapped up quickly in the summer. The beach below the village is a delight and it's possible to arrange a lift over to the sand bar just offshore.

To get here, you need to jump off the Tavira–Vila Real bus on the highway, just before Vila Nova de Cacela, from where it's a fifteen-minute walk down a side road to the village.

Manta Rota, Praia de Alagoa and Praia Verde

Two kilometres further along the coast at **MANTA ROTA**, a group of half a dozen restaurants cluster at the entrance to the beach, all serving platters of sardines and grilled swordfish and tuna. There's not much else to hang about for; the main road is a fifteen-minute walk up from the beach. **PRAIA DE ALAGOA** is more of a resort, backed by white villas and apartments. Here, there's a line of beach umbrellas and beach bars, drinks kiosks and water sports on hand. Just past Algoa, the once attractive hillside above the sands at **PRAIA VERDE** is starting to go the way of neighbouring resorts as building sites replace woodland. However, a walk up the hill will reward you with a splendid panoramic view from the lookout at the top, and the beach below, served by a couple of drinks kiosks-cum-beach-bars, is still much less crowded than others along the coast. Further east, towards Monte Gordo, the beach becomes more unkempt, backed by scrub-by dunes, but the sands are much less likely to be crowded in summer.

Monte Gordo

MONTE GORDO is the last resort before the Spanish border and the most built-up of the eastern holiday towns. White hotels overlook the wide, clean sands, on which are scattered a profusion of beach café-restaurants with studiously similar menus; the *Mota* is not a bad choice.

From the casino on the seafront, the main Avenida Vasco de Gama leads back before turning into Rua Pedro Álvares Cabral, off which on the west side is the **bus stop**, by the parish church. There are **rooms** advertised at various bars in town; out of season, it's worth checking on discounts at the hotels with the **turismo** (summer daily 9.30am–7pm; reduced hours in winter; ☎081/444 95), next to the casino. If you want to stay right on the beach, then the *Vasco da Gama*, Avda. Infante Dom Henrique (☎081/51 13 21, fax 57 16 22; ⑥), is probably your best bet, a nice place with lots of water sports and kids' facilities. Monte Gordo is also site of the last **campsite** (☎081/425 88, fax 51 19 32) on this stretch of the Algarve.

Vila Real de Santo António

The border town and harbour of **VILA REAL DE SANTO ANTÓNIO** has suffered a marked change in character since the completion of a bridge across the Rio Guadiana, 4km to the north of town. Fewer cars and tourists now clog the streets in summer since anyone bound for Spain can now drive (or catch a bus) straight there. Still, you may want to call in anyway, not least because it's one of the more architecturally interesting towns on the Algarve. The original town was demolished by a tidal wave at the beginning of the seventeenth century, and the site stood empty until it was revived in 1774 by the Marquês de Pombal. Eager to apply the latest concepts of town planning, Pombal used the same techniques he had already pioneered in the Baixa quarter of Lisbon and rebuilt Vila Real on a grid plan. The whole project only took five months – a remarkable achievement,

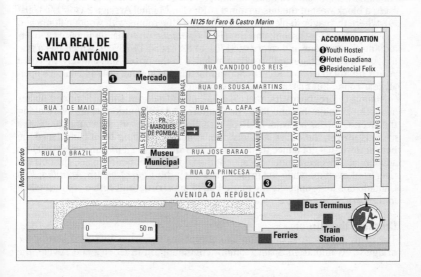

but a startling waste of resources, as it transpired that the hewn stone that Pombal had dragged all the way from Lisbon could have been quarried a couple of miles up the road.

The Town

The central grid built by Pombal radiates out from the handsome square that bears his name, ringed by lemon trees and low, white buildings, a couple of which are pleasant outdoor cafés. In one corner sits the **Museu Municipal Manual Cabanas** (Mon–Fri: summer 11am–2pm & 3–7pm; winter 8.30am–12.30pm & 2–5pm; free), which couldn't really have the cheek to charge entry for its subdued collection of colonial carvings, advertising hoardings, books and engravings. The surrounding streets have a certain low-key charm, bristling with linen shops, electrical retailers and grocers, though sadly the old central **market** – a couple of blocks up from the square – with its Moorish domes, is under restoration; with the help of EU funds it's destined to become a cultural centre.

Admittedly, once you've had a beer and a wander around the shops there isn't a great deal else to do, though head down to the riverside **gardens** before you leave. There are more cafés here, an ice-cream stall or two, some rather touching public notices ("The garden is your friend – respect it"), and fine views across to the splash of white that is Ayamonte in Spain.

Practicalities

Vila Real is the eastern terminal of the Algarve railway, and **trains** pull up at the tatty little station on the riverfront. **Buses** stop at a terminus just in front of here; the turismo closed down long ago, although plans are afoot to open a new one. If you're heading on to Spain (or elsewhere in Portugal come to that), you really shouldn't need to stay. Should you want to, **hotel** choices include the *Residencial Felix*, a block west of the bus terminal at Rua Dr. Manuel Arriaga 2 (☎081/437 91; ②), where the eager-to-please owners oversee little rooms with wooden floors and a clean separate bathroom; and the *Hotel Guadiana* on Avda. da República, overlooking the gardens and river (☎081/51 14 82, fax 51 14 78; ⑤), which has a fine old Art Deco frontage and breakfast included in the price. Alternatively, there's a **youth hostel** in town at Rua Dr. Sousa Martins 40 (☎ & fax 081/445 65); it's open all year round but fills up quickly in summer.

Among the **restaurants**, there's a line of half-a-dozen similarly priced places along the avenida (beyond Rua 5 de Outubro), all with outdoor seats overlooking the river. *Os Arcos* at Avda. da República 45 is pretty good, at around 2000$00 a meal. However, the *Caves do Guadiana*, at no. 90, has long been considered the best in town. It's got a nice tiled, vaulted interior and you'll pay under 3000$00 for a full meal. Prices are much cheaper at the two or three modest places just off the riverfront avenue; while for grilled meats, try the *Churrasqueira Arenilha*, Rua Cândido dos Reis, opposite the market building. **Drinks** and coffee are best taken in the bars on the square.

Crossing the border

Two daily **buses** (morning and late afternoon) run from Vila Real across the bridge to Ayamonte in Spain (15min), continuing on to Huelva and Seville, the total journey taking three hours. **Coming from Spain**, two similarly timed services from Ayamonte run through Vila Real and on to Tavira and Faro. There are timetables posted at the bus terminus.

If you just want to make a day-trip, it's more fun to use the **ferries**, which still cross the river seven days a week (every 30min–1hr; summer 8am–8pm; winter 8am–7pm), from the terminal next to the train station. The ferry trip takes about fifteen minutes and costs 150$00 per person, 650$00 per car.

Inland: along the Rio Guadiana

North of Vila Real, the **Rio Guadiana** forms the border with Spain and provides a little-travelled diversion to some of the less spoiled parts of the region. **Buses** from Vila Real follow the N122, which runs inland of the river, calling at the tiny villages of Castro Marim, Odeleite and Alcoutim, each with a smattering of interest. Best of all, though, is a **boat trip** up the river itself. There are usually summer tourist charters offered in Monte Gordo or Vila Real: at around 7500$00 per person they're not especially cheap, but you do get a barbecue lunch and plenty of swimming opportunities along the way. You should also be able to arrange river trips in Alcoutim, paying around 4000$00 per hour for the boat – talk to the helpful turismo there.

Castro Marim

The little village of **CASTRO MARIM**, tucked away 5km north of Vila Real (several buses daily), was once a key fortification protecting Portugal's southern coast. Marim was the first headquarters of the Order of Christ (1319) and is the site of a huge **castle** (daily 9am–6pm; free) built by Afonso III in the thirteenth century. The massive ruins are all that survived the earthquake of 1755, as well as those of the smaller fort of São Sebastião across the village, but it's a pretty place with fine views of the impressive bridge to Spain. A small museum inside the castle walls (not always open) displays local archeological finds and the like. The **turismo** is in Praça 1º de Maio (Mon–Fri 9.30am–12.30pm & 2–5.30pm, Sat 9.30am–noon; ☎081/53 12 32), just below the castle.

The marshy area around Castro Marim has been designated as a nature reserve, the **Reserva Natural do Sapal**, so there's no danger of its being despoiled; the reserve office inside the castle has more information (Mon–Fri 9am–12.30pm & 2–5.30pm; ☎081/53 11 41). One of the area's most unusual and elusive inhabitants is the extraordinary, ten-centimetre-long, swivel-eyed, opposing-toed, Mediterranean chameleon – a harmless, slow-moving lizard that's severely threatened elsewhere by habitat destruction.

There are several **places to eat** in the village, including the *Eira Gaio*, just up Rua 25 de Abril from the turismo. For drinks and snacks, try either the *Atlantis* or *Casa do Pasto Rodrigues*, both on Rua de São Sebastião, west of Praça 1º de Maio and the turismo.

Alcoutim

If you're feeling particularly energetic, you could walk the 15km north along the riverside road from Foz de Odeleite to **ALCOUTIM**, a beautiful route through unspoilt countryside. The village is extremely attractive, too, with a long history as a river port, dominated in turn by Greeks, Romans and Arabs who all fortified the heights with various structures over the centuries; the **castle** ruins date from the fourteenth century and offer fine views over the town and the River Guadiana. For further diversion, fishing-boat ferries across the river to the **Spanish village of Sanlúcar**, a mirror image of Alcoutim, with its own ruined castle; the local boatmen will take you across for 100$00 or so.

A small **turismo** (summer Mon–Thurs 9.30am–5.30pm, Fri–Sun 9.30am–12.30pm & 2–5.30pm; ☎081/54 61 79) is located in the main square, Praça da República, right in the centre of the village. They're helpful people and can point you in the right direction for **overnight stays**: there are private rooms at *Casa D*, Edifício Turístico near the church (③; breakfast included). There's also a rather nice fifty-bed **youth hostel** (☎ & fax 081/460 04) just out of the village, across the Ribeira Cadavais, with canoe rental among its attractions; cross the bridge beyond Praça da República and follow the signs. Alcoutim's **cafés** and **restaurants** cluster around the praça: the *Afonso* and *Rogério* in the square, and *O Soeiro* a little way down Rua do Município are recommended.

One or two **buses** a day run back down to Vila Real, and there are services north to Mertola (p.426) and Beja (p.421).

THE WESTERN ALGARVE

The **western Algarve** stretches for a hundred kilometres from Faro to Sagres and encompasses Portugal's most intense tourist developments. The most extreme section is between Faro and Lagos, where the beaches and coves are fronted by an almost continuous stretch of villas, apartments and hotels. The purpose-built resorts feature marinas, golf links and tennis centres – all fine if you've booked a holiday, but not especially inviting for casual visitors.

Albufeira is one of the biggest – and most enjoyable – resorts and other decent stops include **Portimão**, nearby **Praia da Rocha** and **Lagos**, the last of which still retains a bit of local character. All of these places are packed to the gills in summer and, particularly if you have transport, you might do better to seek a base inland at the old market towns of **Loulé** or **Silves**, and drive down to the nearest strip of beach. **Caldas de Monchique**, a nineteenth-century spa town, and neighbouring **Monchique** are other inland options, though these are a good forty minutes' drive from the sea.

Until recently, the coast **west of Lagos** was the place to escape the worst of the crowds, but development – in the shape of a fast road and burgeoning enclaves of holiday villas – has been horrifically quick. However, erstwhile fishing villages such as Burgau and Salema still teeter on the edge of complete exploitation. Beyond these villages the road cuts high above the sea, across a cliff-edged plateau, and down to **Sagres**, with its dramatic scenery and busy nightlife.

The coast **north of Sagres**, heading towards Alentejo, is the last undeveloped swathe of the Algarve – partly because the sea is distinctly colder and often pretty wild. If you can brave the climate, you might like to try low-key villages such as **Vila do Bispo**, **Carrapateira**, **Aljezur** and **Odeceixe**, all of which have magnificent local beaches. These attract a rather more youthful and "alternative" crowd than resorts on the Algarve proper; their combination of nude sunbathing, surf and parties is not everyone's idea of an idyll.

Quinta do Lago to Vilamoura

The coast immediately northwest of Faro is unremitting holiday village territory, with little promise for anyone simply in search of a quiet beach and an unsophisticated meal. This is territory for those into "Sportugal" – as the tourist board promotes the lesiure complexes – and none too fussy about a local environment. You have to head inland for even the barest whiff of the old Algarve, best encountered at the historic market town of **Loulé**.

Loulé makes for a pleasant lunchtime or evening break for those staying on the Quarteira strip of coast. Independent travellers may find it the best place for a night away from the crowds, though it's probably more realistic to stay in Faro and see the places below by **bus**; departures are roughly hourly throughout the day.

Quinta do Lago, Vale do Lobo, Almancil and Quarteira

The first of the resorts, **QUINTA DO LAGO** is a vast, luxury holiday village with its own golf course, sports complex and opulent hotel. There's a decent beach, too, the **Praia do Ança0**, and more of the same at **VALE DO LOBO**, next door, with serious-money hotels, golf courses, a riding school, and the David Lloyd Tennis Centre.

Back on the highway, just before **ALMANCIL**, the church of **São Laurenço** (Mon 2.30–6pm, Tues–Sat 10am–1pm & 2.30–6pm; 200$00) comes as a surprise amid the development. Built in the eighteenth century, it survived the earthquake of 1755 and retains its superb fully tiled interior depicting the life of St Laurence – in particular, graphically illustrated panels of his martyrdom. In Almancil itself, the *Pensão Santa Teresa*, Rua do Comércio 13 (☎089/39 55 25, fax 39 53 64; ④), is one of the more reasonably priced places to stay in this entire area.

The first proper town west of Faro is **QUARTEIRA**, 22km away, with a good weekly market and an attractive stretch of sand – though development has overwhelmed most of what was once pleasant about Quarteira. The **bus terminus** (☎089/30 18 23) is a couple of blocks back from the beach, on Avda. Dr. Sá Carneiro, with the **turismo** on the seafront Avda. Infante de Sagres (summer Mon & Fri–Sun 9.30am–12.30pm & 2–7pm, Tues–Thurs 9.30am–7pm; winter Mon & Fri 9.30am–12.30pm & 2–5pm, Tues–Thurs 9.30am–5.30pm; ☎089/38 92 09). They should be able to help with finding accommodation, though if you want to scout around the cheaper **pensões** try the basic *Pensão Triangulo*, Rua Dr. José Pedro 25 (☎089/31 52 37; ②); the very pleasant *Pensão Miramar* at Rua Gonçalo Velho 8 (☎089/31 52 25; ④); or the *Pensão Romeu*, on the same street at no. 38 (☎089/31 41 14; ④). Both streets run back from the seafront avenida. There's also a **campsite** (☎089/30 28 21, fax 30 28 22) 1km east of town; any bus to or from Faro runs right past it.

Loulé

LOULÉ, 11km inland from Quarteira, has a history similar to most of the towns in southern Portugal – Roman and Moorish occupation – and **castle ruins** to match. The castle walls are the best point to begin a look around town. They have been restored as a walkway and enclose a **Museu Municipal** (Mon–Sat 9.30am–5.30pm; free) of vaguely diverting historical bits and pieces. Between the museum and the thirteenth-century Gothic parish church nearby, a grid of white-washed cobbled streets reveals numerous handicraft shops in which you're free to watch the craftsmen at work – lacemaking, in particular, is a flourishing local industry. On Saturdays, the town is transformed as the whole region seems to arrive en masse for a busy **country market**.

Loulé's most curious sight is a beehive-shaped monument on a nearby hilltop, out in the direction of Boliqueime, which you can't help but notice as you arrive in town. It turns out to be the sanctuary of **Nossa Senhora da Piedade**; adjacent is a faded sixteenth-century chapel currently closed for much-needed restoration.

PRACTICALITIES

The **bus terminal** (☎089/41 66 56) is on Rua de Nossa Senhora de Fátima, a couple of minutes' walk from the old town area; there are regular services from Quarteira and from Faro. The **turismo** (summer Mon & Fri–Sun 9.30am–12.30pm & 2–7pm, Tues–Thurs 9.30am–7pm; winter Mon & Fri 9.30am–12.30pm & 2–5.30pm, Tues–Thurs 9.30am–7pm; ☎089/46 39 00) is inside the castle walls, at Largo Dom Pedro I, and can help you find **accommodation**. The cheapest place in town is *Hospedaria Zé Viegas*, Rua Nossa Senhora da Piedade 64 (☎089/46 33 85; ③), or try *Pensão Iberica* at Avda. Marçal Pacheco 157 (☎089/41 41 00; ④), which is a continuation of Avda. 25 de Abril, on the other side of Largo Gago Coutinho. If you have the money, a clear first choice is the comfortable *Loulé Jardim Hotel* at Praça Manuel de Arriaga 23 (☎089/41 30 94, fax 46 31 77; ⑤), a block south of Rua Nossa Senhora da Piedade.

There's a good range of **places to eat**. Among a cluster of restaurants around the parish church, *Las Bons Enfants*, Rua Eng. Duarte Pacheco 116, is known for its carefully prepared and pricey French cuisine (dinner only; closed Sun). There's also the intimate *Bica Velha* at Rua Martim Moniz 17 (closed Sun); or the *Cavaco*, up at Largo de São Francisco 44, where the *cataplanas* are popular. For grilled chicken the place to go is *O Rei do Churrasco* at Rua Assenção Guimarães 84, the street below the park.

Vilamoura

Back on the coast and based around a king-sized marina, **VILAMOURA**, 3km west of Quarteira, is a constantly expanding resort, with a bewildering network of roads signposted to upmarket new hotels and leisure facilities, including some highly exclusive **golf courses**. The beach is impressive – as it should be considering all the development – and, if you're not bothered by the crowds, enjoyable enough. On the outskirts, opposite the Mobil garage on the Vilamoura–Albufeira road, *Kadoc* – the Algarve's biggest **disco** – pulls in even more night-time visitors.

The bus drops you next to the casino, one block from the beach, the **Praia da Marina**. The enormous and luxurious *Vilamoura Marinotel* (☎089/38 99 88, fax 38 98 69; ⑦) is visible, two minutes away, overlooking the marina. Bristling with yachting hardware, the marina makes for an interesting stroll and is really the only other reason to stop off here; you can settle down at one of the cafés and watch the leisured set fooling around on their boats. If you want a go yourself, consider a **cruise** on the *Condor de Vilamoura* (☎089/31 40 70), a schooner which operates out of the marina daily during the summer: tickets cost around 4000$00 for a three-hour trip, more like 7500$00 for a full-day trip and barbecue, up to Albufeira and back.

Albufeira and around

Every inch a resort, **ALBUFEIRA** tops the list of package-tour – especially British package-tour – destinations in the Algarve. It was once an unusually pretty village, with narrow, twisting lanes of whitewashed houses criss-crossing the high grey-red cliffs above a beautiful spread of beaches. These still exist, but they are all but engulfed by hundreds of new apartment buildings strung across the local hillsides. If you're looking for unspoiled Portugal, this isn't it – whatever the brochures might say. Nevertheless, Albufeira is still one of the nicer resorts, attracting a varied mix of holidaymakers: an ageing, well-heeled clientele who frequent the more expensive restaurants, and a younger contingent who seem to devote themselves to downing as much beer as is humanly possible.

There's still a Moorish feel to parts of central Albufeira, as well as the more tangible remnants of a Moorish castle – the original Arabic name of the town, *Al-Buhera*, means "Castle-on-the-Sea". But the 1755 earthquake did for much of the town, and most of the modern centre is nondescript, though enlivened somewhat by a small fishing harbour and by street stalls selling leather, copper, clothes and ceramics.

None of this is of any consequence whatsoever to the summer crowds, who sleep and eat in town but spend their days at one of a dozen excellent cove-beaches in the vicinity. The **beach** fronting Albufeira itself – reached through a tunnel from the main Rua 5 de Outubro – is as good as any of these, flanked by strange tooth-like rock formations. If it's too crowded here, a relatively short bus (or taxi)

ride can open up a number of other possibilities, the best of which are detailed on p.462. At night, the focus switches to Albufeira's central, pedestrianized streets and squares, lined with pavement cafés, bars and restaurants fronted by eager touts and waiters keen to entice you in.

Practicalities

If you're in Albufeira on a package holiday, you might well not be staying in the town at all, but in one of the handful of small resort-villages on either side, like Montechoro, Areias de São João or Praia da Oura. However, all have access to their own beaches and are, in any case, within two or three kilometres of the town centre, which you can reach on regular local buses or by taxi. Everyone else will arrive in Albufeira at the **bus terminal** (☎089/58 97 55) on Avda. da Liberdade, at the top of town, five minutes' walk from the central Largo Eng. Duarte Pacheco, just to the west of which is the main street, Rua 5 de Outubro. At the end of here is the tunnel that's been blasted out of the rock to give access to the town beach. Albufeira's "local" **train station** is actually 6km north of town at Ferreiras; a bus connects it with the bus terminal roughly hourly (7am–8pm).

The **turismo** (summer daily 9.30am–7pm; winter Mon–Fri 9.30am–7pm, Sat & Sun 9.30am–12.30pm & 2–5.30pm; ☎089/58 52 79) is on Rua 5 de Outubro, close to the tunnel.

Accommodation

Finding a room can be difficult in high season since most of the **hotels and pensões** are block-booked by package holiday companies. Those listed below are a few exceptions, which may have "independent" vacancies. Otherwise the tourist office can help you find a **private room**, though they'll charge you for any phone calls they make. Perhaps the best bet, when all is said and done, is to accept the offer of a room from one of the touts who lurk around the bus station; you can always look around on your own later if it's not up to scratch.

The finely appointed (and expensive) **Camping Albufeira** (☎089/58 95 05 or 58 76 27, fax 58 76 33) – complete with swimming pools, restaurants, bars, shops and tennis courts – 2km to the north of town, off the N396, has regular connections from the bus station (any bus to Portimão/Lagos passes it).

Pensão Albufeirense, Rua da Liberdade 16–18 (☎089/51 20 79). Comfortable but drab with fairly reasonably priced rooms, with and without bath. ③.

Hotel Cerro Alagoa, via Rápida, Apartado 2155 (☎089/580 21 00, fax 580 21 90). Extremely comfortable modern hotel on the hill above town, ten minutes' walk from the centre (take the steps at the eastern end of Avda. 25 de Abril), with its own pool, gardens and gym, and courtesy bus to the local beaches. Buffet breakfast included. ⑦.

Residencial Limas, Rua da Liberdade 25–27 (☎089/51 40 25). A good, central choice, though the ten rooms fill quickly. Prices almost halve outside peak season. ④.

Residencial Polana, Rua Cândido dos Reis 32 (☎089/58 71 68, fax 58 68 50). A large, package-tour hotel, right in the thick of things – it's on a very noisy street full of bars. Rooms come with shower. Breakfast included. ④.

Pensão Silva, Trav. André Rebelo, off Rua 5 de Outubro (☎089/51 26 69). Very close to the turismo, in an alleyway to the right as you face the beach. Small, just-about-comfortable rooms with shower, and a toilet down the hall. ④.

Sol e Mar, Rua José Bernardo de Sousa (☎089/586 721, fax 58 70 36). Modern, low-slung, four-star hotel above the tunnel, overlooking the beach. ⑥.

Residencial Vila Bela, Rua Coronel Águas 32 (☎ & fax 089/51 21 01). Situated on the west side of the centre (at the junction with Avda. do Ténis), this is an attractive *residencial* with balconied rooms overlooking a small swimming pool and the bay. Open April–Oct. ⑤.

Residencial Vila Branca, Rua do Ténis 4 (☎089/58 68 04, fax 58 65 92). A three-star *residencial* up in the modern part of town, ten minutes from the beach. Breakfast included. ⑤.

Eating

Albufeira has **restaurants** to match every budget – and most tastes. As well as Portuguese restaurants, there's also a whole range of places serving pizzas, Chinese and Indian food, even fish and chips. Naturally, you tend to get what you pay for (and prices here are ten percent higher than resorts further east), but for the better bargains head for the area behind the fishing harbour, to the east of the main beach. Stand around outside, perusing the menu, and you'll often be presented with enticements in the form of drinks vouchers and the like. The morning-after-the-night-before is well catered for in most restaurants and bars, with massive **English-style breakfasts** available until the sensible hour of 3pm.

Bom Dia, Rua Alves Correira 37–39. Modest little backstreet tourist restaurant with decent, mostly Portuguese food, cheaper-than-usual prices and less predatory waiters than many. Affordable wine, too. Around 2000$00.

Cabaz da Praia, Praça Miguel Bombarda 7. Just up the hill from the main street and overlooking the beach, this serves excellent but expensive meals. The menu is mainly French-inspired, and the roof-terrace offers fine views – for which you're paying higher than usual prices, around 4000–5000$00 a head. Closed Thurs & lunchtime Sat.

Cantinho Algarvio, Trav. São Gonçalo de Lagos 3a. Mid-range restaurant with a large, varied menu where you can fill up on cuts of meat and other standard Portuguese dishes. Around 2500$00.

Louisiana, Largo Cais Herculano 16–20. Drink cocktails on the terrace above the fishermen's beach and then repair upstairs for selections from the grill menu.

Minar, Rua Diogo Cão, off Largo Cais Herculano. Surprisingly good Indian restaurant, where you'll eat for around 3000$00.

O Rei dos Frangos, Trav. dos Telheiros 4, off Avda. 25 de Abril. Common all over Portugal, but hard to pin down in resorts like Albufeira, here's a first-rate little *churrasqueira* – the chicken comes smothered in *piri-piri* and there's also grilled steak, swordfish and a speciality meat *cataplana*. Around 2000–3000$00.

A Ruina, Praia dos Pescadores, Largo Cais Herculano. Rustic old restaurant built into the hillside over the beach, serving fish fresh from the market. Eat on the beach, inside on one of two floors, or on the roof-terrace. Sardines and salad make a reasonably inexpensive lunch, but otherwise you're looking at 3500$00 and up for a full dinner.

Sotavento, Rua São Gonçalo de Lagos 16. Behind the fishing harbour, this small tiled bar-restaurant serves an affordable selection of Portuguese and international standards. Around 1500–2000$00.

OUT OF TOWN

A Curva, Rua da Moinheta 25, Algoz (☎082/57 45 12). Ten kilometres inland of Albufeira, on the other side of the main N125 highway, this village restaurant has a deservedly high reputation for remarkable, good-value country cooking. Closed Sun.

La Cigale, Olhos de Água (☎089/50 16 37). Nine kilometres east of Albufeira, and right on the beach, this renowned restaurant has a lovely terrace and high-quality food, including great seafood. Open for evening meals only; expect to pay around 4000$00.

Drinking and nightlife

Like the restaurants, Albufeira **bars** and **discos** are into promotion. There's not much to choose between them, and you may as well frequent those offering the cheapest drinks at the time – Happy Hour is an extremely flexible concept here. The main areas for carousing are along Rua São Gonçalo de Lagos, around Largo Eng. Duarte Pacheco and – for more of a late-night scene – along Rua Cândido dos Reis, Travessa Cândido dos Reis and Rua Alves Correira. Most bars stay open until around 3am, the discos until 4am or later in summer.

Central Station, Largo Eng. Duarte Pacheco 44. Chic, modern bar which also doubles as a café/restaurant/*gelateria* depending on the time of day.

Classic Bar, Rua Cândido dos Reis 10. Loud and young, outside or in, with rudely named cocktails a speciality.

Jo Jo's, Rua São Gonçalo de Lagos 1. Family-run pub with British soccer and other sports on satellite TV, and London DJs to get the crowd going.

Kiss, Montechoro. Out of town, at the southern end of Montechoro, this is regarded as the best club around. The music is good, but the club tends to be overcrowded and very glitzy; watch for posters advertising events.

Silvia's, Rua São Gonçalo de Lagos 3. Central Albufeira disco on a street full of late-opening bars. The entry price includes one drink.

Sir Harry's Bar, Largo Eng. Duarte Pacheco 36–37. Long-standing tourist institution on the square, with English breakfasts, draught British beer, and live music on occasions.

Sol Dourado, Largo Cais Herculano. Grill-restaurant perched above the square, this has one of the nicer terrace-bars from which to watch the sun set over the water.

Zansi Bar, Rua Miguel Bombarda 7. Live music, karaoke and good-value international food served day and night. It's near the parish church.

The local beaches

The rocky red headlands just to the **west of Albufeira** are beautiful – and were largely inaccessible until the 1980s, when the development of a strip of villa resorts very much changed the landscape. There are no direct buses to these resorts, though the Albufeira–Portimão service drops passengers on the main road, a steep 2km walk distant. The main resorts – **SÃO RAFAEL, CASTELO** and **GALÉ** – spread back from small cove beaches with craggy, eroded rock faces, each place dominated by villa developments. At Praia de Galé is one of the Algarve's most exclusive hotels, the small, Moorish *Estalagem Vila Joya* (☎089/59 17 95; ⑦), which sits right above the beach and includes dinner in its (extremely steep) prices.

Immediately **east of Albufeira**, ochre-red cliffs divide the coastline into a series of bays and beaches, all reached on local buses (6–9 daily) from the bus station. You can walk to the first, **PRAIA DA OURA**, just 2km from Albufeira, by heading up the steps at the end of Avenida 25 de Abril and following the road out of town; signposts point you down to the beach after 25 minutes. This, though, has been extensively developed and you might want to push on by bus to **OLHOS DE ÁGUA**, 7km further east, an erstwhile fishing village with a smaller beach (and *La Cigale* restaurant; see above). If this, too, is crowded, you can walk beyond it to other more isolated coves.

At **PRAIA DA FALÉSIA**, 10km east of Albufeira, and twenty minutes away by bus, the character of the coastline changes to produce one long tremendous stretch of sand, backed by unbroken red cliffs. Just before Falésia, the bus passes through Aldeia das Açoteias, a bewildering chalet and villa complex, from where four daily buses depart for Vilamoura and Quarteira (see p.458).

Inland: São Bartolomeu de Messines and Alte

If you have transport, you can explore further **inland**, though you're not going to get much off the beaten track. Twenty kilometres to the north, the small town of **SÃO BARTOLOMEU DE MESSINES** preserves a sixteenth-century parish church, remodelled in Baroque style and incorporating interior columns decorated with twisted stone rope. There are buses here from Albufeira, Portimão and Silves, with enough services to provide for a day-trip.

From São Bartolomeu, it's 18km southwest to Silves, one possible lunch stop, or only about half that to the pretty village of **ALTE**, to the east, along the winding N124. Tacked across the hillside, a series of narrow, cobbled, mostly pedestrian streets lead up to the Fonte Grande, where there's a small rocky pool, artificially pumped full of water, a stream and an old mill, now converted into a restaurant that caters largely to the "safari" tours that stream out of Albufeira in jeeps into the surrounding countryside in search of the "real" Portugal. Notices by the water warn "No Fishing, Swimming or Washing", though you'd be hard pushed to attempt any in the first place. You can eat better at the *Café Central*, next to the church, back in the centre; and there are **rooms** available at the supermarket, close to the *fonte*, but no earthly reason to stay.

West towards Portimão

Heading west from Albufeira along the main N125, you'll pass through **PORCHES**, about halfway between Alcantarilha and Lagoa. This is where the most famous of the Algarve's hand-made **pottery** comes from. Thick, chunky and hand-painted, it has a good, heavy feel, and if you're looking for thoroughly impractical and ridiculously cheap presents to take home, this is the place to stop. Further on, **LAGOA** is best known for its wine; tours of the vineyards are arranged through local tourist offices.

Armação de Pêra and Praia da Marinha

Off the main road, down on the coast, is the resort of **ARMAÇÃO DE PÊRA**, which claims the largest beach in the Algarve (not a unique claim in these parts) and boasts caves and strange rock formations to the west, around which there are daily boat trips in the summer. It's not the greatest-looking of resorts by any means; modern buildings and apartments straggle along the town's main through-road, tempered only by the terraced gardens and cafés overlooking the central part of the sands. The remains of the town's fortified **walls** are at the eastern end of the seafront road; a terrace in front of a little white chapel provides sweeping views. The town **beach** is fine but if things are terribly crowded, head east along the beach for thirty minutes or so as far as the *Restaurante Salgados*, right on the sands and serving sardines and grilled fish and chicken – it's usually fairly quiet this far out.

There are good things to report about **Praia da Marinha**, too, reached from a turning south between Porches and Lagoa, 8km west of Armação (no bus services). A path leads from a parking area on the clifftop down to an immaculate sandy beach with a string of secluded coves, beautifully warm sea even in winter, and relatively few people with whom to share it. There's a café of uncertain hours on the sand by the path.

Practicalities

Armação de Pêra's **bus terminal** is at the eastern end of the town and there are regular services from Albufeira, Portimão and Silves. Walk up a block to the beach, at the fishing boats, and then head to the right along the seafront road, which changes its name two or three times as it makes for the centre. The **turismo** is along here, around ten minutes' walk from the bus station (summer Mon–Sat 9am–7pm, Sun 9.30am–12.30pm & 2–5.30pm; winter Mon–Sat 9am–1pm & 2.30–5pm; ☎082/31 21 45), and is good for maps and accommodation information.

For **private rooms**, ask at *O Serol* restaurant, Rua da Praia (☎082/31 21 46; ④), overlooking the beach near the fishing boats – you'll pass it on the way in from the bus station – or at the butcher's shop, *Talho Caixinha* (②), a couple of blocks back from here at the junction of Rua Dr. José António dos Santos and Rua Vasco da Gama. If you want something more upmarket, look no further than the *Hotel Garbe* (☎082/31 51 94, fax 31 51 02; ⑦) – just up the seafront road from the turismo – which has a pool and terrace overlooking the beach and breakfast included in the price. The nearest **campsite**, *Praia da Armacão de Pera* (☎082/31 22 60, fax 31 53 79), is out of the centre, a kilometre back up the N269-1, towards the highway.

There are countless **bars and restaurants**, all with more or less the same menus. For a bit more of a dining experience, two places that stand out are the *O Serol* restaurant itself, which sees a fair amount of local people tucking into its daily fish specials; and *A Santola*, in Largo 25 de Abril – adjacent to the old walls and terrace – which serves more expensive seafood accompanied by fine views; expect to pay 3000$00 plus here.

Carvoeiro and Estômbar

Further to the west, the small resort of **CARVOEIRO** can be reached by bus from Lagoa. Cut into the red sea cliffs, it remains quite an attractive place, despite a line of villa-apartments draped across the surrounding hills. The beach, however, is much too small to cope with the summer tourist influx, and rooms are virtually out of the question in high season. The resort also has quite a number of bars and restaurants, a tourist office situated on the beach, and boats offering fishing or beach trips.

Accessible by the coast road, a kilometre east, are the impressive rock formations of **Algar Seco**, where the cliffs form dramatic overhangs above narrow beaches – though there's a monstrous hotel a little further along. By way of contrast, a few kilometres inland is **ESTÔMBAR** (a stop for slow trains on the Algarve line), an unremarkable little town that was the birthplace of the eleventh-century Moorish poet Ibn Ammãr. The town straggles down a steep hill in a confusion of narrow lanes – nothing very special, though at least you feel you're in Portugal.

Portimão, Praia da Rocha and around

Portimão is one of the largest towns on the Algarve, with a population of more than thirty thousand. It has made its living from fishing since pre-Roman times and with its site on the estuary of the Rio Arade, remains today a sprawling port, a major sardine-canning centre, and a base for the construction industries spawned by the tourist boom. Most visitors are just here for a day's shopping, taking time out from the resort of **Praia da Rocha**, 3km south of Portimão. This keeps a highly distinct identity of its own as a fairly upmarket resort. Just across the estuary to the east of Portimão is the workaday town of **Ferragudo**, which has a much smaller and less fancy beach. The coast road west of Praia da Rocha, towards Lagos, has been engulfed by a series of massive and graceless tourist developments of very little interest; only **Alvor** retains any of its original charm at all.

Portimão

As a town, **PORTIMÃO** is fairly undistinguished – most of the older buildings were destroyed in the 1755 earthquake – and it is pedestrianized shopping streets and graceless concrete high-rises that dominate. The mildewed **Igreja Matriz**, rebuilt after the earthquake, could do with a lick of paint, though the encircling streets are pleasant enough, filled with shops catering to the day-trippers – selling lace, shoes, jewellery, ceramics and wicker goods. However, the best part of town is undoubtedly the riverfront gardens, with their outdoor cafés, and fishing **harbour** lined with open-air restaurants, serving grilled sardine lunches. Indeed, the streets just back from here – off Largo da Barca – are Portimão's oldest: narrow, cobbled and with more than a hint of their fishing quarter past. Other reasons to come to town are the huge **market** on the first Monday of each month, held on the Estrada Velha de Praia da Rocha just out of town; and the **flea market** on the morning of the first and third Sunday of each month, which spreads along Avenida São João de Deus.

Practicalities

The **train station** is inconveniently located at the northern tip of town but the bus runs every 45 minutes (Mon–Fri) into the centre; a taxi costs about 600$00 or it's a fifteen-minute walk. **Buses** (including those to and from Praia da Rocha) pull up much more centrally, in the streets around the Largo do Dique, close to the river, from where it's a five-minute walk past the riverside gardens to the **quayside**, which stretches as far as the bridge over to Ferragudo. There's a **post office** in the main Praça Manuel Teixeira Gomes; and the Algarve's only **British consulate** further up the quayside at Largo Francisco A. Mauricio 7-1° (☎082/41 78 00).

The **turismo** at the top of Largo 1° de Dezembro (Mon & Fri 9.30am–12.30pm & 2–7pm, Tues–Thurs 9.30am–7pm, Sat & Sun 9.30am–12pm & 2–5.30pm; ☎082/236 95) might at least point you in the direction of **accommodation**, but it's scarcely worth staying when much nicer Praia da Rocha, Silves or Lagos are so close. Still, if you do get stuck, the better-value options include the *Residencial O Pátio*, Rua Dr. João Vitorino Mealha 3 (☎ & fax 082/242 88; ④), virtually adjacent

PORTIMÃO

ACCOMMODATION
1 Roma
2 O Pátio
3 Arabi

RESTAURANTS
A Dona Barca
B Bom Appetit
C Sateria Sambal
D Casa Ingles

0   50 m

to the turismo, or the spick-and-span *Pensão Arabi*, on Praça Manuel Teixeira Gomes 13 (☎082/260 06, fax 260 07; ④), the main riverside square. Another nice choice nearby is the *Residencial Roma*, at Rua Júdice Fialho 34 (☎ & fax 082/238 21; ④).

For **drinks**, *Casa Inglesa* in the main riverside praça is a thoroughly pleasant place with a bit of character (and a new cybercafé) – unlike any of the dismal "English pubs" which infest the town. Their offerings of steak pie, liver and onions and poor British beer are especially lame when you consider that any of the stalls that line the quayside, underneath the bridge, will serve half a dozen huge, charcoal-grilled sardines, with a plate of chips and half a bottle of the local wine for around 1000$00. On the other side of the road from the stalls, off Largo da Barca, there are a few very inexpensive workers' *tascas*, as well as some more elaborate fish **restaurants**, such as *Dona Barca*, in Largo da Barca. Otherwise, try the friendly *Bom Appetite Restaurant*, Rua Júdice Fialho 21, which serves authentic Portuguese cooking, including a splendid *arroz de marisco*. Or there's always the *Sateria Sambal*, Rua Santa Isabel 14 (closed Thurs in winter), serving a nice range of Indonesian dishes.

Praia da Rocha

PRAIA DA ROCHA, five minutes' south of Portimão by bus, was one of the first Algarve tourist developments and it's easy to see why. The **beach** is one of the most beautiful on the entire coast: a wide expanse of sand framed by jagged sea cliffs and the walls of an old fort built in 1691, the **Fortaleza da Santa Caterina**, that once protected the mouth of the River Arade. The fort itself now houses a café-restaurant, whose terrace offers splendid views at sunset – beach and ocean on one side, Ferragudo and river on the other. Despite the high-rise hotels, discos, sports complex and casino, the rest of Praia da Rocha is more appealing than many other Algarve resorts. Simply because it was one of the first strands to be developed, it looks less of a building site than most, and here and there among the hotel blocks sit *fin-de-siècle* villas that testify to the resort's rather upmarket reputation. Most of the development lies channelled in a strip just two blocks wide, with the beach reached down steep steps from the elevated main street, Avenida Tomás Cabreira; from virtually every bar, restaurant and hotel terrace, all the views are of the sands and sea. It isn't particularly Portuguese of course – there's nothing in town and little in the food offered in the restaurants to lead you to think it is – but it's thoroughly attractive all the same.

Arrival and information

Bus connections from Portimão are excellent, with a bus every fifteen to thirty minutes (7.30am–11.30pm); in Praia da Rocha it stops in front of the *Hotel da*

PRAIA DA ROCHA

ACCOMMODATION
❶ Hotel Jupiter
❷ Hotel Da Rocha
❸ Pensão Oceano
❹ Solar Penguin
❺ Hotel Bela Vista
❻ Hotel Algarve
❼ Hotel Oriental

RESTAURANTS
Ⓐ Safari
Ⓑ La Dolce Vita
Ⓒ La Cabassa

0   150 m

Rocha (see below), on Avenida Tomás Cabreira, and again by the fort. You can pick up the **return bus to Portimão** from here, or from the stop on Rua Eng. José de Bivar, around the back of the *Hotel da Rocha*. If you plan to do much to-ing and fro-ing between Rocha and Portimão, buy a block of ten tickets from the kiosk in Portimão, which will save you around forty percent.

The **turismo** (summer Mon–Fri 9.30am–7pm, Sat & Sun 9.30am–5.30pm; winter Mon & Fri 9.30am–12.30pm & 2–7pm, Tues–Thurs 9.30am–7pm, Sat & Sun 9.30am–12.30pm & 2–5.30pm; ☎082/41 91 32), is also along the main Avenida Tomás Cabreira, near the fort.

Accommodation

Finding accommodation is rarely a problem; ask at the turismo for an array of **private rooms** to rent, or try one of the following **pensões** or (expensive) **hotels**. On the cliffs above the beach you'll find the eccentric *Solar Penguin* (☎082/243 08; ⑤; closed mid-Nov to mid-Jan), just off the main avenue on Rua António Feu – a delightful, old *pensão* with a few rooms overlooking the sea. The showers are hopeless but the place is a joy; in the antiquated lounge look out for the portrait of Queen Elizabeth which was painted by the late husband of the owner. Half the price but not as entertaining, and without the sea views, is the *Pensão Oceano* on Avda. Tomás Cabreira (☎082/243 09; ③). Of the **hotels** on Avda. Tomás Cabreira – all of which offer fine, sea-facing rooms, pools and heavily reduced winter room rates – the *Oriental* (☎082/41 30 00, fax 41 34 13; ⑦) wins hands down for its design, a Moorish-influenced extravaganza of arches, domes and gardens. Other main street choices include the *Hotel da Rocha* (☎082/240 81, fax 41 59 88; ⑦); the luxurious five-star *Algarve* (☎082/41 50 01, fax 41 51 99; ⑦); and the *Jupiter* (☎082/41 50 41, fax 41 53 19; ⑥). However, the most stylish place to stay is the seafront *Hotel Bela Vista* (☎082/240 55, fax 41 53 69; ⑦), a pseudo-Moorish mansion built in 1903 as a wedding gift by the wealthy Magalhães family; the interior is an exquisite mixture of carved woods, stained glass, and yellow, white and blue azulejos.

Eating, drinking and nightlife

Restaurants are plentiful and the half a dozen down on the beach mean that you don't have to leave the sands during the day. Up in town, the *Safari*, next to the *Solar Penguin*, overlooks the beach and serves mainly Portuguese dishes, a few with an Angolan influence – it's around 3000–4000$00 for a good meal, though you could eat for a lot less. The *Penguin* itself has a pleasing terrace-restaurant, serving freshly made dishes and crêpes. Towards the fort on the avenue, *La Dolce Vita* is owned and run by Italians, so the home-made pasta and pizzas are worth eating for once; while further along in a quieter part of town, *La Cabassa*, next to the turismo, has stir-fried Asian dishes and some fairly adventurous Portuguese meals.

For a civilized **drink**, the bar of the *Bela Vista* is open to the public (8.30pm–midnight). More rowdy venues include *Farmers* behind the *Jupiter* hotel and several on the avenida, among them: *On the Rocks* disco bar; *Tropicool*, which spills out onto the street after midnight; and *Shaker Bar* (Happy Hour 4–8pm) – all are loud and libidinous in varying degrees, at various times of the day or night. The *Katedral* **disco** and *Nicho* bar both share the same horrible futuristic building, next to the *Penguin*.

Ferragudo

FERRAGUDO, facing Portimão across the estuary, and connected by a regular bus service (hourly 7.30am–7.30pm), is very different in character from Praia da Rocha. Stuck on the side of a hill, it's a rundown little place of narrow streets and tiny houses that has only recently begun to be dressed up for tourists. It sprawls around a fort – the partner to that in Praia da Rocha – built in the sixteenth century to defend Portimão against attack. The town has a couple of small *pensões* and a few private rooms for rent through the local bars. There are a couple of lively bars and an excellent **restaurant**, *A Lanterna* (closed Sun), which is to be found just across the bridge from Portimão; the smoked swordfish is particularly tempting.

The Ferragudo **beach** is about a kilometre to the south of town. It is popular in a small-scale way, with a windsurfing school and a scattering of restaurant-bars. A large **campsite** (☎082/46 11 21) slouches next to the road ten minutes further to the south of the beach.

Alvor and Quinta da Rocha

Much of the appeal of the ancient port of **ALVOR**, 6km west of Praia da Rocha, has been washed away under a tide of tourists from the surrounding hotels and holiday villages: the town's narrow streets and its multitude of bars and restaurants can hardly cope. Whitewashed houses and lovely views of the estuary are the last vestiges of Alvor's charm. Nonetheless, the **beach** is enormous and, if it's a bit on the dull side, at least you can escape the crowds. The town's **turismo** is at Rua Dr. Frederico Ramos Mendes 4 (☎082/45 81 09). In season, **rooms** at Alvor are hard to come by, but there's a **campsite**: the *Campismo Dourado* (☎082/45 91 78), near the beach. The beach **café** *Rosamar* does good fish and basic meals. Back from the beach, try the *São João* restaurant on Rua Infante D. Henrique, or the more upmarket *Vagabondo*, Rua Frederico Mendes, which has a tree-filled terrace.

The **Quinta da Rocha nature reserve** lies in the peninsula between the mouths of the rivers Alvor and Odiáxere, northwest of Alvor's huge beach. It is an extensive area which, in the parts not given over to citrus and almond groves, consists of copses, salt marshes, sandy spits and estuarine mud flats, forming a wide range of habitats for different plants and animals – including twenty-two species of **wading bird**. A Christian environmental group, A Rocha, runs a bird-ringing programme from a field centre known as Cruzinha, in the middle of the reserve. The centre also has limited full-board accommodation, in shared rooms, though as its aims are to increase the awareness in Portugal of the environment and Christianity, precedence is given to Portuguese visitors. Access to Cruzinha is from a turning south at Mexilhoeira Grande on the coastal N125 highway.

Silves

Eighteen kilometres northeast of Portimão, **SILVES** – the medieval residence and capital of the Moorish kings of the al-Gharb – is one of the few inland towns in this province that really merits a detour. It has a superb castle and a highly dramatic approach, with its red ring of walls gradually revealing their course as you emerge from the wooded hills. Under the Moors, Silves was a place of grandeur, described in contemporary accounts as "of shining brightness" within its three dark circuits of guarding walls. Such glories and civilized spendours came to an end, however, in 1189, with the arrival of **Sancho I**, at the head of a mixed army of Portuguese and Crusaders. Sancho himself was a devout king, at least by the standards of his day, but, desperately in need of extra fighting force, had recruited a rabble of "large and odious" northerners, who had already been expelled from the holy shrine of Saint James of Compostela for their irreligious behaviour. The army arrived at Silves toward the end of June and the thirty thousand Moors retreated to the citadel. There they remained through the long, hot summer, sustained by huge water cisterns and granaries, until September, when, the water exhausted, they opened negotiations.

Sancho was ready to compromise, but the Crusaders had been recruited by the promise of plunder, and were not prepared to accept the king's financial inducements to forgo the pleasure of wrecking the town. The gates were opened after Sancho had negotiated guarantees for the inhabitants' personal safety and goods; all were brutally ignored by the Crusaders, who duly ransacked the town, killing some six thousand Moors in the process. Silves passed back into Moorish hands two years later, but by then the town had been irreparably weakened, and it finally fell to Christian forces in 1249.

The Town

The **Moorish Fortress** (daily 9am–7pm; 250$00) remains the focal point of Silves, dominating the town centre with its impressively complete set of sandstone walls and detached towers. The interior is a bit disappointing: aside from the great vaulted water cisterns that still serve the town, there's nothing left of the old citadel, which is planted with modern gardens. However, you can circuit the walls for impressive views over the town and surrounding hills. There's a "traditional festival" held here on some Friday and Saturday nights in July, and a lively annual **beer festival** in June.

Silves's cathedral, or **Sé** (daily 8.30am–6.30pm, closes at 1pm on Sun), sits below the fortress, built on the site of the Grand Mosque. Flanked by broad Gothic towers, it has a suitably defiant, military appearance, though the Great Earthquake and centuries of impoverished restoration have left their mark within.

Below the Sé, in Rua das Portas de Loulé, is the town's **Museu Arqueologia** (daily 10am–7pm; 300$00). It's engaging enough, despite a lack of English-language labelling, and romps through the history of Silves from the year dot to the sixteenth century with displays of local archeological finds. At the centre of the museum is an Arab water cistern, left *in situ*, which boasts a ten-metre-deep well. Strolling around the rest of Silves is a pleasure. There's a **market** on the riverfront, near the narrow thirteenth-century bridge. This is a fine place to sit out at at one of the grill-cafés (see p.471) and watch life go by.

Practicalities

The **train station** – an easy approach from either Lagos or Faro – lies two kilometres out of town; there is a connecting bus, but it's a pleasant walk if you're not weighed down with luggage. Arriving by **bus**, you'll be dropped on the main road, next to the market near the riverfront at the foot of town.

The **turismo** on Rua 25 de Abril (Mon–Fri 9.30am–12.30pm & 2–7pm, Sat & Sun 9.30am–12.30pm & 2–5.30pm; ☎082/44 22 55), in the heart of the town, will help arrange **private rooms**. Recommended are those with Isabel Maria da Silva at Rua Cândido dos Reis 36 (☎082/44 26 67; ②), which are spotless and share the use of a kitchen and a little outdoor terrace. Alternatively, there are a couple of **pensões**, including the comfortable old *Residencial Sousa*, Rua Samora Barros 17 (☎082/44 25 02; ③), and, across the river, the very pleasant *Restaurante Residencial Ponte Romana* (☎082/44 32 75; ④). Just over 5km out of town, on the road to São Bartolomeu de Messines, the *Quinta do Rio*, Sitio São Estevão, Apartado 217 (☎082/44 55 28, fax 44 55 28; ⑤), is a **country inn** with half a dozen en-suite rooms and garden set within a farm. Breakfast is included in the price and dinner can be arranged too. Closer to town, though on the same road (after the Galp service station), the *Vila Sodre* (☎082/44 34 41; ④) also has rooms and local wines and food on offer.

For **eating** in town, the *Restaurante Marisqueira Rui*, Rua Comendador Vilarinho (closed Tues), continues to attract locals and tourists from all over the Algarve; if you manage to squeeze in – and you should try – order shellfish, the restaurant's speciality. At the other end of the price scale, and just as enjoyable in its way, is the *Ú Monchiqueiro Casa de Pasto*, the best of a handful of grill-cafés on the riverfront road in front of the market. Sit outside and tuck into *piri-piri* chicken, fries, salad and wine for 1500$00. The *Café Inglês*, by the fortress, sells delicious home-made snacks, ice cream and fruit juices, as well as full meals, and also has seats outside; while *Café Rosa*, in the Praça do Município, serves drinks and cakes all day (closed Sun).

Inland to the Serra de Monchique

Nine buses a day leave Portimão for the 24-kilometre, ninety-minute journey north to **Monchique** via **Caldas de Monchique**. Once clear of Portimão's ugly suburbs, the main road crosses the coastal plain, flanked by endless orchards of apples, pears, figs, almonds, pomegranates and citrus fruits. At Porto de Lagos the road divides, east to Silves and north into the foothills of the **Serra de Monchique**, a green and wooded mountain range of cork, chestnut and eucalyptus that provides the western Algarve with a natural northern boundary. It is ideal **hiking country**, or – with a bike or car – a superb route to take if you want to cut across afterwards to the wilder reaches of the western Algarve coast.

Caldas de Monchique

CALDAS DE MONCHIQUE, set in a ravine and surrounded by thick woods, has been a celebrated spa since Roman times. In 1495 Dom João II came here to take the waters (though he nevertheless died soon afterwards in Alvor), and in the nineteenth century the town became a favourite resort of the Spanish bourgeoisie. A casino from these times still stands in the main square, serving now as an excellent **handicraft centre** (summer daily 9.30am–8pm), surrounded by lovely, fading nineteenth-century buildings. The setting is as beautiful as any in the country, though the tiny village's peace and quiet is shattered daily by the busloads of day-trippers who stop for a wander around and a cup of coffee. At times, the buses queue nose-to-tail on the way into the village.

The modern Thermal Hospital sits below the main square, on the edge of a ravine, flaunting its well-kept gardens; below is the ugly Oficina de Engarrafamento where the famous water is bottled for sale around the country. But at least this maintains the town's tradition, and Caldas remains an active spa rather than being simply quaint. Climbing up from the spa, behind the square, you can follow the stream to sit under giant eucalyptus trees and picnic. Take along some of the local arbutus berry-derived *aguardente* (fire water), on sale in the handicraft centre, which nicely complements the spring water.

The only reasonably priced **accommodation** in town is at the *Albergaria do Lageado* (☎082/91 26 16, fax 91 13 10; ④; open May–Oct), which has a pool and garden, and an excellent restaurant where you can eat for around 2500$00, and the *Albergaria Velha* (☎082/922 04, fax 91 39 20; ④), just off the square. A good place to **eat** is the *1692*, on the square, which serves up a range of Algarve fare in its cavern-like 1960s' interior; if you just want a **drink** you can either sit at its outside tables and watch the world go by or try the wine-bodega *O Tasco*, opposite the *Albergaria Velha*. Out of season you may well find most of these places closed.

Not all the **buses** from Portimão call into the centre of Caldas, stopping instead on the main road just out of town before continuing up to Monchique. Note, too, that there's a twice-daily summer tourist service from Albufeira (with connections from Vilamoura, Quarteira and Faro) via Silves.

Monchique and around

MONCHIQUE, 6km to the north of Caldas de Monchique, and 300m higher up the range, is a small market town whose huge market on the second Friday of each month is famous for its smoked hams, furniture and superabundance of emergency vehicles which are forced to double-park in the main square. There's not a great deal else to see, but it's a busy town and makes a nice enough excursion. Of the buildings, the most impressive is the **Igreja Matriz**, the parish church, up a steep cobbled street from the main square, which has a Manueline porch and, inside, a little chapel with a facade of azulejos. The most evocative sight, though, is the ruined seventeenth-century monastery of **Nossa Senhora do Desterro**. Only a roofless shell of this Franciscan foundation survives, apparently quite uncared for, but it's in a great position overlooking the town and shows a beautiful blend of classical Renaissance facade with Moorish-influenced vaulting.

Buses arrive at the terminal in the main square at the bottom of town where Monchique's new **turismo** is located (Mon–Fri 9.30am–12.30pm & 2–5.30pm, Sat 9.30am–12.30pm; ☎082/91 11 89). There are a couple of **places to stay** in town (though it's difficult to see why you'd need to). First choice is the very welcoming *Estrela de Monchique*, Rua do Poco Fundo 46 (☎082/91 31 11; ③), a stone's throw to the right of the bus terminal. Otherwise, the *Bela Vista* (☎082/91 25 81; ③), in the main square, is cheaper but noisier and a bit unappealing. Better by far are the **inns** on the road up to Fóia (see p.473), though you'll need transport to reach them: the *Estalagem Abrigo da Montanha*, on Estrada da Fóia (☎ & fax 082/91 36 60; ⑤), has a lovely garden and views as well as a fine dining room. Nearby, on the same road, there's terrace seating at the *Teresinha* restaurant, where great grills are served.

Monchique itself also has a handful of **restaurants** which soak up the passing tourist trade. *Restaurante A Charrete* on Rua Samora Gil is recommended, while

Café Montanha, Rua do Revez Quente, is fairly inexpensive, serving typical Algarvian meat and fish dishes.

Fóia

Fóia, 8km west of Monchique, is – at nearly 900m – the highest of the Serra's peaks; note that there are no bus services here. At the top there's a concrete obelisk, a radio tower, a few stalls selling knick-knacks and knitwear (it can be cool up here), a *pensão*-café, *O Planalto* (③), and a hotel, the *Estalagem de Santo António* (☎082/91 21 58, fax 91 28 78; ④). There are also lots of bus tours, all attracted by the panoramic view of the Algarve which takes in Portimão, Lagos, the foothills stretching to the Barragem da Bravura, and Cabo de São Vicente. The poet Robert Southey claimed to have caught a glimpse of the hills of Sintra, beyond Lisbon, but that must have been one of those legendary "clear days" – or maybe the air is never as clear now as it was in 1801.

Picota

Reaching 770m, **Picota** comes second in altitude to Fóia, though it's much more interesting in terms of its botany, and easier to reach without transport. You can reach the peak from Monchique in around one and a half hours, a walk that takes in cork trees (and cork collection points), eucalyptus and pines, peach, lemon and orange orchards, and even wild goats scurrying about the heights. At the top there's nothing save a rickety watchtower occupied by a solitary guardian with a pair of binoculars. From here you can see the coastline stretching all the way to Sagres, and take in another magnificent view of the Monchique mountain range.

West to the coast

Back down the road from Monchique towards Caldas, the minor N267 cuts west towards the coast, passing through **MARMELETE** after 14km. There are two buses a day from Monchique, but no real point in coming since, unless you're lucky enough to flag down a lift, you won't get any further – and it's another 20km to Aljezur (p.486) and ten more to the coast beyond that. In a car, though, it's a fine route, heading through tranquil countryside before swinging down through the hills and forests to the west coast.

North to Santa Clara

Heading north from Monchique, the N266 runs through forests of eucalyptus for 20km before reaching the border with the Alentejo province, and then around 20km further on arrives at the huge **Barragem de Santa Clara** – the largest artificial dam in Portugal. After here, the route cuts across the flatlands of the Alentejo to a fork with turnings for Odemira and the west coast, or Beja and the eastern Alentejo. Just west of the dam, **SANTA CLARA-A-VELHA** (1–2 daily buses from Monchique) makes a pleasant break in the journey, a compact little town with a Roman bridge, rooms and a few café-restaurants where you can get a meal of fresh fish from the lake. There's a **pousada** here, the *Santa Clara* (☎083/98 250, fax 083/984 02; ⑥), a tiny place close to the dam, with just six rooms and a swimming pool. Alternatively, there's the truly quiet, relaxing hideaway of *Quinta do Barranco da Estrada*, on the opposite side of the dam and 12km from Santa Clara, just off the Cortelorique road (☎ & fax 083/93 39 01; full board ⑦). During the day you can mess about the lake before enjoying the evening meal prepared by the proprietors. You'll need to book ahead for both places.

Lagos

LAGOS is one of the most ancient settlements in the Algarve, founded by the Phoenicians, who were attracted to its superb natural harbour. Under the Moors it became an important trading post until its reconquest by Christian armies in 1241. Its attractions today are less the historical associations – though there are a couple of fine churches and a circuit of medieval walls – than the fact that it remains a real town: a fishing port and market centre with a sense of independence and a life of its own. It has, of course, over the last two decades, also developed into a major resort (complete with huge new marina), and attracts the whole gamut of visitors, from backpackers to moneyed second-homers. They come for some of the best beaches of the whole Algarve coast: to the east of the town is a long sweep of sand – Meia Praia – where there's space even in summer, while to the west is an extraordinary network of coves, sheltered by cliffs, pierced by tunnels and grottoes, and studded by weird and extravagantly weathered outcrops of purple-tinted rock.

Arrival, information and accommodation

Lagos is the western terminal of the Algarve railway line and its **train station** is across the river, fifteen minutes' walk from the centre via the new swing bridge in the marina; taxis are usually available if you can't face the walk. The **bus station** is a bit closer in, a block back from the main estuary road, Avenida dos Descobrimentos, and almost opposite the bridge to the train station.

The **turismo** is in Largo Marquês de Pombal (summer Mon 9.30am–12.30pm & 2–7pm, Tues–Thurs 9.30am–7pm, Fri 9.30am–12.30pm & 2–7pm, Sat & Sun 9.30am–12.30pm & 2–5.30pm; winter Mon–Fri 9.30am–12.30pm & 2–5.30pm, Sat 9am–noon; ☎082/76 30 31), which is the square adjacent to the central Praça Gil Eanes. It can help with booking private rooms and apartments, as well as dishing out maps, leaflets and timetables.

Accommodation

Most of the town's **hotels** and **pensões** are fully booked through the summer and, unless you turn up very early in the day, your only chance of a bed will be a **room** in a private house, for which you'll pay 3000–5000$00 for a double, depending on the time of year. The tourist office will phone around and try to find you a space, if there's anything left on their books; arriving early in the day you'll probably be met by touts at the bus or train stations. It's a good idea to take whatever's going (as long as it's central), and look round later at your leisure. Out of season, or booking in advance, you could try for space at one of the established *pensões* and hotels, a selection of which are listed below. Prices are comparatively high in season; in winter, however, there are bargains to be had at many of the beach hotels west of town – ask at the tourist office for details. There's a **youth hostel** (see p.476) in town, while Lagos also has two **campsites**, both to the west of the centre, close by the Praia de Dona Ana, whose dramatic rock formations and clear waters provide a far more interesting place to relax than the more popular town beaches.

HOTELS AND PENSÕES IN TOWN

Pensão Caravela, Rua 25 de Abril 16 (☎082/76 33 61). Reasonable rooms on the town's main pedestrianized street. Doubles come with or without bath; breakfast included. ④.

Hotel de Lagos, Rua Nova da Aldeia (☎082/76 99 67, fax 76 99 20). The finest hotel in the centre and boasting a remarkable landscaped, "village-style" design – separate compounds of rooms, bars, restaurants and sports facilities joined by glassed-in corridors and walkways. There's a courtesy bus service to its own beach club at Meia Praia, too; and hefty off-season price reductions. ⑨.

Pensão Lagos-Mar, Rua Dr. Faria e Silva 13 (☎082/76 35 23, fax 76 73 24). Upmarket *pensão*, close to Praça Gil Eanes, and reliable enough for the money. ⑤.

Residencial Marazul, Rua 25 de Abril 13 (☎082/76 91 43). The better establishment on this street, but at the top end of the price scale. A few of the rooms have their own shower and terrace; and breakfast is included. ⑤.

Hotel Riomar, Rua Cândido dos Reis 83 (☎082/76 30 91, fax 76 39 27). Smart, medium-sized hotel tucked into a central street. Most rooms have a balcony – the best overlook the sea on the far side of the hotel. Breakfast included. ⑥.

Pensão Rubi Mar, Rua da Barroca 70-1° (☎082/76 31 65, fax 76 77 49). There are only nine rooms here, but if you can find space it's a treat; some rooms have sea views and breakfast is included. ④.

HOTELS AND PENSÕES AT PRAIA DE DONA ANA

Pensão Dona Ana, Praia de Dona Ana (☎082/76 23 22, fax 78 25 75). Small, white *pensão* situated at Lagos's finest beach, a 20-minute walk from town across the clifftops. In summer, you'll need to book well in advance for one of the 11 rooms. ④.

Hotel Golfinho, Praia de Dona Ana (☎082/76 99 00, fax 76 99 90). Modern hotel on the cliff set a hundred metres back from the beach. Attractive rooms, fine views and a courtesy bus into town. ⑥.

YOUTH HOSTEL

Pousada de Juventude de Lagos, Rua de Lançarote de Freitas 50 (☎ & fax 082/76 19 70). The modern youth hostel has a few double rooms with shower available (breakfast included), though you'll have to book in advance. There's a nice central courtyard too. ③.

CAMPSITES

In season a bus marked "D. Ana/Porto de Mós" runs to the sites from the bus station, while the *Imulagos* site provides its own free bus from the train station (hourly 8am–10.30pm). On foot, follow the main Sagres road around the old town and it's about ten to fifteen minutes from the Forte Ponta da Bandeira to the sites.

Parque de Campismo Imulagos (☎082/76 00 31, fax 76 00 35). The larger of the sites – huge, in fact, with good facilities, lots of shade and access to a private beach.

Campismo da Trindade (☎082/76 38 93). Marginally closer to the town and beach, and much more cramped than the *Imulagos* (though it's only half the price).

The Town

Lagos was a favoured residence of Henry the Navigator, who used the town as a base for the new African trade, to which is owed the town's least proud relic – Europe's first **slave market**, whose arcades survive alongside the old **Customs House** in the **Praça da República** near the waterfront. On the other side of this square is the church of **Santa Maria**, through whose whimsical Manueline windows the youthful Dom Sebastião is said to have roused his troops before the ill-fated Moroccan expedition of 1578. Fired up by militant Catholicism, the dream-crazed king was to perish on the battlefield of Alcácer-Quibir (modern Ksar el Kbir, between Tangier and Fez) along with almost the entire Portuguese nobility. It was a disaster that enabled the Spanish to absorb Portugal for sixty years, but it did Dom Sebastião's reputation a world of good among the aggressively devout. He's commemorated in the centre of Lagos, in **Praça Gil Eanes**, by a fantastically dreadful modern statue – pink, ridiculous and looking like a flowerpot man.

Much of the old town was devastated by the 1755 earthquake, though one rare and beautiful church that survived is the **Igreja de Santo António**. Decorated around 1715, its gilt and carved interior is wildly obsessive, every last inch filled with a private fantasy of cherubic youths struggling with animals and fish. Next door is the **Museu Municipal** (Tues–Sun 9.30am–12.30pm & 2–5pm; 300$00), worth a look if only to discover the true meaning of the word eclectic. Alongside the usual barrowloads of neolithic axeheads, pottery shards, statuary and terrible local religious art are jars containing misshapen animal foetuses, a display of models of Algarvian chimneys, stuffed animals, straw hats, lobster pots and fossils, a locked bookcase of novels, travelogues and English histories, the key to the city (literally), the 1504 town charter, and assorted muskets, swords and cannonballs.

The Praça da República, and the waterfront Avenida dos Descobrimentos, are the best vantage points for the remains of Lagos's once impregnable **walls** and fortifications, which include the squat seventeenth-century **Forte Ponta da Bandeira** (Tues–Sat 10am–1pm & 2–6pm, Sun 10am–1pm; 300$00), guarding the entrance to the harbour.

The beaches

The promontory **south** of Lagos is fringed by eroded cliff faces that shelter a series of postage stamp-sized cove-beaches. All are within easy walking distance of the old town, though the beach tracks are increasingly confused by a multitude of paths leading to the hotels and campsites. In addition, the concentration of resort hotels near the beaches means that you may find the least crowded strand is the **town beach** itself, just beyond the Forte Ponta da Bandeira.

The easiest access on foot to the **cove-beaches** to the south and west is to follow the Avenida dos Descobrimentos up the hill (toward Sagres) and turn left just opposite the fire station, where you see signs to the tiny **Praia do Pinhão**. This is the first of the coves – around a twenty-minute walk from town. Five minutes further, across the cliffs, is the **Praia de Dona Ana** – one of the most photogenic of all the Algarve's beaches, with a restaurant, the *Mirante*, built into the cliffs.

Beyond here, despite the jostling hotels, you can follow a path around the cliffs and coast to **Praia do Camilo** – sometimes a bit less crowded – and right to the **Ponta da Piedade**, the point, where a palm-bedecked lighthouse makes a great vantage point for the sunset.

Beyond the point, the coast sweeps west again and you can continue to follow paths close to the cliff's edge to the beach of **Porto do Mós**, another 45 minutes' walk away, where the *Campimar* bar-restaurant overlooks the sands. The path then moves on as far as Luz (see p.480), another hour away; it's a splendid stretch, high above the ocean, until the obelisk above Luz comes into sight, from where you scramble down the hillside and into the town.

To the **east** of Lagos, flanked by the railway line, is **Meia Praia**, a vast tract of sand that extends for 4km to the delta of the rivers Odiáxere and Arão. A regular **bus service** leaves from the Avenida dos Descobrimentos and travels the length of the beach; alternatively, there's a seasonal **ferry** from Avenida dos Descobrimentos across the river, from which point the beach is a short walk away.

Eating

The centre of Lagos is packed with **restaurants**, most found along ruas Afonso d'Almeida and 25 de Abril. Where the Avenida dos Descobrimentos meets Rua das Portas de Portugal, there's a diverting **fish and vegetable market** (Mon–Sat mornings), in front of which is a line of good fish restaurants. Menus are of a similar standard and price almost everywhere, though Lagos does also have a couple of highly regarded places where it's worth pushing the boat out at least once.

Alpendre, Rua António Barbosa Viana 17. One of the oldest – and more formal – restaurants in the Algarve, serving memorable smoked swordfish and decent *arroz de marisco*. The crêpes are still the best reason to come though – flambéed at your table. At least 4000$00.

O Cantinho Algarvio, Rua Afonso d'Almeida 17. Popular for its wide range of modestly priced Algarvian food. Around 2500$00. Closed Sun lunch.

A Capoeira, Rua 25 de Abril 76. Tiny but accommodating restaurant ("The Chicken Coop") serving a mixture of Portuguese and Continental food – good fish and a fine Mozambican pork dish. Around 3000$00.

Casa do Zé, Avda. dos Descobrimentos. On the corner with the market, this does filling fish dishes at very fair prices. Very much a locals' choice at lunchtime, with the outdoor seating soaking up a brisk trade – daily specials at 800–1000$00.

Dom Sebastião, Rua 25 de Abril 20–22. Arguably the town's finest restaurant, with outdoor seating, a traditional, cobbled-floor interior, good seafood, and a fabulous selection of appetizers. A full meal runs to about 4000$00, though with careful selection you could get away for less.

O Franguinho, Rua Luís de Azevedo 25. Grilled chicken joint with a first-floor dining room – fine greasy chicken and daily specials, too. Good value at under 1500$00.

Galeão, Rua de Laranjeira 1. A little hidden away, but usually packed out with people who recognize good food when they taste it; you may have to wait for a table. All the Algarvian classics and superb steaks at eminently reasonable prices. Under 3500$00.

Italia, Rua Garrett 26–28, off Praça Luís Camões. Bright, cheery restaurant run by Italians: pizzas come from a wood-burning oven; there's Italian wine, pasta and a full menu besides. Around 2000$00 for a pizza or pasta meal, more if you eat the meat/fish specials. Closed Mon.

A Lagosteira, Rua Iº de Maio 20. Upmarket, blue-tiled restaurant with dishes at 1800$00, nice daily specials and pleasant staff.

O Patinhos, Rua Luís de Azevedo 10–12. Friendly, backstreet dining room, basic and local, with most dishes under 1000$00 and cheap wine. Try the baby squid in its own ink. Closed Sun.

Restaurante Piri Piri, Rua Afonso d'Almeida 10. Fresh fish served daily, as well as the spicy chicken dish that gives the restaurant its name. Fairly inexpensive, given its central location, and with a pretty interior. Around 2500–3000$00.

Vai e Volta, Rua Infante de Sagres 40. Stylish little place with some suprises on the menu – bean stew, prawn curry and other ethnic delights. Around 2500–3000$00.

Drinking and nightlife

There are lots of **bars** around town, many of them owned by expatriates – in particular Irish and British. Cocktails are unusually popular in Lagos and measures are almost universally generous; look out for the places offering two-for-one deals and special events. Most bars stay open until at least 2am, some even later if the party is in full swing.

Cervejaria Abrigo, Rua Marquês de Pombal 2. Opposite the turismo, with outdoor tables under the orange trees – beer, cocktails, snacks and meals all day.

Eddie's Bar, Rua 25 de Abril 99. Small, friendly bar with Happy Hour 4–8pm.

Gil Vicente, Rua Gil Vicente 30. Echoing, tiled *pastelaria*-bar with staff who know their way around the vaguely indie CDs on the rack. Beer and sandwiches served to a young, local crowd.

Inoxidavel, Rua Vasco da Gama 37. Club playing alternative, indie and dance sounds four nights a week. Open until 6am; it's on the way to the bus station.

Lords Tavern, Rua António Crisogono Santos 56. Opposite the *Hotel de Lagos*, this British-style pub has live music most nights (dismal crooners – including the chef – a speciality) and sports channel TV for the big games. Open till at least 2am, more like 4am on occasions.

Mullens, Rua Cândido dos Reis 86. The most appealing late-night choice in town, this warehouse-like bar-restaurant serves excellent meals, has *vinho verde* on tap, plays jazz and soul on the sound system, and stays open until 2am.

Phoenix, Rua 5 de Outubro 11. The best club in Lagos; two dance floors play contemporary sounds. Stays open till 4am.

Roskos, Rua Cândido dos Reis 79. Down the road from *Mullens*, an Irish bar with a 7–10pm Happy Hour and fifty serious cocktails. Open till 2am.

Stones, Rua 25 de Abril 101. Split-level bar with a regular local crowd and loud rock.

Vee Jay's Bar, Trav. 1º de Maio 9, off Praça Luís de Camões. Cheap beer, more than fifty cocktails and a dartboard. Open till 2am.

Listings

Banks and exchange Banks are grouped around Praça Gil Eanes and you can exchange money in almost every travel agency, shop and general store.

Bike and motorbike rental *Eddie's Bar*, Rua 25 de Abril 99, organizes mountain bike excursions incuding picnic and evening meal; for motorbikes, Motoride, Rua José Afonso 23 (☎082/76 17 20).

Boat trips Trips around the coast are easy to arrange with the fishing boats that gather around the Forte Ponta da Bandeira.

Buses Travel information for all destinations from the bus terminal (☎082/76 29 44). Note that buses to Portimão leave from Avenida dos Descobrimentos, while buses to most other destinations make a stop along here too.

Car rental Auto Jardim, Avda. dos Descobrimentos (☎082/76 94 86); Avis, Largo das Portas de Portugal 11 (☎082/736 91); Luz Car, Largo das Portas de Portugal 10 (☎082/76 10 16).

Consulate The only British consulate in the Algarve is in Portimão (p.465), at Largo Francisco A. Maurício 7 (☎082/41 78 00). All other consulates are in Faro (see p.443) or Lisbon.

Doctor For an English-speaking doctor, call ☎082/78 98 66; you'll pay for the service.

Hospital Rua do Castelo dos Governadores, adjacent to the church of Santa Maria (☎082/76 30 34).

Police Rua General Alberto Silveira (☎082/76 26 30).

Post office Behind the town hall, just off Avenida dos Descobrimentos; open Mon–Fri 9am–6pm.

Taxis There are ranks in front of the post office or call ☎082/76 24 69 or 76 35 87.

Telephones It's easiest to make long-distance calls at the Telecom office, next to the post office (summer Mon–Fri 8.30am–10pm, Sat 9am–1pm & 5pm–midnight, Sun 6–10pm; winter Mon–Sat 8am–6pm).

Travel agency Tickets (including bus tickets) and tours from Clubalgarve, Rua Marreiros Netto 25 (☎082/76 23 37); and Tourlagos, Rua Infante de Sagres 31 (☎082/76 79 67).

Water sports There's a windsurfing school at Meia Praia (see above). For slides, pools and aquatic fun, take the bus from the bus station (around 9.30am) to the Slide & Splash theme park, N125, Vale de Deus, Estômbar (adults 2800$00, children 1900$00; ☎082/34 16 85), 1hr away. Under your own steam, entrance is 1800$00 (children 1300$00).

West to Sagres

Once one of the least spoiled parts of the Algarve, the coast **west of Lagos**, to Vila do Bispo and Sagres, is currently facing a barrage of development. Villa development along the main highway continues apace and the erstwhile small settlements on the coast itself (Luz, Burgau and Salema) are also seeing an increasing amount of construction. Among them, **Salema** – with a superb beach and still recognizable as a former fishing village – promises most.

In summer there are frequent **bus** services from Lagos to Luz and Burgau, and a regular service to Salema. Connections are less frequent during the winter, but you should always be able to get to at least one of the villages and back in a day-trip, even if it means walking to the highway on occasion to pick up the bus. You could also plan a day that involved **walking** between the villages: Burgau to Luz to Lagos, in particular, is a nice, relatively easy, stretch.

Luz

Five kilometres west of Lagos, the mass of white chalets and villas that is the resort of **LUZ** swamps the old village entirely, disgorging multitudes in summer who, in turn, swamp the fine beach. For all this, it's a handsome enough place as long as you don't mind the crowds or the commercialization. The villas are at least low-rise and many have prime sea views; there's a palm-planted beachside prom-enade; and any number of bar-restaurants with advantageous terraces. Sadly, the food everywhere is almost uniformly overpriced (and often distinctly average), though the *Restaurante Fortaleza*, above the west end of the beach, opposite the church, at least tries hard to match quality with high prices. It's the sort of place that serenades diners with Portuguese "folk music" most nights.

Unless you're booked in to Luz on a holiday, it's really not worth looking for **accommodation** here. There are rooms to be had, and doubtless the Lagos tur-ismo could dig up an apartment vacancy, but you'll do better further west. **Campers** might want to use the large luxury *Valverde* site (☎082/78 92 11), 1.5km or so from the seafront, close to the highway, with the full range of tourist facilities, but it's a charmless place.

Incidentally, the **path back to Lagos** starts at the eastern end of the beach. At the Algarve Sports Club, follow the private road uphill and make the obscenely steep scramble up to the obelisk on the cliffs, from where a gentle path careers along the tops to Porto do Mós, Ponte das Piedade and Lagos (see p.474).

Burgau

It's another five kilometres or so to **BURGAU**, another intensively developed hol-iday spot, though one which still retains vestiges of its former fishing village life. The cobbled main street, with its side alleys and terraces, retains some charm, running right through the village and tumbling down to a wide sweep of sand backed by crumbling cliffs. Out of season, it's truly attractive, the beach desert-ed and the shutters down in most of the shops and restaurants, leaving the streets to echo to your own footsteps and little else. In summer, there's no mistaking Burgau for the out-and-out resort it is, packed day and night.

Again, unless you're here on a pre-booked holiday, you'll find it tough to locate a **room** in summer, though signs scattered around the village provide some hope. There are lots of bars and restaurants, though, including the *Beach Bar Burgau* with a splendid terrace-bar right on the beach (open till 2am). The food isn't all it could be (restaurant closed Mon), but the place also rents out water sports equipment.

Not all the **buses** from Lagos/Sagres call into Burgau itself, though all pass the turn-off on the highway, from where it's a two-kilometre (25min) walk to the vil-lage through arid farming country.

Salema

SALEMA, it seems, is still holding out against the worst of the local excesses. Just 20km west of Lagos, the turn-off from the N125 offers a brief respite from the barrage of development along the main highway, as the road snakes down a delightful, semi-cultivated valley, the sea creeping ever closer. The bus parks just above the fishing harbour, where the slipway is cluttered with brightly coloured boats and fishermen moping in and out of the fish warehouse. Of course, there has been apartment and villa construction, but for the most part it spreads back up the valley from the village in a fairly homogenous white splodge, leaving the sloping central street largely untouched. Here, white terraced houses are split by narrow alleys which run down to the rocky beach on the east side. The western **beach** – a wide, rock-sheltered bay – is magnificent: in winter, the sea comes crashing right up to the edge of the village.

Most of the **accommodation** in Salema is in apartments, though there is a fair-sized and quite attractive hotel, the *Salema* (☎082/69 53 28, fax 69 53 29; ⑤; open March–Oct), plonked rather unceremoniously by the cobbled square just back from the beach, at Rua 28 Setembro. There are cheaper rooms at *A Mare* (④), the white house on the hill, a few metres back up the road from the bus stop, where the rooms have bath, sea views and terraces with sun loungers. Alternatives are private **rooms** in the old village – ask at the bars and the post-office shop, or just stroll along the street and look for signs: you should be able to secure something with a terrace and kitchen. There's also a pleasantly landscaped **campsite**, *Quinta dos Carriços* (☎082/69 52 01, fax 69 51 22), 1.5km back up towards the main highway – the bus passes it on the way into the village.

Best of the **restaurants** is the *Mira-Mar*, signposted off the main street in the village (open 9am–midnight); this serves up barbecued fish and meat on a terrace above the beach. There are three or four others, too, with the *Atlantico* the best sited – right on the beach and with a cheapish menu incorporating sardines and all the usual dishes. The *Atabua*, also on the main street, is a late-opening **bar**.

Figueira and Raposeira

At the village of **FIGUEIRA** on the N125 (the point at which the highway most closely approaches the coast between Lagos and Sagres), there's the very welcoming *Bar Celeiro* by the bus stop. From here, paths lead off to the lovely **Praia da Figueira** (a 20–30min walk), which is often more or less deserted except for a few campers.

Two other worthwhile beaches are accessible by road from the village of **RAPOSEIRA**, 5km further west, now positively overwhelmed by the speeding highway which cuts right through it. There is, though, a decent restaurant, the *Artisanale*, opposite a ceramic shop on the main road. The turn-off to the beach ("Ingrina") is signposted at the traffic lights on the highway: about 1km down the road, take the left fork that passes through Hortas do Tabual and after another 3km or so you'll reach two isolated, craggy beaches – **Praia do Zavial** and **Praia da Ingrina**. These have a minimum of tourist facilities, though there's a **campsite** (☎082/662 42) at Ingrina, 600m from the sea, and with its own bar-restaurant. Zavial is large and sandy, with tumbles of rock at either end and a café-restaurant open daily (except Wed) in season. Ingrina is sandy, too, and good for beachcombing amid the rock pools. There are no public transport connections from the main road.

West of Raposeira the road passes Vila do Bispo and the turn-off for the west coast, before heading across the flattened landscape for Sagres.

Sagres and Cabo de São Vicente

Wild and windswept, **SAGRES** and its cape were considered by the Portuguese as the far limit of the ancient and medieval worlds. It was on these headlands in the fifteenth century that Prince Henry the Navigator made his residence and it was here, too, that he set up a school of navigation, gathering together the greatest astronomers, cartographers and adventurers of his age. Fernão de Magalhães (Magellan), Pedro Álvares Cabral and Vasco da Gama all studied at Sagres, and from the beach at Belixe – midway between the capes of Sagres and **São Vicente** – the first long caravels were launched, revolutionizing shipping with their wide hulls, small adaptable sails, and ability to sail close to the wind. Each year new expeditions were dispatched to penetrate a little further than their predecessors, and to resolve the great navigational enigma presented by the west coast of Africa, thereby laying the foundations of the country's overseas empire.

After Henry's death here in 1460, the centre of maritime studies was moved to Lisbon and Sagres slipped back into the obscurity from which he'd raised it. In the early 1980s, the forlorn one-street village began to attract a growing number of young backpackers and windsurfers from Europe and North America, drawn by the string of magnificent, isolated local beaches. Now, the main highway from Lagos has put Sagres within easy reach and the inevitable trail of villas and apartments is threatening to overwhelm the place entirely. It can still be a great place to stay, especially in winter, when the wind blows hard and there's a bleak, desolate appeal to the scenery, with hardly a tourist to be seen. Throughout the summer, by contrast, the sprawling village draws quite a lively and oddball social scene: the young beachgoers still flock here, well catered for by an ever growing array of rooms for rent, restaurants and bars, rubbing shoulders these days though with families in villas and guests from one of the Algarve's two *pousadas*, which overlooks the village.

Sagres

Sagres village, rebuilt in the nineteenth century over the earthquake ruins of Henry's town, has nothing of architectural or historical interest and is little more than a line of houses connecting the fishing harbour and Praia da Baleeira at one end with the main square, Praça da Républica, at the other. Back from the main road, built to transport tourists straight to the headlands, a virtual new town of white villas and apartments spreads into the distance, much of it still under construction.

Henry the Navigator's **Fortaleza** dominates the whole scene near the village, with Rua da Fortaleza, across the main square, running directly up the headland towards its massive bulk. An immense circuit of walls – only the north side survives intact – once surrounded its vast, shelf-like promontory, high above the Atlantic. With such explicit demands of secrecy and security, together with its wild remoteness, it must have seemed a kind of Aldermaston or Los Alamos of its day.

You enter through a formidable tunnel, before which is spread a huge pebble **Rosa dos Ventos** (wind compass), unearthed beneath a church in 1921 and said to have been used by Henry himself. Historians disagree – and are equally unimpressed by the claims of other surviving buildings to have been part of the prince's house. Still, it is a wonderful, wild setting and the simple, much-restored chapel of **Nossa Senhora da Graça** is at least contemporary with Henry's explorations. A shame, then, that long-term "development" here has done little to enhance the beauty of the site. New buildings within the walls – due to house an interpretative centre – are of ugly concrete, as is much of the reinforcement work done on the walls themselves. Parts of the grounds remain little more than fly-blown wasteground, a situation that's barely changed for a decade or more.

Local beaches

However impressive the fortress, most people's days in Sagres are spent on one of the excellent nearby beaches, five of which are within easy walking distance of the village. Three of them are on the more sheltered coastline east of the fortress: **Praia da Mareta** is just below the square, and the **Praia da Baleeira** is by the harbour, from where it's a five-minute walk to the longest and best beach, the **Praia do Martinhal**, an ideal spot for windsurfing. West of the fortress, the beaches are longer and more impressive, and the one nearest the village is a good spot. It's a longer walk to the beautiful **Praia de Belixe**, 2km down the road from Sagres to Cabo São Vicente, where you are usually guaranteed plenty of sand to yourself.

Whichever beach you choose, the water is cold and swimming must be approached with caution – there are some very strong currents. Before setting off for the more distant strands, stock up with drinks and picnic supplies since there are virtually no facilities. The village supermarket can oblige with most provisions, plus five-litre flagons of the local wine for evening parties.

Practicalities

Buses from Lagos stop on the main village road, just by the square, **Praça da República**. In the other direction to Rua da Fortaleza, which starts acoss the square and leads up to the fortress, it's a ten-minute walk along the village road to the fishing harbour, passing the Praia da Mareta on the way. There's a privately run **information office**, Turinfo, in Praça da República (daily 10am–7pm; ☎082/62 00 03), which can arrange room rental, book you on a local jeep or boat tour, and rent out **mountain bikes** (500$00 per hour; 1200$00 per half-day; 1900$00 full-day), which isn't a bad way to get to the cape and far-flung beaches and back.

Accommodation

There are places to stay everywhere in and around Sagres village, and in high season, at least, it's basically a question of turning up and seeing what you're offered. Generally, you'll be approached by people offering **rooms** (from around 3500$00 a double) and, if you want it, access to a kitchen too. There's little point in giving specific recommendations, since there's not much difference as far as price and location goes. The only alternatives are a scattering of regular **pensões** and **hotels**; as with the private rooms, prices come down considerably out of season. *Residencial Dom Henrique* (☎082/62 00 00, fax 62 00 01; ⑤) is located right on the square – rooms here have bath and some have sea-facing balconies; while for harbour views, the *Hotel da Baleeira* (☎082/62 42 12, fax 62 44 25; ⑥) is the spot. But, best of all – if you your budget will stretch to it – is the *Pousada do Infante* (☎082/62 42 22, fax 62 42 25; ⑦), an attractive clifftop mansion with Moorish elements and splendid views of the fortress from its bar-terrace. It's a wonderful location and offers special rates out of season. Equally upmarket is a small, four-room hotel, the *Fortaleza do Belixe* (☎082/62 41 24, fax 62 42 25; ⑥), an annexe of the *pousada*, perched high on the cliff edge, 2km out of town at Belixe.

The nearest **campsite** (☎082/62 43 51, fax 62 44 45) is 2km north of the village, along (and off) the main road; it is convenient for Praia do Martinhal. Camping rough on the beaches is definitely not an option; the local police don't like it and, given the number of rooms available, you can see their point.

Eating, drinking and nightlife

Sagres's main street, from Praça da República to the fishing harbour, is lined with restaurants and bars, catering for a range of tastes and budgets. For **breakfast**, either *Café Conchinha* or the next-door *pastelaria*, both on Praça da República, open fairly early. **Restaurants** run the gamut from travellers, cafés to more upmarket places specializing in fish. At the fishing harbour end, *A Grelha* is typical of the cheaper establishments, a simple place with a modest menu where you can eat for under 1500$00. Nearby, on the same stretch of road, *Atlântico* and *O Pescador* stand almost opposite each other – fish restaurants, the quality of whose dishes can be a bit hit and miss. At either a full meal will be more like 2500–3500$00, while for the same price you can soak up the harbour views and tuck into the seafood or a *caldeirada* at *A Tasca*, down the steps to the port. At the other end of the village, nearer the square, *Dromedário*, opposite the kiosks on the main street, is an energetic bistro that serves drinks and snacks all day (open until 3am); while *Bossa Nova*, round the corner on Rua Comandante Matoso, is noted for its pizzas, pasta, salads and imaginative vegetarian meals. A short walk north of the village, on Rua dos Mortorios, *O Retiro do Pescador* serves delicious seafood at very reasonable prices. If you can afford it, try and eat at the *pousada*: finely judged French-Portuguese food, with coffee served on the terrace, for around 5000$00 a head.

Of the **bars**, two long-standing favourites, both packed with the travelling youth contingent, are *A Rosa dos Ventos*, on the village square – lively, loud, and drunken – and *The Last Chance Saloon*, around the corner, overlooking the Mareta beach. When it's falling down time, everyone moves on to *Polvo's* bar (open until 4am), just off the square, or to one of the even later-opening **discos** such as *Topas*, just north of the village.

Cabo de São Vicente

The exposed **Cabo de São Vicente** – Cape Saint Vincent – across the bay from Sagres, was sacred to the Romans, who believed the sun sank hissing into the water beyond here every night. It became a Christian shrine when the relics of the martyred Saint Vincent arrived in the eighth century; watched over (some say piloted) by ravens, the remains were transferred by boat to Lisbon in 1173.

It was almost certainly at the cape that Henry established his School of Navigation, founded a small town, and built his Vila do Infante. Today only a **lighthouse**, flanked by the ruins of a sixteenth-century Capuchin convent, are to be seen. The other buildings, already vandalized by the piratical Sir Francis Drake in 1597, came crashing to the ground in the Great Earthquake of 1755, the monks staying on alone until the Liberal suppression of the monasteries in 1834.

The cape is nonetheless a dramatic and exhilarating six-kilometre walk from Sagres, a path skirting the tremendous cliffs for much of the way. This is a wonderful spot for **birdlife** and at the right time of year you should be able to spot blue rock thrushes and peregrines nesting on the cliffs. Walking on the road is easier– it'll take less than an hour and a half, with glorious views all the way. Try to be at the cape for sunset, which is invariably gorgeous, though frequently also very windy.

Vila do Bispo and the coast to Odeceixe

Unlike the southern stretches of the Algarve, the **west coast**, stretching north from Sagres to Odeceixe, is still relatively undeveloped. There are several reasons: the coast is exposed to strong Atlantic winds; the sea can be several degrees cooler; and swimming is dangerous. In addition, the designation in 1995 of the stretch of coast from Burgau to Cabo de São Vicente and up through the Alentejo as a nature reserve – the Parque Natural Sudoeste Alentejano e Costa Vincentina – should go even further to protect this dramatic and rugged scenery from potentially harmful development. If you can brave the climate, you might like to base yourself at low-key resorts such as **Vila do Bispo**, **Carrapateira**, **Aljezur** and **Odeceixe**, all of which have plenty of beach, plus an inexpensive network of private rooms and scope for freelance camping. Like Sagres, these resorts attract a predominantly young and/or alternative crowd. At a few resorts – Odeceixe, in particular – this can be overwhelming, with summer crowds of campervan-hippies strutting about nude on the beach.

Vila do Bispo

VILA DO BISPO, at the junction of the west and south coast roads, is a fairly scrappy little town whose kernel of old white houses centres on a lovely seventeenth-century parish **church** (Mon–Sat 10am–1pm & 2–6pm), every interior surface of which has been painted, tiled or gilded. If you drop enough in the plate in the sacristy, the old custodian on duty will point out the age of everything in the church – you'll get to see the collection of assorted carvings, chalices and ecclesiastical vestments too. That's about all the town has to offer in the way of diversions: have a look over the hills from the church terrace, a coffee in one of the bars by the adjacent town garden, a mooch around the supermarket and you'll be ready to move on.

Nothing much happens here, but the town could make a reasonable base if you have transport for day-trips to the beaches. The nearest beach, the cliff-edged **Praia do Castelejo**, is reached by a rough road – no buses and a tough hike – leading 5km west, across a stretch of bleak moors and hills. In summer, there's a little bar-restaurant here.

Buses from Sagres or Lagos drop you right at the bottom of the village, five minutes' walk from the church. There are **rooms** advertised here and there, or try the *Pensão Mira Sagres*, Rua do Hospital 3 (☎082/661 60; ③) – opposite the church – which has its own bar-restaurant downstairs. Not that Vila do Bispo lacks places to **eat**: down Rua 1º de Maio from the church, *Café Correira* (closed Sat) has a decent menu, while a block further down, along an alley on the left, is the much cheaper *Oasis*, a locals' haunt, where the house speciality is chicken. If neither appeals, Rua Comandante Matoso, the parallel downhill street, has three or four more choices, all modest and acceptable. And there's a small supermarket, bakery and even a couple of **bars** (summer only) that see some late-night action.

Carrapateira

Fifteen kilometres to the north of Vila do Bispo (and connected with it by two daily buses) is the village of **CARRAPATEIRA**, which is better positioned for the beach. It's possible to get a **private room** if you ask around the main square or at the *Bar Barroca*. However, the best accommodation is a couple of kilometres northeast of town at the *Residencial Casa Fajara* (for reservations, see below; ⑤), a spruce modern villa with neat gardens, overlooking an empty river valley. It's in a great location, and is open all year round; breakfast is provided.

Carrapateira's local beach, a kilometre's walk from the *Casa Fajara*, is the **Praia da Bordeira**, a spectacular strand with dunes, a tiny river and crashing surf. The sandbanks provide shelter from the wind for a sizeable community of freelance campers, who seem to be tolerated by the local police. There is a restaurant on the beach, *O Sitio do Rio* (closed Nov; ☎082/971 19); the manager takes reservations for the *Casa Fajara* and also offers horse-riding excusions. A second beach – quieter and with no facilities – is the **Praia do Amado**, 4km south of the Praia da Bordeira, around the Carrapateira headland.

Aljezur and around

The village of **ALJEZUR** (Mon–Fri 2 buses daily from Vila do Bispo; 2–5 daily from Lagos) is divided into two distinct halves: to the west of the river is a rather drab old quarter, Moorish in origin and straggling along the side of a hill below the scant ruins of a tenth-century **castle**, while across the river to the east lies a more modern settlement. More and more surfers are making their way here in summer, attracted by the local beaches; the **turismo** (Mon & Fri–Sun 9.30am–12.30pm & 2–5.30pm, Tues–Thurs 9.30am–7pm; ☎082/982 29), in Largo do Mercado, by the river, does its best to help with private **rooms**. There are also a couple of **pensões** scattered around the vicinity: in the Igreja Nova quarter, just to the northeast of the centre, try the *Residencial Dom Sancho*, Largo 1° de Maio (☎082/981 19; ④), or the rooms above the *Restaurante A Lareira*, Estrada da Cruz (☎082/984 40; ④). The bus from Lagos loops through Igreja Nova on its way out of Aljezur. There are two or three fairly simple **restaurants** in town, too, such as the *Primavera* and *Ruth*, both along the main Rua 25 de Abril.

A kilometre south of Aljezur, a road heads through to the local **beaches** of **MONTE CLÉRIGO** (8km) and **ARRIFANA** (10km). The latter is magnificent, though its small village, perched on the cliffs above, is a rather grubby affair, with a couple of lacklustre bars and restaurants and a supermarket. Midway between the beaches is the **VALE DA TELHA** tourist complex, which has planning permission for expansion to a site of 2500 chalets and villas. At present it's nowhere near that size, nor a great commercial success, with just a modest **hotel**, the *Hotel Vale da Telha* (☎082/99 81 80, fax 981 76; ④), and a **campsite** (☎082/984 44) up and running.

Odeceixe

ODECEIXE, hunched on a hill and cramped by the river, is the last village before the Alentejo. Situated near the head of a delightful curving estuary, it is a fairly quiet little place, at least outside July and August. At this time of year, it seems to attract just about every German hippy on the Algarve, a clientele that creates its own rather exclusive presence. If you hit town outside the hippy season, though, it could be very pleasant, with a couple of simple restaurants, a number of houses offering **rooms**, and some small villas for rent by the beach. There's a campsite here, too.

The beach – **Praia de Odeceixe** – is a high-cliffed cove, stretching north of the estuary. It is one of the most sheltered beaches on this stretch of coast, with a minimum of tourist development and wonderful surf.

travel details

Trains

The Algarve rail line runs from Lagos to Vila Real de Santo António, but only three or four services daily operate along the whole route; you may have to change at Tunes or Faro, depending on your destination. Note that reservations are compulsory on Intercidade and Rápido or "Alfa" trains. For journeys from one end of the rail line to the other, it's worth catching one of the express services rather than the slow local-stopping trains.

Faro to: Albufeira (12 daily; 30–45min); Lagos (7 daily; 1hr 20min–2hr 35min); Monte Gordo (1–5 daily; 1hr 30min); Olhão (10–15 daily; 15min); Portimão (6 daily; 1–2hr); Silves (7 daily; 50min–1hr 45min); Tavira (11–15 daily; 35–50min); Vila Real de Santo António (9–14 daily; 1hr–1hr 30min).

Lagos to: Albufeira (8 daily; 1hr–1hr 35min); Alvor (4 daily; 25min); Faro (8 daily; 1hr 30min–2hr 30min); Loulé (8 daily; 1hr 20min–2hr); Portimão (13 daily; 15–30min); Silves (13 daily; 30–50min); Tunes (13 daily; 50min–1hr 20min).

Tunes to: Lisbon (6 daily; 3hr 45min–6hr 30min), add on 2hr or so for connections from Vila Real, one hour from Faro or Lagos; and to Beja (3 daily; 3–4hr), with connections for Casa Branca (4hr 40min); Évora (2–3 daily; 4hr 30min–6hr 20min).

Buses

Albufeira to: Areias de São João (8–11 daily; 10min); Armação de Pêra (Mon–Sat 9 daily, Sun 5; 25min); Faro (12–15 daily; 1hr 15min); Montechoro (8–11 daily; 15min); Olhos d'Água (hourly; 10min); Portimão (Mon–Fri 8 daily, Sat 7, Sun 4; 1hr 10min); Quarteira (Mon–Fri 15 daily, Sat & Sun 9 daily; 45min); São Bartolomeu de Messines (3–8 daily; 40min); Silves (3–7 daily; 45min).

Faro to: Albufeira (hourly; 1hr 15min); Estói (Mon–Fri 10 daily, Sat & Sun 4 daily; 25min); Loulé (Mon–Fri at least hourly, Sat 8, Sun 6; 40min); Monte Gordo (Mon–Fri hourly, Sat & Sun 6 daily; 1hr 35min); Olhão (Mon–Fri every 15–30min, Sat & Sun roughly hourly; 20min); Quarteira (Mon–Fri hourly, Sat 11, Sun 9 daily; 35min); São Brás de Alportel (Mon–Fri 9 daily, Sat 5, Sun 3; 35min); Tavira (7–11 daily; 1hr); Vilamoura (Mon–Fri hourly, Sat & Sun 9 daily; 40min); Vila Real (6–9 daily; 1hr 40min).

Lagos to: Albufeira (1 daily; 1hr 30min); Aljezur (Mon–Fri 4–5 daily, Sat 1 daily, Sun 1 in summer; 50min); Burgau (8–10 daily, only 4 on Sun in winter; 25min); Luz (9 daily, only 4 on Sun in winter; 15min); Odeceixe (Mon–Fri 3–4 daily, Sat 1; 1hr 20min); Portimão (hourly; 40min); Sagres (7–11 daily; 1hr); Salema (5–8 daily; 40min); Vila do Bispo (7–11 daily; 45min).

Portimão to: Albufeira (5–7 daily; 1hr 15min); Alvor (Mon–Fri hourly; Sat & Sun roughly every 2hr; 20min); Caldas de Monchique (3–4 daily; 30min); Faro (Mon–Fri 2, Sat & Sun 4–5 daily; 2hr 15min–3hr); Ferragudo (hourly; 10min); Lagos (hourly; 40min); Monchique (8–9 daily; 30–45min); Praia da Rocha (every 15–20min; 5min); São Bartolomeu de Messines (4–8 daily; 1hr 15min); Silves (Mon–Fri 9 daily, Sat & Sun 6–7 daily; 35–45min).

Sagres to: Lagos (Mon–Fri 10–12 daily, Sat & Sun 6–7; 1hr); Salema (Mon–Fri 6–7 daily, Sat & Sun 3–4 daily; 35min); Vila do Bispo (6–10 daily; 15min).

Vila do Bispo to: Aljezur (Mon–Fri 2 daily; 45min); Carrapateira (Mon–Fri 1 daily; 15min).

Vila Real de Santo António to: Alcoutim (Mon–Fri 2–3 daily, Sat 1; 1hr 15min); Ayamonte, Spain (2 daily; 1hr 15min); Castro Marim (Mon–Fri 8–13 daily, Sat 2 daily, Sun 2 daily in summer; 10min); Manta Rota (Mon–Fri 4–5 daily, Sat 2 daily; 30min); Monte Gordo (Mon–Fri at least half-hourly, Sat & Sun in winter 10–13 daily; 7min); Tavira (6–9 daily; 40min).

Long-distance buses

There's a long-distance *Linha Litoral* express service which connects Lagos to Vila Real/Ayamonte once daily, the whole route taking four hours; on the Lagos–Albufeira leg of the route, there are more like five daily departures. Several companies also operate regular daily express buses between Lisbon and the Algarve, with approximate journey times as follows: Albufeira (3hr 35min); Faro (4hr); Lagos (4hr 45min); Olhão (4hr 20min); Tavira (4hr 45min); Vila Real (4hr 30min). Ask at any travel agency or bus terminal for details, though note that the Rede Expressos buses are around 700$00 cheaper than the *EVA* bus.

Flights

Faro to: Lisbon (5–6 daily); with connections to Porto.

THE

CONTEXTS

PORTUGAL'S HISTORY

The early history of Portugal – as part of the Iberian Peninsula – has obvious parallels with that of Spain. Indeed, any geographical division is somewhat arbitrary, independent development only really occurring following Afonso Henriques' creation of a Portuguese kingdom in the twelfth century.

EARLY CIVILIZATION

Remnants of pottery and cave burials point to tribal societies occupying the Tagus valley, as well as parts of the Alentejo and Estremadura, as early as 8000 to 7000 BC, and the recently discovered Paleolithic paintings near Vila Nova de Foz Côa in Beira Alta are thought to date back around 20,000 years (see p.292). More, however, is known of **Neolithic** Portugal and its Castro culture based on hilltop forts, a culture that was to be developed and refined after the arrival of Celtic peoples in around 700 to 600 BC. These forts, the first permanent settlements, were concentrated in northern Portugal, and particularly in the Minho, where excavations have revealed dozens of **citânias**, or fortified villages. The most impressive is at Briteiros (p.310), near Braga, with its paved streets, drainage systems and circuits of defensive walls; like many of the *citânias* it survived, remarkably unchanged, well into the Roman era. Settlements in neighbouring Trás-os-Montes, in contrast, reflect less of a defensive

spirit – but all that remains of this more pastoral **Verracos** culture are the crude granite porcas, stone figures venerating wild sows as objects of a primitive fertility cult.

The potential for new trading outlets and the quest for metals, in particular tin for making bronze, attracted a succession of peoples from across the Mediterranean but most of their settlements lay on the eastern seaboard and so fell within "Spanish" history. The **Phoenicians**, however, established an outpost at Lisbon around 900 BC and there were probably contacts, too, with Mycenaean Greeks. In the mid-third century BC, they were followed by **Carthaginians**, who recruited Celtic tribesmen for military aid against the Roman empire. Once again, though, their influence was predominantly on the eastern seaboard and in the south; with defeat in the Second Punic War (218–202 BC) they were to be replaced by a more determined colonizing force.

ROMANS, SUEVI AND VISIGOTHS

Entering the peninsula in 210 BC, the **Romans** swiftly subdued and colonized the Mediterranean coast and the south of Spain and Portugal. In the interior, however, they met with great resistance from the Celtiberian tribes and in 193 BC the **Lusitani** rose up in arms. Based in central Portugal, between the Tagus and Lima rivers, they were, in the words of the Roman historian Strabo, "the most powerful of the Iberian peoples, who resisted the armies of Rome for the longest period". For some fifty years, in fact, they held up the Roman advance, under the leadership of **Viriatus**, a legendary Portuguese hero and masterful exponent of the feigned retreat who, on several occasions, brought the Romans to accept his autonomous rule. He was betrayed after a successful campaign in 139 BC and within two years the Lusitani had capitulated as the legions of Decimus Junius Brutus swept through the north. Still, over a century later, their name was given to this most westerly of the Roman provinces, while in the northern Celtic villages Roman colonization can scarcely have been felt.

Integration into the Roman Empire occurred largely under Julius Caesar, who in 60 BC established a capital at Olisipo (Lisbon) and significant colonies at Ebora (Évora), Scallabis (Santarém) and Pax Julia (Beja). In 27 BC the Iberian provinces were further reorganized under Augustus, with all but the north of Portugal being governed – as Lusitania – from the great Roman city of Merida in Spanish Extremadura. The Minho formed part of a separate province, later added to northwest Spain to create Gallaecia, with an important regional centre at Bracara Augusta (Braga). In general, though, it was the south where Roman influence was deepest. Here they established huge agricultural estates (the infamous *Latifundia* which still survive in Alentejo) and changed the nature of the region's crops, as they introduced wheat, barley, olives and the vine to the area.

There are no great **Roman sites** in Portugal – at least nothing to compare with Spanish Merida, Tarragona, or Italica – though both Évora (p.391) and Conímbriga (p.195) have individual monuments of interest. The mark of six centuries of Roman rule consists more in a network of roads (used well into the Middle Ages) and bridges, many of them still in use today. There is a more basic legacy, too, the Portuguese language being very heavily derived from Latin.

The **decline of the Roman Empire** in Portugal echoes its pattern elsewhere, though perhaps with greater indifference, the territory always being something of a provincial backwater. **Christianity** reached Portugal's southern coast towards the end of the first century AD and by the third century bishoprics were established at Braga, Évora, Faro and Lisbon. But the state was already disintegrating and in 409 the first waves of barbarian invaders crossed the Pyrenees into Spain. Vandals, Alans, Suevi and Visigoths all passed through Portugal, though only the last two were of any real importance.

The **Suevi**, a semi-nomadic people from eastern Germany, eventually settled in the area between the Douro and Minho rivers, establishing courts at Braga and Portucale (Porto). They seem to have coexisted fairly peacefully with the Hispano-Roman nobility and were converted to Christianity by Saint Martin of Dume, a saint frequently found in the dedications of northern churches.

Around 585, however, the Suevian state disappeared, having been suppressed and incorporated into the **Visigothic** empire, a heavily Romanized yet independent force which for two centuries maintained a spurious unity and rule over most of the peninsula. The Visigothic kings, however, ruled from Toledo, supported by a small and elite aristocratic warrior-caste, so in Portugal their influence was neither great nor lasting. And by the end of the seventh century their divisions, exacerbated by an elective monarchy and their intolerance (including the first Iberian persecution of the Jews), resulted in one faction appealing for aid from Muslim North Africa. In 711 a first force of **Moors** crossed the straits into Spain and within a decade they had advanced and conquered all but the mountainous reaches of the Asturias in northern Spain.

THE MOORS AND THE CHRISTIAN RECONQUEST

In Portugal, Aveiro probably marked the northernmost point of the **Moorish advance**. The Moors met with little resistance but the dank, green hills of the Minho held little attraction for the colonizers-to-be and over the following century seem to have been severely depopulated. Most of the Moors were content to settle in the south: in the Tagus valley, in the rich wheat belts around Évora and Beja, and above all in the coastal region of the **al-Gharb**. Here they established a capital at Shelb, modern Silves, and, by the middle of the ninth century, an independent kingdom, detached from the great Muslim emirate of al-Andalus which covered most of Spain.

The Moors in Portugal were a mix of ethnic races – for the most part consisting of Berbers from Morocco, but also considerable numbers of Syrians and, around Faro, a contingent of Egyptians, some of them probably Coptic Christians. In contrast to the Visigoths, the Moors were tolerant and productive, their rule a civilizing influence. Both Jews and Christians were allowed freedom of worship and their own civil laws, while under Muslim law small landholders continued to occupy lands that they themselves cultivated. For most of these **"Moçárabes"**– Christians subject to Moorish rule – life must have improved. Roman irrigation techniques were perfected and the Moors introduced the rotation of crops and cultivation of cotton, rice, oranges and lemons. Their culture and scholarship led the world – though less from al-Gharb than from Córdoba and Seville – and they forged important trade links, many of which were to continue centuries after their fall. Perhaps still more important, **urban life** developed, with prosperous local craft industries: Lisbon, Évora, Beja and Santarém all emerged as sizeable towns.

The Christian "**Reconquista**" began – at least by tradition – at Covadonga in 718, when Pelayo, at the head of a small band of Visigoths, halted the advance of a Moorish expeditionary force. The battle's significance has doubtless been inflated but from the victory a tiny kingdom of the Asturias does seem to have been established. Initially only 65 by 50 kilometres in extent, it expanded over the next two centuries to take in León, Galicia and the "lands of Portucale," the latter an area roughly equivalent to the old Swabian state between the Douro and the Minho.

By the eleventh century **Portucale** had the status of a country, its governors appointed by the kings of León. In 1073 Alfonso VI came to the throne. It was to be a reign hard-pressed by a new wave of Muslim invaders – the fanatical Almoravids, who crossed over to Spain in 1086 after appeals from al-Andalus and established a new Muslim state at Seville. Like many kings of Portugal after him, Alfonso was forced to turn to European Crusaders, many of whom would stop in at the shrine of Saint James in Compostela. One of them, Raymond of Burgundy, married Alfonso's eldest daughter and became heir-apparent to the throne of León; his cousin Henry, married to another daughter, Teresa, was given jurisdiction over Portucale. With Henry's death Teresa became regent for her son, **Afonso Henriques**, and began to try to forge a union with Galicia. Afonso, however, had other ideas and having defeated his mother at the battle of São Mamede (1128), he established a capital at **Guimarães** and set about extending his domains to the south.

The reconquest of central Portugal was quickly achieved. Afonso's victory at Ourique in 1139 was a decisive blow and by 1147 he had taken Santarém. In the same year Lisbon fell, after a siege in which passing Crusaders again played a vital role – though not sailing on to the Holy Land before murderously sacking the city. Many of them were English and some stayed on; Gilbert of Hastings became Archbishop. By now Afonso was dubbing himself the **first King of Portugal**, a title tacitly acknowledged by Alfonso VII (the new king of León) in 1137 and officially confirmed by the Treaty of Zamora in 1143. His kingdom spread more or less to the borders of modern Portugal, though in the south, Alentejo and the Algarve were still in Muslim hands.

For the next century and a half Afonso's successors struggled to dominate this last stronghold of the Moors. Sancho I (1185–1211) took their capital, Silves, in 1189, but his gains were not consolidated and almost everything south of the Tagus was recaptured the following year by al-Mansur, the last great campaigning vizier of al-Andalus. The overall pattern, though, was of steady expansion with occasional setbacks. Sancho II (1223–48) invaded the Alentejo and the eastern Algarve, while his successor **Afonso III** (1248–79) moved westwards, taking Faro and establishing the kingdom in pretty much its final shape.

THE BURGUNDIAN KINGS

The reconquest of land from the Muslims also incorporated a process of **recolonization**. As it fell into the king's hands, new territory was granted to such of his subjects that he felt would be able to defend it. In this way much of the country came to be divided between the church, the Holy Orders – chief among them the Knights Templar – and a hundred or so powerful nobles (*ricos homens*). The entire kingdom had a population of under half a million, the majority of them concentrated in the north. Here, there was little displacement of the traditional feudal ties, but in the south the influx of Christian peasants blurred the distinction between serf and settler, dependent relationships coming instead to be based on the payment of rent.

Meanwhile a **political infrastructure** was being established. The land was divided into municipalities (*concelhos*), each with its own charter (*foral*). A formalized structure of consultation began, with the first **Cortes** (parliament) being held in Coimbra in 1211. At first consisting mainly of the clergy and nobility, it later came to include wealthy merchants and townsmen, a development speeded both by the need to raise taxes and by later kings' constant struggles against the growing power of the church. The capital, which Afonso Henriques had moved to Coimbra in 1139, was transferred to **Lisbon** in about 1260 by Afonso III.

The Burgundian dynasty lasted through nine kings for 257 years. In the steady process of establishing the new kingdom, one name stands out above all others, that of **Dom Dinis** (1279–1325). With the reconquest barely complete when he came to the throne, Dinis set about a far-sighted policy of stabilization and of strengthening the nation to ensure its future independence. During his reign, fifty fortresses were constructed along the frontier with Castile, while at the same time negotiations were going on, leading eventually to the Treaty of Alcañices (1297) by which Spain acknowledged Portugal's frontiers. At home Dinis established a major programme of forest planting and of agricultural reform; grain, olive oil, wine, salt, salt fish and dried fruit became staple exports to Flanders, Brittany, Catalonia and Britain. Importance, too, was attached to education and the arts: a **university**, later transferred to Coimbra, was founded at Lisbon in 1290. Dinis also helped entrench the power of the monarchy, forcing the church to accept a much larger degree of state control and, in 1319, reorganizing the Knights Templar – at the time being suppressed all over Europe – as the **Order of Christ**, still enormously powerful but now responsible directly to the king rather than to the pope.

Despite Dinis's precautions, fear of **Castilian domination** continued to play an important part in the reigns of his successors, largely owing to consistent intermarrying between the two royal families. On the death of the last of the Burgundian kings, Fernando I, power passed to his widow Leonor, who ruled as regent. Leonor, whose only daughter had married Juan I of Castile, promised the throne to the children of that marriage. In this she had the support of most of the nobility, but the merchant and peasant classes strongly opposed a Spanish ruler, supporting instead the claim of João, Grand Master of the House of Avis and a bastard heir of the Burgundian line. A popular revolt against Leonor led to two years of war with Castile, finally settled at the **Battle of Aljubarrota** (1385) in which João, backed up by a force of English archers, wiped out the much larger Castilian army.

The great abbey of **Batalha** (p.157) was built to commemorate the victory. **João I**, first king of the **House of Avis**, was crowned at Coimbra the same year, sealing relations with England through the 1386 Treaty of Windsor – an alliance which lasted into the twentieth century – and his marriage to Philippa of Lancaster, daughter of John of Gaunt, the following year.

DOM MANUEL AND THE MARITIME EMPIRE

Occupying such a strategic position between the Atlantic and the Mediterranean, it was inevitable that Portuguese attention would at some stage turn to **maritime expansion**. When peace was finally made with Castile in 1411, João I was able to turn his resources toward Morocco. The outpost at Ceuta fell in 1415, but successive attempts to capture Tangier were not realized until the reign of Afonso V, in 1471.

At first such overseas adventuring was undertaken partly in a crusading spirit, partly to keep potentially troublesome nobles busy. The proximity of North Africa made it a constant feature of foreign policy, giving a welcome boost to the economy of the Algarve. The first real advances in exploration, however, came about through the activities of **Prince Henry "the Navigator"**, third son of João and Philippa. As Grand Master of the Order of Christ, he turned that organization's vast resources towards marine development, founding a School of Navigation on the desolate promontory of Sagres (then regarded as the end of the world) and staffing it with Europe's leading cartographers, navigators and seamen. As well as improving the art of offshore navigation, they redesigned the caravel, making it a vessel well suited to long ocean-going journeys. **Madeira** and the **Azores** were discovered in 1419 and 1427 respectively, and by the time of Henry's death in 1460 the **Cape Verde Islands** and the **west coast of Africa** down to Sierra Leone had both been explored.

After a brief hiatus, overseas expansion received a fresh boost in the reigns of João II, Manuel I and João III. In 1487 **Bartolomeu Dias** finally made it around the southern tip of Africa, christening it "Cabo da Boa Esperança" in the hope of good things to come. Within ten years **Vasco da Gama** had sailed on past it to open up the **trade route to India**. This was the great breakthrough and the Portuguese monarchy, already doing well out of African gold, promptly became the richest in Europe, taking a fifth of the profits of all trade and controlling important monopolies on some spices. The small cargo of pepper brought back by Vasco on his first expedition was enough to pay for the trip three times over. Meanwhile Spain was opening up the New World and by the **Treaty of Tordesillas** in 1494 the two Iberian nations divided the world between them along an imaginary line 370 leagues west of the Cape Verde Islands. This not only gave Portugal the run of the Orient but also, when it was discovered in 1500, Brazil (though its exploitation would have to wait nearly 200 more years). By the mid-sixteenth century Portugal dominated **world trade**; strategic posts had been established at Goa (1510), Malacca (1511), Ormuz (1515) and Macau (1557), and the revenue from dealings with the East was backed up by a large-scale **slave trade** between West Africa and Europe and Brazil.

The reign of **Manuel I** (1495–1521) marked the apogee of Portuguese wealth and strength. It found its expression at home in the extraordinary exuberance of the "**Manueline**" style of architecture – an elaborately decorative genre which found its inspiration in marine motifs. Notable examples can be seen in the Convent of Christ at Tomar and the monastery and tower of Belém in Lisbon (see pp.82–85), while the best examples of civil architecture are probably the extensions made by Manuel to the royal palace at Sintra.

Enormous wealth there may have been, but very little of it filtered down through the system, and in the country at large conditions barely improved. The practice of siphoning off a hefty slice of the income into the royal coffers effectively prevented the development of an entrepreneurial class and, as everywhere else in Europe, financial matters were left very much in the hands of the Jews, who were not allowed to take up most other professions.

Portugal had traditionally been considerably more tolerant than other European nations in its treatment of its **Jewish citizens** (and towards the Moorish minority who had been absorbed after the reconquest). However, popular resentment of their riches, and pressure from Spain, forced Manuel – who had initially welcomed refugees from the Spanish persecution – to order their **expulsion** in 1496. Although many chose the pragmatic course of remaining as "New Christian" converts, others fled to the Netherlands. This exodus, continued as a result of the activities of the **Inquisition** (from 1531 on), created a vacuum which left Portugal with an extensive empire based upon commerce, but deprived of much of its commercial expertise.

By the 1570s the economy was beginning to collapse: incoming wealth was insufficient to cover the growing costs of maintaining an empire against increasing competition, a situation exacerbated by foreign debts, falling prices and a decline in the productivity of domestic agriculture.

SPANISH DOMINATION

In the end it was a combination of reckless imperialism and impecunity which brought to an end the dynasty of the House of Avis and with it, at least temporarily, Portuguese independence. **Dom Sebastião** (1557–78), obsessed with dreams of a new crusade against Morocco, set out at the head of a huge army to satisfy his fanatical fantasies. They were crushed at the battle of **Alcácer-Quibir** (1578), where the Portuguese dead numbered over eight thousand, including Sebastião and most of Portugal's nobility. The aged **Cardinal Henrique** took the throne as the closest legitimate relative and devoted his brief reign to attempting to raise the crippling ransoms for those captured on the battlefield.

The Cardinal's death without heirs in 1580 provided Spain with the pretext to renew its claim to Portugal. **Philip II** of Spain, Sebastião's uncle, defeated his rivals at the battle of Alcântara and in 1581 was crowned Felipe I of Portugal, inaugurating a period of Hapsburg rule which lasted for another sixty years. In the short term, although unpopular, the union had advantages for Portugal. Spanish wheat helped alleviate the domestic shortage and Spanish seapower helped protect the far-flung empire. Philip, moreover, studiously protected Portuguese autonomy, maintaining an entirely separate bureaucracy and spending long periods in Portugal in an attempt to win popular support. Not that he ever did – throughout his reign pretenders appeared claiming to be Sebastião miraculously saved from the Moroccan desert, tapping a strong vein of resentment among the people. And in the long run, Spanish control proved disastrous. Association with Spain's foreign policy (part of the Armada was prepared in Lisbon) meant the enmity of the Dutch and the British, Portugal's traditional allies, losing the country an important part of its trade which was never to be regained.

Philip's successors made no attempt at all to protect Portuguese sensibilities – cynical and uninterested, they attempted to rule from Madrid while raising heavy taxes to pay for Spain's wars. The final straw was the attempt by Philip IV (Felipe III of Portugal) to conscript Portuguese troops to quell a rising in Catalonia. On December 1, 1640, a small group of conspirators stormed the palace in Lisbon and deposed the Duchess of Mantua, Governor of Portugal. By popular acclaim and despite personal reluctance, the Duke of Bragança, senior member of a family which had long been the most powerful in the country, took the throne as **João IV**.

THE HOUSE OF BRAGANÇA

At first the newly independent nation looked pretty shaky, deprived of most of its trade routes and with the apparently imminent threat of invasion from Spain hanging over it. As it turned out, however, the Spanish were so preoccupied with wars elsewhere that they had little choice but to accept the situation, though they did not do so formally until 1668 under the **Treaty of Lisbon**. João IV used the opportunity to rebuild old alliances and although the Portuguese were often forced into unfavourable terms, they were at least trading again. Relations with Britain had been strained during the establishment of that country's Commonwealth, especially by Oliver Cromwell's particular brand of Protestant commercialism, but were revived by the marriage of Charles II to Catherine of Bragança in 1661.

At home Portugal was developing an increasingly centralized administration. The **discovery of gold and diamonds in Brazil** during the reign of Pedro II (1683–1706) made the crown financially independent and did away with the need for the Cortes (or any form of popular representation) for most of the next century. It was **João V**, coming to the throne in 1706, who most benefited from the new riches, which he squandered in an orgy of lavish Baroque building. His massive convent at **Mafra**, built totally without regard to expense, employed at times as many as fifty thousand workmen, virtually bankrupting the state. Meanwhile nothing was being done to revive the economy, and what little remained from João's grandiose schemes went mainly to pay for imports. The infamous **Methuen Treaty**, signed in 1703 to stimulate trade with Britain, only made matters worse: although it opened up new markets for Portuguese wine, it helped destroy the native textile industry by letting in British cloth at preferential rates.

The accession of João's apathetic son, **José I** (1750–77), allowed the total concentration of power in the hands of the king's chief minister, the **Marquês de Pombal**, who became the classic "enlightened despot" of eighteenth-century history. It was the **Great Earthquake of 1755** that sealed his dominance over the age; while everyone else was panicking, Pombal's policy was simple – "bury the dead and feed the living".

Pombal saw his subsequent mission as to modernize all aspects of Portuguese life, by establishing an efficient and secular bureaucracy, renewing the system of taxation, setting up export companies, protecting trade and abolishing slavery within Portugal. It was a strategy that made him many enemies among the old aristocracy and above all within the Church, whose overbearing influence he fought at every turn. Opposition, though, was dealt with ruthlessly and an assassination attempt on the king in 1758 (which some say was staged by Pombal) gave him the chance he needed to destroy his enemies. Denouncing their supposed involvement, Pombal executed the country's leading aristocrats and abolished the Jesuit order, which had long dominated education and religious life in Portugal and Brazil.

Although Pombal himself was taken to trial (and found guilty but pardoned on the grounds of old age) with the accession of Maria I (1777–1816), the majority of his labours survived him, most notably the reform of education along scientific lines and his completely rebuilt capital, Lisbon. Further development, however, was soon thwarted by a new invasion.

FRENCH OCCUPATION AND THE MIGUELITE YEARS

With the appearance of **Napoleon** on the international scene, Portugal once more became embroiled in the affairs of Europe. The French threatened to invade unless the Portuguese supported their naval blockade of Britain, a demand that no one expected them to obey since British ports were the destination for most of Portugal's exports. Only the protection of the British fleet, especially after the victory at Trafalgar in 1805, kept the country's trade routes open. General Junot duly marched into Lisbon in November 1807.

On British advice the royal family had already gone into exile in Brazil, where they were to stay until 1821, and the war was left largely in the hands of British generals **Beresford** and **Wellington**. Having twice been driven out and twice reinvaded, the French were finally forced back into Spain in 1811 following the Battle of Buçaco (1810) and a long period of near starvation before the lines of Torres Vedras.

Britain's prize for this was the right to trade freely with **Brazil**, which, together with the declaration of that country as a kingdom in its own right, fatally weakened the dependent relationship that had profited the Portuguese treasury for so long. Past roles were reversed, with Portugal becoming effectively a colony of Brazil (where the royal family remained) and a protectorate of Britain, with General Beresford as administrator. The only active national institution was the army, many of whose officers had absorbed the constitutional ideals of revolutionary France.

In August 1820, with Beresford temporarily out of the country and King João VI still in Brazil, a group of officers called an unofficial Cortes and proceeded to draw up a new **constitution**. Inspired by the recent liberal advances in Spain, it called for an assembly – to be elected every two years by universal male suffrage – and the abolition of clerical privilege and the traditional rights of the nobility. The king, forced to choose between Portugal and Brazil, where his position looked even more precarious, came back in 1821 and accepted its terms. His queen, Carlota, and younger son **Miguel**, however, refused to take the oath of allegiance and became the dynamic behind a reactionary movement which drew considerable support in rural areas. With João VI's death in 1826, a delegation was sent to Brazil to pronounce Crown Prince Pedro the new king. Unfortunately Pedro was already Emperor of Brazil, having declared its independence some years earlier. He resolved to pass the crown to his infant daughter, with Miguel as regent provided that he swore to accept a new charter, drawn up by Pedro and somewhat less liberal than the earlier constitution. Miguel agreed, but once in power promptly tore up any agreement, abolished the charter and returned to the old, absolutist ways. This was a surprisingly popular move in Portugal, certainly in the countryside, but not with the governments of Britain, Spain,

or France who backed the liberal rebels and finally put Pedro IV (who had meanwhile been deposed in Brazil) on the throne after Miguel's defeat at Évora-Monte in 1834.

THE DEATH OF THE MONARCHY

Pedro didn't survive long. The rest of the century – under the rule of his daughter Maria II (1834–53) and his grandsons Pedro V (1853–61) and Luís (1861–89) – saw almost constant struggle between those who supported the charter and those who favoured a return to the more liberal constitution of 1822. In 1846 the position deteriorated virtually to a state of **civil war** between Maria, who was fanatical in her support of her father's charter, and the radical constitutionalists. Only a further intervention by foreign powers maintained peace, imposed at the Convention of Gramido (1847).

In the second half of the century, with relative stability and the two warring factions to some extent institutionalized into a revolving two-party system, the economy began at last to recover, with the first signs of widespread industrialization and a major public works programme under the minister Fontes Pereira de Melo. The monarchy, however, was almost bankrupt and its public humiliation over possessions in Africa – Britain and Germany simply ignored the Portuguese claim to the land between Angola and Mozambique – helped strengthen growing republican feelings.

Republicanism took root particularly easily in the army and among the urban poor, fuelled by falling standards of living and growing anger at government ineptitude. **Dom Carlos** (1898–1908) attempted to rule dictatorially after 1906, alienating most sectors of the country in the process, and was assassinated, along with his eldest son, following a failed Republican coup in 1908. Finally, on October 5, 1910, the **monarchy was overthrown** once and for all by a joint revolt of the army and navy. Dom Manuel went into exile and died, in Britain, in 1932.

THE "DEMOCRATIC" REPUBLIC

After a provisional government of Republican Unity, **elections** took place in 1911, showing a marked swing towards Afonso Costa's **Democratic Party**, which remained the most dominant political force in the country until

1926. However, the divisions among the Republicans, the cyclical attempts at violent overthrow of the new regime by the monarchists, and the weakening of the country's economic, social and political structures, kept the Republic in permanent turmoil. Political life was in chaos and the hopes, perhaps unrealistically high, of the Republic's supporters never began to be realized. There were 45 changes of government in 16 years and several military uprisings.

The forces that had brought the Republic were supported largely by the urban and rural poor, yet new electoral laws based on a literacy test led to a smaller electorate than under the monarchy, disenfranchising most of the Republic's strongest supporters. Successive governments failed to fulfil the least aspirations. Anticlericalism had been a major plank of Costa's platform, arousing massive hostility in the countryside. Legalizing the right to strike merely gave workers a chance to voice their discontent in a massive wave of work stoppages, but the new regime proved to be less than responsive to workers' rights and the repression of union activities was a constant theme. Further fuel was given to the reaction by Portugal's economically disastrous decision to enter **World War I** on the side of the Allies in 1916 and by the vicissitudes of the postwar recession. By 1926 not even the trade unions were prepared to stand by the Republic, preferring to maintain "proletarian neutrality" in the face of what at first seemed no more significant a military intervention than any other.

SALAZAR AND THE "NEW STATE"

While the military may have known what they wanted to overthrow in 1926, they were at first divided as to whether to replace it with a new Republican government or a restored monarchy. From the infighting, a Catholic monarchist, **General Carmona**, eventually emerged as president (which he remained until his death in 1951) with the Republican constitution suspended.

In 1928 one **Dr. António de Oliveira Salazar** joined the Cabinet as Finance Minister. A professor of economics at Coimbra University, he took the post only on condition that he would control the spending and revenue of all government departments. His strict monetarist line (helped by a change in the accounting system)

immediately balanced the budget for the first time since 1913 and in the short term the economic situation was visibly improved. From then on he effectively controlled the country, becoming prime minister in 1932 and not relinquishing that role until 1968.

His regime was very much in keeping with the political tenor of the 1930s and while it had few of the ideological pretensions of a **fascist** state, it had many of the trappings. Members of the National Assembly were chosen from the one permitted political association, the National Union (UN); "workers' organizations" were set up, but run by their employers; education was strictly controlled by the state to promote Catholic values; and censorship was strictly enforced. Opposition was kept in check by the PIDE – a secret police force set up with Gestapo assistance – which used systematic torture and long-term detention in camps on the Azores and Cabo Verde Islands to defuse most resistance. The army, too, was heavily infiltrated by PIDE and none of the several coups mounted against Salazar came close to success. Despite remaining formally neutral throughout the **Spanish Civil War**, Salazar had openly assisted the plotters in their preparations and later sent unofficial army units to fight with Franco. Republican refugees were deported to face certain execution at Nationalist hands.

At home Salazar succeeded in producing the infrastructure of a relatively modern economy but the results of growth were felt by only a few and agriculture, in particular, was allowed to stagnate. Internal unrest, while widespread, was surprisingly muted and apparently easily controlled; the New State's downfall, when it came, was precipitated far more by external factors. Salazar was an ardent imperialist who found himself faced with growing **colonial wars**, which proved costly and brought international disapprobation. India seized Goa and the other Portuguese possessions in 1961 and at about the same time the first serious disturbances were occurring in Angola, Mozambique and, later, in Guinea-Bissau. The regime was prepared to make only the slightest concessions, attempting to defuse the freedom movements by speeding economic development.

The government's reign came to an end in 1968 when Salazar's deck-chair collapsed, and he suffered brain damage. Incapacitated, he lived for another two years, deposed as premier

– though such was the fear of the man, no one ever dared tell him. His successor, **Marcelo Caetano**, attempted to prolong the regime by offering limited democratization at home. However, tensions beneath the surface were fast becoming more overt and attempts to liberalize foreign policy failed to check the growth of guerrilla activity in the remaining colonies, or of discontent **in the army**.

It was in the African-stationed army especially that opposition crystallized. There the young conscript officers came more and more to sympathize with the freedom movements they were intended to suppress and to resent the cost – in economic terms and in lives – of the hopeless struggle. From their number grew the revolutionary **Movimento das Forças Armadas** (MFA).

REVOLUTION

By 1974 the situation in Africa was deteriorating rapidly and at home Caetano's liberalization had come to a dead end; morale, among the army and the people, was lower than ever. The **MFA**, formed originally as an officer's organization to press for better conditions, and which had become increasingly politicized, was already laying its plans for a takeover. Dismissal of two popular generals – Spínola and Costa Gomes – for refusing publicly to support Caetano, led to a first chaotic and abortive attempt on March 16. Finally on April 25, 1974, the plans laid by **Major Otelo Saraiva de Carvalho** for the MFA were complete and their virtually bloodless **coup** went without a hitch, no serious attempt being made to defend the government.

The next two years were perhaps the most extraordinary in Portugal's history, a period of continual **revolution**, massive politicization and virtual anarchy, during which decisions of enormous importance were nevertheless made – above all the granting of independence to all of the overseas territories. At first there was little clear idea of any programme beyond the fact that the army wanted out of Africa. Though the MFA leadership was clearly to the left and at first associated with the PCP (Portuguese Communist Party), the bulk of the officers were less political and **General Spínola**, whom they had been forced to accept as a figurehead, was only marginally to the left of Caetano and strongly opposed total independence for the

colonies. Spínola's dream was clearly to "do a de Gaulle" in Portugal, while the army was above all determined not to replace one dictator with another.

In the event their hands were forced by the massive popular response and especially by huge demonstrations on May Day. It was clear that whatever the leadership might decide, the people, especially in the cities, demanded a rapid move to the left. From the start every party was striving to project itself as the true defender of the "ideals of April 25". Provisional governments came and went but real power rested, where it had begun, with the MFA, now dominated by Saraiva de Carvalho and Vasco Gonçalves. While politicians argued around them, the army claimed to speak directly to the people, leading the country steadily left. It was a period of extraordinary contradictions, with the PCP, hoping to consolidate their position as the "true" revolutionary party, opposing liberalization and condemning strikes as counter-revolutionary, while ultra-conservative peasants were happily seizing their land from its owners.

Sudden **independence** and the withdrawal of Portuguese forces from the former colonies – while generally greeted in Portugal with relief – did not always work so well for the countries involved. Guinea-Bissau and Mozambique, the first to go, experienced relatively peaceful transitions, but **Angola** came to be a serious point of division between Spínola and the MFA. When independence finally came, after Spínola's resignation, the country was already in the midst of a full-scale civil war. The situation was even worse in **East Timor**, where more than ten percent of the population was massacred by invading Indonesian forces following Portuguese withdrawal. In Portugal itself the arrival of more than half-a-million colonial refugees – many of them destitute, most bitter – came to be a major problem for the regime, though their eventual integration proved one of its triumphs.

At home, the first **crisis** came in September 1974, when Spínola, with Gonçalves and Saraiva de Carvalho virtual prisoners in Lisbon's Belém Palace, moved army units to take over key positions. The MFA, however, proved too strong and Spínola was forced to resign, General Costa Gomes replacing him as president. By the summer of 1975 more general reaction was setting in and even the MFA began to show signs of disunity. The country was increasingly split, supporting the Revolution in the south, while remaining deeply conservative in the north. The Archbishop of Braga summed up the north's traditional views, declaring that the struggle against communism should be seen "not in terms of man against man, but Christ against Satan". Nevertheless the Revolution continued to advance; a coup attempt in March failed when the troops involved turned against their officers. The Council of the Revolution was formed, promptly nationalizing banking and private insurance; widespread land seizures went ahead in the Alentejo; and **elections** in the summer resulted in an impressive victory for Mário Soares' Socialist Party (PS).

On November 25, 1975, elements of the army opposed to the rightward shift in the government moved for yet another **coup**, taking over major air bases across the country. Otelo Saraiva de Carvalho, however, declined to bring his Lisbon command to their aid; nor did the hoped-for mass mobilization of the people take place. Government troops under Colonel Ramalho Eanes moved in to force their surrender and – again virtually without bloodshed – the Revolution had ended.

DEMOCRACY AND EUROPE: THE 1980S

The period since November 1975 has been one of slow, and sometimes shaky-looking, **retrenchment**. The Socialist Party was still in power at the end of 1975 and won further ground in the elections that followed, helping to shape the post-revolutionary constitution – a mildly Socialist document, though providing for a fairly powerful president. Early fears of a right-wing coup led by Spínola failed to materialize, helped by the election of Colonel Eanes, a man whom the army trusted, as president. Saraiva de Carvalho came in second, despite the fact that no major party supported him – a token of the degree of popular following enjoyed by the MFA during the Revolution.

Although parties of the right and centre have consistently polled higher votes, the Socialists had effective control until 1980 when Dr. Sá Carneiro managed to create the **Democratic Alliance**, uniting the larger groupings on the right. But within a few months he died in a plane crash. His successor as prime minister, Francisco Pinto Balsemão, barely managed to maintain the coalition for the two years of the term remaining and then only because the rightist parties were united in their determination to amend the constitution "to eliminate clauses which were appropriate in the post-revolutionary atmosphere of 1976 but not to today's needs".

The most enigmatic figure throughout this period remained **President Eanes**, a career soldier who supported the MFA in its early days, later led the forces who ended the Revolution, and is now accused by the right of being a "Marxist sympathizer". He above all seemed to be the figure of stability, with enormous popular support though (at least until recently) apparently little ambition, being happy to concentrate on developing Portugal's links with Africa, Asia and Latin America and overseeing a gradual normalization process.

In **elections** held on the ninth anniversary of the Revolution, April 25, 1983, Mário Soares' Socialist Party again became the largest single party in the national assembly, though requiring the support of the Social Democrats to maintain a coalition government. Soares' premiership was dogged by the unpopularity of his **economic austerity measures** (in part insisted on by the IMF) and by constant delays and breakdowns in the talks over Portuguese and Spanish **entry into the European Community**. These problems did have one positive result, namely closer relations with the traditionally hostile government in Madrid. But the government's economic problems led eventually to the withdrawal of Social Democratic support and to the collapse of the coalition.

New elections in October 1985 were barely conclusive: the left-wing vote split three ways and the Socialists lost their position as largest party to the **Social Democrats** (PSD), whose flamboyant leader, **Dr. Aníbal Cavaco Silva**, became prime minister. But the main feature of the election was disillusionment with the government and the choices on offer to the electorate. There was massive, countrywide abstention and, in rural districts (where people worried most about the effects of EC membership), attacks occurred on polling booths.

In the months that followed, the revolutionary leader, Lt-Colonel Otelo Saraiva de Carvalho, was arrested and put on trial in Lisbon accused of being the leader of 73 suspected terrorists in the **FP-25** urban guerrilla group.

Proceedings were postponed following the shooting of one of the key witnesses and it was not until 1987 that Saraiva de Carvalho was sentenced to 15 years' imprisonment (50 others also received prison sentences). He was later conditionally released after a Supreme Court ruling that there had been irregularities at his trial. In February 1990 he renounced the armed struggle and requested an amnesty.

President Eanes, meanwhile – the other great figure at the end of the Revolution – had been forced to resign the presidency on completion of his second term in January 1986. He was replaced by former Socialist Prime Minister **Mário Soares** who, with the reluctant support of the Communists, narrowly defeated the candidate of the centre-right, becoming the first civilian president for sixty years.

Portugal's entry into the **European Community** in 1986 brought with it the most important changes since the Revolution. With the help of a massive injection of funds to modernize infrastructure and increased foreign investment, Portugal enjoyed unprecedented **economic growth**, running at above four percent per year, greater than most of its European partners. For many Portuguese this resulted in greater material wealth, but behind the trappings of the new prosperity remained pockets of deeply entrenched poverty.

Prime Minister Aníbal Cavaco Silva's early attempts to introduce an economic reform programme were hampered by his lack of a majority, but in April 1987 a censure motion defeat caused the prime minister to resign, bringing about general elections. The PSD (Social Democrats) were returned to power in surprising numbers, enjoying the first absolute majority since the 1974 Revolution and the strength to implement real changes. The centre-right government's free enterprise drive for the removal of Socialist structures and privatization did not run unchallenged: the late 1980s were marked by **industrial unrest**. In March 1988, 1.5 million workers took part in a 24-hour general strike in protest against labour reform laws freeing up employers to lay off workers. The law was eventually approved by both the assembly and the president, but strikes continued throughout 1989 in various sectors of the workforce, attempting to bring wages in line with inflation. The government was also able to reach an eventual agreement with the opposi-

tion to remove Marxist-Leninist elements from the constitution in August 1989.

The Portuguese **Green Party** won its first seat in the **European Parliament** elections in Strasbourg in June 1989 and the ruling PSD was successful in retaining most of its own seats, but suffered an enormous set-back six months later in municipal elections. The socialist opposition gained control of the capital, Lisbon; the northern industrial centre, Porto; and other significant cities. Four years of economic growth had benefited a new yuppie class, but voters were aware of accentuated social inequality and the continued inadequacy of health and education structures. Public opinion had also been influenced by **financial scandals** involving government ministers. Aníbal Cavaco Silva, however, avoided any dirt rubbing off on him personally and survived a motion of censure questioning the government's ethics. The ministers involved were summarily replaced in a surprise end-of-year reshuffle, along with three other ministers, in a move which was taken to indicate Cavaco Silva's firm grip on the reins.

THE 1990S

Scandal was also in the air surrounding **President Mário Soares** in early 1990, when the Socialist governor of Portuguese-administered **Macau** (Hong Kong's enclave neighbour), a man personally appointed by Soares, was accused of receiving back-handers from a German company trying to secure the contract for the building of an airport. The incident called Soares' staffs' integrity into question and strained relations with the prime minister, Cavaco Silva. But the president, popular for his down-to-earth image and his dislike of ceremony, retained his public support and won a landslide victory in presidential elections in January 1991. At Cavaco Silva's insistence, the PSD had not put forward a candidate for the presidency, partly in acknowledgement of a successful relationship between the government and the incumbent president and partly to avoid any further humiliation of a figure who was guaranteed to win. In turn, Cavaco Silva won a convincing mandate in the elections of October 1991, when the **PSD returned to government** with over fifty percent of the vote.

The new decade took Portugal into the second stage of its ten-year transition phase for EC entry and into its **presidency of the European**

Community in 1992, the year when (on December 31) all remaining trade and employment barriers were removed and the EC became the EU. The country adopted its EU task with considerable imagination, and expense, staging a superb exhibiton of its culture – Europalia – in Brussels, and building a grand presidency HQ in the Lisbon suburb of Belém. On the domestic front, the PSD continued with privatization and forged plans for the conversion of state-run banks in preparation for joining the European Monetary System in the mid-1990s.

Dealing with **inflation** remained at the top of the government's agenda, during the early 1990s. It had to do this while coping with increased discontent over social issues, as the opposition called it to account for statistics that show Portugal had, and still has, the highest **infant mortality** and **illiteracy** rates in Europe. Unemployment figures, too, hide a high proportion of underpaid and part-time workers and disguise the fact that wages have failed to increase in real terms in spite of impressive economic growth. There are fears, too, that now the European Union has brought down its trade borders completely, fiercer competition is likely to force more Portuguese out of work. Portugal's social security system is incapable of assimilating large numbers of **unemployed**, something which could lead to social unrest. Matters are further strained by the demanding efforts to comply with the Maastricht Treaty's targets and the new GATT agreements.

The **opening up of Eastern Europe** has also exposed Portugal to fiercer competition for trade and investment, although a modernized infrastructure and improved transport networks mean that it continues to be attractive to foreign investors. **Tourism**, which accounts for nearly a tenth of the country's GNP and over a quarter of all foreign investment, has flourished and one challenge will be finding alternatives to the Algarve, where restrictions have been imposed to control the industry's all too disturbingly obvious side-effects.

One of the main headaches for the government, though, continues to be the inefficiency of **Portuguese agriculture**, which employs nearly one-fifth of the workforce but produces only a fraction of the country's wealth. So far, help from Brussels has buffered the less advantageous effects of EU membership, but the honeymoon period is over and although

some modernization has taken place, there is still a huge gap between Portuguese **prices** and European Union prices – a gap that is not likely to be eliminated until the end of the decade and one which will tend to keep Portugal among Europe's poorest nations. A slightly alarming shift, too, has been the takeover of large areas of banking, real estate and the financial sectors by Spanish companies, while EU funds still play a dominant role in Portugal's development, thus blurring the true extent of real economic growth.

General elections in October 1995 brought ten years of Conservative rule to an end and the moderate Socialists came into power under the enthusiastic leadership of **António Guterres**. The Portuguese had tired of Cavaco Silva's austere, secretive style of government and were ready for a change. The Socialists fell just short of an absolute majority, but won a comfortable advantage against a divided opposition. Guterres' programme differed little from that of his conservative predecessors and caused few worries for the business world. He offered a touch more sympathy towards the social welfare budget and a tougher stance towards the European Union, but otherwise pledged to continue to liberalize and privatize the economy and keep the country on target for European monetary union in 1999.

A final nail was banged into the coffin of Cavaquismo by Cavaco Silva's surprise defeat in the presidential elections of January 1996. The leftwing former mayor of Lisbon, **Jorge Sampaio**, whose avuncular, paternalistic style reflects that of his predecessor, Mario Soares, won 54 percent of the votes, against Cavaco Silva's 46 percent. This result gave Portugal a head of state and prime minister from the same – Socialist – party for the first time since the 1974 Revolution. Cavaco Silva, meanwhile, remains active in PSD politics and, should he decide to stand, would be considered a major threat to Sampaio in the next presidential elections, due some time in the year 2000.

But for now, this swing to the left shows a desire in the Portuguese people for a framework of democratic stability and a leaning towards a fresher and more effervescent spirit, particularly among the young. The more uninhibited spirit is no better expressed than in the proliferation of Lisbon's African nightclubs, patronized initially by Angolans, Cape Verdans and others from

Portugal's former colonies, and increasingly by young people from all over Europe. The jumping African rhythms could not be more different from the sad nostalgia of traditional fado and they reflect an increasingly relaxed and cosmopolitan society.

TOWARDS THE MILLENNIUM: THE PROSPECTS

The next major event on Portugal's calendar is **Expo 98** – the last Expo of the millennium – which will take place in Lisbon from May 22 to September 30 and is expected to attract around eight million visitors. Timed to mark the 500th anniversary of Vasco da Gama's arrival in India, the exhibition also coincides with the UN's Year of the Oceans and its theme – "The Oceans, a Heritage for the Future" – will be explored in a variety of pavilions (see p.86), among them, the futuristic **Oceanarium**.

Occupying a five-kilometre stretch along the northern bank of the Tejo estuary, Expo is part of a long-term project (due to be completed in 2015) that aims to transform 3.3 square kilometres of derelict dockland area into a residential and business hub. Radical improvements to the city's **transport infrastructure** have been undertaken, seen to most spectacular effect in the building of the new seventeen-kilometre Vasco de Gama bridge over the Tejo, intended to relieve congestion on the existing bridge and open up the rather sleepy southern bank of the Tejo to speculative development. A brand-new railway station will serve the Expo site, linking up with a new metro line and providing several additional stations in a part of the city hitherto poorly served by public transport. If successful, Expo and its related projects could increase Portugal's economic growth by up to thirty percent over the next few years.

However, away from the big cities and Euro-funded motorways that link them, many of Portugal's rural areas have remained untouched by the transformations of recent years. The northeastern region of the Minho and much of Trás-os-Montes are among Europe's least developed corners and wages are the lowest in the country, with unemployment way above the national average and child labour and illiteracy commonplace. An official report at the end of 1995 found that more than 47 percent of Portuguese between the ages of 15 and 64 have little or no ability to read or do sums, while a more recent report in 1997 indicated that over seventy percent of the adult population had spent less than six years at school. This astounding backwardness – which puts Portugal behind not only the rest of Europe, but also such countries as Paraguay and the Philippines – is a legacy of the Salazar regime, which invested little in education for forty years and even favoured illiteracy as a guarantee against subversion.

As ever, politicians promise much but deliver little, though Portugal's likely adoption of the Euro in line with several other European countries at the end of 1999, will – they hope –bring in the necessary investment and resources. So far, the economic signs are good: inflation, at 2–2.5 percent, is below the EU average; the national debt is below the three percent of Gross National Product allowed by Maastricht, and consumer spending continues to spiral with little negative effect on inflation. However, the government's task of bringing Portugal into the new millennium as a fully integrated EU state depends not only on macroeconomics but their ability to overcome the gulf between the countryside and the towns, whilst staying within a strict budget in accordance with dictates from Brussels. At the moment, massive EU funding in the countryside appears to be reaping its dividends, but what is crucial if this development is to be sustained is that the government remains committed long after EU funds dry up. The outcome of the current debate about the **decentralization of power** (and the December 1997 referendum on the subject) will be crucial in defining the limits and responsibilities of central government.

CHRONOLOGY OF MONUMENTS AND ARTS

2000 BC–1500 BC	**Neolithic** settlements in the north of the country – **Verracos Culture** in Trás-os-Montes.	*Porcas* (stone boars) of Bragança, Murça, etc.
700 BC–600 BC	**Castro Culture** of fortified hill-towns, or *citânias*, concentrated in the Minho; refined by the **Celtic** Iron Age invasions.	**Citânia de Briteiros** (near Braga) and other sites; best collection of artefacts in Museu Martins Sarmento, Guimarães.
210 BC	**Romans** enter peninsula and begin colonization; northern Portugal not finally pacified until 19 BC.	**Conímbriga**, 4th c BC Celtic town near Coimbra, adapted to Roman occupation (survives until 5th c AD).
60 BC	Julius Caesar establishes a capital at Lisbon and towns at Beja, Évora, Santarém, etc.	Walls and other remains at Idanha, in Beira Baixa; temple and aqueducts of Évora; bridges at Chaves, Ponte de Lima, Leiria and elsewhere.
4th c AD	Bishoprics founded at Braga, Évora, Faro and Lisbon.	
409–411	**Barbarian** invasions: Suevi settle in the north.	
585	**Visigoths** incorporate Suevian state into their Iberian empire.	Isolated churches, mainly in the north, include 7th-c São Pedro de Balsemão (near Lamego) and São Frutuoso at Braga.
711	**Moors** from North Africa invade and conquer peninsula within seven years.	Fortresses/walls survive at Silves, Lisbon, Sintra, Elvas, Mértola, Alcácer do Sal, etc.
9th c	**Al-Gharb** (Algarve) becomes an independent Moorish kingdom, governed from Silves.	Moorish legacy also includes azulejos (ceramic tiles), later designed by Muslim (Mudejar) craftsmen for royal palace at Sintra, etc.
868	Porto reconquered by Christian kings of Asturias-León.	
11th c	Country of **Portucale** emerges and (1097) is given to Henry of Burgundy.	Cluniac monks, administering pilgrimage route to Santiago, bring Romanesque architecture from France. 12th-c churches at Bravães, Tomar, etc. Council chamber at Bragança.
1143	**Afonso Henriques** recognized as first king of Portucale at the Treaty of Zamora.	Guimarães castle built.
1147	Afonso takes Lisbon and Santarém from the Moors; followed in 1162 by Beja and Évora and in 1189 (temporarily) Silves.	Fortress-like **Romanesque cathedrals** of Lisbon, Coimbra, Évora, Braga and Porto.
1212	First assembly of the Cortes (parliament) at Coimbra.	1153: Cistercians found abbey of **Alcobaça**; in this and other Cistercian churches, notably at Coimbra, Gothic architecture enters Portugal.
1249	Afonso III completes reconquest of the Algarve.	

1279–1325	Reign of **Dom Dinis** 1297: Castile recognises Portuguese borders.	Over fifty castles built along Spanish border, including Beja and Estremoz. Coimbra University founded.
1385	Battle of Aljubarrota: João I defeats Castilians to become first king of **House of Avis.**	Abbey of **Batalha**, the great triumph of mature Portuguese Gothic, built in celebration of victory. Paço Real built at Sintra.
1415	**Infante Henriques** (Henry the Navigator; d 1460) active at Sagres. 1419: Madeira discovered. 1427: Azores discovered. 1457: Cape Verde Islands discovered.	Navigation School at Sagres; Lagos fort. Painters: Flemish-influenced "Portuguese Primitives" include Nuno Gonçalves.
1495–1521	Reign of **Dom Manuel I** ("The Fortunate"). 1497: Vasco da Gama opens up sea route to India. 1500: Cabral discovers Brazil. 1513: Portuguese reach China.	Late-Gothic **Manueline style** develops, with strong marine motifs and flamboyance anticipating Art Nouveau. Greatest examples at Tomar, Batalha, Lisbon (Belém) and Sintra. By 1530s Renaissance forms are introduced and merged.
1521–57	Reign of João III.	Painters include Grão Vasco (see Viseu).
1557–78	Reign of **Dom Sebastião**. 1578: Disastrous expedition to Morocco, loss of king and mass slaughter of nobility at Alcácer-Quibir.	Important sculptural school at **Coimbra** (1520–70) centred on French Renaissance sculptors Nicolas Chanterenne, Filipe Hodart and Jean de Rouen.
1581–1640	Philip II brings **Spanish** (Hapsburg) rule.	
1640	**João IV**, Duke of **Bragança**, restores independence.	Severe late-Renaissance style: São Vicente, Lisbon (designed by Felipe Terzi), etc.
1706–50	Reign of **Dom João V**. Gold and diamonds discovered in Brazil, reaching a peak of wealth and exploitation in the 1740s.	Baroque palace-monastery of **Mafra** (1717–35). Decoration of Coimbra University Library. High Baroque carved, gilt church interiors. Also simpler, more rustic Baroque style of plaster/granite – **Lamego** and **Bom Jesus**. Rococo Palace of **Queluz** (1752).
1755	**Great Earthquake** destroys Lisbon and parts of the Alentejo and Algarve.	"Pombaline" neoclassical rebuilding of Lisbon (Baixa).
1843–53	Maria II holds throne with German consort, Fernando II.	**Pena Palace** folly built at Sintra.
1908	Assassination of Carlos I in Lisbon.	
1910	Exile of Manuel II ("The Unfortunate") and **end of Portuguese monarchy**.	Cubist painter Amadeu de Sousa Cardoso (d 1918); museum devoted to him at Amarante.
1910–26	"Democratic" Republic.	
1932–68	**Salazar** dictatorship. Goa is seized by India; colonial wars in Africa.	
1974	April 25 **Revolution**.	
1986	**Entry to European Community** (EC).	
1994	Lisbon is European city of Culture.	Permanent gallery of modern Portuguese
1998	Lisbon hosts Expo 98.	artists at Lisbon's Gulbenkian Foundation.

BOOKS

Portugal has been covered very sparsely by British and American writers and publishers, and many of the works that do exist in English are out of print (o/p) and available only from libraries or specialist book dealers. A reliable specialist source for out-of-print books on all aspects of Portugal is Keith Harris Books, PO Box 207, Twickenham, TW2 5BQ (☎ & fax 0181/898 7789, email: *Keith_Harris_Books@Compuserve.com*). For more contemporary publications, it's worth checking the latest books available from the UK publisher Carcanet Press, Conavon Court, 12–16 Blackfriars Street, Manchester, M3 5BQ (☎ 0161/834 8730, fax 832 0084, email: *pnr@carcanet.u-net.com*), who have a fiction series entitled "From the Portuguese" and a non-fiction series entitled "Aspects of Portugal". Some of the titles in these series are reviewed below.

Where two publishers are given for the books listed below, they refer to the UK and US publishers respectively. Books published in one country only are followed by the publisher and UK, US or Portugal; if a book has the same UK and US publisher only the publisher's name is given.

GENERAL TRAVEL AND GUIDES

William Beckford, *Recollections of an Excursion to the Monasteries of Alcobaça and Batalha; Travels in Spain and Portugal (1778–88)* (Centaur Press; Norwood Editions). Mad and enormously rich, Beckford lived for some time at Sintra and travelled widely in Estremadura. His accounts, told with a fine eye for the absurd, are a lot of fun.

Lord Byron, *Selected Letters and Journals* (Pimlico; Belknap). Only a few days of Portuguese travel but memorable ones – beginning with romantic enthusiasm, ending in outright abuse.

Almeida Garrett, *Travels in My Homeland* (Peter Owen; Dufour). A classic Portuguese writer, Garrett was exiled to Europe in the 1820s, came into contact with the Romantics and later returned to play a part in the liberal government of the 1830s. This is a witty, discursive narrative ramble around the country.

Paul Hyland, *Backwards Out of the Big World* (Flamingo, UK). A fascinating and sympathetic account of a journey through Portugal by a man who knows the country's people, history and literature as few foreigners do.

Manfredd Hamm and Werner Radasewsky, *Lisbon* (Nicolai, UK). The strength of this book is its wonderful photographs, which capture the atmosphere and light of the city, its people and its surroundings through all its varying moods.

Marion Kaplan, *The Portuguese: the Land and its People* (Penguin; Penguin, o/p). Published in 1991, this is a readable, all-embracing volume, covering everything from wine to the family, poetry and the land. The style is a bit old-fashioned, but it's the best general introduction to the country available.

Rose Macaulay, *They Went to Portugal* (Carcanet, UK). The book covers British travellers to Portugal from the Crusaders to Byron, weaving an anecdotal history of the country in the process. A serious study if you take it as such; a good read if you just feel like dipping into the stories.

Fernando Pessoa, *Lisbon: What the Tourist Should See (o que o turista deve ver)* (Livros Horizonte, Portugal). Just published, bilingual edition of the great poet's guide to Lisbon, which he wrote in English.

Oleg Polunin and B.E. Smythies, *Flowers of South-West Europe: A Field Guide* (Oxford University Press). The best available guide to the Portuguese flora.

Norman Renouf, *Spain and Portugal by Rail* (Bradt Publications; Globe Pequot). Fairly limited guide containing maps of major stations, lists of hotels near them, and background information on rail passes. Focuses largely on Spain.

Stuart Ross, *Portugal's Pousada Route* (Vista Ibérica Publicações, Portugal; Seven Hill, US). An informative book containing details about Portugal's state-owned hotels and some background history on the surrounding countryside; with photos by Marion Kaplan.

Sacheverell Sitwell, *Portugal and Madeira* (Batsford, UK o/p). Mix of art history, observation and rather pompous upper-class travelogue from the 1950s. Sitwell's great enthusiasm is Portuguese Baroque. He also "discovers" Mateus Rosé wine for the British.

Anne de Stoop, *Living in Portugal* (Flammarion; Abbeville). A glossy coffee-table tome filled with beautifully evocative photographs of Portugal's sights and architectural gems, from palaces and manor houses to rural houses, *pastelarias* and restaurants.

HISTORY AND POLITICS

David Birmingham, *A Concise History of Portugal* (Cambridge University Press). Recommended for the casual reader; concise indeed, but providing straightforward and informative coverage from the year dot to 1991.

Daniel J. Boorstin, *The Discoverers* (Dent o/p; Random House). Old, standard text on the Discoveries that you might find in libraries.

C.R. Boxer, *The Portuguese Seaborne Empire 1415–1825* (Carcanet Press, UK). Entertaining account by a prolific writer on the region.

António de Figueiredo, *Portugal: Fifty Years of Dictatorship* (Penguin, UK o/p). An illuminating study which takes as its starting-point the 1926 military coup that brought Salazar to power and goes through to the 1974 Revolution.

Lawrence S. Graham and Douglas L. Wheeler (eds), *In Search of Modern Portugal: the Revolution and Its Consequences* (University of Wisconsin Press). An academic study published in the early 1980s; heavy-going but ultimately rewarding.

Harold Livermore, *A New History of Portugal* (Cambridge University Press o/p). Covering events through to 1976, this is thorough, if not exactly inspiring, but was revised a little too soon after the 1974 Revolution to be authoritative.

A.H. de Oliveira Marques, *History of Portugal* (Columbia University Press). Accessible general history.

Dan L. Raby, *Fascism and Resistance in Portugal* (Manchester University Press, UK o/p). Scholarly account of the subject.

José Hermano Saraiva, *Portugal: A Companion History* (Carcanet, UK). The most recent of its kind, this is an accessible and concise history of the country written especially for non-specialist foreigners by the author of the bestselling Portuguese original. Includes useful easy-reference glossaries of historical figures and places.

ART AND ARCHITECTURE

Marcus Binney, *Country Manors of Portugal* (Scala Books). The excellent photos are the main reason to buy this solid volume.

Helder Carita and Homem Cardoso, *Portuguese Gardens* (Antique Collector's Club). A huge and beautiful tome, lavishly illustrated with photos and plans, with a scholarly text.

Miles Danby, *The Fires of Excellence* (Garnet Publishing, UK). Magnificent and detailed study of the Oriental architecture of Spain and Portugal, illustrated with specially commissioned photographs.

Júlio Gil and Augusto Cabrita, *The Finest Castles in Portugal* (Beaufort Publishing, UK o/p). A superb illustrated survey of Portuguese castles, let down a little by a highly pedestrian translation/text.

FICTION

António Lobo Antunes, *An Explanation of the Birds, The Natural Order of Things* and *Act of the Damned* (Secker & Warburg o/p; Grove-Atlantic); *South of Nowhere* (Chatto & Windus; Random House; both o/p). Many consider Antunes to be Portugal's leading contemporary writer, notwithstanding the increasing worldwide acclaim for José Saramago (see below). The two writers couldn't be more different, however. Antunes is a psychologist and writes helter-skelter prose, notably in the recent *Act of the Damned*, whose narrative voice changes ceaselessly.

Maria Isabel Barreno, Maria Teresa Horta and Maria Velho da Costa *New Portuguese Letters: The Three Marias* (Readers International). Published (and prosecuted) in 1972, pre-Revolution Portugal, this collage of stories, letters and poems is a modern feminist parable based on the seventeenth-century "Letters of a Portuguese Nun".

José Cardoso Pires, *Ballad of Dog's Beach* (Dent o/p; Beaufort Books o/p). Ostensibly a detective thriller but the murder described actually took place during the last years of Salazar's dictatorship and Pires' research draws upon the original secret-police files. Compelling, highly original and with acute psychological insights, it was awarded Portugal's highest literary prize and made into a film.

Ray Keenoy, David Treece and Paul Hyland, *The Babel Guide to the Fiction of Portugal, Brazil and Africa* (Boulevard Books, UK). A tantalizing introduction to Portuguese literature, with a collection of reviews of the major works of Lusophone fiction since 1945.

Eugénio Lisboa (ed), *The Anarchist Banker and Other Portuguese Stories* and *Professor Pfiglzz and His Strange Companion and Other Portuguese Stories* (Carcanet, UK). A fabulous two-volume collection of twentieth-century short stories, mostly very modern, which gives more than a taste of the exuberance and talent currently proliferating in Portuguese literature. Stories by old favourites – Eça de Queiroz, Pessoa, José Régio and Miguel Torga – are included too, mostly for the first time in English.

Eugénio Lisboa and Helder Macedo (eds), *The Dedalus Book of Portuguese Fantasy* (Dedalus; Hippocrene). A rich feast of literary fantasy comprising short stories by the likes of Eça de Queiroz and José de Almada Negreiros.

José Rodrigues Miguéis, *Happy Easter* (Carcanet, UK). A powerful and disturbing account of the distorted reality experienced by a schizophrenic, whose deprived childhood leads him to a self-destructive and tragic life in Lisbon; evocatively written and a surprisingly gripping read.

Cees Nooteboom, *The Following Story* (Panther; Harcourt Brace). Dutch author Nooteboom successfully evokes the Portuguese melancholy (*saudade*) in a tale of a Classics teacher who falls asleep in Amsterdam and wakes up in a hotel room in Lisbon, the scene of a romantic past that he realizes he can never fully recapture.

Fernando Pessoa, *The Book of Disquiet: a Selection* (Carcanet; Pantheon). The country's best-known poet (see below) wrote just this one work in prose (as Bernardo Soares, one of his six *noms de plume*): a kind of autobiography, set in Lisbon, and posthumously compiled from a trunkload of material. It is regarded as a modernist classic, with the book's admirers including Jorge Luís Borges.

Eça de Queiroz, *The Mandarin and The Relic* (Dedalus; Hippocrene); *The Sin of Father Amaro* (Penguin, UK); *The Maias* (Penguin, UK); *Cousin Bazilio* (Quartet, UK); *The Illustrious House of Ramires* (Quartet; New Directions). Queiroz is the classic Portuguese novelist, responsible for a string of nineteenth-century narratives, recently available in new translations. The two best are *The Illustrious House of Ramires* and *The Maias*, entertaining narratives which give a comprehensive account of nineteenth-century Portuguese society.

Mário de Sá Carneiro, *The Great Shadow* (Dedalus, UK). Sá Carneiro, who committed suicide at 26, writes with stunning intensity and originality about art, science, death, sex and insanity in this series of short stories.

José Saramago, *Baltasar and Blimunda* (Picador; Harvard University Press); *The Year of the Death of Ricardo Reis, The Gospel According to Jesus Christ, The Stone Raft* (Harvill; Harcourt Brace); and *Manual of Painting and Calligraphy* (Carcanet, UK). Saramago has been mooted as a Nobel winner and at last has a number of titles available translated into English. The one to start with is *Ricardo Reis*, a magnificent novel which won *The Independent* foreign fiction award. Its theme is the return of Dr. Reis, after sixteen years in Brazil, to a Lisbon where the Salazar dictatorship is imminent and where Reis wanders the streets to be confronted by the past and the ghost of the writer Fernando Pessoa. In *Baltasar and Blimunda*, Saramago mixes fact with myth in an entertaining novel set around the building of the Convent of Mafra and the construction of the world's first flying machine. In *The Stone Raft*, Saramago describes what happens when the Iberian peninsula begins to drift away from the rest of Europe, both literally and metaphorically.

Antonio Tabucchi, *Declares Pereira* (Harvill; New Directions); *Requiem: a Hallucination* (Harvill; New Directions). A highly-regarded Italian author who lived for many years in

Portugal, Tabucchi has recreated in *Declares Pereira* the repressive atmosphere of Salazar's Lisbon, tracing the experiences of a newspaper editor who questions his own lifestyle under a regime which he can no longer ignore. The book has recently been made into a film by Roberto Faenza. *Requiem: a Hallucination* is an imaginative and dreamlike journey around Lisbon, with Tabucchi engaging in conversations with people as diverse as a barman in the Museu de Arte Antiga and a Pessoa-like writer. The unifying theme, however, is food and drink and the book even contains a note on recipes.

Miguel Torga, *The Creation Days One and Two* (Carcanet, UK); *Tales from the Mountain* (Carcanet; QED Press). Twice nominated for the Nobel Prize before his death in 1995, Torga lived and set his stories in the wild Trás-os-Montes region. His pseudonym "Torga" is a tough species of heather which thrives in this rural, unforgiving landscape, where the fiercely independent characters of his books battle to survive in a repressed society. Torga's harsh views of rural life in *Tales from the Mountain* led to the book being banned under the Salazar regime.

POETRY

Luís de Camões *The Lusiads* (Penguin, UK). Portugal's national epic, celebrating the ten-month voyage of Vasco da Gama which opened the sea route to India. This is a good prose translation.

Fernando Pessoa, *A Centenary Pessoa* (Carcanet; Sheep Meadow). This superlative anthology of poems, prose, letters and photographs is the most comprehensive selection of Pessoa's output yet published in English, and at the moment it's the only substantial in-print translation of the startling, lyrical verse on which his reputation rests.

FOOD AND WINE

Alex Liddell and Janet Price, *Port Wine Quintas of the Douro* (Philip Wilson, UK). Highly erudite account of the wines and history; superb photos put it beyond specialist interest.

Maite Manjon, *Gastronomy of Spain and Portugal* (Garamond o/p; Prentice Hall). A comprehensive collection of classic Iberian recipes, including a glossary of Portuguese and Spanish terms and explanations of traditional cooking techniques. Particularly good on regional specialities and wines, too.

Jan Read, *The Wines of Portugal* (Faber and Faber o/p). Very full descriptions of every region and particularly of soon-to-be internationally recognized wines. Clear explanations, too, of why each region has its own flavour and much interesting social and historical background.

Edite Vieira, *The Taste of Portugal* (Grub Street, UK). A delight to read, let alone cook from. Vieira combines snippets of history and passages from Portuguese writers (very well translated) to illustrate her dishes; highly recommended.

LEISURE AND SPORTS

Bethan Davies and Ben Cole, *Walking in Portugal* (Footprint Guides, UK). New and dependable guide to trekking in the national parks of Gerês, Serra da Estrela, Montesinho, and Serra de São Mamede. An excellent supplement to our own coverage.

Laurence Rose, *Where to Watch Birds in Spain and Portugal* (Hamlyn; Stackpole). Comprehensive guide to some of Europe's finest and most environmentally sensitive wildlife sites, with practical information on how to get there and when to go. Interesting reading for amateurs as well as being invaluable for ardent ornithologists.

John Russell and Nuno Campos, *Golf's Golden Coast* (Vista Ibérica Publicações, Portugal). An attractive, illustrated guide for anyone interested in the Algarve's clubs – of the 18-hole variety.

RESIDENCE

Rachael Robinson and Victoria Pybus, *Live and Work in Spain and Portugal* (Vacation Work; Seven Hills). Invaluable handbook packed with details on permits, business, teaching, health, schools, renting and buying property, etc.

Sue Tyson-Ward, *How to Live and Work in Portugal* (How To Books, UK). Another detailed and practical guide on all aspects of living in the country, including info on how to start a business, open a bank account, find out about schools and, of course, track down ex-pat activities.

MUSIC

Portugal has a rich musical culture, with roots harking back to Provençal troubadours, continuing through ballads and the unique "blues" of the fado and encompassing, more recently, the rhythms of the country's five former African colonies.

Each of these elements has a currency in the sounds that you hear today – from the French Provençal strain in the folk music played at northern festivals, to the cosmopolitan rock and jazz of the larger cities. An additional element is added by the wealth of singer-songwriters, most of them from the highly political "New Song" movement fostered by the dramatic events of the 1970s, as the country threw off the 36-year dictatorship of Salazar and was forced to withdraw from its colonies.

INSTRUMENTS, VOICES AND RHYTHMS

There is a startling variety of Portuguese **folk instruments**: bagpipes, harmonicas, accordions, flutes, assorted drums (*caixas, bombos, adufes, pandeiros, sarroncas*), and countless percussion instruments (*reco-reco, ferrinhos, genebres, trancanholas*). But the country's pride and glory is strings, which include violins, the classic twelve-stringed "Portuguese guitar", and six varieties of "**viola-guitars**", unknown elsewhere in Europe. Each of these has a character, tuning and design of its own. Best known are the little four-stringed *cavaquinho* and the

bigger *guitarra portuguesa*, the standard accompaniments to Lisbon fado. Others range through elaborate combinations of single, double and triple strings.

One of the most common combinations of instruments is the **zés-pereiras**, made up of a large *bombo*, a *caixa* and a bagpipe or fife (depending on whether you're in the Minho or Beiras region) and often used to announce grand occasions. Another traditional combination popular throughout the country is the **rancho**, made up of violins, guitars, clarinets, harmonicas and *ferrinhos*, with the later addition of the accordion.

If the folk traditions are rich in instruments, its **singers** are unrivalled. In every town and district there is an amateur choir. After a good meal someone will start an **à desgarrada** (a cappella) song, followed intuitively by the other guests. It is not at all unusual, if you go to a **fado** performance, to find the entire staff of the establishment taking part, from the owner to the cloakroom attendant. To listen to a vocal ensemble of three women from Manhouce, or a rural male choir from Alentejo, is to hear genuinely popular roots music. Alentejo is home also to the *saia*, sung by women accompanying themselves on the *pandeireta*.

Since Portugal remains for the most part a rural society, a great many **songs** that survive reflect the cycles of nature, such as *natal, reis* and *janeiras* – lullabies and tilling, sowing and harvest songs. They remain very much within a living tradition. Equally authentic, if less harmonious, are the **singing contests** in which rival performers exchange improvizations on a theme, or the fandango, a dance where two men match their footwork. Among other popular **traditional dances** are *modas, despiques, chulas, rusgas, corridinhos, viras*, waltzes and the ritual steps of the *pauliteiros* (stick-dancers) of Miranda in the Douro region.

FADO

The fado is Portugal's most famous – though perhaps also its least accessible – music. Lyrical and sentimental, it is thought to have origins in African slave songs, though the influence of Portugal's own maritime and colonial past is equally apparent. After the 1974 Revolution, when the empire disintegrated, it went through something of a crisis. Today, it has come to be identified with a general sense of frustration and, some would have it, with an endemic and peculiarly Portuguese fatalism.

There are two versions of the fado. That of the humble **Alfama and Mouraria districts of Lisbon** (performed mainly in the Bairro Alto clubs, these days) is highly personal and full of feeling. The more academic strand from **Coimbra** reflects that city's ancient university traditions and is performed mainly by students and Coimbra graduates. In both versions, the theme is usually love, though fados have been composed on all kinds of subjects.

By far the most famous of the fado singers, and arguably its greatest performer, is **Amália Rodrigues**. She can be seen at prestige clubs and concerts in Lisbon, though keep in mind that in recent years she has strayed into other genres, even variety.

Other big traditional names include Florencio Carvalho, Alberto Prado, José de Câmara and Castro Rodrigo. Recent performers have adapted the form to a more modern rhythm, including, most recently, Manuel Osório and (a name to look out for in the clubs) **Carlos do Carmo**. The singer-songwriters, too, have looked toward fado. Following the lead of José Afonso (see below), nearly all the stars have produced one or two of their own interpretations of the form.

THE BALLAD

It was an attempt to update the Coimbra fado that resulted in the modern Portuguese **ballad** and which in turn, in the last years of the dictatorship, gave way to "New Song" (see p.512). This, from the Revolution of April 25, 1974 onwards, became a genuine political song movement, broadening in recent years to a movement known as *Música Popular* – essentially contemporary folk music, composed and performed by an impressive roster of singer-songwriters.

The **lyrics** generated by this movement were – and are – as significant as the music. Many artists turned to modern poetry that dealt with contemporary social and cultural issues. They also drew on music rooted in popular tradition, both rural and urban, that reflected influences of various kinds – colonial, French, English, or Spanish – but avoided the easy rhythms of commercial pop.

One of the forerunners of the genre was the 1956 LP *Canções Heróicas – Canções Regionais Portuguesas* (*Heroic Songs – Portuguese Regional Songs*), arranged by Fernando Lopes Graça and performed by the Choir of the Amateur Musicians' Academy. Although the harmonizations are a long way from New Song, two basic elements are already present: committed lyrics and respect for genuine **regional music**.

Another LP, *Fados of Coimbra* by José Afonso and Luís Gois, appeared in May of the same year. The fado was out of favour in radical circles at the time. It had become just another branch of "national song", with overtones of vulgar soap-opera.

José Afonso gradually abandoned the Portuguese guitar for the Spanish, which allows for more freedom in the accompaniment. His first solo records came out in 1960, including *Balada do Outono* (Autumn Ballad), which gave its name to the new genre and made it respectable. He was soon joined by Adriano Correia de Oliveira and the **poets** Manuel Alegre, Ary dos Santos and Manuel Correia, whose work provided the text for numerous songs.

After the onset of the **colonial wars**, censorship began to wreak havoc. *Menino do Bairro Negro* (*Black Slum Kid*) and *Os Vampiros* (*The Vampires*), both by José Afonso, were withdrawn from the market and only instrumental versions allowed to be sold. Some singers chose to go into exile. Luís Cília released several records in Paris under the general title of *A Poesia Portuguesa de Hoje e de Sempre* (*Portuguese Poetry of Today and All Times*), on which he sung his own arrangements of poems by Camões, Pessoa, Saramago and others.

The release in 1968 of José Afonso's *Cantares do Andarilho* (*Songs of the Road*) marked the coming of age of the ballad. By now Adriano was making his first LPs, as were Manuel Freire, José Jorge Letria, José Mário Branco, Father Fanhais and soon afterwards Fausto, Pedro Barroso and the Angolan Rui Mingas. At the same time, the **social climate** was becoming increasingly suffocating. These singers were banned from television and hardly ever heard on the radio. There were very few venues and permits were granted sparingly, forcing them to take other jobs to make a living.

In today's uncensored climate, a contemporary performer of this style of music is Romantic singer **Paulo Gonzo**, whose ballads are always an instant hit.

NEW SONG

José Afonso's *Cantigas de Maio* (*Songs of May*), José Mário Branco's *Mudam-se os Tempos, Mudam-se as Vontades* (*Changing Times, Changing Wishes*) and Adriano Correia de Oliveira's *Gente d'Aqui e de Agora* (*People Here and Now*) showed an improvement in the quality of the material. The lyrics went further in their reflections on living conditions and were more open in their **protest**, while the music explored new forms, rhythms and means of expression. José Mário Branco made a key contribution as an arranger and producer. Pre-production **censorship**, however, continued to be strictly imposed and some singers stopped recording to avoid it. Others, like José Afonso, resorted to ever more cryptic lyrics.

This was how things stood on the night of **April 24, 1974**. At 10.55pm, João Paulo Dinis of the "Associates of Lisbon" radio programme played *E Depois do Adeus* (*After the Goodbyes*), Paulo de Caravalho's Eurovision Song Contest entry for the year. At midnight came the final signal – Leite Vasconcelos played *Grândola Vila Morena* on Radio Renascença's "Limit" programme. The army captains went into action and on the following day the coup was a reality: Portugal was returning to democracy.

There began an uncertain period during which it was unclear who held power. Singers such as Sérgio Godinho, Luís Cília, José Mário Branco and Father Fanhais returned from exile and, now that censorship had been lifted, New Song gave way to **political song**. Everyone had slogans, analyses and solutions to offer in the process of clarification which followed.

Singers were suddenly in constant demand for the political and cultural events being improvised with a minimum of technical resources all over the country, giving performances in factories, co-operatives and squatters' settlements. They set up various groups according to their political leanings: Free Song (Canto Livre), the October Group (Grupo Outubro), the Group for Cultural Action and Voices for the Cause (Grupo de Acção Cultural-Vozes na Luta, or GAC). The last of these, in mixing traditional songs with its sloganeering political ones, set an unconscious pattern for future developments. Other artists slowly branched out into work with the numerous theatre groups of the time and on soundtracks for films. Some singers and musicians also formed co-operatives, such as Eranova (New Age) and Cantarabril (Sing of April).

FOLK GROUPS

As time passed and things returned to normal, **traditional music** enjoyed a revival, bringing with it the first commercial folk groups. In the 1960s, much work had been done in studying and recording traditional Portuguese music, most notably by Fernando Lopes Graça and Michel Giacometti, who produced a five-volume *Antologia de Música Regional Portuguesa*. Over the last decade, the group **Almanaque** of Lisbon has followed in their footsteps, producing a series of records from the oral tradition, as well as reworking the traditional themes in a more modern form.

The **Brigada Victor Jara** of Coimbra also began by collecting folk tunes but soon turned to new directions, adapting the work of other folk writers. Although none of its original members is still in the line-up, this group is one of Portugal's best, producing well-crafted work based on sound ideas. Other active folk groups, adopting similar approaches, include Raizes (Roots) from Vila Verde (Braga); the Grupo Etnográfico de Cantares e Trajes (Ethnographic Song and Costume Group) from Manhouce; Terra Terra (Land, Land); Vai de Roda, an ethnic arts co-operative from Oporto; Trigo Limpo (Clean Wheat) from Alentejo; and Ronda dos Quatro Caminhos (Crossroads) from Lisbon.

A more **contemporary** and ambitious folk music has also emerged over the last decade. **Trovante**, which was formed in 1975, is highly acclaimed in Portugal and has worked extensively with José Afonso and Fausto. Its work is full of uneven swayings and sudden changes of direction. Interesting, too, though less successful, are Charanga, Pedra d'Hera, Construção, Disto e Daquilo and Rosa dos Ventos.

Música Popular – as more recent folk has become known – owes much of its renewed popularity, however, to the work of some singer-songwriters who have dedicated themselves exclusively to it and to musicians who have made records devoted to individual folk instruments.

Among **instrumentalists**, perhaps the most outstanding figure is the guitarist **Carlos Paredes**. He explores both the folk and the classical sides of the Portuguese guitar, with surprising results; his records are a rare treat.

PORTUGUESE FOLK: THE KEY FIGURES

JOSÉ AFONSO The "father of modern Portuguese popular music" made a key contribution to song from the 1950s onwards and won fame far beyond his country's borders. He was born in Aveiro and as the son of a civil servant visited several colonies as a child, but it was not until later, when he made a trip to Angola as a student, that he became aware of the colonial realities.

His first records were collections of fado made with Luís Góis in 1956. In the 1960s he began to write songs on social issues. His records were censored and he was persecuted by the secret police. His whole life was dedicated to song and his personal crusade against fascism.

After the Revolution, he continued to work prolifically and to consistently high standards, composing music for films and the theatre as well as producing nearly twenty LPs. His work was constantly evolving, yet his first compositions are still fresh today. With their careful attention to music, lyrics, arrangement and voice, any of his records is a miniature work of art. He lived modestly and died after a long illness in 1987.

FAUSTO The work of this singer combines the most diverse influences – modern and traditional, Portuguese and African – with a marked urban slant and a lyrical delivery. His skill lies in the subtlety with which he links African rhythms to Portuguese melodies and instruments and the delicacy of his singing.

His early songs provide a poetic analysis of the uncertain post-revolutionary period. Later ones use tales of the deeds of conquistadores, sailors and other Portuguese heroes 'to reflect on the country's history.

SÉRGIO GODINHO Born in Porto, Godinho went into exile as an economics student to avoid military service in the colonial war. He travelled in France, Switzerland and Canada, working at one time as an interpreter for the musical *Hair* and at another as a member of Living Theatre.

Due to these influences he is one of the more modern, cosmopolitan singers of his generation. His songs are usually narrative and he has a particular knack for affectionate character sketches. When dealing more directly with political issues he employs a fine sense of humour. His music is both loud and cheerful, intimate and sophisticated.

LUÍS CÍLIA Of the new songwriters, Luís Cília is the one who has devoted most attention to setting his poems to music. His work is rigorous and serious, showing a pronounced French influence. He is good at capturing the essence and general atmosphere of a given political moment in his lyrics. Musically, he has worked in two apparently contrasting fields: traditional song and experimental work with synthesizers from which he has produced a solo album.

JOSÉ MÁRIO BRANCO Another native of Porto, Mário Branco's chief contribution has been as an arranger and producer of records, though he has made important records himself, both individually and as a member of the Grupo de Acção Cultural. His skill in the studios has given an added dimension to the records of Portuguese singers.

VITORINO The songs of Vitorino are inextricably linked with the Alentejo region and its farming co-operatives and rural communities, though recently he has made more contact with the city. His early records were uneven in their development, a mixture of Alentejo folk songs, revolutionary anthems and love songs. It is with the latter genre that he has had most success in his recent work.

JANITA SALOMÉ Brother of Vitorino, he also has links with the Alentejo, though he has concentrated increasingly on the Arab heritage there and in the Algarve. His music, full of percussion and gentle touches, also betrays the influence of José Afonso, with whom he worked closely in his last years.

Pedro Cabreira Cabral, very much the next generation after Paredes, also continues the tradition of using indigenous instruments – apart from being an exceptional guitarist and learned musicologist, he also makes and restores instruments and has composed original pieces for the Portuguese guitar. Another excellent instrumentalist is **Júlio Pereira**, who began as a songwriter but became interested in traditional string instruments and has recently experiment-

ed to great effect in combining them with synthesizers, rhythm boxes and samplers in compositions inspired by folk tradition.

JAZZ AND AFRICAN

Though Portuguese jazz cannot even begin to match the maturity of its songwriting tradition, there have been some interesting developments in recent years. An intriguing figure, midway between jazz and "New Age", is the saxophonist **Rão Kyao**. As for jazz proper, there is the great vocalist **Maria João**, the **Lisbon Jazz Sextet**, the experimental trio **Shish**, and the ensembles led by **António Pinho Vargas** and **Mário Laginha**.

The appearance of groups from the former colonies of **Angola**, **Mozambique**, **Cabo Verde**, **Guinea-Bissau** and **São Tomé e Príncipe** has been another exciting development in the Portuguese music scene. Following the colonial wars and independence many African musicians have settled in Lisbon; others spend part of the year based in Portugal, recording and touring Europe, drawn by the comparatively high fees to be made. In recent years, Lisboans have embraced their musical styles with vigour, perhaps because the lively African beat is a complete contrast to the sad, nostalgic tradition of fado.

Staying in Lisbon, you're most likely to get a chance to see Cabo Verde groups, which include among their styles *morna*, similar to the Portuguese fado and the more danceable *moradeira*. The big star of the moment is **Cesaria Evora**, a fabulous diva with an international following. From **Guinea-Bissau** the sounds are an unusual mix of African and Latin, akin to zouk. Big names to look out for that may be in the country include **Justino Delgado**, **Super Mama Diombo**, **Manecas**, **Africa Libre** and **Jetu Katem**. Finally, two outstanding southern African groups to see are **Guem** from **Angola** and **Fernando Luís** from **Mozambique**.

Manuel Dominguez

ROCK, POP AND *PIMBA*

Two names that have been big for some time now are the pop singer **Mafalda Veiga** and the blues singer **Rui Veloso**. However, it wasn't until the beginning of the 1990s that the Portuguese rock and pop music scene started to take off. Up until then, a handful of groups and solo artists struggled to compete with the foreign music pumped out by cable TV and given almost exclusive airplay by radio stations. The national backlash came with the second generation of groups – formed largely of members of the old bands – who concentrated this time on establishing a cult following rather than achieving megastar status. Although slow to react initially, major record companies eventually realized that there was a market to exploit and set about employing the modern marketing techniques of their foreign counterparts.

Although bands such as GNR and Xutos and Pontapes were strongly promoted, **Madredeus** has been the only group so far to achieve international recognition in countries as far afield as the USA and Japan. Other mainstream pop bands to keep an ear out for are **Delfins**, **Rio Grande** and **Santos e Pecadores**.

On a national level, however, it is not the likes of Madredeus but rap singer **Pedro Abrunhosa** who is idolized throughout the country. On its release, his first record, *Viagens*, broke sales records and opened the doors for many groups. One of the main achievements of his music was to make rap more acceptable and its decidedly jazzy feel has provided an alternative to a music scene previously dominated by FM-style hard rock. In fact Portuguese rap and hip-hop now dominate the underground music and club scene – **General D**, **Da Weasel** and **Cool Hipnoise** are the household names, their image and music rivalling anything coming out of the USA or Britain.

Dance music has taken a while to catch on, but in 1991 the first ever Portuguese house track, *Deep Sky* by **Matrix Run**, stimulated a wave of new talent and interest. House and techno rave parties are currently emerging all over the country, attracting thousands of young people to a new club culture.

You're unlikely to get through a visit to Portugal without hearing some **Música Pimba**, – a fashionably tacky music of the sort that usually enters the charts around Christmas time. Despite the wholesale snubbing of this style by the Portuguese media, *pimba* has succeeded in conquering the whole country as well as being big in countries with large Portuguese communities.

Mixing traditional and modern elements, its success was previously limited to the provinces, but the introduction of satirical jokes and sexual references to the lyrics found new support among college students and its popularity has now spread to the main cities. Today, *pimba* is firmly established and, to some extent, its humorous and satirical style reflects a lot of the national character.

The main exponent of *pimba* is the singer/songwriter **Marco Paulo**. Another seasoned performer is **Quim Barreiros**; if you get a chance to see him, take it. Even if you can't speak Portuguese, the atmosphere at the shows is contagious.

Michael Oliveira-Salac

RECORDS

Portuguese music is hard to obtain outside the country, save for a few fado recordings (including some excellent reissues of old classics), so our advice is buy when you're there. CDs are broadly similar in cost to those in the UK, and pricier in the US; records, by contrast, are excellent value. The following is a personal selection of the most interesting.

FOLK
Almanaque *Desafiando Cantigas; Sementes.*
Brigada Victor Jara *Marcha dos Foliões.*
Ronda dos Quatro Caminhos *Fados Velhos.*
Vai de Roda *Vai de Roda.*

FADO
Amália Rodrigues *O Melhor.*
Carlos do Carmo *Um Homem na Cidade; Um Homem no País.*

PORTUGUESE GUITAR
Carlos Paredes *Guitarra Portuguesa; Movimento Perpétuo; Concerto em Frankfurt; Espelho de Sons.*
Pedro Caldeira Cabral *Encontros; A Guitarra Portuguesa nos Salões dos sec. XVIII.*

SINGER-SONGWRITERS
Adriano Correia de Oliveira *Memória de Adriano.*
Fausto *Madrugada dos Trapeiros; Por Este Rio Acima; Despertar dos Alquimistas.*
Janita Salomé *Lavrar em teu Peito; Olho de Fogo.*
José Afonso *Cantigas de Maio; Venham Mais Cinco; Coro do Tribunais; Com as Minhas Tamanquinhas; Fura Fura; Fados de Coimbra e Outras Canções; Como se Fora Seu Filho; Galinhas do Mato.*

José Maria Branco *Ser Solidário.*
Julio Pereira *Cavaquinho; Braguesa; Cadoi; Os Sete Instrumentos; Miradouro.*
Luís Cília *Cancioneiro; Penumbra.*
Sérgio Godinho *De Pequenino se Torce o Destino; Coincidências; Na Vida Real.*
Vitorino *Romances; Negro Fado; Frol de la Mar.*

ROCK/POP
G.N.R. *Os Homens não se querem Bonitos.*
Madredeus *Os Dias da Madredeus.*
Matrix Run *Deep Sky*
Pedro Abrunhosa *Viagens*
Rádio Macau *Rádio Macau.*
Sétima Legião *Mar d'Outubro.*
Trovante *Terra Firme.*

JAZZ
António Pinho Vargas *Variações.*
Maria João *Conversa.*
Rão Kyao *Fado Bailado; Danças de Rua.*
Sexteto de Jazz de Lisboa *Sexteto.*

AFRICAN
Cesaria Evora *Miss Perfumado* (Cabo Verde).
Kaba Mane *Kunga Kungake* (Guinea-Bissau).
Guem *Dans Voyage* (Angola).
Fernando Luís *Bassopa* (Mozambique).

LANGUAGE

If you have some knowledge of Spanish and/or French you won't have much problem reading Portuguese. Understanding it when it's spoken, though, is a different matter: pronunciation is entirely different and at first even the easiest words are hard to distinguish – the sound is more like that of an East European language than of the Romance tongues in which it has its roots. If you're stuck, most people will understand Spanish (albeit reluctantly) and in the cities and tourist areas French and English are also widely spoken. Even so, it's well worth the effort to master at least the rudiments; once you've started to figure out the words it gets a lot easier very quickly.

The pronunciation guide below and the box on p.517 will equip you with the basics. For more detail, check out the *Rough Guide Portuguese Phrasebook*, set out dictionary-style for easy access, with English–Portuguese and Portuguese–English sections, cultural tips for tricky situations and a handy menu reader.

PRONUNCIATION

The chief difficulty with **pronunciation** is its lack of clarity – consonants tend to be slurred, vowels nasal and often ignored altogether.

CONSONANTS

The **consonants** are, at least, consistent:
C is soft before E and I, hard otherwise unless it has a cedilla – açucar (sugar) is pronounced "assookar."

CH is somewhat softer than in English; Chá (tea) sounds like Shah.
J is pronounced like the "s" in pleasure, as is **G** except when it comes before a "hard" vowel (A, O and U).
LH sounds like "lyuh" (Batalha).
Q is always pronounced as a "k".
S before a consonant or at the end of a word becomes "sh," otherwise it's as in English – Cascais is pronounced "Kashkaish," Sagres is "Sahgresh".
X is also pronounced "sh"– caixa (cash desk) is pronounced "kaisha".

VOWELS

Vowels are worse – flat and truncated, they're often difficult for English-speaking tongues to get around. The only way to learn is to listen: accents, ã, ô, or é, turn them into longer, more familiar sounds.

When two vowels come together they continue to be enunciated separately except in the case of **EI** and **OU** – which sound like a and long o respectively.

E at the end of a word is silent unless it has an accent, so that carne (meat) is pronounced "karn," while café sounds much as you'd expect.

The **tilde over Ã or Õ** renders the pronunciation much like the French -an and -on endings only more nasal.

More common is **ÃO** (as in pão, bread – são, saint – limão, lemon), which sounds something like a strangled yelp of "Ow!" cut off in midstream.

A FEW KEY WORDS . . .

Even if you speak no Portuguese at all there are **a few key words** which can help you out in an enormous number of situations.

● **Há** (the H is silent) means "there is" or "is there?" and can be used for just about anything. Thus: "Há uma pensão aqui?" (Is there a pension here?), "Há uma camioneta para . .?" (Is there a bus to . . .?), or even "Há um quarto?" (Do you have a room?).

● More polite and better in shops or restaurants are **"Tem . . .?"** (Do you have . . .?) or "Queria . . ." (I'd like . . .).

● And of course there are the old standards "Do you speak English?" (Fala Inglês?) and "I don't understand" (Não compreendo).

PORTUGUESE WORDS AND PHRASES

BASICS

sim; não	yes; no	grande; pequeno	big; little
olá; bom dia	hello; good morning	aberto; fechado	open; closed
boa tarde/noite	good afternoon/night	senhoras; homens	women; men
adeus, até logo	goodbye, see you later	lavabo/quarto de banho	toilet/bathroom
hoje; amanhã	today; tomorrow	banco; câmbio	bank; change
por favor/se faz favor	please	correios	post office
tudo bem?	Everything all right?	(dois) selos	(two) stamps
está bem	it's all right/OK	sou Inglês/Inglesa	I am English
obrigado/a*	thank you	Americano/a	American
onde; que	where; what	Irlandês/Irlandesa	Irish
quando; porquê	when; why	Australiano/a	Australian
como; quanto	how; how much	Canadiano/a	Canadian
não sei	I don't know	Escocês/Escosesa	Scottish
sabe . . .?	do you know . . .?	Galês/Galesa	Welsh
pode . . .?	could you . . .?	Como se chama?	What's your name?
desculpe; com licença	sorry; excuse me	(chamo-me . . .)	(my name is . . .)
aqui; ali	here; there	Como se diz isto em	What's this called in
perto; longe	near; far	Português?	Portuguese?
este/a; esse/a	this; that	O que é isso?	What's that?
agora; mais tarde	now; later	Quanto é?	How much is it?
mais; menos	more; less		

* Obrigado agrees with the sex of the person speaking – a woman says obrigada, a man obrigado.

GETTING AROUND

Para ir a . . .?	How do I get to . . .?	A que horas parte?	What time does it leave?
esquerda, direita, sempre em frente	left, right, straight ahead	(chega a . . .?)	(arrive at . . .?)
Onde é a estação de camionetas?	Where is the bus station?	Qual é a estrada para. . .?	Which is the road to . . .?
a paragem de autocarro para . . .	the bus stop for . . .	Para onde vai? (Vou a)	Where are you going? (I'm going to)
a estação de comboios	the railway station	Está bem, muito obrigado/a	That's great, thanks a lot
Donde parte o autocarro para . . .?	Where does the bus to . . . leave from?	Pare aqui por favor	Stop here please
É este o comboio para Coimbra?	Is this the train for Coimbra?	bilhete (para) ida e volta	ticket (to) round trip

ACCOMMODATION

Há uma pensão aqui perto?	Is there a pension near here?	É caro, não o quero	It's expensive, I don't want it
Queria um quarto	I'd like a room	Posso/podemos deixar os sacos aqui até . . .?	Can I/we leave the bags here until . . .?
É para uma noite (semana)	It's for one night (week)	Há um quarto mais barato?	Is there a cheaper room?
É para uma pessoa (duas pessoas)	It's for one person (two people)	Com duche (quente/frio)	With a shower (hot/cold)
Posso ver?	May I see/look around?	Pode-se acampar aqui?	Can we camp here?
Está bem, fico com ele	OK, I'll take it	chave	key
Quanto custa?	How much is it?		

DAYS AND MONTHS

domingo	Sunday	*abril*	April
segunda-feira	Monday	*maio*	May
terça-feira	Tuesday	*junho*	June
quarta-feira	Wednesday	*julho*	July
quinta-feira	Thursday	*agosto*	August
sexta-feira	Friday	*setembro*	September
sábado	Saturday	*outubro*	October
janeiro	January	*novembro*	November
fevereiro	February	*dezembro*	December
março	March		

THE TIME

Que horas são?	What time is it?	*dez para as duas*	ten-to-two
é/são . . .	it's . . .	*meio-dia*	midday, noon
A que horas?	(At) what time?	*uma da tarde*	one in the afternoon
à/às . . .	at . . .		(1pm)
meia-noite	midnight	*sete da tarde*	seven in the evening
uma da manhã	one in the morning (1am)	*(dezanove)*	(7pm)
uma e dez	ten past one	*nove e meia da noite*	nine-thirty (pm)
uma e quinze	one-fifteen	*(vinte e uma e trinta)*	
uma e vinte	one-twenty	*meio-dia e quinze*	quarter past noon
uma e meia	one-thirty	*meia-noite*	midnight
quinze para as duas	quarter-to-two	*meia-noite e dez*	ten past midnight

NUMBERS

1	*um*	10	*dez*	19	*dezanove*	90	*noventa*
2	*dois*	11	*onze*	20	*vinte*	100	*cem*
3	*três*	12	*doze*	21	*vinte e um*	101	*cento e um*
4	*quatro*	13	*treze*	30	*trinta*	200	*duzentos*
5	*cinco*	14	*catorze*	40	*quarenta*	500	*quinhentos*
6	*seis*	15	*quinze*	50	*cinquenta*	1000	*mil*
7	*sete*	16	*dezasseis*	60	*sessenta*	2000	*dois mil*
8	*oito*	17	*dezassete*	70	*setenta*	1,000,000	*um milhão*
9	*nove*	18	*dezoito*	80	*oitenta*		

PORTUGUESE WORDS AND TERMS: A GLOSSARY

ARCHITECTURAL, HISTORICAL AND RELIGIOUS TERMS

AFONSINO Relating to the reign of Dom Afonso Henriques, first king of Portugal.

AZULEJO Glazed and painted tile; originally used as geometric decoration around the base of doorways of a church or mansion; by the late sixteenth century whole pictorial blocks were created. From the late seventeenth until the mid-eighteenth century – the main period – tiles were exclusively blue and white.

CAPELA Chapel; Capela-Mor is a chancel or sanctuary.

CITÂNIA Prehistoric/Celtic hill settlement.

CLAUSTRO Cloister.

CONVENTO Convent, though just as often an old church.

CORO Central, often enclosed, part of church built for the choir.

DOM, DONA Courtesy titles (sir, madam) usually applied to kings and queens.

ERMIDA Remote chapel – not necessarily a hermitage.

FORTALEZA Fort.

IGREJA Church; Igreja Matriz is a parish church.

INFANTA Princess.

INFANTE Prince.

MANUELINO Flamboyant, marine-influenced style of late Gothic architecture developed in the reign of Manuel I (1495–1521).

MOÇÁRABE Moorish-Arabic (usually of architecture or a design).

MOSTEIRO Monastery, or just as often an old church since most orders were suppressed in 1834–38.

MUDÉJAR Moorish-style architecture and decoration.

NOSSA SENHORA (N.S.) Our Lady – the Virgin Mary.

RETÁBULO Altarpiece – usually large, carved and heavily gilt.

SALA DO CAPÍTULO Chapter house.

TORRE DE MENAGEM Keep of a castle.

GENERAL WORDS AND TERMS

ADEGA Wine cellar or winery, often also a wine bar or restaurant where wine is served straight from the barrel.

ALAMEDA Promenade.

ALBERGARIA Upmarket inn.

ALBUFEIRA Reservoir or lagoon.

ALDEIA Small village or hamlet.

ARTESANATO Handicraft shop.

BAIRRO Quarter, area (of a town); Alto is upper, Baixo lower.

BAIXA Commercial, shopping centre of town.

BARRAGEM Dam.

CACHOEIRA Waterfall.

CALDAS Mineral springs or spa complex.

CÂMARA MUNICIPAL Town hall.

CAMPO Square or field.

CASA ABRIGO "Open house"; a hut or shelter in natural and national parks for hikers and park staff (free); also 'abandoned house" usually a farmhouse for rent.

CASA DE PASTO Cheap and simple place to eat

CASTELO Castle.

CENTRO COMERCIAL Shopping centre.

CHAFARIZ Public fountain.

CHURRASQUEIRA (spelt variously) Grill house, usually serving chicken.

CIDADE City.

CORREIOS Post office, abbreviated CTT.

CRUZEIRO Cross.

DORMIDA Room in a private house.

ELÉCTRICO Tramcar.

ELEVADOR Elevator or funicular railway.

ESPIGUEIRO Grain shed on stilts, common in the north.

ESPLANADA Seafront promenade.

ESTAÇÃO Station.

ESTALAGEM One step up from an *albergaria*, usually in rural towns, formerly a coach inn.

ESTRADA Road; Estrada Nacional is a main road, designated EN on maps.

FARMÁCIA Pharmacy.

FEIRA Fair or market.

FESTA Festival or carnival.

FONTE Fountain or spring.

FREGUESIA Parish (*Junta da Freguesia* is the local council)

GRUTAS Caves.

HORÁRIO Timetable.

HOSPEDARIA Cheap and basic pension, usually with shared facilities (same as Casa de Hóspedes).

ILHA Island.

JARDIM Garden.

LAGO Lake.

LARGO Square.

MERCADO Market.

MIRADOURO Belvedere or viewpoint.

PAÇO Palace or country house.

PAÇOS DO CONCELHO Town hall.

PALÁCIO Palace or country house; Palácio Real, Royal Palace.

PARAGEM Bus stop.

PARQUE Park.

PARQUE DE CAMPISMO Camping site.

PARQUE NACIONAL/NATURAL National/Natural Park or Reserve.

PASTELARIA Bakery, pastry shop.

PELOURINHO Stone pillory, seen in almost every northern village.

POMBAL Pigeon house.

PONTE Bridge.

POUSADA Luxury state-run hotel, sometimes converted from a castle or monastery.

POUSADA DE JUVENTUDE Youth hostel.

PRAÇA Square.

PRAÇA DE TOUROS Bullring.

PRAIA Beach.

QUINTA Country estate, farm or villa.

RIA Narrow, open-ended lagoon where sand bars block a river's mouth.

RIBEIRO Stream.

RIO River.

ROMARIA Pilgrimage-festival.

SÉ Cathedral.

SENHOR Man, Sir, or Mr.

SENHORA Woman, Madam, Ms or Mrs.

SERRA Mountain or mountain range.

SOLAR Manor house or important town mansion.

SOLARES DE PORTUGAL (formerly "Turismo de Habitação"). A number of organizations use this term to market accommodation in often outstanding buildings, often of historical or architectural importance (see p.30).

TASCA No-frills local bar.

TERMAS Thermal springs or spa complex.

TOURADA Bullfight.

VILA Town.

INDEX

Note: beaches are listed under "Praia" and not the proper name, ie Praia do Guincho, not Guincho.

Stay in touch with us!

ROUGH*NEWS* **is Rough Guides' free newsletter. In three issues a year we give you news, travel issues, music reviews, readers' letters and the latest dispatches from authors on the road.**

direct orders from

Amsterdam	1-85828-218-7	UK£8.99	US$14.95	CAN$19.99
Andalucia	1-85828-219-5	9.99	16.95	22.99
Australia	1-85828-220-9	13.99	21.95	29.99
Bali	1-85828-134-2	8.99	14.95	19.99
Barcelona	1-85828-221-7	8.99	14.95	19.99
Berlin	1-85828-129-6	8.99	14.95	19.99
Belgium & Luxembourg	1-85828-222-5	10.99	17.95	23.99
Brazil	1-85828-223-3	13.99	21.95	29.99
Britain	1-85828-208-X	12.99	19.95	25.99
Brittany & Normandy	1-85828-224-1	9.99	16.95	22.99
Bulgaria	1-85828-183-0	9.99	16.95	22.99
California	1-85828-181-4	10.99	16.95	22.99
Canada	1-85828-311-6	12.99	19.95	25.99
China	1-85828-225-X	15.99	24.95	32.99
Corfu	1-85828-226-8	8.99	14.95	19.99
Corsica	1-85828-227-6	9.99	16.95	22.99
Costa Rica	1-85828-136-9	9.99	15.95	21.99
Crete	1-85828-316-7	9.99	16.95	22.99
Cyprus	1-85828-182-2	9.99	16.95	22.99
Czech & Slovak Republics	1-85828-121-0	9.99	16.95	22.99
Dublin Mini Guide	1-85828-294-2	5.99	9.95	12.99
Edinburgh Mini Guide	1-85828-295-0	5.99	9.95	12.99
Egypt	1-85828-188-1	10.99	17.95	23.99
Europe	1-85828-289-6	14.99	19.95	25.99
England	1-85828-301-9	12.99	19.95	25.99
First Time Europe	1-85828-270-5	7.99	9.95	12.99
Florida	1-85828-184-4	10.99	16.95	22.99
France	1-85828-228-4	12.99	19.95	25.99
Germany	1-85828-309-4	14.99	23.95	31.99
Goa	1-85828-275-6	8.99	14.95	19.99
Greece	1-85828-300-0	12.99	19.95	25.99
Greek Islands	1-85828-310-8	10.99	17.95	23.99
Guatemala	1-85828-189-X	10.99	16.95	22.99
Hawaii: Big Island	1-85828-158-X	8.99	12.95	16.99
Hawaii	1-85828-206-3	10.99	16.95	22.99
Holland	1-85828-229-2	10.99	17.95	23.99
Hong Kong	1-85828-187-3	8.99	14.95	19.99
Hotels & Restos	1-85828-306-X	12.99	19.95	25.99
Hungary	1-85828-123-7	8.99	14.95	19.99
India	1-85828-200-4	14.99	23.95	31.99
Ireland	1-85828-179-2	10.99	17.95	23.99
Italy	1-85828-167-9	12.99	19.95	25.99
Jamaica	1-85828-230-6	9.99	16.95	22.99
Kenya	1-85828-192-X	11.99	18.95	24.99
Lisbon Mini Guide	1-85828-297-7	5.99	9.95	12.99
London	1-85828-231-4	9.99	15.95	21.99
Madrid Mini Guide	1-85828-353-1	5.99	9.95	12.99
Mallorca & Menorca	1-85828-165-2	8.99	14.95	19.99
Malaysia, Singapore & Brunei	1-85828-232-2	11.99	18.95	24.99
Mexico	1-85828-044-3	10.99	16.95	22.99
Morocco	1-85828-040-0	9.99	16.95	21.99
Moscow	1-85828-118-0	8.99	14.95	19.99
Nepal	1-85828-190-3	10.99	17.95	23.99
New York	1-85828-296-9	9.99	15.95	21.99
New Zealand	1-85828-233-0	12.99	19.95	25.99
Norway	1-85828-234-9	10.99	17.95	23.99
Pacific Northwest	1-85828-092-3	9.99	14.95	19.99

In the UK, Rough Guides are available from all good bookstores, but can be obtained from
Penguin by contacting: Penguin Direct, Penguin Books Ltd, Bath Road, Harmondsworth, West
Drayton, Middlesex UB7 0DA; or telephone the credit line on 0181-899 4036 (9am–5pm) and
ask for Penguin Direct. Visa and Access accepted. Delivery will normally be within 14 working
days. Penguin Direct ordering facilities are only available in the UK and the USA. The availability
and published prices quoted are correct at the time of going to press but are subject to alter-
ation without prior notice.

around the world

Paris	1-85828-235-7	8.99	14.95	19.99
Poland	1-85828-168-7	10.99	17.95	23.99
Portugal	1-85828-313-2	10.99	17.95	23.99
Prague	1-85828-318-3	8.99	14.95	19.99
Provence	1-85828-127-X	9.99	16.95	22.99
Pyrenees	1-85828-308-6	10.99	17.95	23.99
Rhodes & the Dodecanese	1-85828-120-2	8.99	14.95	19.99
Romania	1-85828-305-1	10.99	17.95	23.99
San Francisco	1-85828-299-3	8.99	14.95	19.99
Scandinavia	1-85828-236-5	12.99	20.95	27.99
Scotland	1-85828-302-7	9.99	16.95	22.99
Sicily	1-85828-178-4	9.99	16.95	22.99
Singapore	1-85828-237-3	8.99	14.95	19.99
South Africa	1-85828-238-1	12.99	19.95	25.99
Soutwest USA	1-85828-239-X	10.99	16.95	22.99
Spain	1-85828-240-3	11.99	18.95	24.99
St Petersburg	1-85828-298-5	9.99	16.95	22.99
Sweden	1-85828-241-1	10.99	17.95	23.99
Thailand	1-85828-140-7	10.99	17.95	24.99
Tunisia	1-85828-139-3	10.99	17.95	24.99
Turkey	1-85828-242-X	12.99	19.95	25.99
Tuscany & Umbria	1-85828-243-8	10.99	17.95	23.99
USA	1-85828-307-8	14.99	19.95	25.99
Venice	1-85828-170-9	8.99	14.95	19.99
Vietnam	1-85828-191-1	9.99	15.95	21.99
Wales	1-85828-245-4	10.99	17.95	23.99
Washington DC	1-85828-246-2	8.99	14.95	19.99
West Africa	1-85828-101-6	15.99	24.95	34.99
More Women Travel	1-85828-098-2	10.99	16.95	22.99
Zimbabwe & Botswana	1-85828-186-5	11.99	18.95	24.99

Phrasebooks

Czech	1-85828-148-2	3.50	5.00	7.00
Egyptian Arabic	1-85828-319-1	4.00	6.00	8.00
French	1-85828-144-X	3.50	5.00	7.00
German	1-85828-146-6	3.50	5.00	7.00
Greek	1-85828-145-8	3.50	5.00	7.00
Hungarian	1-85828-304-3	4.00	6.00	8.00
Italian	1-85828-143-1	3.50	5.00	7.00
Japanese	1-85828-303-5	4.00	6.00	8.00
Mexican	1-85828-176-8	3.50	5.00	7.00
Portuguese	1-85828-175-X	3.50	5.00	7.00
Polish	1-85828-174-1	3.50	5.00	7.00
Spanish	1-85828-147-4	3.50	5.00	7.00
Swahili	1-85828-320-5	4.00	6.00	8.00
Thai	1-85828-177-6	3.50	5.00	7.00
Turkish	1-85828-173-3	3.50	5.00	7.00
Vietnamese	1-85828-172-5	3.50	5.00	7.00

Reference

Classical Music	1-85828-113-X	12.99	19.95	25.99
European Football	1-85828-256-X	14.99	23.95	31.99
Internet	1-85828-288-8	5.00	8.00	10.00
Jazz	1-85828-137-7	16.99	24.95	34.99
Millennium	1-85828-314-0	5.00	8.95	11.99
Opera	1-85828-138-5	16.99	24.95	34.99
Reggae	1-85828-247-0	12.99	19.95	25.99
Rock	1-85828-201-2	17.99	26.95	35.00
World Music	1-85828-017-6	16.99	22.95	29.99

the perfect getaway vehicle

low-price holiday car rental.

rent a car from holiday autos and you'll give yourself real freedom to explore your holiday destination. with great-value, fully-inclusive rates in over 4,000 locations worldwide, wherever you're escaping to, we're there to make sure you get excellent prices and superb service.

what's more, you can book now with complete confidence. our £5 undercut* ensures that you are guaranteed the best value for money in holiday destinations right around the globe.

drive away with a great deal, call holiday autos now on **0990 300 400** and quote ref RG.

holiday autos
miles ahead